THE
SOCIOLOGY
OF
SOCIAL PROBLEMS

SOCIOLOGY SERIES
Edited by John F. Cuber

THE
SOCIOLOGY
OF
SOCIAL PROBLEMS

Paul B. Horton

WESTERN MICHIGAN UNIVERSITY

Gerald R. Leslie

PURDUE UNIVERSITY

SECOND EDITION

New York

APPLETON - CENTURY - CROFTS, INC.

PRINTED IN THE UNITED STATES OF AMERICA

E-46025

Preface

A TEXTBOOK SHOULD DO AT LEAST THREE THINGS. First, it should present both a body of data and interpretations of those data which will meet the reasonably critical demands of professional colleagues; second, it should fit those data into a framework of theory which the student can use in interpreting data after the course is completed; third, it should present this in such manner as to stimulate and challenge the students who use it.

Built upon the assumption that modern social science provides the tools to permit significant, systematic, and consistent interpretation of social problems data, this book employs three separate, but related, frames of reference which have proved more than ordinarily useful. Social change and resulting social disorganization, the emergence of value conflicts, and the influences of personal deviation are brought to bear upon each problem. This is no "omnium gatherum" of facts and varying interpretations of those facts, nor is it a narrowly particularistic interpretation.

Part I includes a chapter on the nature and definition of social problems, a chapter on logical and statistical problems involved in the interpretation of facts, and a chapter which outlines the three frames of reference. Part II comprises the major part of the book and consists of a series of chapters devoted to various social problems. Each chapter presents a body of the most relevant data bearing on the problem and interprets these data in terms of each of the three approaches. Through such practical application, the concepts of social disorganization, value conflicts, and personal deviation are continuously explained and illustrated. In Part III, one chapter integrates and re-examines the fully developed concepts, while the final chapter projects the completed picture of social problems a short distance into the future.

Most of those who use this book will be lower division students with fairly limited training in sociology. This book has been written with these students in mind. It strives to be readable, and yet sociologically sophisticated. It avoids the use of unnecessary "sociologese" but seeks to provide a thorough explanation of basic sociological concepts. It assumes that a textbook need be neither a "students' book" nor an "instructors' book," but may adequately meet the needs of both.

In preparing this second edition, we have been impressed by the many contributions which only five years have seen in our rapidly changing field. This book is, therefore, much more greatly rewritten than we had anticipated. All chapters have been substantially revised, with the addition of considerable new material on juvenile delinquency, problem families, and the personal pathologies.

The basic approach remains unchanged. We believe that instructors who liked the first edition will be pleased with this one. We hope that those who were less enamored may find some of our errors corrected. We are grateful for many helpful suggestions and criticisms from our colleagues, and we owe a deep debt of gratitude to Dr. John F. Cuber for his encouragement and assistance. In the effort to please, however, we have not diluted controversy to the level of platitude. We have sought to sharpen, not to soften, the contrast of opposing views. The pungent phrase and the ironic twist have a proper place in a textbook. We have sought to make this textbook as interesting as possible so that it may stimulate students to seek for greater understanding of the drama in which they are both actors and audience.

The authors sought to document this book with easily available sources and references wherever practical. Obscure citations and foreign language references may spread the mantle of erudition upon the authors, but are of little use to undergraduate students, often dependent upon meagre library facilities. The descriptions of current social developments draw heavily upon such sources as *Time* magazine and the *New York Times*, since current developments are rarely found in academic journals. The list of Audio-Visual Aids has been shortened, following the authors' conclusion that relatively few films available are very useful for a college audience in this area of study.

We share joint responsibility for the organization of the book, and each chapter is a product of mutual criticism and suggestion. In the actual writing, Horton prepared Chs. 1, 3, 5, 6, 8, 10, 12, 13, 15, 17, 19, and 21, while Leslie prepared Chs. 2, 4, 7, 9, 11, 14, 16, 18, and 20.

P. B. H.

G. R. L.

Contents

Figures

Tables

ORIENTATION TO THE
STUDY OF SOCIAL PROBLEMS

Part I

ORIENTATION TO THE
STUDY OF SOCIAL PROBLEMS

1

Why Study Social Problems?

ᖾᖾᖾ

A group of whites and Negroes stand watching a mechanical cotton picker bring economic, social, and psychic chaos to their lives. A lonely girl permits herself to be picked up by a man. The member of a religious or racial minority turns away in dejection from an employment office, denied again a job because of creed or skin color. A public health report sums up in cold statistics the story of emaciated and scarred bodies ravaged by tuberculosis and syphilis in an overcrowded urban slum or a disintegrating rural area. A juvenile delinquent, raised in an "exclusive" neighborhood, has his thieving or hoodlumism "covered up" by his parents on a promise "not to do it again." A flood rips through homes, factories, and eroding farm land in one of the country's great river valleys. The sun turns a sickly green at noon during a Kansas dust storm, and the people try to wash the earth out of their mouths and keep it from their lungs. And the finest examples of young manhood leave their home to "save the world for Democracy."[1]

THESE ARE THE PERSONAL symptoms of social problems. Their consequences in financial cost and emotional insecurity reach into every home and disturb the life of every community. This year we shall spend at least $20 billion on social welfare measures, admit about 175,000 new patients to mental hospitals, imprison roughly 100,000 new criminals, and pay a national crime bill some four or five times as great as the cost of operating all the nation's schools, colleges, and universities. Whether we like it or not, *social problems affect all of us,* so perhaps we should know something about them. What are they? Why do they exist? Who is responsible for them? How much do they cost? What can be done about them?

To ask these questions takes only a short paragraph; to answer them would require a library with half its shelves filled with books not yet

[1] Alfred McLung Lee and Elizabeth Briant Lee, *Social Problems in America* (New York, Henry Holt & Co., Inc., 1949), p. 3.

3

written. Even the first question, What are the social problems?, is much more complicated than it appears to be.

DEFINITION OF A SOCIAL PROBLEM

Whenever people begin to say, "Isn't it awful! Why don't they do something about it?", we have a social problem. A formal definition might read, "*A social problem is a condition affecting a significant number of people in ways considered undesirable, about which it is felt something can be done through collective social action.*" This definition has four distinct ideas: (1) a condition affecting a significant number of people; (2) in ways considered undesirable; (3) about which it is felt something can be done; (4) through collective social action. Each of these four ideas needs to be examined in detail.

1. "A condition affecting a significant number of people . . ."

One's pet peeves are not social problems unless they also disturb a good many other people. How many people? There is no exact number that must be affected before a condition qualifies as a social problem. But when a condition affects enough people so that many of them take notice and begin to talk and write about it, a social problem exists. One way of measuring public concern about a condition, for example, is to count the number (and length) of magazine articles devoted to it each year as listed in the periodical index. When numerous articles are appearing, it is clear that the condition has attracted widespread concern and has become a social problem.

2. "in ways considered undesirable . . ."

Child labor was no social problem as long as most people thought child labor was acceptable. Only when a considerable number of people decided that child labor was harmful and began saying, "Isn't it awful!"— only then did child labor become a social problem. A social problem involves, therefore, a *value-judgment*, a decision that the condition is "*bad.*" A person's value-judgment may define a condition either as an undesirable situation requiring change or as a proper and acceptable part of the society. During the Reformation period, such instruments of torture as the stake, rack, and thumbscrew were accepted by both Protestant and Catholic as proper means of defending their faith. Consequently, neither Catholic nor Protestant considered religious intolerance or persecution as a social problem. Neither objected to the *use* of the thumbscrew; to each the problem lay merely in the fact that the "wrong" people were being thumbscrewed. In other words, the values of the period approved the use of torture in suppressing heresy, while values differed as to which heresies should be suppressed. The values of Reformation man, therefore, defined the problem not as the achievement of religious tolerance but as the suppression of dissent. The values held by most of us today would define the problem as being exactly the opposite of this.

These examples show how *values may define any condition as a social problem or prevent designation of any particular condition as a problem.* Suicide, drunkenness, narcotic addiction, homosexuality, starvation, kissing on Sunday, beating one's children, not beating one's children—any of these may be defined as a social problem by the values of the society, or they may be defined as nonproblematic because they are acceptable. No condition, no matter how dramatic or shocking to someone else, is a social problem *unless and until* the values of a considerable number of people within the society define it as a problem.

3. "about which it is felt something can be done . . ."

Everybody talked about the weather, but nobody did anything about it until very recently. Conditions that cannot be changed or evaded must be accepted, usually with the aid of a supporting set of rationalizations. In much of the world, until very recently, famine was not a social problem because of the belief that famine was nature's inescapable way of removing surplus population. Flood control became a social problem only when we discovered that floods could be prevented; prior to that time, floods were simply a misfortune to be endured. Now that we may possibly exercise some control over the weather through cloud-seeding, the weather is becoming a social problem, and debate has already arisen over who owns the clouds in the sky and who may say where rain shall fall.[2]

The nature of a problem also changes as techniques of treatment are developed. For centuries, the mental illness problem was purely one of protecting the sane and disposing of the mentally ill; only recently (and to a lesser degree than might be imagined) has the problem become one of treating and curing the mentally ill. This is due not to any hardheartedness of our ancestors, but to their lack of any means of treatment for mental illness.

A condition is a problem when *it is believed* something can be done about it. It is *the belief* in the possibility of treatment that causes people to consider it a problem. Whether this belief is correct can often be determined only by trial. Meanwhile the *hope* of treatment is sufficient to lead people to consider a condition a problem and to seek a means of doing something about it.

[2] See George H. T. Kimble, "Storm Clouds Over Weather Control," *New York Times Magazine* (February 9, 1958), pp. 15 ff.; also "The Weather Weapon: New Race With the Reds," *Newsweek*, Vol. 51 (January 13, 1958), pp. 54-56.

4. "through collective social action."

If a local butcher short-weights his customers or some lunatic dumps arsenic into a water reservoir, this is not a *social* problem, since a simple police action will dispose of it. No general public discussion, crystallization of value-judgments, exploration of alternatives, determination of treatment, or organization of pressure is needed before the situation can be dealt with. Social problems are confined to those situations which are so complex that public concern, discussion, opinion formation, and pressure are needed if a treatment is to be sought.

Social problems are, therefore, *social in origin* ("a condition affecting a significant number of people . . ."); *social in definition* ("in ways considered undesirable . . ."); and *social in treatment* ("about which it is felt something can be done through collective social action").

FALLACIES ABOUT SOCIAL PROBLEMS

Although most people have a certain amount of knowledge about social problems, this "knowledge" is sometimes unorganized, frequently contradictory, and often incorrect. A listing of some of the widespread fallacies about social problems will reveal that much of this popular "knowledge" is superficial and unreliable.

1. That People Agree on What Are the Social Problems

Although many people may agree that housing, poverty, and unemployment are social problems in America, there are many others who emphatically disagree. Important real estate spokesmen have insisted that there has been no real housing shortage. Some religious sects claim that poverty is spiritually beneficial, while some wealthy people argue that poverty is good for people (other people, that is). An occasional employer is heard to remark that a moderate amount of unemployment (three or four million) is a good thing, for it encourages "troublesome" workers to be quiet and work harder. Most people agree that race relations are a social problem in America. To some the problem is how to complete the emancipation of the Negroes, whereas to others the problem is how to put them back in their "place." To a rather small but eloquent minority, cigarette smoking is a major social problem and moral issue. Although there may be considerable agreement upon some problems, this agreement is never complete; on other problems there may be very little agreement as to their nature or, sometimes, their existence.

2. That Social Problems Are Natural and Inevitable

To attribute a problem to "natural law" is a delightfully simple way to dispose of it and avoid doing anything about it. The "natural law" cited usually turns out to be an a priori assumption that has emerged from the depths of an armchair rather than from scientific research. The "natural law" of self-interest, that is, that people work hard only for private gain, is easily disproved by data from dozens of other cultures, and would hardly explain the motivation of Albert Schweitzer, Walter Reuther, or Dwight Eisenhower; yet this "law" is often invoked to sanction the status quo. The "natural law of the survival of the fittest," borrowed from zoology where it has some application, can easily be shown to be quite inoperative in human society where man-made customs and institutions interefere with the survival process; yet this may be cited as a "natural law of society" to sanctify the successful and to discourage sympathy for the unfortunate.

It will be seen in following chapters that social problems are not products of natural law or physical inevitability. In only one sense are social problems inevitable—namely, that *certain social arrangements make certain outcomes inevitable*. But this is a totally different kind of inevitability, because it is somewhat under human control.

3. That Social Problems Are Abnormal

Problems are sometimes discussed as though they were unexpected, freakish, unexplainable things which pop up where they have no business being, like sand in a fruit salad. Thus, the slum problem may be discussed as though the slum were an "abnormal" or "substandard" part of our city, instead of just as "natural" and "normal" a product of urban ecological processes as are the business district, the parks and monuments, and the attractive new suburban developments. Such problems as mental illness, alcoholism, and drug addiction are often discussed purely in terms of personal abnormality, with disregard for the fact that the same traditions and social pressures which make a person competitive, ambitious, and hard-working also produce the insecurities and anxieties which may lead to mental and physical illness. Our high divorce rate is usually described, with much wringing of hands, as a symptom of social breakdown; it is much more accurately viewed as a perfectly logical expression of the high value our society now places on individualism and marital happiness. In short, *social problems are the logical, understandable, and inevitable products of present social values and practices.*

4. That Social Problems Are Caused by Bad People

This is probably the most widespread fallacy of all. In many ways we are conditioned to analyze problems in terms of a simple good-bad dichotomy. Our nursery tales are filled with fair young princes decapitating fiery dragons or evil witches, whereupon all dangers cease and joy reigns forever. Most of our novels and practically all of our movies avoid offending any group by presenting all problems as simple contests between the good people and the bad people; with the defeat of the bad people the matter is ended happily. We shall see, however, that social problems are more often caused by good people who are minding their own business than by bad people who are being bad. For example, when nice people move to the suburbs, they help foster slums. When nice people buy a house in a segregated neighborhood, they maintain the discrimination which forces other races to live in pathetic overcrowded quarters which cause family disorganization and, consequently, increased crime rates. Nice people recoil in well-bred dismay from these squalid homes and the violence surrounding them. Social problems persist because nice people tolerate and support the conditions which produce them.

This conclusion is not easy for us to accept. Our religious training has, in the past, encouraged us to impute evil motives to those who do things we consider evil. To all this conditioning is added the fact that among the people involved in social problems, we constantly see some doing "bad" things—being selfish, brutal, exploitative, lazy, and shiftless. It is easy to jump to the conclusion that the problem exists *because* some people are obviously at fault. When we observe that a drunkard is unemployed, our conditioning leads us to assume that he is unemployed because he drinks, not that he drinks because he is unemployed. Although either possibility may be true, our conditioning prepares us to accept one explanation and to fail even to consider the other.

This makes the average person's study of social problems an elaborate game of "I spy," a search for the villain instead of a search for insight. To many people, "doing something" about a social problem means finding and punishing the "bad" people. The chapters to follow will try to show how *each problem is a product of existing social institutions and practices and not primarily a product of willful wickedness.* We shall see how the "evil" conduct of the persons involved is more properly viewed as a *symptom* of a problem and *not its cause.* We shall also see how merely punishing the "bad" people, although it may relieve our feelings, will have very little permanent effect upon the problem.

5. That Problems Are Created by Talking About Them

This belief takes the form of the suggestion that it is not entirely decent, gentlemanly, or "American" to talk about things like slums, poverty, inadequate medical care, or racial discrimination because ignorant and irresponsible people may become dangerously inflamed. To talk about such things is to "stir up trouble," "foment class hatred," and so on. Such a belief is, of course, completely undemocratic and, therefore, "un-American," for it presupposes that the common people cannot be trusted to use responsible judgment, whereas democracy is based upon the assumption that the common people can be trusted to make wise decisions most of the time.

This fear that talk is dangerous exaggerates the excitability of our people. Most people are more interested in ball games and television shows than they are in social issues. If one doubts this, let him try promoting a local forum or discussion group! Reformers have always found the task of arousing people exasperatingly difficult. Only when the problem deeply affects *them*, or sharply threatens *their* cherished values, are most people concerned enough even to listen, let alone do anything about it.

It is true that talking about a problem may lead to a greater public awareness of it, and this may be what some people fear. But to imagine that people will tell one another about a nonexistent problem until they have manufactured a myth is to exaggerate people's readiness to borrow trouble.

6. That All People Would Like to See the Problems Solved

The belief that everyone would like to solve social problems, disagreeing only on methods, is a naïve illusion. The fact is, that for every problem, there are some *people who do not want the problem solved*. During the war, this writer once talked to a women's group about racial discrimination; the women nodded sympathetic agreement with each remark, but during the tea which followed, many were overheard lamenting because Negro cleaning women were demanding as much money as white workers received! Whatever their professed ideals might be, these women did not wish to surrender their genteel exploitation of Negroes. Certain southwestern farm operators who employ "wet-backs" [3] at very low wages have no interest in doing anything about the "wet-back" problem and strive to prevent effective enforcement of the immigration

[3] *Wet-backs* are Mexicans who illegally enter the United States, generally crossing the Rio Grande at night, to work as seasonal farm labor. Some farm operators employ them at low wages and may even cheat them of their small earnings by reporting them to the government for deportation after they are through with the Mexicans for the season.

laws. "Full employment," with plenty of well-paid jobs for everyone, would cause many of us distress; under such conditions, employers have difficulty in finding good workmen, middle-class housewives cannot get good, cheap cleaning women, and we would be annoyed to find stores understaffed, repair work poorly done, and good "service" hard to obtain.

Plenty of well-paid, pleasant jobs for all would mean that the dirty unpleasant work simply wouldn't get done. [4] Ending residential segregation of Negroes would greatly reduce the income from housing into which Negroes are now crowded at fantastically high rentals; therefore, the owners (some white and some Negro) of this very profitable housing have no interest in reducing residential discrimination. Slum housing, however wretched, is often a highly profitable investment [5]—is it surprising that its owners should be disinterested in slum clearance? The big conventions that put so much money in the cash registers of a city's hotels, restaurants, and stores are more likely to visit a city in which high-class prostitution, exciting floor shows, "honest" gambling, and after-hour taverns are readily available. A too-determined enforcement of the laws governing prostitution, entertainment, gambling, and tavern closing hours would, in any major city in America, probably meet the strenuous opposition of powerful sections of the business community and of many local citizens of all classes who enjoy these attractions. [6]

For any social problem one might mention, a sizable array of groups can be found who do not desire its solution. Either their values do not define it as a problem or a solution would prove costly to them in money, status, power, sentiment, or something else they treasure.

7. That Problems Will Solve Themselves

A central element of the American ethos is a general expectation of progress. Although the formal theory of automatic and inevitable social

---

[4] This situation was to a limited extent true during World War II. It would have prevailed more had it not been for the Negroes, whom we forced to do most of the dirty, unpleasant jobs by excluding them from most of the desirable ones.

[5] Slum property normally earns a rental income far higher than its sale value would justify or, conversely, slum property sells at a price far lower than its rental value would justify. This is due largely to the high risk involved in slum property ownership. Slum property is highly inflammable but often uninsurable, and almost never insurable at a figure that represents its rental earning power. Furthermore, much slum housing would either be condemned or would require costly repairs if the health and safety laws were enforced. Slum housing, then, is a highly profitable investment, as long as it does not burn up or tumble down and local officials can be dissuaded from tearing it down.

[6] For example, Galveston recently elected a new mayor who promised a more wide-open town than his predecessor had run. The only "reform" candidate ran last in a field of six. The winner was supported by ". . . the belief of many leading Galveston businessmen that sin is good for business, that the tourist trade would fall off if gambling and prostitution were suppressed. . . ." (*Time*, Vol. 65, [May 23, 1955], p. 26.)

progress has taken quite a beating in the carnage of recent decades, Americans seem to accept it piecemeal, if not *in toto*. Most discussions of any problem are sprinkled with such sage observations as, "Of course, it's improving, and . . . ," or "It's not as bad as it used to be, and. . . ." These statements are sometimes descriptively true, yet behind them often lurks the unspoken suggestion that such progress comes about naturally with the passing of time, like the growth of a tree or the melting of an iceberg. From this position, it is but a short step to the faith that only patience is needed, for time will solve all problems. And this provides a beautiful rationalization for inactivity; it enables one to make a very creditable display of sympathetic feeling for the unfortunates without requiring the sacrifice of a penny of money or an hour of time. It enables one to be both humanitarian and thrifty.

A belief that problems improve if left alone is based on this theory of automatic, inevitable progress, a theory which no social scientist accepts today. To apply it to social problems is naïve and unsound. Although some problems (for example, the assimilation of the immigrants) may grow less pressing as time passes, others (crime, traffic, housing) seem to grow more serious. To expect problems to solve themselves will remain unrealistic and ineffectual.

8. That "Getting the Facts" Will Solve the Problem

No problem can be treated intelligently without first "getting the facts" about it, but "getting the facts" is no guarantee that people will interpret facts in the same way. Facts in themselves mean nothing and lead nowhere. Facts must be *interpreted* before they have meaning. Does the fact that a manager gets $100,000 a year and his workers $4000 mean the manager is getting too much, or too little? Does the fact that many respectable citizens gamble mean that the laws against it should be repealed so their gambling will be legal, or enforced so their gambling will be discouraged? It is clear that *a fact has meaning only as it is interpreted according to one's values*. When people have the same values, fact-gathering may help resolve their disagreements. When people have differing values, fact-gathering cannot possibly resolve their disagreements; it just helps each individual defend his values more convincingly. Since nearly all social problems involve conflicting value-judgments, it is useless to hope that fact-gathering will solve them. It is difficult enough for people to agree upon *means* when they share the same ends or goals; when their goals differ, agreement on means is impossible.

The process of "getting the facts" does, however, have certain utility. Carefully collected facts can demolish the rationalizations through which some people evade the problem. Statements such as "There is no real poverty in America," or "Everyone who really needs medical care can get it in America," can be contradicted effectively with facts. And large masses of carefully collected and fully digested facts are needed before people (who agree upon values and objectives) can work out any practical modes of treatment. Facts are exceedingly important, but we need a clear understanding of what *can* and what *cannot* be accomplished by fact-gathering.

9. That Problems Can Be "Cured" Without Institutional Changes

Many folk are like the fat man who wants to reduce without giving up any of the things he likes to eat. We would like to solve social problems if we could do so without changing anything. Social scientists are invited to produce some quick, painless social panacea that will solve the problem without anyone's sacrifice of money, power, or sentiment. This is impossible. A complete solution of nearly any problem would require sweeping changes in present institutions and practices. To "cure" the problem of poverty would require such extensive changes in our educational, economic, and governmental institutions that some of them would become unrecognizable. To "solve" the housing problem would probably require either a drastic reduction of building costs through new materials and processes or large government subsidies for housing; either "solution" would involve major institutional changes and exact costly penalties from many vested interest groups. Problems are painful, but so are "solutions"; and then the "solutions" create new problems to be solved.

Since the genuine solution of social problems nearly always involves sweeping institutional changes, and these are costly and difficult to promote, it is unrealistic to expect that these problems will be solved easily or quickly. Institutional changes come slowly, and therefore basic solutions of social problems will come slowly, if at all. Meanwhile, however, considerable *amelioration* or "improvement" may be possible. Although we shall not eliminate poverty or unemployment in the near future, we have already developed moderately successful programs for reducing the personal suffering involved. We shall not eliminate crime, but we may develop more effective techniques of reforming criminals. There is no prospect of eliminating mental illness, but there are excellent prospects for greater success in curing mentally ill persons. Although a universally acceptable solution to most problems in the near future is not possible, considerable success in reducing the personal suffering and social waste due to social problems *is* possible. Any practical proposal must be developed with a foreknowledge of the limitations of social solutions.

ATTITUDES TOWARD SOCIAL PROBLEMS

One's attitudes and values determine the meanings that he finds in the fact he observes. A study of some widespread attitudes toward social problems may help to show why people react to facts so differently.

1. Indifference

Possibly the most widespread attitude is that of unconcern. Few of us become very agitated over anything which does not involve our own welfare. There is never time enough for all the things we want to do, and there are many diversions more entertaining than boning up on the present status of the migrant labor problem. Pressures of home, family, friends, jobs, and other duties keep us so busy that in idle moments we crave amusement and relaxation, not social surveys and research studies. General interest in a problem is likely to develop only when people sense a serious threat to their welfare or a particularly shocking denial of their values.

2. Fatalistic Resignation

Another attitude is the passive acceptance of misfortune. Countless millions have endured great suffering, even starvation, with a calm, stoical resignation. If one believes the way to meet misfortune is to endure it quietly, he does not attempt to "solve" the problem. In fact, there *is* no problem—nothing that we should "do something" about—if one believes misfortune is simply an inescapable fate one must endure. It is not that these people *refuse* to do anything about problems; it is rather that the thought of trying to do something would not even occur to them, just as it would not occur to most of us to react to a sore thumb by chopping it off.

3. Cynicism

To the confirmed cynic, all talk about social problems is a waste of time; the "unfortunates aren't worth getting excited over," and the "do-gooders" are "a bunch of hypocrites secretly grinding their own axes." The cynic believes that people are really a sorry lot, that all people are motivated purely by self-interest and other ignoble motives, and those who are not completely repulsive are either amiable scoundrels or pious frauds. The cynic's pet phrases are, "So what! They like it that way," "Everybody has an angle," "They wouldn't take care of it if they had it," "They are too dumb to know any better," and so on. Since those in trouble are not worth saving, and their "saviors" cannot be trusted, why not just let each person "stew in his own juice"?

4. Religious Retribution

This attitude views problems as God's punishment for man's sin. If there be drought, flood, war, pestilence, depression, high prices, low prices, and other calamities, some proclaim them God's punishment of sinful man. [7] If this is true, the solution for social problems is to be found not in social policy or institutional changes, but in penitence, righteousness, and prayer.

All questions about God's intervention in human affairs and the functions of penitence and prayer relate to philosophy and religion, not sociology. These are questions for which there are no scientific techniques for seeking an answer. In the study of social problems, however, sociologists find it more successful to analyze them in terms of social, rather than supernatural, causation. Furthermore, we now have enough facts about social problems to realize that the theory of religious retribution scarcely does justice to God. It would cast Him in the role of one who uses a punishment that is both unjust and ineffectual. The sacrifices of war, depression, and other problems are never equally divided; there is no evidence that only the "wicked" suffer. Neither is there evidence that those who suffer through being poor, ill, unemployed, or shot at become in general, more godly, righteous, or noble as a result. Instead, there is some evidence that those who endure insecurity and hardship are likely to become selfish, callous, and insensitive. The modern conception of God as a wise, just, and loving Father is not compatible with the theory of religious retribution, but is entirely compatible with the theory that social problems result from imperfectly harmonized social institutions.

5. Sentimentalism

The sentimentalist, whose attitude differs from those already described, is not trying to run away from the problem but is anxious to do something about it. The sentimentalist is deeply moved, saying, "Oh, those poor, poor, people; let's do something quick!" The sentimentalist does not see distressed persons as symptoms of the institutional imperfections of society; he sees them only as suffering individuals who should get help quickly and directly. The sentimentalist is so absorbed in distributing baskets to the poor and in finding a generous physician to sew up

[7] Sometimes this attitude is applied to distressed individuals, and the unemployed or poverty-stricken are seen as being individually punished for their sins. A few generations ago both physical and mental illness were also considered as divine, punishments for sin; this view is no longer widely held in our society.

poor old Widow Brown's rupture that he never stops to wonder whether it might be possible to reduce the number of people who must depend on basket-handing and medical generosity. The sentimentalist often idealizes the distressed, endowing them with a nobility few possess. Upon eventually discovering that the distressed are not saints but ordinary people who are often greedy, shiftless, and "ungrateful," the sentimentalist may become a cynic. Some of the most harsh cynics are disillusioned sentimentalists.

But one should not criticize the sentimentalists too severely. Although their indiscriminate basket distribution doubtless encourages some people to become professional relief clients, there is little evidence to support the accusation that they do more harm than good. And the sentimentalist approach was the forerunner of the social-scientific approach; out of earlier efforts to "do good" and the discovery that these efforts often failed, there came a realization that more knowledge was needed. This led to a more careful study of social problems. The sentimentalist approach to organized social work is now largely abandoned, with professionally trained social workers increasingly replacing the well-intentioned amateurs of the past.

6. Social-Scientific Attitude

This is the attitude of the social scientist and the professional social worker. Although there may be deep sympathy for distressed persons, it is recognized that sympathy is not enough; it must be coupled with expert knowledge and professional insight. As in all science, the social-scientific attitude toward social problems begins by asking, What is the probem? What are the relevant facts concerning it? What are the various value-judgments involved? What are the alternative possibilities for treatment and what is involved in each? Which policies are most likely to produce "desirable" results, as measured by the most widely held values?

This is the most difficult approach of all. Whereas all the foregoing attitudes provide simple, definite answers, the social-scientific approach has none ready-made. These must emerge from the painstaking, objective study of the problem in a field where objectivity is extremely difficult to maintain. Few people can succeed in maintaining it.

OBJECTIVES FOR OUR STUDY

1. Awareness

First of all, students should become aware of the main social problems. Have you ever visited a place and then been surprised at how often you heard or read about that place afterwards? The place had been mentioned just as frequently before you visited it, but you never noticed these comments until you were acquainted with it; thereafter, you noticed each reference because it tied up with something you knew about. In a similar manner, an awareness of a particular problem causes us to notice things we would otherwise overlook. We notice each reference to it in the newspaper, possibly take time to read a magazine article, or prick up our ears when it enters conversation. In this way we may constantly increase our knowledge of a problem and the validity of our judgments about it.

2. Factual Knowledge

All intelligent analysis must rest upon facts. To "discuss" a social problem accomplishes little unless someone in the group knows what he is talking about. Although fact-gathering will not automatically solve any problem, it is entirely impossible to analyze a problem intelligently until large masses of facts have been collected, organized, and interpreted.

3. Understanding of the Sociology of Social Problems

This means to have *a general understanding of why and how problems develop, of how people are affected by them, and what is involved in dealing with them.* These general understandings become a frame of reference within which data may be catalogued and problems studied. If one has a thorough understanding of the sociology of social problems, data on any particular problem can be organized rather quickly and the problem can be analyzed intelligently. These general understandings help one decide which data are significant and which are trivial; they help one to interpret new data correctly and to fit it in place mentally so that he keeps his thinking up to date. The data in this text will become obsolete, and the complexion of many problems may change considerably within a few years; yet, if the student understands the *sociology* of social problems, he will not find it hard to interpret new data and understand new developments.

4. Relation of Theory and Practice

To poke fun at "theory" and "theorists" is as American as hot dogs. Our frontier values, which rated skill with axe and mule team above skill with Latin verbs and metaphysical propositions, are mirrored in the present pride of the average man in being "a practical man, not a theorist."

The naïveté of this anti-intellectual bias is evident when one recalls that in social policy, as in most other fields, theory and practice are inseparable. Every "practical" policy flows from some theory of causation, and every theory carries some implications for control or treatment. One who tries to separate them merely reveals his ignorance of their relation, and most self-styled "practical" men are simply unaware of the theories that underlie their action. For example, the person who says, "Criminals should be punished, not coddled; give them nice long sentences on the rock pile and they would think twice before doing it again," probably imagines that he is expounding "practical common sense" untouched by "mere theory." In truth, however, this man is subscribing to a number of theories. He is applying the 4000-year-old theory that man is a hedonistic creature, determining his actions on a basis of simple pleasure-pain calculations, so that if we make the consequences sufficiently painful, he will refrain from the act. He is also using the theory that man is a purely rational being whose actions are determined not by habit, or training, or emotion, but by coldly rational and logical calculation. Still other theories about the existence of free will, the efficacy of punishment, and the processes of learning influence him. Hundreds of pages would be needed merely to state the theories underlying this man's innocent remark, and thousands of books have been written to explain and debate them. Of all this, our "practical" man knows nothing; he merely "knows" that he has "the answer."

The practical man who imagines he is unmoved by theoretical considerations is, in fact, slave to the theories of some dead economist or philosopher. His stout denial of theoretical contamination only reveals his ignorance of the theories which guide his thinking. Both the "conservative" and the "liberal" are supporting economic policies equally derived from economic theory; their main theoretical difference is that whereas one prefers policies based on the theories of classical economists like Smith, Ricardo, and Carver, the other supports programs based on the newer theories of Veblen, Keynes, and Slichter.

It is, of course, quite true that some scholarly folk become so immersed in theoretical abstractions that they seem innocently unaware of the realities surrounding them. It is from such persons that the stereotype of the impractical theorist probably was drawn. [8] Sound theory is proved by

---

[8] It is important to remember that the stereotype of the impractical college professor grew up at a time when the college curriculum was largely composed of pure science, classical studies, ancient languages, and other content quite remote from everyday life. Today the emphasis is quite different, and it is likely that the modern professor of political science, history, or American literature has at least as practical and realistic an understanding of our social world as has the average businessman, physician, or engineer.

It is also interesting to note that the businessman is rated as "practical" if his business prospers, a physician if his patients survive, and a mechanic if he can fix a car so it runs. A teacher, however, rarely is so classed merely because he can teach well; to be a "practical" man the teacher must also show that he can run a business, treat a stomach-ache, and overhaul his car. It may be that the teacher would be successful in business about as often as the businessman would be successful in teaching. Yet no matter how well a teacher can teach, some people (including some who failed as teachers themselves) will continue to consider him a childish, impractical theorist.

successful application. Not until it is shown that a theory works can we know whether the theory is sound. Vague theorizing or failure to test the theory at every possible point have no place in science, and persons guilty of these errors deserve no defense.

It is equally true that practice divorced from theory is not always practical; it may be merely guesswork, sanctified by precedent. One does not become a "practical" man merely by announcing himself as one. The genuinely practical man, in the field of social policy, is one who knows and understands the theoretical underpinning of his recommendations, who knows how they have worked out elsewhere, and has some factual basis for predicting their effectiveness.

To help the student gain a clear picture of the relation of theory to practice is one of the objectives of this book. To recognize that sound theory is established by successful applications; that no policy is any sounder than the theory from which it flows; that only when one thoroughly understands the theories involved is he qualified to select a practical course of action; that much "practical common sense" is nothing more than guesswork and folklore—to recognize these premises is to clear one's mind of a clutter of myth and misconception that obstructs clear thinking.

5. A Sense of Perspective

Some people find the study of social problems upsetting. Just as many people are frightened by all the diseases they find listed in a medical textbook, some students are disturbed at the great amount of implied criticism of our society in a social problems course. For some others, the awareness of social imperfections may become almost an obsession. They become so impressed with the suffering, frustration, and waste of a problem-ridden society that they fail to see the more encouraging aspects of the total picture. A sense of perspective is necessary if we are to see a problem without exaggeration or distortion.

Present problems should be seen against a background of past realities, not of past myths. The popular complaint that "Things aren't what they used to be" overlooks the fact that they never were! The past was rarely the tranquil, problem-free pastoral scene we sometimes imagine. History books rarely give full details on past problems, and today we are simply unaware of how sharp and bitter they may have been. Some people will probably be amazed to hear that in earlier periods of American history, government was far more corrupt, vote frauds more common, war profiteering far more flagrant, grafting more widespread, business methods less scrupulous, minorities more often mistreated, drunkenness more commonplace, church memberships proportionately less numerous, labor violence more unrestrained, employers incomparably more ruthless, newspaper bias more pronounced, police less efficient and more brutal, and wife beating and cruelty to children more common than they are in America today. Those who deplore today's immoralities and long to return to the pieties of the past merely reveal that they do not know their history well. [9] In fact, some modern problems (for example, prostitution, racial inequality, newspaper bias, "influence peddling" in government, truth in advertising) have become problems because our values now define as undesirable certain behavior which earlier generations accepted without question. A century ago, it was taken for granted that a senator had a personal financial interest in any legislation he sponsored (and he often did). [10] Today, such a revelation usually brings electoral defeat, if not worse, to any senator who is thus compromised. In a very real sense, some modern problems have arisen because our standards of public morality are "higher" than those of our predecessors. This is scarcely a reason for despair.

This text will strive to place each problem in a reasonable perspective, presenting it in its setting of past history, present trends, future prospects, and mitigating circumstances. In this way, the student may be helped to develop an attitude of realistic analysis that avoids the twin extremes of naïve evasion and morbid exaggeration.

6. Appreciation of the Proper Role of the Expert

Americans distrust "experts." We want no one telling us what to do. We readily array the "common sense" of a "plain, practical American" against the "theories" of some "long-hair expert."

Although in a democracy every person is equally entitled to hold his own opinion, it does not follow that those opinions are equally valuable. If we want a useful opinion on why our head throbs or our car stalls, we ask an appropriate expert. But when we wonder why Susie has grown disobedient or how to reduce sex crimes, we disdain to ask the expert and confidently announce our own opinions, perhaps after "discussing" the questions with others who know no more about it than we do.

[9] The sexual license of the later Roman Empire, the Renaissance, and the Restoration are well known. Yet even the Victorian period, supposedly so prim, was in fact quite indulgent. Most wealthy men had mistresses, and prostitutes in eighteenth century London were at least fifty times as numerous, in proportion to population, as they are today. See Cyril Pearl, *The Girl With the Swansdown Seat* (New York, The Bobbs-Merrill Company, Inc., 1956) for a well-documented look beneath the surface of Victorian respectability. For more Victorian horror stories, see Charles Terrot, *Traffic in Innocents* (New York, E. P. Dutton & Co., Inc., 1960).

[10] For example, Daniel Webster, eloquent senatorial defender of the National Bank, saw nothing improper in writing to the bank's director in the midst of senate debate over renewing the bank's charter, complaining that "my retainer has not been received or refreshed as usual." (John F. Kennedy, *Profiles in Courage* [New York, Harper and Brothers, 1955], p. 64.)

Many of these contradictions may stem from failure to distinguish between *questions of knowledge* and *questions of value*. In matters of knowledge there are right and wrong answers, whereas in matters of value there are no right and wrong answers, merely differing preferences. In matters of value the layman [11] and the experts are equals, each entitled to his preferences. But in matters of knowledge the layman and the expert are *not* equals, and for the layman to debate a matter of knowledge with the expert is futile and presumptuous. To illustrate, the question of whether leisure should be used in viewing paintings or prizefights is a matter of value, and all are entitled to their tastes; but the question of whether an alleged van Gogh is authentic is a question upon which expert knowledge is needed while lay opinions are not worth much.

Stated in its simplest terms, *the function of the scientific expert is not to tell people what they should want, but to tell them how best to get what they want.* When experts are *agreed* upon the futility of one policy or the soundness of another, it is sheer stupidity for the layman to disagree. Although it is quite possible that all the experts are wrong, it is so much more probable that the layman is wrong that he would be wiser to keep his silence. When the experts are disagreed among themselves, then it is stupid for the layman to consider any answer as positive and final. To illustrate, since the experts in criminology are agreed that criminal behavior is learned and not inborn, the layman who talks of a "criminal instinct" or a "born criminal" simply reveals his igorance. Since these same experts are not entirely certain as to what measures will most successfully reduce crime, the layman who confidently prescribes a particular treatment simply makes a fool of himself.

In the field of social problems, the function of the expert is to provide accurate descriptions and analyses of social problems and show laymen what consequences will follow each proposed treatment. It is scarcely his task to tell people what kind of a society they should want, but he should show them how to get the kind of society they want, if possible. Since people often want contradictory things (for example, cheap labor and prosperity), it is also the function of the social scientist to show laymen how their values are incompatible, and where they must compromise or choose between them. More simply, to say to the laymen, "If you do this, here is what happens"—this is the function of the social scientist. [12] The task of the student is to learn how to recognize an expert when he

[11] With regard to social problems, the term *laymen* refers to everyone except social scientists. Workers, farmers, businessmen, and government administrators are all laymen where social problems are concerned, just as the sociologist is a layman in the field of farm technology or medical diagnosis.

[12] There are some social scientists who feel that the social scientist should also tell people what they *ought* to do, but they are in the minority. All would agree, however, that the scientist is also a citizen and that he may share in any movements he wishes. Here, however, he acts as a private citizen pursuing his own values, not as a scientific spokesman expressing the conclusions of science.

meets one, and how to guide his own thinking by expert knowled
than by folklore and guesswork.

7. Personal Orientation

In the course of his study of social problems, the student will probably develop a personal reaction to them. Each student will have some
attitude towards social problems, perhaps one of the "attitudes" discussed
a few pages earlier. Many students take a course in social problems not
from any consuming curiosity, but because the course is required, or
comes at a convenient hour, or the instructor is popular, or for some other
reason. No particular interest, sympathetic or otherwise, is necessarily implied. Yet these students nevertheless find themselves developing attitudes
toward the subjects they study. To some, social problems represent a
subject to be completed, a course to be passed, and not vital situations
dramatically and tragically affecting the lives of human beings. To some,
the study of social problems may be a depressing recital of miseries and
woes, whereas to others it may be a catalog of suggestions and encouragement. A great many students may find that the continual emphasis upon
the institutional setting of social problems fills them with a vast sense of
futility—what can one person do? If a problem grows from the pon-
derous movement of impersonal social trends and forces, what use for one
person to try to stem the course of social change?

Granted that one person cannot do much, students who feel impelled
to "do something" should remember that they are never alone. Changes
in social policy grow from changes in the thinking of large numbers of
people. Although a single person does relatively little to affect that
change, each person is an indispensable part of that change merely by
being on one side rather than the other. As a famous clergyman has noted,
one may avoid a depressing sense of personal helplessness by asking, "Am
I part of the problem or part of the answer?" [13] Are you one whose
ignorance, indifference, prejudice, and self-interest are roadblocks in the
path of intelligent social policy? Or are you one whose sympathetic interest, realistic knowledge, and open-minded receptivity place you on the
side of those seeking to promote intelligent social policy? Even though
one may accomplish very little by himself, his belief that he is on the
"right" side is a powerful antidote for despair.

PLAN OF THIS BOOK

This introductory chapter is followed by a chapter presenting the
three common approaches used by sociologists in studying social prob-

[13] Harry Emerson Fosdick, "Are We Part of the Problem or of the Answer?"
National Education Association Journal, Vol. 36 (December, 1947), pp. 621-622.

lems and showing how each will be used in this text. The third chapter discusses the puzzling question of how to know when to believe what you read or hear.

Part II consists of a number of chapters, each exploring a social problem in some detail. For each problem, a considerable body of factual data will be presented, the problem will be analyzed according to each of the three approaches which are described in Chapter 2, and the probable consequences of alternative modes of treatment will be explored.

Part III attempts a reappraisal of the three approaches and of the special contributions of each to a more complete understanding of social problems. A final chapter will indulge in the fascinating but hazardous pastime of attempting to forecast the future development of social problems in America and the general lines of treatment which American society will employ.

SUMMARY

This introductory chapter attempts to give some impression of the nature and scope of social problems and to arouse some interest in them. Social problems are defined as conditions affecting many people in ways thought harmful, but avoidable through social action. Contrary to widespread but fallacious belief, (1) people do not agree upon which conditions are problems; (2) problems are not natural or inevitable; (3) problems are not abnormal, but are normal results of our social arrangements; (4) problems arise from social arrangements, not from "bad" people, and the "badness" of the people involved should usually be viewed as a symptom or result rather than the cause of the problem; (5) problems are genuine and are not illusions created by wild talk; (6) many people do not actually want certain problems solved; (7) most problems do not solve themselves or die out as time passes; (8) "getting the facts" will rarely solve a problem because people hold different values and want different outcomes; (9) problems cannot be thoroughly solved without major changes in present social institutions and practices.

Different persons hold different attitudes toward social problems. Some are *indifferent* and disinterested. Some are *fatalistically resigned*, accepting social problems as unavoidable scourges to be endured with patience. Some are *cynical* in their belief that the victims of problems are not worth helping and that the reformers are corrupt and venal. Some consider social problems as *religious retribution*, as divine punishment for man's misdeeds. All four of these attitudes discourage any attempt at treatment. The *sentimentalist* wants to "do something" but is guided by emotion rather than scientific knowledge, and his efforts are often wasted. The *social-scientific* attitude attempts to apply scientific technique to the analysis of a problem so that effective social policies may be developed.

It is our intent that through the study of social problems the student may develop: (1) *awareness* of present problems; (2) accurate *factual knowledge* about some of them; (3) some *understanding of their sociological origins,* of the general way in which problems develop; (4) an intelligent understanding of the *relation of theory and practice* in which all theory is tested by practical application while all practical policy is based on sound theory; (5) *a sense of perspective* so that a problem is seen in proper relation to the past and present society without distortion or exaggeration; (6) an *appreciation of the proper role of the expert* respecting social problems, with some skill in locating and using expert knowledge and opinions; and (7) *a personal orientation* that is intellectually and emotionally satisfying to the student.

SUGGESTED READINGS

CUBER, JOHN F., *Sociology: A Synopsis of Principles,* 4th ed. (New York, Appleton-Century-Crofts, Inc., 1959), Chs. 2 and 3. A general discussion of the sociological frame of reference. Although not directly addressed to social problems, its treatment of causality, case materials, and objectivity will be helpful in studying social problems.

NORDSKOG, John Eric, McDONAGH, Edward C., and VINCENT, Melvin J., *Analyzing Social Problems* (New York, The Dryden Press, 1956), Ch. 1. A collection of essays defining social problems and discussing the sociological approaches to their study.

Statistical Abstract of the United States (published annually by the U. S. Department of Commerce), and

The World Almanac and Book of Facts (published annually by the *New York World-Telegram and Sun*). These two books are not "readings," but are sources of statistical and factual information. They are the most easily accessible sources for data on practically any subject. Every student should thumb through these books in order to know what kinds of information can be found in them.

STEINBECK, John, *The Grapes of Wrath* (New York, Viking Press, Inc., 1939; Garden City, N. Y., The Sun-Dial Press, 1941; New York, Bantam Books, 1945), Ch. 5. A famous and highly controversial "social problem" novel dealing with the "Okies," the marginal Midwestern farmers whom drought and farm mechanization displaced and converted into migrant farm workers during the 1930's. Chapter 5 raises and gives an answer to the perennial question, Who is to blame?

QUESTIONS AND PROJECTS

1. List a number of modern conditions which we consider to be social problems, but which the values of an earlier period would not have defined as problems. List some, not problems to us, that would have been considered problems in our earlier period.

2. Have there been any continuous problems throughout recorded history? If so, what values, continuously held, define these conditions as problems?

3. Of the problems listed as chapter titles in the Table of Contents of this textbook, which would probably *not* be social problems in the Soviet Union? Why?

4. State some current public controversies that continue largely because of lack of knowledge with which to settle the issue. State some which exist largely because of disagreements upon values. Which group is the larger?

5. Do any social problems arise from our lack of ability to control the factors producing the situation?

6. What "harm," if any, has been done by the sentimentalist approach to social problems? What "good" has it done?

7. What difference does it make whether social problems are viewed as abnormal or as normal aspects of social organization?

8. What is meant by the suggestion that the "bad" people involved in social problems are more symptomatic than causative?

9. Give some examples which illustrate the statement that "certain social arrangements make certain social outcomes inevitable."

10. What kind of controversies can be solved by determining the relevant facts? What kind cannot be solved by fact-finding? Why?

11. Does an "awareness" of social problems and a recognition that their origin lies in our social structure make one a less "loyal" citizen?

12. Is it possible to be "practical" without also being "theoretical"? Can one be "theoretical" without being "practical"?

13. What is meant by a "sense of perspective" on social problems?

14. Read Chapter 5 of John Steinbeck's *The Grapes of Wrath*. Who or what is "to blame" for the situation? Why doesn't Pa fulfill his threat to "shoot the man who's starving" him? What significant insights into the sociology of social problems does this chapter illustrate?

2

The Sociology of Social Problems

┿┿

SOURCE: Special permission of *The Reporter,* New York

An Indian Tsar commanded that all the blind men be gathered together, and when they were collected, he commanded that they be shown his elephant. The blind men went to the stables, and began to feel the elephant.

One felt the leg; another, the tail; the third, the rump; the fourth, the belly; the fifth, the side; the sixth, the back; the seventh, the ear; the eighth, the head; the ninth, the tusk; and the tenth, the trunk.

The Tsar called the blind men to him, and asked them: "What is my elephant like?"

And one blind man said, "Thy elephant is like a pillar." This blind man had felt the leg.

The second blind man said, "Thy elephant is like a broom." This blind man had felt the tail.

The third said, "It is like wood." This man had felt the rump.

The man who had felt the belly said, "An elephant is like lumps of earth."

The man who had felt the side said, "It is like a wall."
The man who had felt the back said, "It is like a hill."
The one who had felt the ear said, "It is like a handkerchief."
The one who had felt the head said, It is like a mortar."
The one who had felt the tusk said, "It is like a horn."
The one who had felt the trunk said, "It is like a stout rope."
And all the blind men began to dispute and quarrel. [1]

EACH OF THESE BLIND MEN was telling the truth. An elephant *is* like a pillar, *and* like a wall, *and* like a rope. Yet, anyone depending upon these blind men for a realistic description of an elephant will undoubtedly be misled and confused. An elephant, like a social problem, may be studied from more than one point of view.

As seen in Chapter 1, the average layman is apt to think of social problems as though they were simply a series of separate trouble spots to be straightened out. He fails to see how each problem has roots which reach far out into the social system. For example, the individual "criminal" who robs filling stations, burglarizes homes, hijacks trucks, or swindles widows out of their life savings is only one part of the crime picture. The tenement district which requires "double" police protection, the police officials who occasionally are "silent partners" in crime, and the "honest" merchant who has two prices for each article of merchandise are also parts of the crime problem. John Doe may become a criminal because of the family life he has had, the school he attended, the groups he joined, the television shows he watched, the business practices he observed—these and many other forces shaped his destiny. To "cure" the crime problem, or any other problem, may involve changes in things as diverse as infant care and corporate finance. Since both the roots and the consequences of each social problem are so extensive, *the study of social problems requires a comprehensive point of view.*

SOCIOLOGICAL FRAME OF REFERENCE

Students who have taken courses in sociology will be familiar with the sociological point of view. For others, it may be helpful to discuss certain aspects of the sociological frame of reference.

Social Change

Change in social life is unceasing. Although the change may be gradual and unnoticed, all societies are constantly changing. Social change

---

[1] Based on Leo Nikolaievich Tolstoi, "The Tsar and the Elephants," in *The Great Fables of all Nations*, selected by Manuel Komroff (New York, Tudor Publishing Company, The Dial Press, Inc., 1928), pp. 439-440.

may be planned, but more often it takes place without plan or intent. Virtually every act of every individual leaves a particular situation different than it was before the act occurred; even when the act is a conscious attempt to prevent change, some kind of change follows. Thus, the attempt of a farmer to resist the federal government's corn acreage allotment controls inevitably affects the government's authority over agriculture. If he can defy the government successfully, its authority is weakened; if he must eventually comply, its authority is confirmed. Either way, he has effected change. Thus, the actions of farmers, whether compliant or evasive, become elements in structuring a social problem. In like manner, people sometimes oppose new industry because they wish to "keep our town as it is now." Without new growth and opportunity, the young people migrate, the buildings age, so the town does *not* remain unchanged. Men may be unaware of helping to change the social group in which they live, but they do so nevertheless.

The fact of continuous social change should be clear enough to students who have grown up amid the rapid social changes of our era. Major and minor wars, the development of the ballistic missile, the approaching obsolescence of manned military aircraft, the appearance of commercial television, the exploration of space, the development of atomic energy, the United Nations, and the married undergraduate college student are just a few of the changes that have developed during their lifetimes.

Not all aspects of a society change at the same rate, however, or even in the same direction. The automobile and our highway system, for example, have given to youth an unprecedented opportunity to escape the watchful eye of their elders. Profound changes in courtship patterns and in criminal behavior are only two of the unanticipated results. The translation of atomic energy into bombs has far outdistanced the development of political attitudes or skills adequate to handle the resultant problems. The implied principle here—that changes in technology often occur more rapidly than changes in customs and beliefs—has led to the formulation of the concept of "culture lag." [2] One eminent sociologist observed that technological change requires that adjustments be made in other (nonmaterial) aspects of the culture and that there is generally a time lag before such adjustments are made. Hence, the development of the automobile encouraged a younger physical involvement of dating couples and showed that new social controls would be needed if the former rules were to be enforced. Whether these adjustments have yet been made is debatable. The time lag involved is the period of *culture lag*; the resulting breakdown in time-honored courtship practices would be called *social disorganization*.

The constancy of culture change and its differential rates are two

[2] William F. Ogburn, *Social Change* (New York, The Viking Press, Inc., 1922).

major principles in the understanding of human behavior; consequently, they are important in the analysis of social problems. We shall soon see how they are important in both the creation of, and in the handling of, social problems.

Cultural Relativity

Social practices are almost infinitely variable. Governments are democratic, republican, oligarchical, or totalitarian; they are elaborate and formal, or they may operate informally under a chief or headman. The means of production may be privately owned and controlled, they may be privately owned and publicly regulated, or there may be substantial public ownership. People may worship one god or many—through fasting, meditation, and self-denial or through feasting, dancing, and orgy. Any of these cultural practices may meet the needs of a given society. This ability of man to devise endless ways of solving group problems stands at the heart of the concept of cultural relativity.

Societies, generally, are ignorant of the principle of cultural relativity. Instead, each society tends to believe that its own ways of doing things are the most logical and proper ways—indeed, that they may be the *only* right and proper ways. The sociologist calls this *ethnocentrism.* He recognizes that ethnocentrism restricts the range of possible solutions that may be found for social problem situations. World-wide perspective on family patterns indicates, for example, that few societies base marriage upon romantic attraction between a man and a woman. The welfare of the larger family unit is often regarded as more important than the whims of the married couple. In such societies, group pressures are brought to bear upon the couple to encourage them to get along amiably with one another. In our own society, high divorce rates are apparently encouraged by the isolation of the young married couple from the guidance of parents and other relatives. Many proposed solutions for high divorce rates in the United States (such as the tightening of divorce laws or requiring premarital sex education) while of possible utility, betray gross ignorance of the fact that high divorce rates may be compatible with other societal goals that they are presumed to threaten.

The concept of cultural relativity implies that *a trait has no meaning by itself; it has meaning only in its cultural setting.* No custom is either "good" or "bad" by itself; it is "good" if it harmonizes with the rest of the culture in which it functions, and "bad" if it clashes with the rest of its culture. Thus, the immolation of the widow upon the funeral pyre of her husband may be "good" in a society which provides no place for widows in its social system. Polyandrous marriage, with several husbands sharing one wife among them, is very practical for a primitive people who *must* keep their population in check or face starvation in their environment. This is the meaning of cultural relativity—every idea or practice must be understood in terms of its relation to the other parts of the culture within which it occurs. This concept helps us to understand some of the stresses within our own society and some of the difficulties in finding agreeable relief from them.

Learned Behavior

The recognition that personality, or behavior, stems largely from the society and culture in which the individual lives is one of man's most important discoveries. Whether one is sad or joyful at the death of a loved one depends on how death is defined by one's culture. Whether one shows his grief by laughing or by crying is culturally defined. In one society, boys are taught to be aggressive and domineering, while, in another society, the male is supposed to be shy and dependent. In the United States, middle-class pupils seek the teacher's approval while lower-class children invite the teacher's censure—both are seeking recognition from their fellow students. Biologically, the human species is one, but human behavior varies strikingly from group to group and from culture to culture.

In the study of social problems, one frequently encounters the argument that proposed changes are undesirable *because* they are contrary to human nature or to the customary ways of doing things. They supposedly will not work because they are new, or different, or "radical." The student who understands the above principles will require more satisfactory evidence than such a priori statements before either accepting or rejecting proposed solutions to social problems.

APPROACHES TO THE STUDY OF SOCIAL PROBLEMS

Due to the tremendous number of, and the involved nature of, social problems, no single approach to their study has proved wholly satisfactory. There are at least three relatively distinct approaches that have proved useful in the study of various problem situations. These three approaches are (1) the social-disorganization approach, (2) the personal-deviation approach, and (3) the conflict-of-values approach. Each of these approaches will be employed in examining the specific social problems treated in Part II of this book.

The Social-Disorganization Approach

All social life occurs in a setting of regulation. The behavior of individuals and groups is controlled through a vast network of "rules" that define which behaviors are permissable, desirable, or mandatory. At the most formal level, that of *law*, the rules are codified, that is, they are written down, and punishments are specified for each violation. Thus the law prohibits the unprovoked killing of another person and specifies death or a long prison term for murderers; the punishment for illegal parking is a small fine; continued unsanitary conditions in a restaurant may lead to its being closed. Most of the "rules" in any society, however, are less formal than laws. They take the form of certain *expectations* about how people will act. We expect the policeman to enforce the law, the mother to love her children, and the worker to get to work on time. Such expectations pervade every aspect of life and operate unobserved —as long as they operate effectively.

This network of socially sanctioned expectations about personal behavior makes up most of what the sociologist calls *social organization*. These expectations are internalized by the members of a society and, except in the face of unexpected or rapid change, ensure the smooth functioning of the society. People usually act as others expect them to act, and moral concepts of "right," "natural," and "good" come to be attached to these customary ways of behaving.

Throughout its history, American society has been monogamous; that is, it has enforced a concept of marriage that permits each man or woman to have no more than one spouse at a time. Monogamy is required by law. In practice, the legal requirements relating to marriage have been supplemented by a whole series of requirements such as the expectation that people will marry as soon as they are old enough to do so; that, once married, they will stay married; that wives will be subservient to their husbands; that they will have children; and that the children will respect and obey their parents. In cases of serious conflict the law has been invoked to determine the degree to which, and the way in which, these expectations should prevail in individual families. But, ordinarily, the informal pressures of public opinion and the expectations of friends and associates have been sufficient to influence people desirably. Enforcement in any direct sense has usually been unnecessary, for people regard the customary way of doing things as being the only right and natural way. They behave according to the rules of society, partly because it never occurs to them to do otherwise, and partly because they tend to be distrustful of that which is new or different.

Not always, though, do rules function efficiently. They are especially vulnerable to breakdown under the influence of social change. People try to adjust to the new conditions by adhering to time-honored ways, but, instead of satisfaction, they reap frustration and unhappiness. The order and predictability of former days are replaced by confusion and chaos. This is the condition of "social disorganization." Note once again the monogamous mores as set forth in the preceding paragraph. This might well be a description of the American pattern of colonial days. Marriages were permanent, stable, and productive unions. The hard task

To put it another way, it is man's ideas that have evolved and changed the world about him. Now, confronted by the lethal radiations of open space and the fantastic speeds of his machines, he has to invent new electronic controls that operate faster than his nerves and he must shield his naked body against atomic radiation by the use of protective metals. Already he is physically antique in this robot world he has created. All that sustains him is that small globe of gray matter through which spin his ever-changing conceptions of the universe. . . .

LOREN C. Eisely, "Was Darwin Wrong About the Human Brain?" *Harper's Magazine*, Vol. 211 (November, 1955), p. 69, by permission.

of farming was aided by the ready manner in which men, women, and children adapted themselves to play the roles designed for them. But conditions have changed considerably since colonial days. Farming as a way of life has largely given way to urban living and mass production. The resulting disorganization of the family is widely regarded as a major social problem. Divorce rates have soared, personal unhappiness presumably is even more widespread, many women want careers *as well as* marriage, parent-child relations are often strained, and some people prefer not to have children. People want to be successful in marriage, but many of the old rules which governed relationships between men and women— which kept women in the home, and which encouraged large families— seem to have broken down. Many private and public agencies now are concerned with the "disorganization" of the family. They see a problem about which something needs to be done. Proposals pour forth ranging from advocating "free love" to demanding stricter divorce laws. Changes in the basic conditions of life have caused a breakdown of traditional rules and have resulted in widespread personal unhappiness.

One of the routes to a competent analysis of social problems is via analysis of the social disorganization that accompanies social change. Whether one is talking about the problems that plague the modern family or the issues that surround racial integration, one needs to understand how the present issues have developed. The social-disorganization approach assumes that, at some time in the past, a problem did not exist or was not recognized. It assumes that a society has once had a fairly stable equilibrium in which practices and supporting values were in harmonious agreement. Then, social change of some kind disrupted this harmonious agreement. Change brought new practices or new conditions in which the old practices no longer worked properly, or new knowledge which made old practices look foolish, or new value-judgments which declared old practices no longer endurable. In the resultant confusion, old rules were both debated and ignored, yet no new rules were generally accepted. Change had *disorganized—disrupted the organization of*—the former system of behavior. Eventually, according to this approach, new rules and practices will develop, a new equilibrium will appear, and will be preserved until disrupted by another round of change.

For example, the development of the trailer, or mobile home, has created some new problems. "Home" normally means a fairly permanent abode enshrined in sentiments and values and embedded in a network of laws, regulations, and tax policies. Within the generation since the mobile home appeared, it has come to house over three million people— more than live in our seven least populous states. The tax laws, sanitary regulations, and other policies developed for conventional homes are not practical for mobile homes and mobile-home courts. Mobile-home dwellers are accused of avoiding their fair share of taxation, of overcrowding local schools and other public facilities, and of depressing real estate values. Many communities have sought to exclude mobile-home residents by legal regulations of various sorts. Yet the mobile-home population is growing constantly. Other communities have sought to revise their tax laws, zoning restrictions, and other regulations affecting housing in such a way as to take into account the different nature of the mobile home. Eventually most communities will come to terms with this new way of living, thus completing the cycle of organization, disorganization through social change, and eventual reorganization. [3]

The assumptions on which the social-disorganization approach is based are considerably modified in actual practice. There are no periods of complete cultural stability separated by cycles of change, for change, disorganization, and re-organization are going on continuously. Yet it is helpful in understanding a particular problem to look for an earlier period of relative stability, out of which the present situation has developed. In Part II of this book many specific social problems will be analyzed. We shall always need to ask "To what extent does this problem stem from social change and social disorganization?" and, "What can the direction of social change tell us about the possible resolution of the problem?"

SPECIFICALLY, IN APPLYING THE SOCIAL-DISORGANIZATION APPROACH TO SOCIAL PROBLEMS, HERE ARE SOME OF THE QUESTIONS WE ASK:

1. *What were the traditional rules and practices?*
2. *What major social changes made them ineffective?*
3. *Which of the old rules have broken down? How completely?*
4. *Is the social change continuing? How fast? In what direction?*

[3] For an incisive analysis of the appearance and public control of mobile-home courts in several California cities, see Edwin M. Lemert, "Is There a Natural History of Social Problems?" *American Sociological Review*, Vol. 16 (April, 1951), pp. 217-223.

5. *Who are the dissatisfied groups? What solutions do they propose?*
6. *How do various proposed solutions fit in with the trend of social change?*
7. *What may become the accepted rules in the future?*

The Personal-Deviation Approach

In employing the social-disorganization approach to social problems, one looks to the rules that have broken down, to the general social change that has accompanied the breakdown, and to the new rules that are emerging. In using the personal-deviation approach, one looks to the motivation and behavior of certain *people* who are influential in causing the problem, in defining its nature, in proposing solutions to the problem or opposing them. These people are deviants whose deviancy is bound up in many ways with social problems. We need to know how personal deviancy develops and what types of personal deviation are frequently involved in social problems.

REASONS FOR PERSONAL DEVIATION. Deviancy does not spring full-blown from germ plasm—at least in the vast majority of cases it does not. Individuals ordinarily become deviant or nondeviant in the process of learning the norms (rules) of their societies. The development of deviancy is literally the development of personality. In the development of deviancy there may be either an inability to follow generally accepted norms or a failure to accept those norms.

Inability to follow generally accepted norms. Some persons are so constituted biologically, emotionally, or socially that they are incapable of adhering consistently to generally accepted standards. They are biologically, emotionally, or socially *deficient.* The socially deficient do not truly violate norms, rather they manifest an inability to learn and to follow the norms. The existence of large numbers of such inadequate persons is, in itself, a social problem.

With the mentally deficient the cause of deviancy is often biological; however, there are several other groups which are totally unable to follow generally accepted norms. Narcotic addicts, alcoholics, and confirmed gamblers, for example, also have little power to alter their deviant patterns. Most of these individuals have internalized society's norms early in life, but they appear, for reasons that are primarily emotional or social, not to have the control over their behavior expected of normal members of society. These deviants constitute social problems, and they also contribute importantly to related problems; for instance, they often require medical treatment or are involved in criminal activities.

Failure to accept generally accepted norms. With alcoholics, drug addicts, and the like there has obviously been a failure in the socialization process. Though many of them have learned the norms and have come

... they are emotional people who throw themselves frantically into a cause—often to make up for some kind of frustration in their private lives. They form the hard core of many religious, nationalist, and revolutionary movements; they have great capacity ... for "enthusiasm, fervent hope, hatred, and intolerance ... blind faith and single-hearted allegiance."

"The Editor's Easy Chair," *Harper's Magazine*, Vol. 212 (March, 1956), p. 22, by permission.

to accept them as bases for judging right behavior from wrong, they cannot follow them. A different sort of deficiency in socialization occurs when a person fails to accept the society's norms in the first place. Some individuals never seem to be able to accept the standards of judgment of the conventional people around them. They never accept the values inherent in fair play, honesty, truthfulness, personal integrity, justice, cooperation, and so on. They remain disposed to lie, to cheat, to defame, to exploit, or even to kill when it suits their purposes to do so. Since they have never accepted society's norms in the first place, their deviant behavior does not produce in them the guilt and shame that would be experienced by more adequately socialized persons. Psychologists use the general term *character disorder* to refer to the variety of symptoms that accompany the failure to develop a normal social conscience. Such people are often deeply involved in social problems. They seek power, wealth, and personal aggrandizement. They may change sides completely on a social issue if it serves their purposes to do so. They care little whether social problems exist or whether they are solved, so long as the existent situation can be used to their own personal advantage.

TYPES OF PERSONAL DEVIATION. The above reasons for personal deviation explain how deviation comes about either through basically unsocializable persons or through failures in the socialization process. When one turns to types of personal deviation one finds both deviation from accepted norms and the existence of deviant subcultures with their own norms.

Deviation from accepted norms. One type of deviation involves a direct, perhaps deliberate, flouting of generally accepted norms. Some Southern whites, for example, condemn the segregation of Negroes, physicians occasionally favor a system of public health insurance, and some wealthy men vote for laws which increase their own taxes. In each instance, such people violate the mores of their own groups and seemingly act contrary to their own best interests. Not all of these people are otherwise maladjusted in their own groups, but many whose deviancy does extend into other areas are deeply involved in the issues to which their deviation "sensitizes" them. Many of them are motivated by extreme personality needs which are neurotic. They are frightened, anxious, insecure people whose interest in particular situations is limited to the satisfaction of their own neurotic needs.

Deviant subcultures. In some cases of personal deviation, cultural factors appear to play a major role. Deviants are frequently thought to be emotionally or socially maladjusted people; many of them are, as we have illustrated above. However, others considered deviant by majority standards may not have rejected the values and demands of *their* associates; they may be deviant precisely because they are well adjusted to the demands of those associates. Much of the criminality common in the slum areas of large cities is of this sort. Though such behavior is condemned by the larger culture, it may be accepted and even expected in the local area. The slum youth may develop a deviant life organization by moving up from petit larceny gangs to hijacking or some other racket as naturally as the middle-class boy moves up from kindergarten through college to a profession. Though the slum youth frequently knows his pattern to be disapproved of by outsiders, they are *outsiders*. Their disapproval may arouse little of the guilt or motivation for change usually assumed to be present in lawbreakers. Wherever there are *subcultures* whose values conflict with those of the larger culture, we may expect to find such patterns of deviant life organization.

Not all subcultures are so universally regarded as deviant as are those of the slums or the underworld. In the preceding section we spoke of Southerners who favor racial integration, physicians who favor compulsory health insurance, and so on. The deviancy in such cases may suggest personality maladjustment or it may indicate simply that these persons have come to identify with other subcultures beyond the ones they apparently belong to—with those of the urban North or of certain labor organizations. In examining personal deviation it is always important to know how the deviation came about and what it means in the life organization of the individual.

IN APPLYING THE PERSONAL-DEVIATION APPROACH TO SOCIAL PROBLEMS, HERE ARE SOME OF THE QUESTIONS WE ASK:

1. *What deviant persons and groups are involved?*
2. *Are deviants, themselves, the problem? Do they help create the problem? How?*
3. *Are the deviants basically maladjusted people? What neurotic needs motivate them?*
4. *What deviant subcultures are involved? What are the norms accepted by these groups?*
5. *What alternatives are there for dealing with the deviants?*

The Value-Conflict Approach

A society's values are its estimates of worth—its preferences and its rejections. A society derives its character from its values whether they be monogamy, democracy, and practicality, or whether they be opposite values, such as polyandry, theocracy, and otherworldliness. Modern societies, moreover, are characterized by diversity and heterogeneity. Rather than *one* set of values each society has *many* sets of values—which results in disagreements about values.

VALUE CONFLICTS HELP PRODUCE SOCIAL PROBLEMS. Value conflicts in modern society help produce social problems in the following two ways. First, they help produce problems through conflicting definitions of desirable social conditions, and, second, they foster moral confusion which encourages personal deviation.

Conflicts over whether problems exist. Many of the most bitter conflicts surrounding social problems arise over whether a given condition is desirable or should be regarded as a problem. Given social conditions do not equally affect all parts of the society. Some groups profit from conditions that produce misery for others. And whether profit or advantage is involved or not, value differences remain that lead to conflicting definitions of social conditions. Prostitution and racial discrimination, for example, are subject to widely conflicting definitions in the United States. Prostitution is denounced from the pulpit, by the medical profession, and by many individuals and groups who deem it a moral threat to the family structure. Others argue that both history and biology amply demonstrate that the sex drive should not be denied. They view prostitution as a necessary evil which provides a temporary solution to sexual frustration. At the same time, some landlords, some tavern owners, and some highly respectable businessmen who want to "entertain" customers find that prostitution is highly profitable. To some, racial discrimination in the United States is a moral blight; to others, it is the inevitable result of inherent differences between the races. Some whites and some Negroes profit more by preserving discrimination than by eliminating it. It is the exception rather than the rule when most groups agree that a given condition represents a problem to be eliminated. A problem is usually compounded because there is no universal acceptance of its existence nor of a definition of its nature.

Value conflicts encourage personal deviation. Not all value conflicts in a society derive from the failure to accept a given condition as a problem. Conflicting values permeate the American social fabric and are internalized within the individual personality during its growth. People are taught that they should be scrupulously honest; at the same time they are taught that it is important to be successful in their occupations.

Yet complete honesty and success are not only *not* the same thing, they are fundamentally incompatible at many points. Similarly, church attendance, a certain humility, and concern with otherworldly things are religious values widely acknowledged in this society. At the same time it is important to amass material goods and to conform to the demands of peers for cocktail parties or for golf on Sunday. One result of conflicts such as these is to create moral confusion in the society which, in turn, encourages personal deviation. [4] Constant exposure to conflicting values may lead to the individual's inability to hold to any values consistently. Such confusion fosters personal irresponsibility; it encourages one to define social problems strictly in terms of personal gain. Such confusion may result in enlarging problem areas due to the desperate efforts of a floundering personality to find certainty and security through pathologically becoming identified with a "cause."

THE NATURAL HISTORY OF SOCIAL PROBLEMS. Value conflicts are involved in the origin, the definition, and the solution of social problems. The late Richard C. Fuller, who was instrumental in developing the value-conflict approach, proposed a regular series of stages which problems pass through in the process of being defined and solved. [5]

Awareness. As indicated in Chapter 1, before any condition becomes a social problem, people must be convinced that the condition is undesirable and that something can be done about it. Typically, conditions which are eventually defined as problems are at first regarded as inevitable or even desirable. At first there are no important conflicts of values. Under the impact of social change, a few people begin to raise questions, to challenge, and to debate. There is agitation for something to be done. Gradually, the awareness first experienced by a few persons or groups spreads to larger segments of the society. In this developing awareness, the social problem (not necessarily the condition defined as the problem) comes into existence.

Policy determination. As awareness of the problem gradually spreads throughout a society, the value conflicts become increasingly sharp and bitter. Solutions and the means of achieving the solutions are discussed. The first agreement comes with regard to what solutions are desirable and possible; then the means of achieving the chosen solutions are debated. Poverty, for example, was at first defined by many groups as natural, inevitable, and even desirable. Eventually, most groups agreed that at least the most serious consequences of poverty should be eliminated. The question then became one of *how* they should be eliminated. We have not progressed much beyond that point even today. Some groups advocate

---

[4] For an aging but classic statement of the value conflicts which permeate American society, see Read Bain, "Our Schizoid Culture," *Sociology and Social Research,* Vol. 19 (January, 1935) pp. 266-276.

[5] Richard C. Fuller and Richard R. Myers, "The Natural History of a Social Problem," *American Sociological Review,* Vol. 6 (June, 1941), pp. 320-328.

slum clearance, others would settle for the establishment of clinics to provide free medical care, while still others hold out for broadening the minimum wage laws. *The emphasis in the policy determination stage shifts from what should be done to how do we do it.*

Reform. As basic solutions and policies for achieving them are decided upon, the problem becomes one of *action.* The remaining questions of policy are likely to be those which lie in the province of experts or specialists entrusted to carry out the will of the people. If slum clearance is to be the answer, ways must be found to control the slum areas and relocate the people who live there. Details of construction have to be worked out. Then, conditions and arrangements for the rent, lease, or sale of the new buildings must be formulated. These are all "technical" problems which the conflicting interest groups generally leave to the experts. *This is the stage of implementation rather than the stage of decision.*

The general logic of this "natural history" is simple enough. Awareness must precede effective discussion of possible solutions, and the debate is apt to crystallize finally into action. It is important to remember, however, that this is a general pattern and an ideal one. Most actual problems will vary from it in greater or lesser degree. In some cases, for example, there are latent or even active conflicts already present in the developing problem area. In other cases, a general awareness of the problem may never develop, especially if it is a local one. In still other cases, legislatures of government agencies may attempt to regulate conditions which are not yet defined as problems by the public. The stages of awareness, policy determination, and reform may be scrambled in order, or even too confused to define clearly. Natural history is a tool for analyzing social problems, but not the analysis itself. [6]

HERE ARE THE QUESTIONS WE ASK IN APPLYING THE CONFLICT-OF-VALUES APPROACH:

1. *What are the values that are in conflict?*
2. *How "deep" is the value conflict?*
3. *What groups in the society hold to each of the competing values? How powerful are they?*
4. *Which values are more consistent with other larger values such as "democracy" and "freedom?"*
5. *What value sacrifices would each solution require?*
6. *Are some problems insoluble at present because of irreconcilable value conflicts?*

---

[6] See Edwin M. Lemert, *op. cit.*, for an example of this point in relation to the mobile home problem.

THE ANALYSIS OF SOCIAL PROBLEMS

Part II of this book analyzes each of a series of current social problems in considerable detail. In each case, the attempt has been to marshal and present the most relevant facts bearing upon the origin and development of the problem, upon its present status as indicated by the findings of scientific research, and upon the various possible lines of future development. These data, when considered in the light of our three approaches, provide a basis for evaluating the already proposed and yet-to-be-proposed solutions to various aspects of problem situations. Rather than advocate given types of solutions the authors try to maintain the role of analysts who foresee and predict certain outcomes according to the policy followed. The student will remember from Chapter 1 that it is consistent with the position of the social science analyst to say, "If these are your values, *then* this solution will work," or that, "This solution which you propose is not consistent with your other basic values," but he generally does not, *as a scientist,* adopt the role of value advocate.

With our present social knowledge it is reasonable to expect that there will be more adequate data available on some problems than on others and that, consequently, more precise and fuller analyses will be possible in some situations than in others. Each problem in Part II is analyzed in terms of its relation to social change and social disorganization, in terms of the deviant behavior patterns involved, and in terms of the conflicts of values among different social groups.

SUMMARY

Social problems are not separate, clear-cut, uncomplicated, readily corrected situations; they are complex phenomena, endlessly interrelated, and difficult to analyze objectively. Their analysis requires that a frame of reference be adopted. Three major approaches—social disorganization, personal deviation, and conflict of values—are used in this book.

The term *social organization* refers to all the organized and customary ways of doing things in a society, and is characterized by order, stability, and predictability of behavior. "Social disorganization," a product of social change, occurs when the customary ways of doing things break down or are no longer adequate. The resulting confusion and disorder are major elements to be considered in analyzing social problems. Analysis begins with a description of the original behavior patterns, traces their breakdown under the influence of social change, and finally moves to the consideration of current proposals for dealing with the situation.

Patterns of social organization and social disorganization have their counterparts in personal behavior. The deviant behavior of individuals is also a factor in social problems. Such deviancy cannot be accounted for solely in terms of institutional maladjustments but must be explained in the context of personality development. In some instances deviant behavior is learned as part of the subculture in which the person participates, while in others it is a product of extreme personality needs that are usually neurotic.

Modern societies show great disagreement within themselves over basic values. These value conflicts create disagreement as to which conditions should be defined as actual problems and encourage moral confusion which leads to personal deviation. There is a kind of natural history in the development of social problems. First, awareness must develop that a given social condition is a problem; second, agreement must be reached as to what should be done about the problem; and, third, this intent must be translated into a program of action or reform.

SUGGESTED READINGS

BROWN, Lawrence G., *Social Pathology* (New York, F. S. Crofts & Co., 1942). An excellent, thorough analysis of the development of personal deviation. Details the influences of heredity, culture, and the unique experiences of the individual.

ELLIOTT, Mabel A., and MERRILL, Francis E., *Social Disorganization,* revised (New York, Harper and Brothers, 1941). A well-established textbook in the field of social problems. Interprets a wide range of problems in terms of the social-disorganization approach.

FULLER, Richard C., "The Problem of Teaching Social Problems," *American Journal of Sociology,* Vol. 44 (November, 1938), pp. 415-435. The original formulation of the conflict-of-values approach to social problems.

———, and MYERS, Richard R., "The Natural History of a Social Problem, *American Sociological Review,* Vol. 6 (June, 1941), pp. 320-328. A fuller exposition of the "natural history" concept of social problems outlined in this chapter.

LEMERT, Edwin, *Social Pathology* (New York, McGraw-Hill Book Company, Inc., 1951). An excellent book on social and personal deviation. For the student with some background in sociology.

LIPSET, Seymour, "The Radical Right: A Problem for American Democracy," *The British Journal of Sociology,* Vol. 6 (June, 1955), pp. 176-209. Though this article stresses ideological change and the ideologies of social groups, it is extremely useful as an illustration of both social change and personal deviation in the creation of social conflict. Intense neurotic needs on the part of members of the radical right is an implicit theme throughout.

OGBURN, William F., *Social Change* (New York, Viking Press, Inc., 1922). An early major treatise stressing the appearance of social disorganization through the process of social change.

QUESTIONS AND PROJECTS

1. Evaluate the statement: "In most cases it is more accurate to speak of *social problem areas* rather than of *the* race problem or *the* crime problem."

2. "Human nature" depends upon the values of one's society as well as upon heredity. Explain.

3. What is meant by the term *cultural relativity?* How is knowledge of the principle of cultural relativity apt to influence one's thinking about social problems?

4. How does the breakdown of rules and customs help to create social problems?

5. How does personal deviation develop? Relate the development of personal deviation to failures in the socialization process.

6. Explain how variability in cultural standards may result in the development of personal deviation.

7. Define the term *values.* How does the multiplicity of values in modern society affect the definition of social problems? the solution of social problems?

8. How do value conflicts encourage personal deviation?

9. Talk to two or three people of the same generation as your grandparents about what family life was like when they were young and what it is like today. Pick out from their discussions what "rules" governing family life seem to have broken down and compare their interpretations of modern family life with your own. Explain how both social disorganization and reorganization occur through social change.

10. Read Margaret Mead's *Sex and Temperament in Three Primitive Societies* and relate its contents and point of view to the nature of human behavior discussed in this chapter. How do you explain the personality differences found among members of these three societies? Relate the principle involved to personality development in modern American culture.

3

The Interpretation of Data

ᵗⱼ

THIS IS THE ONLY SOCIAL PROBLEMS book most students will ever read. Whatever is "learned" about social problems after completing this course will come largely through what is read in newspapers and magazines, heard on the radio, seen on television, and picked up in casual conversations. From these sources one rarely gets an authoritative, objective, and comprehensive analysis of a social problem. Instead he gets bits of gossip, sensational incidents, offhand guesses, wild charges, and various kinds of propaganda. The extent to which one remains intelligently informed about his social world will be largely measured by how skillfully he recognizes and interprets these scraps of social data which come his way. *If this textbook has any enduring value for students, it lies mainly in helping them develop skills in collecting and interpreting the scattered social data which they will continually encounter.*

A certain amount of the social data—the "facts," incidents, charges and countercharges, and so on—which one finds in popular sources is untrue. Other data consist of half-truths, distortions, and exaggerations. And all data need to be related to other data before they have meaning. Therefore, we need to know (1) whether to accept a report as true, and (2) what difference it makes even if it is true.

THE TECHNIQUE OF SUCCESSFUL LYING AS PRACTICED BY TALENTED LIARS

Most people have heard about the laws of libel and slander and have a comfortable feeling that "people wouldn't dare say those things if they weren't true." Accompanying this assurance is the folk belief that "where there's smoke there must be fire," a statement fairly true in a folk society but not necessarily true in a mass society wherein propaganda is practiced like a fine art. There are many ways to plant a lie without running afoul of the laws of libel and slander. [1] A good way to learn how to recognize truth is to discover how liars go about their business. If we know the tricks of the skillful liar, we may be able to detect his half-truths and falsehoods.

1. Lie About a Group

A group cannot sue for libel or slander. A person can sue and under certain circumstances a corporation or organization can sue or prosecute, but an unorganized group of people cannot sue anyone who slanders them. To charge that "John Jones is a robber" would invite a libel suit. But to charge that "the bankers are a bunch of robbers," or "the labor leaders are a bunch of Communists," or "the Jews are a bunch of subversives," is legal in most states. No particular *person* or *organization* has been slandered, so no one can bring a legal action. (Three states now have "group libel" laws, but in the other forty-seven there is still open season.)

2. Lie About a Dead Man

He cannot sue for libel. Neither can his heirs. The death of a public figure often brings forth a rash of scandalous tales, whose publication during his lifetime would have been grounds for libel suits. Some of these stories may be true; others are half-truths or falsehoods.

3. Imply Guilt by Association

This is a modern version of the ancient technique of lying by implication. To say "John Jones is a Communist" would invite a libel suit, but to say "John Jones, who so often follows the Communist party line," is quite safe. (Since the Communist party line has changed and veered so often, there is probably *nobody* who has *not* been in agreement with Communists at some time or other.)

Another way to disparage an individual is to bracket his name with that of several widely distrusted persons. If we say "Joe Doaks, Adolf Hitler, and Joseph Stalin all believed in . . . ," everyone gets the idea that Joe Doaks is not to be trusted. To see just how effectively this device of bracketing names together will color the impression one receives, try comparing the two following hypothetical statements:

Senator Taft, General MacArthur, ex-President Hoover, and many distinguished Americans were highly critical of President Truman's foreign policy.

[1] See Paul R. Ashley, *Say It Safely: Legal Limits in Journalism and Broadcasting* (Seattle, University of Washington Press, 1956), for an explanation of the laws of libel and slander.

Senator Taft, Joseph Stalin, Andrei Vishinsky, and America's enemies throughout the world were highly critical of President Truman's foreign policy.

Another technique is to get the victim before the camera lens next to some disreputable character. If this fails, it is easy with scissors and paste pot to concoct a composite photograph which seems to show the victim surrounded by scalawags. A misleading picture can be worth ten thousand misleading words. Partly by this associative means, suspicions of sympathy for Communism were successfully fastened onto one of the most conservative members of the United States Senate, and a single doctored picture was given much credit for his defeat. [2]

In those instances where two persons are in close *personal* association over some period of time, there is good reason to suspect that they may have had similar ideas. But a purely *verbal* association, in which two people happen to have been on the same side of a particular question at a particular moment, is a very different matter. Consider this syllogism: [3]

> The Pope believes in child-labor laws.
> Khrushchev believes in child-labor laws.
> Therefore, the Pope is a Communist.
> (or)
> Therefore, Khrushchev is a Catholic.

The syllogism works either way. By this weird sort of "logic" one can prove anyone guilty of practically anything.

4. Impute Wicked Motives, Purposes, or Consequences

This is another way to lie by implication. To charge specific *actions* may be dangerous; it is too easy to prove or disprove such charges. Instead, one can be charged with *wishing* to bring about some despicable end. The charge, "Mr. Jones strangled a worker," is too easily checked to be safe unless true; to say, "Mr. Jones wants to starve us workers into submission," is libel-proof, for who can prove in court what Mr. Jones "wants"? So, instead of hearing public charges that "Joe Brown is a Communist," we are more likely to hear that "Joe Brown has aided the

---

[2] *Time* magazine reported, "[Senator] Tydings was up for re-election to a seat he had held since 1926. Franklin Roosevelt in 1938 vainly tried to beat Tydings on the ground that he was too conservative. [Senator] McCarthy, by accusing Tydings of sympathy for Communism, succeeded where Roosevelt had failed. The campaign against Tydings included a faked photograph showing Tydings and Communist Earl Browder cheek by jowl. . . . The Tydings defeat made Joe [McCarthy] a power. If he could successfully smear one of the most conservative and best entrenched Senators, was any man safe from his furious onslaught?" (*Time* [October 22, 1951], pp. 21-22.) For a reproduction of this picture, see *Time* (March 20, 1951), p. 61.

[3] Adapted from Stuart Chase, "Guilt by Association," *New York Times*, October 14, 1951.

Communist cause by . . ." or "Joe Brown expressed the Communist viewpoint in saying. . . ." Such statements are libel-proof ways of implying that Joe Brown is a Communist. *Such inferences may, of course, be entirely true.* The important thing to note is that the mere fact that such statements do not produce libel suits is no *proof* that the charges are true.

5. Use "Weasel" Words

A weasel is a small animal that can wiggle through a tiny opening. "Weasel" words are shrewdly chosen qualifying words that make a statement technically correct but very misleading. Thus the speaker has not actually told a lie; he has just made it easy for you to infer one.

Weasel words abound in advertising. Federal laws forbid the claim that a pill will "cure" an illness unless there is some factual basis for the claim. So the seller must find some way of convincing buyers that it will cure them without actually saying so. He does this by using weasel words which few people will notice or understand. If he says, "Hoakum's Pills will cure your backache," he may be in trouble with the Food and Drug Administration. So he says, "Hoakum's Pills, which have helped so many people . . . ," or "Try Hoakum's Pills and see if you don't feel better!" The television announcer reads, "New Dri-Up is twice as effective as any other deodorant tested," without saying how many others were tested, or how their "effectiveness" was measured. Radio and television announcers who deliver such commercials have developed a technique known as the "throwaway." This consists of sliding over the weasel words and bringing out the others so that the weasel words will not be remembered. One highly successful announcer reports, [4]

Every sponsor has to put some weasel words in his copy that you've got to learn how to handle. Suppose an announcer has to say, "If you use Blank face cream you can hope for a more beautiful complexion." You've got to get that word, "hope" in to keep the lawyers happy, but as much as you can, you'll throw it away.

Occasionally the weasel word is used with a reverse twist. Instead of being an innocent-sounding word which greatly changes the meaning of the statement, the weasel word may be a dreadful-sounding word whose innocent meaning will be missed. For example, a present member of the U.S. Senate was elected after righteously proclaiming to his less sophisticated constitutents that his opponent: [5]

. . . is known all over Washington as a shameless extrovert! Not only that, but this man had to matriculate before he could go to college, and he has a sister who is a Thespian in wicked New York. Worst of all, it is an established fact that Mr. ——, before his marriage, habitually practiced celibacy.

[4] Dick Stark, quoted in *Time*, Vol. 59 (June 16, 1952), p. 72.
[5] See *Time*, Vol. 72 (Sept. 8, 1958), p. 20.

There is no easy way to detect weasel words. Sometimes the qualifying phrases are so obvious that the critical reader cannot miss them, but in other cases some special knowledge is needed to detect them. While an awareness of these verbal pitfalls is helpful, there is no substitute for an intimate and exact knowledge of a subject for spotting the misuse of language.

6. Quote Out of Context

The Bible says, "Let him who stole steal . . ." clearly a subversive doctrine. Of course, if St. Paul's statement is quoted in full, "Let him who stole steal no more" (Ephesians 4:28), the meaning is somewhat changed. By leaving out part of a sentence, or omitting the sentences that precede or follow it, the most innocent remark can be made to sound most damning. For example, in attempting to depict a famous historian as having Communist sympathies, a well-known senator quoted him as saying, "I happen to believe that the Communist party should be granted the freedom of political action and that Communists should be allowed to teach in universities," but the senator did not quote the rest of the sentence—"so long as they do not disqualify themselves by intellectual distortion in the classroom." [6] In this way, by omitting the qualifying words that are attached to a statement, an unscrupulous critic can attribute to his victim damaging remarks he has not made.

Sometimes two separate phrases or sentences are glued together and quoted as a single statement. One supposed "quotation" from Owen Lattimore's writings, cited against him before a senate investigating committee, turned out to be two separate sentences, originally *eleven pages apart*, joined and quoted as a single statement. [7] With scissors and paste pot, a man can appear to have said practically anything!

Equally common is the practice of ignoring the *time* context of one's words or action. During World War II, Charles Lindbergh was attacked and his Americanism questioned because he had accepted a Nazi decoration, although he had received this decoration several years earlier while on a semiofficial mission for our government. Unjustified attacks were also made on the patriotism of many business executives whose firms had exchanged technical information with German firms *before the war*.

Many of us have 20-20 hindsight. As this is written, our wartime leaders are being scolded for not having foreseen that Russia would be troublesome about our access to West Berlin. Tomorrow will bring yet other examples of chastising men for not considering facts which were revealed after their actions. By examining a man's *past* words and actions

[6] *New York Times*, November 2, 1952, p. 84.
[7] Elmer Davis, *But We Were Born Free* (Indianapolis, The Bobbs-Merrill Company, 1952), p. 165.

in the light of *present* knowledge and social attitudes, it is easy to depict practically anyone as either a traitor or a fool. As Sir Winston Churchill, certainly not a pro-Communist, writes in his memoirs: [8]

It is easy, after the Germans are beaten, to condemn those who did their best to hearten the Russian military effort and to keep in harmonious contact with our great ally, who had suffered so frightfully. What would have happened if we had quarrelled with Russia while the Germans still had almost three hundred divisions on the fighting front? Our hopeful assumptions [that Russia would be reasonable] were soon to be falsified. Still, they were the only ones possible at the time.

7. Become a Congressman

This enlarges one's opportunities for libel-free lying. This does *not* imply that most congressmen are liars; on the contrary, the average senator or representative probably compares most favorably with the voters who elect him. But the congressman has an *opportunity* for wild lying such as no ordinary citizen enjoys. Congressmen enjoy "Congressional immunity" which means (among other things) that they cannot be sued for libel or slander because of anything they say on the floor of Congress or in committee proceedings. This limitation is necessary in order to protect a congressman from being sued every time he opens his mouth or being blackmailed into silence by threats of lawsuits. A few congressmen have abused this privilege and have even become notorious for the grave personal accusations they make or hint at with little or no real evidence to support them. The accused persons have absolutely no recourse except to proclaim their innocence and hope that their denial will get as wide publicity as the accusation—but it rarely does.

Once a congressman has made his accusation in Congress or in a committee hearing, it becomes a part of the *Congressional Record* and can be freely reprinted by anybody without fear of libel suits. Consequently, if one wishes to give wide publicity to libel-proof charges against some person or group, he may get a friendly congressman to insert them in the *Congressional Record;* then they can be repeated and reprinted at will and in perfect legal safety.

8. Become a Witness Before a Congressional Committee

Persons who have been maligned cannot sue a witness for any testimony given before a Congressional committee. These committee proceedings become public records, with "Congressional immunity," and can be reprinted at will. Although the witness may be prosecuted for

[8] Sir Winston Churchill, *The Second World War*, Vol. VI, *Triumph and Tragedy* (Boston, Houghton Mifflin Company, 1953), p. 402.

perjury if he lies, this action must be initiated *by the committee, not by the injured victim.* Committees rarely prosecute a "friendly" witness, that is, one who tells them what they want to hear. So although grave charges against persons or groups made before Congressional committees are never successfully refuted, and the accuser is never brought to trial, this does *not* mean that the charges are true. They may be true, half-true, or totally false.

Most Congressional committee work is serious business, in which congressmen conscientiously seek to collect the facts needed to frame effective legislation and discharge their other proper duties. But the power to do this can also be perverted to serve partisan political purposes, pursue a private vendetta, or confuse and distort issues. When this is attempted, truth and fair play are likely to take a beating.

9. Repeat the Lie at Every Opportunity

Hitler argued that the bigger and more preposterous a lie, the more firmly will it be believed, *if it is repeated often enough.* Sometimes it seems as though Hitler were right. An American business executive sadly concedes: [9]

Tell a big lie to millions of people, tell it over and over without bothering about facts or logic, without regard to how preposterous or ridiculous or vicious it sounds at first, and pretty soon it acquires the status of fact with those unhappy people who are not in a position to check the facts.

Pretty soon even the injured and slandered parties, who know better, are panicked into fighting the big lie or negotiating over it, just as if it were the truth.

TESTS OF RELIABILITY IN INTERPRETING DATA

It is clear that many reports cannot be accepted as true. Some are deliberate falsehoods, some are unintentional errors, and some are products of neurotic, irresponsible people who are emotionally unable to distinguish between facts and wishful thinking. Are there any tests or rule-of-thumb ways of evaluating reports and estimating their reliability?

1. Authorship—Who Said it?

Who makes the charge or reports the disturbing facts?

a. Is he an authority on the subject involved? Some people become "authorities" on government, foreign affairs, or practically anything, not through professional training, but through the ingenuity of their press

[9] Philip D. Read, quoted in *The Progressive*, Vol. 15 (October, 1951), p. 8. Mr. Read was Chairman of the Board of Directors of the General Electric Company.

agents. A continuous parade of "diet specialists" collect lecture fees and book royalties without displaying either scientific training or professional experience in dietetics. The counseling field is cluttered with thousands of self-anointed "psychologists,"[10] "counselors," and "human relations experts" who have no professional training in these fields. This misrepresentation is a profitable racket, as long as there are people who do not inquire whether the "authority" is a reputable professional person or a pious fraud.[11]

Many people without college degrees have become recognized authorities through private study and experience, such as Edison, Stefansson, and others. The question is: "Experience makes one an expert in *what?*" The obvious answer is, "Experience makes one an authority in the matter in which he is experienced; in unrelated fields he is not an authority." To repeat such an obvious truth seems unnecessary, were it not that this limitation is so often overlooked. A successful businessman has learned a great deal about the conduct of a business, but his business experience has not necessarily qualified him as an authority on diet, teaching methods, or race relations. The college professor of physics is unlikely to be an authority on the cultural patterning of personality or on the state of competition within the oil industry.

We must also distinguish between the "familiarity with" and "knowledge about" phenomena. A bank cashier who handles millions of dollars does not thereby become an authority on government finance or banking legislation. The girls who bottle pills in a pharmaceutical house have some familiarity with many drugs but have no thorough understanding of their nature or use. A foreman who has bossed many Negro workmen may imagine that he "understands Negroes," when all he really may have learned is how to handle a certain class of Negroes in a particular situation. This may not stop him from speaking confidently on all phases of Negro life. A superficial familiarity with a subject does not make one an authoritative philosopher thereupon.

b. What is the author's known bias? Is the author known to be a liberal, a moderate, or a conservative? Is he an atheist, an agnostic, or a believer? In which faith? *All persons have biases,* but some control them better than others. In interpreting an author's statements, it is helpful to know what his biases are and to know how deeply they color his judgments.

c. Is the author emotionally stable? This is exceedingly important. Most of the extremely violent diatribes against government, against business, against the church, and so on, are the products of neurotic, paranoid,

---

[10] At present, anyone who can spell the word can call himself a "psychologist" and collect fees for his "services"—a situation which reputable psychologists are anxious to correct through appropriate legislation.

[11] See Mrs. Lee R. Steiner, *Where Do People Take Their Troubles?* (New York, International Universities Press, 1945).

MANAGEMENT SAYS

Steelworkers' wages have risen faster than the cost of living.

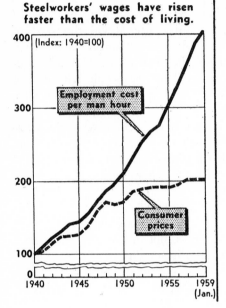

Costs per man hour have surged ahead of output per man hour.

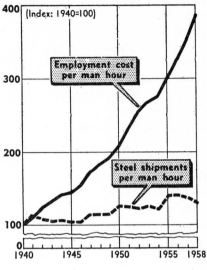

THE UNION SAYS

Price of steel has risen faster than the cost of wages per ton.

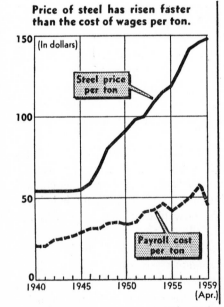

Employe earnings have not risen as fast as profits per man hour.

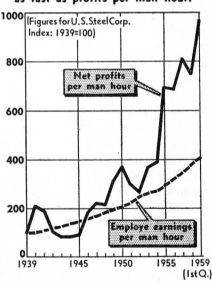

SOURCE: *The New York Times*, June 28, 1959.

FIG. 3–1. Steel wages—too high or too low?
Often the "facts" will support opposite conclusions, for there are many facts in any complex situation, and facts are interpreted according to one's values. Next year, these facts will be different, but will the basic controversy remain?

or otherwise maladjusted personalities. Most extremists, both right-wing and left-wing, are maladjusted people whose bitter attacks stem from their inner emotional problems rather than from the realities of the situations they fret about. [12] Unfortunately, it is not always easy to detect a neurotic personality upon brief acquaintance. Many neurotics are brilliant, engaging people who speak and write convincingly. But when a writer has a reputation for instability—for taking extreme positions, for rapidly changing his story, for changing sides and causes frequently, his claims may be qualified accordingly.

2. Sponsorship—Who Publishes, Distributes, or Sponsors It?

The law generally requires that the publisher of printed material be identified. Reputable publications are unlikely to publish grave charges or shocking reports without making some investigation. An article in the *New York Times* or the *Christian Science Monitor* will be widely accepted by discriminating readers, since these newspapers enjoy an excellent reputation for objectivity, whereas certain other papers are notorious for distorting the news to make it fit their editorial policy. [13] Labor newspapers and trade journals clearly reflect the biases and vested interests of their respective groups; this means that while the *facts* they present will generally be true, the *selection* and *interpretation of* these facts reveals the bias of the publishers.

Sometimes the real sponsor hides behind an apparent, phony sponsor. Certain "labor papers," published by groups of employers, stockholders, or others sympathetic with their interests, have been printed to look like a labor newspaper, so as to be able to criticize union policies more effectively. [14] In political campaigns, it is a common practice for, say, the Democrats to help elect their candidate, Joe Doaks, by organizing a "Republicans-for-Joe-Doaks Committee." If possible, some disgruntled Republicans are rounded up for this committee; if not, a purely "paper" committee is set up as a means of confusing the Republican voters. The Republicans, of course, sometimes use the same tactic by setting up a "Democrats-for-Pete-Zilch Committee."

Sponsors are sometimes stolen without their consent. Communist-front organizations have listed on their "advisory boards" the names of many famous persons who had not given permission for their use. In a recent election, the supporters of one successful candidate for Congress had four pages of flattering news and pictures of him printed in the

[12] See Harold D. Lasswell, *Psychopathology and Politics* (Chicago, University of Chicago Press, 1930); also C. S. Bluemel, *War, Politics, and Insanity* (Denver, The World Press, Inc., 1950); also Eric Hoffer, *The True Believer* (New York, Harper and Brothers, 1951).

[13] See Milton Mayer, "How to Read the *Chicago Tribune*," *Harper's Magazine*, Vol. 198 (April, 1949), pp. 24-35.

[14] Cf. *New York Times Magazine*, November 23, 1952, p. 31.

style of a *Life* article; these inserts were stapled into copies of *Life* and scattered throughout his district. This made it appear that the editors of *Life* had given this candidate a favorable write-up.

Sometimes organizations with similar names have opposing purposes. The *National Education Association* is an organization of educators, whereas the *American Education Association* contains few, if any, teachers and seeks mainly to cut school costs and combat what it views as "radicalism" in the schools. The *American Civil Liberties Union* is composed of people seeking to protect the constitutional rights of all citizens regardless of race, religion, or political belief, whereas the *American Civil Rights Congress* is an organization exploiting civil liberties issues in order to promote communist propaganda. Both communist and fascist organizations invariably hide behind extremely patriotic titles. All organized pressure groups choose impressive titles, dripping with noble words, so it becomes clear that the title of an organization tells little about its purposes. One must know something of the membership and purposes of a sponsoring organization before one can correctly evaluate its publications.

3. Vested Interest—Whose Axe Is Showing?

The vested interest of a spokesman can often be seen peeking between the lines of his arguments. In many attacks upon the "frills" of education the desire to cut school costs is easy to sense, while the vested interests of wealthy people who oppose the "welfare state" are as obvious as are the vested interests of low-income groups who favor it. Of course, it is possible to collect and state facts with complete honesty despite one's vested interest. But in evaluating data we must never forget that the author's selection of data and the interpretation he gives of it are almost inevitably affected by his vested interest.

4. Factual Content—How Specific Is the Author?

Is the report based on established facts or does it consist largely of unproved assumptions, imputed motives, and undocumented accusations? Are the "facts" really facts upon which all qualified observers would agree, or are the "facts" really assumptions and accusations stated as if they were facts? Sometimes a number of people who share the same viewpoint will quote one another's opinions and accusations back and forth until they become accepted as facts. Many crime waves and narcotic drug scares are in this category. One person announces a "crime wave," the next expresses alarm over the "crime wave," a third asks what to do about "the widely-recognized crime wave," and so on until many people accept this "crime wave" as fact.

Is the report filled with vague, sweeping phrases such as "the government honeycombed with subversives," "the thousands of loafers on the public payroll," "monopolistic big business," "needless waste in government," "the Jews getting control of everything," and the like? All such statements are worthless unless accompanied by sufficiently exact, detailed, and complete data to justify them.

5. Verifiability—Can it Be Checked?

Unless one is not only a liar but also a fool, he will be careful about the accuracy of statements which can be checked easily by his audience. The statement that "wages (or profits) doubled last year" could be quite easily checked against the statistics; the statement that "workers today are a bunch of loafers who don't work like they used to" cannot be measured or tested so easily.

The more readily a statement can be checked, the *more likely* it is to be reliable. There is no guarantee that it will always be true, however. The author may make an unintentional error or simply be careless about checking his facts. Or he may lie in the belief that the truth will never catch up with the lie. Yet the general rule is that reliability will vary in direct ratio to verifiability.

6. Relevancy—Do the Data Support the Conclusions?

When confronted by a distressing lack of evidence to prove one's case, an ancient dodge is to prove a different case. A lot of irrelevant evidence can be cited as though it supported the original conclusion. For example, the maker of a well-known mouthwash wishes to promote it as a cold preventative. Since the cold germ has not been isolated and therefore there is no evidence that his mouthwash kills the cold germ, he merely advertises how many millions of other germs his mouthwash kills. Or suppose a propagandist wishes to prove the school responsible for juvenile delinquency. He has no evidence showing that the methods of the school really promote delinquency, so he cites overwhelming statistics documenting the *increase* in delinquency, and many hearers will forget that he has presented no evidence that the school is responsible. Or suppose he wishes to accuse the local relief office of wasting the taxpayers' money. All the evidence shows that the local office is administering the welfare laws efficiently, so he accuses the relief clients of being a bunch of worthless bums—lazy, drunken, and syphilitic—and thus he may convince many people that the local relief officials are criminally incompetent. Fortunately, the test of relevancy can be applied quite easily, merely by asking, how directly are the data related to the conclusions drawn therefrom?

7. Style—Is it Descriptive or Propagandistic?

a. Are the familiar propaganda devices used? Material that employs the standard propaganda devices *may* nevertheless be truthful and accurate, but is still suspect until its exact purposes and content are established. The standard propaganda devices include: [15]

1. *Name-calling*—giving an idea (or person) a bad name, so it will be rejected without examining the evidence—"socialized medicine," "slave labor act," "rich man's tax law," "Communistic idea."
2. *Glittering generality*—associating an idea with noble words which have vague meanings—"The American Way," "sanctity of the home," "the future of America," "patriotic support," "sound program."
3. *Testimonial*—linking a loved or hated person with an idea—"The Jeffersonian principle of . . .", "Washington would be shocked at . . .", "Russia will be happy if . . .", "Our boys overseas pray that . . .", and so forth.
4. *Plain folks*—making one's ideas seem to represent those "of the people." "Your plain Yankee horse sense tells you . . .", "The simple faith of my mother tells me that . . .", "I'm just a simple farm boy, not a corporation lawyer, and . . .".
5. *Card-stacking*—using only those selected facts, true or false, which support one's case. Supporting facts are emphasized, and damaging facts ignored.
6. *Band wagon*—"Everybody's doing it," "Every thinking person now realizes that . . .", "Join the rising tide of protest against . . .", "Unite with that great army of patriotic Americans who . . .".

b. Is the style accusatorial and conspiratorial? Does the material abound in cloak-and-dagger suspense, with a dark plot on every page, and a subversive or a traitor or a bloodsucking capitalist behind every bush? If so, it is probably the work of a crackpot. Dependable, reliable reporting is usually written in sober, precise, and cautious language, and any writing which departs from this should be very critically examined. Of course, a skillful propagandist addressing well-educated minds will assume a dignified style. So, while a melodramatic style suggests unreliability, a sedate style is no guarantee of reliability.

c. Is the style informative or platitudinous and tautological? A platitude is a statement of a truth so obvious as to be inane, such as "Our future lies before us," "The home is the cradle of civilization," or "The race belongs to the swift." Many a speaker's reputation, politician's career, and churchman's eminence rests on the ability to recite old platitudes so eloquently that they sound original and profound. Tautology is the needless repetition of the same idea in other words, such as "audible to the ear," or "visible to the eye." Attributed to Calvin Coolidge are the statements that "When there are not enough jobs for everybody, unemploy-

[15] Adapted from Institute for Propaganda Analysis, *The Fine Art of Propaganda* (New York, Harcourt, Brace & Co., 1939), pp. 23-24.

ment results," and "the cure for unemployment is work." Skillful tautological writing sounds impressive but is devoid of meaning.

   *d. Is the statement cluttered with meaningless words and mystical
expressions?* Father Divine reassures his followers that they "can speak
the words into 'tangibilization' or outer expression 'visibilated,' " [16] and
the Prophet Jones tells Father Divine, "I know that the chassis of your
divine mind has been lubricated with divine lubrimentality." [17] A well-
known promoter of diet fads and dubious food products suddenly recalled
in middle age that he recovered from a usually fatal childhood illness
after eating "green vegetables *saturated with the earthy elements*" (italics
ours). [18] Enigmatic and unprecise prose of this sort is the hallmark of
questionable propaganda.

8. Consistency—Does It Agree with Other Known Facts?

   This is perhaps the most useful test of all, *providing that one knows
the other facts* regarding the matter. Some knowledge of scientific facts
about race should render one immune to most racial propaganda. Those
who express alarm over the rising death rates from cancer and heart disease
might be less disturbed if they realized that these increases are largely
statistical illusions produced by the decline of other death rates. As stated
before, there is no substitute for knowledge in interpreting data.

9. Plausibility—Does It Sound Reasonable?

> How to avoid radar speed traps. Fits all cars. Full instructions en-
> closed. Send $1.00 cash or money order.

   This advertisement appeared in a popular magazine, and some people
were naïve enough to believe that a device which would neutralize a car
against radar waves could actually be made and sold for one dollar. In
return, these people received a small windshield sticker on which was
printed. "WARNING!!! OBEY ALL SPEED LIMITS," and in small print,
"Place in a conspicuous place as a constant reminder." [19]

   Dozens of gadgets are being advertised with careful, weasel-worded
promises to increase gas mileage, boost power, and so on. If they are so
good, why don't auto manufacturers adopt them? Is it reasonable to believe that the inventor can make more by selling them one-at-a-time than
by selling them to car manufacturers?

[16] Quoted in Hadley Cantril, *The Psychology of Social Movements* (New York,
John Wiley & Sons, Inc., 1941), p. 128.
[17] Quoted in *Life* (September 28, 1953), p. 106.
[18] See Spencer Klaw, "Gaylord Hauser, The Blackstrap King," *The Reporter*,
Vol. 4 (March 20, 1951), pp. 31-34. See also *Consumer Reports*, Vol. 16 (February,
1951), p. 86.
[19] See *Motor Trend*, Vol. 10 (March, 1958), p. 6.

The test of plausibility can be made by asking, "If this claim were true, *what else* would be happening?" If Standard Oil had bought up and suppressed a wonderful new gas-saver, would General Motors remain silent? Would not General Motors and Ford be clamoring for a congressional investigation? Would not the Senators from Michigan be making eloquent speeches about public interest? If some of the more colorful toothpaste claims were true, some of the reputable medical organizations would be endorsing them, instead of deflating them with monotonous regularity.

A few years ago, there was a rash of "Negro Bump Day" rumors. People in several cities gravely assured this writer that every Tuesday, Wednesday, or Friday (the tale varied), the Negroes would flock downtown to bump and push white people out of the stores and off the sidewalks. None of the informants *themselves* had been "bumped," but each "knew" of many who had been. If this absurd propaganda had been true, businessmen would have complained, fights and riots would have broken out, police would have arrested hundreds, and a great furore would have resulted.

Many people firmly believe in spiritualism and it is impossible to prove scientifically that there is no communication between the living and the dead. But the "spirits" which the mediums summon insist on appearing only in darkened rooms in prepared quarters and are preoccupied with sighs and groans and tooting trumpets; they present trivial recollections and missing odds and ends, but never locate any important missing documents or have anything of significance to say. Which is more plausible— to accept spiritualism at face value or to conclude that it probably is a pious fraud?

HOW TO LIE WITH STATISTICS[20]

Disraeli once observed that there are three grades of liars—plain liars, d——— liars, and statisticians. This unkind observation springs from the fact that statistics can be manipulated in such a way as to support whatever point of view one wishes. But simply to dismiss statistics as misleading and confusing is pointless, for *statistics mislead and confuse only when one does not know how to interpret them.* There are elaborate statistical formulas for determining the significance and reliability of a statistic, but this text is concerned only with some simple tests which the student can apply.

1. The Underfed Sample

A toothpaste maker breathlessly announces that "scientific tests" prove that his new miracle formula stops tooth decay. The "test" re-

[20] This title, and some of the illustrations which follow, are taken from Darrell Huff, *How To Lie With Statistics* (New York, W. W. Norton & Company, Inc., 1954).

ferred to was conducted on exactly *six* persons. Several small test groups were observed, and all the results were discarded until one of these small groups gave the desired results. Tested in this manner, "scientific proof" can be found for practically anything.

A sample which is *large enough* to rule out chance variations is called an *adequate* sample. It may number from a few hundred to several million, depending upon the rarity of the question under study. A sample is not considered statistically adequate until it is found that the addition of more cases does not alter the percentages established.

2. The Unbalanced Sample

Two pollsters, one at the factory gate and the other at a country club, will report very different findings. A sample is useless unless it is *representative*. This means that each *kind* of person appears in the sample *in the same proportion* that he appears in the total population group under study. One would not get a representative sample by standing on a street corner quizzing passers-by because not all groups will appear on that street at that hour. A student sample collected at fraternity houses and campus hangouts would leave several groups underrepresented. A representative sample of the student body would have the same percentage of freshmen, of males, of science majors, and so on, as found in the entire student body. Occupation, income, education, and, perhaps, religion are very often controlled in order to poll a representative sample.

A very common short cut is the *random* sample, in which, for example, every tenth or every fiftieth name in the telephone book is used. This would give a representative sample of the people in the book, but would not be truly representative of the entire community. If every tenth house in the city is visited, this random sample would also be fairly representative. An *uncontrolled* sample is composed of whomever one comes across, without any system or formula, and is of little value.

All *self-selected* samples are suspect. These are samples in which people become members of the sample through their own actions. Those who attend a particular meeting, read a particular magazine, or write letters on a particular issue are by no means a representative sample of the entire population. California's Governor Brown, in 1960, received thousands of letters urging him, in a ten-to-one ratio, to stay the execution of convicted kidnapper Caryl Chessman; he did so, and promptly found his mail scolding him, by six-to-one, for his action. This does not necessarily show that people are fickle, but that self-selected samples are not representative.

3. The Loaded Base

More women are murdered at home by their husbands than are slain on the street by sexual psychopaths, but this does not prove that women would be safer sleeping on the sidewalks, since there are many more women at home than on dark streets at night. To be comparable, two statistics must have a comparable base. All statistics have some starting point in time or some universe of data on which they are based. A percentage, for example, has no meaning by itself—it is a percentage *of* something. An advertiser's claim that "79 per cent prefer El Faggo cigarettes," has no real meaning as it stands; 79 per cent *of whom* prefer El Faggo *over what?* The fact that women drivers are involved in fewer accidents than men, in proportion to their numbers, in inconclusive; it is not the *number* of women drivers, but the proportion and type of *driving* done by women that is the base against which the percentage of accidents involving women should be compared.

Percentage comparisons can also be misleading when drawn on a very small base. Occasionally one sees a "research" project in which the data consist of a small handful of cases, yet these have been fully anaylzed in terms of percentages and other statistical procedures. A percentage based on two or three dozen cases or informants is not worth much—the base is too small. The same holds true when computing percentage of increase or decrease. The writer knows of a storekeeper who at the close of a year's business showed a net profit of $1.71 for the year; the following year he did little better, clearing $42.34. Since a well-run store of this size was earning about $10,000 a year, to claim that this storekeeper increased his profits by 2476 per cent would be true, but most misleading.

TABLE 3-1. Would an increase of ten percentage points in income tax rates affect everyone alike?

Income Before Taxes	Federal Income Taxes at 1959 tax Rates*	ALL TAX RATES RAISED BY 10 PERCENTAGE POINTS			
		A Taxes at new rates	B Per cent increase in taxes paid	C Income left after taxes	D Per cent drop in income left after taxes
$ 5,000	$ 300	$ 450	50	$ 4,550	3
50,000	18,235	22,885	25	27,115	15
500,000	401,455	450,140	12	49,860	51
5,000,000	4,496,455	4,950,140	11	49,860	90

* Taxes computed for man with wife and three children, using standard deductions.

A percentage of change may be very misleading if the starting point is near zero.

Table 3-1 shows what may happen when a constant percentage is computed on bases of differing size. Suppose that tax revenues were to be increased by adding ten percentage points to the income tax rates on all size incomes. Although such a proposal might have the appearance of "justice," it is clear that it would not impose equal sacrifice upon all groups. Notice particularly how the same set of facts can be used to support opposite conclusions. If one wishes to make this look unfair to the poor man, one will cite the percentages in Column *B*, which show that the "little fellow" has his taxes increased proportionately more than the wealthy person. If one wishes to make this look unfair to the rich man (as it obviously would be), one will cite the percentages in Column *D*, showing how much this tax rate change would reduce the income he had left after taxes. Probably no one has proposed exactly this tax schedule; it is cited purely to illustrate how percentages can be used and misused. Much of the demogoguery in tax debates has made such questionable use of percentages to buttress anguished cries of outrage at such "injustice."

The aircraft industry in 1957 earned profits after taxes at "a whopping 20 per cent" or at "a modest 3 per cent." Both figures are correct, so one may take his choice! Profits ran 3 per cent of sales, and 20 per cent on net assets—total investment in buildings, machines, and so on. Both figures are useful—one for impressing the stockholders and the other for resisting wage demands and tax increases. It makes a difference which base is used.

Often a "loaded" base is chosen because its distortions make good propaganda. For example, the American Tariff League believes in high tariffs, and has used an interesting formula to show that our tariff rates are too low. It measured the "average tariff level" by taking the total value of imports and divided this figure by the customs duties collected. Thus, for 1952, they divided imports of $10,745 million by customs receipts of $575 million, and found an "average tariff level" of 5.3 per cent. By including duty-free imports in the base, the League came up deviously with a misleading set of figures. The purpose of a tariff is to cut down on imports which compete with our own products. A high tariff rate keeps out imports, and therefore results in low customs receipts. If this formula is employed dividing total imports by total customs receipts, it means that the *higher* the tariff rate, the *lower* the "average tariff level." The higher they are, the lower they look! As a propagandist's device, this is hard to beat! [21]

There is an interesting statistical shell game which uses a "wandering"

[21] See "Numbers Racket," *The Reporter*, Vol. 9 (November 24, 1953), p. 4; *New York Times*, July 2, 1952, p. 19; October 23, 1952, p. 47.

base. In this, the propagandist shifts bases in the middle of his argument. Consider this political campaign statement: [22]

When _____ was elected governor in 1942, the minimum teacher's salary in some districts was as low as $900 a year. Today . . . the minimum salaries of teachers in New York City range from $2,500 to $5,325.

This statement shifts the base from "in some districts" to "New York City," thus painting a more glowing picture of achievement. Needless to add, a comparison is valid only if its base remains unchanged throughout the comparison.

THE MOST IMPORTANT THING ABOUT AN AVERAGE IS ITS BASE

TABLE 3-2. Average annual earnings of employees of the Blank Manufacturing Company

MANAGEMENT'S FIGURES

1000 Regular employees @ $5,000		$5,000,000
~~500~~ Trainees and probationary employees @ ~~$2,000~~		
~~500~~ Laid-off and part-time employees @ ~~$1,000~~		
100 Supervisors and foremen @ $8,000		800,000
50 Engineers and technicians @ $13,000		650,000
Bonus payments and overtime pay – $1,600,000		1,600,000
1150	1150 ⌐$8,050,000⌐	$7,000
		Average Earnings

UNION'S FIGURES

1000 Regular employees @ $5,000		$5,000,000
500 Trainees and probationary employees @ $2,000		1,000,000
500 Laid-off and part-time employees @ $1,000		500,000
~~100~~ Supervisors and foremen @ ~~$8,000~~		
~~50~~ Engineers and technicians @ ~~$13,000~~		
~~Bonus~~ payments ~~and~~ overtime pay – ~~$1,600,000~~		
2,000	2,000 ⌐$6,500,000⌐	$3,250
		Average Earnings

Whenever a trend is shown, there must be a starting point. The objective scholar picks a relatively normal or typical year as his base year, while the propagandist tries to find a base year which is particularly helpful for his purpose. For example, if wages [23] and prices are measured

[22] Darrell Huff, *op. cit.*, p. 85.
[23] The problem of accurately comparing wage and price changes is complicated by still other difficulties. *Which* prices shall be included in the price index? Which wages shall be used—wages of *all* wage earners, of *factory* wage earners, or only of *manufacturing production* workers (the one given above)? Shall it be *gross* hourly wages, weekly wages, or "take-home" pay? In deciding which to use, beautiful opportunities for "card-stacking" are presented.

AN AVERAGE TELLS NOTHING ABOUT THE INDIVIDUAL

How To Make $25,000 a Year!

1. Acquire a wife and twelve children
2. Compute the average per capita income (about $1750 in 1957 in the U.S.)
3. Multiply by 14 (you, wife, and 12 children=14; 14× $1750=about $25,000.)

   Adapted from Darrell Huff, *op. cit.*, p. 105.

from 1944 to 1958, wages have risen a modest 20 per cent more than prices; but if 1948 is chosen as the base year, then wages have risen a whopping 153 per cent faster than prices. [24] Most trends show some up and down fluctuations. This makes it possible, by selecting either a peak or a valley as a base year, to show the trend as a sluggish crawl or as a galloping dash, according to one's wishes. This is why, in all comparisons, the base year or starting point must be critically examined. Is it a relatively normal year or a highly abnormal one? Is the base period long enough so that seasonal or annual variations are evened out? Frequently a base period of several years is used in order to get a base which is not distorted by peculiarities of a single year. [25]

4. The Top-Heavy Average

One might say that the average income of his graduating class is $20,000. He might also say that his typical classmate earns about $5,000. Both can be entirely correct, for the "average" is often a top-heavy figure, inflated far above anything which is normal or typical of the group. One could divide last year's baby crop into the number of married women, and find that the average wife had .132 of a baby, which shows that in some cases an average is meaningless. Or one could compute the average height of river vessels in order to decide how high to build a bridge; again, the average is useless. An average is useful only when it is pertinent to the problem.

There are three standard "measures of central tendency." They are

[24] U. S. Bureau of the Census, *Statistical Abstract of the United States: 1958* (Washington, 1958), pp. 227, 332.

[25] For example, the "parity price" formula used to determine federal price supports for farm products is based on a five-year period, 1910-1914. The Bureau of Labor Consumer Price Index was based on prices of selected items for the 1935-1939 period until 1953. Since 1953, the Consumer Price Index has been based on 1947-1949 prices.

computed differently and have different uses. The most common one is the *arithmetic mean*, commonly called "the average," and found by adding all the values and dividing by the number of cases. It is simple to compute, but a few extreme cases can pull this average so high that it is not at all typical. If the graduating class has one millionaire, he pulls the "average" far above what most members earn, which gives a false impression of their wealth. Because of this tendency of the average to become top-heavy, two other measures of central tendency are widely used, and may also occasionally be referred to as "averages." The *mode* is that value in a series which *appears most frequently*, and is, therefore, descriptive of the largest possible number of the cases. The *median* is the *mid-point* in a series of cases, with half the cases above and half below the figure. Both mode and median are easy to compute if the values have been arranged in top-to-bottom order. Finding the value appearing most often will locate the mode, and counting halfway through the series will locate the median.

When a frequency distribution approaches the *normal*, or bell-shaped curve, these three measures come out the same. If the distribution is *skewed*, or lopsided, they diverge, as shown in Table 3-3. Whenever there

TABLE 3-3. Family income in the United States, 1957

Arithmetic Mean—"the average" $5,160
       Total income divided by number of families

Median $4,350
       The middle case—half above and half below

Mode $4,415
       More families at this income than at any other level

SOURCE: *Statistical Abstract of the United States, 1954, pp. 318, 323.*

are a few extreme cases in a series, one knows in advance that the arithmetic mean (or average) will be a misleading figure. The mode and median are coming into increasing use because they give a better picture of normal or typical cases. However, these calculations allow the propagandist some leeway in selecting whatever figures best suit his purposes.

5. The Microscopic Comparison

Several years ago, *Reader's Digest* published some research showing that all popular brands of cigarettes contained about the same amount of tar, and that any differences in tar content between brands were unimportant. A cigarette maker promptly launched a massive advertising campaign on the theme, "——has *less* tar than any other brand." Many people, when it suits their interests, can pump a flood of conclusion from a drop of scientific data. When two groups or cells differ by only a few percentage points, the serious scholar will base no firm conclusions upon a small variation.

6. The Elastic Graph

A graph can be made to distort data somewhat as the mirror in an amusement park makes one look grotesquely fat or incredibly lean. Each graph has two (or three) scales plotted along its axes. For example, time (decades, years, months) may be plotted along the horizontal axis at the bottom edge of a graph, while data (dollars, births, or whatever one wishes to show) are plotted along the vertical axis. Both vertical axes can be used, as in Figure 3 on page 64, where "earnings" are plotted along the left axis and "prices" along the right axis. If the step interval along the vertical axis is great, then a great change will appear as a tiny jog on the graph. By making the step interval very small, a minor change can be blown up into a massive sweep on the graph. The graphs on page 64 show what interesting things can be done by varying the step interval on the scales of a graph. There are many other ways in which graphs and charts can deceive and mislead, but limited space prohibits their description. [26]

This does not mean that the student should dismiss graphs as unreliable, but that he should *study them critically*, to see what they actually show. The student should read the title or heading, study the scales along the axes, and see exactly what is shown and in what way. A graph is a *picture* of a body of data, and the student must determine whether the picture is accurate or deceptive.

7. The Leaning Poll

A complete study of the art of public opinion measurement would fill several volumes. Since public opinion polls are often cited in debates about social problems, students should be able to recognize the more obvious of the pitfalls that impair the accuracy of opinion measurement.

a. *Sampling errors* probably have ruined more opinion polls than any other error. The sample must be adequate and representative, as outlined earlier in this chapter. The first step, therefore, in evaluating any poll, is to take a critical look at the sample.

b. "*Loading the questions*," a second common error, often intentional, means wording them in such a way as to get a desired response. This is done deliberately when the "research" is intended as support for propa-

[26] See Darrell Huff, *op. cit.*, for other examples of graphic deception. For a brief, understandable explanation of various kinds of graphs and charts and their interpretation, see Mary Eleanor Spear, *Charting Statistics* (New York, McGraw-Hill Book Co., 1952).

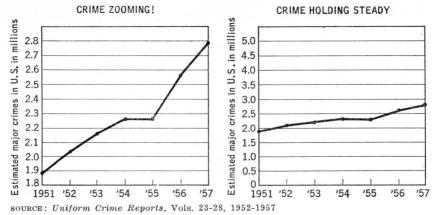

CRIME ZOOMING!

CRIME HOLDING STEADY

SOURCE: *Uniform Crime Reports*, Vols. 23-28, 1952-1957

FIG. 3-2. Is there a crime wave?

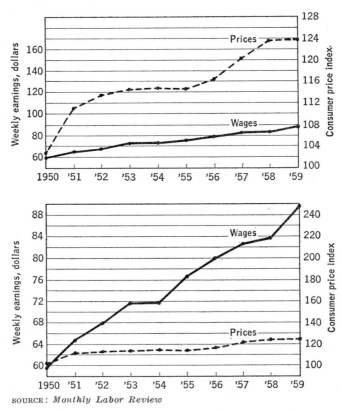

SOURCE: *Monthly Labor Review*

FIG. 3-3. Which rises faster—wages or prices?

ganda but it may also be an unintentional result of carelessness or ignorance. In either case an inaccurate measure is the result. Shortly before the United States entered World War II, one group was polling people on the question, "Should the United States stay out of this foreign war?" while another group was asking, "Would our active participation in this war be preferable to a Nazi domination of Europe?" (approximate quotations). Each question drew an overwhelming majority of "yes" responses, for each was worded so as to invite a positive response.

c. *Limiting of responses.* If responses are to be tabulated, the informants must select one from a series of prepared answers. Among the few answers offered, some persons may find none which suits them. If this happens, the findings of the survey are not valid.

The highly reputable opinion measurement concerns, such as the Gallup Poll, the *Fortune* Survey, or the National Opinion Research Center, generally avoid these errors. Many "opinion surveys" are made by less competent agencies, or are intended to provide support for a publicity campaign, and should be very carefully examined for possible misrepresentation.

8. Statistical Associations and Causation

A favorite method of hunting for "causes" is to hunt for statistical associations. Association, or correlations, [27] have been found between drinking and unemployment, broken homes and juvenile delinquency, smoking and school failures, and many other factors. What does "association" mean?

The first step in evaluating a claimed association (assuming that the statistics themselves appear to be accurate) is to contrast the association with the total universe from which it is drawn. For example, suppose that 50 per cent of the unemployed are "drinkers." This tells us nothing until we know how many of the general population are "drinkers." If 50 per cent of the general population also drink, then there is no true association between drinking and unemployment; whereas if considerably more (or less) of the general population are "drinkers," then an association exists. *We have a genuine association only when the factor we are studying appears much more (or less) often in the observed group than in the general population.* Delinquency is associated with broken homes only if delinquents come from broken homes more often than nondelinquents. Suppose that 50 per cent of the delinquents came from broken homes. If only 25 per cent of *all* children live in broken homes, then there is an association, since the broken homes are contributing more than their

[27] A *statistical association* is a relationship between two pairs of categories, such as drinker-nondrinker and employed-unemployed. A correlation is a statistical measure of degree of association between two sets of quantitative variables, such as amount of education and amount of annual income.

share; but if 50 per cent of all children live in broken homes, then there is no association, since the broken homes are contributing exactly their proportionate share.

This step of contrasting the association with the total universe is one which students often have difficulty in grasping, so some further illustrations are given. The examples in Table 3-4 may clarify the central point, namely, that a genuine association exists *only* when two things appear together *either more frequently or less frequently than would be normally expected.*

TABLE 3-4. When does a percentage indicate a statistical association?

If:	We need to know:	Before trying to decide:
50% of the college girls drink	what per cent of all girls of college age drink	whether college girls drink any more or less than average
25% of fatal accidents involve drinking drivers	what per cent of all cars are driven by drinking drivers	whether drinking drivers contribute more or less than their share of accidents
50% of all cancer victims have a relative or ancestor who had cancer	what per cent of all people also have a relative or ancestor who has had cancer	whether those with cancerous relatives are more likely than average to contract cancer
75% of the delinquent children have fathers who do not go to church	what per cent of all children have fathers who do not go to church	whether paternal church-going is associated with delinquency rates
10% of the relief clients are illiterate	what per cent of all people of similar age are illiterate	whether illiteracy is associated with relief status
20% of the penitentiary inmates are mentally retarded	what per cent of all people of similar age are mentally retarded	whether mental retardation is associated with criminal status
10% of the convicted criminals are foreign-born	what per cent of all persons of similar ages are foreign-born	whether the foreign-born contribute more or less than their share of convicts
40% of the former college athletes die of heart diseases	what per cent of all men die of heart diseases	whether there is any association between athletic activity and heart disease

Above percentages are hypothetical, not authoritative.

Chanticleer, the Cock, crowed each morning and made the sun rise— or so he believed. Cause and effect are easily confused, so when an actual statistical association is found, the next step is to determine which is cause and which is effect. Whenever two factors are associated, there are at least four possibilities:

1. *A* causes *B*.
2. *B* causes *A*.
3. Both *A* and *B* are caused by *C*.
4. *A* and *B* are independent and the "association" is accidental.

To be more specific, consider the well-established association between smoking and poor grades in elementary school. The possibilities include:

1. Smoking among small boys causes poor grades. (It upsets digestion, interferes with mental concentration, and has other ill effects.)
2. Poor grades cause smoking. (Boys who get failing grades smoke to show off, to rebuild ego, and express defiance of school authorities.)
3. Both are caused by a third factor. (Boys who hate school are likely to smoke to express defiance, and get poor grades because they are disinterested; in the lower social class, both early smoking and a disinterest in school are parts of the class culture.)
4. They may be independent variables. (Some boys get poor grades because of limited intelligence and smoke because the gang does.)

This case shows how a statistical association never identifies the cause; it merely states that two factors move together, without indicating why. The difficult question of determining *what causes what* is only begun when a valid association is established.

A coefficient of correlation is a particular kind of measure of association used when associating two or more quantitative variables. For example, if height and weight of a group of people show a coefficient of correlation of +.80, this would mean that in most cases the taller persons are heavier than the short persons. This is called *positive* correlation, for both variables rise or fall together. In *negative* or *inverse* correlation, the two variables move in opposite directions. For example, as people get older, their hearing usually fades; age and hearing acuity, therefore, would show a negative coefficient of correlation, written with a minus sign preceding the coefficient.

How much does a coefficient of correlation mean? A coefficient of less than ±.20 (either positive or negative) is so low as to have scarcely any significance. Those between ±.40 and ±.60 have moderate significance; those between ±.80 and ±1.00 are highly significant. But even a very high correlation between two variables never *proves* that one causes the other; it only suggests that one *may* be the cause of the other and that further study is needed to settle the point.

DEFINITION OF TERMS

The terms *liberal, conservative, radical,* and *reactionary* arise frequently in any discussion of social problems. Since these terms are used in several ways in public discussion, it is well to define them.

As used in this textbook, these terms represent four points along a continuum, with "radical" at one end and "reactionary" at the other, and with "liberal" and "conservative" respectively a little to the left or right of center. The conservative is one who considers the existing society, or status quo, to be quite satisfactory and wishes to preserve it without any great change. The liberal agrees that the existing society is fairly satisfactory, but thinks that quite a number of "improvements" can and should be made. Both agree that *some* "improvements" are desirable, but disagree on the *amount* of improvement and the *kind* of improvement needed. Present American conservatives and liberals agree in supporting a private enterprise system with *some* public ownership and *some* government controls, although the liberals favor *more* public ownership and *different* government controls than do the conservatives. Both approve government expenditure for welfare purposes, but liberals favor further increases in these services, while conservatives hesitate to expand government functions or expenditures. At present, most American liberals favor increased government expenditures for health services, federal aid to education, and conservation of natural resources, and favor federal control of public lands and public development of multiple-purpose river development authorities (like TVA). Most conservatives have far less enthusiasm for such ideas, but favor government economy, less government control over business, and more government control over labor.

Radicals and reactionaries share an intense dislike for the status quo, but disagree in their recommendations. The reactionary (or extreme "right-winger") wishes to return to an earlier, and presumably better, pattern, of social organization. Most American reactionaries would like to return to the sort of relationship between government, business, and labor which existed during the Coolidge, or perhaps the McKinley, administration. Labor unions, the social security system, civil rights legislation, most government welfare services, and practically all other liberal programs are viewed as abominations. The reactionary hates the liberals, distrusts the conservatives, considers the Eisenhower administration almost as "bad" as the Roosevelt and Truman administrations, distrusts democracy, and finds much to admire in fascism.

The radical (or extreme "left-winger") considers the status quo basically repulsive and wishes to replace it with a new social order. He dismisses the conservatives as irrelevant and hates the liberals for trying to improve or patch up the society he wishes to overthrow. Since he wishes to replace and not to reform the society, the policies he is "for" at any given moment are likely to be expedient propaganda rather than genuine objectives. The American radical in the recent past was likely to be either a Communist, a "fellow-traveler," or a "parlor pink." At present, radicalism in America has been forced "underground" to a degree which makes it difficult to locate or to define.

Although these terms may have other acceptable definitions, this is what these terms mean in this volume.

SUMMARY

Data (facts) lead nowhere by themselves; they are quite motionless. Data must be *interpreted* before they have meaning. The first problem is to establish with reasonable certainty if the data are *true*. The popular faith that "they couldn't say those things if there weren't some truth in them" underestimates both the skill of an accomplished liar and the unintended distortion inherent in one's frame of reference. Those who wish to falsify the truth are likely to:

1. Lie about a group.
2. Lie about a dead man.
3. Imply guilt by association.
4. Impute wicked motives, purposes, or consequences.
5. Use "weasel" words.
6. Quote out of context.
7. Find a friendly congressman.
8. Find a friendly witness before a Congressional committee.
9. Repeat the lie until it becomes accepted as fact.

How is a fact to be recognized as authoritative when it is encountered? Among the useful tests for reliability in interpreting data are:

1. Authorship—who said it?
   a. What is his training and competence?
   b. What is his bias?
   c. Is he emotionally stable?
2. Sponsorship—who publishes, distributes, or promotes it?
3. Vested interest—whose axe is showing?
4. Factual content—how specific is the author?
5. Verifiability—can it be checked?
6. Relevancy—do the data support the conclusions?
7. Style—is it descriptive or propagandistic?
8. Consistency—does it agree with other known facts?
9. Plausibility—does it sound reasonable?

In interpreting statistical data, it is easy to employ truthful data to reach false conclusions. Distortion may be suspected whenever a sample is too small to be *adequate,* or too carelessly controlled to be accurately *representative* of the groups and classes of people involved. The *base* upon which a percentage or index number is computed, or which is used as a starting point for a trend or comparison, may be chosen to give a true picture, or may be chosen so as to conceal the truth.

In using averages, the *mean* will always be misleading if based on a lopsided, rather than a normal, distribution, whereas the *mode* or *median* will give a more nearly typical picture. A graph line can be flattened or sharpened by stretching or compressing the scales along the axes, and each graph must be carefully studied for possible distortion. Public opinion polls can be used either to measure or to manufacture public opinion. Sampling errors, loaded questions, or a limited choice of answers may give fallacious results.

Associations and correlations are most useful in suggesting hypotheses and indicating *possible* causes. But an association is significant only when it occurs more often than chance would indicate; therefore, every claimed association between two factors must be checked by asking how often these two factors normally occur together. When it is found that two factors *do* occur together more often (or less often) than can be accounted for by chance, it still remains to be shown whether either one causes the other. Neither association nor correlation proves anything beyond the possibility of causation.

It is no easy adventure upon which the student is invited. The interpretation of data is the most difficult task in social science. It requires a degree of objectivity which not all students have the will or capability to develop; it demands an awareness of the common pitfalls such as those described in this chapter; it requires an accumulation of factual knowledge—a lot of plain, unvarnished, unspectacular, painstakingly acquired facts—without which no intellectual tricks or short cuts will bring that practical understanding of social issues which students presumably desire. Although the study of social problems will never be dull, neither will it be easy. The most difficult task of all will be to recognize and accept the truth when one has found it.

SUGGESTED READINGS

DUNHAM, Barrows, *Man Against Myth* (Boston, Little, Brown & Company, 1947). A critical examination of some of the major myths and intellectual clichés of our time.

EVANS, Bergen, *The Natural History of Nonsense* (New York, Alfred A. Knopf, Inc., 1946). A highly entertaining account of many popular myths and superstitions, which the author demolishes with a rare blend of wit and erudition.

GARDNER, Martin, *Fads and Fallacies in the Name of Science* (New York, Dover Publications, 1957, earlier edition under title, *In the Name of Science*, [New York, G. P. Putnam's Sons, 1952]). An extensive catalog of unscientific and pseudoscientific claims and theories.

GOODE, William J., and HATT, Paul K., *Methods in Social Science* (New York, McGraw-Hill Book Company, 1952). A standard textbook in research methods.

HUFF, Darrell, *How to Lie with Statistics* (New York, W. W. Norton & Company, 1954). A breezy little book on the use and misuse of statistics.

MACDOUGALL, CURTIS D., *Hoaxes* (New York, Dover Publications, 1958; 1st ed., Toronto, The Macmillan Company, 1940). Fakes and frauds in history, science, literature, art, journalism, and politics, engagingly presented and analyzed.

QUESTIONS AND PROJECTS

1. Why not pass a law to prevent the telling of falsehoods and the stating of unjust accusations?

2. Are there any methods, direct or indirect, of telling a lie other than the ones listed in this chapter?

3. How new are these methods of telling lies? Does any group or party monopolize them?

4. Do the people who tell and imply lies believe them themselves? Is most such lying intentional or unintentional?

5. Under what circumstances, if any, is one justified in inferring guilt from association?

6. If Congressional immunity gives a congressman an opportunity for reckless lying, why not abolish Congressional immunity, and hold congressmen accountable under the laws of libel and slander like anyone else?

7. What should be one's first move in reading a serious book or article?

8. Is it safe to assume that any speaker or writer who "takes sides" strongly has a vested interest to defend?

9. Which would require the larger number of people for an adequate sample—a test of a new polio vaccine or a new cold vaccine? Why? How much larger?

10. What is a representative sample? In building a representative sample of your student body, what characteristics would need to be controlled?

11. What are the three measures of central tendency? Which gives the best picture of the typical case? Which may give the least typical picture?

12. What does an association or correlation indicate about causes? Of what use is it?

13. Are you a liberal, conservative, radical, or reactionary? What characteristics identify you as such?

14. On an ordinary week end, about 300 persons are killed in traffic accidents, but on a holiday week end this rises to 400 or more. Is it more dangerous to drive on holiday week ends?

15. One research comparison sought to show that cigarette smoking is harmless by noting that tobacco company employees, who smoke more than the national average, had a death rate one-third lower. Do the data justify the conclusion?

Part **II**

MAJOR SOCIAL PROBLEMS
IN THE UNITED STATES

The sequence of chapters in Part II is unavoidably arbitrary; however, each of the problems treated is a bona fide contemporary American social problem. Some of the problems are traditionally recognized—crime, race relations, and certain aspects of marriage; others have become problems of somewhat general concern more recently—civil liberties, the mass media, and public health. The chapters have been arranged so that the problems judged to be most clearly recognized as such by the student, such as crime, would be studied before the newer and less obvious problems.

4

Vested Interest and Pressure Groups

†††

The N. A. M.'s basic objectives have not changed since McKinley's time—it is today the most important spokesman for manufacturing interests in the country. It has a membership of 18,500 manufacturers whose plants produce more than 80 per cent of American goods and employ more than 75 per cent of American industrial labor. [1]

For a while . . . it looked as if the P. T. A. had a shoo-in proposal. Then the city's Christian Scientists roused themselves in protest. Fluoridation, they insisted, meant enforced medication . . . Seattle's Christian Scientists were joined by the Washington State Council against Fluoridation and a group called the National Nutrition League, Inc. Arrayed against them were the District Dental Society, The Trustees of the King County Medical Society, and a formidable list of other organizations. [2]

The business bloc started with the tariff, before 1800. The labor bloc started soon after the trusts, about 1900. The farm bloc, in its present phase, started with tractors in the 1920's—tractors encourage large-scale commercial farming. It became great and powerful after 1933. Some observers, such as Mr. Kiplinger, think it the smartest, best-turned-out lobby in Washington. [3]

The American Cancer Society, which shares national fund-raisers' love for running their own big campaigns, served a November 1957 ultimatum on 300 . . . local chapters that have joined United Fund-Community Chest drives. The order: get out of combined drives or out of A. C. S. . . . [4]

The C. I. O. leader prepared a 15,000-word statement for the House Labor Committee suggesting removal of practically all major provisions of the present law. "There will be some," said Reuther, "who will say that the sub-

[1] *New York Times*, December 7, 1952.
[2] Reprinted from *Time;* copyright Time, Inc., 1952.
[3] *The Chicago Sun*, February 3, 1945.
[4] Reprinted from *Time;* copyright Time, Inc., 1958.

75

stantial amendments we have proposed amount to actual repeal. To this soft indictment we plead guilty." [5]

Re your brief reference to Governor Adlai E. Stevenson's veto message concerning the notorious anti-cat measure (a bird-lover's bill "to prohibit cats from running at large" in Illinois): I wish to state that the American Feline Society, Inc. played no small part in this legislative battle which could have conceivably cost the lives of 5 million Illinois cats. . . . [6]

"If the peanut program in this country is not basic, there is not one thing in this country that is basic." [7]

EACH OF THE ABOVE QUOTATIONS refers to a special kind of modern group—the pressure group. How many pressure groups are there in the United States? Nobody knows exactly, but the number is already tremendous and constantly increasing.

SPECIAL INTEREST AND PRESSURE GROUPS

Most people believe in a "common good" which everyone should accept and support. People are supposed to play fair and to sacrifice their selfish interests to the welfare of all. Representative government theoretically protects all interests against exploitation by those who would subvert the democratic process. If it worked this way in actual practice, the present chapter need not—indeed, *could* not—be written. The quotations that opened the chapter suggest, however, certain factors that complicate the picture which may change considerably the meaning of "democracy," "fair play," and "proportional representation." We must take into account the existence of "special interest" and "pressure" groups.

Interest Groups

One of the delightful, perplexing, and occasionally frightening things about modern society is its multiplicity of special interests. Some people get deep satisfaction from supporting a symphony orchestra; others form Ricky Nelson fan clubs; some don false mustaches to sing barber-shop-quartet melodies; still others protest against any kind of music being piped into a public transit system or played, for the community's benefit, on church bells. People who could not care less about music may be vitally interested in cats, or peanuts, or local traffic ordinances, or stamp collecting, or right-to-work laws, or in any one of thousands of aspects of modern life.

Most of these people find others with similar interests with whom

[5] *Lafayette Journal and Courier,* March 12, 1953.

[6] Robert Lothar Kendell, President, The American Feline Society, Inc., in *Time,* February 18, 1952, by permission.

[7] Statement attributed to Georgia representative, Elijah Forrester. Reprinted from *Time;* copyright Time, Inc., 1955.

they form an organization. The Philharmonic Society, The Ricky Nelson Fan Club of Chicago, The Society for the Preservation and Encouragement of Barbershop Quartet Singing in America, The American Feline Society, Inc., The Anti-Nicotine League of America, The American Medical Association, The American Legion, The National Association for the Advancement of Colored People, and The National Council for the Prevention of War, the Vine Street P. T. A., and the North Side Neighborhood Association are a few examples of the thousands of special interest groups in American society.

When people band together to further their common interest, they do so theoretically without threatening the interests of other groups. Actually, of course, this is not true. The interests of any group may conflict at many points with the interests of other groups. The interests of the peanutgrowers (who want high prices for peanuts) conflict with the interests of candymakers (who want cheap peanuts to put in their candy bars). And when the American Legion proclaims "Americanism First"—denying the right of individuals to hold unpopular political views—it comes directly into conflict with the American Civil Liberties Union, which seeks to protect the right of individuals to dissent politically and not be persecuted therefor.

Organization into special interest groups is a natural development of life in any complex society. Common interests reflect at least a few shared values, and it is pleasant and profitable to associate with others who share our values. The shared values that encourage comradeship and loyalty within the group, however, may possibly bring it into conflict with other groups. Actual or latent conflict implies that the success of one group in promoting its own interest may have been at the expense of another group's interest. When groups become aware of the possibility, or the necessity, of advancing their interests at the expense of another group's interests, the stage is set for the appearance of pressure groups.

Pressure Groups

When special interest groups actively work to impose their wishes on others, they operate as pressure groups. Pressure groups exist to do exactly what the word *pressure* connotes: to apply strong influence whenever necessary in order to gain their ends.

Perhaps the sharpest examples of pressure group operation are to be found in the field of practical "power politics." Here, pressure groups seek the passage of legislation favorable to themselves, combat unfavorable legislation, and attempt to influence the administration of laws already in existence. Accordingly, they seek the election of particular political candidates, they try to influence the appointment of public officials, they conduct "lobby" operations in local, state, and national capitals, and they conduct extensive "educational" campaigns designed to mold public opinion. Pressure groups are intimately associated with all extensive conflicts of interests in the contemporary scene.

Pressure groups, as well as the special interest groups from which they usually develop, are a natural consequence of the advantages of organization in modern society in which organized power is the most effective kind. Few individuals possess enough power to attain their goals unaided, and the few people who do have such force become still more powerful when they band together. Pressure groups are natural in all areas of activity. The efficient conduct of religious, educational, civic, and business affairs all require organized influence. Pressure groups operate within society's largest enterprises as well as in its most highly specialized and isolated conflicts. This chapter focuses primarily on the operation of pressure groups in a crucial operation in American culture—the economic system.

THE UNIQUE CHARACTER OF PRESSURE GROUPS

Pressure groups, regardless of where they are found, tend to be characterized by: the possession of money, organization, and power; also by the employment of propaganda.

Money, Organization, and Power

The rapid growth of pressure groups in recent decades springs directly from the recognition that small groups, if well organized and financially powerful, can often achieve their interests at the expense of the majority. This is possible because organization makes possible the amassing of capital, especially if the combining interests are moneyed interests to begin with, and the possession of capital enables a group to exert great power over public opinion and eventually over the legislative processes. The group which possesses sufficient capital can pay for radio and television time to present its case to the public. It can also place full-page advertisements in the nation's newspapers or, if it operates shrewdly, it may get its point of view presented on editorial pages, or even on Page One under the guise of being "news" rather than "opinion." It can hire attorneys who give the finest legal advice, consultants of all sorts, and lobbyists to influence the legislators themselves. If it is ruthless enough, it may (and sometimes does) hire thugs and hoodlums to use physical force on those who oppose its plans or interests! In a society dominated by pecuniary values the possessor of wealth (whether an individual or an organization) enjoys strong advantages not shared by the so-called "common man."

The Employment of Propaganda

The operations of pressure groups are generally far more subtle than the open employment of force or the use of financial pressure. It is general knowledge that pressure tends to be most effective when hidden from view, when individuals and groups do not realize they are being pressured but *believe* they are acting in their own best interests. Thus, the fine art of propaganda has become a major pressure group tool. To be successful, the propagandist must, above all, conceal or distort his true motives.

The propagandist denies that he seeks to "indoctrinate"; he insists that he wants to "educate" the public. This clever choice of words is one semantic technique used by the propagandist to sway public opinion. Unless one is sufficiently critical in examining the legitimacy of the use of the terms "indoctrinate" and "educate," it becomes difficult not to accept the propagandist's seemingly logical conclusions. This technique has often been used to oppose liberal education in our nation's schools and colleges. The opponents of liberal education declare that the choice is between "indoctrinating" people with Communism and socialism, or "educating" them to the virtues of capitalism and free enterprise. The possibility of an objective study of the merits and demerits of various economic and political systems is not even considered.

If the student is to guard against manipulation by pressure groups, he must examine some of the other techniques used by them for propaganda purposes. Beyond the general propaganda techniques described in Chapter 3, four such techniques frequently used by pressure groups are: (1) to convince the public that it has the same interests as the pressure group; (2) to soft-pedal its true identity and promote acceptance of its purposes by disguising them; (3) to use emotional, rather than rational, arguments; (4) to employ diversionary tactics to attract attention from the actual issues.

ALLEGED COMMON INTERESTS. Most pressure groups *presume* to speak not only for themselves but for the public at large. Thus, in wage and price disputes, both labor unions and manufacturers' associations claim to represent the public interest against the "narrow selfish interests" of each other. The U. S. Chamber of Commerce has skillfully "sold" slogans to the effect that "a community prospers when its business prospers" and "that which helps business also helps the community." It is true, of course, that there is a correlation between general prosperity and the prosperity of business interests. But equally true is the labor contention that "business prospers when labor prospers." Each group attempts to use the general correlation between the prosperity levels of different segments of the population to demonstrate that anything which helps "its side" automatically aids everyone else at the same time. Thus, from one point of view, a price rise enables the businessman to make a profit which will be reinvested in his business, which provides work for employees who may, in turn, purchase more goods from him. From the other viewpoint, a wage increase enables laborers to buy more goods which results in more profit for businessmen which will be reinvested to produce more jobs and higher wages, and so on.

Both of these arguments obscure the fact that, in the short run at least, the interests of business and labor are by no means synonymous. One group benefits from higher wages, or higher prices, much more immediately and directly than does the other. Modern society is sufficiently complex so that no one pressure group can adequately represent the interests of the entire population. But if a pressure group can *create the illusion* that it is fighting for the interests of all, it has won a marked advantage in the struggle for power.

DISGUISED IDENTITY. Since the arguments of pressure groups tend to be somewhat discounted as the nature and motives of the organizations are revealed, many pressure groups have profited by taking titles which are either ambiguous or which conceal their basic purposes. This technique often succeeds because of ignorance and apathy on the part of the general public. People often make little or no effort to establish the identity and interests of an organization before evaluating its published statements. Pressure groups can be expected to take full advantage of this indifference. Some of the recently formed pressure groups have, without doubt, consciously selected titles which conceal their true identities.

To illustrate the difficulty of accurately assessing the nature of a group from its name consider a few titles which appear frequently in our newspapers. The *American Federation of Labor-Congress of Industrial Organizations* is a respectable labor organization while the *World Federation of Trade Unions* is a tool of Russian policy makers. The *Chamber of Commerce of the United States* is not an official government agency but is a pressure group representing business interests. The *Freedom Forum* also is supported by an impressive array of industrial and business interests, and it serves those interests well in the public forums which it conducts. The *Civil Rights Congress* is listed by the Attorney General as a subversive organization. The *Small Business Economic Foundation, Inc.* follows closely the "big-business" line of the *National Association of Manufacturers*. The student will notice that practically all of these organizations load their titles with words which have a definitely favorable emotional connotation. This emotional appeal warrants further discussion.

EMOTIONAL ARGUMENTS. Pressure groups generally attempt to discourage any critical thought on issues in which they have an interest. Their goal is not to promote analysis of the problem but to induce others

In the Consumer's Interest?

To some extent, the manufacturers of auto polishes may be faced with a problem similar to that of the floor wax people when vinyl tile first came to market. The makers of vinyl tile boasted in their advertising that their product would retain its high gloss without waxing. Now with the new high gloss acrylic, melamine, and like resin finishes for automobiles . . . the same claims of "no waxing necessary" are likely to be made.

In the case of vinyl tile, the floor wax manufacturers won their case hands down. Through the medium of the Chemical Specialties Manufacturers Association, they proved rather conclusively that waxing of vinyl tile is necessary to protect the finish. . . . For auto polishes, the problem might be somewhat more complicated if the carmakers claim "no waxing necessary."

Anticipating that the auto manufacturers who are known for somewhat extravagant advertising claims—probably the understatement of the year—may inadvertently damn waxes and all polishes, we feel the polish people should hop onto this matter now. If the procedure in the case of vinyl tile worked so well, why not follow it in the case of auto polishes?

SOURCE: *Soap and Chemical Specialties*, as quoted in *Consumer Reports*, January 1959, p. 6

to accept the solution which yields maximum benefit for them. One way in which they accomplish this end is by attaching positive word symbols to their own cause and negative ones to that of the opposition. The use of such words as "freedom," "American," "rights," "crusade," and "liberty" in an official title serves, among other things, to encourage outsiders to identify themselves emotionally with an organization and its causes.

Recently, it has become fashionable among some groups to insist that we must return to "basic principles." Whether the complaint is directed toward racketeering in labor unions, influence-peddling in government, federal regulation of prices, or participation in the United Nations, it is cried that we must return to "basic principles." Apparently, the term "principles" refers to those tenets deemed desirable by the pressure group.

Terms such as "socialism," "collectivism," "statism," "Communism," and "bureaucracy," which have acquired unfavorable connotations, are applied indiscriminately to any cause opposed by pressure groups, while those espoused by these interests are identified with "morality," "integrity," and "the American way." It is significant perhaps that at the moment when we are locked in struggle with world Communism, that the term "communism" seems to be devoid of any specific meaning unless the reference is to Russian Communism. Such diverse activities as consumer co-operatives, federal aid to education, school integration, municipal power companies, the United States postal system, and the economic and political theories of Karl Marx have all been called *communist*. This undiscriminating use of the term seriously interferes with our ability to develop any constructive program for dealing with communism as a threat to democracy in our time.

THE RED-HERRING TECHNIQUE. A fourth tactic employed by pressure groups is to divert public attention from vital issues to irrelevant matters. In many instances organized labor has opposed the adoption of labor-saving machinery on the grounds that the resulting products would be inferior and that craftsmanship would be lost. Objective analysis would lead one to suspect that the unions were far more fearful of loss of jobs and income than of the possibility of inferior consumer products— especially since mass production techniques have been instrumental in creating the highest standard of living the world has ever known. But if attention could be concentrated on the possible loss of craftsmanship the unions would have a much stronger case. Similarly, some management groups have sought passage of right-to-work laws [8] that would protect the worker's right "not to join" a union. Regardless of the intrinsic merit of the argument, is it reasonable to assume that management is primarily concerned with the rights of the workers? A union shop contract strengthens a union so that management must bargain with it. If the public was aware of this, it might support the union's desire to maintain its balance of power with management. If management can make it appear that is mainly concerned with the *rights of workers* (to refuse to join unions), then who would disagree with management's conclusion that the union shop is an evil thing? [9]

The four methods discussed above are illustrative of the type and range of techniques employed by pressure groups to propagandize the public into accepting their points of view. This is not, by far, a comprehensive analysis of propaganda techniques, [10] but is intended to stimulate

---

[8] A union shop is one in which the employer by agreement is free to hire nonmembers as well as members of the union but retains nonmembers on the payroll only on condition of their becoming members of the union within a specified time. Right-to-work laws, which have been passed in a number of states, forbid such contracts.

[9] Management is not entirely united in the support of right-to-work laws. Some management officials believe that the union shop stabilizes labor relations and that the open shop drives labor officials to such irresponsible actions as a membership-holding device. See Frederic Myers, *Right To Work in Practice* (New York, Fund For The Republic, Inc., 1959), p. 41.

[10] For a refresher on general propaganda techniques, refer to the discussion in Chapter 3, pp. 43-48.

the student to greater awareness of propaganda patterns, so that he can cope with forces which prevent objective analyses of social problems.

VESTED INTEREST GROUPS

Special interest and pressure groups are not new. They have existed for centuries. What *is* new is the overwhelming number of such groups, the bewildering variety of interests they represent, and the tremendous power that is wielded by some of them. Moreover, some interests have become historically dominant. Some groups have gained enough power that they wish only to consolidate their gains and to prevent any social changes that do not enrich them directly. Such groups, which reap special advantages from the maintenance of the status quo, are called *vested interests*.

A *special interest* group is merely a group of people who share a common interest—bird-watching, hiking, Negro rights, tariff rates—anything! A *vested interest* group is one that benefits in some way from the existing social order in money, power, prestige, and so on. Practically everyone has at least one vested interest. Physicians have a vested interest in the practice of medicine; parents have a vested interest in the local schools; professors of sociology have a vested interest in the curriculum; students acquire a vested interest in the school which may grant their degrees, and so on. Some vested interest groups are well organized and powerful; some are unorganized and virtually powerless.

Are vested interest groups *bad?* This is the same as asking, "Is weather bad?" It is bad when it inconveniences us. Each of us will define a vested interest group as bad when it attacks *our* values or threatens *our* interests. When a vested interest group pursues its own interest, its actions sometimes benefit the public interest and sometimes damage it. When physicians' organizations prevent quacks and untrained people from practicing medicine, both the medical profession and the public are protected from injury. When physicians' organizations oppose mass immunization programs, as they have done in some instances, their action probably benefits the profession, but whether it benefits the community also is debatable.

The true significance of the vested interest concept goes far deeper than appears at first appraisal. This significance derives from the facts that: vested interests owe their position to past social definitions; they have the support of tradition; they usually have a firm basis for wielding power; and they frequently impede social change.

Past Definitions

Vested interests appear whenever a group derives special advantage from the status quo. When our puritan forefathers settled the coasts of

New England they restricted voting rights to male property owners who were church members. Their voting status enabled this group to manage the colonies largely in their own interests and to oppose any changes which would have weakened their position. *A vested interest had been created.* This original definition in the New World, while gradually being modified, has persisted to the present; for example, a substantial proportion of the Negro population is effectively disfranchised by white voters through the use of poll taxes, literacy tests, and other questionable devices. The basis for such obvious, and, occasionally, illegal, discrimination was established by social definitions formulated more than two centuries ago.

To illustrate further, there are, at this time, in the United States, various groups of psychiatrists and clinical psychologists feuding over the right of the latter to receive state licenses to treat emotional illness. From the time of Hippocrates, the professional treatment of bodily pathologies has been limited to accredited physicians. Physicians have had a vested interest in the treatment of disease. Their vested interest in the treatment of bodily pathologies has been defined to include emotional illness and, so far, organizations of psychiatrists (physicians who specialize in emotional disorders) have been fairly successful in frustrating the attempts of psychologists to gain official recognition. However, if the issue were to be decided only on the basis of the nature of emotional illness and of current treatment therefor, the psychiatric position would be considerably weakened. But vested interests have the advantage of favorable *past* definitions, and tradition must be challenged by those who wish to change things.

The Support of Tradition

Ideas of right and wrong, justice and injustice, morality and immorality, are aspects of culture which come to us from the past. Thus, the foundations for our standards of judgment are embedded in the definitions which create vested interests, as discussed above. Not only do these definitions give form to vested interests, but they lend the support of custom and tradition to the maintenance of the advantages thus established. During the first century of this country's existence there was no question of the right of women to vote. The tradition of male authority was so deeply enmeshed in the culture that most *women*, as well as most men, accepted the idea that "woman's place is in the home," and for women to seek a vote was considered ridiculous, presumptuous, unladylike, even immoral. Only after a long and, sometimes, bitter struggle with the tradition-supported male vested interests were women granted full suffrage.

The tradition that supports the right of vested interests to maintain their advantage operates, of course, in concrete as well as abstract ways. Customs and traditions are likely to be supported by law, so an attack upon vested interests is likely to run afoul of the law itself. Agitators may be jailed in accordance with laws that give support to, and are supported by, the vested interests. Furthermore, the legislators who make the laws and the jurists who interpret them tend to favor vested interests against those who challenge them. Negroes in the United States have continuously faced this situation. In almost any altercation between white people and Negroes the law technically and operationally favors the whites. Negroes are jailed and punished on the flimsiest pretexts, while whites are often excused for unprovoked physical assaults on Negro persons. The advantages established by tradition are maintained by present institutions and opinions.

Basis for Wielding Power

The struggle of newborn special interest groups against entrenched vested interests is rendered more difficult because power is traditionally concentrated in the hands of vested interests. On the American scene, holding a financial advantage enables one to "buy" support for his cause. The possessor of wealth may seek to influence the newspaper presentation of an issue by purchasing advertising space, or by withholding advertising if the paper's editorial policy is not "satisfactory." Such coercive measures are not always necessary. The newspaper owners frequently are members of the vested interest groups which seek favorable editorial treatment, since they, too, are employers, businessmen, property owners, and large taxpayers. The theoretical "equal access" which both sides of an issue have to radio and television facilities does not hold when only one side has the necessary means to purchase their use. Concentrated propaganda campaigns involving the use of the mass comunication agencies, the hiring of public halls and speakers, expert legal advice, and preferential treatment under the law are all potent weapons already possessed by vested interests.

Perhaps almost as important as the above is the fact that vested interests are in a better position to mobilize and use effectively the resources they possess. Most vested interest groups are long-established; they usually have formed some sort of organization to further their common goals. They are apt to have formed a "consciousness of kind" which makes it easier for them to join forces when they are threatened from the outside.[11] Conversely, emerging special interest groups are likely to suffer from a

---

[11] For one bit of empiric support for this position concerning the class consciousness of businessmen and labor-union leaders, see Glantz, Oscar, "Class Consciousness and Political Solidarity," *American Sociological Review*, Vol. 23 (August, 1958), pp. 375-383.

lack of "we" feeling, and from the absence of formal machinery with which to implement their ambitions. The consumer movement in the United States is a good example. Although in isolated instances consumer groups have organized concerted campaigns to force prices down, the absence of long-standing common interests among them has frustrated all major attempts at organization.

Opposition to Social Change

Vested interests are often identified with the forces of conservatism and reaction in the community and seldom with those of liberalism and change. Having attained a position of special advantage, these groups attempt to retain that advantage by discouraging any innovation that might weaken it. Among their favorite phrases, therefore, are pleadings for a return to "the good old days" or, more accurately, to the days before the vested interest was seriously challenged. In this way, the psychological tendency for memory to be selective and for past conditions to take on a false golden glow is effectively exploited.

This conservative effect may readily be illustrated in the realm of technology. Time and again vested interests have prevented or delayed the adoption of inventions which were decided improvements over machines already in existence. In relation to the automobile, self-starters, six- and eight-cylinder motors, the "V" engines, four-wheel brakes, low-pressure tires, and automatic transmissions are but a few of the improvements that were accepted only after long periods of delay on the part of automobile manufacturers.[12] The telephone and telegraph companies have sometimes obstructed innovation in the field of communications. Davis, Bredemeier, and Levy report that in 1937 the Federal Communications Commission charged the Bell Telephone System with suppressing thirty-four hundred patents in order to protect itself against competition.[13] Labor history is studded with cases of workers destroying new machines; building codes often exclude new techniques and materials. Examples of the war against change can be found in practically every field of activity.

Vested interests do not always appear as opponents of change, for some changes promise to benefit them. Many proposed social programs are blocked until powerful vested interests redefine their interests and turn from opposition to support. For example, the St. Lawrence Seaway, recommended by every president since Taft, was bitterly opposed by Eastern railroad and shipping interests, while business interests widely viewed it as a wasteful government extravagance. But when the iron ore beds near Lake Superior began to approach exhaustion, the heavy industry

[12] For a fuller development of this general thesis, see Kingsley Davis, Harry C. Bredemeier, and Marion J. Levy, Jr., *Modern American Society* (New York, Rinehart & Company, Inc., 1949), pp. 145-149.
[13] *Ibid.*, p. 148.

. . . natural gas is but one of many targets this year for Washington's corps of 1000 professional lobbyists, most of whom represent business organizations. Whether lobbying helps or hinders the legislative process is a century-old, unsettled question. But there is no doubt that the practice is more widespread than ever. In fact, almost every U. S. citizen is in some way represented or affected by a lobby. The National Association of Letter Carriers is working for higher wages; the Clothespin Manufacturers of America is trying to limit imports of foreign clothespins; the Sioux Indian Tribal Council is demanding compensation for lost agricultural and game land; the American Farm Bureau Federation is pressing the Senate Agriculture Committee to broaden Agriculture Secretary Benson's soil-bank plan. As she has for some fifty years, Miss Alice ("The Little Quakeress") Paul is buttonholing Congressmen in her pursuit of equal rights for women. . . .

of the Great Lakes area was threatened. Improved ocean transport into the Great Lakes area became essential to its industrial survival, and powerful financial and industrial interests swung their support to a project they had long opposed. When Canada threatened to build and control the seaway by herself, shipping and railroad interests decided that American participation was desirable, and the project was approved by Congress. In like manner, when labor unions began bargaining successfully for employer-financed pension plans, employers began to view the federal social security program more favorably. Northern textile manufacturers support increases in the federal minimum wage law when it will protect them from the competition of low-wage Southern competitors. In such fashion, vested interests support changes that enhance their position. The social reformer is most successful when he can persuade a vested interest group to redefine their interests—to discover that the reform will actually benefit *them*—as he will then receive their support.

Special Interests and Vested Interests in Competition

Special interest and vested interest groups continually oppose one another concerning social change. Special interest groups tend to be initiators of action, while vested interest groups are more often opponents of change. Objectively, many advantages are possessed by vested interests. They are protecting what is already theirs by law and custom; they have power, organization and, quite often, the weight of public opinion with them. Yet, the fact that vested interests find it necessary to marshal and employ their resources with ever-increasing skill indicates that the advantages are not completely on their side.

Vested interests compete not only with special interest groups and amorphous, unorganized masses of people who have no particular interests, they also compete with one another. The number of vested interests in the United States, like the number of pressure groups, is unknown but extremely large. Some groups are small and some are huge; some are better organized and more powerful than others. The company which has a contract to supply coal for the boilers of a local institution and the people who manage to get truck traffic routed around their neighborhood, for example, have vested interests that are noncompeting but which bring them into potential conflict with other coal or oil companies and with other neighborhoods. Relief clients and the business community are large and powerful competitive vested interests whose purposes bring them into sharp conflict with many other segments of the community. Recipients of public assistance oppose measures that would interrupt the receipt of, or decrease the amounts of, their monthly checks. Hence, they oppose the enforcement of "need" provisions, economy drives, the opening of welfare rolls to public inspection, and so on. Other vested interests —chambers of commerce, local tax groups, and the like—further their interests by trying to get the welfare rolls cut. Whether the rolls go up or down at any one time often is determined by the relative strength of these and other vested interest groups, such as professional social workers.

The struggles of vested interests must, however, take into account a latent power which is almost always greater than theirs. This is the power of the majority of the people, most of whom are members of various vested interest groups, but who are not immediately interested in a particular conflict. The interest of the quiescent majority may become focused on an issue, and, if it does, its judgment of the worth of the competing vested interest groups may completely shift the balance of power among them. Vested interests compete with each other at times, but they constantly compete—consciously or not—for public support.

Historically, in the United States, the most visible, and one of the most powerful, vested interests was to be found in that segment of the population which is usually referred to simply as "business." The next sections will trace the rise of business as a vested interest and the challenges to that interest that have appeared in recent decades.

BUSINESS: A PRIMARY VESTED INTEREST

In order to understand the role played by business—especially big business—in the current struggle of interest groups we must know something of the historical developments which resulted in the present situation. Briefly, it was the emergence during the eighteenth century of a set of principles concerning the relations of employers to employees and the right of individuals to acquire, hold, and use property which paved the way for business to become a major vested interest.

Free Contract

At the time when business definitions were formulated, industry was still in the handicraft stage and large-scale corporate organization was far in the future. Shops were small; worker and employer worked side by side and talked the same language. Employers and workers had approximately equal bargaining power, so neither could unduly exploit the other. The employer was essential to the workers and the workers were essential to the employer. Each had to bargain with the other. This situation in which buyers and sellers of labor bargained with one another became embodied in the principle of "free contract." The right of workers to seek the best jobs and the best pay they could find and the right of employers to hire them at the lowest wages possible became integral parts of the philosophy of economics and government now known as "laissez faire." Each person was a free agent with the right to enter into any contract. So long as the power wielded by employers and employees was approximately equal, "free contract" did indeed prevail.

Private Property

Owners and workers were free to make the best bargains they could and each claimed the right to hold and to use the fruits of his labors in his own best interest. The acquisition of property was both an end in itself and the means for the acquisition of more property. Thus, the concept of "private property" developed along with that of "free contract." Each worker, through diligence and thrift, might advance himself eventually to the status of owner and/or employer. Then, by paying wages, he would enable others to climb the same ladder. The only restriction placed upon the use of property was that it should not be used to infringe upon the property rights of others. As the doctrine of laissez faire became firmly entrenched in the political and economic life of western European nations, property rights gradually became inviolable. Since property was a means for the acquisition of more property, its permanent possession and free use provided the cornerstone for the growth of modern industry and business.

Born of the twin principles of free contract and private property, business quickly took on the character of a vested interest seeking to maintain intact its parent principles. Further developments were the increased concentration of business power and the separation of ownership from control.

Growth and Concentration

Even before the turn of this century the concentration of business and industrial power had led to the passage of antitrust laws. The Sherman Antitrust Law, 1890, and the Clayton Act, 1914, have been the chief weapons of government in its attempt to prevent the growth of business monopoly. That they did not succeed, however, in preventing the spread of semimonopolistic conditions throughout the American economy is easily established.

Some indication of the amount of industrial concentration in the United States is provided by information compiled by the Temporary National Economic Committee before World War II. This committee found that in the field of transportation and public utilities less than one-twentieth of the total number of corporations owned 93 per cent of the corporate assets. In manufacturing, less than 2 per cent of the corporations owned 66 per cent of the assets. Even in the construction industry and in agriculture, both of which are strongly competitive, the few multimillion-dollar corporations owned over one-fourth of the total corporate assets. The above are not complete monopolies in a strict sense, but neither do they permit free competition. Many industries today are dominated by one, or a few, corporate giants, surrounded in some cases by a number of smaller concerns. The domination of the automobile industry by the "big three," of steel by a few big producers, and the like, are fairly typical of the "bigness" of modern industry.

One of the commercial fields in which consolidation has been occur-

TABLE 4-1. Concentration in American industry

Industry	Per cent of 1947 output accounted for by first four companies
Primary aluminum	100
Electric lamps	92
Locomotives and parts	91
Cigarettes	90
Flat glass	88
Steam engines and turbines	88
Typewriters	79
Soap and glycerine	79
Phonograph records	79
Corn products	77
Sewing machines	77
Tires and inner tubes	77

SOURCE: U. S. Department of Commerce, *Business Report,* December, 1949.

ring rapidly is that of newspaper publication. The number of independent newspapers is growing smaller and smaller and the relatively few papers left are becoming larger and more standardized. One writer estimates that, so far as ownership is concerned, there are approximately one thousand fewer owners now than there were twenty years ago.[14] Over thirty-two hundred newspapers have disappeared from the market, and a single company controls more than three thousand of the remaining ones. Only about one town in eleven in the United States still has competing daily newspapers. Most existing papers depend on one of the two major news services for all but local news and they buy most of their columns from one of the large syndicates. Obviously, bigness extends into the communications field as well as into the more commonly recognized near-monopolies in manufacturing, transportation, and distribution.

Separation of Ownership and Control

An important accompaniment of industrial growth and concentration is the tendency for the control of large corporations to become more and more concentrated in the hands of management officials who own only a small fraction of the corporation stock. Boards of directors and a few important company officials often execute almost complete control over the company, sometimes to the disadvantage of the numerous, heterogeneous, absent stockholders. The significance of this development derives from the fact that the wresting of control from the majority of owners has markedly altered the nature of private property. The purchaser of shares of stock acquires no right to use his property as he sees fit, but surrenders that right to company officers and directors in return for the privilege of receiving dividends. Although, theoretically, directors are elected by the stockholders, they often become a self-perpetuating clique—and the interests of management and stockholders are not completely identical.

More and more actual control of corporations is held by *holding companies*, which are separate corporations that buy up the small fraction of stock needed to control boards of directors. The producing corporation is then forced to pay large shares of its profits to the holding company rather than to its majority stockholders. Occasionally, too, the holding company, because it controls several corporations, may find it advantageous to discourage production in one company in order to benefit the others. Corporation management bitterly opposes any outside regulation of corporations on the grounds that such regulation would violate the rights of private property. It fails to recognize, or finds it expedient to

[14] For the source of these statistics and a fuller treatment of the problem, see Morris Ernst, *The First Freedom* (New York, The Macmillan Co., 1946).

deny, that there has been any alteration in the *nature* of this property itself.

CONTROL OF LIFE CONDITIONS. The rise of great corporations has in another way significantly affected the conditions under which business and industry operate. Following the Industrial Revolution and the appearance of the factory system, the right of "free contract" began to lose some of its original meaning. The worker's freedom of action had been greatly curtailed by the course of events. As industries grew in size, employer and employee ceased to be "equals" in their ability to bargain. Eventually, as a small cog in a vast machine, the worker was subjected to whatever conditions industry imposed on him. His ability to bargain as an individual disappeared along with the individual employer. Once having gained this advantage over the worker, the business world has, typically, sought to retain it. In general, management was, and is, violently opposed to any measures which would give more power to labor groups.

AWAKENING OPPOSITION. There is little question that the course of events till approximately the last decade of the nineteenth century served to favor and strengthen the role of business as a vested interest. It may well be that the last quarter of that century saw business interests at the zenith of their power. The great industrial and financial empires of the Vanderbilts, the Mellons, the Rockefellers, the DuPonts, and the Morgans are all associated with that period. Since then, financial power has been gradually, but steadily, shifting towards favoring other interest groups.

Among the first signs that the validity of the free contract and private property concepts was being questioned seriously was the passage of antitrust legislation by the federal government. The Sherman and Clayton acts, in effect, served notice that other interests, operating through government, had risen to challenge the lofty position of the industrialists. Nor was this the only sign of impending change. At least since 1869, when the Knights of Labor was organized, there had been signs that working groups were actively seeking redress in the balance of power with management. In 1886, the American Federation of Labor appeared on the scene; it was joined by the Congress of Industrial Organizations after 1935. Beginning early in the 1930's, political policies traditionally sympathetic to business interests almost continuously lost ground to the "common man" policies of the New Deal.

Recently a noted American economist advanced the theory that whenever a vested interest arises there are set in motion forces which tend to foster the development of compensatory power in other segments of the population.[15] The appearance of a *countervailing power* in the United States is manifested by the development of the labor movement.

[15] John K. Galbraith, *American Capitalism, The Concept of Countervailing Power* (Boston, Houghton Mifflin Co., 1952).

Let us now examine carefully the status of certain of these newly developed interest groups.

Countervailence: Emergent Vested Interests

BIG GOVERNMENT. The role of the federal government in the clash of special interests and vested interests is twofold: (1) the government, since it represents the people, supports the efforts of emerging interest groups against the established power of vested interests; and (2) the government, itself, which is a big business, has taken on the character of a vested interest.[16]

1. Government efforts to limit the power of industry by means of antitrust legislation have already been mentioned. We might add that such efforts do not end with the passage of legislation; the prosecution of business combinations which practice restraint of trade is regularly carried on by the Department of Justice.

In a more indirect, though not necessarily less effective, fashion, the government offers positive aid to groups attempting to cope with business power. Government support of the rising trade-union movement is a case in point. When the Sherman and Clayton Acts, originally designed to apply to business, were held by judicial interpretation to apply to labor unions also, the Norris-LaGuardia anti-injunction law of 1932 protected the growing unions against this form of restraint. The National Labor Relations Act of 1935 was even more favorable to organized labor and is often credited, by spokesmen for the business world at least, with having given labor a position more desirable than that of industry. It may be that the subsequent passage of the allegedly labor-restrictive Taft-Hartley Law indicates that a new balance of power between business and labor has been achieved and that the government will attempt to preserve that balance. In a similar fashion, the government has favored farmer and consumer groups by giving a special tax status to their co-operatives,[17] thus enabling them to compete with other business.

2. The federal government, in addition to its role as a supporter of emerging interests, is increasingly involved in running its own business. The expansion of its self-operating activities has been accompanied by a tendency for it to become a self-perpetuating and self-aggrandizing agency. It is extremely difficult, even when conscientiously attempted, to eliminate any kind of government service once it has been established. Big government has become a vested interest and business and government

[16] The term, *countervailence*, was coined, but not used systematically, by Galbraith, *ibid.*, p. 118.

[17] The extent of the tax advantage enjoyed by "co-ops" is, itself, a highly controversial matter. Co-ops do not pay corporate income tax, but any other business could avoid this simply by returning their profits to the consumer as co-ops do.

When President Theodore Roosevelt brought his antitrust guns to bear upon J. Pierpont Morgan's Northern Securities Company, Morgan's response was couched in terms that now seem incredibly arrogant. "Send your man to my man," he told the president of the United States, "and they can fix things up."

Nothing was fixed up, however. Northern Securities was, instead, broken up. The kind of power it wielded no longer exists in this country.

This does not mean that there is no place for huge financial institutions. In fact, J. P. Morgan & Company is about to merge with the Guaranty Trust Company because, as the House of Morgan's chairman said, despite its rapid growth since 1940 "our client's requirements for capital have grown even more." The financial giants still serve a purpose, but the operating rules are more in the public interest these days. No one says to the president of the United States, "Send your man to my man."

Editorial, Lafayette *Journal and Courier*, January 1, 1959, p. 6.

---

are engaged in preventing one another from exercising dictatorial control over the lives of the American people.

BIG LABOR. The past two and a half decades have seen organized labor, with the aid of government, join the ranks of the big powers among the vested interests. The number of union members rose from over $3\frac{1}{2}$ million in 1935 to $8\frac{1}{2}$ million in 1940, then to 14 million in 1944. There are now approximately $18\frac{1}{2}$ million trade union members in the United States. The two giants of the labor world, the American Federation of Labor and the Congress of Industrial Organizations have merged at the national level and are now pushing local integration preparatory to embarking on a major drive to gain millions of new members. Moreover, powerful independent unions such as the International Teamster's Union are challenging the supremacy of AFL-CIO. The old stereotype of down-trodden labor hardly fits modern unionism in those parts of the country where unions are firmly established.

Labor now claims the advantages it secured under the National Labor Relations Act of 1935 as inherent rights, while it bitterly opposes the subsequent Taft-Hartley Law as dictatorial, discriminatory, and unjust. Constantly striving to wrest a larger portion of the "profits pie" from business, organized labor is now obviously a vested interest of approximately co-ordinate standing with business and government. In some respects it has ceased to be a disprivileged minority and has become a privileged group with a vested interest in the status quo.

TABLE 4-2. Growth of the federal government

Year	Number of civilian employees in federal government
1929	596,000
1930	611,000
1934	719,000
1935	820,000
1939	969,000
1940	1,078,000
1944	3,337,000
1945	3,569,000
1949	2,101,000
1950	2,081,000
1952	2,612,000
1953	2,567,000
1954	2,424,000
1955	2,402,000
1956	2,415,000

SOURCE: U. S. Bureau of the Census, *Statistical Abstract of the United States: 1958* (Washington), p. 393.

BIG AGRICULTURE.[18] Agriculture is not "big" in the sense that it has 18 million farmers organized into unions as labor does. Nevertheless, over the past few decades, agriculture has become a potent force, demanding its share of the spoils along with business and labor. Agriculture's efforts to gain vested interest status have taken two principal directions. First, co-operative organizations have appeared for the marketing of farm products and the purchase of farm supplies and consumer goods. These co-operatives allow farmers the savings derived from large-scale operation and give them some measure of control over the supply of farm products reaching the market at any given time. The tremendously large numbers of farmers involved and the difficulty of getting all to co-operate, however, have prevented the co-operatives from playing a major role in the development of countervailing power. It is in the second development that the major source of agriculture's power is to be found.

Though such measures were not an innovation, the program of support for farm prices and the establishment of production quotas begun under the New Deal marked the first serious government effort in the United States to help farmers establish a balance of power with industry. Beginning with the Agricultural Adjustment Act of 1933, the government

[18] The discussion in this section and the one following draws heavily upon John K. Galbraith, *ibid.*

Growth of union membership in U. S.

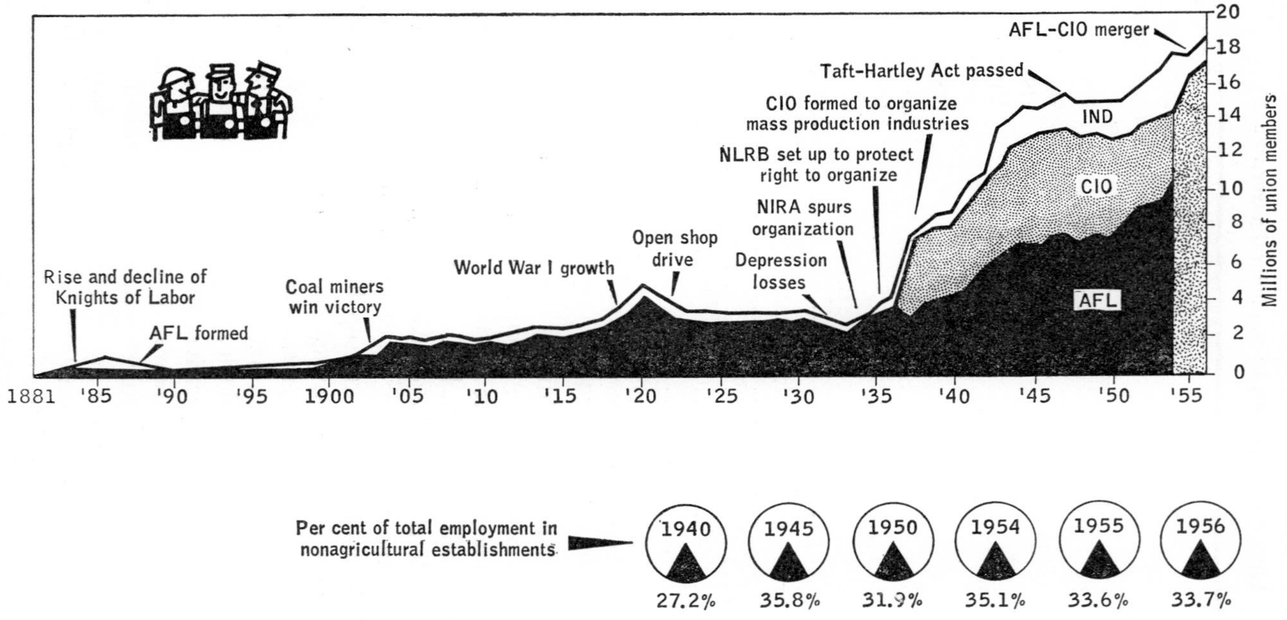

Millions of union members

Rise and decline of Knights of Labor

AFL formed

Coal miners win victory

World War I growth

Open shop drive

NIRA spurs organization

Depression losses

NLRB set up to protect right to organize

CIO formed to organize mass production industries

Taft-Hartley Act passed

AFL-CIO merger

IND

CIO

AFL

1940	1945	1950	1954	1955	1956
27.2%	35.8%	31.9%	35.1%	33.6%	33.7%

Per cent of total employment in nonagricultural establishments

SOURCE: U. S. Bureau of the Census, *Statistical Abstract of the United States* (Washington, D. C., 1958), p. 236

FIG. 4-1.

Clash of Interests and an Appeal to Government for Aid in the Development of Countervailing Power

A serious new conflict is boiling behind the scenes between the American Cancer Society and the cigarette manufacturers over the plans of the society to instruct high school pupils on the dangers of cigarette smoking. . . . Cigarette advertising is being aimed increasingly towards the youth groups—appealing to younger smokers than the cigarette manufacturers have previously dared to address directly. . . .

. . . The American Cancer Society is urging the U. S. Government to co-operate in programming a health approach on smoking that will leave young people free to choose but with an awareness of consequences.

The Wells Newsletter, Vol. 17, December 1, 1958.

has continuously kept "floors" under farm prices and has, itself, drained off excess quantities of various farm products. Government subsidies and payments at present provide about one-half of total farm income. Many people are of the opinion that this is a temporary situation which will disappear "when the time becomes right." Such reasoning ignores two important facts. First, the time was never conceived to be "right" during the past decade, one of the most prosperous periods in American history. Second, and even more important, it is now one of the important functions of government to support the development and maintenance of "countervailing power" against the power of the established interests. Government has aided agriculture in becoming a vested interest and, with the aid of government, a vested interest it apparently will remain.

BIG DISTRIBUTION. Paradoxical though it may seem, certain developments within the business world itself have given rise to a new class of vested interests and have further limited the power of the original business and industry groups. Contrary to general belief, the interests of all large firms are by no means identical. Specifically, there has appeared in the American economy a class of large retailers, for example, the grocery and department store chains, the mail order houses, and the variety store chains, whose primary interest is to obtain goods as cheaply as possible from the manufacturers and then to sell them at low prices to the general public. The very size of these retailers gives them a great deal of power over the manufacturers from whom they buy. The retailers, by threatening to take their business elsewhere or by proposing to set up their own sources of supply, can generally force manufacturer's prices downward. That this situation has resulted in great savings to the consumer can be demonstrated by a stroll through any chain supermarket. Curiously, the function of large retailers in limiting the power of manufacturers is not generally recognized, and there is much sentiment in Congress and in the general public directed toward curtailing the buying power of such organizations. In any event, the chains are a powerful group with which the other vested interests must reckon.

In the preceding sections we have seen how the privileged position allotted to business and industry following the Industrial Revolution has been gradually but surely encroached upon by other emergent vested interests. There is little question that business remains among the most powerful of these vested interests. The weight of tradition, the force of public sentiment, and elaborate protective organization all help to preserve that supremacy. As the government began to challenge industry's domination of the national economy, however, one of its essential functions came to be to aid less powerful groups to buttress their positions against business power. At present, the government itself, organized labor, big agriculture, and big distribution all rank alongside business as important vested interests. Each acts somewhat as a check upon the exercise of power by the others.

THE SOCIAL-DISORGANIZATION APPROACH

The data presented in this chapter are essentially historical data. We have not dealt systematically with current symptoms of the struggles among business, labor, and government, such as labor union racketeering and collusion between business and labor leaders to evade government regulation. We have traced, instead, the significant developments that have led to this situation, so that both present and future forms of these conflicts can be analyzed in perspective. Months or years from now, the details of the conflict will be different. To be interpreted properly they will have to be placed within the larger framework of social change.

The Old Rules

There are really two sets of rules that are important here: one formal and explicit; the other somewhat informal and taken for granted. The United States was founded upon the assumptions that all men should be equal in the sight of the law and that representative government would preserve that equality. These premises are formally embodied in the Constitution, are taught to school children, and are repeated by adults. Yet, even when the United States was founded, a conflicting premise was assumed by the men who wrote the official documents. This premise placed property at the core of society, while government was conceived to occupy merely an auxiliary position. From the production of goods and services, great good presumably was derived—good that was shared equitably (according to worth of the individual's contribution) among all persons. Government could best help the people by aiding the free production and distribution of goods and services, and only harm could follow from governmental action that went beyond, or failed to perform, this proper function.

These assumptions, operating side by side, provided the framework within which industry and business interests became increasingly dominant in American life.

Social Change

The period up to the beginning of the twentieth century brought an extension and consolidation of business power and influence. The economy prospered. The general prosperity was enough to forestall the development of serious value conflicts. There were some challenges to business power, of course, but these were probably more effective in alerting business to the necessity of consolidating its vested interest than in seriously attacking it. By the latter part of the nineteenth century, the position of big business appeared virtually unassailable.

During this entire period, and after it, another significant change had been occurring in politics and economy. Collective action had been discovered by virtually every interest group in the country to be far more effective than individual action. Organized pressure groups increased in number, size, and power. The same form of organization that served business and industry efficiently was created to serve widely diverse interests. The organizational prerequisite for an effective challenge to business power was thus provided.

By the 1880's, the extraordinary power of business was too obvious and too formidable to be ignored. Huge personal fortunes, ruthless use of financial power, and occasional business exposés contributed to a widespread concept of business tyranny. Then, the formal rules set forth in the United States Constitution proved effective and a period of increased regulation of business power began. The government emerged as the primary source of power in the nation and it assisted in the development of countervailing power, particularly in labor unions and in agriculture.

The New Rules

The basic concepts of equality under the law and representative government are as vital today as they ever were. Outwardly, in the Constitution, they appear to be unchanged. Actually, their meaning has been modified through a continuing series of interpretations by the courts. Whereas, formerly, the "rights of individuals" was taken literally and the facts of organized power were ignored (or unknown), today the former is seen increasingly in the context of the latter. Government today seeks to protect the rights of individuals, not alone through the adjudication of personal conflicts, but through maintaining a balance of power among the groups and interests of which the people are members.

The informal rules have changed accordingly. Business and industry are still the core of American society, but they have to share this place with an expanding number of interests. The government, in maintaining the balance of power, has encouraged big labor and big agriculture and has, at least, tolerated big distribution. We might expect, ultimately, that this list of vested interests is not fixed and that others will be added to it.

For many decades one interest group has been struggling for recognition, so far without spectacular success. In the contest of titans in the American economy, the interest that is conspicuously absent is the direct interest of the consumer. Organized labor can guard against many abuses of business power, and business similarly holds the power of organized labor in check. There is nothing in this balance of power, however, to prevent business and labor from co-operating to advance their joint interest in wages and profits at the expense of the consumer. Granted that businessmen and laborers are also consumers, their interests as profit-seekers and as wage earners generally take precedence over their consumer interests. Similarly, the efforts of large distributors to force down manufacturers' prices often work indirectly to the advantage of consumers who, consequently, pay lower prices. When the distributor has consolidated his position, however, the spread between manufacturer's price and retailer's price may become greater. The fact that there are certain indirect protections for the consumer in the competition among interests that are basically opposed to consumer interests is not actually a substitute for an organized, articulate, and powerful consumer movement.

Consumer co-operatives in the United States have a fairly long, but unsuccessful, history. These organizations, which return their profits to their members generally in proportion to the individual purchases made, have not been able to compete with the large retail chains whose efficient operation and abundant resources have often permitted them to undersell the "nonprofit" co-operatives. Until after World War II, co-operatives were about the only significant consumer organizations in the country. The development of a concerted consumer movement in the United States at this point appeared to be improbable.

Following World War II, the consumer movement began to show new signs of vitality. Small scattered groups of consumers organized to protest against inflationary trends in certain consumer prices. Moreover, the general phenomenon of consumer resistance to prices was more widespread than indicated by the organized groups. Conversely, consumer spending appears to have played a significant role in ending ecomic slumps in 1948-49 and again in 1953-54. At times when many experts believed that recessions were apt to be prolonged, consumers, by spending heavily for automobiles, TV sets, and other durable goods, were apparently the most potent force in bringing the recessions to an end. These happenings brought into prominence the potential in consumers' uses of what has been called *discretionary income*. [19]

Until recently, most experts have argued that business investments and government spending were the important factors determining the level of economic activity and that consumers merely responded passively to these influences. The concept of discretionary income implies, however, that large numbers of consumers have significant amounts of income, after basic needs for food, shelter, and clothing have been met, that can be committed to the purchase of goods and services or that can be withheld from the market in the form of savings. How consumers use this income can be a potent force in the total economy.

There is slight evidence both that consumers can stimulate the national economy by widespread spending and that they can slow its expansion by abstaining from purchases if they believe prices to be too high. Economists, university research organizations, and even the U. S. Census are now engaging in attempts to anticipate the future by discovering consumer intentions. Apparently, more than 100,000 United States families subscribe to consumer periodicals which test commercial products and which attempt to advise their readers as to wise patterns of expenditure and saving. It is too early to assert that the consumers are an emerging interest group that will soon challenge business, government, labor, and distribution power, but the possibility does exist. The trend of social change appears to be toward the development of more large vested interests and the consumers' interest may become one of them.

THE VALUE-CONFLICT APPROACH

Major value conflicts between government and business have developed only recently. The potential was always there in the hiatus between the formal ideology that all men should receive equal protection under the law and the informal acceptance of the necessity to favor and encourage business and property. However, not until the latter part of the nineteenth century, when government began seriously to challenge business power and a variety of interests and pressure groups had appeared, did major value conflicts become numerous.

Values began to clash wherever interests competed. Possibly the greatest battle centered around increasing government regulation of

[19] See discussion in *Consumer Reports* (January, 1959), pp. 7-9.

the economy. The basic strife between business and the government has continued and has been augmented by conflicts between government and each new emerging interest. Basically, there appear to be two issues: "Should there be government controls?" and, "If so, in whose interests?"

Should There Be Controls?

This issue is frequently stated as through it were a question either of continuing a set of thoroughly obnoxious controls or of completely freeing the economy from government interference. Such a statement implies that *all* government regulation is "bad" and that the country has nothing to lose if all controls were ended. Even casual reflection will show that this actually is not true.

Government regulation is not new. It is almost as old as the nation itself. The postal system, free public schools, tax-supported universities, and public-utility monopolies are just a few examples of areas where government participation is firmly entrenched and substantially to the advantage of the entire nation. More recently, the regulatory activities of such bodies as the Federal Communications Commission, the Food and Drug Administration, and the Interstate Commerce Commission, all protecting the general public, have received acceptance. In social welfare, the government helps finance unemployment compensation, the United States Employment Service, Aid to the Blind and to Dependent Children, Old Age Assistance, and Old Age and Survivor's Insurance. One should not assume that opponents of government regulation oppose these and all other government aids.

The elimination of *all* government controls would destroy much of what has come to be known as the "American way of life." The opponents of government control really oppose *certain types* of control that they consider harmful to their interests.

In Whose Interests?

Most of the opposition to government regulation of the economy is opposition to *certain types* of regulation *recently instituted* or *threatened* by the federal government. The main conflict is over *which* controls should be strengthened and which ones should be eliminated. The vested interests of business and industry favor one type of controls and emerging vested interests, labor and agriculture, particularly, tend to favor another type of controls.

Neither side really wants a return to a laissez-faire economy. Business generally favors tariff regulations, fast tax write-offs on investments, subsidies to the maritime service, mail subsidies to airlines and railroads, and tax advantages for the holder of corporate stocks. Business is opposed to business taxation, to any tax advantages for co-operatives, to anti-injunction laws, and to the subsidy maintenance of farm prices. On the other hand, labor unions want the government to force management to bargain with the unions and to enter the conflict as mediator whenever an impasse is reached. Labor opposes any limitation on its right to strike, the outlawing of secondary boycotts and jurisdictional disputes, and the right of management to fire union employees without good cause. Farm groups, guarding their interests, look to government to protect the farmer's purchasing power by artificially maintaining parity price levels, by buying up crop surpluses, by limiting the importation of farm commodities from other countries and, at the same time, allowing them to import cheap farm labor from other countries. The basic issue is not whether to have controls, but who should benefit from them.

THE PERSONAL-DEVIATION APPROACH

The broad historical sweep of this chapter indicates that long-term social forces resulted in the government-business controversy, and that the "problem" was not due to the effects of deviant personalities either in the past or in the present. Deviants have not caused this problem and personal deviation is not as relevant to its analysis as either social disorganization or value conflicts. Personal deviation is relevant to the problem in at least two ways, however. First, there are, within each of the major interest groups, extremist minorities who harass their own as well as the opposing interests with their strident demands for a no-holds-barred, no-compromise struggle for complete domination. Second, as in all areas of conflict, there are seriously neurotic persons whose interests in particular outcomes in the struggle for power are secondary to the exercise of their own needs to hate, to blame, to lead, and to bring drama into their frustrated lives.

Extremist Subcultures

Even though their prejudices may clearly favor one or another of the conflicting groups, most people recognize and accept the fact that neither business nor labor nor any other group is apt to gain complete control of the nation's economy. Not all individuals and groups are convinced of this, however.

Using business and labor as examples, it is easy to see that adequate means exist for the perpetuation of subcultures that have their origins in an earlier period. The period when business was completely unchallenged as a vested interest can almost be remembered by some men who are active in business leadership today. In labor unionism the period since inception is even shorter. During this period, each group viewed the opposition as unscrupulous, unprincipled, and immoral scoundrels who must be vanquished at all cost. Gross distortion by both sides is apparent to all who examine the evidence. Not all groups, however, have access to the evidence or are willing to accept it. Some major interest groups have as little communication outside their own organization as any foreign-language-speaking ethnic group isolated within a city. The participation of like-minded people within a small group is more significant in shaping their attitudes and actions than any outside stimuli that impinge upon them.

Such labor union subcultures are apt to point to the "exploitation of the masses" and to urge labor to "fulfill its destiny." They brook no compromises with management—one must be either fanatically prolabor or a traitor to the cause. Comparable business subcultures are intent upon smashing labor unions and reducing the government to the role of hand-maiden to business. They will never settle for the legitimacy of collective bargaining or government regulation; after all, one does not compromise with evil.

These extremist subcultures are generally found today on the margins of special interest group competition. Not only are they rejected by the opposition, they are often rejected by the dominant groups in the factions which they purport to represent. Responsible business and labor leaders know, whether they like it or not, that they must bargain for what they want. The tirades of extremists only stir up animosity and make it more difficult to function. The extremists, sensing their rejection and their ineffectiveness, often become adamant in their refusal to compromise. In time, these extremist subcultures are apt to disappear as their arguments become more and more irrelevant. Until then, they will continue to harass all organized groups.

The Neurotics

Some members of the extremist subcultures described above undoubtedly are neurotics whose emotional quirks feed upon conflict. Most of these subculture members, however, have been normally socialized, but they have been indoctrinated with a different set of norms.

Just as some neurotics are found within deviant subcultures, others are found outside them. Neurotics are always more troublesome than other extremists. Extremists whose convictions are primarily a matter of background, training, and group loyalty may, in the face of continued contrary evidence, be induced to modify their positions somewhat. Extremists whose basic motivations derive from hate, fear, anxiety, or envy, however, can seldom be reasonable on any important point. New evidence does not alter their thinking but tends to force them to even more extreme measures for the defense of their positions. They have no desire to understand issues; they attack irrationally, use emotional labels, and impute questionable motives to the opposition. They play no constructive role in the solution of problems; they are usually to be found intensifying and confusing the issues.

SUMMARY

Pressure groups, which operate in the field of practical power politics, have invaded almost every aspect of American life. Among the propaganda techniques employed by such groups to influence public and governmental opinion are (1) the attempt to convince the public that its interests are identical with those of the pressure group, (2) to soft-pedal its true identity and promote acceptance as something else, (3) to use emotional rather than rational arguments, and (4) to employ diversionary tactics to steer attention away from the important issues. Pressure groups are generally the power instruments of special interest or vested interest groups. Vested interest groups owe their favored position to (1) past definitions, (2) the support of tradition, (3) their firm basis for wielding power, and (4) their opposition to social change.

Big business, traditionally, has been the most powerful of the vested interest groups in the United States. Only within the past few decades has its favored status been seriously challenged. The rise of the giant corporation, however, greatly altered the nature of the "free contract" and "private property" definitions on which the vested interest of business was based, and it is, therefore, losing some of its power to other groups. At least four other groups have attained the status of major vested interests: the federal government, organized labor, big agriculture, and big distribution. At present, these five giants act to checkmate one another in the conflict for power. Considerable disagreement and conflict exists about the role government should play in the struggles among powerful vested interest groups. The problem is further complicated by extremists whose motivations often derive from their own personal inadequacies.

SUGGESTED READINGS

BLAISDELL, Donald C., *Government Under Pressure*, Public Affairs Pamphlet No. 67 (New York, Public Affairs Committee, Inc., 1946). Describes pressure group operations resulting from the concentration of economic power in business and industry. A brief and lucid treatment.

Consumer Reports, published monthly by Consumers Union of the United States, Inc., Mount Vernon, New York. Consumers Union is a nonprofit organization devoted to testing and reporting upon the characteristics of a great variety of commercial products. *Consumer Reports* also contains frequent articles designed to educate consumers to all of their varied interests as consumers.

DAVIS, Kingsley, BREDEMEIER, Harry C., and LEVY, Marion J., Jr., *Modern American Society* (New York, Rinehart & Company, 1949). An excellent book of readings in the area of social problems. See, especially, Part III,

"The Economic Framework." Excellent discussion of impediments to technological change.

GALBRAITH, John K., *American Capitalism, The Concept of Countervailing
Power* (Boston, Houghton-Mifflin Company, 1952). A nontechnical discus-
sion of the development of countervailing power in various segments of
United States economy. A novel formulation by a noted economist.

LYNCH, David, *The Concentration of Economic Power* (New York, Columbia
University Press, 1946). Comprehensive account of concentration in United
States economy during the pre-World War II period. Based on hearings
before the Temporary National Economic Committee.

MILLS, C. Wright, and SCHNEIDER, Helen, *The New Men of Power: America's
Labor Leaders* (New York, Harcourt, Brace, and Company, 1948). Penetrating analysis of the personalities and philosophies of crucial figures in the
vanguard of the American labor movement.

VEBLEN, Thorstein B., *The Vested Interests* (New York, Viking Press, Inc.,
1933). An integrated series of lectures detailing the developing discrepancy
between the definitions underlying the business management of industry
and the conditions engendered by the material conditions under which
modern industry operates.

WARNER, W. Lloyd, and ABEGGLEN, James C., *Big Business Leaders in America*
(New York, Harper and Brothers, 1955). Deals with the origins, education,
occupational mobility, and marriages of 8000 business leaders. Presents
social mobility of business leaders in generally favorable light but contains
considerable discussion of deviation in their personalities.

AUDIO-VISUAL AIDS

1. "America's Biggest Business," United States Rubber Co., Advertising Dept.,
   1230 Sixth Ave., New York, 20, 1946, 18 minutes, sound, black and white.
   $50, free loan. An overview of the farming industry showing reasons for its
   comeback after the depression years. Tells of the importance of education,
   particularly in university extension courses, which helped bring this about.
   Shows the farm as a market for rubber products.

2. "Battle of Wall Street," Workers Education Bureau, American Federation
   of Labor, 1525 "H" Street, N. W., Washington 5, D. C., 1949, 20 minutes,
   sound, black and white, rent $3.00. Produced by the Seafarers International
   Union, Atlantic and Gulf District. The story of the thirty-two-day strike
   of the employees of the New York Stock and Curb Exchanges. Emphasizes
   the role of the militant Seafarers Union which swelled the picket lines
   and organized food and literature dispersals. Documents press coverage and
   police action.

3. "Capitalism," Coronet Films, Coronet Building, Chicago 1, 1948, 10 minutes,
   sound, black and white. $50. Introduces such important aspects of the capi-
   talistic system as private property, profit, competition, free contract and free
   enterprise. The students on a high school radio forum then present conflicting opinions as each tells what capitalism means to him.

4. "Pressure Groups," Encyclopaedia Britannica Films, Inc., 1150 Wilmette
   Ave., Wilmette, Ill., 1952, 20 minutes, sound, black and white. $85, rent $4.50.
   Explains what pressure groups are and reveals that, when democratically

used, they are a necessary instrument for making decisions in a democracy. Illustrates methods used by a representative democratic pressure group to bring about legislation for a desirable civic project. Contrasts these methods with the underhanded and behind-the-scenes manipulation employed by a group attempting to prevent the passage of a bill.

QUESTIONS AND PROJECTS

1. Define the terms, *pressure group, special interest group, and vested interest group.*

2. What vested interests are you as college students majoring in a special field of study now acquiring?

3. Name and illustrate at least three techniques commonly used by pressure groups to disseminate propaganda to the general public.

4. Interpret the statement that "Vested interests tend to admire the past."

5. How were the doctrines of "free contract" and "private property" instrumental in creating a vested interest group of business and industry?"

6. Discuss two important changes in the economic system which served to encourage opposition to complete business freedom.

7. What is meant by the concept of "countervailing power"? What group or organization in the United States has played the most active role in the development of countervailing power?

8. Discuss the proposition that "Government control is not new, and it is not likely to disappear."

9. How does the possession of capital by pressure groups make their efforts more successful?

10. Discuss the proposition that organized labor has become a vested interest.

11. What role or roles do extremists play in the struggle of interest groups to acquire countervailing power?

12. Select from your local newspaper an issue upon which there is considerable public debate and gather the arguments which each side is using to support its position. Subject these arguments to critical analysis in terms of what you have learned about propaganda and the distortion of facts. What techniques are being used by each side in the struggle? Try to arrive at an objective picture of the issue and test the accuracy of each side's position against that objective view.

13. Interview some man of your acquaintance who is in business for himself concerning his attitudes about private property. Note the particular kind of private property he talks about, whether it is land, buildings, merchandise, or corporate stock. Would his arguments apply equally to all kinds of private property? Is he aware that there are important differences among the various kinds of property?

14. Now, interview an acquaintance who is known to be definitely pro-labor. How does he see the conflict of interest between labor and business? Are the assumptions that he makes about business and labor appropriate to the 1960's or to some earlier period? Does he recognize that labor is a vested interest?

5

Crime and Delinquency:
Definition and Classification

ᚦᚦᚦ

Reported crime has been growing four or five times as fast as the popula-tion in the United States during the decade of the 1950's. [1]

Livingston County has started a crackdown on teen-age cigarette smokers. (Michigan) State statute makes it illegal for anyone under twenty-one years of age to smoke or use tobacco in public places. "That's the law and we'll enforce it," said Sheriff Lawrence Gehringer. [2]

Whistling underwater is against the law in the state of Vermont. An Arkansas law provides that school teachers who bob their hair will not get a raise. A Montgomery, Alabama, ordinance forbids sitting on garbage cans. In Iowa a kiss lasting more than five minutes is against the law. [3]

The State of Mississippi in 1958 collected over $23 million in taxes on liquor sales, which are absolutely forbidden by Mississippi law. [4]

In Toledo, onetime Conscientious Objector Charles Cline, 30, who had served two years in a federal prison in Michigan for refusing to shoulder a gun, was given one to three years in Ohio Penitentiary for carrying a concealed weapon. [5]

A salesman was arrested in Medicine Lodge, Kansas, for burglarizing busi-ness places, although he sold them burglar insurance in order to quiet his own scruples of conscience. [6]

New York police arrested fifty-five-year-old Mrs. Beatrice Kam for pos-session of narcotics, and then jailed her son, Herbert, 33, despite her protests.

[1] *Uniform Crime Reports*, various dates.

[2] Associated Press, March 13, 1959.

[3] From "It's the Law," *American Magazine* (April, 1954), p. 72; (October, 1954), p. 133; (December, 1954), p. 126; (January, 1955), p. 119.

[4] *New York Times*, April 12, 1959, p. 55.

[5] *Time*, Vol. 59 (March 17, 1952), p. 12.

[6] *New York Times*, November 23, 1952, p. 54.

"Herbert," said his mother, "is a good son. He never brought me anything but the pure stuff." [7]

In Cedar Rapids, Iowa, a thirteen-year-old who enjoyed leafing through the encyclopedia, was turned over to juvenile authorities after the discovery that he had assembled two-by-fours, a box, and a sharpened steel plate to make a small but serviceable guillotine. [8]

The public seems to be concerned about prison riots only when riots occur—and then wonders why riots occur. [9]

Text accompanying a cartoon: "Before you read this note from teacher, Pop, will you tell me again about the time you put limburger cheese in the school's hot-air register?"

AT FIRST READING, THIS SERIES of items may seem flippant and trivial. Yet each is significant, for each touches upon a different aspect of the crime problem. The first item shows that the crime rate is soaring; the second reflects our confusion over what acts should be termed "criminal"; the third calls attention to the obsolete and foolish laws that clutter up our law books; the fourth shows how our lack of agreement on values results in illogical governmental action; the fifth shows how it is often the *conditions* surrounding the act, not the act itself, which determine whether one is a criminal or a hero; the sixth illustrates one form of the popular practice of "playing both ends against the middle"; the seventh indicates something of the value system of the professional criminal; the eighth shows how education can be used for acceptable or for antisocial purposes; the ninth reminds us that popular indifference is one of the reasons for crime; the last item suggests one of the many ways in which our culture encourages delinquent behavior.

NATURE OF THE CRIME PROBLEM

Definition: What Is "Crime"?

Whenever something impresses us as being dreadful, we say, "Isn't it a crime!" To call any shocking or socially injurious happening a "crime" reveals the popular rather than the scientific use of the term. In technical usage, *a crime is any violation of the law*. Since there are thousands of laws, there are a variety of ways to become a criminal. Some laws define quite harmless acts as crimes. There are so many foolish and obsolete laws that everyone unconsciously violates them indiscriminately; it has been estimated that the average urban citizen violates

[7] *Time*, Vol. 58 (November, 5, 1951), p. 26.
[8] *Time*, 70 (July 29, 1957), p. 84.
[9] W. A. Buckanan, warden of Eddyville, Kentucky, prison, in *New York Times*, October 12, 1952, p. 35.

enough of these laws every day to warrant imprisonment for five years and a fine of nearly $3000. [10]

Meanwhile, many acts which are highly injurious to society are technically legal. If one is quite careful how he does it, it is entirely legal to defraud widows and orphans of their savings, to sell useless and harmful medicines to people who may die unless they find competent medical treatment, to destroy people's self-confidence and mental efficiency by frightening them with a host of imaginary or unlikely ailments, to reduce

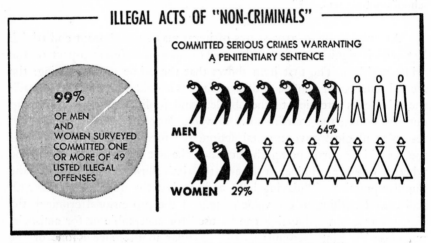

SOURCE: Based on a study reported in *Federal Probation* (April, 1947).

FIG. 5–1. If all criminals were convicted, where would we put them?

the American standard of living by encouraging premature obsolescence through the promotion of endless style changes—these and many other activities fall within the law although they take advantage of people's ignorance, gullibility, and defenselessness. To kill a person by selling him a useless nostrum when he needs medical treatment is legal if done carefully, but to sell him this useless junk for a nickel less than the official "fair-trade" price is a crime in forty-five states. [11]

Although it is the intent of the lawmakers (most of the time) to

[10] See L. M. Hussey, "Twenty-four Hours of a Lawbreaker," *Harper's Magazine*, Vol. 160 (March, 1930). pp. 436-439.

[11] "Last June, Charles Hawkins, owner of a grocery store in French Camp, California, went to jail for twenty days and paid a $1400 fine. His crime; selling a bottle of Alka-Seltzer for forty-four cents." (*Changing Times*, Vol. 13 [October, 1959], p. 36.) During the late 1950's, "fair trade" pricing laws were not enforced in many areas, following several adverse court decisions. As this is written, supporters are making determined efforts to re-enact "fair trade" pricing laws in more enforceable form. (See *New York Times*, March 29, 1959, IV, p. 7.)

ensure justice and protect society from injury, they do not always succeed. Aside from the fact that some lawmakers may be ignorant or venal, *there is no common agreement as to whether many acts are socially injurious.* Are gambling, prostitution, and drug addiction social menaces, or are they matters of private morality which the law should not attempt to regulate? Are holding companies, high-pressure advertising, closed shops, or jurisdictional strikes socially destructive or socially beneficial? Wherever there are conflicting value judgments, each with many passionate defenders, law is relatively ineffective. Law is effective and enforceable only when it reflects the moral attitude of society. As the supporters of national Prohibition learned to their sorrow, law cannot create a moral attitude where none exists.

Even when there is general agreement that a particular act is socially injurious, it is not always practical to try to prevent it *by law.* It is widely recognized that overeating kills many more people than all forms of crime combined, yet as long as people cherish their constitutional right to chew their way into their coffins, a law against overeating would be impractical. Furthermore, there are certain technical difficulties in lawmaking, because any law worded broadly enough to forbid the injurious act often unintentionally forbids other harmless acts or invites abuses. For example, there is general agreement that misleading advertising or the sale of useless "medicines" is socially injurious. But how could a workable law fully control these practices? Any procedure for preventing all dishonest or misleading advertising would be impractical: if the law were worded tightly enough to prevent all misleading statements, it would be unsafe for even an honest advertiser to say anything emphatic lest it be adjudged "misleading"; if the law were phrased loosely enough to allow the advertiser some latitude, the dishonest advertiser would have no difficulty in operating within it.

A legalistic definition of crime as violation of law is, therefore, not entirely satisfactory because it labels much relatively harmless behavior as crime, while it excludes many kinds of behavior that are socially quite destructive. But this legalistic definition is the only definition which is *usable,* for any other definition eventually results in labeling as crime anything a particular writer does not like. Consequently, the definition of *crime* as violation of law is used in this discussion.

Amount: How Much Crime Is There in America?

For this question the sociologist has a prompt and firm answer—*nobody knows!* Not that there is any shortage of crime statistics! Reams of crime statistics are collected by the Federal Bureau of Investigation and published annually in *Uniform Crime Reports,* listing arrests and convictions under twenty-five headings ranging from "homicide" to "suspicion," and classifying crimes by: type of crime, urban-rural rates, states, size of city, age, race, and sex. This source reports that in 1958, crimes reported to the police increased 9.3 per cent over 1957, and ran 26.2 per cent above the 1953-1957 period. One arrest was made for every twenty-two persons in the 1,586 cities for which data were reported. Between 1950 and 1954, reported crime increased four times as fast as the population, but between 1957 and 1958, it increased five times as fast as the population. [12]

Yet statistics such as these cannot give an accurate measure of the amount of crime and present a very rough estimate of crime trends. There are several reasons for this. First, *much crime is never reported* to the police and never appears in the crime statistics. The most successful crime is the one which is never detected at all—the murder that looks like accidental or natural death, the fire that looks accidental, the shoplifting by customers and pilfering by employees that is never noticed, or the frauds in which the victims never realize that they have been defrauded. In other cases, although the victim realizes a crime has been committed, he may be *unwilling to prosecute*. Many sex criminals escape because the victims shrink from the notoriety of a prosecution. Many embezzlements are covered up and the dishonest employee quietly discharged because the firm wishes to avoid unfavorable publicity. Although it is widely believed that store employees steal far more than shoplifters, the dishonest employee is rarely prosecuted. [13] Victims of robbery, theft, or embezzlement often lose interest in prosecution once their money is returned. Hotels do not prosecute their highly "respectable" guests who steal the hotel linen, silver, and anything else small enough to carry, although the practice of quietly billing them for the loot seems to be spreading. [14] Victims of confidence games rarely report the crime, since they are usually swindled while engaged in an effort to turn a shady dollar for themselves. Graft, bribery, extortion, blackmail, and "protection" payments are rarely reported to the police, since secrecy is a basic feature of all these. Much petty crime is not reported because the victims doubt that the police will find the culprit. In some areas, especially rural areas, many known crimes are not reported or officially recorded. [15] It is impossible to know how much crime is unreported, but all authorities agree that the amount is tremendous, probably far greater in dollar cost than the crimes reported to the police.

[12] Federal Bureau of Investigation, *Uniform Crime Reports, 1958* (Washington, Government Printing Office, 1959).

[13] Gene Boyo, "Case of the Vanishing Profit—Chances Are It's an Inside Job," *New York Times,* July 25, 1954, p. 1.

[14] John Kobler, "Souvenir Stealers," *Life,* Vol. 21 (November 4, 1946), pp. 2 ff.

[15] T. C. Esselstyn, "The Social Role of a County Sheriff," *Journal of Criminal Law and Criminology,* Vol. 44 (July-August, 1953), pp. 177-184; also Mabel A. Elliott, *Crime in Modern Society* (New York, Harper and Brothers, 1952), pp. 61, 80, 135, 146, 147.

In the second place, some crimes reported to the police are not officially recorded and included in crime statistics. A survey of four police precincts in Chicago showed that only about one-third of all crimes actually known to the police were included in their crime reports to the FBI. For example, if a stolen car were recovered, it was not officially recorded as "stolen." [16]

Furthermore, *much reported crime remains "unsolved."* Sometimes the police are unable to find the culprit. Figure 5-2 shows that only about one-fourth of the crimes reported to the police were "cleared" by the arrest of a suspect, and these figures pertain to the cities where police are presumably better organized and more efficient than in small towns and rural areas.

NOT ALL CRIMINALS ARE CAUGHT AND CONVICTED

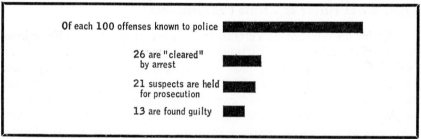

Of each 100 offenses known to police

26 are "cleared" by arrest

21 suspects are held for prosecution

13 are found guilty

SOURCE: *Uniform Crime Reports, 1958, pp. 75, 78.*

FIG. 5–2. Offenses known, cleared by arrest, and persons held for prosecution, 1958, per 100 known offenses, 1,944 cities, total population, 77,469,233.

Finally, *not all arrests result in convictions.* As Figure 5-2 shows, these cities convict about two-thirds of those brought to trial, with wide variations among different cities. The number of arrests made in a particular city is no accurate measure of its amount of crime. A low arrest rate may indicate either a small amount of crime or an inactive police force. A high arrest rate may indicate a police force which makes arrests on slight pretext and is making a great show of combating a "crime wave." In one such "battle" against the underworld, the New York police arrested 652 persons, of whom 152 pleaded guilty to "vagrancy" (having no job or means of support). Of the 500 who pleaded innocent, only three were convicted of anything. [17] Wholesale arrests like this may make the local arrest rate meaningless as a measure of crime.

For the above reasons it is impossible to determine the exact amount of crime actually committed by tabulating crimes reported, arrests, or convictions. Authorities agree that criminal behavior is far more common

[16] *Chicago Sun-Times*, December 9, 1958, pp. 1 ff.

[17] Irwin Ross, "You're Under Arrest," *Coronet*, Vol. 31 (November, 1951), pp. 5 ff.

than most people care to admit. One recent study claims that of 6000 cases of delinquent behavior admitted by a representative group of youths, only 1.5 per cent of these acts were followed by arrest or juvenile court hearings. [18] The same study reveals that of a representative sample of 1698 adults, 99 per cent admitted having committed one or more adult offenses, felonies carrying prison sentences of one year or more. The men in the sample admitted an average of 18 crimes, ranging from a low of 8.2 for ministers to 20.2 for laborers, while the more law-abiding women admitted an average of only 11 penal offenses! If Kinsey's estimates are correct, about one out of each hundred thousand acts of rape, as defined by law, is followed by conviction and imprisonment. [19] It is clear that no existing crime statistics are reliable as measures of the amount of crime committed in America.

Type: What Kinds of Crime Predominate?

Again, no one can be certain. It is conventional to classify crimes into *felonies* (major crimes carrying imprisonment for one year or more) and *misdemeanors* (minor crimes with a maximum penalty of less than a year's imprisonment in a local jail or workhouse). They are also divided into *crimes against persons* and *crimes against property,* and under these headings are classified the specific crimes—burglary, murder, rape, larceny, and so on. These statistics are notoriously unreliable. As already shown, some types of crime are more likely to be reported than others. An arrest on a particular charge is no proof that a crime has been committed by that person. Nor are convictions a reliable measure of the relative frequency of different types of crime. Occasionally a suspect agrees to plead guilty to a lesser crime in a "deal" to avoid prosecution for a more serious crime upon which the prosecutor lacks complete evidence. Consequently, many rapes appear in the statistics as convictions for "disorderly conduct," many "armed robberies" as "carrying concealed weapons," many "murders" as "manslaughter," and much "petty larceny" as "vagrancy." Thus, conviction for a particular crime is sometimes a better indication of ease of conviction than of frequency of commission.

Trends: Is Crime Increasing?

Although criminologists suspect that crime is increasing, it is difficult to be certain about it. It is clear that many "crime waves" are newspaper nonsense, as there is no evidence in statistics or elsewhere to suggest that the actual crime rate changes rapidly or violently. But even

[18] James S. Wallerstein and Clement J. Wyle, "Our Law-Abiding Law-Breakers," reprint from *Probation* (New York, National Probation Association, April, 1947).
[19] Quoted in *Life,* Vol. 43 (September 9, 1957), p. 49.

> The increase of crime is becoming one of the most star-
> tling notices of our daily newspapers. . . . Three, four, five, and,
> in one case, eight murders are announced for New York for
> one week. We are becoming familiar with what, twenty years
> ago, would have shocked the universal conscience.
>
> *Harper's Magazine,* 1853

more gradual changes are difficult to determine, since there is no satisfactory measure of the amount of crime at any given time. Changes in
crimes reported may reflect either a changing frequency of criminal acts
or changed attitudes toward reporting them. [20] The arrest rate is a better
indication of police behavior than of criminal behavior. For example,
more efficient law enforcement would produce more arrests and convictions and would thereby appear to increase the crime rate. The annual
statistics regularly show increases in some types of crime and decreases
in others. To add to the confusion, each new law tends to increase the
crime rate by declaring another act criminal. Auto theft, black-marketing,
and bootlegging were crimes great-grandfather was *unable* to commit!
Many of the opportunities for "white-collar crime" have developed only
within recent decades. All things considered, it is likely that the amount
of crime has been increasing for at least several decades, although the exact
degree of this increase cannot be measured. It is *not* certain, however,
that this apparent increase means that people are growing more lawless,
deceitful, or untrustworthy than they used to be. In fact, there is some
evidence that present standards of private and public behavior are higher
than formerly, [21] and that our rising crime rate may be an indication of
a stricter public conscience rather than of more flagrant misconduct.

Regional, Seasonal, Racial, and Class Variations

None of the above-mentioned variations is particularly important.
There are *slight regional variations,* especially in type of crime; for example, crimes against persons are slightly higher in the South and crimes
against property slightly higher in the North, but regional differences are
quite small. Cities show higher crime rates than rural areas, but it is
probable that rural crime is less fully reported. The city also attracts people intending to commit crimes, as it provides more opportunities for crime
and provides greater anonymity for those seeking an unconventional mode

[20] See Daniel Bell, "What Crime Wave?" *Fortune,* Vol. 51 (January, 1955),
pp. 96 ff.

[21] See Estes Kefauver, "Past and Present Standards of Public Ethics in America:
Are We Improving?" *The Annals,* Vol. 280 (March, 1952), pp. 1-8.

of life. But there is no evidence that country-reared persons are conspicuously less criminal than their city-reared compatriots.

There are *slight seasonal variations* in type of crime, with more rapes and assaults in the summer months, and more thefts and larcenies in the colder months, but these variations are only moderate.

Racial and national variations in crime rates are substantial but misleading. Both Negroes and American Indians show very high arrest and conviction rates. This is partly due to prejudice and injustice, for it has been conclusively shown that these minorities often are more severely treated by police and courts than white criminals.[22] It is likely that much of the remaining Negro-white differential is actually a class variation, since most Negroes are in the less-favored social and economic classes in which the reported and prosecuted crimes are the highest. Shaw found that while juvenile delinquency was high in the slums and low in the prosperous suburbs, Negro and white rates *within* the slum area were approximately the same.[23] There is no evidence, therefore, that Negro crime rates differ very greatly from those of whites in the same area and social class.

Class variations, as indicated by statistics, are spectacular! Arrests and convictions are conspicuously rare in the upper classes and frequent in the lower classes. The Gluecks found that of 1000 juvenile delinquents, about three-fourths were from families below the "level of comfort" (defined as having resources to survive four months of unemployment without going on relief).[24] In Chicago, Shaw and McKay found a correlation of $+.89$ between boy delinquency and proportion of families on relief in each square mile area.[25]

But to criminologists, these and similar studies of adult crime prove only that conventional crime statistics are unreliable as measures of the criminality of the different classes. There is no accurate measure, but there is scattered evidence which casts doubt upon the belief that the lower classes are more criminal than the upper classes. For example, it is the expensive hotels catering to the "best" people which have the heaviest losses from thieving guests—six times as great as the hotels catering to the ordinary trade.[26] One plush hotel placed three hundred expensive

[22] See Guy B. Johnson, "The Negro and Crime," *The Annals,* American Academy of Political and Social Science, Vol. 217 (September, 1941), pp. 93-104; Thorsten Sellin, "The Negro Criminal, A Statistical Note," *The Annals,* 140 (November, 1928), pp. 52-64; Albert Deutsch, "No Glamor," *PM,* July 27, 1952, p. 20; William M. Kephart, "The Negro Offender," *American Journal of Sociology,* 60 (July, 1950), pp. 46-50; William M. Kephart, *Racial Factors and Urban Law Enforcement* (Philadelphia, University of Pennsylvania Press, 1957).

[23] Clifford R. Shaw and others, *Delinquency Areas* (Chicago, University of Chicago Press, 1929).

[24] Sheldon Glueck and Eleanor T. Glueck, *1000 Juvenile Delinquents* (Cambridge, Harvard University Press, 1934).

[25] Clifford Shaw and Henry D. McKay, *Juvenile Delinquency and Urban Areas* (Chicago, University of Chicago Press, 1943).

[26] John Kobler, *op. cit.*

down comforters in its rooms, and exactly one month later the last one disappeared. This is genuine crime, but rarely reported as such. One carefully controlled study, comparing the delinquencies admitted by a high school sample and a reform school sample, found that the boys from different class levels admitted about the same number of delinquencies. [27] The lower class delinquent is more likely to be officially recorded as delinquent, while the middle- or upper-class delinquent is often handled informally. Very often, the upper-class delinquent goes to a clinic while the lower-class delinquent goes to court. All things considered, many criminologists suspect that the lower classes are no more criminal than the middle and upper classes, but are simply less successful in evading punishment. [28]

The upper-class person has a better chance of evading punishment for a number of reasons. (1) He has enough education and sophistication to know something of his legal rights and how to secure them. He is less easily bluffed into a confession or persuaded into pleading guilty. (2) He can usually afford a lawyer who can make a skillful defense. (3) If he lacks resources, he often has friends or relatives who can provide for his legal defense. (4) He can conduct himself with the disarming poise and dignity of a good citizen and a gentleman, and avoid the guilty confusion which suggests the "criminal type." (5) He is sometimes socially superior to the police officers, the jury, and most of the court personnel. He represents a class which they have been conditioned to treat with deference and respect, and whose "story" their class culture has predisposed them to accept. (6) His education, his occupation, and his social life have all cultivated verbal skills that enable him to speak convincingly in maintaining his innocence or in rationalizing his error. (7) He is often able to offer restitution or bribery to the victims to dissuade them from prosecuting. (8) He may be able to offer bribes of money, position, or power to law enforcement officials or jurors. (9) He may have powerful connections —friendship, kinship, or business affiliations with the judge, the prosecutor, or others in a position to influence the prosecution. (10) He can frequently point to a record of community service and occupational success which helps destroy the image of him as a "criminal." (11) He can frequently secure highly respected and prominent citizens as witnesses of his past reputation and character. (12) There is considerable feeling that public humiliation is a great penalty to an upper-class person, making further punishment less necessary than for a lower-class person. (13) For all of the above reasons, the judge is more likely to suspend sentence, to use probation rather than imprisonment, or to impose a very light punishment

[27] F. Ivan Nye, James F. Short, Jr., and Virgil J. Olsen, "Socioeconomic Status and Delinquent Behavior," *American Journal of Sociology,* Vol. 63 (January, 1958), pp. 381-389.

[28] See Edwin H. Sutherland, *White Collar Crime* (New York, The Dryden Press, Inc., 1949), Ch. 1.

in case the accused is found guilty. (14) For all these reasons, the upper-class convict is likely to be paroled at the earliest possible date, whereas less fortunate defendants may serve the full sentence.

White-Collar Crime—The Upper-Class Specialty

Possibly the greatest reason why the middle- and upper-class violators so often escape punishment is because they usually commit a peculiar kind of crime, which is called *white-collar crime.* This is not merely crime committed by white-collar persons; white-collar crime is crime committed by business and professional people *in the course of their occupation.*[29] If a physician shoots his wife, forges a check, or burns his house for the insurance, this is conventional crime; if he commits an illegal abortion, falsifies a prescription for a drug addict, or "pads" a bill, this is white-collar crime. A businessman who systematically short-weights his product, misbrands it, embezzles the firm's funds, manipulates a phony bankruptcy, or falsifies his financial statement is engaging in white-collar crime. When upper-class people engage in crime, it is more likely to be of this sort, rather than the conventional armed robberies, assaults, auto thefts, and the like.

There is no way of knowing the extent of white-collar crime, but criminologists agree that it is tremendous, "probably several times as great as the cost of all the crimes which are customarily regarded as the 'crime problem,' "[30] and producing "infinitely more damage to the community."[31] One estimate places the annual total of kickbacks, payoffs, and bribes at $5 billion, with $500 million embezzled and another $500 million taken in home repair frauds.[32] Another authority cites estimates ranging from $500 million to $3 billion stolen by employees, with only one-tenth of these dishonest employees brought into court when detected.[33] Lie detector tests of all employees of several Chicago banks showed that 20 per cent of them had stolen bank property, and similar tests of a sample of store employees showed that 75 per cent had stolen money or merchandise from the store.[34] A certain chain store systematically short-weighted and overcharged its customers for many years, netting as much as 3.4 per cent profit on its entire capital investment through this policy.

[29] *Ibid.,* p. 9.
[30] *Ibid.,* p. 12.
[31] Morris Ploscoe, "Crime in a Competitive Society," *The Annals,* Vol. 217 (September, 1941), pp. 105-111.
[32] "The Crooks in White Collars," *Life,* Vol. 43 (October 14, 1957), pp. 162 ff.
[33] "Embezzlers, the Trusted Thieves," *Fortune,* Vol. 46 (November, 1957), pp. 142 ff. Similar estimates are given by the head of a large management consulting firm, Norman Jaspan, in *The Thief in the White Collar* (New York, J. P. Lippincott Co., 1960).
[34] F. P. McEvoy, "The Lie Detector Goes into Business," *Reader's Digest,* Vol. 38 (February, 1941), p. 69.

In one year, 456 of its stores showed "stock gains" of more than 2 per cent, meaning that its customers were cheated enough to make up all the stores' losses from spoilage, breakage, and pilferage, and provide a net of two cents on each dollar in addition. [35] Hundred-thousand-dollar robberies are extremely rare, but hundred-thousand-dollar swindles, embezzlements, and stock frauds have become rather commonplace, and hundred-million-dollar frauds are not unknown in American financial history. The Senate Banking and Currency Committee estimated that fraudulent profits of over $500 million were realized by builders who secured federal loans far in excess of the cost of building projects. [36] An estimated $2 billion in counterfeit "name brand" merchandise is sold each year, mainly through respectable retail storekeepers. [37] One great corporation "overcharged" the government by more than $8 million in a single contract by "overstating" its expenses. [38]

Another type of white-collar crime is the violation of state and federal laws which regulate business conduct. These laws, passed to protect consumers, workers, and competitors, are often viewed by a businessman as an unjustified interference in his business affairs. One young business executive complains, "It is impossible to conduct business in the United States today without breaking the law." [39] Without doubt, the law is often broken. Sutherland tabulated convictions for violation of federal laws (restraint of trade, patent infringement, unfair labor practices, illegal rebates, and others) by seventy of America's largest and most famous corporations, finding that they amassed a total of 340 convictions from 1940 to 1948. [40] In a single year, the Department of Labor found 3,049 industrial firms and 1,910 farms hiring child labor in violation of federal law. [41] In the same year, 18,000 firms were found violating wage and hour laws, thereby depriving over 125,000 workers of wages due them. [42] White-collar crime is popular, profitable, and seldom punished by arrest and conviction. As one popular magazine put it: [43]

Take an active, if concentrated, day in the life of a reputable New York State businessman. . . . As he walks to his downtown office after leaving his car resting snugly in a "No Parking" zone, he warmly greets the veteran cop on the beat, who thanks him for his recent annual present, a case of good blended whiskey (penalty for attempting to influence a police officer with a

[35] *Consumer Reports,* Vol. 15 (February, 1950), p. 84.

[36] *New York Times,* July 4, 1954, p. 1.

[37] Stanley Frank, "Do You Know What You Are Buying?" *Saturday Evening Post,* Vol. 228 (July 9, 1955), pp. 28 ff.

[38] *Time,* Vol. 70 (August 5, 1957), p. 68.

[39] *Fortune,* Vol. 58 (September, 1958), p. 116.

[40] Sutherland, *op. cit.,* Ch. II.

[41] *New York Times,* February 25, 1957, p. 75.

[42] U. S. Department of Labor, *They Are America* (Washington, D. C., Government Printing Office, 1957), p. 64.

[43] "The Crooks in White Collars," *Life,* Vol. 43 (October 14, 1957), pp. 167 ff.

gift: $5,000 fine and/or 10 years in jail). After a few routine desk chores the businessman has a profitable late morning session with his personal income tax consultant, who has found a happy device for distorting repair and depreciation costs on some rental property he owns (penalty for filing a fraudulent income tax return: $10,000 fine and/or five years in jail). By this time he has worked up an appetite for a good expense-account meal, so he entertains his wife and two close friends at a lavish lunch, all on the company tab (a misdemeanor under Section 665 of the State Penal Law, subject to a $500 fine and/or one year in jail).

Back in the office, he reminds one of his assistants to "take care of" the building inspector with jurisdiction over their new plant site, thus getting as much red tape out of the way as possible (penalty for bribing a public officer: $5,000 fine and/or 10 years in jail). He then dictates a letter to an executive of a small concern with which he has just signed a contract, thanking him for *his* thoughtful gift of a new model portable TV set (penalty for secretly accepting a gift in return for corporate favors: $500 and/or one year in jail).

At a late afternoon conference he congratulates the controller on a new bookkeeping device that handily pads a few of the firm's more controversial assets (penalty for concurring in a bookkeeping fraud: $500 and/or one year in jail). He later tells the head of his company's advertising agency to disregard a recent Federal Trade Commission cease-and-desist order about misleading TV commercials, at least until after the fall sales drive (this ultimately puts the company in line for an embarrassing and costly federal court action).

As the day closes, he asks his secretary to wrap up one of the new company desk sets, which will be just the thing for his den at home (penalty for appropriating company property to one's personal use: $500 fine and/or one year in jail). Safe at home, he advises his wife not to worry about the maid's social security payments because she is leaving soon anyway (penalty for willful nonpayment of employer's social security contributions: $10,000 fine and/or five years in jail). Laying aside the cares of the day, he settles down to watch the news on his souvenir TV set—and fulminates about the dishonesty of the "union racketeers" he sees on the screen.

Attitudes toward white-collar crime. Public indignation at conventional crime contrasts sharply with public tolerance of white-collar crime.[44] To most people, many forms of white-collar crime are not viewed as being "real crime." They are not defined as genuine crime either by the public or by the perpetrators. The business executive who is convicted of violating the antitrust laws generally assumes not the guilty manner of a criminal caught in the act, but the righteous indignation of a victim of government tyranny. Many of his business associates sympathize with his martyrdom. The newspaper editors and radio commentators—those of them who raise their voices at all—usually raise them not

[44] One study shows that a sample of citizens would punish violators of the Food and Drug laws more severely than the courts punished them, but shows no tendency to class these violators with conventional criminals. See Donald J. Newman, "Public Attitudes Toward a Form of White Collar Crime," *Social Problems,* Vol. 4 (January, 1957), pp. 228-232.

in condemnation of the criminal for violating the law, but in condemnation of the government for enforcing it. This merely illustrates that many forms of white-collar crime are not generally considered to be actual crime, but, instead, are viewed as merely technical errors, or perhaps even as courageous opposition to government meddling. There are substantial groups which are strenuously opposed to much of our regulatory laws—antitrust laws, labor-relations legislation, wage-hour laws, securities and exchange laws, and others regulating business conduct. Lacking any strong body of supporting public opinion, the government finds it politically difficult to enforce them very enthusiastically. It is also protested that there are so many confusing and contradictory regulations that a businessman can scarcely follow all of them—an argument for which there is considerable justification. The argument is rarely used, however, to excuse the violations of lower-class offenders jailed for vagrancy, nonpayment of alimony, or some other offense which, in many cases, the offender may have no desire to commit, but be unable to avoid.

This lack of any strong condemnation of many forms of white-collar crime, by the public or by one's business associates, helps to account for the popularity of white-collar offenses. This attitude that white-collar crime is not real crime is further expressed in the mode of its treatment. Violators are usually dealt with not in the ordinary criminal courts, but by special quasi-judicial commissions and agencies—the Federal Trade Commission, the National Labor Relations Board, the Securities and Exchange Commission, and other agencies. These agencies are empowered to determine facts, make settlements, and recommend criminal prosecution in federal courts when they think it advisable. They rarely do so. Usually the violator is permitted to sign a consent decree (a promise not to break the law any more) and allowed to go free. Sometimes he is required to give some of the money back. In cases of especially flagrant violation, or where the accused maintains his innocence, the case may enter a federal court, where the accused is aided by all the advantages of status mentioned above. If found guilty, the penalties are in sharp contrast to those given conventional criminals. Insofar as the writer can determine, no violator has ever gone to prison for violating the antitrust laws, the labor relations laws and many other regulatory laws. Fines are usually nominal and are often assessed to the corporation rather than to the officers personally, meaning that if the officers break the law, the stockholders pay the fine. It has been suggested that the antitrust laws be enforced by dissolving any corporation which repeatedly violates them, or punishing any corporate officer involved in repeated violations by prohibiting him from holding any corporate office thereafter. Such proposals have received little support from businessmen, the press, or the public. This lack of severe penalties for white-collar violators of regulatory law is often excused by the doctrine that the object of these quasi-judicial agencies is not to punish the offenders, but to gain compliance with the law. This point—that law enforcement should seek to gain compliance rather than to inflict punishment sounds reasonable and humane. Curiously enough, however, it seems to be reserved for white-collar offenders rather than for ordinary criminals.

In summary, then, there are few significant variations in probable actual crime rates of different regions, seasons, races, or classes in America. Most variations are due largely to statistical illusions and imperfections, and any genuine variations which remain are of little significance in analyzing the causes or treatment of crime. For it is not of much value to know that one group commits 10 per cent more crime than another; what is important is to know why either commits crime at all!

SOME POPULAR FALLACIES ABOUT CRIME

1. The Fallacy of the Criminal Class

We hear frequent references to the "criminal class," the "criminal type," or the "typical criminal." There is no such person! There is perhaps no other category in society whose members differ so greatly in motive, in background, and in conduct as the "criminal class." The confirmed drunkard, the professional racketeer, the confidence man, and the abortionist have remarkably little in common. It is absurd to speak of the "typical criminal," for he does not exist.

2. The Romantic Stereotypes of the Criminal

Around such highly dramatic but little understood behavior as crime, it is inevitable that a number of highly romantic stereotypes should develop. One is the stereotype of the "mad killer" who murders without reason or remorse. Such psychotic killers are rare, but their high publicity value encourages an exaggerated notion of their numbers. Another is the "Robin Hood" stereotype who robs the rich to feed the poor, a type whose popularity in fiction is matched by his rarity in real life. Another is the "tough softie," a Damon Runyon type, whose menacing exterior conceals a heart of gold that melts at the mew of a kitten or the quaver of somebody's dear old mother. Opposed to this is the "insensitive clod" stereotype, a passionless, unfeeling creature who cares not what anyone thinks of him and has abandoned all hope of status or respectability. Complete ignorance of the manner wherein status and recognition are actually secured by professional criminals is necessary to believe in this type. Then there is the "gay desperado," a soldier of fortune, whose life of crime is an adventuresome flirtation with death. There is the "secret society" stereotype of the underworld as a vast brotherhood united by eternal oaths of loyalty, practicing a chivalrous code of "honor among thieves," and united in eternal warfare against the forces of law and order. Finally, there is the "master brain" stereotype of the king of the underworld, a commander-in-chief of a vast criminal network which he rules with iron hand.

All of these florid conceptions are largely untrue, some entirely untrue. All are romantic oversimplifications of highly complex phenomena. None of them is consistent with the known facts about the actual organization and operation of crime, and none contributes anything to an understanding of the behavior of criminals.

3. The Fallacy That Criminals Are Abnormal

Many people believe that criminals are the physical, mental, or psychological inferiors of the general population. Many early studies seemed to support this conclusion; but these early studies suffered from two serious defects. First, they were based upon convict samples, and the prison population is overloaded with the failures in the criminal profession —the clumsy beginners, the stupid bunglers, the impulsive and careless, and so on. Presumably the more intelligent and skillful criminals are successful in staying out of prison. Although studies of prison samples have some value, they cannot be the basis of generalizations for all criminals. To study a sample of businessmen who go bankrupt would provide useful knowledge about business failures, but would tell nothing reliable about businessmen as a whole. Any studies of prison inmates must be interpreted with equal caution. Secondly, many early studies did not compare their convict samples with a control group from the general population; the scholar often compared his survey findings with what he *assumed* to be true of the general population. Consequently, the theory of the inferiority of the prison population rested upon an inflated and inaccurate notion of the characteristics of the general population. Inasmuch as there is no way to define, locate, and measure criminals who have not been convicted, it is impossible to determine accurately their qualities. Most criminologists are now of the opinion, however, that criminals, taken as a group and including those not in prison, probably form a relatively representative cross section of the general population physically, mentally, and psychologically. [45]

4. The Fallacy of the Born Criminal

It is a common habit of mankind to attribute to instinct any behavior for which he has no other explanation. Lacking any satisfactory explanation for criminal and other perverse behavior, further perplexity can be neatly avoided by assuming that some instinct was responsible. This as-

[45] Cf. Harry Elmer Barnes and Negley K. Teeters, *New Horizons in Criminology* (Englewood Cliffs, N. J., Prentice-Hall, Inc., 1951), pp. 247-250.

sumption is buttressed by the observation that criminal behavior often "ran" in certain families and was absent in others. It might be observed, however, that membership in the Catholic Church, preference for large breakfasts, or the use of correct grammar also run in certain families without being considered instinctive.

No reputable American criminologist today accepts the notion of a "criminal instinct," for they are agreed that *criminal behavior is learned*, a conclusion most biologists share. [46] An *instinct* is an inborn, relatively inflexible and specific behavior pattern, rigidly uniting a specific stimulus with a specific response. But a given pattern may be a crime in one period or one society and a noble benefaction in another. The criminal act could scarcely be an inborn pattern, for Nature has no way of knowing which acts will be deemed criminal and, hence, cannot know which compulsions to implant in human heredity. Furthermore, a given act may be criminal in some circumstances and legal in others. Under some circumstances we hang the man who kills another; in other circumstances, we hang medals on him. It is obviously impossible to attribute to heredity those acts which will, when committed, be defined as criminal, so the notion of a criminal instinct becomes fantastic nonsense.

It remains fashionable to maintain that although crime may not be actually instinctive, "criminal tendencies" may still be inherited. This is merely a diluted version of the original proposition. If Nature cannot know what acts to implant, how can she know what "tendencies" to implant? Furthermore, exactly what is a "criminal tendency"? It cannot be an inclination toward a particular act, since the criminality of an act is a constantly changing matter of social definition. It cannot be a general resistance to social expectation since, as will be shown later, actual criminals are as hungry for status and social recognition as other people. In fact, the term *criminal tendency* illustrates the "naming fallacy" wherein a suitable name serves as a substitute for knowledge. Unable to find any firm evidence of an hereditary basis for criminal behavior, but feeling that there ought to be one, hereditarians use the term *criminal tendency* to conceal their lack of exact knowledge upon the matter. In other words, if you can't prove it, just call it a "tendency!" Meanwhile, no one has yet defined a "criminal tendency" or proved that one exists, and the term remains scientific nonsense.

5. The Poverty and Broken-Homes Fallacies

Many people firmly believe that crime and delinquency are often caused by poverty and broken homes. Although it is true that most people convicted of conventional crimes are in the low-income class, this does

[46] Cf. M. F. Ashley-Montagu, "The Biologist Looks at Crime," *The Annals*, Vol. 217 (September, 1941), pp. 46-57.

not prove that poverty is a *cause* of crime, since there are many facts about the distribution of conventional crime which poverty cannot explain. For example, an equal number of boys and girls suffer poverty and broken homes, yet boy delinquents outnumber girl delinquents by four or five to one. Many poverty-stricken groups in the slums, such as the Chinese, have very low crime and delinquency rates despite their poverty. Certain immigrant groups with historically low crime rates have developed high crime rates in America, even though they are more prosperous than before. [47] Fluctuations in crime rates show little or no association with variations in the level of national prosperity. [48] Poverty, by itself, is a negligible factor in crime.

The "broken-homes" cliché is almost religiously believed by many people. Numerous studies have been made and have disagreed widely—finding from 20 to 60 per cent of delinquents coming from broken homes. [49] These figures cannot be interpreted without knowing what proportion of all children live in broken homes, and this figure is not accurately known. Earlier studies underestimated the proportion of children living in broken homes, and therefore made it appear that the broken homes were more common to delinquents than to the general child population by a large ratio. Later studies, using more scientific methods of determining how many children are exposed to broken homes, have found only slight associations.[50] The broken home may be expected to show a somewhat higher incidence of *official* delinquency, since a child is more likely to be referred to the court as an official delinquent if his home is broken, but returned to his parents if his home is unbroken; thus he stays out of court, and is not included in the statistics. [51] It is likely that broken homes are *not* contributing greatly more than their share of actual delinquents, and recent research has shifted from study of the physically broken home to study of the psychologically disrupted home, a factor of far greater importance. One recent study finds that a sample of children from unhappy unbroken homes shows more delinquent behavior than a sample of children from homes broken by divorce. [52]

[47] See Pauline V. Young, *The Pilgrims of Russian Town*, (Chicago, University of Chicago Press, 1932).

[48] Thorsten Sellin, *Research Memorandum on Crime in the Depression* (New York, Social Science Research Council, 1937).

[49] Edwin H. Sutherland and Donald R. Cressey, *Principles of Criminology* (New York, J. B. Lippincott Company, 1955), pp. 174-175.

[50] Clifford R. Shaw and Henry D. McKay found a ratio of 1:18 to 1, which they consider insignificant. ("Social Factors in Juvenile Delinquency," National Commission on Law Enforcement and Observance, *Report on the Causes of Crime*, No. 13, Vol. II, pp. 261-284.) Other studies find associations ranging no higher than 2 to 1. (Sutherland and Cressey, *op. cit.*, pp. 175-176.)

[51] Sutherland and Cressey, *ibid.*

[52] F. Ivan Nye, "Child Adjustment in Broken and Unhappy Unbroken Homes," *Marriage and Family Living*, Vol. 19 (November 1957), pp. 356-361.

6. The Fallacy That Violent, Dramatic Crime Constitutes the Crime Problem

From reading newspaper headlines, one would infer that the problem of crime is largely concerned with such offenses as murder, armed robbery, rape, and other sex crimes, for these are the ones which crowd the front pages. For every woman killed by a "sex fiend," several are slaughtered by their husbands; but the sex crimes attract more interest and arouse far greater anxiety. For every person murdered in calculated detective-story fashion, dozens are killed by drunken and reckless drivers (negligent homicide, if it can be proved). For every dollar taken in armed robbery, hundreds or thousands are taken quietly by gamblers, racketeers, and white-collar criminals. The corruption of police and government officials by organized and white-collar crime wreaks an injury to public life and public morals beside which the depredations of pickpockets, shoplifters, bank robbers, and homosexuals are of minor importance. Yet these crimes rate the headlines. It would be only slightly exaggerated to say that the genuine social destructiveness and financial cost of a form of crime varies *inversely* with the publicity it receives and the public concern it arouses.

A REALISTIC CLASSIFICATION OF CRIMINALS

As already indicated, a classification of criminals according to type of crime is of little value. It tells nothing of the criminal's motives and contains no suggestions for effective treatment. A useful classification should give some insight into the purposes of the criminal and be of some practical aid in analyzing different methods of treatment. For this, criminals should be classified not according to type of crime, but according to personality orientation of the criminal. [53]

1. Legalistic Criminals

a. Some persons become *criminals through ignorance.* Feeble-minded persons, because they are unable to understand the nature of their actions may, in certain instances, be dangerous, but they are problems for custody, not for punishment or treatment. Anyone convicted of an act done in complete ignorance of its illegality is a "criminal," even though he had no criminal intent and obviously presents no difficult problem for treat-

[53]The classifications that follow are not commonly used by sociologists, except perhaps the last three terms—*situational, habitual, and professional.* Although these classifications used here are unconventional, the writers consider them practicable. There is some overlapping of categories, as is unavoidable in any typology of complex behavior.

ment. Some laws are so unclear that it is difficult to know whether a specific act is legal or illegal. Businessmen often complain that there are so many confusing and overlapping regulatory laws that they cannot be certain what is legal. Sometimes the only way to tell whether a particular act is prohibited by the law is to commit it and invite the government to try to get a conviction. If it succeeds, the act was illegal! There are hundreds of such test cases every year, many resulting in convictions. These convicts are not criminals in the usual sense, nor do they require any conventional "treatment."

b. Other legalistic criminals include the *victims of unjust law enforcement.* In any kind of court system, an innocent person of good reputation will occasionally be convicted, either through a freak, mistaken identity, circumstantial evidence, or perhaps through a frame-up. Although such cases are relatively rare, each year a number of convicts are cleared when *another* person confesses or new evidence is discovered. [54] In other cases the police and prosecutor may "hang" a crime on an innocent suspect whose bad reputation or limited resources make it difficult for him to defend himself. [55] A record of misdemeanors—drunkenness, tavern brawls, nonpayment of bills, and so on—prejudices the police, prosecutors, and jurors to reject one's protestations of innocence. Negroes, Mexicans, and other racial or foreign minorities are usually handicapped due to prejudice, poverty, and ignorance when they are suspected of crime. Quite a few are convicted on incredibly flimsy evidence, or are easily frightened into signing false confessions. One Negro was convicted of "assault by leering" at a white woman from a distance of sixty feet! [56] While this particular conviction was reversed by a higher court, not a year passes without several cases of similar "justice" appearing in the liberal press (*The Nation, New Republic,* and so on). Such cases rarely receive wide publicity in the conventional press.

c. Still another group of legalistic criminals are those whose *alleged crime is merely the pretext for action* against them because they hold unpopular social or political ideas. In a few instances, of which the Sacco-Vanzetti case is a celebrated example, [57] political radicals are convicted of a conventional crime on very flimsy evidence by a court whose lack of judicial objectivity results in nothing less than a legal lynching. Labor organizers have been arrested for "loitering" while waiting for a street car; while talking to one another, they have been arrested for "obstructing

[54] See Erle Stanley Gardner, *The Court of Last Resort* (New York, William Sloane Associates, Inc., 1952), for popularized accounts of such cases; also Jerome N. Frank and Barbara Frank, in association with Harold M. Hoffman, *Not Guilty* (New York, Doubleday and Company, 1958).

[55] See Milton Mayer, "The Case of Roger Touhy," *The Reporter,* Vol. 13, (November 17, 1955), pp. 12-20.

[56] *New York Times,* November 13, 1952, p. 22; January 29, 1953, p. 29.

[57] See Felix Frankfurter, *The Case of Sacco and Vanzetti* (Boston, Little, Brown & Co., 1927).

the sidewalk"; while passing out handbills, they have been arrested for "littering the sidewalk."

Legalistic criminals have little in common with conventional criminals. Granted some of them may be very poor citizens, they generally lack criminal intent, lack criminal orientation, and need no special treatment. If convicted and punished, they are likely to become worse citizens than before.

2. Moralistic Criminals

Moralistic criminals are violators of laws forbidding certain vices that rarely injure anyone except possibly the criminal himself. The moral views of a powerful segment of the community, possibly a hundred years earlier, have written into law many regulations of matters involving private morality as well as public protection. These include laws forbidding gambling, prostitution, illegal use of liquor or narcotics, homosexuality, adultery, fornication, and other sex offenses. All of these laws are of debatable effectiveness. The attempt to suppress gambling and prostitution, despite a great market for these services among "law-abiding" citizens, tends to result in widespread violation of the law and in corruption and demoralization of law enforcement agencies through protection payments and political pressures from "respectable" citizens. Laws forbidding adultery are violated by perhaps half the male population,[58] and those forbidding fornication by possibly nine-tenths of the male population.[59] These laws are usually enforced only when the police want to convict someone of something, or when an offended third party wishes to make trouble. For all practical purposes, adultery and fornication are crimes only when somebody wants to make an issue of them. Kinsey has shown that if existing sex laws were strictly enforced, 95 per cent of the male population could be imprisoned, while not less than 60 per cent of the male college graduates could be imprisoned for certain illegal techniques of love-making in which they engage with their own wives.[60] Such laws, which make criminals of nearly the entire adult population, are pointless.

Although many who are engaged in the illegal sale of narcotics are professional criminals, it is useless to class the drug addict as a criminal. The main direct effect of narcotics is to quiet him, and if he commits a crime, it is usually in an effort to insure his supply of drugs. He plays no part in organized crime, for a drug addict is untrustworthy. There is good reason to control the sale of narcotics, but many criminologists agree that to make the use of drugs by an addict a crime serves only to aggravate a

[58] Alfred C. Kinsey, Wardell B. Pomeroy, and Clyde E. Martin, *Sexual Behavior in the Human Male* (Philadelphia, W. B. Saunders Co., 1948), pp. 249, 585.
[59] *Ibid.*, p. 552
[60] *Ibid.*, pp. 392, 576.

difficult problem. Despite determined enforcement of narcotics laws, drug addiction remains a real problem, [61] while the drug addict commits perhaps 25 per cent of all conventional crime in the nation. [62] Treating the addict as a criminal is not proving effective, for the addict is a problem in medicine and psychiatry, not in criminology.

The moralistic criminals are, as a group, a relatively harmless lot. Although much of their behavior is highly offensive to others, they have little in common with professional criminals. Neither their motives nor their life organization is basically criminal. Their successful treatment should be viewed primarily as a problem in public morality rather than in criminology.

3. Psychopathic Criminals

In the psychopathic class fall all criminals who are unable to control their behavior in a legally acceptable way because of a major emotional maladjustment—this includes not only the legally insane but all others with more or less permanent complexes, phobias, manias, and other instabilities or disturbances which result in criminal acts. In some cases, the behavior is of a wildly erratic sort which may result in any one of a wide variety of crime. In other cases, the psychopath suffers an uncontrollable compulsion to commit a particular act which he does not want to perform, and may receive no enjoyment from doing, yet must do to find psychic relief. The kleptomaniac is a compulsive thief, often specializing in a single kind of merchandise for which he has no use, whose stealing has symbolic meaning for him. In one case, a lonely, unattractive girl accumulated a trunkful of costume jewelry, as the act of stealing jewelry became a substitute for gaiety and companionship. In another, a timid, ineffectual housewife found a temporary sense of power and accomplishment in the act of stealing. The kleptomaniac should not be confused with the ordinary shoplifter who steals for profit, nor should the arsonist who burns his barn to collect the insurance be confused with the pyromaniac who cannot resist setting fires. The pyromaniac gains nothing from the fire except a sense of power, excitement, or revenge on society and the temporary release from a driving compulsion he is powerless to understand or subdue. The sexual psychopath is not merely one caught in a sex act that offends the moral or esthetic sensibilities of the community; he commits an illegal act under uncontrollable compulsion, not because it brings enjoyment, but because it brings relief. These "crimes" range from window peeping and lingerie-stealing to knifings and murderous assaults. The

[61] A Senate Judiciary Subcommittee estimates that drug addiction has trebled in the United States since the end of World War II. (*Time*, Vol. 40, January 1956, p. 18).

[62] *Ibid.*

sexual psychopath finds sexual excitement and sexual relief through these acts rather than through normal sex activities.

All these psychopathic criminals have little in common with professional criminals. They do not seek profit, status, or recognition, but release from uncontrollable impulse. Punishments are futile, for their acts are irrational. Imprisonment gives them no aid and eventually they are released uncured. To view them as criminals is both ineffectual and medieval. Many sexual psychopaths are not curable and must be kept in permanent custody in an appropriate institution if society is to be protected. Some may respond to psychiatric treatment, after which they can be released.

4. Institutional Criminals

Institutional crime refers to certain criminal acts which are repeated so often that they become a part of the normal behavior of the group, yet are so perfectly rationalized that these acts are not defined as crime by those committing them, or perhaps even by the community. These offenders are not professional criminals, for crime is not a career, only incidental to a legitimate career.

The slot machines in American Legion halls and private clubs, and the bingo parties and raffles which certain churches sponsor are examples of institutional crime. They are actual crimes as defined by law but are not viewed as such by those promoting them, by the law-enforcement officials, or by most of the general public. Instead, they are standard, customary practices of these groups and are likely to be testily defended with the argument that "the law is foolish," or that "the law isn't intended for this," with the added comment that it isn't polite to mention the matter.

Longshoremen on the New York waterfront engage in systematic pilfering as a means of supplementing their irregular earnings. This practice is encouraged both by their actual need and by their awareness of the huge "take" of the waterfront mobsters.

"If five per cent of everything moving in and out is systematically siphoned off by the mob, why shouldn't I take a few steaks home for the wife and kids?" a longshoreman figures. "Taking what you need for your own table is never considered pilferage," it was explained to me rather solemnly. Shortly before Thanksgiving a longshoreman who could double for Jackie Gleason noticed barrels of turkeys being unloaded from a truck. He was not working that day but he simply got in line and waited for a barrel to be lowered onto his back. Everybody in his tenement got a free turkey. Another longshoreman . . . in a whole year . . . made less than $1500, and he had kids to feed. "We couldn't have made out if I hadn't scrounged the groceries on the dock," he said. [63]

[63] Budd Schulberg, "Joe Docks, Forgotten Man of the Waterfront," *New York Times Magazine*, December 28, 1952, pp. 3 ff. See also, "Last of the Business Rackets," *Fortune*, Vol. 43 (June, 1951), pp. 89 ff.

Income tax frauds are popular among all groups which have an opportunity to conceal part of their income from the tax collector: business proprietors, doctors, dentists, farmers, writers, gamblers, waitresses, cabdrivers, and others. The National Bureau of Economic Research estimates that no taxes are paid on at least 25 per cent of the taxable income of these groups. [64] Few storekeepers report as personal income all the merchandise they take home for family use as is required by income tax law. It is said that some businessmen rarely eat a meal, light a cigar, or see a show except on an expense account where part of the cost can be shifted onto other taxpayers. [65] Many of these chiselers do not define this as "real" crime, but as a game of wits with the government. It therefore fits the definition of institutional crime—criminal acts which are widespread and generally tolerated by an occupational group but not treated as actual crime either by them or by most of the community.

In the American Southwest, most large growers employ Mexican labor, partly contract labor brought in by agreement with the Mexican government, and partly wet-back labor consisting of Mexicans who illegally cross the border at night. Some growers prefer the wet-backs, as they are not protected by contract, can be hired more cheaply, and can sometimes even be cheated out of their meager earnings. It is no secret that some growers connive at violation of the immigration laws and strongly oppose their rigid enforcement. The Immigration Service has accommodated these growers by staging "roundup" raids near the end of the work season, "so they haven't interfered seriously with the farm labor force." [66]

Dozens of other examples of institutional crime can be cited. An investigation of forty farm-labor camps in New York found only three who kept the payroll records required by law, so there is no way of knowing how many were violating the child labor laws or cheating the migrant laborers. [67] Violation of the highway weight laws by commercial truckers is a widespread practice, and some haulers consider it more profitable to pay the fines than to stay within the "unrealistic" legal weight limits. [68] Violation of fire, sanitary, and building regulations is standard practice for many owners of slum property. In Chicago, a survey showed

[64] John L. Hess, "The Gentle Art of Tax Avoidance," *The Reporter*, Vol. 20 (April 16, 1959), pp. 12-15; also *The New York Times*, December 9, 1959, p. 31.

[65] Richard A. Girard, "They Escape Income Taxes—But You Can't," *American Magazine*, Vol. CLVI (December, 1952), pp. 15 ff.; also V. Henry Rothschild and Rudolph Sobernheim, "Expense Accounts for Executives," *Yale Law Journal*, Vol. 67 (July, 1959), pp. 1363-1392.

[66] *Farm Journal* (September, 1952), p. 34.

[67] Paul Jacobs, "The Forgotten People," *The Reporter*, Vol. 20 (January 22, 1959), pp. 13 ff.

[68] *New York Times*, March 21, 1954, p. 21. See also *Time*, Vol. 64 (December 20, 1954), p. 61, for a report of Illinois' unsuccessful effort to bar from its highways a trucking company with 157 overweight violations. *Time* concludes, "Most of them [the truckers] count fines as simply another routine cost of doing business."

one owner who had accumulated a total of 418 violations, but, since half of all violation suits were dropped, and the fines averaged only $10 each, and half the fines assessed were never collected, it was more profitable to continue to violate the law than to repair the property. [69] Institutional criminals have little in common with conventional criminals, or even with each other, for the tax evader, the longshoreman, and the wet-back employer differ greatly from one another. "Treatment" would not be a conventional effort to reform criminals, since no one considers them criminals. Institutional crime is not a problem in conventional criminology, but a problem in social organization, in jurisprudence, and in public morality.

5. Situational Criminals

Every prison contains a number of persons who, under pressure of overpowering circumstances, have committed a criminal act entirely out of harmony with their basic life organization. A melodramatic illustration is the clerk or cashier who embezzles to pay for his wife's operation. A high proportion of murders are committed by husbands, wives, or in-laws who are caught in an intolerable domestic conflict from which they see no escape and which they eventually "solve" with a shotgun or meat axe. Many a normally law-abiding businessman, faced with ruin through adverse circumstances, will consider a profitable fire or a fraudulent bankruptcy. The debts from a single gambling spree may involve one so deeply that he tries a little larceny as a way out. Many an honest employee becomes dishonest when he acquires an expensive girl friend. Occasionally a thoroughly respectable citizen commits a serious crime while intoxicated. In rare cases a timid, mousy employee, taunted once too often, flares into towering anger and parts his tormentor's hair with a sledge hammer. Such situational criminals as these form a moderate share of our prisoners, because they are fairly easy to detect and prosecute. Courts are inclined to be lenient if his prior life was exemplary, but when the offender's past life has been somewhat unsavory, he may find the judge inclined to treat him severely as an "example."

No social purpose is served by *punishing* most of these situational criminals. Inasmuch as their basic life organization is not criminal, they are in no need of the treatment or reformation needed by conventional criminals. They may be no more likely to commit another crime, in most cases, than are their neighbors. Imprisonment serves only to satisfy the community's sense of "justice" and usually embitters and brutalizes the offender.

[69] *Chicago Sun-Times*, May 28, 1953, p. 16; June 9, 1954, p. 28. See also William Manchester, "The Life and Times of a Slum Landlord," *The Reporter*, Vol. 15 (November 15, 1956), pp. 24-26, for an account of how to make slums a profitable investment.

6. Habitual Criminals

There are criminals whom circumstances overpower very easily—who yield to temptation over and over. Such people repeatedly get into financial crises from which a little larceny is needed to extract them. Or they are easily provoked to violence. Or, while they may not deliberately seek opportunities for thievery, when one arises they readily seize it. They do not view themselves as criminals and defend each lapse with a succession of excuses. Although they are chronic offenders they have not adopted crime as a career or organized their lives around it. Therefore, they are habitual, rather than professional, criminals.

Unlike the situational criminals who are frequently sober and industrious, the habitual criminals contain a high proportion of shiftless ne'er-do-wells. Individuals who lack vocational skills and industrious working habits or who lead the irregular life of marginal workers may be more likely to engage in many forms of petty mischief. Many habitual (not professional) criminals have a long record of petty offenses—disorderly conduct, drunkenness, traffic violations, nonpayment of bills, vagrancy, nonsupport, perhaps minor sex offenses, arrests "on suspicion," and the like. Lacking a dependable source of income, without any long-term goals in life, and having little "respectability" to sacrifice, the borderline between criminal and noncriminal behavior becomes faint and easily breached.

This group probably provides the major share of our prison inmates. Lacking the training, skills, and "connections" necessary to pursue crime successfully, they are easily apprehended and convicted. They play no important role in organized crime and receive scant profit from their efforts. For these, it is true that "crime does not pay." Crime "pays" only those who pursue it systematically and intelligently.

7. Professional Criminals

These are the career criminals. Although there are important differences between "con" men and hijackers, all professional criminals have many common characteristics. They all define themselves as criminals and consciously organize their lives around a criminal career. They prize professional competence, are contemptuous of amateurs, and value their standing among their fellow professionals. They crave status and respectability and secure it through demonstrated skill in criminal behavior. Flashy clothes, jewelry, and expensive cars are prized as symbols of status, just as in polite society. To go to prison is humiliating because it is inconvenient, because it is a confession of professional failure, because one's skills and "connections" get rusty, and because possible partners lose faith if one gets caught too often. To have to sell the pawn ticket to one's "hock piece" (a large diamond which can be pawned when sudden cash is needed) is a humiliating symbol of professional decline.

The professional criminal is the least likely to get caught of all criminals. His crimes are not impulsive, but planned as carefully and often as skillfully as a military campaign. Professional criminals prefer not to undertake any criminal activity unless the "fix is in"—unless protection has been arranged by making a deal with law-enforcement officials. The professional criminal plans so as to receive a minimum punishment if caught; thus he never kills or resorts to violence unless actually necessary. The professional "second-story man" (house robber) never carries a gun; he would be a fool to use it, and it increases his "rap" if he is caught with it. If the professional is caught, an expert "mouthpiece" (lawyer) obstructs the wheels of justice with a skillful delaying action, aided perhaps by bribery or intimidation of witnesses or jurors. If convicted, the professional becomes a model prisoner and is usually paroled in the shortest possible time, with his "connections" sometimes applying fiscal grease to the wheels of the parole machinery. It is easy to see why professionals comprise a relatively small part of the prison population.

The mental outlook of the professional criminal is somewhat like that of the professional soldier. He kills without passion, but only when there is something to be gained by it. He takes calculated risks, carefully weighed against the objective to be gained. He has a set of firm beliefs that justify his career. The professional criminal believes that "only saps work" and that "everybody has a racket." He attributes his choice of career to his superior perception, not to any lack of moral sensitivity. He may use the "I'm a victim of society" or the "My parents abused me and the street was my home" arguments in a shrewd bid for sympathy if it will help him escape punishment, but he does not really pity himself for being a criminal—only for being caught. [70]

It is doubtful if *all* career criminals develop this system of professional skills, attitudes, and associations, [71] but there is no question that some criminals have made crime a profession.

Some romantic notions of criminal chivalry are quite inaccurate. Professional crime is a business, not a fraternal order. No chivalrous code of honor binds the professional criminal. He generally keeps his word because it is professionally and personally unwise to break promises, yet the double-cross is well known. Sharing a common contempt for the police, professional criminals will ordinarily give them no assistance and will occasionally "cover up" for a stranger whom they recognize as a fellow professional, but not to the extent of endangering themselves. The profes-

[70] See Chic Conwell, *The Professional Thief*, annotated and interpreted by Edwin H. Sutherland (Chicago, University of Chicago Press, 1937).

[71] Edwin M. Lemert, "The Behavior of the Systematic Check Forger," *Social Problems*, Vol. 6 (Fall, 1958), pp. 141-149, questions the "professionalization" thesis.

sional sometimes disposes of competitors by betraying them to the police; when caught by the police himself, he occasionally will "sing," betraying his partners in exchange for a promise of leniency.

ORGANIZED CRIME

Professional crime varies in degree of organization. Some kinds, such as picking pockets, armed robbery, or confidence games (swindles) do not lend themselves to large-scale organization, and are ordinarily handled singly or by groups of two or three. In other operations, such as gambling, prostitution, and narcotics peddling, large-scale organization has certain advantages.

Successfully organized crime operates smoothly and quietly, rarely rating headlines, whereas unorganized and nonprofessional crime fills the front pages and gives the public an incorrect notion of its relative importance. But all authorities agree that the cost of organized crime greatly exceeds that of unorganized crime and that organized crime is largely responsible for the corruption of public officials.

A number of journalistic descriptions have fairly accurately pictured the structure and functioning of organized crime, [72] and these popularizations are generally supported by more scientific sociological investigations. [73] The investigations of the "Kefauver Committee" focused national attention upon organized crime and brought wider public recognition of the tie-up between crime, business, and government, but the Kefauver investigations added nothing new to our knowledge of organized crime beyond certain up-to-date details. [74] The general pattern of organized crime was well known to sociologists, journalists, and public officials long before Senator Kefauver helped to popularize it.

Connivance of Law-Enforcement Agencies

The term *organized crime* is not applied to small roving bands of robbers, pickpockets, shoplifters, confidence men, and the like. Organized crime is crime conducted by quite large, organized groups of criminals, who operate in more or less clearly defined territories and maintain constant connections with law-enforcement officials. Elaborately organized crime is found in gambling and prostitution. In these instances, there is a large market among "respectable" people who have no interest in seeing the law enforced. This large and highly profitable market, combined

[72] For example, Courtney Ryley Cooper, *Here's To Crime* (Boston, Little, Brown, & Company, 1937); Martin Mooney, *Crime Incorporated* (New York, McGraw-Hill Book Company, Inc., 1935).

[73] William Foote Whyte, *Street Corner Society* (Chicago, University of Chicago Press, 1943).

[74] See Estes Kefauver, *Crime in America* (Garden City, Doubleday & Company, Inc., 1951).

with considerable public opposition to law enforcement, guarantees the development of organized crime and provides a ready-made rationalization for the law-enforcement officials who must co-operate. For *without exception, organized crime cannot exist long without the connivance of law-enforcement officials.* When a "book" or a house of prostitution opens, the police almost invariably know about it within a short time. For it is a patrolman's duty to know what goes on in his district, and even a sudden increase in the number of cars parked before a building or in the number of people entering it calls for an investigation. As onetime gambler Mickey Cohen remarked, ". . . none of these operations would operate for five minutes if it wasn't for the co-operation of the powers." [75] It is safe to conclude that wherever large-scale gambling or prostitution exist for long, it is with the knowledge of our public officials.

This does not mean that *all* the public officials are corrupt; in fact, it would be too costly to "pay off" all of them. Only a few strategically placed officials need to be "reached" in order to provide effective protection. A few judges, one or two assistant district attorneys, and a few police captains are enough to guarantee that the business can operate with only occasional minor annoyances. There are many subtle ways to avoid effective prosecution while going through all the motions of determined law enforcement, and there are many points at which one corrupt public official can neutralize the integrity of a dozen honest companions and frustrate honest law enforcement. The "honest cop" soon learns who is under protection and discovers the futility (and the danger) of attempting to molest them. So the honest cop concentrates on catching traffic violators, pickpockets, and other small fry and closes his eyes to the things he can do nothing about. It is, therefore, quite possible to have a "wide-open" town even though most of the police are honest. [76]

The "connections" of organized crime reach high and wide. When a New York bookie "talked" a few years ago, 450 policemen, of all ranks, either resigned, retired, or were dismissed. [77] Mayors of great cities and district attorneys by the dozen have been revealed as having amiable relations with the "mob." Even federal judges and state supreme court judges sometimes owe their appointments to the mobsters. A famous telephone conversation in which Thomas A. Aurelio thanked gangster Frank Costello for arranging his nomination as Justice of the Supreme Court of the State of New York is one of the best authenticated of many such cases. [78]

[75] *Saturday Evening Post,* Vol. 231 (October 11, 1958), p. 116.
[76] See Albert Deutsch, "The Plight of the Honest Cop," *Collier's* Vol. 132 (September 18, 1953), pp. 23 ff; Vol. 133 (May 28, 1954), pp. 29 ff; Vol. 134 (July 23, 1954), pp. 33 ff.
[77] See Norton Mockridge and Robert H. Prall, *The Big Fix* (New York, Henry Holt & Co., Inc., 1954).
[78] *New York Times* (September 1, 1943), pp. 1, 31.

Role of Respectable People in Organized Crime

Is it possible to suppress organized gambling and prostitution when there are so many customers for these services? It is difficult to suppress organized gambling while permitting private organizations to raise funds through gambling operations, yet former Governor Stevenson of Illinois has described the opposition of many "good citizens" when he instructed his state police to remove the slot machines from veterans' post and private clubs. [79] This widespread toleration of gambling, coupled with the powerful connection of "the syndicate," makes it extremely difficult to suppress gambling even when officials are determined to do so. Whether such laws should be repealed or enforced is a moot question. Most attempts at enforcement are only temporarily successful, and the existence of these laws, forbidding what many people want and will pay for, leads directly to the corruption of law-enforcement officials. Yet, Nevada's experience with legalized gambling is anything but encouraging, and the question remains unresolved. [80]

Can labor racketeering be suppressed as long as there are many businessmen who would rather deal with labor racketeers than with an honest but aggressive union? In some cases, the businessman is a victim of labor racketeering, but in other cases, he is a partner. [81] Organized theft and burglary could not operate without dishonest businessmen who sell stolen merchandise through normal trade channels.[82] As in the days of piracy when pirate loot (mostly merchandise) was marketed through dishonest

[79] Adlai E. Stevenson, "Who Runs the Gambling Machines?" *Atlantic Monthly* Vol. 189 (February, 1952), pp. 35-38.

[80] Virgil Peterson, "Gambling—Should It Be Legalized?" *Journal of Criminal Law and Criminology* Vol. 40 (September-October, 1949), pp. 259-329; Joseph F. McDonald, "Gambling in Nevada," *The Annals*, Vol. 269 (May, 1950), pp. 30-34; Estes Kefauver, *op. cit.*, Ch. 16, "Nevada: A Case Against Legalized Gambling"; Albert Deutsch, "The Sorry State of Nevada," *Collier's*, Vol. 135 (March 18, 1955), pp. 74 ff.

[81] See *Hearings Before the Select Committee on Improper Activities in the Labor and Management Field*, 85th Congress, Second Session (Washington, D. C., Government Printing Office, 1958). For a popular account, see Robert F. Kennedy, *The Enemy Within* (New York, Harper and Brothers, 1960), in which the committee's counsel writes, "Although we exposed improper activities on the part of at least fifteen attorneys and fifty companies and corporations around the country, with the exception of the bar of the State of Tennessee, no management group or bar association has taken any steps to clean house. The only group that has tried to maintain standards and clean out their corrupt elements has been the A.F.L.-C.I.O." (Quoted in *New York Times Book Review*, February 28, 1960, p. 22.) See also Daniel Bell, "Nate Shefferman, Union Buster," *Fortune*, Vol. 57 (February, 1958), pp. 120 ff; also "Waterfront Priest Accuses Employers," *New York Times*, February 12, 1956, III, p. 10.

[82] See Robert Rice, *The Business of Crime* (New York, Farrar, Strauss and Cudahy, Inc., 1956), for case histories of businessmen who co-operated with criminals for profit.

merchants under the benevolent eye of conniving government officials, [83] organized crime is not profitable without the co-operation of supposedly honest persons.

National or Regional Organization

We are occasionally entertained by lurid tales of a national crime syndicate, run by the Mafia, which reaches into every city and hamlet. [84] Although the Mafia bogeyman is popular with Congressmen seeking headlines, writers with stories to sell, and police administrators justifying their budget requests, there is no firm evidence that a national Mafia-run crime syndicate exists. At least one serious effort to find such evidence was unsuccessful. [85] A number of American gangsters are of Sicilian extraction, and some Sicilian immigrants are said to have been members of the Mafia before their migration. This does *not* prove that the Mafia, as a functioning organization, exists in the United States, just as the fraternity men in business do not prove that American business is run by the Interfraternity Council. There is also an element of national chauvinism in the Mafia myth, which conveniently blames our crime problem on a foreign minority group.

There *is* organized crime in the United States, but the role of the Mafia in it is uncertain and probably unimportant. There is no national syndicate, directing local crime operations as a board of directors runs a great corporation. There are local gangs, organized into a loose network, and local or regional syndicates, which mark out territories through negotiation and intimidation. The power of these groups is enforced by occasional beatings or killings, and occasional outbreaks of gang warfare when arrangements are in dispute. An informal network of acquaintanceship provides a means of communication, serves to identify new arrivals, and is used in arranging deals and co-operative arrangements among the syndicates.

Although gambling and prostitution form the backbone of organized crime, other activities include narcotics, hijacking, bootlegging, smuggling, labor racketeering, "protection" rackets, and possibly others. Rack-

---

[83] Cyrus H. Karraker, *Piracy Was a Business* (West Ridge, N. H., Richard R. Smith, Inc., 1953); Patrick Pringle, *Jolly Roger: The Story of the Great Age of Piracy* (New York, W. W. Norton & Company, Inc., 1953).

[84] Frederick Sondern, Jr., *Brotherhood of Evil* (New York, Farrar, Strauss, and Cudahy, 1959), "Old Style Mafia and Its Heirs, the Calculators," *Life*, Vol. 46 (February 23, 1959), pp. 20-27.

[85] California's Governor Brown engaged a special investigator to determine the extent of Mafia activities in California. The report concluded that, "The significance of the Mafia on the American scene has never been clearly defined, and its existence is yet to be objectively proven." *New York Times*, May 3, 1959, p. 46. Virgil Peterson, executive director of the Chicago Crime Commission says, "I have never seen any convincing evidence of the existence of the Mafia as an organization which governs organized crime today." (*Chicago Sun-Times*, August 7, 1959, p. 6.)

eteers have also moved into a number of legitimate businesses: hotels, restaurants, bars and night clubs, linen supply, jukeboxes and vending machines, liquor distribution, trucking, and so on. The usual objective is to eliminate competition, by "strong-arm" methods if necessary, and jack up prices. [86] Here, other businessmen have sometimes been willing partners. Whether organized crime is growing or shrinking at present is not definitely known.

SUGGESTED READINGS

Since Chapters 5 and 6 form a unit, the analysis, Summary, Suggested Readings, and Audio-Visual Aids for both chapters will be found at the end of Chapter 6.

QUESTIONS AND PROJECTS

1. What is a crime? Why is it difficult to find a fully satisfactory definition of crime?

2. Why is it difficult to determine the amount of crime or the direction of crime trends? If informed of a "crime wave," what information would be needed to determine if the report were accurate?

3. Approximately 100,000 prisoners are released each year from state and federal penitentiaries, most of them under thirty years of age. Try to compute how many people you would pass on the street before meeting an ex-convict.

4. What is meant in saying that the difference in Negro-white crime rates is better explained in terms of social class than in terms of race?

5. How does the presence of foreign-born people in our population affect our crime rates?

6. What reasons are there to doubt that crime statistics accurately measure the "criminality" of the different social classes? In what ways is the middle- or upper-class offender helped to avoid punishment?

7. What comment would you make at hearing a reference to "the criminal class"?

8. In early studies of the association between crime and physical type, emotional disturbance, poverty, or broken homes, what methodological error led to overestimates of their importance?

9. Exactly what would an "inherited criminal tendency" be? Of what special inborn reflexes, drives, or urges would it consist, and how would it operate to produce criminal behavior?

10. Is the moral criminal, as described in this chapter, a product of conflicting social values or of personal moral weakness?

11. What is the main distinction between the professional and other types of criminals?

12. Discuss the proposition: "Every community gets the kind of police force it deserves."

[86] *New York Times,* May 12, 1957, IV, p. 9.

13. In what ways do decent, respectable people contribute to the crime problem?

14. Why do some businessmen co-operate willingly with labor racketeers? Why do you think this aspect of labor racketeering has received so little attention from Congress or the press?

15. How does the Mafia myth serve the interests of politicians? Of police administrators? Of the press, radio, and TV? Of the gangsters themselves?

6

Crime and Delinquency: Causes and Treatment

ᖴᖴ

THE ANALYSIS OF CAUSES

WHAT CAUSES CRIME? This is the first question many students would ask about crime. But the classification of crime shows that much criminal behavior is properly a problem in jurisprudence, or public morality, or in education and social organization rather than a problem in criminology. It is the habitual and professional criminals whose behavior needs to be explained in terms of crime causation, together with that of the juvenile delinquents, whose behavior may seem even more perplexing.

1. Biological Theories

Early attempts at the scientific study of crime tried to establish physical differences which would identify the "criminal type." No distinct criminal type has been found, although some physical peculiarities are claimed. The Gluecks compared 500 delinquent boys with 500 carefully matched nondelinquents, and found that the solid, muscular boys were significantly more delinquent. [1] They do not claim that body type *causes* delinquency, but that the energetic, muscular boys seem to be more likely to relieve their tensions in ways that are delinquent. No physical feature causes crime; but a physical characteristic may be socially defined and treated in ways which encourage criminal behavior.

[1] Sheldon and Eleanor Glueck, *Physique and Delinquency* (New York, Harper and Brothers, 1956); see also George B. Vold, *Theoretical Criminology* (New York, Oxford University Press, 1958), Ch. 4, "Physical Type Theories," pp. 43-74.

2. Psychological Theories

There have been many attempts to link crime with some type of psychopathy. Although often considered the basis for criminal behavior, neuroses and psychoses are, in fact, comparatively rare among prison inmates [2] or juvenile delinquents. [3] It is claimed that delinquency often springs from emotional disturbance, and that delinquent behavior can be predicted from psychiatric observation; however, there is little agreement upon the traits which lead to delinquency with practically every trait being labeled predictive by one psychiatrist or another. [4]

Only a limited amount of crime and delinquency can be attributed to psychological factors. The Gluecks found some emotional disturbance among 51 per cent of their delinquents and 44 per cent of their control group of nondelinquents—not a very significant difference. [5]

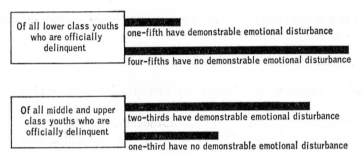

SOURCE: Adapted from data by Walter B. Miller, "Some Characteristics of Present-Day Delinquency of Relevance to Educators," Paper presented at meeting of American Association of School Administrators, Feb. 18, 1959.

FIG. 6–1. Does emotional disturbance cause delinquency?

3. Sociological Theories

The search among environmental factors for causes of delinquency seemed more promising. Shaw found that certain slum areas maintained extremely high delinquency rates quite consistently over many years. Although a succession of racial or ethnic minorities might have occupied an area, the delinquency rates remained constant regardless of the group

[2] Daniel Silverman, "The Psychotic Criminals: A Study of 500 Cases," *Journal of Clinical Psychopathology*, Vol. 8 (October, 1946), pp. 301-327; James C. Coleman, *Abnormal Psychology and Modern Life* (New York, Scott, Foresman & Company, 1959), p. 349.

[3] Michael Hakeem, "A Critique of the Psychiatric Approach to the Prevention of Juvenile Delinquency," *Social Problems*, Vol. 5 (Winter, 1957-1958), pp. 194-205.

[4] Michael Hakeem, *op. cit.*

[5] Sheldon and Eleanor Glueck, *Unraveling Juvenile Delinquency* (New York, The Commonwealth Fund, 1950), p. 239; also George B. Vold, *op. cit.*, pp. 109-140.

living in it. [6] Obviously, crime was not a product of the kind of people in the area but a product of the physical and social life of the area. Other studies showed some association between juvenile delinquency and broken homes, parental neglect, school failure, parental alcoholism, and other social circumstances. But these studies did not indicate *causes,* for in each instance the statistical associations were too low. Furthermore, in some cases, such as delinquency and school failure, it is difficult to determine which is cause and which is effect. Instead of listing environmental factors as causes, it is more correct to list them as "risk factors," since they increase the risk of coming into contact with and learning criminal behavior. For criminal behavior is *behavior,* and like other social behavior, *criminal behavior must be learned.* This discovery has led to the formulation of a *differential-association theory of crime.*

a. The *differential-association* theory states that *most criminal behavior is learned through contact with criminal patterns which are present, are acceptable, and are rewarded in one's physical and social environment.* As Sutherland states: [7]

The hypothesis of differential association is that criminal behavior is learned in association with those who define such behavior favorably and in isolation from those who define it unfavorably, and that a person in an appropriate situation engages in such criminal behavior if, and only if, the weight of the favorable definitions exceeds the weight of the unfavorable definitions.

In a "delinquency area," where perhaps one-fourth or more of the youths are officially delinquent each year, and many more are delinquent without being caught, it is no exaggeration to say that *delinquency is normal.* Although not every youth is delinquent, most of them are delinquent some of the time, some of them are delinquent most of the time, and delinquent behavior is an integral part of the area culture. Since such areas have a high adult crime rate, an easy and natural graduation to a criminal career is provided for the juvenile.

Yet not all children living in a delinquency area become delinquent, and not all juvenile delinquents become adult criminals. Although criminal patterns are an integral feature of the area culture, even the delinquency area is not totally isolated from noncriminal patterns and anticriminal definitions. In many cases a stable family life, strongly integrated around the conventionally approved values, may insulate the child against the criminal patterns of the area, while an unsatisfactory home life virtually throws the child into the streets. The Gluecks, after carefully controlled studies of hundreds of delinquents, believe that the family life of the child is very nearly the all-important factor in delinquency. They believe

---

[6] Clifford R. Shaw and others, *Delinquency Areas* (Chicago, University of Chicago Press, 1929).

[7] Edwin H. Sutherland, *White Collar Crime* (New York, The Dryden Press, Inc., 1949), p. 234.

they can predict a delinquency with 90 per cent accuracy from the "five highly decisive" factors in family life: father's discipline (harsh, erratic, unsympathetic); mother's supervision (indifferent, unconcerned); father's affection (lacking); mother's affection (cold, indifferent, even hostile); cohesiveness of the family (unintegrated, devoid of warm companionship). Where all five of these factors are favorable, serious delinquency is practically unknown. [8]

In some instances the church or school may acquaint the child with noncriminal ambitions and values, but it is rare for these institutions to affect children very deeply unless supported by a constructive home environment. Life in a deteriorated area of drab, crowded housing and dubious business enterprises offers the child many contacts with criminal patterns. In a high delinquency area, these factors—unsatisfactory home life, unsolved emotional problems, and the influences of a deteriorated neighborhood—all work together to increase the child's contacts with criminal patterns, while reducing or neutralizing his contacts with noncriminal patterns and anticriminal values.

This holds true not only for the slum delinquent but for the middle-class delinquent as well. Since middle-class and upper-class delinquents do not live in deteriorated neighborhoods, delinquent behavior is much less a normal part of their cultural world. In a certain sense, delinquency is normal for the slum child and abnormal for the middle-class child. The middle-class child has less contact with delinquent patterns and more contact with anticriminal evaluations than has the slum child. Yet the middle-class child is not isolated from contact with criminal behavior, for he reads about it, sees it portrayed in movies and on television, and observes a certain amount of unreported crime in his social world. As long as there is no serious rupture in his emotional life, his close and frequent association with anticriminal definitions is likely to keep him from criminal behavior. But if his emotional life is seriously disturbed—by parental conflicts, by social difficulties with his age group, or by other unsolved emotional conflicts—he frequently grows immune to the anticriminal evaluations and becomes delinquent.

This differential-association theory is equally applicable to white-collar crime. The discovery that a great many of one's associates are chiseling on their income tax, and that they view it as "smart" rather than shameful, is a powerful temptation to follow suit. The employee who sees his boss entertaining relatives on the company yacht, and receives from his boss detailed instructions on how to cheat the government, may wonder why he should not cheat his boss now and then.

The differential-association theory does not explain all criminal be-

[8] Sheldon and Eleanor Glueck, *Predicting Juvenile Delinquency* (Cambridge, Mass., Harvard University Press, 1959). See also Walter C. Reckless, Simon Dinitz, and Ellen Murray, "The Good Boy in a High Delinquency Area," *Journal of Criminal Law, Criminology, and Police Science*, Vol. 48 (May-June, 1957), pp. 18-25.

havior. It does not cover crimes of impulse or passion, or those delinquencies which spring from emotional maladjustment. [9] It does not explain the original *causes* of crime, but describes a process whereby crime is transmitted and perpetuated.

b. Group-conflict theories. There are some theories which attempt to explain criminal behavior in terms of some kind of group conflict. Minority groups, defeated by discrimination and inequality, may turn to crime in frustration and bitterness. Many criminal acts take place in the course of other kinds of group conflict—battles between unions and management or between rival unions, contests between conservative and radical political groups, and so on. The nineteenth-century range wars between cattlemen and settlers are an historic example. Within each group, its vested interests are sanctified and its grievances nursed until violent reprisals seem morally justified even when they are in violation of law.

Group-conflict theories help explain some crimes, but not all of them. Some minorities, for instance, have high official crime rates, but the crime rates of others, such as the Chinese and Japanese, are very low. And many individual crimes are difficult to connect with any kind of group conflict or group interest. [10]

c. Delinquent-subculture theories. These theories note that most officially delinquent youths associate mainly with other delinquents, [11] and that many of them become adult criminals. [12] Several studies also show from 50 to 90 per cent of official delinquents coming from homes with a record of crime in the home. [13] Between 25 and 50 per cent of all household units in lower-class subcultures of major urban centers are irregular families with the "parents" not married to each other. [14] While 98 per cent of the Glueck's persistently delinquent boys associated mainly with other delinquents, only 7 per cent of the nondelinquent boys from the same area associated with delinquents. [15]

Clearly there is a delinquent subculture which is shared by most of the persistent delinquents but by few nondelinquents. This delinquent subculture rejects middle class values as expressed by teachers, ministers,

[9] Cf. James F. Short, Jr., "Differential Association and Delinquency," *Social Problems,* Vol. 4 (January-March, 1957), pp. 233-239.

[10] Vold, *op. cit.,* Ch. 11, "Group Conflict Theories as Explanation of Crime," pp. 203-219.

[11] Marshall B. Clinard, *The Sociology of Deviant Behavior* (New York, Rinehart & Company, Inc., 1957), pp. 180-181.

[12] Vold, *op. cit.,* p. 295.

[13] Edwin H. Sutherland and Donald R. Cressey, *Principles of Criminology* (Philadelphia, J. B. Lippincott Co., 1955), pp. 174-175.

[14] A. B. Hollingshead, *Elmtown's Youth* (New York, John Wiley & Sons, Inc., 1949), p. 117; U.S. Senate, Subcommittee on Low-Income Families, 84th Congress, *Characteristics of Low-Income Population* (Washington, D. C., Government Printing Office, 1955), p. 48.

[15] Sheldon and Eleanor Glueck, *Delinquents in the Making* (New York, Harper and Brothers, 1952), p. 89.

police, and, perhaps, parents. Its members express masculinity by rejecting maternal influences. Their crimes are nonutilitarian, malicious, and negativistic. The *act* of stealing is more important than the object stolen. Boys outside this subculture, as well as disapproving adults, are "squares," unworthy of serious consideration. One graduate of the subculture recalls an incident: [16]

"Thirteen arrests." The judge shook his head over my file. "Gang-fights, shootings, burglary, stealing a car . . . I don't know what to make of you. . . . Why do you do these things?"

I shrugged. What a dumb question! Every boy I knew did these things. Maybe I just did more of them and better.

One sociologist attributes the delinquent subculture to the frustrations of the working-class boy who is competing unsuccessfully for status in a middle-class oriented society. [17] Whether this is correct or not, a delinquent subculture *does* exist and helps promote delinquency. This theory is less helpful in explaining delinquency among girls, among middle-class youth, and among the emotionally maladjusted.

None of the above-mentioned theories of crime causation is completely satisfactory. All help show how criminal behavior is transmitted and rationalized, but none of them explains what *causes* crime in the first place. The basic causes of crime are unknown and probably unknowable, perhaps because they are inseparable from the same drives and motives that impel all other behavior. A search for understanding of the conditions under which criminal behavior appears and spreads has proved to be far more useful.

THE PERSONAL-DEVIATION APPROACH

This approach views a social problem as an outgrowth of certain individuals who, for one reason or another, fail to absorb and internalize conventional attitudes, habits, goals, and values. The criminal is viewed as a deviant person who has failed to form the normal value judgments, ambitions, and habits, and instead has developed socially disapproved ones.

Such an approach does not fit slum delinquents, since delinquency is a normal part of their cultural system. It would be inapplicable to "legal," institutional, situational, and at least some of the "moral" criminals, for in none of these cases have the offenders rejected the conventional value system. They have, in some way, become criminals despite the conventionality of their value system and life organization.

But some of the "moral" criminals (those who engage in sex perver-

[16] "A Gang Leader's Redemption," *Life*, Vol. 44 (April 28, 1958), pp. 69 ff.
[17] Albert K. Cohen, *Delinquent Boys: The Culture of the Gang* (Glencoe, The Free Press, 1955). See also John I. Kitsuse and David C. Dietrick, "Delinquent Boys: A Critique," *American Sociological Review*, Vol. 24 (April, 1959), pp. 208-215.

sions, for example) are deviant personalities, as are many habitual and professional criminals. In these cases, the individual has rejected major portions of the conventional value system and consciously identifies himself as different from other people in this respect.

The reasons for criminal deviation are probably similar to the reasons for any other form of personal deviation. *Any factor in inheritance, environment, or social experience can become either a factor in a conventional or in a deviant personality organization.* Lack of maternal affection drives one child to the streets, another to books, still another to church. A number of biographical studies have shown how the influences of a deteriorated neighborhood interact with an unsatisfactory home life in producing many juvenile delinquents who graduate into adult criminals. [18] Yet even a "desirable" characteristic may be defined and interpreted in social experience in such a way as to contribute to a deviant personality orientation, as seen in this case: [19]

School was always easy for me. By just sitting and listening to what happened I could always learn enough to pass the examinations pretty well. I never bought a textbook and never studied one single lesson throughout high school. My grades were never high but I never failed a course and my grades averaged more than satisfactory. . . . I also learned quite young that if one is smart he can outwit the ordinary suckers who are really pretty dull. Only dopes work for a living. I've never really done a day's work in my life and I don't intend to. I have always found it possible to work out some kind of a racket and you can always be sure to find some sucker who will do the work for half the gain. I live on the other half. . . . I am now 40 years old and in this scrape which will probably land me in jail. I just overstepped a little—didn't cover up too well. My lawyer tells me I won't get over four years and I may be out in two and a half for good behavior. You can bet that my behavior will be —— good. And the guys who sent me up will be working for me yet.

This deviant of extremely high native intelligence, whose parents and teachers never required him to do any real work, developed a pattern of "getting by" without work. His home life failed to cultivate conventional ambitions and values, but did provide him with poise, vocabulary, and refinement which were helpful to him in his criminal career. As this case shows, high intelligence, a pleasing personality, and a "good" home background can be incorporated into either a deviant or a conventional personality organization.

No one knows exactly how large a proportion of criminals are emotionally maladjusted. It is clear that some prison inmates show evidence

[18] See Clifford R. Shaw, *The Jack-roller; A Delinquent Boy's Own Story* (Chicago, University of Chicago Press, 1930); Clifford R. Shaw and M. E. Moore, *Natural History of a Delinquent Career* (Chicago, University of Chicago Press, 1931); Clifford R. Shaw, H. D. McKay, and J. F. McDonald, *Brothers in Crime* (Chicago, University of Chicago Press, 1938).

[19] Quoted from John F. Cuber, *Sociology*, 4th ed. (New York, Appleton-Century-Crofts, Inc., 1959), pp. 217-218.

of emotional maladjustment, although genuine neurotics and psychotics are quite rare. But those who harbor intense resentments, who are erratic and unstable, or who have other serious emotional problems, are likely to have difficulty in conforming to social expectations.

The study of criminal deviation is, then, only a phase of the larger study of personality development in general. In any society, a number of persons develop badly adjusted personalities or fail to internalize the conventional values and are therefore deviant; some, but not all, of these come from bad environments. Among the possible behavior outlets for deviant persons are a number which are criminal. The specific study of criminal careers in terms of personality deviation helps one to understand crime but will not fully explain it. Intelligent treatment for criminals is impossible without this understanding.

THE VALUE-CONFLICT APPROACH

The value-conflict approach analyzes the problem in terms of the conflicting values of our society. Values differ both on the questions of what acts are crimes and what should be done about them. In "moral" and institutional crime, the value conflict is obvious. These are widespread crimes because the value judgments of certain groups have been written into law, forbidding acts which the value judgments of other groups tolerate. Gambling and prostitution become problems purely because of such value conflicts. If everyone disapproved of these activities there would be no question of what to do about them, and suppression would be less difficult. Or if everyone accepted these activities, there would be no problem, since no critical judgments would define them as situations needing correction. But wherever there is a substantial number of people whose values define acceptably a form of behavior forbidden by law, widespread violation of the law and persistent corruption of law-enforcement officials are inevitable.

There is another manner in which value conflicts function as a "cause" of crime. This is through the corrosion of personal morality by the value conflicts inherent within the culture. At home, church, and school the child learns a set of moral values—truth, honesty, loyalty, and so on, and a set of copybook maxims—"honesty is the best policy," "crime does not pay," "truth wins out in the end," and the like. Eventually he discovers that these are only half true. He comes to realize that a considerable amount of business or professional success is based upon a subtle betrayal of trust. [20] He learns that a salesperson's job is to sell not necessarily what the customer needs but what the store has to sell. He realizes that much advertising depends upon the cautious half-truth, and upon a calculated pandering to the vanities, fears, and weaknesses of the potential

[20] See Donald R. Cressey, *Other People's Money: A Study in the Social Psychology of Criminal Violation of Financial Trust* (Glencoe, Ill., The Free Press, 1953).

customers. [21] He learns about politicians who practice graft, about physicians who split fees and collect kickbacks from pharmacists and opticians, about the bribery of purchasing agents, about falsification of financial statements, about the many legal and semilegal ways of avoiding tax obligations, about padded repair bills, and dozens of other forms of fraud. If he is in business, he soon learns that his customers are as dishonest as he is, or perhaps even worse! He realizes that a customer's claim for damaged property is nearly always inflated. "We've never yet damaged an *old* piece of luggage," says an airline executive. [22] Automobile insurance companies estimate that one-fourth to one-half of all the money paid out in claims goes into secret commissions and padded charges. [23] He generally comes to accept those forms of sharp practice which are common to his occupation, [24] along with the rationalizations which justify them, and he is constantly reminded of the many other forms of exploitation and fraud going on around him. Meanwhile, according to this theory, his moral sensitivity is blunted and his lofty moral principles are relegated to a remote island of life, available for ritualistic repetition when needed, but carefully insulated from any controlling influence upon his economic practice. Some criminologists consider this process to be a primary explanation of the prevalence of crime in modern society. [25]

This indictment is, however, in some respects an exaggeration. Although in practically every business or profession there are certain questionable or dishonest practices that are common, it is probably true that the dishonest acts are vastly outnumbered by the honest acts, and false statements outnumbered by truthful ones. After some experience with the business world, one learns to expect scrupulous honesty in some activities and dishonesty in others. For example, it is likely that most people do not expect complete truth in advertising and are calmly prepared to discount what they read. Meanwhile, they do expect a businessman to be honest in weighing hamburger or making change, and in these respects businessmen are probably more honest than their customers. In securing a proper perspective, one must not assume that most business activity is dishonest or fraudulent, for this would be highly unjustified. But it is true that there is enough misrepresentation, exploitation of ignorance and gullibility, and deliberate fraud in the business world to make the maintenance of a strict moral conscience more difficult.

The role of cultural values in producing crime, however, goes be-

[21] See Vance Packard, *The Hidden Persuaders* (New York, David McKay Co., Inc., 1957).

[22] Morris B. Baken, "There's Larceny in the Air," *Flying*, Vol. 64 (March, 1959), pp. 56 ff.

[23] *New York Times*, March 1, 1959, p. 43. See also Thomas Meehan, "The Case of The Insurance Detective," *New York Times Magazine*, March 6, 1960, pp. 51 ff.

[24] For example, see "Confessions of an Appliance Salesman," *Consumer Reports*, Vol. 23 (October, 1958), pp. 546-547.

[25] Harry Elmer Barnes and Negley K. Teeters, *New Horizons in Criminology* (Englewood Cliffs, N. J., Prentice-Hall, Inc., 1951), p. 22.

yond the tendency for shady practices to beget criminal ones or for white-collar crime to encourage shirt-sleeve crime. It also involves the basic ethos of our culture. There are good reasons to suspect that *the basic values of our competition-success-seeking culture must inevitably produce a high crime rate.* No other culture has so persistently trained people to want so many things that most of them have no remote possibility of ever getting. No other culture has so strongly conditioned them to view themselves as failures unless they attain status and living standards that most of them cannot ever attain. It is not surprising that many of the people in this bitter struggle for status and respectability should overstep the line of legality, especially when that line of legality is so vague.

It may be that there is no prospect of a low crime rate in a society which pays greater attention to the possession of status and wealth than to the means used in gaining them. It is unlikely that America can achieve a greatly lowered crime rate without major changes in American values. In place of the present Cadillac-and-country-club measure of success, it might be necessary to measure status and respectability in terms of some values more readily attainable by all who put forth a reasonable effort. For only when the rewards of status and respectability represent attainable probabilities to all those who are willing to strive for them—only then will the resort to shady short cuts be discouraged.

There is little prospect of any such sweeping change in American cultural values. The entire American value system would need to be overhauled and most of the present incentives of our economic system would need to be revised. Even to blueprint these value changes, together with the other institutional changes they would produce, would be a task few sociologists would care to attempt. Furthermore, values do not change at the suggestion of a sociologist; values emerge from the social life of a people and change only as it changes. Therefore, to call for a revolution in American values is unrealistic; we must recognize that part of the cost of our present competition-success value system will be paid in high crime rates.

THE SOCIAL-DISORGANIZATION APPROACH

The social-disorganization approach studies the crime problem as a product of social change. A stable, well-integrated society has very little crime. Those habits and practices that are necessary and useful will have become institutionalized and thoroughly supported by the moral values of the culture. In time, an objectionable practice will be dealt with in a stable culture, either by a gradual change of values so as to approve it, or by suppressing it through the compelling system of social control found in such a society.

Social change disorganizes the existing network of arrangements and values of a society. Many old norms become inapplicable and numerous value conflicts appear. Children are allowed to develop expectations which do not fit the realities they eventually find. Traditional standards seem remote and meaningless, and traditional behavior controls lose power. Change produces new groupings with special interests to advance and new situations and pressures to reconcile. Such rapid and sweeping changes as Western civilization experiences mean that before adjustment to one set of changes is completed, new changes rush upon it.

A social-disorganization analysis of crime emphasizes how change from a rural agricultural society to an urban industrial society has revolutionized our values and disorganized our traditional social control machinery. The hard-work-and-thrift value orientation of a peasant people has been replaced with live-it-up materialism. The informal controls of neighborhood and community are less effective in our anonymous urban civilization. Parental supervision of children and adolescents suffers due to modern transportation, commercialized recreation, the smallness of homes and apartments, employment of mothers, and the daily scattering of the family for work and play. Modern employment schedules, with work at all hours of day or night, disrupt the traditional family routines and subject millions of families to temptations unknown to our grandparents. In numerous subtle ways the conditions of modern life tend to break down traditional controls and to increase temptations; for example, the mere fact that one passes jewelry stores and auto salesrooms instead of brooks and fences on the way to work probably serves to increase wants and temptations. For the first time in history, a society is expending great energies, through advertising and salesmanship, in deliberately encouraging the people to want more than they can possibly get. Although advertising and salesmanship doubtless are necessary parts of our economic system, this mass promotion of unlimited wants is a development of which the impact is only beginning to become apparent. Many of the traditional values, such as thrift, simplicity of life, and pride in craftsmanship, become increasingly remote as the urge for conspicuous consumption is nursed into full bloom.

Social change produces many new situations and practices for which the traditional mores have no clear-cut guide. Although the existing mores clearly condemn murder or rape and openly support private property and marriage, they provide no positive definitions concerning the propriety of labor unions, selling watered stock, or the set-back requirements for a skyscraper. In order to regulate such technical matters, thousands of laws which are not tied in with any strongly entrenched mores have been passed. There are too many such technical matters; they have developed too rapidly and are too complicated for any coherent set of moral definitions to have crytallized and preceded the passing of the law. Such laws, which are not buttressed by a strong supporting morality, are difficult to enforce; neither the violator, the enforcement officials, nor the public view these violations very seriously, but are likely to dismiss them lightly as minor administrative errors instead of criminal acts. Severe punishments for such technical violations probably would be unwise, yet it remains likely that widespread violation and lax enforcement of certain laws tend to break down the habit of obedience to law in general.

Social change also produces new interest groupings of people and alters the complexion of old ones. New occupations appear, new industries arise, new recreational groups develop, and new pressure groups of all sorts are constantly being organized. A constant battle rages for position and power in which the law is often violated. Again, the existing morality often provides no clear-cut guides. Is the wire-tapper, who secretly (and illegally) records telephone conversations for the use of police, politicians, business competitors, suspicious husbands, or sometimes blackmailers, a menace or a benefactor? Should corporations or labor unions be permitted to make contributions to political campaign funds? Should the closed shop and industry-wide bargaining be viewed as labor rights or labor abuses? The rise of new interest groups always produces considerable new legislation and considerable confusion.

Another disorganizing feature of American life is its ethnic hetero-geneity—the variety of racial and national backgrounds represented among the American people. Settled by a mixture of peoples, America has never possessed an integrated cultural tradition. Immigration during the past century brought a heavy infusion of Slavic and Latin elements into the predominantly Anglo-Saxon culture, resulting in increased cultural conflict and confusion. Many of our value conflicts stem from the clash of cultural backgrounds—for example, Catholic-Protestant disagreement over gambling, or over relations of church and state. In the clash of cultural backgrounds, each cultural tradition loses some of its power to control the behavior of individuals. The high crime rates of most second-generation immigrant groups reflect the assimilation problems which they confront. With parental authority undermined by the clash of cultures, the immigrant's child readily absorbs the delinquent patterns of the slum areas in which most immigrants live. With the virtual disappearance of immigration, this problem rapidly fades, but the lack of a single coherent cultural tradition will continue to create moral confusion for generations.

The lack of any important role for adolescents is a prime defect in our social organization. In most societies, children and adolescents have had important, productive things to do, giving them a real share in adult life and responsibility. Although often monotonous and sometimes re-sented, their work was important and worthwhile. In our society, the task of the child and adolescent is to grow, to learn, and to wait. He has no really important *work* to do, and is excluded from the important adult life of the society. He has no clearly defined role to fill, with a clearly defined set of privileges and duties for each age level, but is expected to alternate between adult responsibility and childlike dependence at the whim of adults. Just how to replace the delays, confusions, and trivialities of our present adolescent roles with a more functionally significant adolescent role in our highly complex society is not clear. Perhaps delinquency and the adolescent problem are part of the price we must pay for our dynamic, complex culture.

Of all the approaches to the crime problem, sociologists have made most use of the social-disorganization approach. It provides a very plausible explanation for much criminal behavior. The high crime rates of disorganized groups, such as second-generation immigrants or the American Indians, and the increase of crime in war-devastated countries, clearly show how social disorganization is accompanied by a high crime rate. Yet no one approach gives a complete picture. The social-disorganization approach indicates the conditions under which crime may be expected to increase or decrease; the value-conflict approach reveals how people may rationalize and justify their criminal behavior; the personal-deviation approach helps explain why some people are more inclined to be criminal than others.

SOME POPULAR PROPOSALS FOR TREATMENT

1. Severe Punishment

Each "crime wave" produces a backwash of clamor for more severe punishment. A string of murders arouses a cry for the death penalty among people who do not realize that the homicide rate has been falling, [26] or that the homicide rate in states having the death penalty is approximately three times as high as in states without it. [27] This clamor for punishment is understandable, if not scientific. *There are three conventional reasons for punishment: revenge, reformation, and deterrence.* Although punishment for revenge may have been abandoned in theory, the popular thirst for revenge is brutally apparent whenever a highly revolting crime captures public attention. It is entirely respectable, however, to believe in punishment for reformation or deterrence, and meanwhile vent one's hostilities very effectively. Consequently, many people see the crime problem as simply a matter of imposing more severe punishments.

The facts about the frequency with which criminals revert to crime after being punished are revealing, if not exactly encouraging. Glueck

[26] The homicide rate, despite possibly more accurate reporting in recent years, has fallen from 7.1 murders per 100,000 people in 1933 to 4.7 in 1958, according to *Uniform Crime Reports.*

[27] Karl F. Schuessler, "The Deterrent Influence of the Death Penalty," *The Annals,* American Academy of Political and Social Science, Vol. 284 (November, 1952), pp. 54-62.

quotes a number of studies showing that from half to three-fourths of the convicts in penal institutions have a record of at least one earlier conviction, [28] and that from two-thirds to four-fifths of them became officially delinquent again within five years after release. [29] Since these records are an incomplete measure of later criminality, it is reasonable to estimate that somewhere between three-fourths and nine-tenths of all criminals commit further crimes after they have been punished. There is no evidence that states with more severe penalties have lower crime rates or recidivism rates than states with lighter penalties.

The "practical" people who continue to advocate punishment seem unaware that their proposal has had several thousand years of trial without conspicuous success. The severity of ancient and medieval punishments is beyond the comprehension of most students today. A long list of offenses were normally punished by amputation of ears, noses, hands, genitals, tearing off scalps, tearing out tongues, branding, and by other mutilations. Severe and often fatal floggings were commonly used for relatively trivial offenses. One decree of William the Conqueror stated: [30]

> We decree that no one shall be killed or hung for any misdeeds, but rather that his eyes shall be plucked out and his feet, hands, and testicles cut off, so that whatever part of his body remains will be a living sign to all of his crime and iniquity.

No historical movie begins to depict the brutality of medieval punishments, for it would sicken the patrons. These cruel punishments were finally abandoned by civilized societies and replaced with imprisonment when it became apparent to eighteenth- and nineteenth-century critics that they were ineffective. [31] One of the arguments against mutilation was that the sight of mutilated convicts had become so commonplace that it was no longer a deterrent. One of the arguments leading to the abolition of public hangings was the claim that, at the very moment when the trap was being sprung, and the observers presumably being deterred from crime by the awesome spectacle—at this moment of fascinated concentration, the pickpockets and thieves were the busiest. It almost seemed as though public hangings produced more crime than they prevented.

It becomes more clear why punishment is relatively ineffective if the different kinds of criminals are again considered. Since legalistic criminals

---

[28] Sheldon Glueck, *Crime and Justice* (Boston, Little, Brown & Co., 1936), pp. 207-209.

[29] Numerous recidivism studies are summarized in George B. Vold, "Does the Prison Reform?" *The Annals*, Vol. 293 (May, 1954), pp. 42-50, with the conclusion that from 60 to 80 per cent of the offenders receive further convictions after leaving prison.

[30] Barnes and Teeters, *op. cit.*, p. 344.

[31] Cf. Dr. Benjamin Rush, *An Inquiry into the Effects of Public Punishments upon Criminals and upon Society* (Philadelphia, 1787). Quoted in Barnes and Teeters, *ibid.*, p. 346.

have no criminal intent, deterrence is impossible and reformation unnecessary. Severe punishment of moralistic criminals (excepting certain sex offenders) is impractical, for our society will not tolerate strict enforcement of these widely violated laws. Punishment of psychopathic criminals is repugnant to all who realize that the psychopath is emotionally incapable of directing his behavior and that punishment will neither reform nor deter him. The institutional criminals form another group which society will not allow to be severely punished; furthermore, since this "criminal" and his associates agree in justifying his behavior, punishment will not make him not penitent, but bitter. The situational criminals need no reformation, since their life organization is not criminal and their crimes are committed only under desperate circumstances wherein it is unlikely that any threats of punishment would deter them. The habitual criminals are generally ineffectual, unstable personalities, repeatedly surrendering to impulse or getting into "desperate" jams; they are unlikely to be deterred by some remote punishment, nor will punishment transform them into well-integrated or responsible personalities. The professional criminal discounts the likelihood of punishment. There is no evidence in the life histories of professional criminals to indicate that they gave much thought to the possibility of punishment during their apprenticeship; nor do the life histories of law-abiding folk show that they ever seriously considered a criminal career and recoiled from it through fear of punishment. Neither is there any convincing evidence that many criminals of any kind have actually reformed because of punishment, and criminals who have reformed are said to be unanimous in believing that their punishment did not help them. [32] It would seem that an examination of the values, motivations, and life organization of each type of criminal reveals none for which punishment is likely to prove either deterrent or reformatory.

This misplaced faith in punishment may rest upon the unrealistic assumption that people consciously *decide* whether to be criminal—that they consider a criminal career, rationally balance its dangers against its rewards, and arrive at a decision based upon such pleasure-pain calculations. It supposedly follows that if the pain element is increased by severe punishments, people will turn from crime to righteousness. A little reflection reveals the absurdity of this notion. How many of the readers of this textbook can recall when they seriously considered a criminal career, not as a vague daydream but as a concrete possibility? How many weighed this possibility and, after balancing all the considerations, "decided" against it? For most law-abiding citizens this decision is not a conscious, rational choice, thoughtfully made at some crucial moment; it is an unconsciously developed way of life, a set of values, and a group of expectations, all emerging from the thousands of events and incidents

[32] See John Resko, *Reprieve* (New York, Doubleday & Company, Inc., 1956); also Sutherland and Cressey, *op. cit.*, p. 318.

forming their social experience. Nor is it any more likely that the professional criminal ever makes such a conscious choice. For him, too, the "decision" is a gradual, imperceptible crystallization of habits and values which emerge from the totality of his social experience. For him, the question of *whether* to commit crimes has never arisen; the only question is one of *which* crimes to commit and *how* to commit them most profitably. Just as most people "decide" whether to be Catholic or Protestant without having to think it over at all, so do most people decide whether to be criminal or noncriminal. Since a rational choice between criminal and noncriminal careers is rare, deterrence is unnecessary for the law-abiding and ineffective for the criminal.

For all these reasons, criminologists and penologists generally agree in doubting the effectiveness of punishment either as a deterrent or as a means of reformation. One distinguished criminologist even draws the startling conclusion that punishment leaves a man seven times more likely to commit further crime than those convicts treated in some other manner. [33] This conclusion is supported by the informal testimony of many criminals, of which the following, related by a famous warden, is typical. [34]

Before Morris Wasser's execution, when I told him the governor had refused him a last-minute respite, he said bitterly: "All right, Warden. It doesn't make much difference what I say now about this here system of burning a guy, but I want to set you straight on sometł ing."

"What's that?" I asked.

"Well, this electrocution business is the bunk. It don't do no good, I tell you, and I know, because I never thought of the chair when I plugged that old guy. And I'd probably do it again if he had me on the wrong end of a rod."

"You mean," I said, "that you don't feel you've done wrong in taking another man's life?"

"No, warden, it ain't that," he said impatiently. "I mean that you just don't think of the hot seat when you plug a guy. Somethin' inside you just makes you kill, 'cause you know if you don't shut him up it's curtains for you."

"I see. Then you never even thought of what would happen to you at the time."

"Hell, no! And lots of other guys in here, Harry and Brick and Luke, all says the same thing. I tell you the hot seat will never stop a guy from pullin' a trigger." That was Wasser's theory, and I've heard it echoed many times since.

2. Better Law Enforcement

The popular faith in punishment is coupled with an equally strong faith in law enforcement as a means of reducing crime. The *immediate* effect of better law enforcement, however, would be to increase crime

[33] Thorsten Sellin, quoted in Barnes and Teeters, *op. cit.*, p. 74.

[34] Lewis E. Lawes, *Meet the Murderer* (New York, Harper and Brothers, 1940), pp. 178-179.

rates, since many unreported crimes and unidentified criminals would be added to the crime statistics. The long-run effects are more difficult to measure.

It is possible that the popular faith in law enforcement is not entirely misplaced. It is a fact that organized crime cannot long survive determined law enforcement. It is probable that the apparent immunity enjoyed by many professional criminals helps encourage youths to follow suit. The wholesale violation of many rarely enforced laws may tend to undermine respect for law in general. It is quite likely, therefore, that more effective law enforcement would eventually reduce the amount of crime committed while perhaps increasing the number of criminals apprehended and under treatment. A *certainty* of punishment would probably be a more effective deterrent than severity of possible punishment. [35] If prompt punishment were absolutely certain, there might be few crimes except those of accident, compulsion, or passion.

The unreality of this proposal lies in the difficulty of securing better enforcement. The many legal and constitutional rights of the accused make the work of the police more difficult, and these rights of the accused are often violated in the process of his conviction. [36] Even so, many suspects who are guilty escape conviction, so one way to increase convictions is to reduce the rights of the accused. This would involve a value sacrifice many of us would be reluctant to make.

Other difficulties hamper law enforcement. There are many laws which the public is unwilling to repeal, yet unwilling to enforce. The public calls for honest officials, but gives them little support. [37] The public desires a competent police force, but is unwilling to bear the financial cost of one. Our localistic bias prevents us from organizing our 40,000 competing and overlapping police agencies into more effectively integrated regional units. We are concerned about police corruption, but not concerned enough to provide a form of city government that makes a politically independent police force more easily attainable. Although better law enforcement might prove effective, there is little prospect of any sudden changes. Meanwhile, "police science" has appeared in the college curriculum, professional police administrators are replacing untrained ones, and police operations are steadily becoming more efficient.

[35] John C. Ball, "The Deterrence Concept in Criminology and Law," *Journal of Criminology, Criminal Law, and Police Science,* Vol. 46 (September-October, 1955), pp. 347-354.

[36] See *Secret Detention by the Chicago Police* (Chicago, Illinois Division, American Civil Liberties Union, 1959); also Subcommittee on Constitutional Rights of the Committee on the Judiciary, Senate, 85th Congress, 2nd Session, *Confessions and Police Detection* (Washington, D. C., Government Printing Office, 1958).

[37] See Anonymous, "Are You Sure You Want an Honest Mayor?" *Collier's,* Vol. 132 (October 30, 1953), pp. 64 ff.

3. Education

The plea to "build schools instead of jails" is doubtless a fine one, but it offers a doubtful cure for the crime problem. *More* education of the conventional sort will not reduce crime, for there is no conclusive evidence that poorly educated people are more criminal than high-school or college graduates, even though the highly educated are less frequently caught. It is possible, however, that the *kind* of schools we have may affect delinquency and crime. It is plausible to argue that a school with an indifferent staff, a dull and unchallenging curriculum, and a slender program of activities offers no help to an unadjusted child and may drive him to truancy and the influences of street life. There can be no doubt that a fully adequate school has many opportunities to aid in the development of well-adjusted personalities and in the guidance of poorly adjusted ones. [38] Since the school has regular supervision of nearly all children, it is the institution through which guidance and counseling can most easily be arranged. The effectiveness of such services in reducing delinquency and the degree of success with which schools are employing them are not known. Concrete evidence of the effectiveness of superior schools in controlling delinquency is lacking, except in a few isolated instances. Meanwhile, the overcrowding and understaffing of our public schools at present is less than encouraging. The proportion of students taught in substandard schools by substandard teachers remains high, so the possible contributions of the school will for some years remain largely unrealized.

4. Religion

Many assert that our crime rates rise because we have "forgotten God," and that only a "return to faith" will lower them. Just how we have "forgotten God" is not clear, since church membership, participation, and financial support appear to be at record levels.

Few doubt that if all Americans were good Christians (or good Jews, or good humanists) all of the time, there would be little crime. It is equally clear that no church has succeeded in getting all of its members to act like good Christians all of the time. In fact, it is not certain whether church members are more law-abiding than nonmembers. One investigator, after giving thousands of lie-detector tests, is of the opinion that conventionally religious people are no more or less honest than those with no faith. [39]

[38] Paul H. Bowman, "Effects of a Revised School Program on Potential Delinquents," *The Annals*, Vol. 322 (March, 1959), pp. 53-61. See also William Kvaraceus and others, *Delinquent Behavior; Principles and Practices* (Washington, D. C., National Education Association, 1959), for a handbook of school strategy and tactics in preventing and treating delinquency.

[39] John Edward Reid, in Herbert Brean, "Everybody Is Dishonest," *Life*, Vol. 45 (November 24, 1958), pp. 70 ff.

There is a remarkable lack of carefully controlled comparisons of the behavior of members and nonmembers. The famous Hartshorne-May studies of the honesty of children found no significant behavior differences between children who attended Sunday School and those who did not. [40] Although this study is neither recent nor conclusive, it does raise questions about the effectiveness of traditional religious education as a behavior control.

Religious education as a means of crime control is limited in at least two ways: *first*, the church is unable to reach half of each generation of children at all and has only fleeting contact with many of the remaining half; *second*, there is no clear evidence that the church has effective techniques of preventing delinquency among those it does reach. While it is known that church-connected children are less likely to be recorded as delinquent, this does not prove that their actual delinquency is less than that of other children of the same social class. Neither does it separate cause from effect—it does not indicate whether the "good" children are good because they go to church, or whether they go to church because they are good children. In other words, church people may have lower crime rates because the church *attracts* the conventional and orderly folk rather than because it *produces* them. In the absence of more detailed and carefully controlled research, nothing conclusive is known about the relation of church membership and criminal behavior.

The suggestion that religious education be promoted by, or in cooperation with, the public schools is attracting considerable interest, and is often presented as a means of delinquency control. There is an almost total lack of evidence to support this belief, and few, if any, criminologists are convinced that such a program would have much effect upon delinquency.

SOME PROFESSIONAL PROPOSALS FOR TREATMENT

1. Legal Reforms

Criminologists, penologists, and leaders in the legal profession are in considerable agreement upon a number of suggestions for reform, including the following:

a. Revision of the criminal law. Present laws make crimes of many trivial and harmless acts, and most people agree that the legal code should be cleared of a considerable clutter of outmoded legislation. Laws that treat alcoholics and drug addicts as conventional criminals are outmoded. Some progress has been made in treating drug addicts as medical and

[40] Hugh Hartshorne and Mark A. May, *Studies in Deceit* (New York, The Macmillan Co., 1930), p. 15. They conclude: "Attendance at Sunday School or membership in at least two organizations which aim to teach honesty does not seem to change behavior in this regard, and in some instances there is evidence that it makes children less, rather than more. honest."

psychiatric problems, but alcoholics are still ordinarily given a futile succession of jail sentences. All experts agree that special provision should be made for all psychopathic offenders—pyromaniacs, kleptomaniacs, sex deviants, and others. Only a few states have such laws, and even these often fail to follow the special procedures provided for such offenders.

b. Revision of the jury system. It is widely felt that whatever justice we enjoy is secured not because of the jury system but in spite of it. It is argued that the method of selecting and excusing jurors now operates to eliminate most of those who are well educated, who have important business, or who impress the lawyers as uncomfortably intelligent and critical, leaving the average jury overloaded with average or below average persons, semiliterates, and loafers. This jury views an elaborate stage show, with carefully rehearsed witnesses, and with every possible appeal to the vanities, prejudices, and gullibilities of the jury serving as substitutes for a rational weighing of evidence. [41] To correct this travesty, one of these two means is suggested: (1) the replacement of the jury by one or more judges who weigh evidence and render decisions, or (2) a revised method of jury selection to insure a higher proportion of educated and intelligent members. Either method would probably be an improvement, for although juries probably convict few who are innocent, there is little doubt that they free many who are guilty.

c. The indeterminate sentence. Since no judge can possibly know how long it will take to reform a convict, the *indeterminate sentence* (such as one-to-five years, or three-to-ten years) is used in about three-fourths of our states with about half our prisoners. [42] This permits a prisoner to be released after serving the minimum term, or to be held for the full term if prison and parole officials think it advisable. But even under the indeterminate sentence the prisoner must serve the minimum term whether he needs it or not, and he must be freed at the end of the term whether reformed or not. Penologists believe that for every prisoner who is ever worthy of release, there is a certain moment in his development when he is ready to be released; to release him before this moment, or retain him after it is reached, is to invite failure. So there is some support for a completely *indeterminate* sentence, under which a convict is committed for no specified period, to be released whenever prison and parole officials consider him ready for release.[43] Since such a program could easily be abused, it would require a professionally trained prison staff

---

[41] See Barnes and Teeters, *op. cit.*, Ch. XIV, "The Jury Trial"; J. Warren Madden, "Is Justice Blind?" *The Annals,* Vol. 280 (November, 1952), pp. 60-66; Sutherland and Cressey, *op. cit.*, pp. 385-387.

[42] Sutherland and Cressey, *op. cit.*, p. 552.

[43] *Ibid.*, pp. 550-563; Karl Menninger, "Verdict Guilty—Now What?" *Harper's Magazine,* Vol. 219 (August, 1959), pp. 60-64.

and an incorruptible, politically independent parole board for its success-ful operation.

2. Penal Reforms

There is no such thing as a really *good* prison. To remove a man from all stabilizing contacts with family, friends, job, and community [44] and isolate him among a choice selection of our poorest citizens in an environ-ment to which he can adjust only by forgetting most of the habits neces-sary to normal adjustment on the outside—to do all this and then hope that the convict will somehow purge himself of bitterness, adopt a con-ventional value system, and be prepared to resume family life and useful citizenship upon his release is to expect a miracle. One can scarcely learn conventional behavior patterns by being isolated from them. The facts are that prison tends to brutalize convicts. Their vocational skills deterio-rate, their family life is interrupted, and all the routine habits of living and taking care of one's self become inoperative. Instead, the inmate receives a graduate course in criminal skills and attitudes, often develops homosexual practices or other sexual deviations, and ordinarily learns nothing that will be useful in a noncriminal career. [45] Upon release, he must forget prison habits, resume the forgotten ones necessary to making a living and operating a family, and meanwhile overcome the great handi-cap of the sigma of "ex-convict." [46] Silverman examined five hundred psychotic prisoners, finding that relatively few were psychotic before imprisonment, but by the end of the first year of prison life, 80 per cent were psychotic. [47] The demoralization of prison life is further suggested by the fact that much recidivism takes the form of petty crime instead of major crime. [48] It seems that long imprisonment unfits one to be either a good citizen or a good criminal. All prisons are bad, and their futility is widely recognized. The public continues to support them because it can think of nothing else to do with its criminals. That locking them up is no

[44] One questionnaire study of 500 penitentiary inmates shows 70 per cent saying they had a "happy" home life with an "average" standard of living, while 66 per cent claim that no other family member had ever been in trouble with the law. Published in *Atlantan*, edited by inmates of Atlanta Penitentiary, reported in *Chicago Sun-Times*, September 26, 1959, p. 39.

[45] See Victor Nelson, *Prison Days and Nights* (Boston, Little, Brown & Co., 1932); Norman Hayner and Ellis Ash, "The Prison as a Community," *American Sociological Review*, Vol. 5 (August, 1950), pp. 577-583; Robert Neese, #24933, *Prison Exposures* (Philadelphia, Chilton Company, 1959), for descriptions of prison life.

[46] See Frank O'Leary, "The Twilight World of the Ex-Convict," *The Reporter*, Vol. 10 (June 8, 1954), pp. 38-40.

[47] Daniel Silverman, "Psychoses in Criminals: A Study of Five Hundred Psy-chotic Prisoners," *Journal of Clinical Psychopathology*, Vol. 4 (October, 1943), pp. 703-730.

[48] Sheldon and Eleanor Glueck, *Later Criminal Careers* (New York, Harper and Brothers, 1937), pp. 121, 350.

solution, however, is clear when we remember that in an average of less than two years each prisoner will be released, [49] often worse than when he entered, while even those sentenced to "life imprisonment" are released after an average of ten years. [50]

All prisons are bad; some are incomparably worse than others. Wretched food, filthy quarters, indifferent medical care, brutal and sadistic guards, lack of any educational or training program, and a demoralizing system of convict "self-government" by the more vicious of the convicts—all these conditions are still common in many American prisons, although considerable improvement has occurred. To most people, "prison reform" means providing these things—good food, decent medical care, humane guards, clean quarters, and an educational program. Adequate financing and enlightened administrators can easily accomplish these things, yet many prisons still lack them, and there is scarcely a prison in the country which is not so overcrowded as to place any serious attempts at reformation under a severe handicap.

But there are certain basic features that make prison life demoralizing no matter how good the food or humane the treatment. The sex starvation, monotonous routine, isolation from conventional behavior patterns, lack of opportunity for self-direction, and stigmatizing of the convict as "criminal"—all these are unchangeable features of prison life. For the vast majority of inmates, prison brings a demoralization which the most enlightened warden cannot possibly change.

Since prisons do not reform, it would seem logical to abolish them, at least for those whom there is any hope of reforming. It would seem sensible to use conventional prisons only for those whom there is little hope of reforming, imprisoning them permanently for the protection of society. Since prisons are more likely to corrupt and demoralize than to reform, it would seem to follow that *no one who is expected to reform should remain in prison for any great length of time.* If not prison, then what? There are at least two practical alternatives: probation or parole, and various sorts of minimum security institutions.

Under *probation* the convict's sentence is suspended provided he stays out of trouble for a specified period of time during which the probation officer checks upon his activities. The probation officer supposedly functions as a guide and counselor, helping the convict to work out a more successful life organization. This task requires a person who combines professional social casework training with certain qualities of personality that relatively few people possess. Inasmuch as many communities pay their probation officers less than they pay their janitors and truck drivers,

[49] Mabel A. Elliott, *Crime in Modern Society* (New York, Harper and Brothers, 1952), p. 730.
[50] Alfred M. Harries, "How Long Is a Life Sentence for Murder?" *Proceedings,* American Prison Association (1939), pp. 513-524.

it is not surprising that the probation officer is sometimes a political hack, a semiliterate ignoramus, or a well-meaning but incompetent busybody. In other instances a well-trained probation officer is given such a heavy case load that he can do little more than keep an address file of his probationers. Since it costs several thousands of dollars to convict each criminal and costs ten or twenty times as much to keep him in prison as it costs for probation or parole supervision, [51] our niggardly probation and parole programs are revealed as penny-wise-and-pound-foolish. Success is claimed for about 75 per cent of probationers, [52] meaning that they do not get into any known difficulty during the period of probation. It is not established whether success on probation is due to the effectiveness of probation or to "self-curing" on the part of those persons selected for probation. [53] Carefully controlled evaluation studies are necessary before drawing any sweeping conclusions.

Parole is a conditional release of a prisoner who will be supervised by a parole officer for the remainder of his sentence. If any misconduct occurs during parole he will be returned to prison to serve the rest of his sentence. Over half our prisoners are paroled before serving their full sentences. Parole operates very much like probation, except that it follows rather than precedes imprisonment.

Minimum security institutions are those in which walls and locks are partly replaced by the cultivation of intelligent self-direction by the convict. Prison farms and work camps are the most familiar examples, but any institution that places emphasis upon self-direction and personal responsibility instead of locks and iron bars is a minimum security institution. Whereas a conventional (maximum security) prison concentrates upon keeping the prisoners from escaping, the minimum security institution must emphasize rehabilitation, for the inmates will walk away if they see no reason for remaining. Minimum security institutions do have gates and fences, but anyone who wants to break out has little difficulty in doing so.

Since minimum security institutions are not pervaded with the prevention-of-escape atmosphere, it is simpler to arrange brief furloughs or temporary releases for visiting one's family, thereby enabling the prisoner to keep contact with his family and community and helping prevent the loss of routine life habits. Many variations of part-time custody are possible in a minimum security institution, although such plans are not yet widely used. Most of the inherent defects of a conventional prison

[51] Sutherland and Cressey, *op. cit.*, p. 440.

[52] According to a United Nations survey of probation in Britain, Denmark, Norway, Sweden, The Netherlands, and the United States, *New York Times*, August 29, 1954, p. 19; also Sutherland and Cressey, *ibid.*, p. 437.

[53] Ralph W. England, "What Is Responsible for Satisfactory Probation and Post-Probation Outcome?" *Journal of Criminology, Criminal Law, and Police Science*, Vol. 47 (March-April, 1957), pp. 667-676.

can be either eliminated or greatly reduced in the minimum security institution.

There are other suggestions for improving penal treatment. The *classification program* aims to separate the vicious prisoners from those for whom there are prospects of reform. Although the suggestion for classification and segregation of hardened offenders is at least a hundred years old, the perennial overcrowding and understaffing of most penal institutions means that the classification program is often little more than a pious hope. An *educational program* is nonexistent in some institutions and chronically neglected in many others. Realistic vocational education is expensive, so prison workshops are operated mainly to supply the needs of the prison, not to train the prisoners. Academic education is cheaper but is not highly appreciated by most convicts. The *local jail*, often a filthy, vermin-ridden dungeon, and nearly always a human wastebasket filled with all kinds and degrees of offenders—thieves, murderers, sex deviants, and bums, mixed with traffic violators, drunks, wide-eyed first offenders, and suspects awaiting trial—is widely regarded as a source of criminal contagion. [54] The need for, and means of, dealing with the jail nuisance [55] are as obvious as is our general failure to do anything about it.

3. Guidance and Counseling Programs

Since many adult criminals were more or less delinquent as children, the suggestion for a comprehensive guidance and counseling program is a logical one. Educators, psychiatrists, and some criminologists recommend programs ranging from sympathetic assistance by the classroom teacher to intensive psychotherapy. The anxious, fearful child may gain increased assurance, and the lonely, rejected child may be helped to gain group acceptance. Well-meaning parents may achieve increased insight. A child's drift towards a major emotional disturbance may be arrested through psychotherapy.

The effectiveness of such counseling programs has not been determined. Several delinquency prediction tests attempt to select the child who is in need of help, but they have not proved to be very reliable. [56] There have been a few follow-up studies in which a group of delinquents who have received extensive guidance or psychiatric treatment are compared with a control group of delinquents who received no such treat-

[54] See Joseph F. Fishman, *Crucibles of Crime* (New York, Cosmopolis Press, 1923); Austin H. McCormick, "Children in Our Jails," *The Annals*, Vol. 261 (January, 1949), pp. 150-157.

[55] *Proceedings*, American Prison Association (1937), p. 320; Roy Casey, "Catchall Jails," *The Annals*, Vol. 293 (May, 1954), pp. 28-34.

[56] William C. Kvaraceus, "Prediction Studies of Delinquent Behavior," *Personnel and Guidance Journal*, Vol. 34 (November, 1955), pp. 147-149. The reliability of the Gluecks' recent prediction test (Sheldon and Eleanor Glueck, *Predicting Juvenile Delinquency, op. cit.*), has not yet been established, although preliminary reports claim a high degree of accuracy. *Time*, Vol. 74 (October 12, 1959), p. 62.

ment. The findings are inconclusive. Some studies report a reduction in delinquency as compared with the control group, [57] while others find no significant difference in the behavior of the treatment and the control groups. [58] A recent experiment at Highfields, a boys' training school, uses "guided group interaction" sessions in treating delinquent boys. After daily outdoor work, the boys discuss their problems in small groups under the guidance of trained workers who are careful not to monopolize the discussion. Preliminary reports seem to show that the project has had some success. [59]

It is uncertain how guidance and counseling programs affect juvenile delinquency or adult crime. Not much can be expected when delinquency is a normal aspect of the local culture, as in the high-delinquency slum. Delinquency in a slum child does *not* denote maladjustment; delinquent behavior is a normal adjustment pattern in his social world. The counseling program rests upon the assumption that delinquency stems from compensatory strivings of the frustrated, maladjusted child, groping for some means of release or satisfaction. This assumption correctly applies to many middle-class delinquents, but not to those in whose social world delinquency is normal. Nor can the counseling program be expected to prevent much institutional or white-collar crime, or any other form of crime indulged in by normal, well-adjusted people. It is only where crime is a compensatory response of frustrated people that the counseling services are likely to be effective. "Problem" children in school, incipient sex deviants, drug addicts, chronic alcoholics, and certain other emotionally disturbed offenders represent the most promising opportunities for guidance and counseling, from various sources ranging from the classroom teacher to the psychiatrist.

4. Social Group Work

Boy Scouts, Girl Souts, Y.M.C.A., Y.W.C.A., summer camps and playgrounds, and other organized activities are widely considered as ways of delinquency prevention. There have been few evaluative studies, [60] and it is not known to what extent these activities actually prevent delin-

[57] William Healy and A. F. Bronner, *Treatment and What Happened Afterward* (Boston, Judge Baker Foundation Center, 1939), p. 42.

[58] Joan McCord and William McCord, "A Follow-up Report on the Cambridge-Somerville Youth Study," *The Annals*, Vol. 322 (March, 1959), pp. 89-96; Michael Hakeem, "A Critique of the Psychiatric Approach to Crime and Correction," *Law and Contemporary Problems*, Vol. 23 (Autumn, 1958), pp. 650-682.

[59] H. Ashley Weeks and others, *Youthful Offenders at Highfields* (Ann Arbor, University of Michigan Press, 1958); Lloyd W. McMorkle, Albert Elias, and F. Lovell Bixley, *The Highfields Story: An Experimental Treatment Project for Youthful Offenders* (New York, Henry Holt & Co., Inc., 1958).

[60] See Helen L. Witmer and Edith Tufts, *The Effectiveness of Delinquency Prevention Programs*, U. S. Department of Health, Education, and Welfare, Children's Bureau Publication, No. 350 (Washington, D. C., Government Printing Office, 1954); Roscoe C. Brown, Jr. and Dan W. Dodson, "The Effectiveness of a Boy's Club in Reducing Delinquency," *The Annals*, Vol. 322 (March, 1959), pp. 47-52.

quency or merely attract the nondelinquent. Nevertheless, these activities are widely supported by both laymen and specialists.

Aside from their other possible values, social-group activities under the leadership of a skilled leader offer strategic opportunities for aiding in personality development and, indirectly, in crime prevention. Such activities provide the leader with many opportunities to locate children with problems and to help them develop ways of meeting them. The leader can gently draw the shy, inadequate child into more active group participation; he can help the rejected child find better ways of seeking group acceptance; he can manipulate the group in such a way that the bully and the prima donna are trapped and disciplined by the group, and thus taught the necessity for consideration and self-control; he can guide the normal energies and exploratory interests of young people into acceptable and constructive activities. To the extent that the group leader is able to do these things, he helps develop well-adjusted personalities. To do this, however, requires not merely an athletic director or a well-intentioned adult, but a skilled social worker who has both the personal qualities and the professional training for his task.

A quite new development is the street club worker, a trained social worker who is assigned to a particular boy's gang, and attempts to guide them away from illegal activities. Often he is a young man who was raised in a similar area, and he seeks to gain the gang's confidence and convince the boys of his sympathetic interest. He does not preach or scold, but fills the role of an interested, understanding adult. This approach recognizes that the gang exists because it fills real needs for its members. Instead of trying to break up the gang and treat its members individually, it seeks to reach the gang as a unit. This approach is sociologically sound, and preliminary reports claim some success for it, [61] but, as yet, no fully satisfactory evaluative studies have been made.

5. Area Rehabilitation

It is difficult to reform individuals when they live in a community the basic characteristics of which encourage crime. This recognition has led to attempts to change the area culture so that it will be easier for its members to behave acceptably. Area rehabilitation may be of two kinds.

a. Physical Rehabilitation. The effort to change area culture may focus upon the physical aspects of the area, especially housing. Although

---

[61] George Barrett, "West Side Report: No Incidents," *New York Times Magazine*, February 8, 1959, p. 10 ff; Walter B. Miller, "Preventative Work with Street-Corner Groups: Boston Delinquency Project," *The Annals*, Vol. 322 (March, 1959). pp. 97-106; John M. Gandy, "Preventative Work With Street-Corner Groups: Hyde Park Youth Project," *The Annals*, Vol. 322 (March, 1959), pp. 107-116; Gertrude Samuels, "Why The Assassins Can't Be 'Punks,'" *New York Times Magazine*, August 16, 1959, pp. 13 ff. Harrison E. Salisbury, *The Shook-Up Generation* (New York, Harper and Brothers, 1958), Ch. 11, "The Street Club Worker."

Courtesy of the New York Life Insurance Company

Social case work sometimes prevents delinquency.

housing is not the "cause" of delinquency, every study yet made shows a striking association between substandard housing and delinquency rates. There is also considerable evidence that when slum people are moved into adequate housing, delinquency rates decline significantly. When large slum areas were cleared in the Central South Side of Chicago, the district's crime rate fell 50 per cent. [62] Another study showed crime falling 44 per cent in a clearance project area while crime rose 21 per cent in a comparable control area. [63] Another study reveals delinquency rates for a group of 317 slum families dropping almost one-half after the families

[62] *Chicago Sun-Times*, January 8, 1957, p. 6.

[63] William L. J. Dee, "The Social Effects of a Public Housing Project on The Immediate Community," in Meyer Weinberg and Oscar E. Shabat, *Society and Man* (Englewood Cliffs, N. J., Prentice-Hall, Inc., 1956), pp. 329-339.

moved into a project. [64] One very carefully controlled study showed delinquency to be 21 per cent lower in a project than in adjacent comparable slum areas. [65] These and similar studies show quite clearly that slum clearance is accompanied by a substantial reduction in delinquency rates. Whether slum clearance can best be accomplished through public or private housing is a separate question, and one upon which there is bitter disagreement. But there can be little doubt that slum clearance helps to reduce delinquency.

The Urban Renewal Program of the Housing and Home Finance Agency now gives federal assistance to local communities which improve an area by clearing its slums while preserving and rehabilitating the rest of its housing and improving the streets, parks, and other area facilities. Another program—ACTION—promoted by the American Council to Improve Our Neighborhoods, has had some success in stimulating the people of certain areas into a voluntary, organized effort to arrest urban blight in their neighborhoods. [66]

b. Social Reorganization. A different approach aims to unite the *people* of an area in a joint effort to reduce delinquency and improve area life. The Back of the Yards Neighborhood Council in the stockyards area of Chicago represents a successful attempt to promote neighborhood welfare through uniting its existing groups and agencies. The Roman Catholic Church (in an area 90 per cent Catholic) and the labor unions which were the main forces, were joined by the local Chamber of Commerce, veterans' organizations, athletic groups, and fraternal groups. The Council is made up of persons living in the area, not of outsiders; and the program is developed by them, not imposed upon them by outside agencies. Expert personnel are used as advisors, and the members of the area have developed greatly in leadership ability and in their understanding of the area's problems.

One of the eight committees works with delinquency prevention at the common-sense level. If a boy needs a job, they help him find one. Recreation centers have been established, numerous littered vacant lots have been turned into small parks and playgrounds, and young people have been invited to organize and join with older people in seeking to meet common problems. The Council has not made the mistake of promoting amateur psychiatry or amateur counseling, but it has unified an area in a successful approach to its problems on a practical level. [67]

[64] Naomi Barer, "Delinquency Before, After Admission to New Haven Housing Development," *Journal of Housing,* Vol. 3 (January, 1946), p. 27.

[65] Newark Housing Authority, *Public Housing in Newark* (November, 1944).

[66] "ACTION to Fight Slums and Neighborhood Blight," *American City,* Vol. 69 (December, 1954), p. 23; M. Hickey, "Toward Better Housing," *Ladies Home Journal,* Vol. 73 (May, 1956), pp. 35 ff; C. F. Palmen, "ACTION," *Rotarian,* Vol. 94 (April, 1959), pp. 28-29.

[67] See Saul D. Alinsky, "Community Analysis and Organization," *American Journal of Sociology,* Vol. 46 (May, 1941), pp. 797-808.

The Chicago Area Project operates in a somewhat similar manner, concentrating primarily upon delinquency prevention. One writer summarizes it as follows: [68]

The Chicago Area Project is founded on the idea that the roots of delinquency are to be found in the deteriorated area and that social workers (or psychiatrists and psychologists) cannot prevent delinquency. They can help in lending professional advice, but the motivation and the effort to improve a community must come largely from the people themselves. Those who live in the community set the community standards and these cannot be imposed from without. Hence, the Area Project has enlisted the support of local leadership, which is organized into neighborhood committees for an orderly attack on problems. The local leaders include professional people (usually neighborhood boys who return to practice medicine, dentistry, or law in their old community), clergy, teachers, truck drivers, butchers, grocers, druggists, factory workers, and housewives.

The Area Project provides trained personnel, usually a sociologist who is interested in helping the local residents provide their children with a decent and attractive place in which to live. By and large the committee is composed of citizens whose children are growing up in the community.

Local institutions, the church and the school, parks, and health and welfare agencies are enlisted in the co-operative project, in which the social workers advise but do not direct. They are merely members of the committee. Where practicable, local trained persons are recruited for dealing with delinquents, whether as probation, parole, or truant officers.

Many activities are sponsored by the neighborhood committees of the project. Some are purely recreational, in the shape of community centers, camps, sports tournaments, etc. But the committees have also tried to build up the community in other ways, by promoting housing projects, community forums, adult education classes, etc. A major activity has been the rehabilitation program for delinquents or adults who are returned to the community from courts, correctional institutions, or prison. Here there is an attempt to help the child (or adult) readjust by reintegrating him into the life of the community and helping him help himself. The Chicago Area Project maintains that constructive leadership of the residents can do more to prevent delinquency than any diagnostic skills of psychiatrists or social workers. . . .

The Chicago Area Project is now organized in 10 different high-delinquency areas with 28 separate projects. . . . [In one of these projects] volunteer committees were organized, some 11 neighborhood centers and clubs were established, recreational programs were initiated, funds were recruited from public and private sources. The project itself was an experiment in democracy.

What the Chicago Area Project is doing is converting the values of a delinquency-ridden community to concepts of social responsibility and an acceptance of standards of conduct which are approved by the middle class.

[68] Mabel A. Elliott, *Crime in Modern Society* (New York, Harper and Brothers, 1952), pp. 788-789. See also, Saul D. Alinsky, *op. cit.*, pp. 797-808; Solomon Kobrin, "The Chicago Area Project—A Twenty-Five Year Assessment," *The Annals*, Vol. 322 (March, 1959), pp. 19-29.

These area-rehabilitation programs represent a highly practical approach to certain aspects of the crime problem. Although no approach or combination of approaches is likely to eliminate criminal behavior, delinquency rates in the areas concerned appear to be substantially lower than would normally be expected. In high-delinquency areas, such area-rehabilitation programs are probably the most effective approaches yet developed.

SUMMARY

Crime is a problem the exact extent of which is not known. It probably exists in much the same degree in nearly all areas, races, and classes in the United States, although it is mainly the lower-class violators who are caught and convicted and the prevalence of white-collar crime has only recently become recognized. Popular thinking about crime is confused by a number of fallacies, including the notions that there is a criminal type, a wide variety of romantic stereotypes of the criminal, the view of the criminal as necessarily abnormal, the notion of the born criminal, the idea that poverty and broken homes cause most crime, and the assumption that the dramatic crimes are the serious ones.

A classification of criminals in terms of their motivation reveals several types—legalistic, moralistic, psychopathic, institutional, situational, habitual, and professional. As these differ greatly in motivation, each poses a different problem of treatment. The "causes" of crime seem to be mainly environmental. The *biological* theories have failed to identify any criminal type, and where there are any associations between physical type and criminal behavior, the causes of this association seem to lie in social experience. The *psychological* theories sound plausible, but carefully controlled comparisons reveal few psychological differences between offenders and other people. The *sociological* theories are more helpful. Sutherland's *differential-association* theory holds that a person acts largely according to his contact with other people's approving or disapproving definitions of criminal behavior. The *group-conflict* theory sees crime as a result of frustration and the bitterness of conflicts between groups—racial, national, economic, religious. The *delinquent-subculture* theory holds that much criminal behavior is simply an expression of a subculture in which crime is normal.

The *personal-deviation approach* reveals the criminal as a deviant person who has failed to develop the conventional codes of behavior or as a maladjusted person who is unable or unwilling to follow them. The *value-conflict approach* notes that many common actions are defined as crimes because of the conflicting values of different groups, and that an effective system of social control is constantly being undermined by the many value conflicts in our poorly integrated society. The *social-dis-*

organization approach shows how social change has produced these value conflicts, and has undermined the traditional morality and control system of an earlier society.

Popular proposals for crime reduction are of dubious practical value. Punishment has proved ineffectual in both deterrence and reform. Better law enforcement might reduce crime, if it could be secured. Neither education nor religion, of the conventional sort, is likely to reach and reorient many of those who actually commit crimes.

Professional proposals include: (1) legal reform, with revision of laws, jury system, and system of sentencing; (2) penal reform, recognizing that all imprisonment is inherently injurious, and using probation, parole, and minimum security institutions for all those who are believed reformable; (3) guidance and counseling programs, especially at the school level; (4) social-group work, mainly with children and youth; and (5) area rehabilitation in deteriorated areas where criminal behavior is a normal part of the area culture. At present, crime appears to be increasing, and may continue to increase unless research, experimentation, and professionalized treatment are greatly accelerated.

SUGGESTED READINGS FOR CHAPTERS FIVE AND SIX

BLOCH, Herbert A., and FLYNN, Frank T., *Delinquency: The Juvenile Offender in America Today* (New York, Random House, 1956). A comprehensive textbook on juvenile delinquency.

COHEN, Albert K., *Delinquent Boys: The Culture of the Gang* (Glencoe, Ill., The Free Press, 1955). An interpretation of the delinquent subculture.

ELLIOTT, Mabel A., *Crime in Modern Society* (New York, Harper and Brothers, 1952). A comprehensive, readable textbook in criminology.

GLUECK, Sheldon, and GLUECK, Eleanor, *Predicting Juvenile Delinquency* (Cambridge, Harvard University Press, 1959). An ambitious attempt at a reliable prediction test.

———, *The Problem of Delinquency* (Boston, Houghton Mifflin Company, 1959). A collection of 186 articles and legal decisions covering the field of delinquency.

———, *Unraveling Juvenile Delinquency* (Cambridge, Harvard University Press, 1951). A study of juvenile delinquents, especially of the kinds of family experience which encourage the development of antisocial attitudes.

KEFAUVER, Estes, *Crime in America* (Garden City, N. Y., Doubleday & Co., Inc., 1951) A popular summary of the findings of a famous Senate investigation into organized crime.

KEVE, Paul W., *Prison, Probation, or Parole? A Probation Officer Reports* (Minneapolis, University of Minnesota Press, 1954). The warmly human accounts of thirty cases which the writer handled as a probation officer.

KVARACEUS, William C., and others, *Delinquent Behavior* (Washington, D. C., National Education Association, 1959). A brief, simply written summary of the delinquency problem, with special reference to the program of the school.

NEESE, Robert, # 24933, *Prison Exposures* (Philadelphia, Chilton Company, 1959). Photographs and description of prison life by an inmate.

"Prevention of Juvenile Delinquency," *The Annals,* Vol. 322 (March, 1959). Describes a number of programs intended to prevent or reduce delinquency.

"Prisons in Transformation," *The Annals,* Vol. 293 (May, 1954). A number of articles on prisons, their operation, effects, costs, and alternatives.

SHAW, Clifford R., *The Jack-roller; A Delinquent Boy's Own Story* (Chicago, University of Chicago Press, 1930); or (with M. E. Moore), *Natural History of a Delinquent Career* (Chicago, University of Chicago Press, 1931); or (with H. D. McKay and J. F. McDonald), *Brothers In Crime* (Chicago, University of Chicago Press, 1938). Intensely interesting biographical accounts of delinquents, showing the interaction of social factors in producing delinquent behavior.

SUTHERLAND, Edwin H., *White-Collar Crime* (New York, The Dryden Press, Inc., 1949). A classic analysis of white-collar crime.

SUTHERLAND, Edwin H., and CRESSEY, Donald R., *Principles of Criminology* (New York, J. P. Lippincott Co., 1955). An authoritative standard textbook in criminology.

VOLD, George B., *Theoretical Criminology* (New York, Oxford University Press, 1958). An authoritative summary of criminological theory.

WHYTE, William Foote, *Street Corner Society* (Chicago, University of Chicago Press, 1943). An absorbing analysis of an urban slum, showing the interaction of criminal and noncriminal activities in an area where organized crime is an accepted part of the area culture.

AUDIO-VISUAL AIDS

Boy with a Knife (International Film Bureau, 57 East Jackson Boulevard, Chicago), 24 minutes, sound, black and white. Shows how disturbed boys cloak their insecurity with "toughness" and seek reassurance in the gang.

Criminal Man (Audio-Visual Center, Indiana University, Bloomington), series of 20 films, 30 minutes each, sound, black and white. A condensed television course in criminology; filmed lectures and discussions, with illustrative dramatized episodes and interviews.

Hard Brought Up (Potomac Films, 1536 Connecticut Avenue, N.W., Washington, D.C.), 40 minutes, sound, black and white. Two very different delinquents are aided by casework services.

Prison with a Future (McGraw-Hill Book Company, Inc., Text-Film Department, 330 West 42 Street, New York), 18 minutes, sound, black and white. Shows how one reformatory seeks to rehabilitate its inmates.

Raw Material (International Film Bureau, 57 East Jackson Boulevard, Chicago), 27 minutes, sound, black and white. Pictures work of the John Howard Society in aiding ex-convicts.

Searchlights on Delinquency (Audio-Visual Center, Indiana University, Bloomington), series of 13 films, 29 minutes each, sound, black and white. A condensed television course in juvenile delinquency; filmed lectures and discussions, with illustrative dramatized episodes and interviews.

Step by Step (International Film Bureau, 57 East Jackson Boulevard, Chicago), 20 minutes, sound, black and white. Shows the efforts of the street club worker.

Why Did He Do It? (Center for Mass Communication, Columbia University Press, New York 25), series of six 15-minute, 16-inch, 33⅓ r.p.m. transcriptions. Impressive documentaries giving life stories of six delinquents and criminals.

QUESTIONS AND PROJECTS

1. Why should substandard housing and disorganized family life be classed as "risk factors" rather than as "causes" of crime?

2. There is some evidence that solid, muscular youths are more often delinquent than other physical types. What hypotheses about crime causation may be drawn from this association?

3. Find a detailed case history of a persistent delinquent, such as one of Clifford Shaw's accounts. Analyze the boy's experiences in terms of each of the three sociological theories of causation presented in this chapter. Analyze them in terms of the biological and psychological theories. Which do you think best interprets the case?

4. Explain the delinquency of the boy or girl from a "good" home and neighborhood in terms of each of the three sociological theories of causation. Which most easily interprets delinquency of this kind?

5. Could all three of the approaches—social-disorganization, personal-deviation, value-conflict—be used to explain the criminal behavior of the same person? Illustrate.

6. What theories lie behind the "practical" proposal to curb crime through severe punishment? Could punishment be successful even if the theories were unsound?

7. What do you think of the argument that delinquents who commit acts of physical brutality need a severe beating to "teach them what it feels like?"

8. How would you distinguish between "individualized treatment" and "coddling" of delinquents? Is there a difference?

9. What defects are inherent in the prison system? What defects can be eliminated by adequate funds and enlightened administration?

10. What reasoning lies behind the indeterminate sentence? Does this reasoning also support the completely indeterminate sentence? What are the objections to this practice?

11. What can be gained through area rehabilitation which cannot be accomplished through guidance and counseling programs? Would this make guidance and counseling programs unnecessary?

7

Problem Families and Family Problems

ๅๅๅ

Among the 41,000 families under care of St. Paul agencies in November, 1948, about 7000—7 per cent of the community's families—were dependent, nearly 11,000 had problems of maladjustment, well over 15,000 had problems of ill-health, and almost 19,000 were being served by public and private recreation agencies. It can be seen at a glance that some families had more than one kind of problem. Seventy-seven per cent of the dependent families also had problems of ill-health or maladjustment. Fifty-eight per cent of the families with problems of maladjustment were known to agencies in the other service fields. Thirty-eight per cent of the families with health problems also had other problems. The most dramatic evidence of the vicious circling of problems in St. Paul families came with the discovery that a group of 6,600 families—about 6 per cent of the city's families—were suffering from such a compounding of serious problems that they were absorbing well over half of the combined services of the community's dependency, health, and adjustment agencies.[1]

SINCE THERE IS NO REASON to think that St. Paul families have more problems than families in other sizable cities, it appears possible that 7 per cent of the nation's urban families have severe problems of economic need; 11 per cent evidence major symptoms of crime, delinquency, child neglect, and emotional disturbance; and 15 per cent have serious medical problems. Add to this the facts that each year nearly 400,000 United States couples are divorced, 100,000 men desert their families, and over 600,000 families are broken by death. In untold thousands of homes, husbands and wives are unable to meet their partners' needs, and children grow up perplexed and hostile in the presence of parents who cannot make the grade as mothers and fathers.

[1] Bradley Buell and associates, *Community Planning for Human Services* (New York, Columbia University Press, 1952), p. 9, by permission.

SOME TYPES OF PROBLEM FAMILIES

Family problems are ubiquitous. As we shall see later on, certain family problems can be traced to recent changes in the larger society. To find the roots of such problems one must look to the changing norms governing behavior in the society. But some families have more problems and more serious problems than others—so many problems and such serious problems, in fact, that they merit the use of the special title "problem families."

Broken Families

Divorce and desertion are widely recognized as problems. They are not problems in all societies for they do not exist in all societies—on any large scale at least. In the Western world marriage has been generally regarded as a permanent and indissoluble union. Some Western nations—particularly those where Roman Catholicism prevails—still make no regular provision for divorce. In other Western nations, including our own, the situation has been changing. Under the influence of Protestantism, marriage is no longer regarded as a sacrament but as a civil status, ordained, perhaps, by God but administered by man. What man creates he can set asunder. The United States has gone further than any other modern nation in defining marriage as "a terminable situation." [2]

There are approximately 400,000 divorces granted in the United States each year, [3] and the probability is that one out of every four marriages occurring today will wind up eventually in the divorce courts. [4] Many persons in all walks of life consider these figures appalling and claim that something should be done to stem the tide of divorce. Others claim that, while something needs to be done, there is no point in simply attempting to prevent divorces, for divorce is the result rather than the cause of broken marriages. Divorce is not the death of a marriage but rather its funeral ceremony. [5]

Divorce does not occur randomly over the span of married life, nor is it distributed randomly throughout the population. The risk of divorce is considerably greater during the first years of marriage than at any time thereafter. More divorces are granted during the second or third years of

[2] Margaret Mead, "What Is Happening to the American Family?" *Journal of Social Casework*, Vol. 28 (November, 1947), p. 325.

[3] Derived from National Office of Vital Statistics, *Monthly Vital Statistics Report*, Annual Summary for 1957, Part 1, and Annual Summary for 1958, Part. 1.

[4] John Sirjamaki, *The American Family in the Twentieth Century* (Cambridge, Harvard University Press, 1953), p. 165.

[5] See Mable A. Elliott, "Divorce Legislation and Family Instability," *Annals of the American Academy of Political and Social Science*, Vol. 272 (November, 1950), pp. 145-147.

marriage than any others [6] and half of all divorces occur within the first six years of marriage. [7] Apparently there are major adjustments that have to be made in early marriage when couples are learning to live together harmoniously, and many couples simply do not make the grade. Similarly, having made the early adjustments satisfactorily seems to increase the likelihood that adjustments in the later years will be made successfully— or at least that if divorce is not resorted to in the early years of marriage it is less likely to result later on, no matter what other adjustments might be required.

Divorce has long been considered to be much more probable in childless marriages than in marriages where there are children. The reasoning runs that unhappy marriages are less likely to produce children in the first place and, once born, children tend to deter their parents from seeking divorce. Recent research, however, calls these generalizations

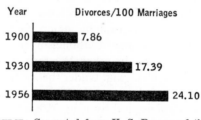

SOURCE: Computed from U. S. Bureau of the Census, *Statistical Abstract of the United States:* (Washington, D.C., 1958), p. 56.

FIG. 7–1. The increase of divorce.

into serious question. At the present time about forty per cent of all divorces involve minor children present in the home. [8] One recent study of divorce in Philadelphia has indicated that the alleged greater prevalence of divorce in childless marriages may be partly a reflection of the short duration of marriages ending in divorce. [9]

It has also been assumed until recently that divorce was apt to produce severe trauma in children. There has been ample impressionistic evidence to indicate that parents and children both sometimes reacted to divorce with other obvious symptoms of maladjustment. [10] In a recent study of divorce in metropolitan Detroit, however, the vast majority of 425 mothers, who had been divorced for periods ranging from two to twenty-six months, believed both themselves and their children to be better off than

[6] Paul C. Glick, *American Families* (New York, John Wiley & Sons, Inc., 1957), p. 140.

[7] *Ibid.*

[8] *Ibid.*, p. 42.

[9] Thomas P. Monahan, "Is Childlessness Related to Family Stability?" *American Sociological Review*, Vol. 20 (August, 1955), pp. 446-456.

[10] Willard Waller, *The Old Love and the New* (New York, Liveright Publishing Corp., 1930).

before the divorce. [11] This may indicate that as divorce becomes more common and less stigma is attached to it that the more serious emotional reactions to divorce will become less common.

The risk of divorce is greater in low-income families than in higher income families. This finding came as something of a surprise to social scientists who had long assumed that lower class families lacked the know-how and the financial resources to make divorce common among them. In the recent Detroit study, divorce rates were highest among the lowest ranked occupational groups and lower among higher ranks. [12] A second study, using occupation as the criterion, also indicated that the highest divorce rates are associated with lower status occupations. [13] There are at least two plausible lines of explanation for these findings. One is that insufficient income and the lesser status rewards of lower ranked jobs are themselves serious problems that tend to be reflected in the inability of men and women to separate their marital adjustments from financial and status adjustments. The other explanation is that divorce reflects the

Table 7-1. Index of proneness to divorce by occupation, Detroit study

Occupational Category	% divorced husbands in occupational group
	% males in that category in metropolitan Detroit
Professional and proprietary	67.7
Clerical, sales, service	83.2
Skilled, foremen	74.1
Semiskilled, operatives	126.1
Unskilled	179.7

SOURCE: William J. Goode, *After Divorce* (Glencoe, Ill., The Free Press, 1956), p. 47, by permission.

general disregard for the importance of marriage among lower class groups. There is a stereotype of lower class persons that has them entering and leaving nonlegally sanctioned marital relationships at will, which is extended to a tendency to break legally sanctioned relationships whenever they prove more troublesome than rewarding. While there do appear to be elements of stereotyping in this conception, it seems likely that divorce is not considered to be as serious a step at lower income levels as it is among middle-class persons.

If awareness of the prevalance of divorce among lower class persons is a recent development, it has long been recognized that desertion is common among them. In fact, desertion is widely referred to as the "poor

[11] William J. Goode, *After Divorce* (Glencoe, Ill., The Free Press, 1956), p. 342.
[12] *Ibid.*, p. 343.
[13] William N. Kephart, "Occupational Level and Marital Disruption," *American Sociological Review*, Vol. 20 (August, 1955), pp. 456-465.

man's divorce." The husband or father simply leaves his family and does not return. There are no really adequate statistics on the number of desertions in the United States for wives are often reluctant to report that they have been deserted by their husbands and it is obvious that the deserting husband is not going to call his action to anyone's attention. It is variously estimated by social scientists that there may be about one-fourth as many desertions as divorces or, at the present rate, about 100,000 annually. [14] Most records of desertions are provided by social agencies to whom the deserted family turns for help. Social workers estimate that 4,500,000 women and children may be without financial and personal support from fathers at any one time.

TABLE 7-2. Percentage distribution by occupational category of male deserters and divorcees: native white first marriages, Philadelphia, 1950

Occupational Category	Divorce Sample (N=939)	Desertion Cases (N=922*)
Professional	4.9	3.1
Proprietors	4.4	8.7
Clerical and sales	20.4	14.8
Skilled	20.0	21.6
Semiskilled	38.6	37.0
Labor-service	11.7	14.8
	100.0	100.0

* Including 75 unemployed and 55 cases in which the occupation was not reported.

SOURCE: William N. Kephart, "Occupational Level and Marital Disruption," *American Sociological Review,* Vol. 20 (August, 1955), p. 462, by permission.

By and large, society has been unable to cope with the financial and relationship problems created by desertion. Until recently the only recourse, other than continued dependence on social agencies, was to seek to locate the deserting spouse and to return him to his family under criminal indictment. Besides being time-consuming, expensive, and inefficient, this procedure effectively spoiled the father's chances in his new community and spoiled any chances of effecting a satisfactory reconciliation with his family. He was often put in jail—at considerable cost to the state—until he agreed to fulfill his obligations to his family; he was then released. Soon he would disappear and the whole process would start again.

In 1949, a more constructive approach got under way in the state of New York when the Family Location Service, headed by Jacob T. Zukerman, and other groups got together to sponsor a uniform dependent's support law which has been subsequently adopted in every state and

[14] Ray E. Baber, *Marriage and the Family* (New York, McGraw-Hill Book Co., 1953), pp. 493-494.

territory except for the District of Columbia. The new law permits a wife to go into a family court instead of a criminal court. The court then sends papers on the case to a corresponding court in the state where the errant husband has been found. The court in that state determines what the husband should pay, collects the money, and forwards it to the wife through the court in her own state. The husband and wife may also be referred to counseling agencies who work with them toward reconciliation. This procedure is too new for its effectiveness to be evaluated adequately but at least it approaches the problem constructively.

This kind of true desertion should not be confused with another kind of *fictitious* desertion which is often a prelude to divorce. In states where divorces are granted for desertion or gross neglect, many couples agree to live apart for the prescribed period in order to have legal grounds for divorce. There are reported instances of "deserted" persons living "across the hall" or "down the street" from their spouses. That many cases of so-called desertion do not involve actual physical disappearance of the husband is indicated by the findings of a recent study that, ". . . husbands and wives were still living in the same household in about one-third of Philadelphia desertion and nonsupport cases." [15] The same study also reports that over the past thirty years, the number of new desertion and nonsupport cases in the Philadelphia courts has been almost double the number of divorces granted during that period. [16] There is unquestionably a great deal of overlap between bona fide and fictitious desertion and between desertion and divorce cases, but many cases of desertion never reach the divorce courts.

Together, desertion and divorce account for the breakdown of approximately a half million American marriages each year. To get an accurate picture of the total number of marriages broken each year, however, there would have to be added an undetermined number of marriages where the spouses agree to separate without any intention of either going back together again or ever securing a divorce. One insurance company estimated, in 1947, that two million spouses were separated from one another without having been divorced. [17] Middle class and professional people often resort to such separation in order to avoid the scandal of divorce. Also, some religions prohibit divorce but do permit separation when the marital situation becomes intolerable. Approximately half our states provide for formal *legal separation* under the supervision of the courts. Such legal separation may be instituted at the request of the married couple or upon the order of the court. The couple are still married to one another but they are forbidden to live together and the husband

[15] William N. Kephart and Thomas P. Monahan, "Desertion and Divorce in Philadelphia," *American Sociological Review*, Vol. 17 (December, 1952), p. 719.

[16] *Ibid.*

[17] Harriet F. Pilpel and Theodora Zavin, *Your Marriage and the Law* (New York, Rinehart & Company, Inc., 1952), p. 300.

must contribute a specified amount for the support of the wife and children. Neither in such separations nor in desertion has the marriage actually been dissolved, but families are certainly broken when their members no longer live together.

Some 600,000 families in the United States are also broken each year by the death of husband or wife. The broken families that result in this case differ from those discussed above in that separation, divorce, and desertion usually follow the severance of emotional ties, while death often leaves the remaining spouse emotionally bound to the departed partner. The death-broken family is apt to experience, in varying proportions, two kinds of problems—problems of inadequate income, and problems of emotional readjustment.

The magnitude of the income problem is heightened by the fact that men, who do most of the earning, usually die before their wives. Some of these deaths occur early in life. Each year, for example, there are more than 42,000 accidental deaths of men between the ages of 15 and 64 years. [18] Death at this point in life is apt to leave not only the widow but dependent children. Except in the relatively few cases where there is sufficient wealth for the wife and children to live on for several years, their financial problems are apt to be acute. The younger the children and the more of them, the more difficult it is for the widow to earn a living for them. In recent years the federal income tax law has given a slight tax advantage to these women but it does not begin to compensate them for the expenses involved in having their children cared for while they work. The plight of this group is partly reflected by the 650,000 families who receive an estimated $700 million in aid to nearly 2 million dependent children annually. [19] Moreover, the widow's chances for re-marrying, ordinarily quite good at the younger ages, decline markedly with the presence of young children in the home.

Most death-broken families, of course, involve older people. There are some eight million widows in the U. S. whose average age is nearly 65 years. [20] The financial problems of these older women are often less acute because of the absence of dependent children and because property accumulated in the marriage, insurance, and Social Security are apt to be more adequate. Many such women return to employment which helps to occupy their time along with providing additional income. The cases of women who are left without financial resources and who may be unable to work, however, are particularly desperate. Even if financial problems are solved, the emotional situation faced by these older women may be

[18] Metropolitan Life Insurance Company, *Statistical Bulletin,* Vol. 40 (January, 1959), p. 8.
[19] United States Department of Health, Education, and Welfare, *Annual Report* (Government Printing Office, 1957), p. 77.
[20] Metropolitan Life Insurance Company, *Statistical Bulletin,* Vol. 39 (November, 1958), pp. 1-2.

New Role for Grandma?

. . . Once the exception, the working grandmother is becoming an important part of the work force.

If women keep taking jobs at the rate they have been for the last five years, 17,460,000 married, widowed, or divorced women between 35 and 64—about half the women in this age group—will be working by 1975. . . . Nearly 60 per cent of those in this group will be serving business and industry twenty years from now if recent growth rates continue.

Bureau of the Census

very difficult. Their chances of remarriage are poor: most otherwise eligible men are already married and they are usually outlived by their wives. The more fortunate women may have married children and grandchildren in whose lives they may participate at least occasionally. For many others, the growing commercial institution of baby-sitting may provide occasional entree into the lives of younger people. It would be interesting to try to measure the relative importance of monetary reward and emotional gratification for older women who baby-sit regularly.

Conflict Families

Many families that remain legally intact are broken emotionally. Their members live together but there is a constant atmosphere of discord and tension. The relationships may not be very different from relationships in other families that lead to divorce or desertion, but these families continue to exist nominally.

There are several different reasons why conflict families may not resort to separation. For some, religious doctrine forbids divorce and this may be reinforced by personal definitions that subordinate personal happiness to religious precept. For many persons occupational and social status make divorce hazardous. It is commonplace that divorce may threaten the careers of ministers, public officials, teachers, and other groups who are in the public eye. The threatened loss of prestige and social status may be even greater among middle class groups to whom prestige is important. Still other persons, where religion, occupation, and social status are not relevant, appear emotionally incapable of dissolving a conflict-ridden marriage. Socially, these are people who accept their unhappiness as inevitable and, psychologically, they often appear to derive masochistic satisfaction from their plights.

Roughly, conflict families can be divided into two groups—the marriages which begin in conflict, and those which begin in harmony and conflict develops later. One theme in American culture has all marriages beginning in bliss. Falling in love and being married are counted among life's most delightful experiences. But many marriages begin under conditions that are far from ideal. Some people marry not to build a highly desirable relationship with the marriage partner but to escape a less desirable situation elsewhere. Many persons who grow up in conflict families or other inadequate families become desperate to escape their lots, and marry to get away from unhappiness. According to folklore, such persons richly deserve happiness and marriage should be their salvation. Too often, however, the undesirable home conditions have made deep impresses upon their personalities and they are capable neither of giving nor receiving love adequately. Instead of remedying the situation, such marriages often perpetuate it through succeeding generations.

For some persons, being married and having a family has nothing to do with happiness anyway. One aspect of American culture defines relationships between men and women as essentially competitive and exploitative. Men and women are drawn together by sexual need and forced together by social pressure until they find themselves trapped in marriage. Marriage to the woman means too much childbearing, unending drudgery, and an unfaithful husband. To the man it means inadequate income, too much responsibility, and too many limitations on his personal freedom. Children are the inevitable by-product—lovable, perhaps, but troublesome and expensive. And the children are soon caught up in the frustrations and dissatisfactions of their parents.

The feeling of being trapped in marriage symbolizes these relationships which virtually begin in conflict. Sometimes the entrapment is more direct and less subtle than it appears above and sometimes there is more than a single kind of entrapment involved. The discovery of pregnancy often springs the trap—it being estimated that at least one marriage in every eight in the United States follows a premarital pregnancy. [21] Even couples who might subsequently have married anyway may lament the fortune that forced their marriages and be somewhat more inclined to find unhappiness in their relationships. This hunch is borne out by the finding that marriages following pregnancy result in higher divorce rates than do other marriages. [22] Marriages may be essentially "shotgun" even where pregnancy is not involved. Parents may pressure a young man or woman into marriage, to the hurt, anger, or bewilderment of one or both partners. Or the pressure may come from one of the partners them-

[21] Harold T. Christensen, "Studies in Child Spacing: I, Premarital Pregnancy as Measured by the Spacing of the First Birth from Marriage," *American Sociological Review*, Vol 18 (February, 1953), p. 55.

[22] Harold T. Christensen and Hanna H. Meissner, "Studies in Child Spacing: III, Premarital Pregnancy as a Factor in Divorce," *American Sociological Review*, Vol. 18 (December, 1953), pp. 641-644.

selves, with the pressuring partner being hurt by the reluctance of the other, and the reluctant partner being hurt by his seeming lack of freedom of choice.

In all these cases the conditions for conflict are laid down even before the marriages occur. The marriage begins in suspicion, mistrust, and resentment. Sullen anger usually erupts into quarrels. Quarreling becomes chronic. Many such marriages soon break up. In others, the conflict becomes a spreading sore, gradually infecting all family members.

Most marriages—even those that become conflict families—begin in relative harmony. Studies generally have shown the vast majority of young married couples to be fairly well satisfied and only 20 or 25 per cent to be definitely unhappy. [23] Yet if some 25 per cent eventually seek divorce, logic and common sense suggest that the number who become unhappy must be far greater. One possibility is that, when reporting to investigators, people overestimate their happiness and underestimate the seriousness of their problems. If people thus fool themselves, however, they must also fool their friends, for estimates of the happiness of a marriage by the couple's friends tend to correlate highly with the couple's own ratings. Another distinct possibility is that the degree of happiness in marriage is not a constant. Most people expect to be happy in marriage and most do achieve some happiness. But as marriage continues, new adjustment problems keep cropping up. After a couple have ironed out their initial differences and worked out a *modus operandi*, along come children, aged and infirm parents, and with the demands created by these, recognition of insufficient income. In each new adjustment lie the seeds of potential conflict. Some families learn successful problem-solving techniques, but others find bitterness and frustration that family members are then likely to take out on one another. Marriages that began in harmony may ultimately become as conflict-ridden as those that began in strife.

Multiproblem Families

This chapter began with a graphic account of the compounding of serious problems in a relatively small proportion of St. Paul families. Divorce, desertion, conflict, dependency, illegitimacy—any of these things alone is a serious enough problem. But evidence mounts that perhaps one family in twenty has *all* of these problems and more. Social workers are rapidly discovering that in most communities there is a "hard core" of multiproblem families that act as breeding grounds for almost every conceivable human pathology and that absorb an amazingly high percentage of all community protective and welfare services.

[23] Ernest W. Burgess and Leonard S. Cottrell, Jr., *Predicting Success or Failure in Marriage* (Englewood Cliffs, N. J., Prentice-Hall, Inc., 1939), p. 32.

Such multiproblem families thrive in ignorance and incompetence. In large cities they are generally to be found in the worst slum areas. In smaller cities and towns they often live in shacks along railroad tracks or rivers, and next to the community dumping grounds where they have taken up "squatter's rights." In rural areas they exist in abject poverty and filth on the backroads where they may scratch out bare livings from impoverished soil and where, like their urban counterparts, they often supplement their resources by the fruits of petty—or even major—crime.

Perhaps their outstanding feature as families is that they fail to perform virtually every function that is normally associated with family life. Instead of affectionate mutually supporting relationships between the parents, the relationships are frequently exploitative. Wives frequently work outside the home in unskilled jobs and associate being at home only with additional drudgery. Tavern-hopping is apt to be a favorite form of recreation, implying both habitual drunkenness and the absence of any concept of responsibility for self and others. Children can hardly be properly indoctrinated with community norms when the parents themselves have never learned them. By example, if not by design, children are soon taught truancy, lying, theft, and a general distrustful, indifferent attitude toward others. Physical, as well as emotional, health problems are common and serious. Poverty, ignorance, unsanitary conditions, and dissipation combine to produce illness and disability and to make effective medical care unavailable. Ill-health and indolence reinforce the inability to earn a decent living, bitterness at seeming discrimination reinforces the antisocial attitudes, and so on in an increasingly vicious circle of incompetence and pathology.

In some of the larger cities, concerted efforts now are being made to break into this vicious circle and to set it spiraling in the direction of rehabilitation rather than in that of continued disorganization. Skilled social work teams are seeking to help men develop minimum occupational competence, are teaching women housekeeping skills, are helping families find decent places to live, and are working with youngsters to help them accept and find places for themselves within the larger community's value structure. These efforts at rehabilitation are tremendously expensive, require large numbers of highly skilled personnel, and are of uncertain effectiveness. Moreover, only a very small fraction of multiproblem families can be reached by this means. Yet the financial and social costs of permitting multiproblem families to remain unhelped are incomparably higher and in some instances, at least, rehabilitation has been accomplished. The long-run hope for eliminating multiproblem families probably lies in what can be learned both about them and how to help them through combination rehabilitation-research programs such as that which exists in St. Paul.

Less than one per cent of the 2,000,000 families in this city (New York) produce more than 75 per cent of its juvenile delinquents, a survey indicated yesterday. . . . From 20,000 "multi-problem" families came three-quarters of the 35,000 children taken into custody each year as juvenile delinquents. . . .

Virtually all of these families are now, or have been recently, among the case load of the city Department of Welfare or of private philanthropies. In fact, they represent about one-third of the total 60,000 families on public and private relief.

"These 'hard core' families are not only poor but are oppressed by a 'constellation' of social problems," said Ralph W. Whelan, executive director of the Youth Board.

For example: 20.3 per cent of the fathers and 7.4 per cent of the mothers suffer from alcoholism or drug addiction or both . . . while 15.8 per cent of the mothers and 7 per cent of the fathers are mentally ill. More than 32 per cent of the mothers and 15 per cent of the fathers are crippled by physical illness.

Twenty-eight per cent of the fathers had deserted their families. . . . Eleven per cent of the fathers and 12 per cent of the mothers were guilty of abusing their children by brutal beating or other cruelty. Nearly 15 per cent of the mothers were said to be sexually immoral. . . .

To cure this "focal point of social infection" Mr. Whelan is now negotiating to pay eleven leading family service agencies $150,000 a year to do remedial work with these 20,000 families. . . . In addition, the Youth Board is asking the Board of Estimate for an additional $100,000 to concentrate its own aid directly on these "hard core" 20,000 families with more than 60,000 children.

The New York Times

Inadequate Families

Multiproblem families, conflict families, and broken families are all easily visualized and have obvious undesirable effects on their members. Some other families whose inadequacies are not so easily recognized may, however, have almost equally devastating effects upon parents and children.

Families are, ideally, primary sources of affection and emotional security for old and young. Parents who are affectionate toward one another and who show insight and understanding into themselves and each other are thereby better equipped to deal satisfactorily with persons and situations outside the home. They also provide appropriate role models to help their children grow into adequate adults. Conversely, some parents cannot, or do not, show affection, show little insight into the needs of others, and fail completely to provide the kinds of adult models with which children can identify. Just as emotionally adequate families foster good health and adequate adjustment, inadequate families encourage physical illness and deviant behavior. These inadequate families can be described in terms of the emotional atmospheres that they produce in the home. [24]

Atmosphere of dislike. In these families the problem is that no one likes anyone else very much. Parents not only do not love one another, they actively dislike each other. Probably they tend to dislike people in general, as well as disliking each other. They are not able to like their children very much either and the children soon acquire the habit of disliking others. No one feels wanted or necessary. No one feels that he is worth being loved. Everyone is "stupid," or "silly," or "worthless," or "lazy," and everyone resentfully feels that way.

Kill-joy atmosphere. Pessimism reigns in these families. They see the worst in everything that happens and everything that will happen. If they get a new car, it is bound to be a lemon. If the husband gets a promotion, the added responsibility will probably break his health. If the child makes a friend, the friend will prove to be false. Their gloomy outlook pervades everything that they do and every relationship that they have. Consequently, other people do not like to be around them very much and soon they are lonely, isolated people. By the time children reach adolescence they are apt to be so entrenched in gloom and doom that they fail to develop the normal contacts of youth and turn their dour attitudes inward on themselves and their families. These families probably are prone to hypochondria, for every bodily twinge becomes an omen of disaster to come. They live out their lives in isolation and self-generated misery.

Critical atmosphere. Everybody criticizes everybody else. The other person is always wrong and is to blame for everything that happens. Mothers, according to fathers, "don't know how to rear their children properly" and children "don't do well enough in school." It does not matter if mother manages a house with three small children and works part time on the side, or if the children bring home 60 per cent *A's* and 40 per cent *B's* on their report cards; nobody does well enough. Soon the family members begin to wonder, what's the use? No matter how hard they try, they cannot please. It is only a short step from these feelings

[24] John A. Schindler, *How to Live 365 Days a Year* (Englewood Cliffs, N. J., Prentice-Hall, Inc., 1954), pp. 127-133.

to believing that, indeed, one cannot do anything right. Everyone feels inferior and everyone criticizes others to mask his own feelings of inferiority. Or the resentment against criticism may be turned in other directions. If it is turned outward it may appear in fighting or lying, in stealing, in sexual exploitation, in speeding or reckless driving, in drinking, or in a host of other outlets. If it is turned inward it may result in whining or in feelings of inadequacy and depression.

Atmosphere of excessive piety. This atmosphere, while superficially very different, has effects very much like the critical atmosphere just discussed. The excessive piety may or may not be connected with religion. In either event the parents are apt to take a holier-than-thou attitude toward their children and toward all outsiders. They have rigid standards of behavior that are heavily overlaid with moral sanction. When the child commits even a minor infraction—as he must do frequently—he is made to feel sinful or, at the very least, to feel unworthy of parents who are such paragons of virtue. Outsiders who find themselves being treated almost as morally delinquent children are likely to keep their contacts with these families both formal and distant. The children who—while they remain children at least—cannot so easily escape the excessive piety may resort to any or all of the "escapes" discussed above. When the children become adult they may break all ties with their families in order to escape the potentially overwhelming guilt or, if they have been more completely indoctrinated, they may unwittingly perpetuate the stifling piety in their own families.

Atmosphere of selfish egotism. In some families that otherwise appear normal, one or more members—usually one of the parents at first—is able to think only of his own wishes and is completely insensitive to the needs of other family members. Outwardly, there may appear to be affection and regard for others but actions reveal selfishness and egocentrism. There are mothers, for example, who are active in virtually every community organization, who are on the go many hours each day, and who are widely respected, but who simply could not imagine that they are depriving their families of companionship and joint recreation. Similarly, there are fathers who spend most of their time at work or with the "boys," completely oblivious to the deprivation experienced by their families. Not all busy mothers and fathers, of course, are lacking in sympathy, helpfulness, and sensitivity to group needs. Some such parents, however, cause their partners and children to feel rejected and unloved. Any or all of the possible reactions to frustration may then follow and the family may be caught in an increasing spiral of rejection and rebellion.

The effects of unhealthy atmospheres. These family atmospheres are important because of the causal link between them and physical illness and deviant behavior. It seems reasonably well established that whenever basic needs for affection and security are continuously thwarted that some physical or emotional impairment results. Illnesses ranging from ulcers and asthma to hypochondria, neuroses, and psychoses, may appear. Obviously such illnesses are accompanied by deviant behavior, and there are other cases where, in the absence of diagnosable illness, inappropriate behavior is the chief clue to the frustration. Antisocial behavior—stealing, lying, fighting, and so on—is one possibility, while others involve behavior that in most contexts is considered desirable. A child may seek the love and approval he needs by conforming to every demand of others. Co-operation and congeniality in children are generally approved, but in this case they are a symptom of unhealthy relationships and, in the long run, they are apt to have very unhealthy consequences for the child. A father may attempt to relieve his frustrations in being more successful in his occupation and a mother may turn her needs for affection too concentratedly on her children. Whatever the nature of the emotional inadequacy in the family, it manifests itself in these and comparable symptoms and threatens to perpetuate the pattern from parents to children to grandchildren and so on indefinitely. While perhaps less graphic than overt family breakdown, the price exacted in human misery may be far greater.

OTHER FAMILY PROBLEMS

Not all families are problem families and many families produce in abundant measure the satisfactions that are traditionally associated with family life. While much family life may be rewarding, however, it is usually anything but that which is nostalgically—and erroneously—associated with the "good old days." Possibly no other institution has been so profoundly affected by social change, in the last century or so, as the family. Family change is reflected in the changed and uncertain roles which face men, women, and children as they move through the life cycle.

Changed Roles for Women

Man's traditional right to "wear the pants in the family" shows signs of being replaced by a "His-hers" arrangement such as that found on guest towels and pillow slips. The uncertainty as to who should play what role is possibly greatest in the husband-wife relationship, but similar problems plague other family members from teen-agers to grandparents.

Woman's place today is in the office and factory as well as in the home. Nor is this true only of single women, for by 1949 over half of all employed women were married. Not that single women are being less employed, for the number of single women in industry has increased steadily. But the number of married women working has increased even

TABLE 7-3 . Marital status of employed women

Marital status	Per cent of all Women workers
Single	19
Married	63
Widowed or Divorced	18

SOURCE: Women's Bureau, "Handbook on Women Workers," Bulletin, No. 266, 1958, p. 31.

faster. Working *before* marriage has been modified to include working *after* marriage and, in some cases, working *instead of* marriage.

The revolution in women's roles goes far beyond the mere facts of women working, however. Women no longer have to fit into the wife-and-mother role, but face a bewildering number of alternatives. The most basic choice of all permits women to marry or to avoid marriage if they prefer. Financial independence of males is possible for most women, and at least that broad group of women whom we generally label as middle-class are consciously prepared in high school and college to earn a living after graduation. Given this possibility, some few women deliberately choose not to marry. Many others never actually choose to remain single, but, because of their financial independence, are able to reject specific suitors until, largely by default, they have drifted into spinster-hood.

Within marriage many different roles are possible. The ever-present concern of young people to know whether it is possible to combine marriage and a career attest to the wife as an economic partner in marriage. It is probable again that most of the wives who work are not career women in the conventional sense. Most young women now work during the early years of marriage but drift into a fairly conventional housewife pattern following childbirth. Some of these women go back to work, part or full time, after their children are in school or after they have grown up and left home. Gradually rising life expectancies mean more years of active life beyond the childbearing period and more and more middle-aged women find themselves with too little useful work to do.

From the very beginning, the working wife faces a dilemma. Employers are reluctant to hire her for occupations with a future because of the probability that she will soon be having children and the time and money spent training her will be wasted. Consequently, even professionally trained young women often are forced to settle for positions as stenographers, clerks, salespersons, and similar fill-in jobs. After a few years of this work and from six to twenty or more years spent rearing their children, very few women can quickly pick up and use their earlier professional training. After all the effort in high school and college, women

Modern Woman: The Forward Sex

Travelers who returned to certain parts of North Africa in the mid-1940's discovered that there had been a social revolution there during the war. Previously, when local Arabs trekked between their villages, their wives had walked twenty yards behind them; now their wives walked twenty yards in front. Research showed that the change had occurred about 1943, when allied troops were advancing across the country. The reason for the change was that, at that time, there were a lot of land mines about.

"The Happy Science" in *The Economist,* December 22, 1956, as reprinted in *Harper's,* March, 1957, p. 61.

with grown families find themselves a drug on the labor market and prepared only for the most menial jobs.

Whether she works or not, the modern wife is apt to find that she faces multiple expectations in marriage for which she is only partly prepared. Moreover, many of her roles are flatly contradictory. She is taught that she must be a good wife but that she has equal rights with her husband, that she should bear children but that she should keep her figure, that she should like to sew and wash dishes but be capable of entering a profession, that she should be a homebody but also a clever hostess, that she should be modest and unassuming but able to keep her husband's interest, that she should be frugal and thrifty but dressed in excellent taste. How are such contradictions to be reconciled and what role or roles can married women play? How well adapted will the clever, glamorous college girl be to scrubbing floors and changing diapers? For that matter, how well adapted is she to play *any one role* in life? She is likely to have some desire, or compulsion, to follow in her mother's footsteps. Also she will likely have acquired notions that her mother's role is old-fashioned, or degrading, or just plain boring. She probably will want to "make something of herself" but also to have children, to stand on a par with her husband but to expect chivalrous courtesies from him. She will probably be ambivalent no matter what role she plays!

The conflicts in women's roles also create problems for men. When his wife shows little disposition to make herself available for the pipe-and-slippers routine, the husband must make adjustments also. He, too, may be torn between the intellectualized belief that men and women should be social equals and nostalgic longing for the deference which "mother showed to father." The husband is perhaps more likely to feel comfortable in the traditional male-dominant role than is his wife in the female-sub-

> The children now love luxury. They have bad manners, contempt for authority, and they show disrespect to their elders. They no longer rise when elders enter the room. They contradict their parents, chatter before company, gobble up dainties at the table, cross their legs, and are tyrants over their teachers.
>
> SOCRATES

ordinate role, but again ambivalence is probable. His wife's independence is a sign of disrespect and her acquiescence makes him feel guilty. Not only has the husband's role been challenged but he must suffer with the confusion in women's roles.

Changed Notions of Morality

Modern America can scarcely be said to have *a* moral code. Rather, it has at least several such codes flatly contradicting one another at numerous points. The most widespread and best known is the Judaeo-Christian code requiring chastity before, and faithfulness in, marriage, but punishing females much more heavily for transgressions. We frequently act and talk as though this code were the only one and apply it alike to all groups in the society. [25] Discussions of morality generally hinge upon how widely the Judaeo-Christian code is adhered to and whether violations of it are on the increase.

In the present century, with the advent of two world wars and the roaring Twenties in between, discussions of sex became fashionable and it became common knowledge that violations of the code are much more widespread than formerly had been admitted. People quickly jumped to the conclusion that violations were increasing rapidly and, consequently, that the moral code was breaking down. Not until the middle 1940's was this conclusion seriously challenged.

When analyzing changed sex patterns it is a mistake to consider men and women together. Men, contrary to expectations, are not having more premarital experience than they have in decades past. A comparison of the total amount of premarital experience for older and younger men show them to be almost identical. Because of their greater freedom men have generally been much more active than women. For women there has been

[25] Actually sex patterns and moral standards vary widely from one society to another and among different social and educational levels in American society. Compare George Murdock, *Social Structure* (New York, The Macmillan Co., 1949), pp. 260-322, and Alfred C. Kinsey and associates, *Sexual Behavior in the Human Male* (Philadelphia, W. B. Saunders Co., 1948), pp. 327-393.

a definite increase in premarital sex experience. Whereas only about 40 per cent of women who were born before 1900 had sexual intercourse before marriage, 60 per cent of those born between 1900-1909 had done so, [26] and it is confidently predicted that by the time all the women born after 1920 are married the figure will also have climbed to approximately 60 per cent.

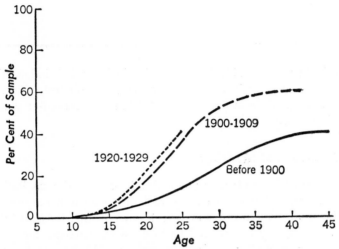

SOURCE: After A. C. Kinsey and associates, *Sexual Behavior in the Human Female* (Philadelphia, W. B. Saunders Co., 1953), p. 299, by permission.

Fig. 7–2. Premarital sex relationships in three groups of females, according to decade of birth.

What conclusions can be drawn from this comparison? First, the increase in premarital experience even among women has not been large, and considerable experimentation occurred in past generations. Predictions that premarital sex relationships are becoming universal are not borne out. How can we account for such widespread misbelief? Undoubtedly, one factor is our greater freedom to talk about sex. For the first time boys and girls discuss sex freely and demand to have some academic preparation for sex adjustment before they marry. Until recently, such demands were unheard of. Consequently, older people who grew up under rigid taboos upon any mention of sex equate the breakdown of taboos in this one area with the breakdown of moral standards in general. It does not occur to them that open consideration of sex matters might be coupled with a pattern of reserving full sexual involvement for marriage. Furthermore, older persons constitute a kind of vested interest in the relations between succeeding generations. Tendencies to "forget" what their own early experiences were like, coupled with enough

[26] Alfred C. Kinsey and associates, *Sexual Behavior in the Human Female* (Philadelphia, W. B. Saunders Co., 1953), pp. 298-299.

remembrance to make them fear for their children's safety, and the habitual resistance to change itself encourage oldsters to take a dim view of their offsprings' behavior. Some of the adult reaction is a direct effort to control the behavior of specific youngsters against dangers with which the adults themselves are familiar.

In addition, the failure to find any increase in premarital sex relationships for boys, together with the increase for girls, suggests that there may be less relative promiscuity now than formerly. Sexual experiences seemingly now are confined more to couples from similar social groups who are potential marriage partners. These couples reject the notion that their relationships should be asexual up to the point of marriage and drastically changed immediately thereafter. Their standards of morality include the gradual progression of intimacy as part of the total relationship.

Changed Roles of Older Persons

Middle age and old age are often periods of tragedy. It seems that suddenly there is nothing to do. Aged men and women sit and rock on porches or wander about the neighborhood waiting out their lives. The problems of age often begin before the period of physical disability, however. Two events are crucial in initiating them: the marriage of children, and retirement.

"No mother ever delivered a child at adolescence with less pain than at the hour of birth." [27] The sudden exodus of grown children from the home is often a distinct shock. Mothers, especially, find that all at once they have little or nothing to do during the many hours each day that they formerly spent in looking after their children's needs. Superficially, one might say, "What an opportunity for leisure!" "What a chance for Mother to do the things she has always wanted to do!" Fine, except that twenty or more years of caring for her offspring probably have destroyed the desire for many of the things she once wanted and, more important, she is left to do them alone! Her children, who are her chief affectional outlet, are building new ties for themselves—which means weakened ties with the parents. She is largely left out of the lives she formerly shared.

Nor is her own marriage prepared to fill the void. Often during the child-rearing period, fathers become more and more engrossed in earning a living and mothers become more and more engrossed in their children. Though the affectional ties between them may continue to be strong, large parts of their daily lives are built apart from one another. When the children leave, the father, to assuage his own frustration, may become even

[27] John Levy and Ruth Munroe, *The Happy Family* (New York, Alfred A. Knopf, Inc., 1938), p. 9.

more involved in his work and even less available to his wife. She is left even more alone. Without existing habits to fall back upon, many women tend toward one of two extremes: a pattern of idleness, self-pity, and despair; or a frantic cycle of activity in almost any group that will accept them and serve as partial outlet for their unmet needs.

At retirement, "the shoe switches to the other foot" frequently. The husband and father faces the more serious problems of adjustment. Enforced retirement at the age of sixty-five or at any other age will be unwelcome to many men who are physically able to continue working. Moreover, even those who look forward to retirement often find it a disappointing experience. The status of adult males is very largely their status as breadwinners. Take away the job and you take away the status. For a man to think, "I am retired," is often equivalent to, "I am no longer useful." He tends to an orientation of "I was . . ." and finds in that orientation no place for the present. His wife can at least cook and clean house and baby-sit for the grandchildren, but what is there for a retired grandfather to do? The few alternatives most available, such as caring for the lawn and garden and household repair, often require more strength and agility than he can muster. There are not even any "men's clubs" for him to join. Retirement often turns still capable men into helpless, useless creatures in a remarkably short period of time.

THE SOCIAL-DISORGANIZATION APPROACH

The Old Rules

The American family that adapted to colonial and frontier life was a strong and stable organization. It was a rural family, oriented toward agriculture. Families were large, for children were highly valued, not much additional expense, and they were a chief source of labor. The husband and father was the undisputed head of the household. The biblical admonition that "husbands should be the head of their wives" was interpreted quite literally and children were supposed to be "seen, not heard." Divorce was rare. Marriages were contracted to meet the necessity for earning a living and rearing a family. A lack of compatability between the spouses was no reason for destroying an otherwise good marriage. The family raised most of its own food, made its own clothing, furniture, and other household goods, and often built its own house. It was a large, patriarchal, stable group which performed numerous functions for its members.

It was not difficult either for men or women to decide what they would do in life. By and large they did what their parents had done. Boys learned to farm, to carpenter and to assume their place as caretakers and disciplinarians for women and children. Girls learned to do all the things required of a farmer's wife, to expect marriage, and to bear large families. For neither were there any real alternatives. Farming is a family business. Men could not run their farms without the help of wives and children, and for women the only alternative to marriage was to live in the home of a relative with a status somewhere between that of a hired servant and that of a child who needs special attention. Family unity also had its positive side. Men, women, and children shared the same basic values in addition to the many tasks required to make a living. Each performed services for the other and each was rewarded in turn. Parents provided apprenticeships for their children and gradually turned over property and responsibility to them. As their vigor declined, the parents withdrew to part-time work without fear of economic deprivation or social isolation. The clearly defined roles for family members fit together smoothly and provided security for all.

The Transition

The Industrial Revolution had profound effects on the family. It displaced farming as the principal occupation, it brought the growth of cities, and it was accompanied by the development of a much more secular outlook on life.

As we have seen, prior to the Industrial Revolution farming was the chief occupation, and what little industry was carried on was organized under the "cottage" system. Small producers fabricated goods in their own homes with the aid of family members and one or two hired workers. On the farm and off, the family was an economic unit with production activities helping to build up and maintain its solidarity. The appearance of the factory changed all this. No longer was work carried on in the home and no longer did all of the family members participate. The husband or father was likely to be employed at some distance from his home and to be effectively removed from contact with other family members throughout most of the waking hours. Both the satisfactions and the frustrations encountered on the job came to have less and less meaning for the remaining family members who were similarly intent on going their separate ways.

The appearance of factories required large numbers of laborers to be congregated near by. Stores and other retail businesses sprang up to cater to the needs of the factory workers and, all at once, the modern city was in the process of development. Land close to the factories became expensive and living space scarce. Families crowded into smaller quarters and spent less time in the home. Children became economic and social liabilities, expensive to raise, and troublesome in the city environment. They went out of the home to the school and church and to centers of commercialized recreation.

It was not only the material aspects of life which changed, however. Customs and traditions which formerly had been accepted as eternal God-given verities became the objects of rational scrutiny. Just because it had always been done that way was no reason for continuing it, if a better way could be found. People began to look for new and better ways of regulating their personal lives as well as for producing goods. Marriage assumed the character of a humanly sanctioned relationship from which the sanction could be withdrawn by divorce or separation. The requirements and expectations which formerly held families together began to give way to a new pattern.

The New Rules

To compile a complete and accurate list of the new rules governing family behavior is not possible for the transition is not yet complete. Though the large patriarchal family has largely given way, vestiges of it remain and the character of its successor is not fully established. From past changes and present trends, the following observations, at least, seem well founded.

The primary goal of marriage (and the family) is happiness—with the emphasis on the personal happiness of each family member. The family is subordinate to its members' needs and is modified or dissolved when individual needs are not met. Permanence of a marriage is no longer a wholly satisfactory criterion of success, and family responsibility does not require a large number of children. Parents consider their own happiness as well as that of their children and plan the size of their families to provide the maximum benefits for all concerned. More stress is placed on the quality of child care than on the number of children. Parents strive to achieve wholesome, well-adjusted personalities in their children as well as to feed, clothe, and educate them.

No longer are husbands the undisputed masters and neither men nor women know beforehand what to expect in marriage. Though women largely have gained equality with men, the nature of that equality remains vague and undefined. To some it is equality based upon the traditional division of labor between the sexes, the husband being bread-winner and the wife, the homemaker. To others it means that beyond bearing children the division of labor should be worked out according to the temperaments and needs of the spouses. To still others it means something intermediate between these two extremes. Above all, it means confusion and dissatisfaction because there is no one role for which persons are trained and in which they can feel comfortable. Perhaps a satisfactory set of new roles will appear, but more likely not. Rigid, unvarying roles for men and women may be incompatible with our highly individualistic, technologically advanced culture. Rather than develop any one set of satisfactory roles, we appear to be moving toward the acceptance of various role patterns. Flexibility of attitude toward roles for men and women with several possible alternatives for each may be about as much uniformity as can be achieved in the equalitarian family group.

Parents, though they may continue to aid their children, are forced to let go of their offspring at marriage. The marriage of children demands again the equivalent of the prechildbearing relationship between the mother and father—and the problems of adjustment are often more difficult at fifty than they were at twenty. Parents are expected to be emotionally self-sufficient and to prepare for financial independence during their old age. Modern homes are small and efficient. They assume the presence of only one set of parents and children. About the only entree into the childrearing family for grandparents is in the role of babysitter or occasional visitor. The independence of the young family requires also the independence of the grandparents.

Many families have been unable to adjust to these new rules and to the urban setting in which they operate. The failure of husbands and wives to find satisfactory roles for themselves and one another contributes to the high incidence of separation, divorce, and desertion. Parents also are puzzled about how to deal with their children and what to expect from them; and youngsters, as they grow up, are confused about their own behavior. Urban living has brought with it the anonymous conditions that permit the development of extreme disorganization illustrated by multiproblem families. Thus social disorganization and change in the larger society has contributed to family disorganization, directly, through the resulting confusion in roles and, indirectly, through providing the setting in which extreme disorganization can develop and flourish.

Many groups bitterly oppose some or all of these changes in the family. Even when the changes are not actively opposed, people are disoriented by them. They are torn between loyalty to the values of old and acceptance of new, supposedly better ways. The conflict rages between groups and within individual personalities.

THE VALUE-CONFLICT APPROACH

Permanence vs. Adjustment

History is replete with accounts of unsatisfactory marriages. Biblical heroes, European monarchs, and American presidents have succeeded or failed because of, or in spite of, the sharp tongues of their wives. Noble women of all countries have assumed increased stature in comparison to the incompetence and debauchery of their husbands. Outsiders have, for centuries, admired and pitied these (un)fortunate men and women. Only recently, and mostly in America, has anyone had the temerity to try to

do anything about it. And rarely have efforts at change met such concerted opposition.

Self-sacrifice has never been the least highly regarded of virtues and
permanence of the family somehow is supposed to compensate for any
sacrifices made by its members. The basic assumptions underlying this
position are at least two: (1) family life itself is "sacred" and not to be
trifled with; and (2) protection of the family against dissolution is necessary for the well-being of all its members. Husbands and wives who
remain together, even if unhappy, reputedly are building "character" in
themselves and will be "better men and women" for the tribulations they
have undergone. Children similarly need their parents. Even though the
home be strife-ridden its continuance is presumed to be better than having
the parents separate. For persons who hold these beliefs, the only solution
to family problems is to seek a return to the stable family of the past.
Generally they advocate stricter divorce laws, or no divorce at all, a clearly
defined set of obligations for husbands, wives, and children to follow,
and punishment for those who disobey.

These "permanence" values are opposed by the emerging "happiness,"
or "adjustment," goals in family life. Many people now deny that benefits
inevitably or automatically result from preserving marriages. On the
contrary, they claim that continuance of conflict-ridden marriages may
be harmful both to parents and children, and that such marriages had best
be dissolved so that other more satisfactory relationships may be formed.
Presumably, unhappy parents are in no position to provide the necessary
affection and security for their children. Moreover, the emotional trauma
resulting from the unhappy parental relationship may be greater than that
involved in experiencing divorce. In support of this position, it is true that
most divorced persons remarry and that second marriages are often happy
ones. [28] Very few of these persons actually favor divorce. They merely
regard it as less undesirable than the existence of unhappy marriages.

Charity vs. Rehabilitation

Widespread knowledge of the increasingly high costs of welfare
services provided to families is sharpening another value conflict—the
issue of public responsibility for providing financial support for families
which cannot provide for themselves. Mirrored in professional social work
is the philosophy that the financial and social costs of failing to provide
maximum aid to these families are far greater than the admittedly high
costs of attempting to rehabilitate them. Not only must the money and
services be provided, they argue, but the goal of getting families off the
welfare rolls as soon as possible must often be sacrificed to the long-range

[28] Jessie Bernard, *Remarriage* (New York, The Dryden Press, Inc., 1956), pp. 44-
70, p. 268, and *passim.*

goal of making them self-reliant, responsible members of the community. Welfare recipients should be accorded as much privacy as possible in their personal and financial dealings just as self-supporting citizens are. That occasional families will take advantage of the situation to sponge unnecessarily on public funds is part of the price that must be paid to provide a favorable rehabilitation climate for the others.

The contrary view, more often presented in the public press, is that in the unprecedented prosperity since World War II there should be virtually no need for long-term support of families by public welfare. Yet welfare costs have risen astronomically because well-meaning, but misguided, social workers favor providing endless financial support for families who show no interest in providing for themselves. Untold thousands of families which actually have adequate incomes continue to draw welfare payments which they use either for debauchery or to provide luxuries for which other families must work and save. Other families, which legitimately need temporary aid, are encouraged in shiftlessness by the unsound philosophy of demanding nothing in return for welfare support. The protagonists of these views would make welfare payments a matter of public record and would coerce rapid rehabilitation under the threat of withdrawal of welfare support.

These are issues that are not easily resolved. Many social workers and their supporters see the need for placing more effective limits on the public support of indigence. And many of their opponents, who feel strongly the pressure of increasing taxes, recognize that public support which destroys self-respect may be worse than no support at all. The most hopeful efforts to resolve the controversy probably are not those that pertain to it directly, but those efforts to develop more effective techniques for modifying the attitudes and skills of dependent families. The recent discovery of a hard core of multiproblem families already may be leading to more effective co-ordination of the efforts of various public agencies. The systematic research now under way on how to deal with chronic dependency may soon make these co-ordinated efforts more effective.

THE PERSONAL-DEVIATION APPROACH

The United States is both a much married and a much divorced nation. A larger proportion of the adult population is married today than ever before, but one out of every eight persons is in a second or subsequent marriage. [29] High marriage and divorce rates in the United States are not new, nor do they show any real signs of declining. Apparently they are a fundamental part of modern American culture. Yet the vast majority of people maintain that the situation is "abnormal" and should

[29] Harold T. Christensen, *Marriage Analysis* (New York, The Ronald Press Company, 1958), p. 572.

be remedied as soon as possible. Only a small group which is convinced that the instability is here to stay have the temerity to suggest that it is man's ideas and expectations of marriage which must change rather than the nature of marriage itself. They are deviants who believe that the individualistic, materialistic values of modern society require that institutions, the family included, be flexible enough to fit themselves to individual needs. It is yet near heresy to proclaim that divorce may serve socially useful purposes, that some marriages may cause or aggravate personality problems for the spouses, and that divorcees and remarried people should not automatically be suspected of having special personal difficulties. The few persons who take this extreme position may themselves lead quite conventional family lives, [30] but they are deviant in the attitudes they take toward family problems. They are important because their ideas are so directly contrary to prevailing family traditions. If these deviants are correct in the assertion that a universal permanent monogamy is incompatible with modern conditions, they may prove to be the vanguard in a movement to reorient our thinking about the family.

Ordinarily, deviant behavior is considered to be the unusual—or atypical—behavior deriving from motivation which differs in kind or in force from that experienced by most people. But this is not always true. For example, sex relationships before marriage are regarded as deviant behavior in the United States. Yet more than half of all boys and a sizeable proportion of girls eventually have such relationships. [31] Premarital relationships are then the majority pattern! The forces that give rise to them are deeply rooted in biology and culture. The deviancy in this case is from a verbal norm, not a behavioral one. Premarital sex relationships are still so strongly disapproved of that most young people are forced to attempt to justify for themselves behavior that they condemn in anyone else.

It would not be correct to assume, however, that premarital relationships result inevitably from biological and cultural forces with individual personalities not playing an important role in them. Especially among boys, the need to prove they can carry it off and, thereby, assure themselves and others of their adequate masculinity is an important factor. Boys who feel inferior to and hostile toward girls frequently use sex conquests as a means of getting even with the girls to whom they feel inferior. Both boys and girls unwittingly use sex relationships as weapons against parents and others in authority. In addition to indicating complete de-

[30] An interesting parallel case is to be found in Sigmund Freud with whose name is associated a very permissive attitude toward sex expression. Freud, himself, was far more conventional in his family and sexual behavior than were many of his contemporaries. See Ernest Jones, *The Life and Work of Sigmund Freud*, Vol. 1 (New York, Basic Books, Inc., 1953), p. 139.

[31] Kinsey, *op. cit.*, *Sexual Behavior in the Human Male*, p. 550, and *Sexual Behavior in the Human Female*, pp. 330-331.

fiance of authority, if these relationships are discovered they cause parents great anguish or concern. Girls who do not receive sufficient feelings of security and being loved in their families sometimes resort to sex relationships for the temporary feelings of being loved and desired which these relationships provide. In all the cases mentioned here, premarital sex relationships are furthered by failure of the individual to establish satisfying relationships with other people.

Divorced persons are generally regarded as deviant, and frequently with good reason. Certainly not all divorces, however, involve maladjusted persons. Differences in social background or temperament of the spouses may be so extreme as to thwart adjustment and indicate divorce, even though each of the spouses might be quite successfully married to some other person. Such divorced persons cannot realistically be considered to be personality deviants. The really deviant divorcees are those who would probably not make good marriage partners no matter whom they married. They are the persons whose needs—for security, affection, approval, to dominate, or be dominated—are too great a burden for almost any marriage partner to bear. After failing with one partner, they often seek out a second and a third and destroy each of these relationships by their insatiable demands. In a minority of cases the neurotic need appears to be for the notoriety of marrying and divorcing itself. Such people go through a series of marriages, attracting a great deal of attention to themselves on the way.

To some extent divorce itself *creates* deviancy. Even though it may be anticipated for months or years, the experience of divorce is frequently traumatic. Habit patterns and personal relationships of long duration are suddenly uprooted. The person must finally face up to having failed in marriage and having been rejected by the marriage partner. Extreme bitterness and despair often follow. To assuage the hurt and to cope with the frustrations of suddenly being unmarried again, the individual often enters a more or less promiscuous series of sex relationships. Gradually as he reorients himself, these symptoms of deviancy are replaced by a more conventional pattern. Some persons, of course, never completely recover from the divorce experience, and divorce may be expected to remain at least temporarily disorganizing in the foreseeable future.

Personal deviation shows up in a variety of family symptoms other than divorce. All of the problems discussed under the heading "Inadequate Families" dealt with the effects of emotionally impaired personalities upon marital and parent-child relationships. The theme of the discussion was that absence of normal affection and emotional security in childhood leads to hostility, selfishness, and feelings of inferiority in adulthood that are then passed on to succeeding generations. The deviant behavior perpetuates itself until, somehow, someone is able to break the chain.

At least two kinds of deviancy have been found associated with multiproblem families. First, the absence in these families of all skills normally associated with earning a living stands out. Not only are there no manual skills but there may not even be the ability to read and write. Actual mental deficiency is suggested in some cases and extremely inadequate social backgrounds have been found in others. The second kind of deviancy appears related to relatively recent migration. Many multiproblem families in urban areas are found to be recent migrants from depressed rural areas and from the isolated hill regions of the Appalachian and Ozark mountains. These people may have no salable skills and, even more significantly, they may not wish to develop any. Uprooting this kind of deviancy presents a formidable challenge to modern society.

PROPOSALS FOR IMPROVING FAMILY LIFE

"Good Old Days" Proposals

Unsophisticated people often argue that the way to solve family problems is to encourage men to become men again and to encourage women to be glad of it! Men, after all, are bigger and stronger so that they can care for women, who presumably will attain real contentment only when they are free to indulge their emotional whims under the protective care of some practical man. From the Scriptures onward there are many admonitions for the "husband to be the head of the wife," and, supposedly, what worked two thousand years ago ought to work today. Men restored to their rightful places as undisputed, but kindly, masters of the household and women who concentrate on bearing and rearing broods of healthy children will not have the needs or conflicts that lead to quarreling, separation, desertion, or divorce. Family problems virtually will disappear if only we return to the family patterns of the good old days.

Two things that are wrong with this proposal are that the good old days never were so ideal, [32] and we stand just about as much chance of recreating the family of several decades ago as we stand of reversing the forward march of time itself. There is a widespread belief—but not one shred of evidence—that families were happier in the days of the horse and buggy. Buggy rides in the moonlight seem romantic, but a very conservative computation of the moonlight-buggy-riding time for at least moderately amorous persons might amount to about three-tenths of one per cent of their lifetimes. Moreover, as the owner of any modern convertible can attest, much of that time must have been spent fleeing rain and cold, to say nothing of slogging through muddy, rutted country roads. Nor does this romanticized picture take into account that personal

---

[32] William Goode emphasizes the fictional character of our conceptions of the nineteenth-century family by referring to it as "the classical family of Western nostalgia." See his *After Divorce*, pp. 3-4.

preferences were long considered largely irrelevant to the selection of a marriage partner; that if the husband turned out to be a brute, a drunk, or incompetent, or if the wife turned out to be lazy, a shrew, or a recluse, they were nevertheless stuck with one another for the rest of their lives. "The rest of their lives" may not have been too long, however, for many more men than today died in their prime due to accidents and infectious diseases, and several times as many women died in childbirth as do now.

The quality of family life cannot easily be measured even today, [33] and virtually nothing is accurately known about the family life of earlier decades. Expert opinion, however, agrees widely to the effect that a large part of contemporary family problems derive not from the fact that to-day's family life is inferior to that of earlier periods but to precisely the opposite—that we are no longer willing to settle for standards of family compatibility and happiness that would have satisfied our forefathers. [34] Thus, the problem is not that family life has worsened but that we expect it to be much better. Consequently, when we are interested in bettering family life it makes no sense at all to yearn for a return to a time when standards of successful family life were lower than they are at present.

If seeking a return of the good old days is not a sensible proposal for improving family life, however, there are other proposals which appear to have some merit.

Family Life Education

Modern American society is unique in that nearly a whole generation is now seeking formal education for marriage. All societies prepare their young for marriage but most do it indirectly and by example. Ours is the first to separate preparation for family living from the family itself and to do it by formal instruction in the classroom. Family life education in the United States has several roots but had its direct beginnings in the early 1920's when colleges began to offer courses in preparation for marriage. At first these were offered as noncredit courses but students proved so enthusiastic about them that soon they were introduced into the regular curriculum. By the late 1940's some six hundred family courses were being

[33] Scales that measure the degree of satisfaction with which persons regard their marriages, and scales that predict the amount of satisfaction to be expected from contemplated marriages do exist. Unfortunately, these scales cannot be applied retroactively to the marriages of earlier generations. For a summary of marriage prediction and marriage adjustment studies and for the most sophisticated and recent prediction effort, see Ernest W. Burgess and Paul Wallin, *Engagement and Marriage* (New York, J. B. Lippincott Co., 1953).

[34] Many modern textbooks on the family either directly or indirectly reflect this point of view. Among others, see Ray E. Baber, *op. cit.*; Ernest W. Burgess and Harvey J. Locke, *The Family: From Institution to Companionship* (New York, American Book Company, 1953); Ruth S. Cavan, *The American Family* (New York, Thomas Y. Crowell Company, 1953); and Joseph K. Folsom, *The Family and Democratic Society* (New York, John Wiley & Sons, Inc., 1943).

offered over the country, and by the middle 1950's the number probably exceeded twelve hundred. [35] Gradually, instruction has been filtering down to the high schools and some school systems are now developing integrated programs that make preparation for family living a continuing part of the program from the first to the twelfth grade. Other community groups—particularly religious groups—have taken up the challenge and YMCA's, YMHA's, and the Cana Conferences of the Roman Catholic Church all seek to strengthen family life by placing preparation for marriage within a religious framework.

The goals of family life education are obvious—to develop the skills, attitudes, and values that promote harmonious family relationships. But one reasonably may ask, "How effective is such education?" Can half a dozen lectures, or a semester's classroom work, or even a curriculum-wide program be effective in counteracting all of the social forces that work against successful family life? And what can reasonably be taken as the criteria of success? If some students who have taken and passed family life courses later seek divorce, does this mean that they did not learn how to make happy marriages or does it mean that they learned not to settle for unhappy marriages? Or if they remain permanently married, does this mean that the relationships within their families are emotionally healthy ones? Professional family life educators are aware that the task of discovering just how valuable family life education is in the lives of its consumers is a formidable one.[36] What evidence is available, however, overwhelmingly supports its value. [37] The consumers themselves, whether they are asked immediately after having taken family life courses, or years after having taken them, are virtually unanimous in agreeing that the courses are valuable and that more students should take them. [38]

The trend in American society may well be toward making some formal preparation for family living universal and a prerequisite for marriage. As it stands now, we require more evidence of competence before we permit an individual to drive an automobile than we do before we permit him to marry and rear children. Some professional persons—often judges, ministers, and physicians rather than professional family life edu-

---

[35] Extrapolated from figures provided in Judson T. Landis, "The Teaching of Marriage and Family Courses in Colleges," *Marriage and Family Living*, Vol. 21 (February, 1959), pp. 36-40.

[36] See John F. Cuber, "Can We Evaluate Marriage Education?" *Marriage and Family Living*, Vol. 11 (Summer, 1949), pp. 93-95.

[37] Donald S. Longworth, "Critique of Attempts to Evaluate Marriage Teaching," *Marriage and Family Living*, Vol. 15 (November, 1953), pp. 308-312.

[38] The possibility should not be overlooked that the students who take family life courses, and who evaluate them favorably, may be the ones who need them least. The courses are often elective courses and they may tend to be selected by people whose basic values encourage harmonious family living and who would be well prepared for marriage even without having taken marriage preparation courses. Similarly, students whose attitudes and values are opposed to successful family living may also tend to shy away from courses on the family.

cators—have begun to suggest that young persons should be required to attend classes in preparation for marriage before they become eligible to apply for marriage licenses. Whether such proposals will receive widespread public support in the near future is doubtful, but American society does seem to accept the principle of formal preparation for family living as desirable public policy.

Family Counseling

Just as family life education is designed to forestall family problems by preparing people to avoid problems, professional family counseling is designed to aid them to resolve problems that do develop. Scientific family counseling has developed wholly within the present century and has major roots in family life education and social science, in social case work, and in medicine and psychotherapy. [39] Social science counselors probably operate mainly in university communities, doing some counseling in connection with their teaching and in special marriage counseling clinics operated by some of the larger universities. They tend to work with marital problems more than parent-child problems and they serve mainly the university staff, employees, and students. Family counseling received marked emphasis from social agencies as they shifted away from providing "charity" and toward "casework" early in the century. By tradition, social agencies have catered to lower income and education groups but many agencies are now seeking to extend their clientele to include middle income groups. Though agency practice has tended to focus on the mother-child relationship it is coming increasingly to involve all family members. Psychotherapy and psychiatry have for the most part provided family counseling services for middle, and upper, income groups.

One of the greatest problems in relation to family counseling is the tremendous need in proportion to the services available. Legitimate counseling agencies seldom advertise their services but most of them have waiting lists and often a wait of several months is necessary before counseling can be secured. Since most people do not seek counseling until their problems become acute, the long wait often may be disastrous. Yet for every family that does not get service in time there must be dozens more who get no service at all, either because they do not know of the possibility of it or because they are afraid or ashamed to seek help.

[39] In its broadest sense, family counseling may be as old as man himself. Sympathetic persons who would listen to the problems of others without immediately condemning or giving advice have been known for thousands of years and today would include persons from such varied occupations as bartender and pharmacist to fortuneteller. This "professional listening" was early institutionalized into the roles of minister and physician and much "counseling" is done by these groups today. The discussion in this section, however, focuses upon recently developed family counseling with a basically scientific *modus operandi*, as contrasted with theological or common-sense *modus operandi*.

The success or failure of family counseling is as hard to evaluate as that of family life education. Is the problem "cured" when a family decides to stay together or is the cure sometimes divorce? How do we know whether the situation would have turned out differently had the family not sought counseling at all, and how do we know that they will not soon be in trouble again? Simple and final answers to these questions are not possible and perhaps the questions themselves are not fair. Physicians, for example, do not question the efficacy of medical practice simply because they cannot always restore patients to full health or because a patient cured of tuberculosis later develops heart disease.

Most specialists believe that family counseling does considerable good and that counseling services should be greatly expanded so that far more people can be helped. Most of them also agree that, in the long run, counseling must place far more emphasis on prevention of problems and less upon alleviating problems that already exist. Emphasis upon prevention, of course, will tend to merge family counseling with family life education, a development that both counselors and educators consider highly desirable.

PROPOSALS FOR LEGAL REFORM

The tangle of legal hazards facing married couples today might well discourage marriage altogether were the forces of love not so imperious! Some of the common practices of at least 90 per cent of all married persons are illegal, and a majority of couples face possible criminal prosecution for behavior that they regard as right and proper, but concerning which the law takes a different view. [40]

Family Planning

American families are small. The modal number of children per family is two. There is no reason to believe, however, that couples are less capable of reproduction than they have ever been. Today people plan their families, or at least try to. Certainly families are successfully limiting the number of children they have. Such limitation has been made possible by modern techniques of contraception. Perhaps nowhere is contraception more widely condemned or more widely practiced than in the United States.

Between 80 and 90 per cent of American women believe that birth control knowledge should be made available to them. Devices for the prevention of conception are sold in an estimated 300,000 retail outlets. [41] The Planned Parenthood Federation of America has over seven hundred

[40] Harriet F. Pilpel and Theodora Zavin, *op. cit.*, p. 213.
[41] *Fortune Magazine*, Vol. 17 (February, 1938), p. 85.

centers scattered throughout the United States. The American Medical Association promotes medical school instruction on various factors affecting fertility; the American Federation of Women's Clubs, the Federal Council of Churches, and countless other groups have endorsed the principle of family planning. Yet powerful groups forbid contraceptive practice and many aspects of it are illegal.

In 1873, a man named Anthony Comstock was influential in getting Congress to pass a law prohibiting the transportation or sale of obscene literature and, though it apparently was not the intent of Congress to do so, articles for the prevention of conception were included in the ban. Later about half the states passed similar laws which came to be known as "Little Comstock laws." Massachusetts and Connecticut both have par-

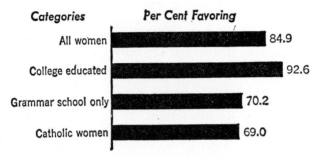

SOURCE: Redrawn by special permission of the editors from the August, 1943, issue of *Fortune*, pp. 24, 30.

FIG. 7–3. American women believe that birth control knowledge should be available to married couples.

ticularly stringent anticontraceptive legislation. The Massachusetts law forbids a physician to provide contraceptive information even though a pregnancy would mean the certain death of his patient. The Connecticut law that forbids only the "use" of contraception is enforced chiefly by prosecuting doctors and nurses as "accessories to the crime." Despite wholesale violation all but one of the original laws still remain on the statute books. Attempts on the part of legislators to repeal these laws have amounted to political suicide. Most of the "teeth" of the federal law have been removed by Supreme Court decisions rendering physicians and druggists relatively safe from prosecution. Ironically, several of the states which have Little Comstock laws have since established state-supported planned parenthood clinics, often providing free of charge information and devices the sale of which is illegal.

The practical effect of existing legislation has been to make contraceptive information available to upper income groups who can afford the services of private physicians but to deny it to the lower income groups who may feel the greatest need. It also increases the use of the least reliable devices which generally do not require medical prescription and decreases the use of the more reliable methods that do require such prescription. Despite the discrepancies between law and practice, it seems unlikely that any of the laws will be repealed. Any future changes are likely to come about through court decisions which modify application of the laws while permitting them to remain unchanged on the law books.

Migratory Marriage and Divorce

The fact that some states have more lenient laws than others encourages people to migrate temporarily to secure the advantages of marrying and divorcing under the easier laws. Some states require that there be a waiting period between the time of application for a marriage license and the marriage itself. That this requirement serves to discourage hasty, ill-considered marriages is demonstrated by the experience of California where in the first full year following the institution of a three-day waiting period there were ten thousand fewer marriages. [42] The states also vary in requirements, such as certification of freedom from venereal disease and the minimum age at which people may legally marry.

Desire to escape the stricter requirements of some states has led to the development of many "Gretna Greens" or marriage-market towns, especially along state borders. In these towns, license bureaus may remain open twenty-four hours a day to catch the "night trade," and the securing of a blood test, marriage license, and the marriage ceremony itself can all be completed in a few hours. Mercenary ministers and justices of the peace co-operate by providing quick ceremonies with none of the frills attached.

In relation to migratory divorce, an even more obvious situation exists. The length of residence required before a divorce can be secured varies from six weeks in Nevada and Idaho to five years in Massachusetts for persons who were not married in that state. New York accepts one legal ground for divorce, while other states recognize a dozen or more grounds. Actually only about 6 per cent of United States divorces are migratory, [43] but this amounts to approximately 24,000 migratory divorces each year. According to precedent, such divorces are valid even though they obviously violate the intent of the laws of the states in which the persons actually live.

Recently in cases where residence was obviously established for divorce purposes the courts have shown some tendency to declare the divorces invalid. Where such divorces stand now seems to depend on whether anyone decides to contest them. Many persons remarry after securing migratory divorces. At present such persons cannot be sure if they are legally single, or married, or, perhaps, bigamists. Such confusion

[42] Ray E. Baber, *op. cit.*, p. 62.
[43] *Ibid.*, p. 473.

will exist until the courts take a firm stand one way or the other. Many jurists and social scientists believe that the only way to resolve the problem is for the courts to take a unified stand and, at the same time, to grant amnesty to all persons whose present statuses would be jeopardized by the decision.

Divorce Laws

All states in the United States now grant divorces. The number of *legal grounds* upon which divorce may be secured ranges from one to more than a dozen. The legal grounds for divorce are generally not, however, the actual *reasons* or *causes* for divorce. The grounds for divorce are the reasons the courts will accept, so whatever the actual reasons, people pretend to seek divorce for "adultery," or "desertion," or some other reason recognized by the law. Actually, most people seek divorce because they are no longer willing or able to live together. Generally they are agreed, if reluctantly, that the divorce should take place. Yet if it should come to the official attention of the court that both partners want a divorce they cannot legally get one.

American law is such that in any litigation there must be two parties, the plaintiff (or accuser) and the defendant (or accused). One of the parties must have committed some act contrary to the law; there must be a guilty party. Though a legal violation may not have occurred, the fiction must be maintained that it has. Consequently, one spouse must agree to be charged with some offense that is legal ground for divorce in the state in question. For the spouses to make any such agreement is known technically as *collusion* and evidence of it requires the judge to throw the case out of court. In sum, the law which requires that there be a guilty party and that there be no agreement between husband and wife concerning the divorce means that if the law were adhered to, very few divorces would be granted. In actual practice the law is winked at, and judges, lawyers, and clients conspire to prevent the law from interfering with the divorce procedure. It is estimated that collusion is involved in at least 75 per cent of American divorces.[44]

There are at least two other interesting legal fictions in current divorce practice. The first of these is the noncontestant petition whereby collusion is made less obvious. By not appearing in court to defend himself, the accused spouse is held to be guilty by default. His absence is supposedly an admission of guilt. This is a popular technique because it does not require any lengthy airing of the charges in court. The second legal fiction is the counter-petition wherein the spouse who is the defendant in a divorce case files another suit and himself brings suit for divorce. The

---

[44] See the figures cited in Pilpel and Zavin, *op. cit.*, p. 299.

court then maintains the fiction that these are separate cases and grants the divorce to the partner with the better case.

There is some awareness of this ridiculous situation and isolated efforts are being made to deal with it. Two states, New Mexico and Alaska, now grant divorce for "incompatibility," which is a rather radical departure from traditional American practice. It is the first recognition that two normal, essentially law-abiding people might have reason for divorce. As yet, no state grants divorce for "mutual consent" (as do Sweden and Norway) which would simply legalize current practice. Although accepting nonjudgmental grounds for divorce would not eliminate the problem, it would reduce the inconsistency between legal practice and current values.

PROPOSALS FOR INSTITUTIONAL CHANGES

Several writers have pointed out that there may be a basic incompatibility between the traditional forms of stable family life and the demands of the urban, technologically oriented society in which we live. [45] These writers tend to conclude, by implication at least, that fundamental changes in the family are in process and are, indeed, inevitable. Much of what has been covered in preceding sections of this chapter deals with these changes. There are, however, several other kinds of minor institutional changes which often are suggested to reduce the incompatibility between family and economy as they are presently constituted. These include proposals for more widespread use of day nurseries, development of more adequate part-time employment for women, extension of cooperative child care arrangements, and occasional pleas for the use of some system of family allowances.

The day nursery movement reflects the fact that most of the working wives in the United States apparently work because of economic necessity more than because of inner conflict which they may have over women's roles. Income figures show that the proportion of married women who work outside the home varies inversely with the husband's income— the lower the income the greater the possibility that the wife will also be a breadwinner. Historically, lower income families also have had more children than higher income families. This means that the wives who most need to work also are the most burdened with child care. The day nursery is an arrangement designed to provide a place where working mothers can leave their preschool children under expert paid supervision while they go off to work. The children are supervised in play, in educational activities, and also are fed nutritious meals. The cost is kept low, often

[45] Talcott Parsons, "The Social Structure of the Family," in Ruth Nanda Anshen, ed., *The Family: Its Function and Destiny* (New York, Harper and Brothers, 1959), pp. 211-274.

by municipal subsidy, so that lower income families can afford it. The most comprehensive system of day nurseries in the United States probably is to be found in New York City. The day nursery, of course, is an urban phenomenon but it is one that might be more widely dispersed over the country than it is at present.

Proposals to encourage more part-time employment of women are also designed to permit women to combine motherhood with helping to earn the family's living. Since school takes up at least six or seven hours of the child's time during the day, many women would like to find employment during those hours and to be home again when their children return from school. Factory hours and those in retail sales and clerical work, however, seldom coincide with school hours, forcing women either to remain unemployed or to leave their children unattended for varying periods of time. Traditionally, there have been a few occupations for women, such as schoolteaching and nursing, that can be combined satisfactorily with raising children. Not all women can be schoolteachers or nurses, however. In fact, these are essentially middle-class occupations requiring extensive educational preparation. What is needed is a wide variety of part-time jobs that do not require elaborate professional training. Perhaps, before this can become a reality, society will have to be willing to pay a much higher economic price for supporting family stability than it has been willing to pay thus far. Either that, or occupations must be found that women can perform more efficiently than men, and these must be in industries that can operate profitably upon part-time or split-shift bases.

The parent-co-operative nursery school appears to be more of a middle-class than a lower-class phenomenon. Parents of children of nursery school age band together to form their own nursery school-child care arrangement, with or without professional help. Professional nursery school educators feel strongly that at least one full-time professional person should direct such nursery schools. [46] The parents then take turns in assisting at the school. In return for caring for all of the children a fraction of the time, they are freed from caring for their own children most of the time. Formal co-operative nursery school goals are stated positively in terms of providing desirable social and educational experiences for the children but an important motivation of many parents seems to be to free the mother from at least some of the onerous burden of caring for small children. The mothers are freed, briefly, to indulge themselves in professional training and pursuits of the sorts that appeal also to their husbands. Or they may simply escape for a while the delightful, but tiring and intellectually stultifying, world of children. Co-op nursery schools

[46] Katharine Whiteside Taylor, *Parent Cooperative Nursery Schools* (New York, Teachers College, Columbia University, 1954), pp. 2, 25-30.

have had a tremendous rate of growth over the past fifteen years but they show few signs of being other than a middle-class institution.

There is not much clamor now for direct financial relief to child-bearing families but occasional proposals still are heard. Some European countries long have used family allowances that were paid to families directly for the birth of children or in the form of additions to the husband's salary. [47] Other arrangements include priorities on housing, lower rents, or lower taxes for families with children. [48] The United States provides a slight tax advantage in the form of the $600 deduction for each dependent child and also grants a slight advantage to certain women heads of household. The United States, however, has never embarked on a comprehensive policy of encouraging family life by making special financial provision for it. It is questionable whether programs in other countries have been very effective in attaining the goals set out for them. The subsidies, however provided, have never been adequate to cover the expenses of rearing an additional child and basic social conditions and family values do not appear to have been importantly influenced by them.

SUMMARY

There are both problem families and family problems in the United States. Families that are broken by divorce, desertion, and separation are widely recognized as problems, but families may also be broken emotionally, whether or not they are broken physically. Some emotionally broken families exist in continuous conflict and some that show outward harmony include emotionally inadequate people who frustrate the needs of other family members for affection and security. Increasingly, it is being recognized that there is a relatively small but hard-core group of multiproblem families who absorb the lion's share of all public welfare funds and who present formidable barriers to rehabilitation.

Considerable dissatisfaction with marriage and family life stems from far-reaching changes in the accepted roles for various family members. Women's roles have changed most drastically. A woman may now work, and/or marry, and/or bear children, and/or choose any one of several other roles. Whatever the role she selects, it is likely to cause adjustment problems both for her and her husband. Adolescents and young adults are questioning openly the validity of a moral code which has, in the past, been observed in the breach as well as in actual practice. Mothers and fathers today live long past the usual childbearing period, often without sufficient interests and opportunities to round out their lives.

[47] See the discussions in Joseph K. Folsom, *The Family and Democratic Society* (New York, John Wiley & Sons, Inc., 1943), pp. 193-208, 606-607; and Clifford Kirkpatrick, *The Family: As Process and Institution* (New York, The Ronald Press Company, 1955), p. 573.
[48] *Ibid.*

Changes resulting from the Industrial Revolution and the shift to urban living underlie modern family problems. A new equalitarian, happiness-centered family is emerging. Powerful groups oppose the transition. Particularly, they oppose the assumption that marriages should be dissolved if happiness and personal satisfaction are not forthcoming. Very few persons can accept, completely, present family instability as being an integral part of modern family life. Conflict also exists over the extent of public responsibility for problem families and over the best way to rehabilitate them. Personality problems both create and are created by the new patterns. Immature and neurotic people swell the ranks of those involved in family conflict and divorce, and conflict and frustration bring deviancy into being. Deviant families often are recent newcomers to the social environments where they are defined as deviant.

Various proposals have been advanced for solving family problems. In addition to unrealistic yearning for a return to the large, stable, patriarchal family of yesteryear, much has been and can be accomplished through more widespread education for family life and through marriage and family counseling for those with problems. Extensive legal reform is called for. Some form of birth control practice is practically universal and, more often than not, illegal. Though each state establishes its own marriage and divorce laws, evasion is generally an easy matter. One has only to cross a state border to change jurisdiction. Divorce is widespread, but the nature of our divorce laws forces most applicants to become liars and perjurers as well as serving to embitter further the already embattled spouses. Current proposals are to clarify the status of migratory divorce and to institute divorce for "mutual consent." Finally, the more widespread use of day nurseries and the development of more part-time jobs for women would aid many lower income families to be more fully self-reliant.

SUGGESTED READINGS

BUELL, Bradley, and associates, *Community Planning for Human Services* (New York, Columbia University Press, 1952). Presents results of the St. Paul, Minnesota, survey of multiproblem families and concludes that existing social services often are not equipped to rehabilitate these families.

CUBER, John F., *Marriage Counseling Practice* (New York, Appleton-Century-Crofts, Inc., 1948). The first systematic treatise on the new field of marriage counseling. Treats both the theory of marriage counseling and the professional status and problems of the field.

GLICK, Paul C., *American Families* (New York, John Wiley & Sons, Inc., 1957). Provides nationwide data on marriage, family composition, and other significant aspects of family life in America. Traces historical trends and anticipates future population changes. Based primarily upon the 1950 Census and upon annual sample surveys of families.

GOODE, William J., *After Divorce* (Glencoe, Ill., The Free Press, 1956). Report of a major field study of divorced women in metropolitan Detroit. Deals with the social backgrounds of divorced persons, the divorce process, and post-divorce adjustment.

KINSEY, Alfred M., POMEROY, Wardell B., and MARTIN, Clyde E., *Sexual Behavior in the Human Male* (Philadelphia, W. B. Saunders Co., 1948). The most exhaustive study of the sexual behavior of American males. The data are analyzed in terms of relevant social variables.

KINSEY, Alfred M., and associates, *Sexual Behavior in the Human Female* (Philadelphia, W. B. Saunders Co., 1953). Companion volume to the earlier volume on sexual behavior among American males. Weighted toward the better educated segments of the population.

MEAD, Margaret, *Male and Female* (New York, William Morrow & Co., 1952). Synthesis of twenty-five years of study by an anthropologist of problems of masculine and feminine roles in various cultures including modern American society.

PILPEL, Harriet F., and ZAVIN, Theodora, *Your Marriage and the Law* (New York, Rinehart & Company, Inc., 1952). An excellent nontechnical treatment of the legal problems surrounding marriage in the United States. Interprets the law and points the way toward a more rational legal philosophy.

NOVELS

ABAUNZA, Virginia, *Sundays From Two to Six* (Indianapolis, The Bobbs-Merrill Company, Inc., 1957). This is a novel which treats perceptively and movingly a 16-year-old girl's reactions to the discovery that her supposedly happily married parents are about to seek a divorce.

MAUROIS, André, *The Art of Being Happily Married*, trans. from the French by Crystal Herbert (New York, Harper and Brothers, 1957). A series of scenes, in dialogue form, between a couple who are followed from courtship to their silver anniversary. Thoughtful, witty, realistic.

AUDIO-VISUAL AIDS

1. *Date of Birth* (Seminar Films, Inc., 347 Madison Ave., New York), 16 minutes, sound, color. Produced by the National Film Board of Canada for the Department of Labour of the Government of Canada. Presents the actual record of employees in the over-forty-five age group, indicating that there is less absenteeism, a lower turnover rate, and an equal standard of production among older workers.

2. *Jealousy* (McGraw-Hill Book Company, Text-Film Department, 330 West 42 St., New York), 16 minutes, sound, black and white. A young wife learns that her jealous misunderstanding of her husband is really an expression of her dissatisfaction with her role as homemaker, and her tendency to distort events in her own imagination.

3. *Life With Grandpa* (McGraw-Hill Book Company, Text-Film Department, 330 West 42 St., New York), 17 minutes, sound, black and white. Produced by March of Time. Discusses the problems of old age including degenerative diseases and economic insecurity. Various remedies are suggested to

these and other problems including the feelings of loneliness and uselessness that so often come with old age.

4. *Marriage and Divorce* (McGraw-Hill Book Company, Text-Film Department, 330 West 42 St., New York), 15 minutes, sound, black and white. Produced by March of Time. Surveys the problems of broken homes and the increasing divorce rate by examining the effects of mechanization on present-day family relations. The opinions of several experts as to what should be done are included.

5. *A Planned Parenthood Story* (Mayo-Video, 113 West 57 St., New York), 18 minutes, sound, black and white. Produced for the Planned Parenthood Federation of America, Inc. Deals with a young couple who lost two babies in rapid succession because the wife had not regained her strength after the birth of their third living child. They learn of the service of "Planned Parenthood" and are able to space the arrival of their next baby. During the clinic scenes, the action shows how other services of "Planned Parenthood" are carried on.

6. *Social-Sex Attitudes in Adolescence* (McGraw-Hill Book Company, Text-Film Department, 330 West 42 St., New York), 22 minutes, sound, black and white. Shows how teen-agers meet, and are helped to meet, the problems in becoming aware of and adjusted to the opposite sex. Takes a boy and girl through their entire adolescent experiences, culminating with their marriage.

QUESTIONS AND PROJECTS

1. Define the terms: *divorce, desertion,* and *legal separation.* Why is the divorce rate, alone, an inadequate measure of the rate of family breakdown?

2. Not all problem families are broken families. What are "inadequate families," and "multiproblem families"? What social costs are connected with such families?

3. Indicate how changed roles for young adults, for husbands and wives, and for older persons have contributed to disorganization in the American family.

4. How are changes deriving from the Industrial Revolution basic to most of today's family problems?

5. Debate, with some other student in the class, the desirability of "permanence" values in marriage as opposed to "adjustment" values.

6. Evaluate the statement that, "there are many otherwise normal people among the ranks of the divorced."

7. How does variation in marriage and divorce law among the separate states encourage violation of the laws? What dangers are inherent in these procedures for the persons involved?

8. Relate the hackneyed expression, "The younger generation is going to the dogs," to the fact that we have not one but several moral standards in modern society.

9. Which of the several proposals for improving family life appears to you to have the most merit? Why? Can you see any difficulties in the way of implementing this proposal?

10. Investigate your community to see what resources it provides for the

welfare of older persons. Evaluate the programs of church groups, fraternal societies, and community agencies. How much are these agencies doing to provide meaningful goals and interpersonal relationships. What is the prevailing attitude within the community's families upon the place of grandparents within them? What can be done to provide more satisfactory arrangements for both the older and younger generations?

11. Interview the judge in your county who is responsible for administration of the divorce laws. What does he think are their major strengths and weaknesses? What changes does he recommend in existing laws? Do you agree with him on what changes are needed? Why?

8

Religious Problems and Conflicts

╈╈

AT NO TIME IN AMERICAN HISTORY has the institutional status of the church in America been more secure than it appears to be today. When we became a nation, only one American in fifteen was a church member. [1] Today, three out of five are members, and church membership during the past quarter-century has been growing twice as fast as the general population. [2] Church contributions are at an all-time high and have been rising faster than the cost of living in recent years. [3] Organized opposition to religion is weaker than it has been in generations. Not a single widely known professional atheist or agnostic carries the mantle of the Robert Ingersolls and Tom Paines of earlier generations, and popular interest in atheism appears to have faded. The leadership of the American labor movement, once sharply anticlerical, is now composed of leaders who are either devoutly religious or discreetly silent. No American president today dares, like Lincoln, to remain unaffiliated with any church, and one president within recent decades was hastily baptized and enrolled after his nomination.

Despite such evidence of institutional stability, however, religion remains an area of conflict and discontent. Religious bodies expend much of their energy in rivalries with one another, while a host of unheeded Jeremiahs call for repentance. After a long period of comparative religious toleration, it seems possible that America is drifting into a period of intensified religious strife. What is the nature of these conflict areas? Why have they developed?

[1] William W. Sweet, "The Protestant Churches," *The Annals*, Vol. 256 (March, 1948), p. 50.
[2] National Council of Churches, *Yearbook of American Churches*, 1959, (New York, National Council of Churches, 1958), p. 294.
[3] *Ibid.*, pp. 289-291.

RELIGIOUS PROBLEMS IN AMERICAN LIFE

Alleged Lack of Religious Faith

Despite the record level of church membership, there is a continuous chorus of lament over the "lack of faith," the "godlessness," and the "falling away from the faith" of the American people. Church membership alone is not a satisfactory measure of functional religious faith, and something beyond mere membership is insistently demanded. Statements that "the world crisis is basically a *moral* crisis," that "the only hope for our nation is in a rebirth of religious faith," and that "the only way to solve national and world problems is to seek God's way" pour from the pulpit and the lecture platform. All such views hold that some sort of religious inadequacy is basic to (or even the sole cause of) our national and international problems. It follows that no solution is possible unless it involves these religious elements. In its more naïvely uncritical form, this viewpoint proposes personal religion as a substitute for political or sociological approaches. In its more sophisticated form, this viewpoint insists that economic and political reforms must spring from religious motivations and be guided by profound religious convictions if they are to be fully effective.

Such anxieties about our faith are nothing new. Every period in recent history has heard denunciations of godlessness and exhortations to repentance. At one time in the early nineteenth century it was seriously charged that only three students at Yale University professed to believe in God. Although it is impossible to determine just how godly our ancestors were, it is clear that certain of them were deeply disturbed about the godlessness of the rest of them.

It is difficult to determine whether religious faith and devotion are actually declining. There is some scientific evidence that people no longer accept certain traditional religious beliefs (belief in a personal God, Heaven as a physical place of reward, Hell as a physical place of torment, and so on) as widely as formerly. [4] But is this a *lack* of faith or a *change* in faith? There is some disagreement on this question.

If it is uncertain whether religious faith is declining, why is the alleged lack of religious faith a social problem? Simply because a number of people *view it* as one. When a considerable number of people think a condition poses a problem, express concern over it, and discuss ways of meeting it, then it *is* a social problem. In this instance, it may be a problem to only a minority of people, but to them it may be the most serious of all problems—may even be the only problem they recognize.

[4] James H. Leuba, "Modern Man and Religious Faith," *Survey Graphic,* Vol. 28 (April, 1939), pp. 277-279.

The problem of "irreligion," however, is unique in at least one respect. Among most of those who consider it a problem, there is little uncertainty about the solution. But there are *disagreements* about the solution. Some groups call for a great "revival" similar to those of the past; some urge the socializing and modernizing of the program of the churches, with emphasis upon group activities and attention to current social issues;

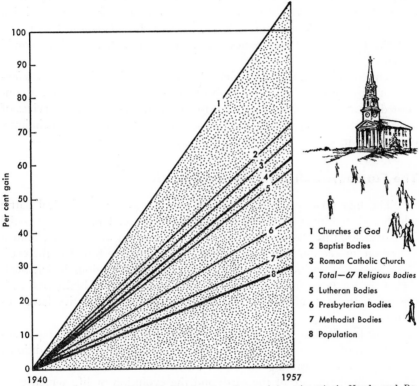

SOURCE: Adapted from J. Frederic Dewhurst and associates, *America's Needs and Resources: A New Survey* (New York, Twentieth Century Fund, 1955), p. 422. 1957 data from *Yearbook of American Churches*, 1959, pp. 268-273.

FIG. 8-1. Percentage increase in membership of major religious bodies and in population, 1940-1957.

some feel that their present church program is entirely adequate and needs only to be promoted with greater zeal and enthusiasm. The holders of each view seem to be thoroughly convinced that their approach is correct. Among many religious groups there is a relative lack of interest and an almost complete lack of research into alternative methods of evangelism. For each group the solution lies in continuing to do what it is already doing, and no "search for the answer" is necessary.

The problem of irreligion may never be solved, since the problem is inherent in the nature of Christianity. The Christian religion is a universal religion, demanding that its members not rest until every soul has been won, but also teaching that one's acceptance of Christianity must be an act of personal faith, voluntarily and willingly taken according to one's own heart and conscience. It is inevitable that some will remain unbelievers and that there will always be the "godless" to save. It is also inevitable that, as believers follow their private consciences, a number of religious sects will arise, some of which view the others as corrupters of the faith. Even if *all* persons were devout followers of some Christian church, there would be many who considered the others still "unsaved," and the problem of "godlessness" and "lack of a saving faith" would remain.

This problem, however, is one with which social scientists, *as scientists*, are not deeply concerned. Most of the groups who are the most concerned with this problem have neither sought nor accepted the services of social scientists in analyzing the problem or evaluating their techniques of meeting it.

The Fundamentalism-Modernism Battle

The first quarter of the twentieth century saw a theological battle which still continues as a sort of guerrilla warfare. Unlike many social controversies, this was not deeply rooted in changing technology, human migration, or economic interest clashes; its causes were found in the clash of increasing scientific knowledge with intrenched religious belief. Such a clash is not new, for intellectual history since Galileo is littered with the remnants of cherished beliefs which scientific discoveries have demolished.

The last half of the nineteenth century, however, saw a rapid accumulation of scientific fact and theory which impinged upon traditional theology with devastating effect. From natural science came facts and theories about the age of the earth and the evolution of life which conflicted sharply with the biblical account of creation as it was generally interpreted at that time. From psychology and the infant field of sociology came insights into human motivation and behavior that cast doubt upon the traditional religious interpretation of "good" and "bad" behavior as results of an individual's voluntary "free-will" choices between good and evil. From anthropology there came some fairly complete and sympathetic pictures of primitive life which caused some people to wonder whether it was entirely civilized to consign all the unsaved heathen to eternal damnation. A developing school of "higher criticism" arose which began to study the cultural background of the biblical writings, with a suspicion that bits of mythology and tribal folklore may have crept into the Bible.

Many church leaders were appalled at these heresies and rallied to defend the faith. The battle lines were drawn between those who wished to accommodate their biblical interpretations and church doctrines to the discoveries of science, and those who denounced as "false science" all claims and theories which conflicted with traditional religious doctrines. These rival camps came to be known as "modernists" and "fundamentalists." The *fundamentalists* generally agreed: that all parts of the Bible are divinely inspired and unalterably true; that man was created by God in his present form without intermediate stages; that Christ was born of a virgin and was a Divine Being who died on the cross to atone for our sins; that only those who accept and profess these (and other) beliefs can enter Heaven, a physical place of eternal reward, whereas all others must go to Hell, a physical place of eternal torment. With only minor changes, these views are retained by fundamentalist groups today. The *modernists* (or "liberals" as they often prefer to term themselves) generally believed that the Bible contained the word of God along with bits of literature and folklore, and that not all parts of the Bible were true in a literal sense; that earth and man developed through a long evolutionary process; that Christ may have been a mortal man, of natural conception and birth; that Christ's crucifixion was a symbolic rather than a literal atonement for our sins; that the acceptance and professing of religious belief is less important than the living of a Christian life; that little is positively known about Heaven and Hell, and that the idea of eternal punishment for unbelief is revolting; that religious beliefs should be revised whenever they conflict with the studied conclusions of science.

These opposing positions gradually crystallized during the closing decades of the nineteenth century, and the battle reached its peak during the first quarter of this century. Within each major Protestant denomination, the issue was debated at their periodic conferences, in their colleges and theological seminaries, and sometimes in their local congregations. Modernists were accused of being atheists, agnostics, agents of the Devil, and other assorted kinds of villains. Fundamentalists were accused of being narrow-minded bigots and ignorant reactionaries. In several states, fundamentalists secured the passing of laws forbidding the teaching of evolutionary theories in the public schools. These led to the 1925 "monkey trial" in Tennessee, when a teacher, John Scopes, was tried for the teaching of evolution. Few trials in American history have excited such intense national interest. William Jennings Bryan and Clarence Darrow, possibly the most famous lawyers of their day, met in what became less a trial of Scopes than a trial of the law itself. The fundamentalists won the battle but lost the war. Scopes was convicted and later freed on a technicality, but Darrow succeeded in picturing the law as undemocratic and its supporters as ignorant bigots. The attempt to prevent by law the teaching of evolutionary theories quickly collapsed, and acceptance of evolutionary ideas soon became practically universal among scientists and others fully familiar with the evidence.

The modernists also won the war within most of the major Protestant denominations. They captured the leadership of most denominations, but not without a struggle which left the churches deeply divided. In several instances, groups of dissatisfied fundamentalists withdrew and organized separate denominations. Many ministers and laymen drifted away to join denominations which had remained fundamentalist or to join one of the new fundamentalist denominations which appeared. The battle within each denomination has subsided, leaving a considerable realignment of religious bodies in America. [5]

The Roman Catholic Church itself was not deeply involved in this controversy. There were opposing schools of liberal and conservative thought among Catholics as among Protestants, for increasing scientific knowledge affected both faiths. But the Catholic Church succeeded in keeping its disagreements "within the family." No basic church doctrines have been repudiated, but there have been some changes of emphasis and reinterpretations of church doctrines.

Before the fundamentalism-modernism battle was finished, a new theological movement, *neo-orthodoxy*, was already gaining momentum. Led by such men as Barth, Tillich, and Niebuhr, neo-orthodoxy arose largely as a reaction against the easy optimism which was swept away in the disillusionment of two world wars and the depressions and tyrannies which followed them. Neo-orthodoxy agrees with the fundamentalists that man is self-centered and tyrannical and in need of divine salvation, that sin is real, and that social progress must come through God's grace. Neo-orthodoxy agrees with the liberals that the Bible should be criticized like any other human document, that traditional religious beliefs should be revised as scientific knowledge requires, and that the "good" society can be attained in this world and need not be postponed until the next. Neo-orthodoxy represents a partial *rapprochement* between fundamentalism and liberalism. It appears to be the dominant theological movement at present and may have helped reduce the sharpness of theological controversy.[6]

If this is largely a past battle, wherein is it a present social problem? Guerrilla warfare continues both between denominations and *within* denominations. The American Council of Christian Churches, comprising

[5] For an account of this controversy, see John Dillenberger and Claude Welch, *Protestant Christianity Interpreted Through Its Development* (New York, Charles Scribner's Sons, 1954).

[6] For statements of the fundamentalist, modernist, and neo-orthodox positions, see, respectively, Edward J. Carnell, *The Case for Orthodox Theology* (Philadelphia, Westminster Press, 1959); L. Harold DeWolf, *The Case for Theology in Liberal Perspective* (Philadelphia, Westminster Press, 1959); William Hordern, *The Case for a New Reformation Theology* (Philadelphia, Westminster Press, 1959).

fifteen national fundamentalist denominations, is sharply critical of the more liberal National Council of Churches of Christ in the United States, which includes thirty Protestant and five Eastern Orthodox churches with over 30 million members. Relations between the two councils are far from cordial. The fundamentalist churches maintain a continuous drum-fire of attack upon the liberal or modernist churches as traitors to the faith. The more extreme fundamentalists believe that the liberal churches are not only mistaken but are positively pernicious, since people may fail to find salvation because of its false teachings. Some even consider the modernist a greater menace to true religion than the atheist or agnostic. The liberal churches tend to ignore these charges, having apparently concluded that further argument is pointless.

For this determined fundamentalist minority, the task of recapturing the faith from the modernists and propagating it remains the *only* important social problem. If this could be done, and all people could be won to the true faith, they believe that all ordinary social problems would be easily solved, not through social reforms, but as a natural by-product of religious faith. This leads the fundamentalist to reject both the attempt to reform society through legislation and the "social gospel."

The Social Gospel Controversy

The roots of Christianity extend far back into the history of an agricultural people living in small groups within which all relations were primary group relations. Most of the Bible is written in the language of the primary group association of person with person. Little is said about impersonal group relations of the sort rare in a primitive agricultural society but important in an urban industrial society. A half century or more ago it became increasingly apparent that many men who were moral and generous in their relations with other individuals were thoroughly ruthless and amoral in dealing with impersonal groups. A number of churchmen concluded that the teachings of the Bible and the church must be reinterpreted in the language of impersonal, secondary group relations in order to fit the needs of the present society. This would mean that, in addition to such personal sins as murder, theft, greed, or lust, the church must also *define* and condemn such "social sins" as economic exploitation, racial injustice, and fraudulent business practice.[7]

Another root of the social gospel is found in the insights of social

---

[7] For statements of the social gospel, see Henry F. May, *Protestant Churches and Industrial America* (New York, Harper and Brothers, 1949); Walter G. Muelder, *Foundations of the Responsible Society* (Nashville, Abingdon Press, 1959); John C. Bennett, *Christians and The State* (New York, Charles Scribner's Sons, 1958). For Catholic statements, see John F. Cronin, *Social Principles and Economic Life* (Milwaukee, The Bruce Publishing Company, 1959); Benjamin L. Masse, "A Half-Century of Social Action," *America*, Vol. 101 (April 11, 1959), pp. 138-147.

science. Nineteenth-century folklore held that each person consciously and freely chooses whether he will be good or evil, Christian or pagan, lazy or ambitious, honest or deceitful. Poor people were poor because they were lazy, and the evil man was evil because he wished to be evil. Social scientists began to cast doubt upon these assumptions, showing how a man may be lazy and unmotivated because he has experienced only poverty and lack of ambition in his environment, and how the "choice" between good and evil is usually a more or less mechanical response to the balance of environmental influences surrounding him.

Whereas the traditional approach was to seek converts and assume that a better society would eventually follow, [8] the social gospel seeks to improve the institutions and practices of society directly in the belief that they are obstacles to Christian life. In 1910, the social gospel included support of labor's right to organize and bargain collectively, and opposition to the twelve-hour day and the seven-day week. Today, the social gospel calls, for example, for slum clearance and equal rights for Negroes and other minorities. The exact content of the social gospel changes along with changing social needs and issues.

The social gospel has been hotly attacked ever since its appearance. The fundamentalists charged that reforming society was no proper business of the church, and was a betrayal of the church's real purpose of saving souls. Vested interests sought to forestall clerical criticism by urging that the church confine itself to "spiritual" matters and stay out of "politics." Still others feared that the church would be torn with dissension if it became involved in social controversies. The social gospel debate accompanied the fundamentalist-modernist battle, with much the same participants and outcome. The leadership of the liberal churches accepts the social gospel, whereas the fundamentalist bodies generally reject it. The National Council of Churches tends to promote the social gospel while the much smaller American Council of Christian Churches strongly opposes the social gospel and lends tacit support to the economic status quo. These positions having crystallized, there is not much debate today about the social gospel within any denomination.

It is uncertain just how effectively the liberal churches are applying the social gospel approach. Many official resolutions about social issues produce little activity in the local congregations. Possibly the most effective promoter of the social gospel in America today is the Roman Catholic Church, which has combined a fundamentalist theology (differing somewhat from Protestant fundamentalism) with a social gospel. [9] Catholic participation in the Back of the Yards Council in Chicago and the

---

[8] Some religious groups are totally uninterested in a better society, believing that society is unalterably bad and that the church should concentrate upon the rescue of individuals from sin through personal salvation.

[9] See Cronin, *op. cit.*; Masse, *op. cit.*

Rural Life Association are examples of Catholic applications of the social gospel, although Catholics usually use the term *social action*. Their purposes are both ameliorative and evangelistic; through identifying the church with the economic needs and social problems of Negroes, workers, and other *groups*, the Catholic church hopes both to improve social conditions and to develop a rapport with these groups which will lead to individual conversions.

Among those who accept the social gospel, the question of how to apply it is not an easy one. If the church uncritically supports the status quo, it invites the charge that it is an instrument of exploitation. If it promotes extensive reforms beyond those for which its membership is prepared, it ceases to lead anyone. If it develops detailed programs of social action, it tears itself apart in controversy over them. It cannot make a frontal attack upon vested interests, for it depends upon them for support. Most important of all, both the clergy and the membership are products of our culture. For all these reasons, the social action program of the church consists mainly of repeated reminders of unsolved problems and a quiet insistence that the Christian conscience should not rest while they remain untreated.

The Controversy Over Religion in the Schools

The American Constitution provides for the separation of church and state and forbids the state to use any public funds for the support of religious bodies or sectarian religious education. In a country of multiple religious bodies, each desiring that *its* beliefs be taught, the public school can avoid giving offense only by refraining entirely from the teaching of sectarian religious doctrines.

In recent years there has arisen a determined and well-organized effort to get the public schools to co-operate in the teaching of religion. [10] This is accompanied by an equally determined effort to prevent "sectarian invasions of the public schools." [11] The courts have held that any use of public funds or public school facilities for sectarian religious instruction is unconstitutional, but forms of co-operation involving no use of public funds or facilities are permissible. Under the "released time"

[10] See Nicholas C. Brown, ed., Committee on Religion and Education, *Study of Religion in the Public Schools* (Washington, American Council on Education, 1958); V. T. Thayer, *The Attack on the Secular School* (Boston, Beacon Press, 1951), Ch. IX, "Religion in the Secular School: Religious Instruction on Released Time"; Robert Gordis and others, *Religion and The Schools* (New York, Fund For The Republic, Inc., 1959).

[11] One organization, "Protestants and Other Americans United for Separation of Church and State," seeks to check any growth of Catholic power or influence in any directions, and seeks federal legislation to protect children against "sectarian invasions of the public schools." See *New York Times*, September 6, 1959, p. 5; January 3, 1960, p. 44; February 10, 1960, p. 16.

plan, children may be released during school hours to receive religious instruction away from the school premises. Supporters are convinced that the benefits of such religious training far outweigh any possible inconveniences or objections. Opposition comes partly from those who doubt that such religious training is as effective as claimed and partly from those who maintain that the school should not be expected to assemble classes for the church. Opposition also comes from school personnel who object to the disruption of the school's schedule. To release part of the children while retaining the rest creates a dilemma for the school. If, for those children who do not elect to take the religious training, the school arranges an interesting activity, then it draws children away from the religious program; if the school does not plan an interesting activity for those remaining, a discipline problem develops.

In some communities this has become a bitter issue. Dispute becomes intense; neighbors attack one another's character and impugn one another's motives. In an earlier period when the church functioned as a community center, no such problem arose. But in recent decades the school has increasingly become a center of community life and has absorbed a growing share of the children's time. It is perhaps not surprising that some in the church should move to reclaim a portion of that time which they feel the school has usurped. At present only a minority of communities have responded. Whether the released time program will become general is doubtful. [12]

There are other questions of church-school relations which may provoke disagreement. Should the candidate's religion be considered in engaging public school teachers? Should there be any "devotionals" in the classroom? Should the teacher simply read a few biblical verses? From which Bible? Should clergymen be invited to address assembly programs in the public schools? Clergymen from which churches? What about religious programs at Thanksgiving, Christmas, and Easter? Should Jewish children be expected to sing about the "little Lord Jesus?" Each of these questions has arisen in many places, and no answer can possibly satisfy everyone. [13]

The Uneasy Course of Catholic-Protestant Relations

Of all religious tensions in America, the one which seems most likely to disrupt orderly social life is the suspicion and distrust between Roman

---

[12] Robert L. Anderson, "Religion in the Michigan Public Schools," *School and Society*, Vol. 87 (May 9, 1959), pp. 227-229; Jordan L. Larsen and Robert B. Tapp, "Release Time for Religious Education" (debate), *National Education Association Journal*, Vol. 47 (November, 1958), pp. 572-574.

[13] See A. E. Sutherland, "Public Authority and Religious Education: A Brief Summary of Constitutional and Legal Limits," *Religious Education*, Vol. 52 (July, 1957), pp. 256-264.

Catholics and Protestants. Relations between Catholics and Protestants in America have never been entirely cordial. Since the Catholic Church was mainly composed of working class immigrants, [14] a variety of nationalistic and class prejudices were intermingled with religious prejudices on the part of each group. Organized anti-Catholicism appeared at times, as with the Know-Nothings of the 1830's, 1840's, and 1850's and the Ku Klux Klan of the 1920's. [15] These were short-lived and localized protests and attracted little following among Protestants of education and responsibility. In recent years, however, there is evidence of increasing tenseness and anxiety among both Catholic and Protestant leaders. [16]

1. Catholic Evangelism

Throughout most of its history in the United States, the Roman Catholic Church was fully occupied in caring for an immigrant membership. Many of the priests were foreign-born and trained and would have found little response among non-Catholics. With the ending of mass immigration and the gradual assimilation of the immigrants, the Catholic Church has now become aggressively evangelistic and has announced its desire to win America for the Church.

This increase in Catholic evangelistic activity has been paced by a mounting Protestant anxiety lest these efforts prove successful. There is no evidence that Catholics are overtaking Protestants in church membership statistics, which, if accurate, show the Catholic Church to be about holding its own in proportionate membership. [17] But church membership statistics are notoriously unreliable, as not all churches define a "member" in the same way, nor are all churches equally prompt to prune duplications and inactive members from the roll. And the mere fact of aggressively evangelistic efforts by the Catholic Church, together with a number of highly publicized conversions (for example, Henry Ford II, Clare Booth Luce) still arouses anxiety among Protestants, for they consider

[14] Some earlier Catholic colonists, mainly around Baltimore and New Orleans, were of aristocratic origin, but the great mass of American Catholics are of Irish or of central and southern European origin, and became members of our working class upon arrival.

[15] John Higham, *Strangers in The Land: Patterns of American Nativism, 1860-1925* (New Brunswick, Rutgers University Press, 1955), pp. 77-87, 175-183.

[16] John F. Kane, "Protestant-Catholic Tensions," *American Sociological Review*, Vol. 16 (October, 1951), pp. 663-672.

[17] Between 1926 and 1957, total membership reported by all Protestant churches in the United States grew by 90 per cent, while the Roman Catholic Church reported membership gains of 96 per cent. The Roman Catholic Church includes children as members, while many Protestant churches do not. If the Protestant membership count included children, it is likely that the Protestant gains would equal or exceed the Catholics' 96 per cent, since there is evidence that the Catholic birth rate has fallen and the Protestant birth rate has risen since the 1920's. (See Albert J. Mayer and Sue Marx, "Social Change, Religion, and Birth Rates," *American Journal of Sociology*, Vol. 62 (January, 1957), pp. 283-290).

that more than merely religious doctrines are involved. A clue to Protestant fears is found in an analysis of the content of 188 unsolicited letters sent to the author of a book which criticized the Catholic Church. Most of the letters contained dire predictions of Catholic destruction of our democratic institutions, with warnings that the Catholic Church will use any means, fair or foul, to gain power. [18]

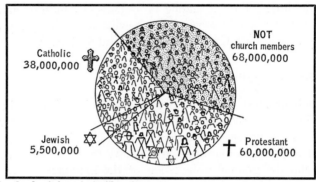

SOURCE: *Yearbook of American Churches.*

FIG. 8–2. Membership in major religious faiths, 1957.

While these letter writers may be extremists, their fears are probably shared in some degree by a great many Protestants. For Protestants have long assumed that this would remain a Protestant country and are now disturbed to discover that their assumption is being challenged. A great many Protestants feel that the Catholic Church in America has never really accepted the principles of religious liberty and of separation of church and state. [19] They fear that Catholic ascendancy in America would mean persecution of Protestants, church domination of the state, religious censorship of the movies, radio, and press, and suppression of free inquiry and expression in many areas of life. They cite the reported existence of some of these conditions in present Catholic countries in evidence. [20] To

[18] Gordon C. Zahn, "The Content of Protestant Tensions: Fears of Catholic Aims and Methods," *American Catholic Sociological Review,* Vol. 18 (October, 1957), pp. 205-212.

[19] The Protestant "doctrine" of separation of church and state has, like the Catholic position, usually been governed by practical power considerations. Where a Protestant group has been dominant, it has generally sought church-state union, which now exists in several Protestant European countries. As an example, the seventeenth century Congregationalists advocated separation in England to keep the state from the Presbyterians, but sought church-state union in New England, where they were dominant. (See Thomas F. Hoult, *The Sociology of Religion* [New York, The Dryden Press, Inc., 1958], pp. 215-216).

[20] See Paul Blanshard, *American Freedom and Catholic Power* (Boston, Beacon Press, Inc., 1958); "Soft Answer Doesn't Work: Persecution of Protestants in Colombia," *Christian Century,* Vol. 74 (October 9, 1957), pp. 1189-1191; *New York Times,* Jan. 21, 1958, p. 12; April 6, 1958, p. 7; May 21, 1959, p. 26; May 3, 1959, p. 21. See also John Wicklein, "Catholics Ending Colombia Strife," *New York Times,* Octo-

these charges, American Catholics reply that the practices of the Catholic Church always reflect the cultural setting in which it functions, that American fears of loss of liberties through Catholic action are completely unwarranted, and that a strong Catholic Church in America strengthens American freedom. [21] Yet Protestant fears continue, leading to charge and countercharge, hostility, and resentment.

2. Differing Mores: Divorce, Birth Control, Gambling

In an earlier period when divorce was rare and strongly condemned by all church folk and birth control was virtually unknown, there was no reason for Catholics and Protestants to disagree. But among the social changes of the past half century, divorce has become commonplace and birth control a widespread practice, each with a measure of carefully qualified approval from most Protestant churches. The Catholic Church does not recognize divorce for any reason [22] whatsoever and condemns all chemical or mechanical devices for preventing conception. Catholics have sought to impose these views upon our entire society by law and in some states have been partly successful. [23] Most Protestants have no objection to Catholics applying these views to themselves, but bitterly resent the attempt to impose them on non-Catholics by law. Catholics believe that these practices are contrary to *natural law*, and that this law is binding upon all people, whether Catholic or not. Natural law is not something invented by Catholics; it is (according to Catholics and preceding philosophies) part of God's natural order of the universe, like the law of gravity. If one violates natural law, for instance, by committing suicide, he will suffer. The basic issue, therefore, is not whether divorce or birth control are approved by the majority, but whether they are contrary to natural law as interpreted by the Catholic Church. This question cannot be answered *scientifically*, since it is not a scientific question. No settlement or satisfactory compromise is possible unless one side surrenders its beliefs.

Protestants get very indignant at this Catholic effort to impose Catholic mores upon non-Catholics by force of law, yet Protestants have fre-

---

ber 18, 1959, p. 71, for a report of recent Catholic Church efforts to prevent mistreatment of Protestants.

[21] James M. O'Neill, *Catholicism and American Freedom* (New York, Harper and Brothers, 1952); Currin V. Shields, *Democracy and Catholicism in the United States* (New York, McGraw-Hill Book Company, 1958); John Cogley, "The Catholic and The Liberal Society," *America*, Vol. 101 (July 4, 1959), pp. 492-495.

[22] A Catholic may secure a legal divorce, but the church considers that the marriage still exists as long as both parties live; therefore to remarry would be a sin, and the new marriage invalid in the eyes of the church.

[23] For example, Connecticut law forbids the use of contraceptives or the giving of contraceptive information. Repeated attempts to pass a law permitting physicians to prescribe contraceptive devices for married women when their health was endangered "have failed because of strong Roman Catholic opposition," *New York Times*, April 19, 1953, p. 52.

quently imposed religious bans themselves! Numerous Sunday blue laws, expressing Puritanical notions of Sunday behavior, are still legally extant, although seldom enforced. The Eighteenth Amendment (Prohibition) was a mighty Protestant effort to impose Protestant mores upon Catholics (also Episcopalians, and some Lutherans) who viewed drinking as a matter for private moderation rather than legal restraint. Protestant churches today are practically unanimous in supporting laws which forbid all forms of gambling, while the Catholic Church believes that certain games of chance, such as bingo or lotteries and raffles, are harmless when conducted by religious or benevolent organizations. [24] In a number of states, the question of legalizing "charity bingo" and certain other games of chance has provoked bitter political controversy. [25] This issue generally arrays Catholics against Protestants, issuing critical and self-righteous remarks about each other. Since differences in mores can rarely be resolved by discussion or compromise, extreme bitterness is sometimes provoked by this issue.

3. Parochial School Aid

The Catholic Church is educating a growing proportion of its children in Catholics schools, which are controlled and entirely financed by the church. In 1938, the nonpublic schools, mainly Catholic, enrolled one-tenth of the nation's pupils; by 1953, this had risen to one-eighth and reached one-seventh by 1959. [26] At a time when most students quit school early, when equipment was limited, and teachers needed little training, the costs of a private school system were not too burdensome. As the school term lengthened, as students prolonged their education, and as standards of equipment and teacher training were raised, the burden of supporting parochial schools mounted. Catholics are now seeking public funds for the partial support of these schools. They state that their taxes help support public schools, that they are being "doubly taxed," and that the parochial schools relieve the taxpayer of much expense. They ask for tax assistance of various forms; that school taxes be refunded to Catholics, that their schools share in state or federal aid payments, that their children be transported in public school buses, and that certain other expenses be assumed by the state. [27]

[24] Thomas N. Munson, S.J., "Gambling, a Catholic View," *Christian Century*, Vol. 69 (April 9, 1952), p. 437; also, Robert Daley, "Bingo Binge is Big Business," *New York Times Magazine* (December 8, 1957), pp. 61 ff.

[25] See *New York Times Index*, any issue, under heading, "Lotteries," for citations upon gambling controversies.

[26] *New York Times*, April 12, 1953, IV, p. 11; *United Press International*, March 28, 1959.

[27] R. E. Wise, "Right to Educate: The Role of the State," *National Catholic Education Association Bulletin*, Vol. 55 (August, 1958), pp. 303-306; E. A. Fitzpatrick, "Federal Government and the Schools," *Catholic School Journal*, Vol. 59

Relations between public school leaders and Catholic educators are, on the whole, amiable and co-operative. But there are questions of value which cordiality does not erase. Since state aid to parochial schools would presumably aid Catholic evangelism, those who fear the spread of Catholicism are opposed to all such proposals. Opposition also comes from those who fear the destruction of the public school system through its atomization into a series of church-controlled school systems which they predict would follow. They consider the public school system an essential unifying agency in a democracy and fear that multiple school systems would foster divisiveness and lack of mutual understanding. [28]

4. Censorship

When the Catholic Church in America was busy with its immigrant membership, it paid little attention to the newsstands. Today, the Catholic Church keeps a watchful eye on the newsstand and the movie screen. [29] The Legion of Decency urges that all Catholics boycott movies that, in its opinion, are obscene or critical of the church. Since movie makers seek to avoid offending any group, this often results in deleting from the movie script any material that may offend the Catholic Church. In certain localities, Catholics have provided strong backing for censorship ordinances and boards that seek to remove "obscene" material from the newsstands. Protestants are divided upon the question of censorship, [30] but even some Protestants who do not object to censorship per se are bitterly critical of *Catholic* censorship activities. Opposition also comes from those who object to censorship by *any* private group because they believe that all censorship is oppressive or self-defeating, and this resentment is directed strongly toward Catholics.

For all of these reasons, it appears to some observers that relations between the Catholic and non-Catholic segments of our society are growing more tense than they have been in the recent past. Since present social trends promise to aggravate rather than to eliminate these sources of hostility, it seems possible that these antagonisms may become still more

(March, 1959), pp. 67-69; *New York Times*, April 9, 1959, p. 31; April 10, 1959, p. 24. Neil G. McCluskey, S. J., *Catholic Viewpoint on Education* (Garden City, Hanover House, 1960).

[28] V. T. Thayer, *op. cit.*; James B. Conant, "Education, Engine of Democracy," *Saturday Review*, Vol. 35 (May 3, 1952), pp. 11-14; S. M. Brownell, "Positive Values in our Public Schools," in Educational Conference, 1958, *Positive Values in the American Educational System*, (Washington, American Council on Education, 1959).

[29] "Bishops Speak on Censorship," *America*, Vol. 98 (November 30, 1957), p. 263; "Text of Bishop's Plan to Fight Obscenity," *New York Times*, November 17, 1957, p. 58; Msgr. Thomas J. Fitzgerald, "NODL States its Case," *America*, Vol. 97 (June 1, 1957), pp. 280-282; J. M. O'Neill "Nonsense About Censorship," *Catholic World*, Vol. 187 (August, 1958), pp. 349-355.

[30] H. G. Cox, "Obscenity and Protestant Ethics," *Christian Century*, Vol. 76 (April 8, 1959), pp. 415-417.

bitter as time passes. While no blood bath is even remotely probable, a lengthy period of tenseness and distrustful hostility seems likely. Many nonreligious issues will become complicated by religious antagonisms. Political campaigns will continue to have religious overtones, with the religion of the candidate taking precedence over other qualifications for many voters. Such programs as "federal aid to education" will be complicated by disagreements over public aid to parochial schools. Periodic outbursts will betray inner tensions for both groups appear at times to be abnormally distrustful of each other.

THE SOCIAL-DISORGANIZATION APPROACH

Although religious conflicts have never been absent in America, most of them have developed as a result of some change in the religious status quo—either an invasion by a new religious group or the rise of a dissenting local group threatened the security of existing religious institutions. Insecurity breeds anxiety and distrust of the character and motives of one's rivals.

The religious problems here presented are not exceptions. The religious heterogeneity of America gives many opportunities for conflict, while the American tradition of religious liberty and tolerance has been relatively effective in minimizing these conflicts. With so many religious faiths, each claiming to know the absolute and exclusive truth, it is remarkable that conflict has been so limited. But the rise of an energetic Catholic evangelism in a traditionally Protestant country will place a heavier strain upon the American tradition of tolerance than it has borne for some time. In some Catholic countries, where Protestants appear to be gaining strength,[31] Catholic anxieties are revealed in scattered acts of violence and suppression directed at aggressively evangelistic Protestants.[32] Should

[31] According to *Gentes*, missionary organ of the Jesuits, Protestant membership in Latin American countries has increased 500 per cent in the last twenty-five years. (Reported in *Christian Century*, Vol. 69 [April 23, 1952], p. 484). See also, "Protestants in Italy," *Time*, Vol. 69 (April 22, 1957), pp. 68-70.

[32] See footnote 20. It appears that in Catholic countries, Protestant churches are not likely to be disturbed unless they engage in active, public efforts to gain members, thereby threatening to disorganize the status quo. One Catholic writer, describing certain Protestant bodies which have long existed in Spain without molestation, states that they "have loyally co-operated. They abstain from proselytizing and open propaganda. Unfortunately certain smaller sects use political means and large funds of foreign origin for their propaganda by which they seek to undermine Church and State." (Archduchess Adelaide of Austria, "Cardinal Segura and the Protestant World," *Catholic World*, Vol. 175 [July, 1952], pp. 266-272.)

In a predominantly Catholic country, the propaganda of a small Protestant minority, largely inspired and financed by foreigners, arouses a reaction somewhat similar to that aroused in many Americans by Communist propaganda. In each case, it appears to be an attack upon both God and country. It is also possible that, at least in some cases, Protestant missionaries may have been unnecessarily provocative and insulting in a (conscious or unconscious) desire to invite persecution. A

the Catholic Church make substantial membership gains in the United States, increased anti-Catholicism would probably develop.

The march of science has been perhaps the most disorganizing single factor; it was primarily responsible for the fundamentalist-modernist battle and the social gospel controversy. It is unlikely, however, that the discoveries of natural and social science will be as disorganizing in the future as in the past. The liberal church has already adapted a theology which can readily accommodate itself to any further discoveries that are likely to appear. The fundamentalist churches have quite effectively insulated themselves from the impact of science upon theology and will confine their membership to those who accept such a divorcement.

Urbanization, industrialization, and secularization have had an impact upon the church which it has not yet fully recognized. The Protestant churches are still largely rural institutions insecurely transplanted into an urban environment. The oft-lamented "loss of influence" of the churches, to the extent that it is a genuine loss, may be a result of the churches' relative isolation from many of the real problems of people in an urbanized, specialized, impersonal, secondary group society. The Catholic Church, with its membership mainly among urban workers, has been more prompt to recognize this than most Protestant churches. Both Catholic and Protestant churches have elaborated their programs of activities in an attempt to cater to the diversified interests of people today. But whereas the Protestant churches still appear to consider the individual mentality to be the proper unit for evangelistic effort, the Catholics also direct their appeal to "collectivities"—the Negroes, the workers, ethnic groups—in what represents a rational adaptation to the structure of modern society.

THE VALUE-CONFLICT APPROACH

In a number of respects, value disagreements enter into religious conflicts. The clash between the sacred and the secular values which our scientific progress and our economic materialism have encouraged lies at the root of the problem of "godlessness"—certain people are more secular-minded than other people think they should be. A *secular-minded* person is one who is inclined to be preoccupied with worldly goals and interests and to seek explanations in terms of physical cause-and-effect sequences instead of in terms of divine influence. Both fundamentalists and liberals consider secularism a threat to religion, possibly an even greater threat to religion than communism or atheism.

---

little persecution may be highly beneficial to an obscure sect struggling for recognition.

Many American Catholics regret the occasional mistreatment of Protestants in some Catholic countries, feeling that such treatment, though exaggerated by American critics, is nonetheless uncharitable and ineffectual. See "Protestants under Franco," *Commonweal*, Vol. 70 (May 15, 1959), pp. 171-172.

That secularism and materialism are enemies of religious faith cannot be denied, but it is not clear even to churchmen how they are to be overcome. Our scientific and mechanical civilization encourages secularism, as people are conditioned to look for physical rather than supernatural causes for events of all sorts. Most daily "problems" consist of the malfunctioning of some human contrivance—the car breaks down, traffic jams up downtown, a government policy works out badly, and so on. When faced with such problems, we call a mechanic, engage some traffic engineers, or revise government policies. We do not pray about these, for both the causes and the cures are well within human understanding and control. The urban factory worker, operating a machine which he can touch, control, and perhaps repair, is less likely to feel a constant sense of dependence upon supernatural forces than the primitive hunter or the farmer. Knowledge—sometimes superficial knowledge—often leads to secularism, a point which some faiths have recognized by attempting to discourage the spread of knowledge.

Materialism—a preoccupation with worldly possessions and interests—competes with religion for man's time and money, but how is materialism to be curbed? Our economic system rests squarely upon the deliberate cultivation of materialism, and there is no immediate prospect that this will change. Our status system is largely sparked by material symbols. The core of our system of incentives lies in an appeal to man's carefully stimulated thirst for possessions and conspicuous consumption. Materialism is too deeply rooted in our culture to be easily replaced, and the clash of materialistic with religious values is not likely to diminish.

Other value clashes, real or imaginary, are central to the tension between Catholic and non-Catholic. Many non-Catholics do not believe that the Catholic Church in America has really accepted the principle of religious liberty and separation of church and state. There is no definitive and binding papal pronouncement on these questions, and the statements of individual Catholic spokesmen reflect a variety of opinions on religious liberty. This makes it easy for anxious Protestants to remember only those Catholic statements which confirm their fears that a Catholic America would bring religious persecution and domination of the state by the church. The overwhelming trend of modern Catholic thought, however, is toward the acceptance of religious liberty, not just as a temporary expedient, but as a universal principle.[33]

Sociologists would readily predict that a Catholic America would differ greatly from Catholic Ireland, Spain, Italy, or Peru even as these countries differ from one another. The American cultural heritage will continue to shape American values and practices, regardless of which

[33] For a documentation, from authoritative Protestant sources, of the impressive Catholic support of religious liberty, see Angel F. Carillo, *Roman Catholicism and Religious Liberty* (New York, Commission on Religious Liberty, World Council of Churches, 1960).

religious group gains ascendancy. It is also true that the profound differences between the Catholic and Protestant churches would significantly affect our culture, should one supersede the other. No sociologist can predict exactly what these effects would be, or to what degree these Protestant fears may or may not be justified. But the *existence* of these Protestant fears is a fact, and mutual distrust and resentment is their inevitable product.

Multiple faiths do not *necessarily* create religious conflicts. No religion is a threat to freedom merely because it claims to profess the absolute truth and announces its superiority over all others. As long as it relies upon persuasion in promoting its views, there need be no conflict. But when a religious group seeks, by *coercion* to impose any of its views upon non-members, conflict is inescapable and religious liberty is imperiled. Both Catholics and Protestants in America have repeatedly sought to win by police power the debate they could not win by pulpit persuasion. Each time either group attempts this, the brotherhood of man is again divided.

THE PERSONAL-DEVIATION APPROACH

To what extent are deviant persons involved in religious problems? To a great degree, in the opinion of most observers. Every minister has suffered with the parishioner who, with great professions of religious devotion and divine guidance, proceeds to wreck his church by stirring up trouble. Such persons are not usually hypocrites; they are simply neurotics who happen to be religious. For a neurotic who belongs to the church is still a neurotic. He still imagines slights and insults; he defines all disagreement as personal opposition; he insists on having his own way, impugns the religious sincerity of any who block him, and finally leaves to disrupt another congregation.

The number of people who are seriously mentally ill is vastly exceeded by those who are in a state of neurotic adjustment. These persons are oriented to reality, but their reactions to reality are considerably distorted by their unconscious fears, hostilities, insecurities, and unsatisfied longings. Such people are likely to be oversensitive, overcritical, jealous, aggressive, uncompromising, and very intense in their opinions and dislikes. Frequently they are prodigious workers, but their labor is often wasted because others find them so hard to work with for long. Religious activity is one of the many possible outlets for such people. Religion has certain advantages as an outlet, for the members of a religious body are required to welcome the newcomer, to refrain from sharp criticism, and to avoid ejecting even the troublesome member. Furthermore, the neurotic may find through religion an effective rationalization for his motives. Where else can one sanctify his selfish and petty impulses and raise them above reproach by attributing them to the will of God? The Protestant tradition of the "priesthood of the individual believer" [34] means that each person's prayerful conclusion as to the will of God must receive respectful recognition from others. Most ministers need no study of psychology to arrive at the suspicion that sometimes a member's "divine commands" arise not from the voice of God, but from the depths of his own unconscious compulsions and yearnings. Usually these people are intensely earnest and deeply hurt at the suggestion that their inner motives are other than purely spiritual.

Every church is plagued with some of these maladjusted trouble-makers. The Catholic Church, with its authoritarian structure, can control them with a minimum of confusion. The maladjusted troublemakers appear to be most numerous not among the major Protestant denominations but among the marginal Protestant sects and fundamentalist bodies. [35] These groups are somewhat unconventional and therefore may attract the deviant person. They are bitterly and vocally critical of the major denominations, and provide the neurotic with an approved outlet for his hostilities. Being relatively small congregations, they offer many opportunities for leadership. Aggressively evangelistic, they offer an approved opportunity to lose one's self in purposeful activity. There would appear to be much more to attract and hold the interest of the deviant or the neurotic in these groups than in the sedate downtown churches. It is *not* suggested that most of the members of these bodies are neurotics, but merely that those persons who are neurotic may tend to gravitate to them.

Neurotic behavior appears to play an important part in religious conflicts, as in most conflicts of any sort. In most such controversies, the extremists on both sides appear to be neurotic persons who are more interested in making issues than in resolving them and taking greater pleasure in scoring points than in settling them. The most bitter anti-Catholicism among Protestants is found not among the leaders of the major liberal denominations but among the most narrowly fundamentalist sects, who merely include Catholics in their violent condemnations of all who disagree with them. And the Catholic Church felt it necessary to suspend an intolerant priest who attracted a following of "scowling fanatics." [36] It is clear that much neurotic behavior is expressed through religious activity and that much of the bitterness of many religious controversies stems from the compulsions and emotional maladjustments of the more violent participants. Even if all doctrinal disputes, power struggles, and value conflicts among religious groups were resolved, it is likely that the emotional compulsions of the neurotic minority would still provoke a measure of religious controversy.

[34] All Protestant churches teach that the believer may approach God directly, without any intermediary priests or officials, and that God may reveal His will directly to the believer. Some Protestant bodies (for example, Jehovah's Witnesses, Friends) operate largely or entirely without a professional clergy.

[35] William R. Catton, Jr., What Kind of People Does a Religious Cult Attract?" *American Sociological Review*, Vol. 22 (October, 1957), pp. 561-566.

[36] *Time*, Vol. 53 (May 2, 1949), p. 67; Vol. 60 (October 13, 1952), p. 78.

SUMMARY

Religious problems may be unique among social problems in several respects. For almost no other problem are so many people confident that they have the "answer." Since each group already has the "answer," no search for an answer is necessary. As each group's "answer" often consists of converting all the others, it is clear to the sociologist that these "answers" provide no solution in the foreseeable future. Meanwhile, there is little point in suggesting new answers to groups who are complacent about their present ones. There are other groups, of course, to whom the problem is not this simple, and which are actively seeking ways and means of resolving religious differences.

With few, if any, other problems is there so great an opportunity to use *tolerance as a solution.* To "tolerate" crime, ill-health, or waste of natural resources would be no solution, for the social effects of these conditions would remain unaffected but still be defined as undesirable by our values. But intolerance is itself the cause of much of our religious tension, and "a decent respect for the opinions of mankind," which includes a respect for the "wrong" opinions we cannot accept, would relieve much needless conflict. If all persons, however firm in their own religious convictions, sought a tolerant understanding of the views of others, it would be far easier to confine the problem to those issues which actually require an agreement.

Although no genuine solution for religious problems is in immediate prospect, considerable progress has been made in certain areas. The fact that many different faiths exist in the United States with practically no violence is a substantial achievement. The ecumenical movement, seeking to unite similar churches into common denominations, has brought several mergers and may bring still more. Co-operation between denominations in areas where they can work together is being promoted at the national level by the National Council of Churches, and at the regional and local levels by appropriate church councils and ministerial associations. Friendliness and understanding between religious groups is cultivated with a dedicated zeal by the National Conference of Christians and Jews. Although in certain areas, religious tensions appear to be growing, there are others in which discord and rivalry are being replaced by amity and co-operation. The sharpness of religious conflicts in the future will be highly affected by the strength of the American traditions of religious tolerance and democratic regard for the rights and beliefs of others, and there is reason to believe that these may become stronger than ever.

SUGGESTED READINGS

CRONIN, John F., *Social Principles and Economic Life* (Milwaukee, The Bruce Publishing Company, 1959). A Catholic statement of how religious principles should be expressed in social and economic life.

GORDIS, Robert, and others, *Religion and the Schools* (New York, Fund For The Republic, Inc., 1959). A brief treatment of the issues in church-school relations.

HOULT, Thomas F., *The Sociology of Religion* (New York, The Dryden Press, Inc., 1958). A sociological analysis of the nature and function of organized religion in American society.

MUELDER, Walter G., *Religion and Economic Responsibility* (New York, Charles Scribner's Sons, 1953). A statement of the social gospel—attempting to interpret Christian principles in terms of the structure and problems of modern society.

PFEFFER, Leo, *Creeds in Competition* (New York, Harper and Brothers, 1958). An analysis of the differences and problems separating Catholic, Protestant, and Jew in the United States.

ROSTEN, Leo, ed., *The Religions of America* (New York, Simon and Schuster, Inc., 1955). The beliefs and practices of sixteen religious bodies in the United States, presented by their spokesmen.

QUESTIONS AND PROJECTS

1. How can an intangible like "lack of religious faith" be a social problem?

2. Is it possible to resolve religious disagreements scientifically? Why, in an age of steadily increasing knowledge, do religious controversies persist?

3. What conflicts of value enter into Catholic-Protestant tensions?

4. Why has the assimilation of the Catholic immigrant group failed to bring an end to tension between Protestants and Catholics?

5. In what way is the social gospel a product of social change?

6. How have Catholics justified the attempt to impose their mores upon nonmembers by force of law? How have Protestants justified their efforts to do so? What are the consequences of such efforts?

7. Which of the differences between Catholics and Protestants can be quite easily tolerated? For which differences is toleration no solution? What sort of settlement is possible for those differences where toleration or compromise are not acceptable?

8. Jews receive little mention in this chapter, but receive considerable attention in the chapter on Race Problems. Why, since the Jews are not a race, do you believe they are discussed in that chapter rather than in this one?

9. Read Marshall Wingfield, "One Preacher in Politics," *Christian Century*, Vol. 69 (September 24, 1952), pp. 1094-1096. Do you think these are proper activities for a Christian minister?

10. The article by David S. Burgess, "Place: A Georgia Town. Time: 1952," *Christian Century*, Vol. 69 (August 27, 1952), pp. 971-973, raises a num-

ber of questions about the role of the church in labor-management controversies. Should the church remain aloof? Should it defend the interests of its
larger contributors? Should it encourage the unionization of workers? Is there
any way for the church to avoid taking sides in economic conflicts?

9

Population Problems: National and International

There are many serious problems facing the world all the time, but . . . the most serious of all . . . is the [problem] of overpopulation. . . . If increases should go on at the present rate for only a thousand years there would not be standing room for the human race on the Earth.[1]

[A whimsical suggestion] that interplanetary travel might alleviate the earth's population pressures. But merely moving people on the earth itself is costly. . . . Assuming that an individual could be moved to another planet for the ridiculously low cost of one million dollars, it would take $45,000 billion to get rid of the earth's current increase for one year—a sum exceeding the earth's total income.[2]

Speculations on how many people the earth will be able to feed in the future as a result of scientific developments are futile. Better than half the people now on earth are underfed. . . .[3]

In Japan, which supports 91 million people in an area the size of Montana, a nine-year-old birth control program has already cut the birth rate almost in half. . . . The free world's most extensive contraception campaign is expected to achieve similar results in less industrialized India.[4]

Admittedly, nobody can predict future populations with certainty. The world's inhabitants in the year 2000 may exceed six billion or may number only a few thousand sufferers from nuclear radiation.[5]

WHILE YOU HAVE BEEN READING the five quotations above, the earth's population has grown by ten people. By the time you finish reading this

[1] Sir Charles Darwin, "The Pressures of Population," *What's New*, Vol. 210 (Late Winter, 1959), p. 2.
[2] Kingsley Davis, "The Other Scare: Too Many People," *New York Times Magazine*, March 15, 1959, p. 112.
[3] "The Population Bomb," the Hugh Moore Fund, New York, p. 6.
[4] Reprinted from *Time;* copyright, Time, Inc., 1957.
[5] Kingsley Davis, *op. cit.*, p. 13.

chapter, it will have grown by approximately 5400 people. And by this time tomorrow there will be 129,600 more people in the world. [6] Many people are gravely concerned about the effects of continued high birth rates and, as indicated by the quote on Japan's birth control program, many people are trying to do something about it. Other people and other groups are concerned about different kinds of population problems. Organized groups are promoting new homes for refugees from Soviet dominated states, for Jews in Israel, and for Arabs displaced from what is now Israel. Other groups oppose the contamination of existing populations by immigration. Some groups are worried because the "less desirable elements" in the population seem to have most of the children, while the "better stocks" fail to reproduce themselves. All of these positions suggest different population problems.

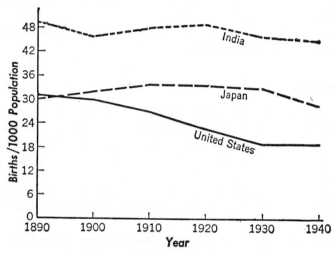

SOURCE: New York, The Ronald Press Company, 1949, p. 34; and Kingsley Davis, *The Population of India and Pakistan* (Princeton, Princeton University Press, 1951), p. 69, by permission.

9-1 Crude birth rates in Japan, India, and the United States.

THE PROBLEMS

Population problems may be summed up under three words: size, distribution, quality.

Size

The world's population has been characterized by irregular but continuous growth ever since the appearance of man on earth. Moreover, as

[6] Based upon statistics from the *United Nations Demographic Yearbook*, 1957.

time passes the average rate of growth increases. The world's people are multiplying faster now than ever before.

Demographers estimate that man has been on earth for a hundred thousand years or so. During the first 98,000 years (more or less), or up to the time of Christ, the population increased to between 200 million and 300 million people. In the next 1650 years the population doubled to approximately 550 million, a rate of growth almost sixty times that which existed before. In the last three hundred years the population of the world has quintupled again—to 2,700,000,000. According to the United Nations the next forty years may see another 100 per cent increase, to 5,400,000,000. [7] Though it is impossible accurately to predict the size of the population fifty or a hundred years from now, the estimates vary only in the *rate* of increase predicted. Population growth in the past has been accompanied by both high birth rates and high death rates. Both rates remain high in most of the world today. Since a drop in the death rate generally precedes a lowering of the birth rate, large population increases seem inevitable in the near future.

Distribution

The approximate 2¾ billion people who populate the earth are not distributed equally over its surface. Nor are all nations or continents equally capable of supporting large populations. Differing ratios of population to resources and techniques of food production mean that population pressures are quite severe in some areas and practically nonexistent in others. In general, population pressures are greatest in Asia and the Near East and least in the United States, Canada, Australia, and in parts of Europe.

In 1950, Asia contained approximately 60 per cent of the world's population; Europe had 17 per cent; North America, 9 per cent; Africa, 8 per cent; and Australia, less than one per cent. India, with a total land area of 1,353,364 square miles, has nearly 406 million people; Japan, with only 152,357 square miles, has 83 million; the Soviet Union has 208 million people in a 8,400,000 square mile area; England has 44 million people in 58,343 square miles; and the United States has more than 179 million people in 3,022,387 square miles. [8]

Within the United States, New York state has a density of 309 persons per square mile, Rhode Island has 748 people per square mile, Nevada has 1.5, and Wyoming has 3 people per square mile. In New York City the density is almost 25,565 persons per square mile of land while in some parts of rural Montana it is less than 1 person per square mile. [9]

[7] *Ibid.*

[8] All figures taken or computed from *United Nations Demographic Yearbook,* 1951, pp. 91-109.

[9] All figures taken or computed from *The World Almanac,* 1959, p. 269 and *passim.*

Bound up with these differences are problems of war and peace, famine and plenty, disease and health. Tens of millions of people have migrated from China, India, Japan, and Korea without materially reducing the size of their populations. The shrill cry for *Lebensraum* (space for living) threatens the world with future disasters.

Quality

Ever since Darwin, the notions of "struggle for survival" and "survival of the fittest" have emphasized the idea of inequality within both animal and human species. Theoretically, the fittest do survive, and the inevitable result of natural competition within the species should be to produce a constantly improving biological stock. A major difficulty with the theory, however, is that among human beings competition is not the simple biologic process that it is among lower species. Human competition is complicated by the existence of *culture*. Rarely do human beings meet in mortal combat. And when they do, the meeting is not likely to be a chance occurrence. Each combatant is likely to be a chosen representative of his group, specially armed and trained for the purpose. Each is equipped with weapons designed to minimize physical advantage. Wars are fought and won through technological superiority rather than through the quality of the germ plasm. High mortality rates among infants and children generally are considered bad, and efforts are made to save the weak as well as the strong. Within human groups, *social* selection is as important as *biological* selection.

It is widely feared that human interference with the operation of biological selection means a lowering of population quality. If the inferior and incompetent are protected against extinction will they not go on to perpetuate their kind? May they not gradually lower the quality of the entire population and, perhaps, eventually bring about its destruction? Such fears have given rise to eugenics, a movement which deals with influences which improve population quality. Eugenics is based on two principles: (1) discouraging reproduction of the hereditarily unfit; and (2) encouraging reproduction of the "better" biological stocks.

POPULATION GROWTH

The rapid rate of world population growth has already been noted. The figures themselves are staggering. But what do they mean? If the world already holds nearly 2¾ billion people, is it not capable of holding twice as many, or even more? If there are limits that may not be surpassed, what are they? And how do they operate? A partial and classic answer to some of these questions was provided a hundred and fifty years ago by Thomas R. Malthus in his famous work, *An Essay on the Principle of Population.* [10]

[10] *First Essay on Population,* 1798 (New York, The Macmillan Co., 1926).

The Malthusian Theory

According to Malthus, population tends to grow faster than the food supply can be increased. Population tends to increase in geometric fashion (1, 2, 4, 8, 16) while the food supply increases only arithmetically (1, 2, 3, 4, 5). In other words, population *multiplies* with each increase thereby furnishing the basis for a further increase, whereas food production cannot be multiplied nor endlessly increased. Consequently, at any given time, the size of a population is limited by the amount of available food. So long as they can be fed, additional children will live. Most of the world population exists at a minimum subsistence level, barely staying alive and ready to be wiped out by a variety of possible calamities.

Malthus went on to define the nature of the calamities which result when population size presses too closely upon the food supply. These he called *positive* and *preventive checks*. The term *positive checks* refers to those means of population limitation that operate through the taking of human life. Chief among them are war, disease, and famine. Up until the time of Malthus these had been the principal forces holding down the rate of population growth. They result from the blind operation of societal forces, relatively independent of human control. The *preventive checks* reduce population size not through taking lives but through preventing additional births. They depend primarily upon the exercise of human will power. To Malthus this meant chiefly that people should delay the time of marriage. The longer they waited and the older they were at the time of marriage, the fewer children would result. He did not, as is often assumed, advocate birth control in marriage. Modern contraception had not come into existence at that time and, even if it had, it is not likely that Malthus, who was also a minister, would have regarded it as desirable. He placed great emphasis on the exercise of "moral restraint" through delay in the time of marriage.

Malthus' theory was the first comprehensive one to foresee great danger to standards of living, to political freedom, and even to human survival in too rapid population growth. Drawing his illustrative material from the experience of the United States, which was growing rapidly through immigration and natural increase, Malthus postulated that under ideal conditions populations would double in size about every twenty-five years. In the absence of moral restraint, this could mean only increased dependence on the undesirable positive checks: war, disease, and starvation.

Is Malthus' theory applicable today? Instead of there being a real shortage of food in the United States, the government is holding millions of pounds of surplus butter, farmers are being urged to limit the size of crops, and millions of bushels of grain are being "dumped" into foreign countries. Here, at least, population does not seem to be pressing very hard upon the means of subsistence. Important changes have occurred since Malthus' time which must be taken into consideration in evaluating his theories.

England at the beginning of the nineteenth century was still very much an agricultural nation and was beset by a series of ever lengthening economic recessions. It was in this atmosphere that Malthus wrote. Poverty was widespread and was being rendered more acute by population increases. Malthus did not live to see the tremendous changes which were wrought by industrialization. The Industrial Revolution in Europe and the United States transformed agricultural nations into manufacturing ones, and food production increased at an almost unbelievable rate. Un-

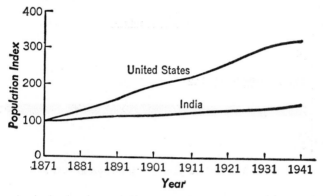

SOURCE: Adapted from Kingsley Davis, *The Population of India and Pakistan* (Princeton, Princeton University Press, 1951), p. 27, by permission.

FIG. 9–2. Relative population growth in India and the United States, 1871–1941.

paralleled growth and expansion followed. Population increased rapidly but the food supply increased even faster. Especially in the United States, Malthus' theory seems to have been invalidated by the course of social change. But before asserting that such is necessarily the case, let us examine more closely the current picture in the world at large and then in the United States.

The World Picture

Over one-half of the world's population is concentrated in Asia. China, India, Japan, Java, the Philippines—all have exceedingly large populations and all are threatened with inadequate food supplies. The Industrial Revolution has not been a world-wide revolution, since many of these areas have been relatively untouched by it. Undoubtedly, industrialization could relieve the situation somewhat. But whether even full-scale industrialization could accomplish what it has in the United States is open to serious question. The United States is blessed with a large, fertile land area and relatively low population density. The world at large is much more crowded. According to one estimate it takes a minimum of two and one half acres of arable land to provide a minimum adequate diet for each person. There are now less than two acres for each person in the world. [11]

In Asia, especially, populations are characterized by exceedingly high birth rates and are held in check only by extremely high death rates. Malthus' positive checks seem to be in full operation. Poverty, malnutrition, and even starvation are widespread. Contrary to widely held opinion, not all Asian populations are increasing rapidly. Near saturation points were reached decades ago and increases have been limited to the additional

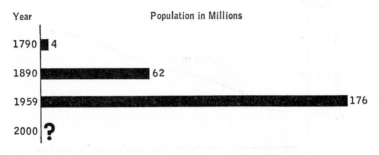

FIG. 9–3. United States population growth.

persons who could be supported by the slight technological advances that have occurred. Unfortunately, accurate data for most of these countries are lacking. Adequate censuses are unknown and only estimates are available. The most reliable information comes from India where the population has been under intensive study for a number of years. Since 1870, the rate of population growth in India has been only about one-fifth that of the United States. Yet the birth rate in India has been nearly twice as high. In Asia, generally, the positive checks continue to operate with undiminished fury.

United States Population Growth

American population experience up to the present has been that of rapid and almost continuous growth. From approximately 4 million people in 1790, the United States grew to 151 million in 1950, and the total has now passed the 179 million mark. This represents an increase of 3900 per cent in 160 years. For analytic purposes, United States population growth may be considered in three separate stages: before 1900, 1900-1940, and from 1940 onward.

[11] Fairfield Osborn, "Crowded Off the Earth," *The Atlantic Monthly*, Vol. 181 (March, 1948), p. 18.

Before 1900. Superficially, population growth would appear to be due to high or increasing birth rates. Equally important, however, are the size of the death rate and the amount of migration. These latter factors have been of great importance in the United States. Until very recently, the trend in American birth rates was steadily downward. Past gross reproduction rates [12] are shown in Figure 9–4. But American death rates have been dropping even faster. Between 1880 and 1950 the death rate dropped by 60 per cent while the birth rate decreased only 43.4 per cent. The decreasing death rate means a larger population *in spite of* a declining birth rate.

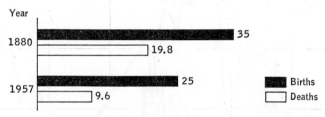

SOURCE: U. S. Bureau of the Census, *Statistical Abstract of the United States: 1958* (Washington, D.C.), p. 56.

FIG. 9–4. The decrease in birth and death rates in the United States.

Some forty millions of the United States population were gained through immigration, coming primarily from Europe. During most of the nineteenth century the United States government looked with favor upon immigration and did little to discourage it. Land was to be had almost for the taking and immigration was a means of developing and strengthening the country. Most of the immigrants were coming from the countries of northwestern Europe such as England, Ireland, and Germany. Similar in cultural background to those who were already here, the immigrants adjusted easily and were rather quickly accepted by the "Americans."

Before the turn of the century, the population policies and problems that were to characterize the next period were becoming evident. Birth rates were dropping rapidly and the government began to curb immigration from the Orient. Spurred on by the fear of "unfair" competition from Chinese laborers who were accustomed to very low living standards, first Chinese laborers, then all Chinese, and, finally, all Japanese were excluded.

1900-1940. Though the population continued to grow during the early decades of the twentieth century, the increment added each decade was smaller than the one before. Reproduction dropped below replacement requirements and by the 1920's immigration virtually ceased. The prolonged depression of the 1930's depressed birth rates even further,

[12] The number of births per 1000 population.

and from 1931-1935 for the first time the number of persons emigrating *from* the United States exceeded the number migrating *to* the United States. [13] The steady decline in birth rates led demographers to predict that soon the population would stop growing. That very thing had already happened in Europe, for instance, in France and Scandinavia. Even-

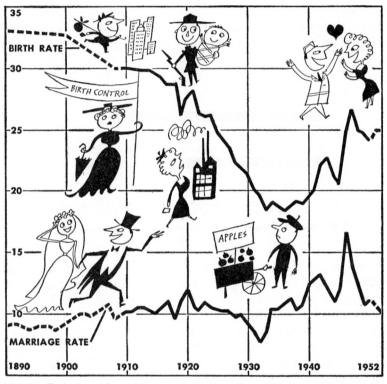

FIG. 9–5. Births and marriages in the United States over the past six decades.

tually, they predicted, the population would even start to decline. At first, it was believed that a stable population size would be reached by 1970 or 1975. But then World War II loomed on the horizon, the nation began to come out of the depression, and things began to happen to the birth rate.

Since 1940. Fluctuations in the birth rate from 1938 to 1945 can be ascribed almost wholly to the war. Birth rates rose at first and then dropped as more and more men left their homes and the country. Beginning in 1946 the number of births increased rapidly, reaching an all-

[13] U. S. Bureau of the Census, *Statistical Abstract of the United States: 1952* (Washington), p. 95.

time high of 3,786,000 in 1947. The figures for the years 1948-1950 were only slightly lower. Demographers generally "stuck to their guns," maintaining that no real reverse had occurred. We were simply experiencing, they said, the effects of the backlog of marriages which had built up

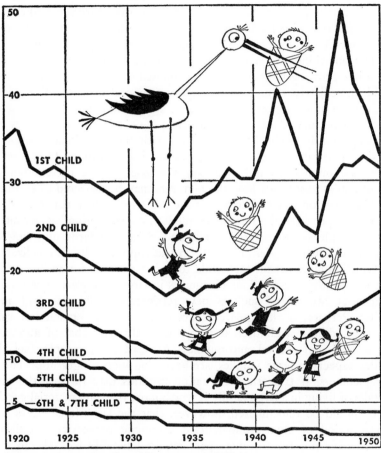

Births per thousand native white women aged 15-44.
SOURCE: Reproduced from *Life,* copyright Time, Inc., 1952, by permission.

FIG. 9–6. Family size in United States since 1920. Higher order births are increasing.

during the depression of the 1930's and the war in the early 1940's. They pointed out that most of the births were of first or second children—the result of the formation of new families rather than an indication that families were getting larger. The birth rate would drop soon, and drastically. It did not. In 1953 the number of births totaled approximately 3,900,000, a new high.[14] Since then, the annual number of births has

[14] U. S. Bureau of the Census, *Statistical Abstract of the United States: 1958* (Washington), p. 56.

passed 4,000,000. The marriage rate reached its peak in 1946 and has declined gradually since that time. Not as many new families are being formed, yet the number of births continues to remain high. People are having more children! The number of first births has declined somewhat since 1952; second, third, and fourth births are becoming more numerous. [15] Even the percentage increase in fourth order births is higher than that for first order births. What has happened to the predictions of a continuing decline in birth rates and, eventually, a stable population?

The one thing which is certain is that the United States population will still be growing long after it was supposed to stop. Even if birth rates should immediately resume their lengthy temporal downward trend the present crop of youngsters would ensure continued growth till about the end of the century. And, at present, there is no sign that birth rates will drop importantly again. Demographers, with the traditional caution of scientists, generally have adopted a wait-and-see attitude. They are revising their predictions and examining the bases for the present bumper crop of babies to see how long the high rate may be expected to continue.

The question is whether or not we are witnessing a real reversal of the long temporal trend. Heretofore, modern contraception has permitted, and the emphasis on material goods and rising standards of living has encouraged, small families. The pattern was supported by rationalizations that "small families permit each child to be better cared for and to receive more of the *advantages*." The advantages in large part were construed to be material advantages, such as new refrigerators, bicycles, and automobiles. Perhaps, if the apparent reverse is real, the satisfaction value of having additional children is rising relatively with that of automatic dish-washers and second automobiles. At least some people feel that families, especially large families, are becoming increasingly important to their members. If true, the new rationalizations may be that the give-and-take of living in a large family is worth more than any material goods."

It should be remembered, however, that the last fifteen years have been a period of almost unparalleled economic prosperity. Additional children have not for the most part required families to "take in their belts." It has been possible to have additional children *and* luxuries. The real test may come when and if living standards drop. Continued large families in the face of some financial hardship might well mean that a new cycle of growth is under way, and that perhaps the validity of some of Malthus' original formulations needs to be re-examined.

[15] *Ibid.*, p. 57.

DISTRIBUTION: PROBLEMS OF MIGRATION

Immigration

For over two hundred years the United States immigration policy was officially an open-door policy. The inscription on the base of the Statue of Liberty, presented to the United States by France, indicates how this policy was received abroad:

> ... "Give me your tired, your poor,
> Your huddled masses yearning to breathe free,
> The wretched refuse of your teeming shore,
> Send these, the homeless, tempest-tossed to me:
> I lift my lamp beside the golden door."

The United States was a haven of refuge for the surplus population of Europe and, to a very slight extent, for that of Asia. She became known as the melting pot where diverse peoples and cultures were fused into a new entity of great vigor and promise. Culturally and politically the new nation remained tied to northwestern Europe. English-speaking people outnumbered other immigrants and established their prejudices in the new land. The first restrictions which barred the poverty-stricken, the insane, the disabled, and the criminal from entering the country, included also the first of a series of bans against Orientals, who were believed to threaten the "native" population. Until after World War I, no further restrictions were imposed.

The stage for the drastically altered policies that followed World War I was set by the changed character of immigration during the last of the nineteenth and the first of the twentieth century. During this period, immigration from northwestern Europe had virtually ceased and increasing numbers came from southern and eastern Europe—Italy, Greece, and the Balkans. There were language barriers to be overcome, ethnic communities multiplied in the cities, and whereas the original migrants had been predominantly Protestant, the newcomers were more often Catholic. [16] The antagonism and resentment first directed against Asiatics were

---

[16] There is substantial evidence that the United States never was a true melting pot in the sense of uniformly assimilating immigrants, regardless of religious and national backgrounds. One study has shown three distinct melting pots—one for Catholics, one for Protestants, and one for Jews—in one American city. There is considerable intermarriage between persons of the same religions but differing nationality backgrounds, but relatively less marriage across religious lines. See Ruby Jo Reeves Kennedy, "Single or Triple Melting Pot? Intermarriage Trends in New Haven, 1870-1940," *American Journal of Sociology*, Vol. 39 (January, 1944) pp. 331-339. Other evidence shows increased willingness of persons to marry across religious lines. See Judson T. Landis and Mary Landis, *Building a Successful Marriage*, 3rd ed. (Englewood, New Jersey, Prentice-Hall, Inc., 1958), pp. 241-242, 253; and John L. Thomas, "The Factor of Religion in the Selection of Marriage Mates,"

extended to the south Europeans. The situation came to a head after 1918. There was much clamor "to keep America for Americans" and to protect American jobs by halting the flood of immigration.

Laws passed in 1921 and 1924 laid down the basic policy which is still with us today. The concept of national origins underlies this legislation. Nations are allotted immigration quotas on the basis of the proportion of the United States population that is made up of persons from those nations. The 1921 law stated that immigration from any country in any one year should be limited to 3 per cent of the persons of that nationality who were residents of the United States in 1910. The law of 1924 was even more drastic in that the proportion was reduced to 2 per cent and the base year was moved back to 1890. The practical consequence of this immigration policy has been virtually to cut off immigration to the United States.

TABLE 9-1   Immigration quotas to the United States

GREAT BRITAIN	65,361
GERMANY	25,841
GREECE	308
INDIA	100
CHINA	100

SOURCE: Immigration and Nationality Act of 1952.

Since the northern Europeans were the first to migrate to the United States, the national-origins system gives them very large quotas. People from central and southern Europe who had begun to migrate in large numbers only from about 1870 have very small quotas. Moreover, unused portions of one country's quota cannot be used by other countries, and unused portions cannot be carried over into subsequent years. Large parts of the quotas for England and other northern European countries remain unused while southern Europeans who seek admittance are refused. There seems to be little question that prejudices against the Italians, Poles, Greeks, and others were instrumental in the formation of this policy and were furthered by it. The "land of the free" is freer to northern than to southern and eastern Europeans!

Though the national-origins theory was established in the 1920's, it should not be interpreted as being solely a product of the past. In 1952, the question of immigration policy came up before the Congress again. The law that was passed, the Immigration and Nationality Act (popularly known as the McCarran-Walter immigration law), did little to remove existing inequities; it simply consolidated and simplified the provisions of earlier laws.

American Sociological Review, Vol. 16, (August, 1951), pp. 487-491. Perhaps the idea of a single melting pot, which did not accurately describe the situation for which it was developed, is becoming increasingly applicable to American society.

Internal Migration

The Puerto Rican Migrant. Most people, when they think of international migration, probably envision assimilation problems involving differences of language, religion, and, possibly, skin color. When they think of internal migration, they probably think of people much like themselves who are simply moving to another geographical area generally similar in culture where the problems of readjustment should not be great. In at least two major instances, this oversimplified notion of migration does not fit modern American experience.

Though immigration from other nations has been drastically curtailed, the Commonwealth of Puerto Rico is not included in the ban. Puerto Rico, traditionally having one of the western world's lowest living standards, is just a few hours flying time from New York City, and since the end of World War II nearly 50,000 Puerto Ricans have been entering the continental United States each year. [17] There are approximately 750,-000 first and second generation immigrant Puerto Ricans in the United States today, an increase of nearly 250 per cent since the 1950 census was taken. Nearly 80 per cent of these migrants live in New York City, though the proportion of new immigrants settling there is declining and Puerto Ricans are living in all forty-eight states of the central continent. In skin color they range from white to very dark. Their native tongue is Spanish. Like generations of immigrants before them, the Puerto Ricans tend to move into slum areas, particularly in New York City.

Most of them find jobs at what seem to them to be relatively high wages, but the cost of living, they find, is also high and the temptations to buy unwisely are formidable. They cannot protest effectively when they are gouged by unfeeling landlords because their frequent lack of schooling and language difficulties make them easy prey. If they try to settle personally with their persecutors, as would be permissable in their former homes, they run afoul of the law—a law that always appears to be loaded against them. Irresponsible merchants, who promise payments of only a few pennies a day, urge naïve migrants to purchase automobiles, television sets, furniture, and a host of other items that they would dearly love to have but which they cannot afford. When these items must be repossessed, the merchants confirm their stereotypes of untrustworthy Puerto Ricans and the migrants have one more bit of evidence of the hostility and unfairness of the world around them.

The great importance assigned to skin color in the United States results in most Puerto Ricans being subjected to economic and residential segregation, a type of discrimination many of them have never experienced before. The one way by which an other-than-white Puerto Rican can

[17] "Puerto Ricans in the Continental United States," 1950 *Census*; Special Report P-E, No. 3D, 1953; and Clarence Senior, "Patterns of Puerto Rican Dispersion in the Continental United States," *Social Problems*, Vol. 2 (October, 1954), pp. 93-99.

demonstrate to those around him that he is not Negro is through his use of the Spanish language. Consequently, the same process of speaking another language that holds him back occupationally, and complicates his life in countless other ways, becomes functional to him in this area. Studies have shown a marked correlation between darkness of skin color and reluctance to give up Spanish for English. [18]

The family lives of Puerto Rican migrants also suffer. Many of them who come from the lower socioeconomic levels have little tradition of family stability to begin with. Whatever stabilizing influence the family in Puerto Rico had becomes lost in the anonymity of the American city. Relatively high wages, loneliness, racial discrimination, and bewilderment combine to encourage the formation of casual associations between men and women, although families both on the continent and in Puerto Rico try to protect their members against them.

In at least two ways the Puerto Rican migration to the United States appears unique among large scale human migrations. First, there is unprecedented travel back and forth. Major airlines advertise economy flights (more passengers to an airplane than the regular flights carry) that will whisk the Puerto Rican out of the turmoil of city life back to homeland and family in a few hours. Many migrants return home for visits whenever possible, some saving their money solely for that purpose. The visits may be as short as a week end or they may last for months or even years before return to the continent. Never before have so many migrants been able to return to their homeland so fast or so often. And never before has the need to become assimilated to the new home been interfered with so regularly by the existence of this kind of escape.

The Puerto Rican migration is also unique in that, for the first time, the migrants' government is attempting to aid their assimilation in their new homes. The Migration Division of the Puerto Rican Department of Labor maintains offices in the continental United States where employment, social welfare, and educational services are provided. Research into assimilation problems is encouraged and a deliberate policy of encouraging Puerto Ricans to disperse over the country is followed. It is probably too early to evaluate this program properly but it represents a radical departure in the history of human migration.

The Negro Migrant. The migration of Negroes in the United States has frequently been a three stage process—from a depressed southern farm area to newly industrialized southern cities, and then on to the generally better job opportunities in northern cities. In the cities the Negroes crowded together in the slums—the only places where they were permitted to live and where they had friends. The poverty, the overcrowded conditions, lack of preparation for urban living, and sheer ignorance

[18] Clarence Senior, "Research on the Puerto Rican Family in the United States," *Marriage and Family Living,* Vol. 19 (February, 1957), p. 36.

contributed to high rates of family breakdown, alcoholism, crime, and indolence. The migrants were unwelcome to residents of surrounding areas, to municipal authorities, and to much of the general public who saw in them competitors for jobs and potential threats to property values and even to personal security. As early as 1918, and sporadically ever since, there have been outbreaks of violence against Negroes in northern cities. These have ranged from large-scale riots in Chicago and Detroit to neighborhood opposition to a single Negro family entering a formerly all-white residential area.

In recent years the relative abundance of jobs has lessened the direct economic threat somewhat and heightened the threat to the superior *social* status of middle-class whites. Just as the large-scale race riot symbolized the racial tensions of the 1920's and 1930's, the tensions of the 1950's more often concerned the efforts of Negroes to acquire housing outside of completely segregated residential areas. This also reflects the movement of Negroes into middle-class occupations that formerly were held almost exclusively by whites.

The White Hillbilly Migrant. Since the 1930's there has also been an increasing migration of whites from the economically depressed mountain areas of the upper South to the cities of the Midwest. [19] So-called hillbillies from West Virginia, Kentucky, Missouri, and Tennessee have fled their worn-out farms and worked-out mines for the rumored high wages in the North. According to American folklore, these migrants should have been desirable additions to their new communities. After all, they were, almost without exception, Americans of old Anglo-Saxon stock— exactly the kind of people to whom proponents of the national-origins theory say the country rightfully belongs. Municipal authorities, landlords, employers, social workers, and ministers, however, have found these migrant whites almost impossible to cope with. They congregate in slum areas as thickly as any racially segregated group. Their disregard for, and suspicion of, law and order is reinforced by a social code that encourages casual sex contacts, hard drinking, and the settling of disputes by resort to fists, knives, or guns. Employers often find them unreliable, creditors find them evasive, and landlords run the risk of losing their furnishings along with the rent that is often due. For one thing, many of these hillbilly migrants have a tendency to maintain primary allegiance to their communities in the South rather than to their new homes in the North. When they get into a scrape or lose their jobs or get behind in their rent, they sometimes just quietly pack up and go back home until the whole thing blows over. Needless to say, this is disconcerting to law enforcement officers, landlords, and creditors.

Moreover, the migrants probably find northern cities as hard on them

[19] Albert N. Votaw, "The Hillbillies Invade Chicago," *Harper's Magazine*, Vol. 216 (February, 1958), pp. 64-67.

as they are on the cities. With their typically large families, they are usually unable to find housing that they can afford outside of slum districts. Because of this, many landlords exploit them unmercifully and use the law to coerce payment. Merchants encourage these people, as they do the Puerto Ricans, to use credit in ways that they have no experience with, and then repossess the merchandise when it cannot be paid for. The law sometimes punishes migrants for behavior that is normal and acceptable in their home environment. The city must appear to the migrants to be a very inhospitable place where they can expect fair or predictable treatment only from their own kind.

How soon these migrants will make their peace with the city remains to be seen. Social workers are attempting to teach them vocational and housekeeping skills and to induce the children to attend school regularly. Most of all, they are attempting to cultivate the attitudes that would make successful accommodation to the city possible. In this they may be aided by the church, if a compromise between revivalist and standard denominational churches can be found that will encourage assimilation rather than simply re-enforce their isolation. One thing is certain. The economic base of the border South from which these people come will not permit them to remain in the South. Assimilation into city life appears to be the only probable outcome, no matter how long it takes.

QUALITY

The Differential Birth Rate

A society's birth rate is an average of the higher birth rates of some groups and the lower rates of others. The higher-birth-rate groups account for a larger proportion of succeeding generations than do the lower-birth-rate groups. To paraphrase a beatitude: . . . the high-birth-rate groups . . . shall inherit the earth. People have long speculated on the meaning of such differential birth rates. Any special characteristics of the high-birth-rate groups would appear more and more frequently in future generations. If these characteristics are desirable, the quality of the population would be improved; if they are undesirable, quality would be lowered. Eugenics is founded on these premises and attempts to encourage reproduction of the hereditarily fit and to discourage reproduction of the hereditarily inferior.

Within the United States two instances of birth-rate differentials have received considerable attention. Rural birth rates are higher than urban ones, and birth rates vary inversely with socioeconomic status. Rarely is it contended that the rural population is either markedly superior to, or inferior to, the urban. The rural-urban differential generally is considered to be of primary social significance. Therefore, it will be treated in the chapter on urban and rural problems rather than here. Birth-rate differences according to socioeconomic status, on the other hand, are frequently conceived to have social *and* biological significance.

It is widely known that the economically disprivileged segments of the population tend to have large families, whereas white-collar business and professional groups are more likely to be childless, or to limit the number of children to one or two. The general inference is not that the lower economic groups are biologically more capable of having children, but that the upper economic groups marry later and make more successful use of birth control. Typically, the higher the income, the more respected the occupation, the higher the educational level, and the lower the birth rate. That portion of the population which is college-educated has never, in

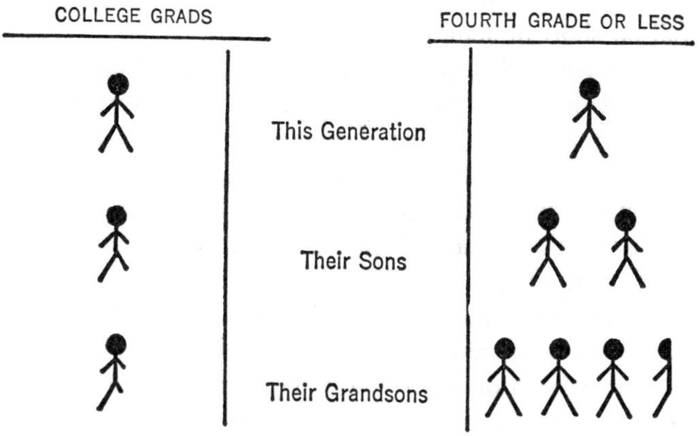

FIG. 9–7. The uneducated have most of the children.

SOURCE: Especially prepared by the Population Reference Bureau, Washington, D.C.

the past, had enough children even to replace itself, while groups with little or no formal education over-reproduce themselves.

How does this affect population quality? The arguments advanced stress biological factors, social factors, or both.

Biological factors. Francis Galton, the English biologist, was among the first to recognize and systematically explore the possible consequences of birth-rate differentials. His conclusions have since been taken over in more or less modified form by large numbers of scholars and laymen. Galton assumed that the biological struggle for survival and natural selection result in persons with greater innate ability or superior genetic endowment rising to the top of the social ladder while the less talented remain on the lower rungs. Hence, the upper classes of society should be the superior biological stocks. The fact that these groups do not adequately reproduce themselves presupposes that the quality of the population is reduced accordingly. The human race, thus, might be breeding itself into mediocrity and, perhaps, eventually out of existence.

To many persons these conclusions have come to represent unquestioned fact, and, though it would be an error to assert that the eugenicists have uncritically accepted them, many eugenics proposals do, in fact, rest upon them. That which is commonly called "negative" eugenics calls for the sterilization of certain classes of people *believed* to have defective heredity. Since 1907, over two-thirds of the states have passed laws permitting or requiring the sterilization of certain groups. Most commonly, the laws call for sterilization of the feeble-minded, but some laws include the psychotic, the epileptic, certain criminal classifications, and certain types of hereditary malformation. The goal, of course, is to prevent the multiplication of hereditarily inferior types. However desirable the goal, the laws fall far short of achieving it.

The basic error in this approach is in its original assumptions, namely, that feeble-mindedness, psychosis, epilepsy, and criminality are completely hereditary and that they can be eliminated or even markedly reduced through sterilization. The difficulties are twofold. First, the role of hereditary factors in causing these difficulties has been greatly overestimated. Probably not more than half of all feeble-mindedness is strictly hereditary, the other half being the product of extremely adverse environmental conditions, birth injuries, disease, and still other factors. [20] Adverse social conditions, as well as genetic factors, can produce feeble-mindedness in generation after generation with whole families being affected. Similarly, only a part of all epileptic cases are hereditary, and even fewer cases of mental illness are entirely genetic in origin. With regard to criminality, hereditary factors now are regarded as negligible. It is the consensus of social scientists that wholesale sterilization of such groups would result in sterilizing large numbers of people who are not organically defective but it would do little to reduce the number of defectives in the next generation.

The second difficulty derives from the fact that most defective organisms are produced not by defectives but by the so-called normal population. At least some of the genes that cause conditions such as organic feeble-mindedness are carried recessively so they may be present even when there are no observable symptoms in the individual. They may remain hidden for several generations, only to reappear. According to a reliable estimate, there are ten times as many normal persons as morons carrying a simple recessive "black" gene for mental deficiency. Most of the carriers of recessive harmful genes cannot be identified; but if they

[20] For a balanced, readable account of the role of heredity in mental deficiency and mental illness, see Amram Scheinfeld, *The New You and Heredity* (Philadelphia, J. B. Lippincott Co., 1950).

could be, and sterilization were recommended, *"Almost every one of us would have to be sterilized!"* [21]

Social factors. Galton and his followers generally failed to recognize the role of *social selection* in determining the placement of individuals within the socioeconomic structure. They assumed, but could not demonstrate, that it is superior innate ability which accounts for the movement of people upward in the class system. It is probable, however, that such nongenetic factors as motivation, shrewdness, and ruthlessness play a role in determining who gets to the top. Moreover, the class system itself exerts a major selective influence. A given class status, once attained, becomes somewhat hereditary. The upper classes may contain many persons of decidedly inferior ability who are able to stay there simply because of the competitive advantages which upper-class status provides them. Similarly, there is believed to be a vast reservoir of potential ability among lower socioeconomic groups which is not tapped because of unfavorable social environment. On these assumptions, a somewhat more realistic eugenics program has been developing.

Poverty-stricken adults beset by malnutrition and illness and living in ignorance, whether or not there be any organic inferiority, are not the best-fitted to bear and raise the young. The upper economic groups, however, with their higher standards of housing, nutrition, medical care, education, and awareness of personal and social responsibility have traditionally had few children. Beyond the question of biologic capacities, large numbers of children have had the cards stacked against them *socially.* Consequently, eugenicists advocate larger families among the upper economic groups and lower birth rates among the economically disprivileged. The expansion of planned-parenthood facilities including adequate and inexpensive birth-control information is basic to the latter. Legal implications of such a program are discussed in Chapter 7. Efforts to raise the birth rates of middle- and upper-income groups have been less widespread. Reports by occasional public and private agencies have stressed the low reproduction rates among college graduates and have urged that these rates be raised. By and large, however, not much has been done. Yet family size among these same middle- and upper-income groups seems to be on the increase. A disproportionate part of the baby boom since World War II has been concentrated in the great middle-income group. Other recent statistics indicate that college graduates are now having enough children to replace themselves for the first time in recent history. [22] To further this trend seems to be the chief eugenic possibility. Little is known about, and even less control can be exerted over, the biological quality of the population. Within existing biological limits, however,

[21] *Ibid., p.* 549. italics in original.
[22] Wilson H. Grabill, Clyde V. Kiser, and Pascal K. Whelpton, *The Fertility of American Women* (New York, John Wiley and Sons, Inc., 1958) p. 388.

considerable use might be made of the superior cultural advantages possessed by upper-income groups.

An Aging Population

Ordinarily we think of "population" as including persons of all ages and we seldom stop to think that some populations may be "younger" or "older" than other populations. Expanding populations with high birth rates tend to be "young" because of the large proportion of infants and children in them. Stable or decreasing populations tend to be "older" because of their low birth rates and smaller numbers of children. Traditionally, the United States has had a young population, but more recently there has been a rapidly increasing proportion of older persons.

During its early history the average age of the United States population was kept down by high birth and immigration rates. The effect of high birth rates has already been mentioned, and immigrants are primarily people in the young adult ages. Married immigrants also tend to have high birth rates. But birth rates have dropped steadily, at least since 1790, and immigration from Europe has virtually ceased. In 1800, the median age was sixteen years; in 1920, it was approximately twenty-five years; in 1945, it was almost thirty years. The average life expectancy increased from 49.2 years in 1900 to 67.5 years in 1950, and has now reached seventy years for the white population. In 1900, there were only 3 million people in the United States who were over sixty-five years of age. The number had increased to 12 million in 1950, is more than 15 million now, and will reach 22 million by 1980. This great increase in the number of aged persons will have extensive repercussions for the population at large.

Before discussing the effects of an aging population, however, the post-World-War-II birth rate again needs to be brought into the picture. Up to 1940 the increased proportion of older persons was accompanied by steadily decreasing proportions of younger persons. The baby boom has again raised markedly the numbers of children under ten years of age. If the birth rate remains high, the *proportion* of older persons will not increase as rapidly as the *number* of older persons. If the birth rate should begin to drop again, the proportion, as well as the number, of older persons will increase rapidly. The additional number of older persons to be expected is already known. What we do not yet know is how many young people there will be to balance the older ones.

In any event, the presence of a large number of older people poses a variety of problems. In many industries, sixty-five years is the compulsory retirement age. Persons beyond this age are largely a dependent population—dependent for even the barest living upon their children and other younger adults. As the proportion of older dependent persons becomes larger, the burden of support will fall more heavily upon each younger adult. Thus, the birth rate is most important. If the birth rate remains high, the proportion of young adults will rise considerably beginning about 1960 and will remain relatively high. If it falls, the burden will be greater. With rare foresight, the federal government anticipated this situation during the 1930's and instituted the Social Security program to help care for the increasing numbers of aged. Widely misunderstood, this

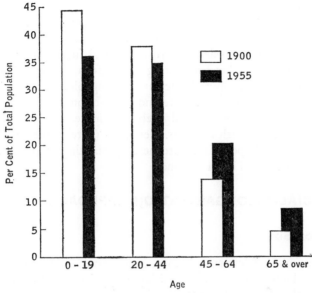

SOURCE: Reproduced from *Progress in Health Services,* Health Information Foundation, June, 1956.

FIG. 9–8. Per cent distribution of United States population, by age, 1900 and 1955.

program has been subjected to continuous criticism as needless taxation. Up to the present, social security taxes *have* built up a considerable surplus (on paper, for, actually, the government has spent the money for other purposes) *but* that surplus will be quickly exhausted and a deficit will result when the number of persons over sixty-five increases. Labor unions, and, increasingly, business, are emphasizing retirement and annuity programs as one way to help meet the needs of the aged. The next twenty or thirty years will probably see considerable expansion of such efforts. It is questionable, however, whether the country can afford to continue its arbitrary retirement philosophy no matter how great its old age assistance efforts. When the number of aged persons was very small, their retirement did not materially reduce the size of the effective labor force. But when the number of persons over sixty-five years of age exceeds 10 per cent of the total population, as it well may within another twenty-five years, their enforced retirement might mean lower standards of living for the entire nation. Certainly per capita production would suffer. Many persons of sixty-five years and more are still capable of performing their jobs efficiently and many physically undemanding tasks now performed by younger men might well become the province of older persons. In managerial and executive positions the value of increased maturity and experience has long been recognized. These same traits should be useful at least in many lesser jobs.

Beyond its employment significance, the changing age structure of the population will have other consequences for the economy. The bright young man of today who desires a rosy financial future should not overlook the expanding market for hearing aids, bifocals, wheel chairs, canes, crutches, and other products in demand among older persons. Clothing manufacturers will need to devote more attention to the conservative styles and colors. Contractors will likely find increased demand for one-floor plan bungalows with no stairs. Geriatrics (care of the aged) may be the coming medical speciality. Attorneys specializing in probate matters (wills and estates) will be in demand.

THE SOCIAL-DISORGANIZATION APPROACH

Population Size

During most of human existence, populations were small, techniques of food production were crude, and large populations were not possible. Though Malthus did not write until the beginning of the nineteenth century, the principles that he expounded probably had been operating through the millenniums—population growth up to the maximum permitted by the level of technology, then relative stability until some new technological advance permitted growth to be resumed. As growth continued, the rate of growth accelerated. The greatest of all stimuli to population growth—the industrial and agricultural revolutions—ushered in a period of change that provides a classic example of social organization yielding to disorganization. And the prospect of reorganization in terms of new norms looms on the horizon.

The relatively slow growth of population up to the Industrial Revolution resulted from a particular balance between birth rates and death rates. Birth rates were high and the average number of children born to married couples was relatively large. Population did not grow rapidly, however, for death rates also were high. In fact, the high death rate actually required a high birth rate, for the average size of the *surviving* family was small! This situation persisted until after the Industrial Revolution.

The Industrial Revolution lowered the death rate by providing modern sanitation and improved medical care, and it also resulted in greatly increased food supplies. With the death rate down, and no increase in the birth rate, population began to grow by leaps and bounds. This is the situation that exists today. In our sentimental fondness for the large families of our grandparents' time, we have been slow to realize that large *surviving* families actually were rare. And we have not yet fully recognized that the birth-rate levels that were functional before the Industrial Revolution have been turned into a major cause of population problems by changes in the death rate.

A well-organized society has birth and death rates adjusted to each other so that a stable society is possible. If population growth outstrips production, or if population shrinks, the traditional social arrangements of the society are disrupted. The present combination of high birth rates and low death rates *cannot long continue*. At the present rate of world population growth, the death rate will inevitably rise again as increased numbers in many parts of the world face starvation. The change in death rates and greatly increased world population calls for reorganization in terms of a lowered birth rate which will restore the historic balance between births and deaths.

Population Quality

Modern technology not only has permitted population figures to push up into the billions, but it possibly has provided a basis for the first large-scale interference with population quality. With increased knowledge of human genetics on the one hand and of human society on the other, a twofold approach to population quality is possible. One possibility is to identify persons of superior heredity and to encourage them to marry and reproduce. Reproduction of the hereditarily unfit would be discouraged. Such a program, however, probably will not be realized until the distant future. Not only is our knowledge of human heredity inadequate to the task at present, but such a program would raise grave questions about the rights of individuals, particularly in democratic societies.

In the form of birth control techniques, technology has so far worked against the reproduction of the groups who probably are best fitted socially to rear the young. Whether or not the middle- and upper-income groups which practice birth control most successfully have any biological superiority, the sociocultural advantages that they possess are not being used to fullest advantage. Perhaps the changes in birth rates since World War II foreshadow another pattern of social change that will see more of the reproduction burden assumed by those who are socially best fitted to assume it.

THE VALUE-CONFLICT APPROACH

International Conflicts

Many people in the United States are prone to assert that "if other nations just were not so backward, we wouldn't have to worry about populations getting too large." The implication is that science has now provided the means for population limitation and sensible persons (or nations) would not hesitate to use them. People who make such statements generally are not aware, of course, of their ethnocentric implications; namely, that any system of values may be unreasonable to persons reared in a different value context. American values typically ascribe great worth to life itself and to high living standards, subordinating most other values to these goals. In some other nations, India is perhaps the best example, human life and welfare must yield to more sacred values. India's economic capacity is greatly reduced by having to support large numbers of sacred cattle and monkeys. The fact that Americans would say, "Slaughter these animals," is of little help when "these animals" are worth more than the people who would do the slaughtering. The unrealism of arbitrarily attempting to impose our values in such situations may become more evident when we realize that a somewhat similar situation exists *within* the United States. Though most Americans favor the limiting of family size to preserve at least minimum adequate living standards, the religious values of some groups define any attempts at limitation to be one of the gravest of sins. The "logical" conclusions of the majority make little difference if the behavior they advocate is believed to be *wrong* or *sinful*. Nor are there any ready solutions when the conflict is between nations where even a clear majority belief does not exist.

There is an additional factor making it difficult to reach agreement at the international level—the power that is latent in numbers. So long as there is a struggle for supremacy among nations, numbers will be a factor in that struggle. Numbers and technological superiority are crucial. With them wars are won and without them wars are lost. When some nations, such as the United States, have definite technological superiority, less advanced nations are forced to rely upon the *size* of their armies. Programs for population limitation have little appeal when survival itself may depend on size.

Birth Control and World Population Policy

Many Americans complain because the economic aid supplied to other nations does so little to raise economic levels or living standards in those countries. Virtually everything goes, ultimately, to feed the continually

. . . it is really very disappointing that the whole problem [of birth control] is being so little studied as it seems to be at present. Contrast it for example with the vast amount of work that is being done on cancer. It is granted that this work is important for the relief of suffering, and also that it is scientifically very interesting indeed, but even if a perfect cure for all forms of cancer were discovered, it would not really make much difference to the future of the world, for the main result would be that there would be a good many more elderly people, past the reproductive age, who would be able to end their lives in comfort.

It would make much more difference to the world if a really good contraceptive drug or something of the kind could be found, and its use adopted on a world-wide scale.

Sir Charles Darwin, "The Pressures of Population," *What's New*, No. 210, (Late Winter, 1959), p. 3.

---

growing populations. Yet the United States, and agencies such as the World Health Organization, are partly responsible for this situation. The very aid that they provide is a major factor in lowering death rates and in increasing the rate of population growth. These increases soak up the additional aid that can be provided and effectively prevent the economic development that is urgently needed. Many governments, including those of India, Japan, and Puerto Rico, want help in establishing birth control programs to cut their birth rates. The United States government, however, avoids any discussion of promoting birth control because of the domestic political repercussions that would surely result. American society is deeply divided upon the morality of artificially preventing conception, and, in many areas, for politicians to take a stand in favor of birth control is tantamount to political suicide. Thus it appears that we will go on indefinitely subsidizing self-defeating rates of population growth.

Homogeneity vs. Melting Pot

"To preserve the national character!" "To maintain our homogeneity!" "To exclude the inferior, the subversive, the unwanted!" "Discrimination!" "Racism!" "Fascism!" "Ignorance of the facts!" These are some of the most frequent battle cries. The issue is immigration, its extent, and its character. The battle is being fought in local communities, in the press, on radio and television, and in Congress.

Proponents of the national-origins theory urge that the United States is no longer a developing country in need of population but a mature nation whose distinctive character has made it the leader among nations. They urge further that the existing composition of the population be maintained; that fairness to the people of the United States and to future citizens requires protection against our being overwhelmed by "foreign" elements. They maintain also that "the realities" of international struggle must be recognized and the United States must exclude all persons who might possibly subscribe to subversive ideologies. All these views are supported by the Immigration and Nationality Act of 1952 (the McCarran-Walter Act).

Opponents of the national-origins theory do not regard the battle as lost, however. They declare that the present policy is un-American, autocratic, and unrealistic. Democracy in the United States, they insist, is built upon the recognition of differences and the faith that out of the free mingling of diverse peoples and philosophies a vigorous nation can develop. They see in the doctrine of national-origins the implicit assumption that southern Europeans and Asiatics are "less desirable," and compare this reasoning to the former Nazi German notion of "Aryan superiority." They assert that the leading national exponent of representative democracy is behaving shamefully like the fascist nations it fought to suppress. Just what the provisions of acceptable immigration legislation would be have not been spelled out in detail. So far, the struggle has been limited to the fight against national origins. But the arguments used indicate a desire to allot immigration quotas on the basis of need and desire to immigrate, with far larger quotas going to non-English speaking nations and the elimination of categorical restrictions against Asiatics. Feelings run high on both sides of the issue and it will likely be reopened in future sessions of Congress.

Freedom vs. Responsibility

Does everyone have the right to reproduce? Or, should everyone have the right to bear children? Is the freedom to bear children dependent on the ability to bear normal healthy children who are not likely to become wards of the state? Should such freedom and responsibility be contingent on one another? One set of values assumes that reproduction is a basic human right which cannot be abridged, no matter what the eugenic implications. According to this view, one might encourage some groups to have children and discourage others, but the decision is ultimately a personal one. Often this reasoning is buttressed by our admittedly limited knowledge of human genetics. Though in some cases the quality of potential offspring may be predicted, in many cases it cannot. Especially when sterilization is recommended to prevent the reproduction of the unfit, the holders of these values see an intolerable interference with a basic human right. The situation is further complicated by the problem of adequate safeguards. Even should one grant the eugenic desirability of

Dr. George W. Beadle, Nobel-Prize-winning geneticist of the California Institute of Technology, said at a forum on "resources of the future" in Washington last week that society would have to decide soon whether individuals should retain the right to determine how many children they will have. He observed that the world population will increase from 2,500,-000,000 in 1950 to 6,250,000,000 in the year 2000. Former Vice-President Henry A. Wallace, an expert on plant genetics, who participated in the forum, said he doubted that "we now have or will have within fifty years knowledge which would enable a genetic dictator to avoid the most serious mistakes."

New York Times.

selective sterilization, how could its unintentional or, perhaps, calculated misuse be prevented? The possible benefits, they say, could never be worth the inherent risks in such a program.

Opposing factions, on the other hand, claim that the right to reproduce may be withheld when the exercise of that right would knowingly be detrimental to the group at large. They see, even in our limited knowledge of genetics, the possibility of greatly reducing the financial and social burden of caring for large numbers of mental and physical incompetents. Frequently they point to selective sterilization surrounded by "adequate" safeguards as the most humane, and only rational, approach to the problem. About half the states, today, have sterilization laws and the *principle* of sterilization has been upheld by the Supreme Court. The actual number of sterilizations performed, however, has been quite low, and more than a third of the total have been performed in one state—California. [23] The California program is both looked to for leadership and is a chief target in the maneuverings and conflicts of other states.

THE PERSONAL-DEVIATION APPROACH

The Genetically Inferior

One of the most difficult problems facing biological and social scientists is to define the role played by heredity and environment in the production of defective, deficient, and deviant organisms. The problem is difficult because in many instances it is not heredity *or* environment but heredity *and* environment which bring the undesirable condition into being. Frequently, an hereditary potential or "tendency" will not appear unless the environmental conditions are adverse, and adverse environ-

[23] Scheinfeld, *op. cit.*, p. 544.

mental conditions will not bring the condition about unless there is some hereditary tendency present. To be hereditary or genetic, the condition must definitely be tied to the operation of one or more genes. The genetic composition is determined at the moment of conception and normally cannot be changed by anything that happens during the lifetime of the individual. But the presence of unfavorable genes does not always produce a deviant organism. Geneticists estimate that practically all persons carry some unfavorable genes. Because it generally takes two or more such unfavorable genes, the deviancy does not appear unless unfavorable genes from the father "match up" with similar genes from the mother. Thus the deviancy may appear several generations apart, in seemingly unpredictable fashion, and still be hereditary. In other instances, the condition may repeat itself in successive generations. Certain recurrent physical abnormalities as, for example, the presence of additional or fewer than the usual number of fingers and toes is known to be hereditary. Blindness, deafness, gross physical deformities, and mental deficiency are *often* hereditary. It is further believed that some family lines carry greater than ordinary susceptibility to certain diseases such as tuberculosis and schizophrenia. The difficulty as we move down this list is that environmental factors come to play larger and larger roles. Between those conditions which are purely hereditary and those which are purely social lie an intermediate group of constitutional deviancies.

The Constitutionally Inferior

Not all conditions that are present at birth are hereditary. Some of these "congenital" conditions are produced by the intra-uterine environment and some are contracted during the birth process. In hemolytic disease, for instance, the genetic combination of an Rh-negative mother and an Rh-positive fetus permits development of the disease *when and if* there is sufficient transmission of antigens and antibodies between mother and child. Hereditary factors alone will not produce the condition and yet, when found, it is present at birth. Syphilis is a good example of a disease frequently believed by the uninformed to be hereditary. Syphilis cannot be inherited but it may be transmitted to the child during birth by a syphilitic mother. Birth injuries, particularly to the head and to the central nervous system, occasionally produce defective and deficient persons for whom little can be done. Such conditions are *congenital* and organic, yet they are not hereditary. In still other cases there may be no abnormality present at birth but there may be a proneness toward diabetes, tuberculosis, epilepsy, and other conditions. The genetic structure may be such that the individual is constitutionally weak in one or more regards, not having inherited any specific diseases but being especially susceptible to them. At the present state of scientific knowledge, however, it has not been definitely proved what constitutional susceptibilities can be inherited.

The Socially Inferior

Research tends to ascribe continually increased importance to social-environmental factors in the production of deviants. Many conditions that were once thought to be purely or principally hereditary in origin are found instead to be socially transmitted. It is now recognized that merely because a given condition tends to run in certain families is not sufficient reason to label it as biological. Many of the ills associated with lower population quality can be reduced through the bettering of environmental conditions alone. Slum conditions, poverty, malnutrition, and filth are capable of producing as much havoc in *physical* functioning of human beings as are genetic factors. Among the diseases, tuberculosis is an excellent illustration. In 1900, tuberculosis resulted in more deaths in the United States than any other disease. Now, thanks largely to improved sanitary conditions, the tuberculosis death rate is only about one-sixth what it was then. To illustrate further: Negroes are widely *believed to be* more susceptible to tuberculosis than whites. True, Negro death rates from tuberculosis are generally far higher than white tuberculosis death rates. *But* Negroes generally live under economic and social conditions far inferior to those of the whites. Examination of the situation in the city of Milwaukee in 1940 revealed that:

The tuberculosis mortality rate among Negroes living in a slum area was fifteen times as high as for whites of the city. But a generation before (in 1915), the rate among whites, mostly foreign-born, who lived in the same depressed environment *had been almost exactly the same as it now was among the Negroes who succeeded them there.* And among descendents of those same whites, now living elsewhere and under much better conditions than their forebears, *the tuberculosis mortality rate had dropped to one-fifteenth*—to the same rate current for other whites in the city. [24]

Not all diseases result so directly from environmental conditions as does tuberculosis, of course, but much of the deviancy in any population is less closely tied to physical factors than is true in the case of physical disease. Adverse environmental conditions play an even larger part in the development of mental and emotional malfunctioning. Fuller discussion of these factors will be reserved for the chapter on personal pathologies.

[24] Amram Scheinfeld, *op. cit.,* p. 172. Italics in original.

SUMMARY

Population problems are chiefly those associated with size, distribution, and quality.

The tremendous size of modern populations is a relatively recent development. The world's population has more than quintupled in the past three hundred years. Throughout history, however, operation of the Malthusian principle—that population size tends to press upon the available means of subsistence—has been applicable. Most of the world today has too many people in proportion to the available resources. The United States and part of Europe have escaped the struggle, temporarily at least, through the tremendous production advances which followed the industrial and agricultural revolutions.

The United States has shown a continuous pattern of growth ever since its founding. Though both birth and death rates have dropped steadily, immigration sustained the pattern of growth until approximately 1920. The period beginning about 1940 saw a reversal in the birth rate with a trend toward larger families. How long this trend will continue is not yet certain.

Since 1921, the United States has followed a policy of drastic limitation of the volume of immigration according to the theory of national origins. This policy, in effect, discriminates against southern Europeans and Asiatics and has virtually cut off immigration to this country.

The United States also has a number of problems related to migration within the country. The migrations of Puerto Ricans to the mainland, of Negroes from South to North, and of whites from the southern mountain areas to northern cities provides examples of groups which are unprepared for urban living. The assimilation of these groups has been handicapped by the possibility of their making frequent visits to their former homes.

The quality of the United States population has been affected by the tendency for lower economic groups to have the highest birth rates, and by the gradual aging of the population. While the lower economic groups may not be biologically inferior, the upper economic groups probably are best fitted to care for large families. The problems created by the aging of the population will depend greatly on whether the birth rate remains high. In any event the production of goods and services will have to take cognizance of the changing age structure.

Rapidly growing populations disrupt the entire social organization. High birth rates, that were functional while death rates were high, now need to be lowered. Conversely, the upper economic groups probably are fitted to have a larger proportion of the children than they now do. The various nations do not agree upon what are desirable population policies and how these may be achieved. Within the United States bitter conflict rages over the morality of birth control, over immigration policy, and over the legalized sterilization of people believed to be hereditarily unfit.

Among the deviant persons in any population may be distinguished the genetically inferior, the constitutionally inferior, and the socially inferior. The socially inferior are probably the largest of these three groups and offer the quickest and surest route to improvement of population quality.

SUGGESTED READINGS

DAVIS, Kingsley, *The Population of India and Pakistan* (Princeton, N.J., Princeton University Press, 1951). The most thorough analysis, to date, of the population of India and Pakistan. For the serious student.

DRAKE, Joseph T., *The Aged in American Society* (New York, The Ronald Press Company, 1958). Includes discussions of attitudes about older people, problems of older workers, problems of retirement, and the social position of older persons.

HANSEN, Marcus L., *The Immigrant in American History* (Cambridge, Harvard University Press, 1940). A readable account of the role played by European immigrants in American history.

MEIER, Richard L., *Modern Science and the Human Fertility Problem* (New York, John Wiley & Sons, Inc., 1959). Explores the growth of human population and surveys developments in physiology and medicine relevant to the control of human fertility.

OSBORN, Fairfield, *Our Plundered Planet* (Boston, Little, Brown & Co., 1948). Neo-Malthusian treatise, highlighting wastage of the world's resources and predicting dire consequences for the world's population.

OSBORN, Frederick, *Preface to Eugenics* (New York, Harper and Brothers, 1940). An able introduction to the eugenics field by a leading United States authority.

TAEUBER, Conrad, and TAEUBER, Irene B., *The Changing Population of the United States* (New York, John Wiley & Sons, Inc., 1958). A survey of population changes in the United States, from 1790 to 1955. Based upon census data.

AUDIO-VISUAL AIDS

Food for Asia (British Information Services, 30 Rockefeller Plaza, New York), 10 minutes, sound, black and white. Produced for the British Foreign Office. Shows that in a war-stricken world the Far East is the greatest sufferer from lack of food. Tremendous efforts are being made to increase the acreage for growing rice and to step up production so that through trade the people may get the food they so desperately need.

Heredity and Environment (Coronet Films, Coronet Building, Chicago), 10 minutes, sound, black and white. Visual examples are shown of heredity and environment at work. An overview is given of cultural inheritances, genetics, environmental influences, and their interrelationships.

Immigration (Encyclopaedia Britannica Films, Inc., 1150 Wilmette Ave., Wilmette, Ill.), 11 minutes, sound, black and white. Photographs and animated maps show how the United States became populated, and why Europeans left the Old World for the New. Scenes of families leaving their homes for this country present the human side of the story.

QUESTIONS AND PROJECTS

1. Why can we not consider American population problems in isolation from world population problems?

2. Describe the Malthusian theory of population growth. What are the *positive* and the *preventive* checks? How applicable are Malthus' theories today? in the United States? in Asia?

3. Explain how the tremendous growth of the United States population was accompanied by a steadily falling birth rate.

4. Why is it not possible to state definitely that a real reversal in birth rate trends has occurred since 1940?

5. What is "the differential birth rate"? Evaluate the belief that the differential birth rate is leading to a lowering of the quality of the United States population.

6. What kinds of problems are likely to be augmented due to the increasing proportion of oldsters in the population?

7. Evaluate the usefulness of the argument: India would have no excess population problem if only the Indians would kill off all the sacred cows and monkeys.

8. In what ways is the national-origins theory consistent with American traditions? In what ways is it contrary to basic American values?

9. Write a short paper on the topic, "Resolved: the unrestricted freedom to reproduce *is not* a universal human right." Then write a second paper on the topic, "Resolved: the unrestricted freedom to reproduce *is* a universal human right."

10. Distinguish among the genetically inferior, the constitutionally inferior, and the socially inferior. Which type or types of inferiority can be most easily eliminated?

11. Major medical break-throughs on cancer, heart disease, and arthritis would lengthen the life-expectancy of older persons by perhaps ten or fifteen years. What effects would this have upon the proportion of aged in the population? Upon pension and retirement systems? Upon family life? Upon political life?

12. It might be possible, through artificial insemination, to improve human stock somewhat as we have improved cattle. What values would interfere with such a program? Should it be promoted despite these values?

13. Read Fairfield Osborn's *Our Plundered Planet*. Now relate the point of view of this book to Malthus' original theory of population growth. Why is this book described as Neo-Malthusian? Evaluate the validity of its arguments.

14. Check the number of births for your county for the years 1934-1938 and for 1954-1958. What is the proportion of increase? To what factors do you ascribe the increase? What effects are the increased numbers of births having upon the community? What are community institutions, schools, and hospitals, doing to adjust to the higher birth rate?

10

Educational Problems and Conflicts

꿔꿔꿔꿔꿔꿔꿔꿔꿔꿔꿔꿔꿔꿔꿔꿔꿔꿔꿔꿔꿔꿔꿔꿔꿔꿔꿔꿔꿔꿔꿔꿔꿔꿔꿔꿔꿔꿔

Recently Mrs. Franklin D. Roosevelt was making friends, as she does, with people of other lands. These people happened to be residents of Moscow. One member of the family was studying Tagalog.

Do we know what Tagalog is? It is a language spoken in the Philippine Islands.

"Surely you have no need to study this tongue," Mrs. Roosevelt commented.

"Not now, but we will later," the Soviet student replied.

The Communists are planning ahead, way ahead.

WILLIAM H. STRINGER
Christian Science Monitor, October 18, 1958

I tell you we don't educate our children in school; we stultify them and then send them out into the world half-baked. And why? Because we keep them utterly ignorant of real life. The common experience is something they never see or hear. All they know is pirates trooping up the beaches in chains, tyrants scribbling edicts, oracles condemning three virgins to be slaughtered to stop some plague. Action or language, it's all the same; great sticky honeyballs of phrases, every sentence looking as though it has been plopped and rolled in poppyseed and sesame.

GAIUS PETRONIUS
The Satyricon, A.D., First Century

FROM SOCRATES DRINKING THE HEMLOCK to last night's PTA, schools have been attacked and defended, teachers have been blessed and damned. At no time in history have we all agreed upon what the schools should be and do. Today is no exception.

THE CHANGING TASK OF EDUCATION

Schools were invented several thousand years ago to prepare a select few for leadership. A century or more ago, public schools were created to teach the three R's to the masses. Today, we are in the midst of a third educational revolution. In the atomic era, education is no longer merely a stairway to personal advancement, but has become a weapon of national survival. At present, one brilliant mathematician may be more valuable than a destroyer, and one radio technician more useful than a platoon of semiliterate infantrymen. The next war will be won—or perhaps averted —by the nation with the best schools, for the nation with the best educational system will, in all likelihood, have the best military weapons.

Early generations had few educated brains and a lot of brawn, which was what most of the work required. Today the situation is reversed. Mechanization and automation are destroying the jobs of the unskilled at an accelerating rate. Between 1910 and 1957, the group engaged in jobs which generally call for some education or training (professional and technical; proprietors, managers, and officials; clerical; skilled workers and foremen) rose from one-third to one-half of all workers. [1] At this moment, there is mass unemployment in the midst of "prosperity," along with severe labor shortages in almost every kind of skilled labor. Those who are unemployed for very long at this time [2] are mainly the uneducated and untrained *for whom there will never again be enough jobs to go around*. In most cases, the boy or girl who leaves school early, fails to learn what has been taught there, or who has no good school to attend, will be condemned to a lifetime of low wages, periodic unemployment, and relief-check living.

Our economic and industrial system cannot continue its growth without great numbers of professionals and technicians of many kinds. *We cannot waste half our brains and survive as a nation or grow as an economic system.* From one-third to one-half our children do not learn to read or write well enough for it to be of much value to themselves or to society. Fewer than half our youths with the intellectual capacity for higher education ever enter a college or professional school, and almost half of them never graduate. If this continues to be true, industrial stagnation and national decline are almost a certainty. Merely to educate a growing number of children as well as we have been doing is not enough to insure national survival.

[1] Rockefeller Brothers Fund, *The Pursuit of Excellence: Education and the Future of America* (Garden City, N. Y., Doubleday & Company, Inc., 1959), p. 7.
[2] In mid-1959, with employment at an all-time peak, over 500,000 had been continuously unemployed for more than twenty-six weeks. (*Monthly Labor Review*, Vol. 83 [February, 1960], p. 196.)

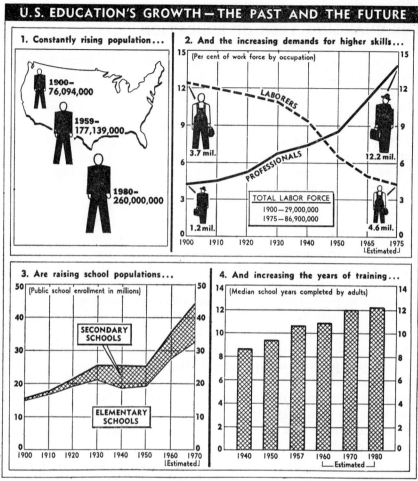

FIG. 10–1. The growth of education in the United States—1900–1980.

PROBLEM AREAS IN AMERICAN EDUCATION

1. Costs: Education Is Expensive

One out of four persons in the United States is attending school this year. In the 1958-1959 school year, we spent about $14 billion on our public schools. This equals $340 for each child, and does not include the parent's cost of keeping the child in school, nor does it include the costs of private and parochial schools, or of colleges and universities. Education is costly, and the cost is steadily mounting. Just how good is the education provided at such great cost?

1. SCHOOLS ARE OBSOLETE AND OVERCROWDED. During the past decade, schools have been built at a record rate, yet they are still overcrowded. There was a twenty-year construction lag between 1930 and 1950, due to the depression and the war, so the postwar tide of children found the schools already overaged and overcrowded. We now need about 45,000 new classrooms a year to provide for growing enrollment, another 20,000 to replace those becoming obsolete each year, and perhaps 2,000 more to replace those destroyed by fires and so on. Los Angeles, for example, will need to open one new thirty-two room school a week for the next fifteen years, just to keep up with growing enrollments. [3] As we are currently building only about 70,000 classrooms a year, we are barely keeping up with growing enrollments and making little dent in the backlog of 140,000 classrooms needed to replace obsolete rooms and relieve overcrowding. [4]

Why cannot a prosperous society which strongly believes in education build enough schools for its children? Perhaps because schools are "low men" on the governmental totem poles. Schools are the only major item of governmental expenditure upon which voters must vote directly to tax themselves. If, for example, voters were asked to tax themselves $100 per family to maintain farm price supports at their present level, the program might not last long! Taxes are at a level which provoke strong protests and widespread evasion. Candidates who are elected to office on a promise to try to cut taxes find that the voters wish to retain most of the governmental services and handouts, and that no great tax reductions are politically possible; meanwhile, the voters fret with a confused sense of helpless frustration. In this frame of mind, the voter may be asked to approve a bond issue and an increased school tax for a new building, and he may express his irritation at taxes in general by voting a thunderous "No!" For most citizens, the school budgets provide almost their only opportunity to vote *directly* against higher taxes. Even many who claim to believe in schools appear to be so resentful of high taxes in general that they seize the first opportunity to register a protest, even at the expense of their own children's future. As long as school construction is financed by bond issues and local property taxation, it is unlikely that we shall ever catch up with building needs, and many children will still attend classes in antiquated buildings, basements, and other substandard accommodations.

2. THE INCREASING TEACHER SHORTAGE. In recent years, despite strenuous efforts to attract more young men and women into teaching, the teacher shortage has not diminished. The number of teachers with incomplete training, teaching on "emergency" certificates has been rising (from 70,000 in 1952 to 95,000 in 1959), and 30,000 additional teachers would

[3] *Time*, Vol. 70 (July 15, 1957), p. 31.
[4] *Fall, 1958, Statistics on Enrollment, Teachers, and Schoolhousing*, U. S. Department of Health, Education, and Welfare, Circular, No. 551, 1959, p. 5.

be needed to relieve oversize classes and half-day sessions. Yet we are making no dent in this accumulated shortage of 135,000 teachers, a figure which has shown no significant decline in over a decade. [5]

In higher education, the shortage is even greater, and will grow greater still! College enrollment is expected to double between 1958 and 1970, calling for 350,000 new college teachers, even with allowance for some rise in student load per teacher. This means that we shall need 25,000

BUILDING CONSTRUCTION $115   OIL & GAS PRODUCTION $120   PRINTING & PUBLISHING $101   STEEL PRODUCTION $124   ALL MANUFACTURING $97   TEACHERS $95*

* $113 a week if year's salary paid in 10 months

SOURCE: United States Department of Labor and National Education Association.

FIG. 10–2. Average weekly earnings by occupation—1959.

to 35,000 new college teachers each year; yet in 1958-1959, only 9,000 entered college teaching. [6] The proportion of new college teachers holding doctor's degrees has already fallen by almost one-third since 1953, while the proportion with *less* than a master's degree has increased. Even if a monumental and entirely successful effort to attract more competent people into college teaching were made at once, a spectacular decline in the qualifications of college teachers, extending into the mid-1960's, is a predictable certainty, since a college teacher cannot be created overnight.

Why do such shortages exist? The work is not unpleasant; one who is temperamentally fitted for teaching finds it to be a stimulating and emotionally rewarding task! The work is socially useful, and the vacations are the envy of other occupations. Yet a recent survey found only about half the men in public school teaching reporting that they would enter

[5] National Education Association, Research Division, "Teacher Supply and Demand in Public Schools," *Research Report*, R-6 (Washington, The Association, 1959), p. 19.

[6] *Ibid.*, "Teacher Supply and Demand in Universities, Colleges, and Junior Colleges, 1957-58 and 1958-59," *Research Report*, R-10, pp. 12, 13, 16, 51.

TABLE 10-1. How does the relative economic status of American teachers compare with that of teachers in other countries?

Country	Ratio of teachers' average annual salaries to per capita income
Syria	10.2
Colombia	9.6
Philippines	8.5
Union of South Africa	6.8
Israel	5.8
Chile	5.6
France	5.1
Austria	5.0
Germany	4.7
Ireland	4.7
Belgium	4.5
Peru	3.9
India	3.6
Sweden	3.6
Cuba	3.5
Ceylon	3.4
Switzerland	3.3
Yugoslavia	3.3
Denmark	3.2
Italy	3.1
Netherlands	3.0
Norway	2.7
Scotland	2.7
England	2.5
New Zealand	2.0
UNITED STATES	1.9
Canada	1.8
Iran	1.7
Australia	1.6

Yearbook of Education, 1953 (Yonkers, N. Y., World Book Company, 1953), p. 106.

teaching again if they had it to do over. [7] The income of teachers does not compare very favorably with that of other occupations which demand far less training, ability, and self-discipline. The average teaching salary of $4792 paid to public school teachers in 1958 is less than the $4911 received by the average factory worker. [8] College teachers did a little better, averaging $6015 in 1958, one-half to one-third the incomes averaged by lawyers, dentists, and physicians. [9] Although differences in working year, regularity of employment, and other factors make a direct comparison somewhat misleading, it is clear that teachers receive meager

[7] National Education Association, *Journal,* Vol. 48 (April, 1959), p. 45.

[8] National Education Association, Research Division, "Economic Status of Teachers in 1958-1959," *Research Report,* R-3 (Washington, The Association, 1959, p. 17; *Monthly Labor Review,* Vol. 82 (July, 1959), pp. 221 ff.

[9] *Ibid.,* "Salaries Paid and Salary Practices in Universities, Colleges, and Junior Colleges, 1957-1958," *Research Report,* R-1 (Washington, The Association, 1958), p. 9.

What price teacher do you want for your son or daughter?

At $2500—you probably will get persons who have not finished college or who have little training for any special kind of work. Semiskilled labor comes higher.

At $5000—a mixture of those with and those without talent for teaching, of those who have graduated from college and those who have not. Many of the best will quit teaching after a few years.

At $7500—assurance of fairly strong college graduates and a good chance of able persons with master's degrees. Emergency teachers could probably be eliminated at this level. At this salary, teaching begins to compete for real talent.

At $10,000—virtual certainty of quality teachers, the majority with two or three degrees. At this level, teaching competes for the best talent available.

National Education Association Journal

financial reward for the extended training, the exemplary character, the pervasive insight, and the unwavering dedication they are expected to display.

Other factors also help explain the teacher shortage. Teachers are overloaded; over 85 per cent of the nation's classes are over the ideal limit of 25 members, and a fifth are over 35 members. [10] Excessively large classes not only make teaching more tiring; they also prevent good teaching and imbue the teacher with a sense of futility. The burden of extracurricular responsibilities grows heavier as more and more tasks are piled onto the school. Some of the 75,000 teachers who leave teaching for other jobs each year complain about lack of administrative support and co-operation, and some even complain that the vigilante activities of self-styled patriots have made it unsafe to teach realistically in certain areas. [11]

The greatest shortage appears to be in the sciences and the industrial arts, perhaps because teachers in these fields can so easily make more money by leaving teaching. Since it is these fields which are most closely connected with technological progress and national defense, this shortage has sobering implications.

The results of the teacher shortage are not hard to recognize. Overcrowded classrooms and neglect of individual needs of pupils may be the most obvious consequences. But in other, less spectacular ways, the quality of teaching is impaired. Many schools, especially those in the poorer states and in the lower paying towns and rural areas, must accept teachers with little college training and with *no professional training* whatever. While

[10] *Ibid., Research Bulletin*, Vol. 36 (April, 1958), p. 51
[11] See "Why I Quit Teaching," as told to Victor Boesen, *The Reporter*, Vol. 11 (July 6, 1954), pp. 18-20; "The Last Brake?" *Time*, Vol. 69 (April 22, 1957), p. 54.

some of these persons may become good teachers anyway, many are not really *teachers* but are merely collective baby-sitters! Many failures continue to teach because there is no better candidate to replace them. As with any profession, some beginners prove to be temperamentally or emotionally unqualified. Some are too erratic or unstable to teach; some cannot keep discipline; some can do no more than keep discipline; some have no understanding of children; some do not like children; some are simply dull and ineffectual. But in today's teaching market, especially in the lower paying systems, a teacher will be retained as long as she can keep the classroom from explosion and the parents from revolt. The normal process of weeding out the incompetents has virtually ceased. It is very rare today for a teacher to be let go for any reason other than immorality, "subversion," or utter failure to keep discipline.

At the college level the results are much the same—fewer fully qualified professors, oversize classes, impersonality, excessive dependence upon textbooks and objective tests, and the acceptance of mediocrity. Students sit, listen, fill out test forms. They never know their professors, rarely talk, rarely write. Courses are hurdles to surmount, not doorways to exciting fields of inquiry. In the elementary school, poor teaching often leads to classroom chaos; at the college level, students just go to sleep, physically and intellectually.

There is little likelihood that the teacher shortage will disappear in the near future. It is doubtful that teaching salaries will be increased enough to attract a greater number of suitable persons into the teaching profession. Some communities show little interest in raising salaries or improving teaching conditions as long as they can staff the schools with baby-sitters. Teachers themselves show little interest in organizing themselves into the aggressive kind of teachers' organization which might succeed in improving their financial status. In fact, our school enrollment is growing so rapidly that the question becomes not, How soon will the teacher shortage be relieved? but, How much worse will it get before it gets better?

3. FEDERAL AID TO EDUCATION: THREAT OR PROMISE? For American youth, "success" begins with picking the right state to be born in. The average Mississippi child in 1959 had a teacher who received $3070 a year, while $181 covered the entire public expense of his year's education. The average New York child had a teacher who was paid $6200 and had $535 of public funds spent on his year's education. [12]

Although the amount of money spent is not an *exact* measure of the quality of education, there is some relation between educational expenditures and educational achievements. In New York State, 13 of each 1000 draft registrants were classed by the armed services as "educationally deficient"; in Mississippi, ten times as many were so classed, and the war

[12] *Ibid.*, "Ranking of the States," *Research Report*, R-4 (Washington, The Association, 1959), pp. 18, 20.

fronts had to wait while the army tried to educate them. In 1957, one of six New York men failed to pass the Selective Service mental test, while one-half the Mississippi men failed to pass. [13] After enlistment, emotional disturbances were more common among these poorly educated soldiers, and the least educated were four times as likely to be ineffective soldiers as the well educated. [14]

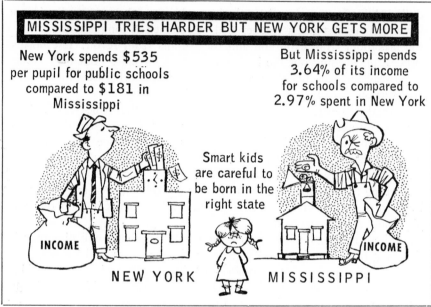

SOURCE: Adapted from *Labor's Economic Review*, Vol. 2 (March, 1957), p. 22

FIG. 10–3. How well can states with high birth rates and low incomes support their schools?

Does this situation exist because Mississippi is *unable* or because it is *unwilling* to afford better schools? Mississippi spends a larger share of its total personal income for schools than does New York—3.64 per cent of Mississippi's income as against 2.97 per cent for New York State. [15] In the ten years before 1958, Mississippi increased its per pupil expenditure on schools by 135 per cent, as against New York's 88 per cent, a greater increase than shown by any other state. [16] Due to its higher birth rate and lower income, Mississippi has only $3,420 of personal income to each

[13] *Ibid.*, p. 9. See also Eli Ginzberg and Douglas W. Bray, *The Uneducated* (New York, Columbia University Press, 1953), Ch. 6, "The Military Performance of the Uneducated."

[14] Columbia University Conservation of Human Resources Project, *The Ineffective Soldier: Lessons for Management and The Nation* (New York, Columbia University Press, 1959).

[15] National Education Association, "*Ranking of The States,*" *Research Report*, R-4, *op. cit.*, pp. 26-27.

[16] *Ibid.*, p. 20.

school age child, while New York has $12,167—almost four times as much. [17] Mississippi, along with a number of other poorer states, cannot afford equally good schools because it has *more children to educate and less wealth with which to pay the costs.*

The vicious circle of educational inequality now becomes apparent. The low per capita income of these states is both the cause and effect of inferior schools. The low incomes make it a practical impossibility for these states to provide schools equal to those of more prosperous states, even though some of the states with the poorest schools are spending a *larger proportion* of their income on education than many states having the highest per pupil expenditures. The inferior schooling, in turn, helps to keep the income of the region low by failing to help children increase their earning power. Thus, the circle of low productivity and inferior education is completed—and perpetuated.

These educational deficiences affect the national interest in time of war, both by reducing the productivity of our economy and by reducing the efficiency of our armed forces. In peacetime the national interest is also involved, since the "graduates" of substandard schools do not stay home. Those states with the lowest school expenditures are also the states with the highest birth rates. It is these states which provide a great many of the migrants to the industrial towns and cities of the North and West. These migrants are, then, coming from the areas where the schools are least able to prepare them to migrate, to enter the urban labor market advantageously, and to become useful citizens of their new communities. In these and other ways the people of New York and Illinois share the results of poor schools in Mississippi and Alabama, whether they wish it or not. Since our need for unskilled workers is falling so rapidly, large numbers of functionally illiterate workers from educationally impoverished areas will not be of much use in the kind of economy we are developing.

The National Education Association has called for a "massive infusion of federal funds" in the form of grants to the states for school construction and teachers' salaries. [18] Such proposals have been repeatedly rejected by Congress, although more modest proposals have been enacted. Land-grant colleges have received federal aid for nearly a century. Several hundred school districts whose schools were overrun by defense workers' children have received federal aid. The National Defense Act of 1958 provided one billion dollars over four years for a number of grants, including scholarships for college students. The question is not *whether* there will be federal aid, but *how much there should be,* and *how it should be allocated.*

Opponents charge that federal aid to education is unnecessary, waste-

---

[17] *Ibid.*, p. 30.
[18] *Michigan Education Association Journal*, Vol. 36 (December 1, 1958), p. 175.

ful, and socialistic [19]—charges which are quite easily refuted. [20] Opposition comes from several sources, including people who are more interested in reducing federal taxes than they are in improving education, and those who fear that federal aid would bring federal control. Whether a measure

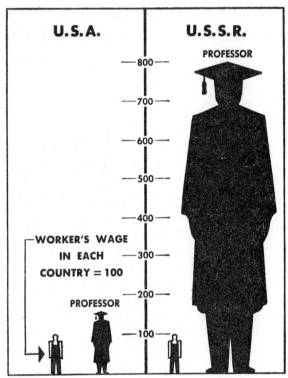

SOURCES: Center For International Studies, Massachusetts Institute of Technology: National Education Association; McGraw-Hill Department of Economics.

FIG. 10–4. The Russian professor earns 8 times as much as an average Russian factory worker. Professors in the United States make only 1½ times our average factory worker's pay.

of federal control of education would be harmful or beneficial might be debated, but it is clear that we already have considerable federal aid

[19] Roger N. Freeman, *School Needs in the Decade Ahead* (Institute for Social Science Research, 1958); Government Economy Committee, *Does Public Education Need Federal Aid?* (New York, National Association of Manufacturers, 1956.)

[20] National Education Association, Research Division, *Can Our Public Schools Get By With Less?* (Washington, The Association, 1958); "Critique of Chamber of Commerce Federal Aid Policy," *School and Society*, Vol. 85 (May 11, 1957), pp. 170 ff; National Education Association, Legislative Commission, *Federal Funds For Schools: Facts vs Fallacy* (Washington, The Association, 1957).

which has *not* been accompanied by federal control. [21] Since neither Congress, nor educators, nor the states, nor localities *want* federal control, it is difficult to see just how it would materialize.

The problem of the cost of education will never be settled to everyone's satisfaction for not everyone has the same values. How important *is* education, after all? Several recent surveys have called for a doubling of our expenditures on education within a few years. [22] This would require that we increase our educational contribution from about 3.5 per cent to 5 or 6 per cent of our national income. How much *should* we sacrifice to improve education—or, perhaps, to keep it from deteriorating any more than it already has? The Soviet Union is reportedly spending between 10 and 15 per cent of her national income on education, [23] as part of her massive effort to nose us out of world leadership. What odds would you give on her chances?

2. The Curriculum: What Should American Schools Teach?

Neither educators nor laymen are agreed upon what the school should be and do. One survey of pressures upon school superintendents reports that 59 per cent were under community pressure to concentrate upon the three R's, 64 per cent were under pressure to offer a greater variety of courses, and some were obviously under pressure to do both. Some 39 per cent of the superintendents reported protests against addition of new school services, such as guidance and health programs, while 63 per cent had demands for such services. Twenty-nine per cent of them were pressed to introduce new teaching methods, while 43 per cent faced protests against such innovations. Forty per cent faced demands for less emphasis on athletics; 58 per cent reported pressure for more emphasis on athletics. [24]

At least three different kinds of curricula are in use in American schools. *The classical curriculum* is the traditional one, emphasizing foreign and ancient languages, history, literature, mathematics, and pure science. This was once useful in preparing a limited number of selected young men for college and the professions and in preparing a limited number of selected young women to be highly ornamental. This curricu-

[21] Benjamin Fine, "Federal Aid for Schools Has Not Resulted in Federal Control in Cases Studied," *New York Times*, June 14, 1957, IV, p. 9; H. Zeitlin, "American Pattern of Education Control and Authority: Some Perspectives Provided by the Experience of the New Deal Period," *Educational Record*, Vol. 40 (April, 1959), pp. 108-112.

[22] Rockefeller Brothers Fund, *op. cit.*, p. 34; *New York Times*, May 24, 1959, p. 1.

[23] Office of Education, U. S. Department of Health Education, and Welfare, *Soviet Commitment to Education: Report of The First Official U.S. Educational Mission to the U. S. S. R.* (Washington, Government Printing Office, 1959), p. 13.

[24] Neal Gross, *The Pressures and Dilemmas of the School Superintendent*, summarized in *New York Times*, May 2, 1954, IV, p. 9.

lum although quite practical for the select few who went to college, was less useful for the great masses who began crowding into high school after the turn of the century. Yet, outside of the larger cities and more progressive towns, a basically classical curriculum, called a college preparatory curriculum, continues to be the primary curriculum emphasized in a great many of the high schools. Ironically, it is often those towns with the smallest proportion of students going to college which emphasize the college preparatory course most heavily, often because they have nothing else to offer.

The vocational curriculum abandons such ornamental material in favor of preparing the student for a job. To many students, the vocational curriculum brought a chance to learn something which appeared useful to them in place of studies which had little meaning in terms of their interests and values. Many students have had their interests stimulated, their school adjustment transformed, and their adult earning power developed as a result. But often there is little relation between the vocational training offered and the job opportunities available in the locality. In many an agricultural village, more boys study auto mechanics than study agriculture. Many high schools crank out a dozen "secretaries" or "bookkeepers" each year in villages where only one secretary or bookkeeper is hired each decade. Much allegedly vocational training is offered not because that particular training is needed by the students, but because many students will not accept the college preparatory curriculum. Students of limited ability or of lower-class origin who have little interest in a college preparatory course are herded into vocational courses in order to keep them occupied until they may legally drop out of school. [25] For these students the vocational curriculum is just an educational waiting-room rather than an avenue to employment.

The life-adjustment curriculum describes a third curricular approach. Consisting of a wide variety of courses and combinations, this is the approach most widely supported (and least widely employed) by educators. Emphasis is placed on the personality development of the student and the social usefulness of what he studies. Many traditional course titles may remain, but course content is vastly changed. Although much traditional subject matter is covered, much of it is learned through projects and group activities rather than through traditional recitation and drill. Personality characteristics such as initiative and self-confidence, and social skills such as ability to participate in a discussion, organize a work project, or conduct a parliamentary meeting, are considered to be at least as important as the ability to parse a sentence or prove the binomial theorem. This is an eclectic approach, drawing from many sources and seeking to functionalize all learning areas and levels. [26]

[25] A. B. Hollingshead, *Elmtown's Youth* (New York, John Wiley & Sons, Inc., 1949), Ch. 8.

[26] For a concise statement of the life-adjustment curriculum, see National Association of Secondary School Principals, *Planning for American Youth: An Educa-*

Critics of the life-adjustment curriculum charge that pupils are not required to work but are permitted to loaf and bluff, that basic factual learnings and intellectual skills are neglected, and that much school time is wasted in noneducative activities and frivolities. [27] Some very sweeping indictments of present school practices have been issued, based largely on the technique of generalizing on single cases. [28] (For example, a charge that "schools waste students' time" is "proved" by describing a single school where the students spent several days making a stage set.) When Russia beat us to the stratosphere with the first earth satellite, there were renewed demands that our schools quit fooling around and get busy on solid subject matter. [29]

Charges that pupils are not learning basic subject matter as well as formerly are easily disproved by dozens of surveys of comparative learning achievements, all showing that the present generation of children know as many or more basic facts than their parents did at the same grade level. [30] There is little doubt, however, that *in some instances* charges of wasted time, aimlessness, and sloppy standards are justified. Like most new developments, life-adjustment education has sometimes carried a practical approach to an impractical extreme. [31] As in every field, there are some teachers and administrators who go off the deep end with each innovation. And it probably requires far more judgment and teaching skill to develop an integrated unit of meaningful activities than to conduct a spelling drill. In some instances, the language of life-adjustment education has been invoked to excuse aimlessness and inefficiency.

The progressive education movement formed the main guide for the changes taking place in the curriculum during much of the second

---

tional Program for Youth of Secondary-School Age (Washington, National Education Association, 1944). This pamphlet is a condensation of Educational Policies Commission, *Education for All American Youth* (Washington, National Education Association, 1944). See also National Education Association, "Life Adjustment Education," *Research Bulletin,* No. 35, Part IV (December, 1957), pp. 141-148.

[27] Arthur E. Bestor, "Life Adjustment Education: A Critique," *American Association of University Professors, Bulletin,* No. 38 (Autumn, 1952), pp. 413-441; *Ibid., Educational Wastelands: The Retreat From Learning in Our Public Schools* (Champaign, University of Illinois Press, 1953); Albert Lynd, *Quackery in the Public Schools* (Boston, Little, Brown & Co., 1953); R. T. Flesch, *Why Johnny Can't Read* (New York, Harper and Brothers, 1955); Hyman G. Rickover, *Education and Freedom* (New York, E. P. Dutton & Co., Inc., 1959).

[28] See E. G. Pogue, "How To Become an Education Critic in Ten Easy Lessons," *Education Digest,* Vol. 24 (November, 1958), pp. 32-33.

[29] Hyman G. Rickover, *op. cit.*

[30] See A. Conrad Posz, "We Just Want the Facts, Sir," *Michigan Education Journal,* Vol. 31 (March, 1954), pp. 316-318, for a summary of numerous such studies; see also Louis E. Raths and Phillip Rathman, "Then and Now; Some Research Findings on the Effectiveness of Teaching the Three R's," National Education Association, *Journal,* Vol. 41 (April, 1952), p. 214.

[31] For a development of this viewpoint, see Paul B. Horton and Rachel Y. Horton, "False Dichotomies and Educational Perspective," *Michigan Education Journal,* Vol. 29 (September, 1951), pp. 5-8; condensed in *Education Digest,* Vol. 17 (November, 1951), pp. 19-21.

quarter of this century. Finding its original inspiration in John Dewey, progressive education sought to replace mechanical drill and memorization of unrelated facts with purposeful integrated learning. It sought to make education a process of pupil growth *through learning activities which appear interesting and worth while to the pupil now,* rather than making education a process of storing away information for use in some remote future. Thus motivated, it was believed that pupils would not only learn subject matter more quickly but would also develop a set of study methods, social skills, attitudes, and other personality outcomes vastly superior to those developed by the traditional school.

The basic viewpoints of progressive education have been widely accepted (and somewhat less widely applied) in American education. The progressive education movement, as an organized movement, has recently languished for lack of spirited opposition *among educators.* The Progressive Education Association has disbanded as its major principles, shorn of their more extreme enthusiasms, have ceased to be controversial *among educators.* Most educators and teachers feel that they have incorporated the enduring contribution of progressive education into their thinking and that the label has become meaningless. *Laymen,* however, often invoke the term *progressive education* in making their criticisms of whatever they dislike about the school system. Progressive education often gets the blame for everything that goes wrong in the school, whether it is actually a part of the philosophy of progressive education or not.

The athletic program is another highly controversial aspect of the curriculum of the school. Should the athletic program of the high school or college be primarily an activity program, which urges *all* students to develop a number of athletic interests and skills? Or should it emphasize the production of winning teams and sporting events in which highly trained specialists perform while the student body and townspeople watch, identify, and cheer? Recent exposés have made common knowledge of the commercialization of athletics, especially by many of the larger colleges and universities. It is no secret that academic standards are sometimes corrupted, student athletes exploited, coaches reduced to nervous wrecks, and college finances jeopardized so that the students and others may enjoy a spectacle. [32] It is no secret that many, possibly most, big-time football teams are composed of professional players, secretly paid through devious subterfuges which enable them to maintain the pre-

---

[32] Cf. Virginius Dabney, "The Ivy-Covered Fraud," *Reporter* (November 27, 1951), pp. 38-40; Excerpts from Judge Streit's, "Comments on College Basketball Fixing Scandal," *New York Times,* November 20, 1951, pp. 1, 26; Jeff Cravath and Melvin Durslag, "The Hypocrisy of College Football," *Collier's,* Vol. 132 (October 30, 1953), pp. 30-33; Jack Newcombe, "Athletes Tell How Illicit Pay-Offs Destroy the Amateur Code," *Life,* Vol. 40 (April 30, 1956), pp. 113 ff; Don Faurot, "Is College Football Worth Saving?" *Saturday Evening Post,* Vol. 231 (October 18, 1958), pp. 36 ff.

tense of amateur status. Both the athletes and the rest of the student body receive a liberal education in the art of "getting around" the laws and regulations one pretends to honor—a point which has provoked caustic comment about the campus as a center of moral and spiritual growth and about football as a builder of character.

Although the subsidization problem affects mainly the larger universities, the small college and the high school face the question of whether to sacrifice the general athletic program in a bid for a winning team. Seldom is there money and staff enough to do both. And, more important, emphasis on the winning team means that both students and faculty come to feel that this is important, while ordinary participation is less important. The promotions and the testimonial banquets go to those who coach winning teams, not to those instructors who instill in masses of students a fondness for archery or handball. The wealthy alumni, who are often said to control college athletics, are unlikely to excuse a coach's failure to have a winning team because of his success in encouraging intramural sports.

If an occasional high school principal or college president attempts to shift emphasis from competitive athletics, he may not last very long. Many educators severely criticize the emphasis upon winning games and would like to encourage general student participation in athletic activities, [33] but they cannot easily challenge the status quo. Alumni are powerful, and alumni good will is necessary. Private colleges would close without the contributions of loyal alumni, and public institutions need loyal alumni to lobby for them in the legislature. High school coaches seldom forget that the townspeople are more interested in seeing spectacular games than in knowing how many students have learned how to swim. Manufacturers of sporting goods remember that a football team will wear out a gratifying number of suits, balls, and footwear in an active season. The students themselves, who have never been offered any real choice in the matter, appear to be well satisfied with the status quo. So the educator who is dissatisfied (and not all are) finds it expedient to invoke the folklore of sportsmanship to sanctify the athletic status quo and direct his attention to matters he can more easily control.

3. Academic Freedom: How Much Freedom Do We Want?

Socrates was neither the first nor the last teacher to suffer because he persisted in teaching ideas that other people disliked. For, in most times and places, the teacher has been commanded to be not a searcher for truth but a propagandist for the approved values. During only a few brief moments in history have teachers been permitted to encourage students to search for truth, regardless of where the search might lead. These

[33] See Educational Policies Commission, *School Athletics: Problems and Policies* (Washington, National Education Association, 1954).

> Academic freedom and tenure do not exist because of a peculiar solicitude for the human beings who staff our academic institutions. They exist, instead, in order that society may have the benefit of honest judgment and independent criticism which otherwise might be withheld because of fear of offending a dominant group or transient social attitude.
>
> Clark Byse and Louis Joughin, *Tenure in American Higher Education: Plans, Practices, and the Law* (Ithaca, N. Y., Cornell University Press, 1959).

islands of rationality represent, in part, the achievement of those for whom truth itself comprises a worthy value, and who believe that truth is best protected from corruption by maintaining an atmosphere of freedom of speech and inquiry. Jefferson, founder of the first state university in America, the University of Virginia, expressed this faith in writing: "This institution will be based on the illimitable freedom of the human mind. For here we are not afraid to follow truth wherever it may lead, nor to tolerate error, so long as reason is left free to combat it." [34]

But truth is costly. It often demolishes cherished beliefs and hallowed traditions. It often undermines comfortable vested interests and threatens a profitable sinecure. The scientific truth about the composition of Jewish and gentile blood would have undermined Hitler's political propaganda, so German scientists dared not publish this truth. The true biographies of the persons who are Russian heroes and villains at any particular moment would not always fit the roles in which they are cast, so Russian biography must be rewritten as individuals rise or fall in official favor. The truth about the relative nutritional qualities of butter and oleomargarine was most unpopular with those who wished to protect the market for butter, and some professors who published objective nutritional studies soon faced demands for their dismissal. For every truth, there are usually a number of people whom it will distress and who may wish to suppress it.

Still more dangerous to the search for truth, however, may be those people who lack Jefferson's faith in the ability of truth to defend itself, but feel it necessary to protect truth by suppressing error. To suppress error requires that books and magazines be censored, that movies and television shows be censored, that textbooks and teaching materials be inspected and approved, and that teaching be purged of all who harbor unconventional thoughts. It is a determined effort to do just this which has provoked what many educators are calling the greatest academic freedom battle of American history. [35]

[34] Jefferson to William C. Jarvis, September 28, 1820, in *The Writings of Thomas Jefferson*, Vol. XV, (Library Edition, Washington, 1903), p. 278.

[35] See Robert M. MacIver, *Academic Freedom in Our Time* (New York,

What is academic freedom? By *academic freedom* is meant *the freedom to seek and impart knowledge without any limitations except those inherent in the search for knowledge.* [36] If one really searches for knowledge, he must accept facts honestly, he must consider *all* the relevant facts, he must welcome honest debate and be willing to revise his conclusions in the light of new-found facts. These limitations are inherent in the search for knowledge. Other limitations—that one must not shock students with material for which they are too immature, that one must operate within the standards of good taste and personal discretion, that one must not propagandize for pet ideas but must present objectively all sides of controversial issues—these limitations inhere within the task of *imparting* knowledge. Academic freedom does *not* include the right to do or say whatever one wishes. Academic freedom includes the right to reach conclusions through scholarly investigation, but does not include the right to *act* in accord with these conclusions if such action is against the law. Academic freedom is not license.

Academic freedom demands the freedom to seek and impart knowledge *without any external authority* telling teachers what they may or may not teach. Academic freedom grants neither the church, nor the state, nor any private organization the right to tell teachers what books they may not assign or what ideas they may not teach. The state may properly require that certain *subjects* be taught but may not decree *how* they must be taught, or which ideas must be taught. For example, the state may legitimately require the teaching of American history; but for the state, or a newspaper, or a "patriotic" society to insist that teachers depict the

---

Columbia University Press, 1955); Louis Joughin, "The Current Questionings of Teachers: Notes for a Social Pathology," *Social Problems*, Vol. 1 (October, 1953), pp. 61-65; Paul F. Lazarsfeld and Wagner Thielens, Jr., *The Academic Mind: Social Scientists in a Time of Crisis* (Glencoe, Ill., The Free Press, 1958).

[36] The American Association of University Professors defines academic freedom as:

(*a*) . . . full freedom in research and in the publications of the results, subject to the adequate performance of his other duties. . . .

(*b*) . . . freedom in the classroom in discussing his subject, but he should be careful not to introduce into his teaching controversial matter which has no relation to his subject. . . .

(*c*) The college or university teacher is a citizen, a member of a learned profession, and an officer of an educational institution. When he speaks as a citizen, he should be free from institutional censorship or discipline, but his special position in the community imposes special obligations. As a man of learning and an educational officer, he should remember that the public may judge his profession and his institution by his utterances. Hence he should at all times be accurate, should exercise appropriate restraint, should show respect for the opinions of others, and should make every effort to indicate that he is not an institutional spokesman. (From "1940 Statement of Principles," as printed in *American Association of University Professors Bulletin*, Vol. 39 [Spring, 1953], pp. 122-123.) See also pamphlet, *Academic Freedom and Academic Responsibility* (New York, American Civil Liberties Union, 1953); M. Mark, "Meanings of Academic Freedom," *American Association of University Professors Bulletin*, Vol. 43 (September, 1957), pp. 498-506.

United States as a saint and Great Britain as a villain would be an invasion of academic freedom.

There have been many such invasions in our history. [37] Every great crisis in American thought—the Revolution, the sedition controversy between Federalists and Republicans, the slavery question, the evolution debate, the temperance issue, the surge of nationalism following World War I—each provoked determined efforts to control the ideas taught in schools and colleges. Earlier periods allowed far less academic freedom than is enjoyed today, for it was generally assumed that teachers should reflect the conventionally approved opinions of the period. The slavery question, for example, resulted in wholesale firings of teachers, college professors, and ministers in both North and South, together with the burning of some newspaper publishing offices. For more than a half century following the Civil War, two sets of history books were published—Northern and Southern—for neither the Grand Army of the Republic nor the Daughters of the Confederacy would allow an objective history textbook to be used.

The present invasions of academic freedom. At no time in American history has academic freedom aroused such a controversy as rages today. While earlier periods tolerated little academic freedom, a great many Americans today expect and treasure the academic freedom which many other Americans seek to curtail. There has been widespread popular acceptance of the idea that schools should study controversial issues, should present both sides, and encourage students to think things through. Recently, however, many groups who claim to intend no attack on academic freedom are nevertheless doing a number of things that tend to make academic freedom impossible to exercise. A series of Congressional investigations have located no *present* Communists among college professors, but of those professors who admitted *past* membership, or refused to co-operate with the investigating committee, two-thirds have been dismissed. [38] Of a representative national sample of 2450 college professors, four out of five felt that outside pressures were greater than a few years earlier, and two-thirds of these felt that education had been damaged. [39] By a two-to-one majority, they felt that in filling vacancies at their institutions, a meritorious candidate who was somewhat unconventional would lose out to the candidate of lesser merit but greater conventionality. [40] Two-thirds of those with an opinion felt that students had become less willing to join student organizations concerned with possibly unpopular beliefs. [41] Many of the professors in this survey were fearful lest

[37] See Howard K. Beale, *A History of Freedom of Teaching in American Schools* (New York, Charles Scribner's Sons, 1941); also, Howard K. Beale, "Teacher as Rebel," *The Nation*, Vol. 176 (May 16, 1953), pp. 412-414.
[38] Paul F. Lazarsfeld and Wagner Thielens, Jr., *op. cit.*, p. 70.
[39] *Ibid.*, pp. 36, 377.
[40] *Ibid.*, p. 390.
[41] *Ibid.*, p. 386.

The inclusion of a Russian folksong in the repertoire of the glee club at the Berry Hill Grade School here was just a mistake in judgment, the Board of Education said today.

After a special Saturday meeting, school officials cleared the music teacher . . . of any subversive intent. His patriotism was vindicated . . . (after he) had apologized for introducing the song and had admitted "an error in judgment."

The song, "Moscow," written in 1942 by a Russian composer, had been included in the program for a recital scheduled next month. The Glee Club . . . had planned to sing patriotic songs from the United States, France, England, and Russia.

The disputed song was banned this week after parents complained.

The New York Times, May 25, 1958, p. 4.

their interview schedules fall into the hands of Congressional investigators and make trouble for them or their institutions. [42] A rash of loyalty oaths, some of them so vaguely worded that they might apply to almost anything, have caused the more independent teachers to wonder what may be the test of "loyalty" tomorrow. A few years ago, alleged Communism was the main cause of dismissals; today, racial integration is replacing it, and teachers are being dismissed in some areas if they belong to an organization (for example, National Association for the Advancement of Colored People) which urges obedience to the orders of our federal courts respecting segregation. [43]

Not only the teacher, but also his teaching materials are under suspicion. According to a *New York Times* survey a few years ago: [44]

A concerted campaign is underway over the country to censor school and college textbooks, reading materials, and other visual aids. Voluntary groups are being formed in nearly every state to screen books for "subversive" or un-American statements. . . . Librarians are intimidated by outside pressures in their choice of books and other materials. Unwilling to risk a public controversy, they meekly accept the requests of the self-appointed censorship groups. Several textbooks and other materials have already been removed from school or college libraries and are effectively on the "blacklist."

This drive has continued, with textbook censorship laws under consideration by the legislatures of twenty-four states in 1959. [45] Several organ-

[42] *Ibid.*, pp. 279-280.
[43] See *Chapter Letter* No. VI, 1959, American Association of University Professors, July 27, 1959.
[44] Benjamin Fine, "Textbook Censors Alarm Educators," *New York Times*, May 25, 1952, p. 1.
[45] *Chicago Sun-Times*, June 8, 1959, p. 8.

izations, including the Daughters of the American Revolution, publish lists of "approved" textbooks, with only one in five high school social science books meeting DAR standards. [46] Any textbooks containing any criticisms of the private enterprise system, or saying anything favorable about publicly owned power plants, socialized medicine, the welfare state, or the United Nations, is likely to be rejected. [47] Any textbook which surveys our institutions in an atmosphere of critical appraisal instead of one of resounding admiration is under suspicion.

Any textbook censorship or textbook evaluation law is an insult to the teaching profession, for it implies that teachers are either disloyal, incompetent, or both. More serious, however, is its exposure of the school system to the pressure of private groups to exclude any but their own views from the schools. A certain road to a politics-ridden, demoralized school system is to allow textbook approval to become the football of private pressure groups.

The consequences: who loses when academic freedom suffers? It is widely agreed among educators that academic freedom suffered during the "McCarthyism" of the postwar era. A number of surveys during the early 1950's showed teachers to be timid, cautious, and fearful of dealing with controversial issues lest they be attacked personally. [48] Anxiety appears to have somewhat subsided, but a legacy of loyalty oaths and play-it-safe attitudes remains. Professors are loath to act as faculty advisors to student organizations dealing with controversial or unpopular ideas, and students are wary of joining any group which might be suspect in a security clearance investigation years later. The vigorously argumentative campus atmosphere of the 1930's and 1940's has given way to one which is safe, conventional, and unimaginative. Possibly the preoccupation with trivialities, of which the college is so often accused, [49] may be in part due to the diversion of students' interests from dangerous ideas to campus nonsense.

It is clear that *academic freedom is not merely a convenience for the teacher, but a necessity for a free society.* When academic freedom is

[46] *Ibid.*

[47] See E. Merrill Root, *Brainwashing in the High Schools: An Examination of Eleven American History Textbooks* (New York, Devin-Adair Co., 1958), which surveys eleven widely used textbooks, finding them all hostile to the free enterprise system and tinged with subversion; this book has been generally dismissed by scholars as prejudiced and dishonest. See reviews in *New York Times Book Review*, November 23, 1958, p. 20; *Social Education*, Vol. 23 (March, 1959), p. 138; T. Ebensen, "How Far Have the Book Burners Gone?" *School Executive*, Vol. 76 (May, 1957), pp. 69-71; condensed in *Education Digest*, Vol. 23 (October, 1957), pp. 10-12; M. Hamburg, "Case of the Subversive Text," *School Executive*, Vol. 77 (April, 1958), pp. 59-61.

[48] "New York Times Survey Shows Liberalism Declining under Current Political Tensions and Pressures," *New York Times*, May 10, 1951, p. 1; May 11, 1951, pp. 26, 29; *Time*, Vol. 63 (April 5, 1954), p. 46.

[49] For example, Jerome Ellison, "Are We Making a Playground out of College?" *Saturday Evening Post*, Vol. 231 (March 7, 1959), pp. 19 ff.

impaired, the main casualties are *not* the teachers, most of whom form a quite conservative group who can easily accommodate themselves to the prevailing orthodoxies. The real casualty is *independent, critical thinking.* The dominant note in nearly all discussions of academic freedom in educational journals is concern over "the growing paralysis of thought in the nation's classrooms. The play-safe attitude in teaching, induced largely by the activities of fanatical vigilantes, has been one of the main concerns of national educational organizations." [50]

The real issue. The issue is not whether Communism should be taught, or whether Communists should teach. Every major educational organization in America has agreed that Communist Party members, having abandoned the objective search for truth by submitting to the discipline of an absolute faith, are unfit to teach. No responsible person familiar with the facts believes that any significant number of true Communists remain among American school and college teachers, and in this most critics agree. [51] Any Communist can remain a teacher in the present atmosphere only by refraining from all communistic propagandizing. The real issue is not Communism, since it is no present ideological threat and has no influential defenders in American education. The real issue in the academic freedom controversy is between (1) those who believe that truth can protect itself and those who believe that truth must be helped out by suppressing the expression of error; and between (2) those who want an objective treatment of social issues and those who want special treatment for their ideas. There are some people who label as "Communism," "socialism," or "subversion" almost any ideas which disagree sharply with their own. In attacking subversion, these people are really insisting that no ideas but their own should be taught. Their ideas seem so unmistakably right to them that they do not realize the bigotry of their position. Like an Illinois congressman who was surprised when people criticized his statement that the purpose of a proposed antisubversive bill "was not to prohibit exploration of ideas but to prevent people from reaching the wrong conclusions," [52] they are puzzled and hurt when critics suggest that they have no understanding of democratic freedom. But their benign intentions make them, nonetheless, the enemies of academic freedom. And whether, in coming decades academic freedom will regain the ground it has lost, or lose still more, is a question few social scientists would care to answer.

[50] Malvina Lindsay, "Intimidating Teachers," reprinted from *Washington Post* (D.C.) in National Education Association, *Journal*, Vol. 41 (October, 1952), p. 411. Even the textbooks have assumed a "gray flannel cover," according to the textbook analyst for the New York City Board of Education, who says that they avoid controversy by articifially "balancing" issues so as to please the partisans on every side. (*New York Times*, February 14, 1960, IV, p. 9.)

[51] See Robert W. Iverson, *The Communists and The Schools* (New York, Harcourt, Brace & Co., 1959).

[52] Quoted in *Civil Liberties*, monthly newssheet of American Civil Liberties Union, September, 1953, p. 3.

4. . . . and Still Other Educational Problems . . .

There are many other educational problems that might be explored, although there is space to mention only one or two. *The financial plight of the private colleges* in a period of rising costs has attracted widespread concern. [53] To meet this crisis, the private colleges within a region often band together for co-operative fund-raising, with a strong appeal for contributions from corporations. A number of business leaders have responded, saying that American business should support the private colleges which educate so many business executives and which serve as insurance against the possibility of a politically dominated government's monopoly of higher education. Business concerns donated over $136 million to private American colleges in 1958, plus additional funds for equipment and research. This increasing dependence of private colleges upon corporate contributors gives rise to still another problem: will this dependence result in subtle pressures to teach only those points of view most agreeable to business interests? The generous provision of free pamphlets, films, and other materials by business concerns, trade associations, and, to a lesser extent, labor organizations, also raises the question of how schools and colleges shall use such free materials without becoming propagandists for the donors. [54]

In a society in which agriculture becomes steadily more specialized and is highly dependent upon migrant, seasonal labor, *the education of the children of migrant laborers* is a growing problem. Yet the federal government spends more to protect migratory birds than it spends to educate migratory children. This is a problem to which a chapter could easily be devoted. [55] *The problem of social class and education*—of the manner in which social class affects pupil motivation, classroom behavior, and school organization and administration—is worthy of attention. [56]

The question of *who should go to college* is receiving growing interest. The National Manpower Council finds that there is a serious national shortage of nearly every kind of well-educated manpower; yet only half the students who are mentally capable of going to college ever

[53] See Beardsey Ruml and Donald H. Morrison, *Memo to a College Trustee: A Report on the Financial and Structural Problems of the Liberal College* (New York, McGraw-Hill Book Co., 1959).

[54] J. Austin Burkhard, "Big Business and the Schools," *The Nation*, Vol. 173 (November 10, 1951), p. 401.

[55] See Lester Velie, "The Americans Nobody Wants," *Collier's*, Vol. 125 (April 1, 1950), pp. 13 ff; Jerome C. Manis, *A Study of Migrant Education: Survey Findings in Van Buren County, Michigan* (Kalamazoo, Western Michigan University Press, 1958).

[56] See A. B. Hollingshead, *Elmtown's Youth, op. cit.*, Chs. 6, 8, 13; Lloyd A. Cook and Elaine F. Cook, *Sociological Foundations of Education* (New York, McGraw-Hill Book Co., Inc., 1950), Ch. 11.

enter, and only one out of twenty-five who are capable of earning a doctoral degree ever complete one. [57] It would be easily possible to persuade many more of our young people to go to college and graduate school, but to do so would cost money and might also involve some changes in the class system. Either of these would arouse bitter value controversies.

THE SOCIAL-DISORGANIZATION APPROACH

Change and disorganization are involved in some way in each educational problem. The recent rise in the birth rate has swelled the child population just after a long depression and a major war curtailed the building of schools. Add to this the fact that the costs of the recent wars and the present defense program have kept taxes at record peacetime levels, and the origin of the classroom shortage is clear.

The existence of a continuing teacher shortage is a clear symptom of social disorganization. A well-organized society includes means of attracting sufficient workers to do the work believed necessary. In a free society, a continuing and disproportionate shortage of workers in a particular occupation means that the society is failing to reward them well enough to attract the right number and type of workers. [58] Although our society rewards teachers fairly well in terms of vacations and working conditions, it rewards them rather poorly in terms of status [59] and still worse in terms of income. Between 1939 and 1958, a period of acute teacher shortage and widely publicized teachers' salary raises, their salaries increased by 6 per cent less than the incomes of "all persons working for wages or salaries," and 23 per cent less than the average earnings of factory workers, leaving them about $100 a year below factory workers. [60] Three-fourths of the men teachers and one-sixth of the women teachers supplement their incomes by taking additional part-time jobs, often to the detriment of their teaching. College teachers fare even worse. Between 1930 and 1957, while the average American's purchasing power rose 75 per cent, that of the college professor dropped 15 per cent. [61] Fifty years ago, top professional salaries of $5,000 were fairly common; today's equivalent, merely to restore 1908 status, would be about $20,000, a salary practically unknown

[57] National Manpower Council, *A Policy for Scientific and Professional Manpower* (New York, Columbia University Press, 1953); summarized in *New York Times*. May 24, 1953, IV, p. 10.

[58] Provided there is no artificial restriction upon entrance, as exists in some trades and professions.

[59] A survey of 199 communities by the New York Citizen's Committee for the Public Schools finds only 24 per cent of the adults saying that they admire teachers, and only 18 per cent of the parents saying they would like to see their sons enter teaching. (*Time*, Vol. 68 [October 15, 1956], p. 83.)

[60] National Education Association, *Research Report*, 1959, R-3, *op. cit.*, p. 17.

[61] From "The College Teacher: 1959," special feature carried in alumni publications of about 250 colleges in Spring, 1959.

today. [62] Even if professorial salaries are doubled by 1967, as urged by the American Association of University Professors, they would still have gained less than the "average" American. For a society to prize education so highly, yet support it so poorly—to be so emphatic about *wanting* teachers, yet so unwilling to pay enough to get them—is prime evidence of social disorganization.

The curriculum controversies can be very neatly analyzed in terms of social disorganization. A changing society imposes upon its schools a set of changing responsibilities. A curriculum that very successfully prepares a small and selected class for college entrance and professional careers may work very poorly in preparing *all* classes of people for effective citizenship. Our changing patterns of work, of play, of family life, of mass communication, of political behavior—all require constant revisions of the curriculum if the school is to be an active guide to effective social living and not merely a museum of ancient lore and ornamental refinements. But none can be entirely certain just what sort of adaptations a changing society requires, and this makes the curriculum an area of constant debate, experimentation, and compromise.

The academic freedom battle, although it is a continuous one, has been intensified by recent changes. The rising tension with Russia and a growing recognition of the totalitarian nature of Communism have strengthened the hand of those who have never really believed in academic freedom, and increased the number of those who feel that academic freedom may have become a weakness we must correct. Many have accused the schools and colleges of encouraging the liberalism of the New Deal-Fair Deal era, and consider the present, more conservative period as a fine time to comb "socialistic thinking" out of the textbooks and classrooms. The school desegregation controversy has brought to many teachers and administrators the virtual certainty of dismissal unless they oppose school integration with proper enthusiasm. On this topic, academic freedom is not merely threatened in many areas; it is dead, embalmed, and buried— at least for the present. [63]

While a social-disorganization analysis does not fully explain all current educational problems, neither can they be understood without reference to the changing social setting in which they grow.

THE VALUE-CONFLICT APPROACH

A conflict of values is basic to every one of these educational problems. From the question, How much is education worth? to the question, Who is worth educating?, it is clear that people disagree partly because

[62] Beardsley Ruml and Stanley G. Tickton, *Teaching Salaries Then and Now* (New York, Fund for the Advancement of Education, 1955), p. 18.

[63] S. H. Smith, "Academic Freedom in Higher Education in the Deep South," *Journal of Educational Sociology*, Vol. 32 (February, 1959), pp. 297-308.

they do not want the same outcomes. In school tax balloting, parents of school-age children generally vote about two to one for school improvements, whereas elderly people and owners of rental properties often vote about two to one for low taxes instead of school improvements. Although nearly all people desire "good schools," they are not equally intense in their desire for good schools or in their willingness to sacrifice for them.

The factual case for federal aid to education is overwhelming. It is clear beyond debate that (1) there is no practical possibility that certain states will be able to provide first-class education to all their children at any time within the near future through their own resources; (2) these educational deficiencies help to retard the economic and cultural development of these areas and inflict economic and military burdens upon the entire nation. *But a number of value choices are involved.* Federal aid means more taxes to be paid by somebody, striking at the nerve center of many a person's value system. Federal aid would tax the more prosperous states for the direct benefit of the poorer states. Although circumstances may force us to be our brothers' keepers, few of us seem to enjoy the privilege. Federal aid would enlarge the function and possibly control by the federal government, and the values of many are furiously opposed to this. Among the seldom discussed issues are the changes in social structure that federal aid would promote. Better schools for southern Negroes and "poor whites" would make them less docile as workers and would accelerate the decline of the plantation and tenancy systems of agriculture. Better education probably would encourage farm mechanization and industrialization and encourage the organization of co-operatives and labor unions. Since federal aid would almost certainly have some sort of non-discrimination provision, it would be a powerful lever for equalizing educational and occupational opportunities for Negroes. Better education would accelerate the trend toward Negro voting and might also weaken the one-party system in the South. In short, better education would tend to alter the social structure and power system of the South in many respects. There are people in both the South and the North who do not enjoy the prospect of such changes.

The academic freedom controversy is, above all else, a conflict of values. Some prize the *unrestricted search* for knowledge and object to any authoritarian labeling of truth and error; some desire an authority in which to find confidence and security and want all "wrong" and "right" ideas officially labeled, for they dislike confusion, uncertainty, and debate. Some desire change and "progress" secured through constant examination and debate; some prefer stability of thought and social structure and seek to insure it through an educational indoctrination of the young. Some prize the average citizen's ability to study data, analyze competing propagandas, and arrive at valid conclusions; some doubt that the average citizen can develop any such ability and prefer that he be trained to believe and obey his leaders. As to the child of average ability who has been trained to think independently, ask questions, and join with his neighbors in forming an action organization when he is dissatisfied—some would consider him an educational achievement; others would view him as a social menace. The academic freedom controversy is, therefore, more than a debate over whether indoctrination or critical analysis is the better way to preserve social order; *it is also a debate over what kind of a social order is to be preserved*—a society of loyal, united, obedient, intolerant believers, or a society of inquiring, discussing, quarreling, relatively tolerant searchers for truth.

The most inescapable fact about each educational problem is the existence of such irreconcilable value conflicts. The value conflicts of the society become the problems of the school, since the members of the society cannot agree upon what the school should be and do. Not only differences upon *means*, but differences upon *ends* are involved. People who disagree about the kind of society they want must also disagree upon how children should be trained to live in society. As long as such value conflicts persist—and they will persist at least as long as our society continues to change—educational controversies are inevitable.

THE PERSONAL-DEVIATION APPROACH

Educational problems are ones in which deviant persons are incidental rather than major factors. If there were no value conflicts involved, deviant persons would be unable to transmute their private grudges into social issues. Since there *are* important value conflicts, plus many misinformed people, it is possible for deviant persons to play a major role in mobilizing people for school battles. People who have closely observed local school battles have been impressed by the large number of hostile, aggressive, resentful, hate-filled persons who appear at mass meetings. [64] Many persons who, throughout an adult lifetime, have shown no particular interest in the school suddenly become bitter participants in a school battle. It would appear that these are maladjusted people who have displaced their inner emotional conflicts upon the school or upon some group of school people. Of course, the success of an attack requires that many ordinary, well-adjusted citizens be induced to join, but the contagious intensity of the neurotic core helps to build such a mass following.

Not all who criticize the school, of course, are neurotics. Some are cynical opportunists, planning to cut school costs or to capture the school as an instrument for their propaganda. Some are honest critics, calling attention to the genuine failures and dubious aspects of the school's

[64] Dorothy Frank, "I Was Called Subversive," *Collier's*, Vol. 131 (March 28, 1953), pp. 68 ff; Carey McWilliams, "The Enemy in Pasadena," *Christian Century*, Vol. 68 (January 3, 1951), pp. 10-15.

operation. And not all the neurotics are found among the attackers. Educators and teachers have their share of eccentric and maladjusted personalities, apparently in about the same proportion as other professions. [65] Although the neurotic person appears more likely to join the free-swinging attackers, he may also turn up among the defenders. The cause of academic freedom has suffered greatly from neurotic, exhibitionistic, and Communistic teachers who have invoked academic freedom to evade legitimate criticism. Although a genuine Communist is prevented by his doctrine from accepting the responsibilities of academic freedom as a teacher, when he is discharged he almost unfailingly raises the cry that academic freedom has been despoiled. In each instance, it is important to determine whether a real interference with academic freedom has occurred, or whether there are entirely proper reasons for the teacher's dismissal. [66]

In each educational problem, then, deviant persons play a similar role. They do not *cause* educational problems, but can *greatly aggravate* them. The basic causes of educational problems are found in the value conflicts of a changing (disorganized) society. Since there are value conflicts that produce tension and misunderstanding, a small band of neurotics can capitalize on this to organize an attack. Many local school battles, textbook controversies, and dismissal quarrels *would* not occur if they were not promoted by aggressive neurotics, and they *could* not occur if basic value conflicts had not provided the background of controversy. In this way, deviant persons may function as precipitating factors in educational controversies.

FUTURE PROSPECTS

Since educational problems are rooted in the value conflicts that a changing society inevitably produces, no complete or final solutions are possible. Whether the immediate future brings a relaxation or aggravation of tensions depends partly upon developments in other fields. If no major war develops, it is likely that the classroom shortage will be considerably relieved after a decade or so. A major depression would quickly end the teacher shortage, however unpleasantly. A relaxation of international tension and the reduction of military expenses would make it easier to pay the salaries necessary to help alleviate the teacher shortage. If most teachers

[65] Lloyd A. Cook and Elaine F. Cook, *op. cit.*, p. 435.

[66] The Committee on Academic Freedom and Tenure of the American Association of University Professors investigates complaints to determine whether academic freedom has actually been infringed, although it has no powers beyond those of publicity and persuasion. Each issue of the AAUP *Bulletin* publishes a list of "censured administrations" where "unsatisfactory conditions of academic freedom and tenure have been found to prevail," a list currently numbering twelve colleges and universities. State education associations and the NEA also seek to offer public school teachers some protection against arbitrary discharge.

were to join an aggressive union—which appears unlikely—they perhaps could raise salary levels and increase the teacher supply. [67] If a genuinely peaceful accord with the Soviet Union were to develop, the anxieties which lead to a fear of academic freedom would greatly subside. Such external developments as these can have great effects upon educational problems.

Even if final solutions for educational problems were possible, further social change would soon produce new problems. All major educational problems—curriculum, teaching methods, finances, academic freedom— are *permanent problems* in that social changes will continue to excite debate and call for readjustment. The prospect is for a continuing process of *accommodation* through which conflicting wishes and pressures of a democratic society can be compromised. Wherever ultimate solutions are unavailable, accommodation provides democracy's alternative to chaos, and nowhere is this more true than in education. This is a far from gloomy prospect, since most of us consider the argumentative and wordy compromises of democracy far preferable to the orderly discipline of monolithic authority.

SUGGESTED READINGS

American Library Association and American Book Publishers Council, "The Freedom to Read," *American Association of University Professors Bulletin,* Vol. 39 (Summer, 1953), pp. 209-214. An eloquent plea that book publishing and circulation should be free from censorship, labeling, or other restrictions on freedom to read.

Association for Supervision and Curriculum Development, *Forces Affecting American Education* (Washington, National Education Association, 1953), Ch. 3, "Groups Affecting Education," by Robert A. Skaife. A survey of national pressure groups interested in the school, with several brief case histories of local school controversies.

CONANT, James B., *The American High School Today* (New York, McGraw-Hill Book Co., Inc., 1959). A proposal for sweeping reorganization of the high school.

HUNTER, Evan, *Blackboard Jungle* (New York, Simon and Schuster, Inc., 1954); condensed in *Ladies Home Journal,* Vol. 71 (October, 1954), pp. 60 ff. A highly readable and disturbing novel which portrays many of the problems of the school in an underprivileged neighborhood.

LAZARSFELD, Paul F., and THIELINS, Wagner, Jr., *The Academic Mind: Social Scientists in a Time of Crisis* (Glencoe, Ill., The Free Press, 1958). A research study of the effects of the loyalty crisis upon higher education in the mid-1950's.

Rockefeller Brothers Fund, *The Pursuit of Excellence: Education and The*

---

[67] Few teachers belong to teachers' unions, although a Gallup Poll (February 17, 1959) shows the public favoring unions for teachers by two to one. See also American Federation of Teachers, *Organizing the Teaching Profession* (Glencoe, Ill., The Free Press, 1955).

Future of America (Garden City, N.Y., Doubleday & Co., Inc., 1958). A brief forecast of educational needs and a program for meeting them.

RUML, Beardsley, and MORRISON, Donald H., *Memo To a College Trustee* (New York, McGraw-Hill Book Co., 1959). A provocative proposal for reorganization and finance of the college.

SCOTT, C. Winfield, and HILL, Clyde M., *Public Education Under Criticism* (Englewood Cliffs, N.J., Prentice-Hall, Inc., 1954). A collection of many short articles dealing with criticisms of the school system; stimulating and readable.

AUDIO-VISUAL AIDS

Children Must Learn (New York University Film Library), 15 minutes, sound, black and white. Depicts a poverty-stricken rural family and the inadequate one-room school which cannot meet the needs of life in the area.

Crowded Out (National Education Association, Washington, D.C., or from state education associations), 29 minutes, sound, black and white. Dramatizes the effects of school overcrowding on teachers, children, and parents.

Freedom to Learn (National Education Association, Washington, D.C., or from state education associations), 27 minutes, sound, black and white. A charge of teaching Communism in the classroom, hurled at a high school teacher, raises the issue of freedom to learn. Asks whether the freedom to study and evaluate can be controlled or restricted and still be deemed freedom.

Who Will Teach Your Child? (McGraw-Hill Book Co., Text-Film Department, 330 West 42 St., New York), 24 minutes, sound, black and white. Presents the opportunities and responsibilities of the good teacher.

QUESTIONS AND PROJECTS

1. Why is the cost of education a problem during a period of unprecedented national prosperity?

2. What are the causes of the teacher shortage? How does the shortage illustrate the social-disorganization approach? The value-conflict approach?

3. Why has federal aid to education been proposed? Why has there been opposition to it? Are the disputes mainly over facts or over values?

4. Nearly everyone seems to "believe in" athletics in the school, so what is the argument about?

5. How would one "prove" whether a private school education is generally superior to a public school education, or vice versa? What variables would have to be controlled in making any comparisons?

6. What is academic freedom? Whom is it supposed to benefit? Is academic freedom threatened? By whom?

7. What responsibilities does academic freedom place upon the teacher? Upon the school administrator? Upon the citizen?

8. Is the "freedom" of the schools endangered only by those who do not "believe in" education?

9. How would you distinguish between "constructive" and "destructive" criticism of the schools? Do you think educators and administrators have generally received criticism less fair-mindedly or more fair-mindedly than have other professional groups (such as lawyers, physicians, or businessmen)?

10. Should schools and colleges accept free pamphlets, films, and other teaching materials from corporations and trade associations, labor organizations, or other sources which may have an ax to grind?

11. Read Robert Maynard Hutchins' essay, "What Price Freedom?" (in John Eric Nordskog, Edward C. McDonagh, and Melvin J. Vincent, *Analyzing Social Problems* (New York, The Dryden Press, Inc., 1950), pp. 438-441; also in American Association of University Professors' Bulletin, Vol. 35 [Summer, 1949], pp. 211-215). If the viewpoints in this statement are accepted, what present tendencies and practices in America would need revision?

11

Social-Class Problems

ᝣᝣ

"The" June debutante party—the James Floods' ball for their daughter Judy in Woodside Saturday night—is only a memory this morning—but one that will not soon be forgotten.

Over 500 people drove up the Flood's long driveway to the great circular oak-studded courtyard in front of their English-style country home, which was ablaze with lights. They came from dinner parties in Woodside, Burlingame, and San Francisco. The Floods and Judy had dined first at the Charles Gillespies!

Alighting from cars (which attendants took off to a parking area), guests walked into the spacious entrance hall, where Judy's orchid gifts were tied to a great madrone tree, set in the curve of the staircase.

. . . [Judy] was graduated from Crystal Springs School for Girls the day before the party and will enter Connecticut College. At Christmas she will make her debut at the Debutante Cotillion. . . . [Included among the guests were] the Graeme MacDonalds and their son Kirk, a Yale student, and the Charles Thieriots and their son Dick, who has just graduated from St. Marks.

A number of guests just back from Europe, among them the Richard Hydes . . . the Polk Dodsons [who] had returned from the Continent Friday. . . . The G. Willard Somers [were] talking about plans to return to Rome and their penthouse apartment on September 14. . . . Mrs. Paul Browne [was] talking about the round-the-world trip her daughter, Mrs. Daniel Walcott, is taking with her husband . . . [1]

"I wish that I could have a doll for Christmas. If I could I would also like to have a new suit. This is about all I think I would like for Christmas. I never had a doll before, so I'd like to have one this Christmas. Some day I wish I could have a lot of dolls." (Ten-year-old Chicago girl's reply to question put by an inquiring reporter). [2]

[1] *San Francisco Chronicle*, June 15, 1959, p. 15.
[2] *Chicago Sun-Times*, October 18, 1950.

Practically every Spanish kid—all the poor ones it's safe to say—dream of becoming bullfighters . . . in a land of rigid social stratification, bullfighting can lift the kid from the wrong side of the tracks onto a level with the horsiest set in Spain . . .[3]

Tom Brown, the ordinary boy, is ten years old and in the fifth grade. His father owns and runs a grocery store in Hometown. The family lives in a large well-kept house in the "better" part of town. Tom's mother is proud of her home but she recognizes that their part of town is inferior to the Hillcrest region where the Peabodys and families like the Peabodys reside. . . .
The Peabodys are "one of the town's old families," and their kind are often referred to in Hometown as "our Four Hundred," or, by those hostile and often envious, as "small-town aristocrats." Tom's mother and father, while respected as pillars of society, are never spoken of in such terms.
Neither Tom's nor Kenneth's [Peabody] father knows or has heard of the Jones family. Tom's father knows of Joe Sienkowitz's big brother, who was a great football player, and he says, "That Sienkowitz boy's football career goes to show how everybody who wants to, and who tries, can go places in this country." Kenneth's father thinks too many people now go to high school. His interest in football is confined to the annual game between Yale and Princeton.[4]

"ALL MEN ARE EQUAL" is a favorite cliché of many Americans. But what does it mean? And is it true? If we add the phrase, ". . . in the sight of God," it means that *to the Almighty* one human soul is as important as another. Such propositions, which are a matter of faith, cannot be scientifically proved or disproved. If we limit the question to whether all men are equal *here on earth* a much more definite answer is possible. It is ridiculous to assert that all men are equal without qualifying the phrase. They are certainly not equal in height, intelligence, in the ability to drive a car, or in ability generally. Neither are they equal in what they get from society. Some men drive Cadillacs; more men drive Chevrolets; many have no automobiles at all. Houses range from twenty-room mansions to converted chicken coops. Debutantes have coming-out parties, and slum youth quit school to help support their families. Cities maintain welfare departments, and civic organizations distribute baskets at Christmas.

CLASSES AND DEMOCRACY

The American Ideology

In their enthusiasm for democracy, many people imagine that there are no important social distinctions in the United States. A moment's sober

---

[3] *True*, The Man's Magazine, August, 1952, p. 59, by permission.
[4] W. Lloyd Warner, Robert J. Havighurst, and Martin B. Loeb, *Who Shall Be Educated?* (New York, Harper and Brothers, 1944), pp. 2-3, by permission.

reflection will show that this is not true. The United States since its beginning has had great social inequality, and, indeed, our free enterprise system assumes that extraordinary initiative and ingenuity should be rewarded by wealth, power, and prestige. The American dream does not picture an undifferentiated mass society but rather holds out to each person the prospect of climbing the class ladder. American history specializes in stories of the "poor boy who made good," of the "office boy who became president of the firm," and of the open road from "log cabin to White House." The United States is founded not on the idea of a classless society, but upon the notions of an "open" class system. A chance to change class position in accord with one's ability is the essence of such a system.

The kind of equality which is admired in this country is *equality of opportunity*. Men are supposed to be *equal at birth* if not at any time thereafter. Given the same initial advantages, one person should have as much chance to succeed as any other. It is conceded that some persons may be more favored biologically than others, but aside from the uncontrollable aspects of heredity, success is regarded largely as a matter of ambition, hard work, and, perhaps, a little luck. Prestige, wealth, and power are the rewards for diligent application of one's talent's and are equally available to all who strive for them.

This faith in unlimited opportunity is, to some extent, justified by the facts of American history. Two factors have been instrumental in supporting the pattern of extensive interclass mobility. These are (1) the expansion of the economy, and (2) the differential birth rate.

1. EXPANSION OF THE ECONOMY. One of the striking features of American life has been the stimulus provided by the western frontier and our rapidly growing population. The frontier served at least two functions. It acted as a kind of safety valve, draining off excess population and goods from the East, and it constantly added to the material wealth and natural resources of the nation. Ever expanding markets gave tremendous impetus to production. In a mere century and a half the United States changed from a group of semiautonomous colonies to the world's most highly industrialized nation. Expansion created new jobs by the thousands. New businesses developed and a whole new class of entrepreneurs was created. It was relatively easy for a man to go into business for himself and eventually to become the head of a large business organization. This is, perhaps, the kind of *vertical mobility* most highly valued in the United States.

Not all upward movement was of this type, however. In fact, much of the mobility occurred within the ranks of workers who were not, themselves, owners of businesses. Large-scale corporate organization with its intricate specialization and complex problems of financing and management brought into being a great new middle class, midway between the "laborers" and the "bosses." This army of white-collar workers, technicians, scientists, and managers was recruited mainly from the ranks of the lower economic groups. The more rapidly the economy developed, the more new positions were created. Either by striking out on their own or by rising through the occupational hierarchy, the sons of working class families could outstrip their fathers and raise their standards of living.

2. THE DIFFERENTIAL BIRTH RATE. Throughout most of western European culture, upper-class groups are known for their low birth rates. Their failure to have enough children to replace themselves again results in some interclass mobility. The groups at the top of the class structure are always in the process of slowly dying out and being replaced by new blood from the lower classes. In most cases it is not a matter of individuals rising from the lowest to the highest class in a single generation, but it is felt as a gentle upward pressure upon whole segments of the population. [5] Advances up the ladder are generally made a rung or two at a time, rapidly enough to keep alive the American's faith that at least his son, if not himself, can achieve a higher class status.

The Nature of the Problem

One might well ask at this point, What, then, is the sociological problem of social class? If an expanding economy and the differential birth rate assure continued mobility, and if the American people are confident that the system is fair and equitable, is there "... a situation believed to be undesirable by a large number of people ... "? To answer these questions, certain other facts must be noted. One set of facts is concerned with the question, Are conditions *today* the same as they were during the early part of our national history? and the other with, Does the class system itself prevent real *equality of opportunity?*

HAVE CONDITIONS CHANGED? The role of economic expansion in maintaining the pattern of upward mobility has led many persons to speculate on the possible effects of the disappearance of the Western frontier. There is at least a strong possibility that the rate of expansion had passed its peak by the early part of the present century, and that the American economy is losing some of its dynamic character. In terms of the class structure, such a slow-down would be apt to increase the rigidity of present class lines and to discourage large-scale upward mobility. Middle- and upper-class groups would be forced to consolidate their positions and lower-class persons would find it more difficult to escape their present lot. Since *mobility, rather than the absence of social classes,* has been the key to the American system, this turn of events would be cause for re-examination of the whole system in terms of its significance for the continuance of our democratic pattern.

[5] Joseph A. Kahl, *The American Class Structure* (New York, Rinehart & Company, Inc., 1957), pp. 260-262.

CLASSES AND EQUALITY OF OPPORTUNITY. Increasingly, thoughtful people are questioning whether there is not a basic incompatability between the ideal of equal opportunity and the existence of social classes. By protecting persons from any *legal disabilities,* as the Constitution does, do we actually guarantee them an equal chance to get ahead in the world? On purely logical grounds, it appears that those who have some power, wealth, and prestige find it easier to get more. The clichés, "It takes money to make money," and, "Them as has, gits," are tacit recognition of this tendency. Though education and technical training are available to everyone, it is easier to take advantage of these opportunities if one's parents can afford to support a member who is not contributing to the family income. But the children of upper-class families have a far more important advantage. To become a member of the middle or upper classes one must acquire the attitudes, values, manners, and social graces characteristic of those groups. Children who are reared in upper-class surroundings will acquire these traits with no great effort. Mobility for lower-class persons requires both the unlearning of behaviors established in childhood and the learning of new patterns in place of them. Having lower-class parents may take much of the meaning out of equality of opportunity!

Thus, there are at least two points of view concerning the operation of social class in the United States. One group stresses relatively free mobility and opportunities for advancement; the other faction points to increasing rigidity of class lines and the advantages possessed by the upper classes. With these two viewpoints in mind, let us examine the available data before attempting to draw any conclusions. First of all, just what is the class structure in the United States? Is it open and fluid or are there elements of rigidity? Do people identify with class groups? What is the objective evidence concerning class placement? How much mobility is there? Is mobility becoming more or less frequent? Do some groups have "most of the advantages"? Are there any trends which can be discerned? These are the questions we shall try to answer.

THE AMERICAN CLASS STRUCTURE

The United States is a large and diversified country. With large rural and urban populations and regional differences from North to South and East to West no single class picture will accurately describe the total society. Class interaction is influenced by the history of the community and by its degree of economic specialization. There are, however, certain broad outlines which are sufficiently typical that, with some modification, they can be applied to each local situation. The student of the American scene must recognize that there are both "class" and "caste" aspects to be considered.

Caste Aspects

One of the most glaring inconsistencies between the American dream and the real situation is to be found in what have been called "caste aspects" of the American system. A caste system differs from a class system in that, once born into a given caste, there is no possibility of rising above or falling below that caste. Placement is hereditary and mobility is nonexistent. Premodern India is frequently offered as a good example of a caste system. The rigid distinctions and the great social distance between castes from the Brahmin down to the Untouchable are fairly well known.

Ordinarily, one would not consider caste to be relevant to the American class structure, but the charge has been made that certain aspects of the system do *approximate* a caste system. It is charged that the 10 per cent of our population who happen to be Negro are impressed into a caste apart from the rest of the class structure from which they cannot escape. In most sections of the country, strong taboos forbid any kind of intimate contact suggesting equality between Negroes and whites. White persons are taught that Negroes are inferior and are to be "kept in their place." Especially in the South, any white man, no matter how poor, ill-educated, and incompetent, considers himself above the most eminent Negro business and professional men. A rigid barrier separates the highest ranking Negroes from the lowest ranking whites. [6] This means that all Negroes are denied certain opportunities available to every white. Negroes, even if they acquire professional training, wealth, and prestige within the Negro group, are forced to recognize the superior position of lower-class whites.

Defenders of the open-class theory in the United States point out that Negro-white relations are really not caste relationships and they point to such persons as Dr. Ralph Bunche, highest ranking American in the United Nations, as evidence that Negroes can overcome the handicaps of their race. There are social classes in Negro society and there is possibility of mobility within the Negro group. Moreover, the caste aspects of Negro-white relations are probably more marked in the South than in other areas of the country. Even there, the castelike suppression of Negroes is breaking down somewhat as it becomes more difficult for the American people to reconcile "discrimination" with "democracy." [7] Eventually, there may be no special class distinctions between the white and Negro groups. Some groups such as the National Association for the Advancement of Colored People are working to bring this about. Other groups, predominantly white, see the gains made by Negroes in recent years as dangerous trends leading to the breakdown of segregation, to

[6] Allison Davis, Burleigh Gardner, and Mary Gardner, *Deep South* (Chicago, University of Chicago Press, 1947), p. 10.

[7] *Ibid.*

intermarriage, and eventually to the deterioration of the population. It appears that the special restrictions on the freedom and upward mobility of Negro persons are tending, in the long run, to break down. Nevertheless, it is evident that the vast majority of Negroes are a disprivileged group in the struggle for status. The success achieved by a mere handful of Negroes serves only to accent the plight of the many.

Class Aspects

The emphasis on equal opportunity and upward mobility has discouraged the development of any real *class consciousness* on the part of the American people. The prospect of better things, at least for one's children, encouraged people to identify themselves with the prosperous and powerful elements in the community rather than with the so-called common man. Conscious recognition of class has generally been confined to vague differentiations between the "business class" and the "working class," or to casual references to upper, middle, and lower classes. It is not surprising, then, that the class distinctions made by ordinary people in ordinary speech do not mirror very clearly the actual status differentials that exist within the population. Consequently, one may look at the class system either in terms of the *identifications* made by individual persons or in terms of *objective differences* that exist among them.

SELF-IDENTIFICATIONS. Most Americans identify themselves with the middle class. *Fortune* some years ago conducted a survey in which people were asked to identify the class to which they belonged. Seventy per cent of the respondents called themselves middle class, 7 per cent claimed upper-class status, and 22 per cent identified themselves with the lower class. This pictures the population as a remarkably homogeneous one in terms of social class, with seven out of every ten persons belonging to the middle class, two to the lower class, and one to the upper class.

Rather than accept these identifications at face value, it would seem prudent to ask *why* people overwhelmingly conceive of themselves as middle class. The explanation probably is to be found in the peculiar American attitude toward class. The prevalent belief that one's present status is temporary encourages lower-class persons to identify with the middle class toward which they aspire. Schoolteachers and some other low paid white-collar workers, for example, who, as far as income is concerned, might well be lower class, are prone to identify themselves with middle-class business and professional interests. Upper-class persons, too, find it advantageous to support these beliefs and are reluctant to admit, at least to others, that they hold positions of special benefit. This upper class largely controls the media of mass communication—press, radio, television—and uses these to cultivate the myths and legends which support the class system, meanwhile denying its existence. Thus, in spite of wide differences in income, wealth, and prestige, most people seem to believe they are middle class. Now let us compare these self-identifications with some other indices of class placement.

OBJECTIVE PLACEMENT. Fifty per cent of United States families and individuals in 1956 received less than $4300 total money income, [8] some 16 million people belonged to labor unions, and up to one-third of the nation was said to be ill-housed. [9] Offhand these do not sound like characteristics of the great middle class. Moreover, the class identifications discussed above are not consistent with the results of many comprehensive studies of the class system in various American communities. Research has generally shown five or six identifiable classes with the bulk of the population concentrated in the lower half of the class structure. The class system revealed by research in a New England city is shown in Table 11-1.

TABLE 11-1. The class system of Yankee City

Class	Number	Per Cent
Upper-upper	242	1.44
Lower-upper	262	1.56
Upper-middle	1715	10.22
Lower-middle	4720	28.12
Upper-lower	5471	32.60
Lower-lower	4234	25.22
Unknown	141	.84
Total	16,785	100.00

From W. Lloyd Warner and Paul S. Lunt, *Social Life of a Modern Community* (New Haven, Yale University Press, 1941), p. 203, by permission.

Note that each of the conventional three classes has been subdivided, and that over 50 per cent of the population fall into the lower two classes. Slightly under 40 per cent are middle class and some 3 per cent belong to the upper classes. A number of criteria, including family background and the patterns of association within the community, were used in

[8] U. S. Bureau of the Census, *Statistical Abstract of the United States: 1958* (Washington), p. 319.

[9] Considerable caution needs to be exercised in the presentation and interpretation of statistics on income. The census regularly presents income statistics for "families and individuals," and for "families." Family income is always higher because it excludes many older persons and others who are not living in conventional family situations, and it often includes the incomes of two or more family members who are working for pay. The situation appears even more confused when, for example, magazines report that "43 per cent of all nonfarm families have after-tax cash incomes between $5000 and $10,000." (*Fortune*, May, 1959, p. 107.) Not only are individual incomes excluded here, but farm families, which traditionally have had lower incomes, are also excluded. Thus, one can make it appear that Americans have generally high incomes or generally low incomes, depending upon which statistics are selected for presentation.

identifying these classes, but it is interesting to see how this alignment parallels that provided by the distribution of money income among the population. The comparison is made in Table 11-2. One-fourth of the population in 1950 had less than $1500 cash income and 60 per cent had incomes of less than $3500. The income picture and the Yankee City data show the major part of the population to be concentrated in the lower half of the socioeconomic structure, with the proportions getting steadily smaller as one moves toward the upper-class and upper-income brackets. *By their own assertion,* most people are middle class. *But according to other evidence,* much of this "middle class" is concentrated in the bottom half of the income and prestige structure.

TABLE 11-2. Money income and social class

Total Money Income, 1950	Per Cent		Yankee City Classes
Under $500			
$ 500-999			
1000-1499 . . . . .25.4%	25.22%	. . . .	Lower-lower
1500-1999			
2000-2499			
2500-2999			
3000-3499 . . . . .35.4	32.60	. . . .	Upper-lower
3500-3999			
4000-4499			
4500-4999			
5000-5499			
5500-5999 . . . . .27.3	28.12	. . . .	Lower-middle
6000-6999			
7000-7999			
8000-8999			
9000-9999 . . . . 9.1	10.22	. . . .	Upper-middle
			Lower-upper
$10,000 and over 2.7	3.0	. . . .	Upper-upper

Income data from U. S. Bureau of the Census, *Statistical Abstract of the United States: 1952* (Washington, Government Printing Office), p. 264.

People in the United States apparently believe, or want to believe, that status differences are at a minimum and that most people are middle class. Objective studies, however, show status differentials to be greater than believed and a class structure with a broad base which narrows to an almost needlelike top. The popular conception of a great middle class ignores the fact that there is an even larger lower class in which incomes and living standards are very low. The opportunities provided by the

American technology and by whatever equality of opportunity prevails have not been enough to eliminate problems of gross inequality in the class system. We still have a large lower class which is potentially capable of challenging the prerogatives of the middle- and upper-class groups. To date, the development of any real class consciousness among the lower class seems to have been forestalled by the widespread hope of climbing into the middle class. Whether this situation continues indefinitely may well depend upon the reality of the hope of upward mobility.

MOBILITY AND THE CLASS STRUCTURE

Being able to move freely from one class to another has been an important part of the American class picture. The expanding economy and the differential birth rate, at least formerly, made widespread upward mobility possible. But now we need to know: Do people have equal chances to acquire upper-class status? Is mobility decreasing?

Equal Chances?

The American ethos proclaims that all children regardless of origin, whether from upper- or lower-class families, shall have equal opportunities to prove themselves and to make good. To that end we have a free public school system and the competitive filling of openings in business and industry. But does this system, in fact, guarantee equality of opportunity? Let us examine the available data in the areas of *education* and *occupation*.

EDUCATION. Since education has been one of the chief routes to upward mobility, equal opportunity depends upon the school system

TABLE 11-3. Number of College Graduates, 1870–1956

Year of Graduation	Number of Graduates
1870	9,371
1880	10,353
1890	14,306
1900	25,324
1910	34,178
1920	48,622
1930	122,484
1940	186,500
1950	432,058
1952	329,986
1954	290,825
1956	311,298

U. S. Bureau of the Census, *Statistical Abstract of the United States* (Washington); 1952, p. 121; 1958, pp. 122, 129.

The study, "Background for a National Scholarship Policy," published by the American Council on Education . . . found that half of the top 25 per cent of high school graduates do not attend college even though the United States has a markedly inadequate supply of highly educated people in many fields. . . .

The study reached these conclusions:

(1) Secondary school graduates from professional homes are much more likely to attend college than are those from non-professional homes.

(2) A higher percentage of high-ability boys than girls continue in post-secondary education.

(3) High school graduates attend college in higher proportions when they live close to a college than when they live at a distance.

(4) A higher percentage of high school graduates attend college from the higher economic levels than from the middle or lower economic groups. Estimates of the odds favoring higher income groups over the lower range as high as ten to one.

New York Times, October 28, 1956.

remaining equally open to children from all social classes. *Legally,* of course, all children are guaranteed a public school education. College attendance is not quite so free since some fees must be paid, books and supplies purchased, and living costs met, even at the tax-supported universities. Especially in recent years, however, more and more scholarships have been made available to help needy and deserving students finance their educations. All these provisions are meant to be a bulwark protecting and maintaining the avenue to improved social position.

Education, particularly higher education, is more widely received today than ever before. The number of persons attending college and doing postgraduate work has grown by leaps and bounds. Unfortunately, national information is not available to indicate how these persons attending college are distributed in the class structure. Probably it can be assumed that college enrollments represent largely middle- and upper-class backgrounds. For a time the GI bill probably encouraged more lower-class persons to attend both private and state universities, and the pattern thus established may be continuing to a certain degree. At least some of the evidence points to ever-widening use of the educational system, but evidence to the contrary also exists.

Much of our information indicates that the educational system, itself, operates as a selective mechanism tending to discourage the continuance of

TABLE 11-4. College attendance of high school graduates in Old City

Class	Per cent of each class attending college
Upper	72
Upper-middle	69
Middle	58
Lower-middle	16
Lower	0

Adapted from W. Lloyd Warner, Robert J. Havighurst, and Martin B. Loeb, *Who Shall Be Educated?* (New York, Harper and Brothers, 1944), p. 59, by permission.

lower-class children and encouraging those from the middle- and upper-class groups. In one study of an anonymous Southern city identified as "Old City," Warner, Havighurst, and Loeb found (Table 11-4) that 72 per cent of the high school graduates from the upper class, 16 per cent from the lower-middle class, and none from the lower class attended college. These figures do not suggest a fully "democratic" educational system. Table 11-5 portrays the situation discovered in one Pennsylvania school system. Some 910 students with IQ's of 110 or above were classified by economic status into two groups. *Though the two groups were of equal ability,* the below-average economic group showed a higher proportion of dropouts at every grade level, and a much larger percentage of the above-average economic group eventually attended college. How can we explain this situation?

Apparently, the theoretical opportunity to complete one's education is in certain ways abridged for many lower-class children. Some of the relevant factors are to be found in the way of life of the lower class and some of them are to be found in the school system. Much of the lower

TABLE 11-5. Effect of economic status on educational achievement of students with IQ's of 110 or above

Educational advance	Socioeconomic status above average	Socioeconomic status below average
Dropped school at eighth grade or below	.7%	7.9%
Completed ninth, tenth, or eleventh grade but did not graduate from high school	6.2	20.2
Graduated from high school but did not attend college	36.3	59.0
Attended college	56.8	12.9

Adapted from W. Lloyd Warner, Robert J. Havighurst, and Martin B. Loeb, *Who Shall Be Educated?* (New York, Harper and Brothers, 1944), p. 52, by permission.

class has not been thoroughly indoctrinated with the ideals of success and mobility that characterize middle-class groups. Instead, large families and low, uncertain incomes combine to create a resignation and apathy which tend to perpetuate the lower-class pattern. Boys and girls are encouraged to quit school, as soon as they can legally do so, to help support their families. Moreover, because they can see little use for education in their way of life the children often *want* to quit school. Defenders of the traditional American system cite this lower-class disinterest in school to prove that lower-class children really are not discriminated against. The opposite viewpoint maintains that the desire for education must be learned and that many *lower-class children never really have a chance to want to go to school!*

TABLE 11-6. Social class distribution of teachers

Class	Hometown Per cent	Yankee City Per cent	Old City Per cent
Upper-upper	0	2	2.5
Lower-upper	0	1	2.5
Upper-middle	26	76	72.5
Lower-middle	72	21	20.0
Upper-lower	2	0	2.5
Lower-lower	0	0	0.0
	100	100	100.0

From W. Lloyd Warner, Robert J. Havighurst, and Martin B. Loeb, *Who Shall Be Educated?* (New York, Harper and Brothers, 1944), p. 101, by permission.

Within the school system, too, there are pressures which operate against lower-class and in favor of middle-class children. The school itself is a middle-class institution. School boards and schoolteachers are both drawn primarily from the middle class. Middle-class teachers, even without realizing it, are prone to reward middle-class children for their clean faces, tidy clothes, nice manners, and interest in pleasing their elders. To lower-class children, whose social world rewards a quite different mode of behavior, and who see in school work only a compulsory and not very pleasant task, the teacher's lack of understanding and encouragement reinforces a latent hostility toward schools and teachers. Taken together, these pressures that operate in the home and in the school deprive lower-class children of much of their "opportunity."

OCCUPATION. Occupational mobility probably is as good a single index as we have of the amount of class mobility in the United States. Davidson and Anderson, in analyzing the data from a California sample in the 1930's, reported that over 40 per cent of the sons of a group of unskilled workers became unskilled workers themselves; 16 per cent became semiskilled; and

27 per cent became skilled workers or clerks. Ten per cent of the sons became proprietors and 4 per cent entered the professions. [10] Thus, slightly over half of the sons remained in lower-class occupations, some 27 per cent moved into middle-class occupations, and 14 per cent into occupations which might be either middle or upper class. Rogoff compared the occupations of two samples of central Indiana men, in 1910 and 1940, with those of their fathers, finding that, "The most likely occupational destination of all the sons was the occupation of their fathers." [11] More-

TABLE 11-7. Occupations of the sons of unskilled workers, Indianapolis, 1940

Professional and Semiprofessional	3.89%
Proprietors, Managers, and Officials	2.78
Clerical and Sales	13.06
Skilled	15.42
Semiskilled	30.00
Unskilled	28.61
Protective and Personal Service	5.97
Farming	.28
	100.01%

SOURCE: Adapted from Natalie Rogoff, *Recent Trends in Occupational Mobility* (Glencoe, Ill., The Free Press, 1953), p. 119, by permission.

over, much of the movement to occupations other than the fathers' was to occupations at roughly the same class level. Most of the upward and downward mobility that did occur was to adjacent rather than widely separated class levels. A relatively small amount of mobility involved movement far upward or downward in the class system. Two other studies conducted after World War II yielded essentially similar results. [12] Judging from these data, lower-class boys have a better than average chance to remain lower class. On the other hand, a substantial number of them will move up to the middle class and a few may even attain upper-class status.

[10] Percy E. Davidson and H. Dewey Anderson, *Occupational Mobility in an American Community* (Stanford, Calif., Stanford University Press, 1937).

[11] Natalie Rogoff, *Recent Trends in Occupational Mobility* (Glencoe, Ill., The Free Press, 1953), p. 106.

[12] National Opinion Research Center, "Jobs and Occupations: A Popular Evaluation," in Reinhard Bendix and Seymour Lipset, *Class, Status, and Power* (Glencoe, Ill., The Free Press, 1953), pp. 424-425, and Richard Centers, "Occupational Mobility of Urban Occupational Strata," *American Sociological Review*, Vol. 13 (April, 1948), pp. 197-203.

Are Class Lines Blurring in the United States?

Only ten years ago, the following description of an American family's style of life would have enabled one to form some fairly firm impressions about the father's occupation and the general social "rank" of the family:

> The parents, who are about forty, live with their two boys in a comfortable six-room suburban house outfitted with a full line of appliances, a television set that is in more or less constant use, and a car in which the father drives to work. The car is also used for camping trips in the summer. The mother shops at a local supermarket and at several local department stores; the boys attend the good local public schools; and on weekends the family often goes swimming at the local beach, although recently the father and mother and their older son have begun to take an interest in golf.

... Given these same facts in 1959, one could deduce practically nothing about the family's social rank or the father's occupation. For the fact is that in the past few years the broad style of life described above has become available, not only to an identifiable "middle class," but to a great mass of Americans, perhaps even a majority. The family head today might be a truck driver earning $5500, a college professor earning $7000, a life-insurance salesman earning $8000, a skilled production worker earning $9000, an airline pilot earning $15,000, or an executive earning $18,000. In the new American society, it is increasingly difficult to tell the players apart without subpoenaing their tax returns.

Daniel Seligman, "The New Masses," *Fortune*, May, 1959, pp. 106-107, by special permission.

Is Mobility Decreasing?

The American dream assumes fairly free interclass mobility and, as we have seen, some mobility does take place. However, since lower-class youth most frequently seem to remain at the same class level as their parents, it is important to ask whether it is becoming more difficult to move upward in the class system. During the decade of the 1930's, and apparently as a consequence of the prolonged depression, many authorities believed that the rate of upward mobility was slowing down. Warner reflected this point of view when he said, "Such economic mobility as now exists in our society is made possible largely by the fact that people in the upper classes do not have enough children to replace themselves." [13]

There were at the time some empirical data to support this belief. Taussig and Joslyn had collected data on the occupations of fathers of present leading businessmen and then separated the businessmen into old and young age groups. If mobility was decreasing, the fathers of the young men should have had higher ranking occupations than the fathers of the older men. It was found that a considerably larger proportion of the younger men had fathers who were major executives. The only other large difference, for farmers' sons, was complicated somewhat by the fact that the proportion of farmers in the population had been declining steadily. Thus, what evidence there was, seemed to point toward a decreased amount of mobility.

It was soon recognized, however, that the Taussig-Joslyn study provided no adequate test of whether mobility in American society was increasing or decreasing. These researchers had used data for only a single generation and their results might have been due only to the fact that the sons of major executives achieve executive status faster than the sons of nonexecutives. Eventually, the mobile sons of men who were not business leaders might catch up. [14]

Warner and Abegglen subsequently repeated and expanded upon the Taussig-Joslyn study, securing data from 8300 major executives in 1952. [15] By comparing the occupations of these executives with those of their fathers, and by comparing their data with Taussig and Joslyn's data, Warner and Abegglen discovered that there had been no decrease in mobility into executive positions over the past quarter century, at least. [16] In fact, they concluded that mobility to the top is slowly increasing.

Rogoff's study of the occupations of Indianapolis men and their fathers in 1910 and 1940 provides the most adequate and complete investigation of trends in occupational mobility that has yet been made. [17] She, for the first time, was able to discover not only how much upward mobility was occurring but also how much of the upward mobility was due to broadened opportunities resulting from the increased number of higher status jobs in the society. Briefly, she found that opportunities for upward mobility in 1940 were about the same as in 1910, even after changes in the occupational structure had been taken into account. [18] Since

---

[13] W. Lloyd Warner and others, *op. cit.*, p. 153.

[14] Bernard Barber, *Social Stratification, A Comparative Analysis of Structure and Process* (New York, Harcourt, Brace & Co., 1957), pp. 446-447.

[15] W. Lloyd Warner and James C. Abegglen, *Occupational Mobility in American Business and Industry, 1928-1952* (Minneapolis, University of Minnesota Press, 1955).

[16] *Ibid.*, p. 36.

[17] *Op. cit.*

[18] *Ibid.*, p. 106.

the proportion of high status positions in 1940 was greater than in 1910, this actually means that there was *more* mobility in 1940 than in 1910.

To sum up the evidence on social class and social mobility in the United States, we have neither the completely open-class system claimed by some groups nor the downtrodden proletariat postulated by some others. The United States has a large middle class based upon income and material possessions, a large lower class with depressed living standards, and a relatively small upper class founded on current or former wealth and family lineage. The actual lines drawn will vary with the local community but the basic pattern is never very far removed. *Mobility*

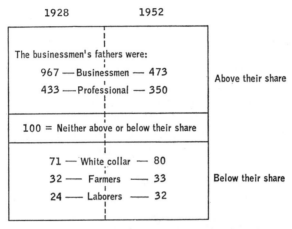

FIG. 11–1. Who got their share in 1928 and 1952?
Those occupations above 100 have a higher per-
centage of business leaders than their percent-
ages in the general population of America;
those below have a smaller percentage.

SOURCE: W. Lloyd Warner and James C. Abegglen, *Big Business Leaders in America* (New York, Harper and Brothers, 1955), p. 27, by permission.

from one class to another is a fairly frequent occurrence and may be becoming easier, but the surest way to attain upper-class status is to be born of upper-class parents. From "office boy to president" is greatly admired, but from "president's son to president" is more certain.

THE SOCIAL-DISORGANIZATION APPROACH

Many people deplore open discussion of class differences and class consciousness. Such talk implies that there is something wrong and that somehow the system is at fault. Sociologically, it means that social change has created new conditions to which people have not yet become fully adjusted. Many of the old familiar definitions are being challenged or denied altogether; many of the new ones seem strange, incongruous, and radical. These are the familiar symptoms of social disorganization. Some of the old rules have broken down; new ones are beginning to emerge. Which are the old rules that no longer function effectively? What groups are dissatisfied? And, what solutions are proposed?

The Old Rules Challenged

Most people apparently believe there is a substantial amount of upward mobility in the United States. Growing numbers, however, are coming to recognize that class status tends to persist; that mobility is possible, but that remaining in the same social class is more probable. Perhaps for the first time, many people are beginning to act and think not only as participants in the American way of life but also as members of a given social class. Such class consciousness encourages at least some awareness of *conflicts of interests among the classes.* Many manual and white-collar workers find it more difficult to identify themselves with business and professional interests. They become less inclined to seek middle- and upper-class status for themselves, and more inclined to demand middle- and upper-class prerogatives for all the members of their class. Labor unions, for example, have grown tremendously and have found support among such white-collar groups as schoolteachers and clerical workers. The recent political affinity of Negroes, farmers, and white-collar workers for New Deal and Fair Deal national administrations also suggests a developing class alignment at variance with the traditional American pattern. Articulate groups at all social levels vigorously deny both the basis for and the existence of such trends. But the argument continues and grows louder. From widespread denial of even the existence of classes, the focus is shifting to the limits on upward mobility and the prospect of a more open class conflict.

The Dissatisfied Groups

Much of the stimulus to increased class consciousness has come directly or indirectly from the intelligentsia. Scholars and academicians have long debated among themselves the extent to which society is organized along class lines and the benefits and injustices that derive therefrom. Nonetheless, not until recently has this concern spread to the general population. The new public awareness is tied to political and economic conditions that have brought it to the fore.

One of the effects of the great depression of the 1930's was to shatter some of the American's naïve faith in the inevitability of progress. Long hard years of unemployment and breadlines made people susceptible to new and radical social philosophies. It remained for the government to do what private enterprise could not—to pull us out of the depression. The idea of government responsibility for individual welfare gained favor and grew in popularity. Two radical economic philosophies—Socialism and Communism—received eager attention from the adventurous, the liberals, and the disgruntled. Both of these philosophies stress the conflict of interests between the "masses" and the "bourgeoisie." Subsequent events in the form of elaborate government regulation of the economy in World War II and the cold war were heartily applauded by some groups and bitterly opposed by others.

Probably, the most vociferous and articulate of the dissatisfied groups are the liberals. As far as class is concerned, the liberals are a heterogeneous lot. For the most part they appear to be drawn from the better-educated segments of the society though they include persons from all economic levels except perhaps the very lowest. A principal requirement for liberal status seems to be the ability to conceptualize *class* and to sympathize with the lower classes. As a group, the liberals are not effectively organized. Being drawn from such varied backgrounds, they have little in common other than their liberality.

Intellectuals, and particularly social scientists, are often thought to be in the vanguard of the liberal movement. In one sense they are, and in another sense they are not. Social scientists are the most persistent critics in any society. Their social science training frees them from the narrow perspective which people generally have of their own society. The social scientist recognizes conflicts among the society's basic values and is apt to lend his authority to reconciling them. However, just as he cannot share the conservative's naïve acceptance of the status quo, the social scientist generally cannot accept the liberal's naïve faith in alleged panaceas. Consequently, conservatives tend to regard him as dangerous and radical while liberals eventually find him stodgy and conservative. As in the matter of class, social scientists through their teaching and research have done much to arouse awareness, but only in rare instances have they been actively involved in liberal movements.

Just as liberals are the vocal chords of the opposition, the lower classes are its muscles. The liberals are likely to be heard, but as a group they wield relatively little power. The lower classes on the other hand are handicapped by their inability to conceptualize the problem. Theirs is more of a latent than an actual awareness. They are prone to see the problem in terms of their individual inability to get ahead rather than as a collective problem requiring collective action. Potentially, they have the power inherent in large numbers, and should they become aroused to a "class" interest, fundamental changes would likely follow. Largely leaderless and only partly aroused, the lower classes are at present not a major threat to the existing order. But some persons in both groups envision the time when the liberals and the lower classes will "get together."

Proposed Solutions

Among the dissatisfied groups, only a few of the intellectuals seem unwilling to accept the inevitability of a rigidly stratified society. These academicians who want to preserve the benefits of the original system ask, How can we ensure that people will be given advantages in accord with their abilities rather than because they belong to certain class groups? The obvious, but not easily achieved, answer is to make education and technical training available on the basis of IQ scores or some other measures of ability. *Availability of educational opportunity* would have to mean much more than just a free public school system, however. To *guarantee* equal opportunity, lower-class children of superior ability would have to be given a type of education that might seem meaningless both to them and their families—education based on middle-class rather than lower-class values. Whether such goals could be achieved within the structure of existing social institutions is doubtful. Many children would soon be destined for social levels either above or below that of their parents; consequently, families would be disrupted. Probably few persons really imagine that such wholesale changes will be effected. An important step toward more equality of opportunity would be taken, however, simply by reducing the middle-class bias of the existing educational system. Teachers would need to become familiar with lower-class culture patterns and to become aware of their own tendencies to discriminate in favor of middle-class children. They would have to learn to interpret the goals and values of an education in terms that lower-class children can understand and appreciate. Some progressive school administrators are already aware of this situation and are attempting to put the above recommendations into practice. Only the barest beginning has been made, however.

Both the lower class and most of the liberals tend to orient their solutions toward improving the position of the lower class *as a class*. The emphasis is on securing new benefits for the class rather than aiding people to escape the class. Many workers have come to accept labor unions as a major weapon in this struggle and their goals are largely identified with those of the unions—higher wages, shorter hours, improved working conditions, unemployment insurance, retirement plans, and paid vacations. The liberal emphasis, on the other hand, attacks much more directly the prerogatives of the upper classes. The liberals favor such measures as excess-profits taxes and higher tax rates on larger incomes to reduce the inequalities in wealth and living standards. They see a need to end the "exploitation of the masses" by restricting the privileges of the "elite." Because their attack is a direct and frontal one, the liberals are most bitterly opposed by the upper classes. The lower class demands for higher wages and better living conditions seem relatively nonthreatening by comparison. One effect of the presence of an articulate liberal group may be to aid lower-class efforts by making them seem to be the lesser of the two evils.

THE PERSONAL-DEVIATION APPROACH

Class conflicts cannot be explained solely in terms of economic interests. Though there is an observable alignment along income lines, certain groups seem to act in a fashion contrary to their own best interests. It is easy to see why the lower-class persons might want to challenge the existing order, but it is not so easy to see why many prosperous middle- and upper-class persons should be involved. Most of these persons stand to lose, financially, if the reforms they propose are adopted. Moreover, they are frequently scorned and regarded as traitors by their own class. Some few radical persons have gone far beyond rejecting upper-class values in favor of lower-class ones, and have flirted openly with Communist and socialist movements. Knowledge of this fact brings condemnation not only by the upper classes but by the majority of people at all social levels. People do not reject the approval of class or society without paying heavy penalties. How can we explain the actions of these deviants in the class structure?

To state that such persons are disloyal to the traditional and customary values tells only part of the story. For our purposes, we may divide these deviants into two groups: (1) those who take different positions than other members of their class; and (2) those whose motivations are complicated by extreme personal maladjustment.

(1) Anyone who takes a position differing from the ones that are usual in his class is more or less a deviant. Thus, the son of a businessman who favors the expansion of trade unionism or the steeply graduated income tax is deviant if only because his family and associates generally believe these things to be undesirable.

It seems likely that even lower-class persons in the United States typically give lip-service to upper-class values, and that the lower-class person who is aggressively antagonistic to upper-class values is a deviant even among lower-class persons. While the aggressive proletarian leader has long been a widely recognized type in Europe, the United States emphasis on fluidity of class lines and frequent upward mobility has prevented his becoming common here.

The failure of a person to accept the values of his own class group may come about in two ways. First, it may come about through his exposure to the influence of social norms that are quite different from those of his parents. Through boyhood gangs or later peer groups, from schoolteachers, through literature, or through a hundred other sources he may become a participant in a different subculture from that of his parents. He may not specifically reject the norms espoused by his parents so much as he accepts an alternative, and conflicting, set of norms presented to him by the society. Or, secondly, his deviancy may involve outright rejection of the parental values. Psychoanalysts have pointed out guilt feelings, father-son rivalries, and the like as bases for rebellion against the parents.

(2) Aggressive, maladjusted, hate-filled persons are found in all areas of life, including class struggles. These people despise the alleged injustices against which they contend with a special fervor. Politically, they are apt to be either reactionary or radical. No matter which extreme they choose, they will not accept any compromise short of the total destruction of the opposing groups, and their hostilities are easily displaced into espousal of fascism or communism. Though they take the directions of their hates from the culture in which they live, such persons are candidates for psychotherapy or institutionalization rather than for re-education.

THE VALUE-CONFLICT APPROACH

The Original Values

The American economy traditionally has been a free economy—free from unwarranted interference by government or other outside agencies. This free economy unquestionably has produced the greatest volume of goods and the highest standard of living the world has ever known. It is not necessary to assert that the free economy *caused* the high production, for it is apparent that other factors—abundant resources, a vast land area, a vigorous young population, and occasional government subsidies—were also involved. But neither can we be sure that a different economic system would have used these factors so effectively. The simple historical fact is that *American prosperity has been associated with a free economy.*

The American free economy, as stated earlier, was built, not upon equality, but on a *relative* equality of opportunity. The system has always embraced—in fact, even assumed—wide differences in income and living standards. According to our traditional values, there is nothing morally wrong with low standards of living. Humble beginnings and the chance to rise above one's origins have been considered to be compatible with our other concepts of "democracy" and "freedom." What has been re-garded as morally suspect is remaining in a lower-class position when one has the opportunity to escape it. According to this traditional view, the responsibility for one's status lies with the individual! The responsibility of society ends with the maintenance of a free economy, so that the individual may rise *if* he is capable of rising. Within this framework, a sizable lower class becomes natural and even inevitable. Each man should profit according to his own merit and the class structure should accurately reflect individual differences in ability.

This free economy, along with its supporting theory of class placement according to individual ability, has, to many Americans, become almost synonymous with freedom itself. *Freedom* has meant the freedom to rise above the masses and become wealthy. Supposedly every man has an inherent right to become as prosperous as he possibly can. Whether these inherent rights are God-given or man-made, justice presumably depends upon their being maintained. Traditionally, the point of view of society as a whole, the maintenance of freedom to rise in the class structure and to amass wealth is perhaps becoming the limited value position of the relatively conservative middle and upper classes. Accordingly, another set of values is gradually rising to challenge it.

The Ideology of Minimum Standards

Increased awareness of the tendency for lower-class status to be self-perpetuating has encouraged people to question the whole set of assumptions on which the class structure is built. It is now widely recognized that income and class status are not distributed simply on the basis of ability alone. People have begun to ask such questions as, Is it ability alone or is it also vices such as ruthlessness and greed, that enable people to get ahead? Should some people be permitted to receive several million dollars per year while almost one-fourth of the population earns less than two thousand dollars per year? Is any man worth five or six hundred times as much as any other man? Should "freedom" include the freedom to live in poverty—to be underfed, ill-housed, ill-clothed, and to be without adequate medical care? Can true democracy exist side by side with filth and squalor?

Few serious people would argue that the answer lies in the elimination of all class differences. Relatively few people see the issue in the extreme form of "freedom" versus "equality," but many people feel that the harsher effects of the class system need to be lessened through raising the living standards of the lowest classes. This position is sometimes referred to as "the ideology of minimum standards." The growing numbers of people who hold these values advocate such measures as minimum-wage laws, guaranteed annual wages, publicly financed health insurance, vacations with pay, retirement programs, and the like. The student will recognize that these are among the hottest issues on the American scene. These are measures which reactionaries, in an effort to forestall their acceptance, label as socialistic or communistic and which liberals ardently support. Theoretically, such gains might come, over the years, out of increased production alone without taking anything directly away from the upper classes. Practically, the conflict of values is too deep for this solution to be really satisfactory to either side. Middle- and upper-class reactionaries bitterly oppose any measures which would put a floor under living standards. Raising the floor for the lower classes would mean, directly or indirectly, lowering the ceiling on the upper classes. The liberals, especially, and probably the lower-class groups, would applaud this philosophy. They favor limiting the freedom of the wealthy to become more wealthy in order to help the poor to become less poor! The fundamental nature of the conflict underlying these two positions must be recognized. For at least twenty years now, the whole issue of social welfare measures to aid the lower classes has occupied a central place in American politics. Elections are being fought, won, and lost over it. To date, the United States has been less disposed to accept the minimum standards ideology than have been many European nations. Reactionaries, and even conservatives, maintain that any further steps in this direction will result in considerable loss of freedom for all; liberals argue that freedom and dire poverty cannot exist together. In any event, resolution of this conflict will have to be part of any solution to existing problems of social class. For now, one may safely predict that the same issue will be a factor in many future elections.

SUMMARY

American democracy is built, not upon the notion of a classless society, but upon an open-class system, under which all persons should have equal opportunity to get ahead so that the more capable individuals will be those who achieve upper-class status. The low birth rates of upper-class groups and the expanding nature of the American economy have favored considerable upward movement in the class structure.

There is considerable evidence, nevertheless, to suggest that there is a basic incompatability between the existence of *social classes* and *equal opportunity*. In the American scene, for example, the one-tenth of the population which happens to be Negro is forced into an almost castelike position beneath the white group. Although most whites tend to identify themselves with the middle class, objective studies reveal the existence of a large lower class. Identification with the middle class is apparently based upon the hope of being able to rise into that group. Again, objective studies show that while mobility is possible it is less probable for lower-class than for middle-class persons.

Some liberals, intellectuals, and members of the lower class have begun to challenge the justice of the original system and are agitating for change. They advocate either opening wider the channels for mobility or improving the lot of the lower classes as a whole. The actions of the opposing groups reflect a basic conflict of values—the freedom of the individual to become wealthy or to live in abject poverty against the right of all people to at least a minimum standard of living. Deviants are defined in terms of failure to assume the class biases of the groups to which they belong. Deviant values may be learned, normally, in the socialization process or they may be associated with parental rebellion or other emotional compulsions.

SUGGESTED READINGS

BARBER, Bernard, *Social Stratification: A Comparative Analysis of Structure and Process* (New York, Harcourt, Brace & Co., 1957). A comprehensive treatment of stratification in the United States, stressing the integration of research findings with general sociological theory.

CENTERS, Richard, *The Psychology of Social Classes* (Princeton, N. J., Princeton University Press, 1949). Penetrating analysis of social class structure in the United States. Stresses class consciousness as a variable in social stratification.

CUBER, John F., and KENKEL, William, *Social Stratification in the United States* (New York, Appleton-Century-Crofts, Inc., 1954). The first systematic textbook in the field of social stratification. A good introduction to both theoretical analysis and empiric research.

DAVIS, Allison, GARDNER, Burleigh, and GARDNER, Mary, *Deep South* (Chicago, University of Chicago Press, 1947). A comprehensive study of class patterns in a city in the deep South. Includes both the white and Negro populations.

KAHL, Joseph, *The American Class Structure* (New York, Rinehart & Company, Inc., 1957). Organizes and evaluates research on social class in the United States. Special attention to how the evidence was collected and the population groups to whom it applies.

MILLS, C. Wright, *White Collar* (New York, Oxford University Press, Inc., 1953). An extensive treatment of the white-collar portion of the American middle classes. Relates the rise of the white-collar classes both to historical trends and to economic forces.

WARNER, W. Lloyd, and ABEGGLEN, James C., *Big Business Leaders in America* (New York, Harper and Brothers, 1955). A study of over 8000 top leaders in American business and industry. Analyzes their occupational origins, their careers, their personalities and their families.

WARNER, W. Lloyd, HAVIGHURST, Robert J., and LOEB, Martin B., *Who Shall Be Educated?* (New York, Harper and Brothers, 1944). Impressive analysis of social class influences on the operation of the American educational system.

WARNER, W. Lloyd and LUNT, Paul S., *The Social Life of a Modern Community* (New Haven, Yale University Press, 1941). A comprehensive picture of the social class structure of a New England city. Includes several chapters on the techniques used to determine a community's class pattern.

AUDIO-VISUAL AIDS

Again Pioneers (Broadcasting and Film Commission, 220 Fifth Ave., New York, 1 hr. 10 minutes, sound, black and white. Produced by the Protestant Film Commission. Shows the efforts of leading citizens in an average American town to rid the community of a group of migrants settled in shacks on the outskirts of town which they feel threatens health and welfare. A home-missions field worker helps the citizens see the needs of these, their neighbors, and to see something of the total task of the church in relation to the underprivileged of the nation.

One Tenth of Our Nation (International Film Bureau, Suite 308-316, 57 East Jackson Blvd., Chicago), 26 minutes, sound, black and white. A picture of the education of Negro children in the rural South, from one-room shacks to high schools and colleges.

Two Views of Socialism (Coronet Films, Coronet Bldg., Chicago), 15 minutes, sound, black and white. Specially designed to stimulate an intelligent discussion on the difference between socialism and capitalism. The basic charges levelled by socialists against capitalist society are made and answered.

QUESTIONS AND PROJECTS

1. How accurate is the unqualified statement. "All men are equal"? What kind of equality is highly valued in the United States?

2. Define the concept "open-class system." What two factors have been important in maintaining a relatively open-class system in the United States?

3. Differentiate between the concepts of "class" and "caste." Where are there castelike elements in the United States stratification pattern?

4. With what social class group do most Americans identify themselves? How do you explain this identification?

5. How do the results of community studies and the distribution of cash income compare with the self-identifications referred to in the previous question?

6. How does class status influence one's chances to acquire higher education? professional status?

7. Explain the "ideology of minimum standards."

8. List as many pro's and con's as you can for each of the value positions involved in the issue, "Freedom versus Minimum Standards."

9. Interview two young men in college or who have just graduated and two middle-aged men who have college degrees, concerning what life goals a young man should select for himself. Are the young men more security-minded and less adventure-minded? Do the young men feel that they have more or less chance for upward mobility than their middle-aged counterparts had? How does this square with the evidence on mobility trends in this country?

10. Map out roughly the main lines of class division in your home community. Are there a few fairly well-defined classes or does there seem to be

a continuous range of variation? How large is your community? How does
this factor of community size influence the precision with which class lines
can be drawn?

11. Suppose all talented youth could be given the ambition and opportunity
for higher education. What changes in the class system would follow?

12. Name some social or political issues that are basically class conflicts
even though they are debated in quite different terms.

13. Does the Marxian theory of a property-owning class arrayed against
a working class describe the American scene? Why or why not?

12

The Race Problem:
From Folklore to Science

ʕʕ

The woman with the pink velvet poppies wreathed round the assisted gold of her hair traversed the crowded room at an interesting gait combining a skip with a sidle and clutched the lean arm of her host. . . .

"Listen," she said. "I want to meet Walter Williams. Honestly, I'm just simply crazy about that man. . . . Oh, when he sings! When he sings those spirituals! Well, I said to Burton, 'It's a good thing for you Walter Williams is colored,' I said, 'or you'd have lots of reason to be jealous.' I'd really love to meet him. I'd like to tell him I've heard him sing. Will you be an angel and introduce me to him?"

"Why, certainly," said her host. "I thought you'd met him. The party's for him. Where is he, anyway?"

"He's over there by the bookcase," she said. "Let's wait till those people get through talking to him. Well, I think you're simply marvelous, giving this perfectly marvelous party for him, and having him meet all these white people, and all. Isn't he terribly grateful?" . . .

"Now, me, . . . I haven't the slightest feeling about colored people. Why, I'm just crazy about some of them. They're just like children—just as easygoing, and always singing and laughing and everything. Aren't they the happiest things you ever saw in your life? Honestly, it makes me laugh just to hear them. Oh, I like them, I really do. Well, now, listen, I have this colored laundress, I've had her for years, and I'm devoted to her. She's a real character. And I want to tell you, I think of her as my friend. That's the way I think of her. As I say to Burton, 'Well, for heaven's sakes, we're all human beings!' Aren't we?" . . .

They reached the tall young Negro standing by the bookcase. The host performed introductions; the Negro bowed.

"How do you do?" he said. "Isn't it a nice party?"

The woman with the pink velvet poppies extended her hand at the length of her arm and held it so, in fine determination, for all the world to see, until the Negro took it, shook it, and gave it back to her.

"Oh, how do you do, Mr. Williams," she said. "Well, how do you do. I've just been saying I've enjoyed your singing so awfully much. I've been to your concerts, and we have you on the phonograph and everything. Oh, I just enjoy it."

She spoke with great distinctness, moving her lips meticulously, as if in parlance with the deaf.

"I'm so glad," he said.

"I'm just simply crazy about that 'Water Boy' thing you sing," she said. "Honestly, I can't get it out of my head. I have my husband nearly crazy, the way I go around humming it all the time. Oh, he looks just as black as the ace of—er. Well, tell me, where on earth do you ever get all those songs of yours? How do you ever get hold of them?"

"Why," he said. "There are so many different—"

"I should think you'd love singing them," she said. "It must be more fun! All those darling old spirituals—oh, I just love them! Well, what are you doing now? Are you still keeping up your singing? Why don't you have another concert sometime?"

"I'm having one the sixteenth of this month," he said.

"Well, I'll be there," she said. "I'll be there, if I possibly can. You can count on me. Goodness, here comes a whole raft of people to talk to you. You're just a regular guest of honor! Oh, who's that girl in white? I've seen her someplace."

"That's Katherine Burke," said her host.

"Good heavens," she said, "is that Katherine Burke? Why, she looks entirely different off the stage. I thought she was much better looking. I had no idea she was so terribly dark. Why, she looks almost like— Oh, I think she's a wonderful actress! Don't you think she's a wonderful actress, Mr. Williams? Oh, I think she's marvelous. Don't you?"

"Yes, I do," he said.

"Oh, I do, too," she said. "Just wonderful. Well, goodness, we must give someone else a chance to talk to the guest of honor. Now, don't forget, Mr. Williams, I'm going to be at that concert if I possibly can. I'll be there applauding like everything. And if I can't come, I'm going to tell everybody I know to go, anyway. Don't you forget!"

"I won't," he said. "Thank you so much."

The host took her arm and piloted her firmly into the next room.[1]

THIS INCIDENT, NOTABLE FOR THE SUBTLETY of the prejudice it reveals, suggests but a few of the many facets of the American race problem. Of all social problems, there is perhaps none more serious, and certainly none more unnecessary, than the race problem. If the first terrestrial expedition to Mars should find that the Martians (if any) have a social structure stacked into layers according to length of proboscis or coloration

[1] Dorothy Parker, "Arrangement in Black and White," *The Portable Dorothy Parker* (New York, The Viking Press, Inc., 1952), pp. 41-47.

of antennae, we should think this very odd. And if the Martians, because of slight variations in structure or coloration, worried themselves into neuroses, drifted into rioting, lynching, and warfare, and excluded many of their members from doing useful and valuable work, we would think this incredibly wasteful and inefficient (and conclusive evidence of Martian inferiority and unfitness to rule themselves!). Would the conclusions of a Martian visitor to our globe be greatly different?

How could such a situation have developed into a genuine and serious problem in America? What is the nature and extent of the race problem? How does it affect all the groups involved? What are the current trends in treatment? Will they prove effective?

THE SCIENTIFIC FACTS ABOUT RACE

The facts about race are no longer a mystery to social scientists. They are well established by scientific research and are easily summarized. Most social scientists believe that, *in biological inheritance, all races are alike in everything that really makes any difference.* There are differences in coloration and slight differences in facial features and bodily proportion but, according to all evidence available, these have no effect upon learning or behavior. With the exception of several very small, isolated, inbred primitive tribes, *all racial groups seem to show the same distribution of every kind of ability.* All races learn in the same way and at the same average speed under the same circumstances. *All important race differences in personality, behavior, and achievement are purely a result of environmental factors.* Such differences (for example, ignorance and shiftlessness among Negroes) are cited by the majority group to justify its discrimination which, in turn, perpetuates those very differences. Thus a vicious circle is completed, and an illusion of innate race differences is preserved.

These are the conclusions of science. Vast numbers of people are unaware of them and of the evidence upon which they rest, and many other people are unable to accept them. For those who wish to study them, the scientific facts about race differences are easily available. [2] This chapter will not attempt any further review of these facts, but will assume that the student has some awareness of them.

[2] See Ruth Benedict and Gene Weltfish, *The Races of Mankind*, Public Affairs Pamphlet, No. 85 (New York, Public Affairs Committee, 1943), for a brief, popularized treatment of race differences and race prejudice, or for a more thorough treatment, see Ashley-Montagu, *Man's Most Dangerous Myth: The Fallacy of Race* (New York, Columbia University Press, 1945). See also Otto Klineberg, *Race Differences* (New York, Harper and Brothers, 1935), for a comprehensive analysis of scientific research about race differences.

Cost of the Problem

1. *The financial cost* of the race problem will surprise most people, who are unaware of the many ways in which they pay for the luxury of enjoying their alleged race superiority. Although there is no fully satisfactory way of measuring the direct and indirect cost of the race problem, there are a number of things which suggest that the total cost is enormous.

Race riots with their destruction of life and property give most dramatic evidence of the cost of the race problem. The 1919 Chicago riot killed 38 persons, injured 537, destroyed the homes of nearly a thousand, and caused over $250,000 destruction. [3] "The newspapers in 1942 and 1943 reported more Negro casualties from racial friction in the United States than [Negro] casualties in the World War for the same period." [4] Disorders in Chicago, where whites sought to keep Negroes out of a public housing project in 1953-1954, caused over $200,000 property damages, and resulted in total costs (for police protection, etc.) of over $2,000,000. [5]

But these losses are as pennies compared to the cost of economic inefficiency which the race problem produces. Since scientists are in general agreement that whites and Negroes have *equal native abilities*, it follows that *all important differences in group behavior are due to prejudice, discrimination, and lack of opportunity and encouragement*. This means that if Negroes work less energetically, receive less income, have more illness, spend more time on relief, commit more crimes and spend more time in jail than whites, all such differences are part of the cost of discrimination. The indirect economic loss from these 15,000,000 people, so many of whom are ignorant, poor, and unmotivated, reaches an impressive total. The President's Committee on Employment Policy estimates that unused Negro talent costs us over $12 billion a year, while the total economic cost is officially placed at $30 billion. [6] A former cabinet officer explains, "Individuals who suffer discrimination cannot be full partners in an economy of plenty. They cannot afford to purchase their share of the goods we produce nor pay their potential share of the taxes for the common good." [7]

Lack of education, lack of motivation, and denial of employment work together to keep the Negro's productivity low and his income small. Median family incomes in 1959 show this distribution:

White $4,569
Negro 2,652

[3] Chicago Commission on Race Relations, *The Negro in Chicago: A Study of Race Relations and a Race Riot* (Chicago, University of Chicago Press, 1922), p. 1.

[4] A. Clayton Powell, *Riots and Ruins* (New York, Richard R. Smith, 1945), p. 17.

[5] "Racial Problems Trouble Chicago," *New York Times*, July 25, 1954, p. 50.

[6] *Time*, Vol. 66 (November 7, 1955), p. 31.

[7] Oveta Culp Hobby, former Secretary, Department of Health, Education and Welfare, in *New York Times*, March 3, 1954, p. 25.

Although the average Negro family has more members at work than the average white family, [8] the Negro family has slightly over half the income (58 per cent) of the white family. Why is this true? The Negro worker is educationally handicapped by having an average of 6.4 years of schooling, compared with 9.3 years for whites (persons over 14 years of age, 1950 Census). He is often barred from the jobs where he could make his greatest contribution. Although 24,000 Negro veterans worked as carpenters in the armed forces, they were barred from the trade as civilians during a period of acute shortage of skilled labor. [9] Although teaching is the principal Negro profession, Negroes have only about half the representation in the teaching profession that they have in the general population. Failure to use Negro talent, and failure to provide opportunities and rewards that stimulate his efforts and ambitions have helped keep the Negro unmotivated and unproductive.

2. *The political costs* cannot be measured in dollars, but must be measured by the degree to which unsolved race problems disrupt democratic processes and impair national unity. Although Negro voters have rapidly increased, millions of Negroes are still prevented from voting through such devices as the poll tax, by white primaries, by various "tests" of voting fitness which local officials permit few Negroes to pass, and sometimes by threats and even violence. [10] In no part of the country can Negroes be confident that they will receive the equal protection of the law, and frequency of charges of police brutality toward Negroes are "proof that improper conduct by police is still widespread." [11] The Negro's constitutional right to a fair trial is often violated, and Negroes are not infrequently convicted on evidence on which no white person would even be tried. One Negro was convicted of "assault" for having "leered" at a white girl from a distance of 50 feet, [12] and a Negro was lynched in 1955 for whistling at a white woman.[13] Virginia executed seven Negroes in 1951, bringing to forty-five its total of Negroes executed for a crime

[8] Eli Ginzberg, *The Negro Potential* (New York, Columbia University Press, 1956), p. 16.

[9] Elmo Roper, in R. M. MacIver, *Discrimination and National Welfare*, Institute for Religious and Social Studies (New York, Harper and Brothers, 1949), pp. 21-22.

[10] The number of registered Negroes in the South has grown from 595,000 in 1947 to 1,240,000 in 1957; this is about 25 per cent of all southern Negroes of voting age, whereas about 60 per cent of the southern whites are registered to vote, according to the *38th Annual Report of the American Civil Liberties Union, 1957-1958*, pp. 51-52. For a description of ways of preventing Negroes from registering to vote, see United States Commission on Civil Rights, *With Liberty And Justice For All* (Washington, Government Printing Office, 1959), pp. 23-83.

[11] President's Committee on Civil Rights, *To Secure These Rights* (Washington, D. C., Government Printing Office, 1947), p. 25; also, "U.S. Sifts Charges in Negro Deaths," *New York Times*, June 15, 1958, p. 68.

[12] *Time*, Vol. 60 (November 24, 1952), p. 22.

[13] *New York Times*, September 2, 1955, p. 37; September 18, 1955, IV, p. 7; September 23, 1955, p. 15; November 10, 1955, p. 31.

(rape) for which no white man has ever been executed in Virginia.[14] In Texas an all-white jury in 1958 condemned a seventeen-year-old Negro to death and sentenced a nineteen-year-old white man to life imprisonment after identical testimony had convicted them both of raping the same white woman.[15]

One celebrated case was tried not in the South but in New Jersey. where six Negroes were condemned to death on exceedingly flimsy evidence in a flagrantly unjust trial, and did not gain their freedom until several years had passed and many thousands of dollars had been spent.[16] Although such cases are unusual, the monotonous regularity of their appearance shows that Negroes are still far from receiving equal treatment from courts and enforcement officers. In *no* respect—the right to vote, to hold office, to buy and own property, to travel about the country, to be arrested justly and tried fairly when suspected of crime, and even to be buried when dead—do Negroes fully enjoy the promises of the Fourteenth Amendment, reading in part: "No State shall make or enforce any law which shall abridge the privileges or immunities of citizens of the United States, nor shall any State deprive any person of life, liberty, or property without due process of law, nor deny to any person within its jurisdiction the equal protection of the laws. . . ."

It is ironical that the political inequities imposed upon Negroes should often prove even more costly to the whites themselves than to the Negroes. The poll tax, a device to prevent Negroes from voting, actually disfranchised an even greater number of whites in some Southern states. In allowing the maintenance of white supremacy to dominate its political life for nearly a century, the South sacrificed all hope of electing another president from the South, curtailed its national political influence, and largely destroyed its power to resist three-quarters of a century of commercial exploitation by the North. Her preoccupation with white su-

[14] Henry Lee Moon, "The Martinsville Rape Case," *New Leader*, Vol. 34 (February 12, 1951), p. 18.

[15] *38th Annual Report, op. cit.*, p. 54.

[16] In this case of the "Trenton Six," the only evidence consisted of "confessions" from the suspects secured by long interrogation and use of drugs. The New Jersey Supreme Court reversed the verdict and ordered a new trial, at which four were acquitted and two convicted, four years after the original arrest. One of these two died while further appeal was pending, and the other, finally pleading "no defense," was sentenced and paroled after serving six months. It is likely that all were entirely innocent. For numerous citations covering this lengthy case, see *New York Times Index* (heading, "Murders; New Jersey," W. Horner), 1948, p. 688; 1949, p. 665; 1950, p. 729; 1951, p. 704; 1952, p. 719; 1953, p. 696. See also Claire Neikind, "The Case of the Trenton Six," *Reporter*, Vol. 4 (May 1, 1951), pp. 31-34; (May 29, 1951), pp. 33-38.

A significant sidelight is the fact that the Communist-front Civil Rights Congress successfully exploited this miscarriage of justice to raise an estimated $300,000 defense fund, most of which was diverted to other party uses. The eventual release was secured mainly through the efforts of the NAACP and the American Civil Liberties Union.

premacy prevented serious discussion of other issues. Candidates for public office who sought to present a constructive program for dealing with critical problems of the South were likely to be defeated by candidates who posed as saviors from a terrifying nightmare of Negro revolt. Beneficiaries of the political and economic status quo found the white-supremacy issue an easy device for diverting attention from possible reforms, and thus political interest was largely diverted from the discussion of economic issues to the ritualistic exorcism of racial bogey-men.

The political costs of prejudice are not confined to the South. By keeping its Negroes poor and half educated, the North has made them prime subjects for political bossism. The seat of a boss's power rests in a group of voters so poor, so ill informed, and so neglected that a few small favors will buy their support. Negro politics is often corrupt politics, for wherever there is poverty, ignorance, and limited opportunity, political corruption appears. Both the North and the South have, as one critic observed, "sold their political birthright for a mess of racial pottage."

3. *The psychic costs* of the race problem are less tangible but no less important. For Negroes, the race problem means a variety of anxieties, fears, and frustrations which the remainder of this book could not fully describe. [17] These differ among regions and individuals, ranging from the fear of violence to the fear of embarrassment, from anxiety over finding a job to anxiety lest a remark be misunderstood—the list is endless. The Negro's dilemma is that *no matter what he does, he irritates some white folks*. If he is docile and easygoing, that only proves his inferiority; if he seeks a nice house and good car, he is an "uppity nigger"—if he doesn't, he is "content to live in filth." He gets along best with whites by appearing to be stupid, unambitious, and contented, but this pattern conflicts with the competition-success ideology of our culture. Thus the Negro, particularly the better-educated Negro, is constantly frustrated by the contradictory pressures imposed upon him. The more successful Negroes often find that increasing frustration is the reward of their efforts, for success fails to bring the Negro the full rewards of status, acceptance, and freedom to spend his money where and as he wishes—the rewards success brings to white folks.

Whites, too, harbor fears, anxieties, and above all, bad consciences. Whites are fearful of Negro violence, especially in the South where a long succession of bloody slave revolts disprove the myth that Negroes were ever very contented.[18] Many whites fear Negro invasions of their

[17] See Richard Wright, *Black Boy* (New York, Harper and Brothers, 1945); Allison Davis and John Dollard, *Children of Bondage: The Personality Development of Negro Youth in the Urban South* (Washington, American Council on Education, 1940); Bertram J. Karom, *The Negro Personality* (New York, Springer Publishing Company, 1958).

[18] See Katherine M. Jones, *The Plantation South* (Indianapolis, The Bobbs-Merrill Company, 1957); Kenneth M. Stampp, *The Peculiar Institution: Slavery in*

jobs, their schools and neighborhoods, even their resorts and clubs. Many whites fear sexual aggression by Negro men against white women, a fear which may spring from the white's own guilt feelings.[19] Lillian Smith has suggested that white men have impoverished their own sexual life with white women through their sexual affairs with Negro women. She suggests that the white man's morbid preoccupation with Negro sexual aggression (and the tendency for every racial discussion to arrive at the "would-you-want-your-daughter-to-marry-a-Negro" rhetorical question) may be only a displacement of the white man's own guilt feelings and his sternly repressed fear that white woman may also find Negro men attractive.[20]

In a hundred lesser ways the race problem afflicts the white man's peace of mind and makes him uncomfortable. He does not really want to give up the many discriminations and subtle forms of exploitation from which he thinks he benefits, and yet he is not always comfortable with them. As Myrdal has pointed out, a moral conflict rages within him, for "even a poor and uneducated white person in some isolated and backward rural region in the Deep South, who is violently prejudiced against the Negro and intent upon depriving him of civic rights and human independence, has also a whole compartment of his valuation sphere housing the entire American creed of liberty, equality, justice, and fair opportunity for everybody." [21] The white who believes both in democracy and in white supremacy, and reconciles the contradiction with a set of artful rationalizations, is sometimes bedeviled by an uneasy awareness that they *are* rationalizations. Whites cannot enjoy the luxury of professing democracy and practicing discrimination without paying a price, either in guilt feelings or in double-talk which they can only half believe.

4. *International costs.* When the Nazis invaded Russia, many of the people welcomed them as liberators. If they had treated the Russian

---

the *Ante-Bellum South* (New York, Alfred A. Knopf, Inc., 1956). One historian writes, "The advertising columns of the newspapers bristled with notices of runaways; and no detailed plantation record which has come to my hand is without mention of them." (Ulrich B. Phillips, *Life and Labor in The Old South,* [Boston, Little, Brown, & Co., 1929], quoted in Irwin T. Sanders, ed., *Societies Around the World* (New York, The Dryden Press, Inc., 1956), p. 577.

[19] Simpson and Yinger write, "Most of the sex contacts between Negroes and whites are initiated by white men; most of the violence is used by whites against the Negroes; yet there is an emotionally vivid belief in the violent and sexually aggressive nature of the Negro. This belief is needed, not only to rid many white people of a sense of guilt for having violated their own standards, but to help them resist the impulses toward violation. The Negro, a designated inferior group, symbolizes the repressed impulses one must not admit are still motivating him." (George E. Simpson and J. Milton Yinger, *Racial and Cultural Minorities* (New York, Harper and Brothers, 1958), p. 82.

[20] Lillian Smith, *Killers of the Dream* (New York, W. W. Norton & Company, Inc., 1949).

[21] Gunnar Myrdal, *An American Dilemma* (New York, Harper and Brothers, 1944), p. xliv.

Colored Asia and colored Africa will never look to us for leadership, will never accept our professions of freedom seriously, until we solve the problem of racial discrimination and segregation. We are on the way to do it. But we may not have time before Asia and Africa are lost to the free world.

Sidney Hook, *New York Times Magazine*, April 5, 1959, p. 108.

people as human beings, Russia might have been defeated, and Hitler might have become master of all Europe. Instead, guided by the "master-race" theories of Hitler, the Nazis' contemptuous brutality united the Russian people and helped insure German defeat. [22] It is well known that Nazi persecution of Jewish scientists largely explains why we, and not the Germans, first developed the atomic bomb. There are times when a people's notions about "race" can be their destruction or their salvation.

In this sense, the future of America rests in the hands of foreigners, for it is doubtful that we can remain free and democratic if the rest of the world embraces Communist totalitarianism. With roughly a third of the world's people under Communist rule, perhaps a fifth of the world's people democratic, and the remainder undecided, the eventual outcome depends largely upon whom this undecided half of the world's people choose to follow. Since *most of the undecided half of the world's peoples are colored*, they are much more interested in our treatment of our Negroes than they are in statistics about our plentiful telephones and bathtubs. For example, when Ethiopian Princess Sybel Desta visited Chicago, she "immediately" asked about racial disorders at Trumbull Park housing development and even knew the name of the Negro whom the whites were seeking to expel. [23] Tom Mboya, perhaps the most influential Negro in all Africa, remarks: [24]

It must be understood that we feel a special kinship with American Negroes, and that we see our struggles as closely related. Segregation robs the United States of the moral standing she needs if she is to give effective leadership to the free world. All the good that she does—even the existence of Supreme Court judgments and other efforts to secure integration—is hardly noticed, whereas Little Rock or a Mississippi lynching receives front-page publicity.

[22] J. A. Lukacs, "Story Behind Hitler's Biggest Blunder," *New York Times Magazine*, June 17, 1951, pp. 10-11 ff; see also Alexander Dallin, *German Rule in Russia, 1941-1945: A Study of Occupation Policies* (New York, St. Martin's Press, 1957).

[23] *Chicago Sun-Times*, July 7, 1954, p. 44.

[24] Tom Mboya, Chairman, All-Africa People's Conference, "Key Questions for Awakening Africa," *New York Times Magazine*, June 28, 1959, p. 39.

It may shock Americans to realize that much of the world considers us insincere, cynical hypocrites whenever we talk of democracy. They ask, "How can you really mean what you say when you treat your Negroes as you do?" In many such ways our international influence is impaired. Our delegates to the United Nations are repeatedly put on the defensive. We must overlook many acts of Russian injustice to minorities because we, too, are to some degree vulnerable to a similar charge. Thus, many opportunities to discredit Communism must be sacrificed, while our denial of equality to Negroes has provided Communist propagandists with a most effective theme.

Many have predicted that the final outcome of the world contest between Communism and democracy will be determined not on battlefields but in the minds of men. If the colored peoples of the world come to feel that their best chance for a better life lies in following Communism, neither American talk nor American guns will long delay the outcome. We cannot garrison the whole world. Only if the people of the world feel that democracy offers a practical solution of their problems of poverty, insecurity, and injustice will they follow America's lead. This is why they watch American treatment of Negroes with such avid interest.

In all these ways and in still others, the race problem is costly to whites and Negroes, to North and South. A Southern sociologist writes, in words also applicable to the North: [25]

The South pays dearly for the economic bondage and the political impotence of its black folk. For, in one way or another—in inefficiency, in waste, in poor health, in low moral standards, in excessive rates of dependency and delinquency—the Negro has levied a tax on the South just as surely as if the states themselves had levied it.

SOME FACTS ABOUT RACE DISCRIMINATION

From his birth to his death the Negro knows discrimination in countless forms. In many parts of the country, he has his choice of being born at home or in a second-class hospital. North or South, he attends schools that are often inferior to those of white children. Whatever test is used —expenditures per pupil, salary of teachers, pupils per teacher, adequacy of school plant and equipment, length of school term—Negroes in many states are at some disadvantage and in some states are at a great disadvantage. Some colleges will not admit him at all; others he can enter only by squeezing into a quota. Upon graduation, the Negro finds most of the jobs open to him are the jobs nobody else wants. Nearly half the employee orders placed by Chicago firms with private employment agencies be-

[25] Guy B. Johnson, "Does the South Owe the Negro a New Deal?" *Social Forces*, Vol. 13 (October, 1934), pp. 100-103.

tween 1955 and 1958 contained discriminatory stipulations. [26] As the business cycle spins, he is "last hired and first fired." [27] Although he earns lower wages, he generally pays a much higher rent than whites pay for comparable housing, because of the limited supply of housing available to Negroes. [28]

If a Negro is highly successful, he cannot buy a home in the better parts of town without facing the certainty of discourtesy and humiliation and the possibility of violence. In no city can he patronize first-class hotels, restaurants, and theaters and be confident of the respectful service which whites receive. If he takes a vacation trip, his itinerary is limited to those resorts and lodges—rarely first-class—which accept Negroes, and all sight-seeing is attuned to the urgent need to reach a town which allows Negroes to stay overnight. In some places, when he dies he is buried in a segregated cemetery. [29]

In hundreds of ways Negroes and other "racial" [30] minorities endure discrimination based not upon their qualities as individuals but upon their status as Negroes, Jews, Indians, and so on. Most of this discrimination rests on the theory of segregation—"separate but equal" facilities. In practice, most segregated facilities are neither fully separate nor fully equal. *Completely* separate facilities—schools, churches, stores, hotels, theaters, buses, waiting rooms, and so on—are impractical because of the cost of duplicate accommodations. In many places there are not enough Negroes to support separate Negro accommodations, especially first-class ones.

[26] *Chicago Sun-Times*, April 4, 1959, p. 3.

[27] In April, 1959, a "recession" period, Negroes formed 10% of the labor force but 20% of the unemployed; only 19% of the whites were on part-time (under 35 hours a week) compared with 30% of the Negroes. (From *Economic Trends and Outlook*, monthly newsletter of the AFL-CIO Economic Policy Committee, May-June, 1958).

[28] A Chicago comparison saw plush Edgewater Beach apartments renting for less, at two rooms for $74.50 a month, than rat-infested Negro tenements, at $78 a month. ("Edgewater Beach Units Cheaper than Ratty Flats where 10 Burned to Death," *Chicago Sun*, October 17, 1947, p. 5). A New York survey found over-crowded rooming houses on Manhattan's blight-infested West Side bringing nearly twice the rental ($2.30 per square foot) that well-maintained elevator apartments bring ($1.30). (Reported by New York City Planning Commission in *House and Home* Vol. 16 [July, 1959], p. 49).

[29] Even his pet dog is unacceptable for burial in one of the plush pet cemeteries which accept pets only from white, gentile owners. Apparently, one can't be too careful!

[30] Jews are generally considered as a race, although, being biologically a highly mixed group, they are not a genuine racial group. Neither are they a religious group, as many Jews have left the Jewish faith. Nor are they a cultural group, since many "emancipated" Jews have abandoned traditional Jewish rites and behavior and are fully assimilated. Jews, then, are a group defined by cultural myth—Jews are a group composed of whomever is generally considered as and treated as Jewish. (See Arthur Miller's novel, *Focus* [New York, Reynal & Company, Inc., 1945], for the story of a gentile who was forced to become a "Jew" when he started wearing glasses which so altered his appearance that people decided he was Jewish.) Since Jews are generally thought of as a race, anti-Semitism is race prejudice, even though Jews are not actually a race.

This cartoon, drawn by Jack Hamm, a white Texan, appeared in the Kansas City Call. Asbury Howard, a Negro leader in Bessemer, Alabama, commissioned a white sign painter, Albert McAllister, to make a large copy of the cartoon for hanging inside the hall of a Negro voters' league. Both men served six-month jail sentences for this "crime," and Howard was severely beaten by a white mob while police looked on. Howard's son, who sought to aid him, was the only one arrested.

SOURCE: See Jeffrey Fuller, "The Duping of Asbury Howard," *The Reporter*, Vol. 20 (April 16, 1959), pp. 23-24.

HANDS THAT STILL CAN PRAY

Strict separation of races is often inconvenient for whites, so segregation is constantly being breached and compromised by whites for their own convenience (for example, the Negro servant traveling with a white family and sharing their accommodations). Nor are the facilities fully equal. It would be unrealistic to expect that whites who insisted upon separation from their "inferiors" would always be concerned about equality of accommodations. In practice, Negro housing, schools, and other segregated facilities have often consisted largely of hand-me-downs, leftovers, and makeshifts.

Patterns of segregation and discrimination differ for different minorities and are very rapidly changing. Most Southern states have been sharply reducing the gap between Negro and white schooling. Between 1940 and 1960, school expenditures for each Negro child in the South grew from 43 to 81 per cent of that spent on each white child. [31] By 1960, very few state colleges or universities remained closed to Negros. Twenty years ago, no industry in the South (and not many in the North) followed nondiscriminatory employment policies. In 1958, a survey of 402 firms in the South showed 53 which claimed to hire strictly on merit, and 114 more which followed merit-hiring in filling some jobs. [32] This is far from full equality, but it is rapid change. Any description of discriminatory practices will need frequent revision to keep up with current change.

[31] Anthony Lewis, "Human Background of the Civil Rights Issue," *New York Times Magazine*, February 14, 1960, pp. 10 ff.

[32] *Time*, Vol. 72 (October 20, 1958), p. 94.

FACTS ABOUT RACE PREJUDICE

Prejudice is not the same as discrimination. Prejudice refers to one's *judgments* of others, whereas discrimination refers to one's *actions* toward others. A prejudice is, literally, a *prejudgment*, a judgment arrived at before having really examined any evidence about the case or person involved. *A racial prejudice is any judgment of a person based upon knowledge of his race rather than upon knowledge of his individual qualities.* Both the teacher who expects the Negro boy to be dull in algebra and the teacher who expects him to be gifted in music are showing their race prejudices, for both impute qualities to him because he is a Negro instead of discovering his qualities by observing him as a person. A prejudice is a stereotyped image, favorable or unfavorable, which one "sees" in place of the actual individual.

1. *Prejudices are learned.* No one is born with prejudices. Small children show no race prejudices until they begin to observe them in their elders. [33]

2. *Prejudices are largely unconscious.* Several studies have offered informants a checklist including many prejudiced statements and have asked them to indicate how highly "prejudiced" they considered themselves to be. In general, those who accepted the largest number of prejudiced statements rated themselves as "unprejudiced," whereas those who checked the fewest prejudiced statements classed themselves as somewhat prejudiced. Apparently those who have the most prejudices are unaware of them—to them, their prejudices are "facts"—while those with the fewest prejudices are acutely aware of them and feel somewhat guilty about the few which they hold. This unconscious quality of prejudice makes it possible for many kindly, humanitarian people to remain unconcerned with race problems, for if one considers it a fact that Negroes are naturally dirty and shiftless, then an announcement that many Negroes are living in squalor suggests to him not a problem to be treated but simply another illustration of the Negro's nature.

3. *Prejudice is learned through contact with prejudice, not contact with other groups.* It is firmly established that there is very little relationship between the amount of contact one has had with a particular group and his attitudes toward that group. Although in certain cases, the *kind of contact* has an important bearing upon attitudes, it is safe to say that, in general, race attitudes are based far more on contact with the *attitudes* of others around us than upon contact with the other race or group. Studies have shown no important differences between the race attitudes of children in towns where no Negroes or Jews live and chil-

[33] Bruno Lasker, *Race Attitudes in Children* (New York, Henry Holt & Co., Inc., 1929), pp. 4-6, 39.

dren in towns having Negro and Jewish residents. Radke found that children who had *no* personal experience with Negroes and Jews had strong and definite prejudices against them. [34] A *Fortune* survey found that resentment of Catholic and Jewish economic and political power was greatest in areas where such "power" was the weakest, and that "Jews evoke the greatest hostility in the areas where there are very few of them." [35] Hartley dramatically showed the irrelevance of personal contact in a study in which three *imaginary* groups—the Danireans, the Wallonians, and the Pireneans—were included in a list of races and nationalities.[36] Informants made much the same responses to these nonexistent groups that they did to other actual groups, with coefficients of correlation ranging from .78 to .85. People who disliked Negroes and Jews also disliked the fictitious Danireans and Wallonians. From such data it is clear that prejudices are learned mainly through contact with prejudiced people rather than through contact with the group toward whom prejudice is felt. The prejudiced person may defend his views with a string of unpleasant anecdotes, but it is likely that his vivid memory of these experiences is a *result of his prejudice, rather than its cause*. For those experiences which dominate our recollections are those which our attitudes define as significant.

4. *Prejudice is unrelated to reality*. Since prejudice is learned mainly through contact with prejudice rather than through contact with the people concerned, prejudice need bear no relationship whatever to the real characteristics of the group concerned. [37] Once a prejudice has been absorbed, the prejudiced person can readily "see" in another person whatever his prejudice tells him must be there to see. Like attitudes, prejudices are subject to a *circular reinforcement*. This enables one to interpret *any* evidence in such a way as to confirm the prejudice. A classic illustration is General J. L. DeWitt's remark on the "need" for interning Japanese-Americans during the war: "The very fact that no sabotage has taken place to date is a disturbing and confirming indication that such action will be taken." [38] Only a tremendous ability to rationalize one's prejudice

[34] Ronald Lippitt and M. Radke, "New Trends in the Investigation of Prejudice," *The Annals*, Vol. 244 (March, 1946), pp. 167-176.

[35] "The Fortune Survey," *Fortune*, Vol. 36 (October, 1947), pp. 5 ff.

[36] Eugene Hartley, *Problems in Prejudice* (New York, The King's Crown Press, 1946), p. 26. Similar conclusions were reached by David Gold, "Is Ethnic Prejudice a Unitary Variable?" *Midwest Sociologist*, Vol. 17 (Spring, 1955), pp. 39-43.

[37] This is illustrated in an experiment wherein informants were shown a number of stereotyped and nonstereotyped situations involving Negroes; they perceived the Negroes according to the situation they were shown in, not according to their individual appearances. (Alice B. Riddlegerger and Annabelle B. Motz, "Prejudice and Perception," *American Journal of Sociology*, Vol. 62 (March, 1957), pp. 498-503.

[38] United States Army Western Defense Command and Fourth Army, *Japanese in the United States, Final Report: Japanese Evacuation From the West Coast* (Washington, Government Printing Office, 1943), p. 34.

can explain a responsible official's interpreting a *lack* of sabotage as "evidence" of *disloyal* intent!

Circular reinforcement enables a person to find in Negroes or Jews whatever traits his prejudice prompts him to look for, and having thus found them, his prejudice is reinforced. To one who thinks Negroes stupid, a cloddish Negro confirms his prejudice. An intelligent Negro, however, is an "exception" who also confirms the prejudice, for, if *he* is an "exception," then *all the rest must be stupid*. Thus, the "exception" proves the rule and confirms the prejudice, and the prejudice becomes totally divorced from the reality it supposedly describes. Perhaps this is why many people remain in undisturbed possession of a set of prejudices which are not even consistent with one another. One study found that most of those who claimed that Jews were too "pushy" (trying to force themselves upon gentiles), were the same informants who reported that Jews were too "clannish" (refusing to mix with other people).[39] Jews are said to be invariably rich and grasping, and, at the same time, to be a bunch of Communists and radicals intent on confiscating all wealth; Negroes are "contented and easygoing" and "getting out of hand"; Negro athletes are second-raters who "blow up in a pinch," but who are so good that they "are taking over athletics"; Jews are instantly recognizable by their "Jewish" features, yet have successfully "concealed themselves in industry, finance, the professions, and everywhere else." Such contradictory absurdities remind one of the well-known comedian who specializes in contradiction (for example, "A tall short little fellow stood running down the street . . ."). Only by remembering that prejudices are unrelated to reality can one understand how a person can hold prejudices that contradict one another so flatly.

5. *Prejudice exists because it is satisfying.* People hold prejudices because they enjoy them. Some may feel a bit guilty about them, but people enjoy many things which bring feelings of guilt. Prejudice can bring many emotional satisfactions—a feeling of superiority, an excuse for failure, an outlet for aggression and hostility—and can be a very useful weapon in power struggles between groups. Some of the emotional values of prejudice are implied in the following section.

THEORIES OF THE CAUSES OF PREJUDICE

The causes of prejudice are hard to evaluate, for there appear to be several causes, often operating in combination with one another. The following are the principal theories of the causes of prejudice.[40]

[39] D. J. Levinson and R. N. Sanford, "A Scale for the Measurement of Anti-Semitism," *Journal of Psychology*, Vol. 17 (April, 1944), pp. 339-370.

[40] As outlined in Brewton Berry, *Race and Ethnic Relations* (New York, Houghton Mifflin Co., 1958), pp. 377-388.

1. Economic Theories

a. The Economic-Competition Theory. This theory assumes that when groups compete, hostilities and prejudices often arise. If the competing groups differ in race or religion, the prejudice takes the form of race or religious prejudice. The more highly identifiable the two groups are (or are imagined to be), the more easily such prejudice can be focused on the differences which identify them—race, religion, or nationality. Thus, prejudice against the Irish, once intense, largely disappeared as the Irish immigrants became assimilated, whereas prejudice against the easily recognized Japanese remains.

There is considerable evidence to support this theory. Both in Hawaii and on the West Coast, little prejudice against Japanese developed until the Japanese immigrants began to enter types of work which competed with white occupations. Medieval anti-Semitism in Europe increased greatly when banking and finance, previously left to the Jews, grew profitable enough to be attractive to gentiles. Yet, although one can cite many instances of prejudice following competition, it is unlikely that competition is the sole factor in prejudice. The intensity of prejudice is not exactly proportionate to the strength of competition or the strength of the competing minority. Furthermore, as Mydral points out, the economic ambitions of the Negro meet much less white verbal opposition than the Negro's social and political aspirations. [41]

b. The Economic-Exploitation Theory. This theory maintains that prejudice is very helpful in maintaining economic privilege. It is much easier to keep Negro wages low if Negroes are believed inferior. As Margaret Halsey wrote in her "Memorandum to Junior Hostesses" serving in a nondiscriminatory servicemen's canteen during the war: [42]

> The real reason back of the refusal of some of you to mingle with Negroes at the canteen isn't nearly so romantic and dramatic as you think it is. The real reason has nothing to do with rape, seduction, or risings in the night. The real reason can be summed up in two extremely unromantic little words: cheap labor. As long as you treat Negroes as subhumans, you don't have to pay them so much. When you refuse to dance with Negro servicemen at the canteen, you are neither protecting your honor nor making sure that white Southerners won't have their homes burned down around their ears. All you are doing is making it possible for employers all over the country to get Negroes to work for them for less money than those employers would have to pay you.

There is considerable evidence to support this exploitation theory. Modern race theories first appeared when European nations established

[41] Gunnar Myrdal, *op. cit.*, pp. 60 ff.
[42] Margaret Halsey, *Color Blind* (New York, Simon and Schuster. Inc., 1946). pp. 56-57.

colonial empires and needed a theory to sanction their exploitation of the native peoples. Prejudice against the Japanese-Americans appears to be, at least in part, a result of agitation by vested interests. [43] The use of white supremacy as a political issue in the South long served to keep Negroes and poor whites in hate and fear of each other, and prevented them from discovering their common interest in modifying an economic status quo that impoverished them both. The conversation at many a bridge luncheon shows that middle-class housewives are quite aware of the relationship between "equality of opportunity" and the wage rate for Negro cleaning women. There is ample evidence that prejudice has often been used, both consciously and unconsciously, as a mask for privilege, but since prejudice also exists between groups where there is no exploitation, there must be other causes as well.

2. Symbolic Theories

A great many theories, some of them fantastic, claim that prejudice arises because we see in another group certain traits which become symbols of what we hate, fear, or envy. Therefore, we hate Negroes because their (supposedly) uninhibited sex life symbolizes a freedom we envy; or we see in their lazy, easygoing life a symbol of a wish that our ambitions force us to renounce. The symbolic theories have most often been applied to anti-Semitism. The Jew is seen as a symbol of urbanism and of the impersonality and sophistication which rustic folk envy and distrust. Other theories see the Jew as a symbol of internationalism, of capitalism, of communism, or of "nonconformity," and accordingly the Jews are hated by the nationalists, the communists, the capitalists, and the worshippers of conformity. [44] Such symbolic theories, although difficult to prove or to disprove, find some acceptance among students of prejudice.

3. Psychological Theories

a. The Scapegoat Theory. Nearly two thousand years ago Tertullian wrote, "If the Tiber rose to the walls of the city, if the heavens did not send rain, if an earthquake occurred, if famine threatened, if pestilence raged, the cry resounded, 'Throw the Christians to the lions.'" After the Christians became the majority, Jews took their place as scapegoats. During the great plague of the fourteenth century, some three hundred and fifty Jewish communities were exterminated within a

[43] See Carey McWilliams, *Japanese-Americans: Symbol of Racial Intolerance* (Boston, Little, Brown & Co., 1944).
[44] See Arnold Rose and Caroline Rose, *America Divided* (New York, Alfred A. Knopf, Inc., 1948), pp. 285-292.

two-year period on the charge that they had already poisoned, or might poison, the water supply and spread the plague. [45]

People have always sought to blame something or someone else for their troubles. The ancient Hebrews each year loaded their sins onto a goat and chased him into the wilderness; [46] this goat, allowed to escape, came to be known as a "scapegoat," and the term came to be applied to anyone forced to bear blame for others' misfortunes. Most minority groups have, at some time or other, served as convenient scapegoats. According to one analysis,[47] a suitable scapegoat should be: (1) easily recognizable, either physically or through some trait of dress or behavior; (2) too weak to fight back; (3) available near at hand; (4) already unpopular; (5) a symbol of something that is hated and despised.

The scapegoat theory helps to explain German anti-Semitism under Hitler, as the Jews were blamed for the loss of World War I and for the postwar difficulties. Hitler actively cultivated the scapegoating tendency, for without the Jews to fill the role of devil, the Nazi movement might have failed. [48] Scapegoating is evident in American anti-Semitism also, as the great depression, the war, the wartime shortages and rationing inconveniences, and the postwar inflation were successively blamed on the Jews by certain groups of people. Prejudices against Negroes are less easily explained by scapegoating, since Negroes are hardly powerful enough to have created our troubles.

b. The Frustration-Aggression Theory. There is some experimental evidence showing that aggressive impulses arise when one is frustrated. [49] All persons, children and adults, are often unable to do the things they wish to do, and their frustration produces aggressive impulses which can find a socially approved outlet through race prejudices and hatreds. The abuse and mistreatment of a minority serves to drain off these irrational, latent hostilities which the frustrations of social living produce. Thus the poor white, prevented by custom and by the power system from any attack upon the landlord or the industrialist, vents his hostilities upon the Negro. The businessman, struggling to survive in a competitive system but

[45] Isaque Graebner and S. H. Britt, eds., *Jews in a Gentile World* (New York, The Macmillan Co., 1942), p. 95.

[46] Lev., 16:5-26.

[47] Gordon W. Allport, *ABC's of Scapegoating* (New York, Anti-Defamation League of B'nai B'rith, 1948), pp. 42-43.

[48] When asked whether the Jew should be destroyed, Hitler replied, "No . . . we should then have to invent him. It is essential to have a tangible enemy, not merely an abstract one." (Herman Rauschning, *Hitler Speaks* [New York, G. P. Putnam's Sons, 1940], p. 234.) When a member of a Japanese mission studying the Nazi movement in 1932 was asked what he thought of the movement, he replied, "It is magnificent. I wish we could have something like it in Japan, only we can't, because we haven't got any Jews." (Fritz August Voigt, *Unto Caesar* [New York, G. P. Putnam's Sons, 1938], p. 301.

[49] John Dollard and others, *Frustration and Aggression* (New Haven, Yale University Press, 1939), especially pp. 151-156.

enjoined from hating his competitor and fellow-Rotarian, hates the Jew instead. The incompetent, unsuccessful person would be particularly tempted to find in racial prejudice a compensation for his own failures.

This theory is not easy to prove or disprove. There is some evidence that unsuccessful people show greater than average amounts of prejudice. One study finds that veterans who were downwardly mobile expressed more aggressive attitudes than those who were moving into better jobs and improved status. [50] The same study reports that those who believed they had received a "bad break" in the army were inclined to be anti-Semitic. The spectacular growth of organized anti-Semitism during the New Deal era, mainly among groups bitterly opposed to New Deal policies, suggests that many who were frustrated by "that man in the White House" may have found an outlet for their anger in anti-Semitic hostilities. [51]

The theory, however, overlooks the fact that aggression is only one of the several possible consequences of frustration (including identification, conversion, repression, retreat into fantasy, and others), and that aggressions need not be directed at a minority group. Nor does the theory explain why one group rather than another becomes an object of abuse.

c. The Social-Neurosis Theory. There are several versions of the social-neurosis theory which views race prejudice as a *symptom of a maladjusted, neurotic personality*. According to this theory, people who are insecure, troubled, and discontented find refuge in prejudice. As Ben Hecht says, "Prejudice is our method of transferring our own sickness to others. It is our ruse for disliking others rather than ourselves. . . . Prejudice is a raft onto which the shipwrecked mind clambers and paddles to safety." [52]

The high proportion of maladjusted persons among race agitators and fanatics has often been noted. [53] Not one student leader joined in a student walkout in protest against desegregation in Little Rock, Arkansas. [54] Of the eleven student leaders of another school strike against

[50] Bruno Bettelheim and Morris Janowitz, *Dynamics of Prejudice, A Psychological and Sociological Study of Veterans* (New York, Harper and Brothers, 1950), p. 59.

[51] Donald S. Strong, *Organized Anti-Semitism in the United States* (American Council on Public Affairs, 1941), records five anti-Semitic organizations founded between 1915-1932, nine in 1933, and 105 between 1934-1939.

[52] Ben Hecht, *A Guide for The Bedeviled* (New York, Charles Scribner's Sons, 1944), p. 31.

[53] See John Roy Carlson, *Under Cover* (New York, E. P. Dutton & Co., Inc., 1943); John Roy Carlson, *The Plotters* (New York, E. P. Dutton & Co., Inc., 1946); Leo Lowenthal and Norbert Gutterman, *Prophets of Deceit* (New York, Harper and Brothers, 1949); Elton Mayo, "Routine Interaction and the Problem of Collaboration," *American Sociological Review*, Vol. 4 (June, 1939), pp. 335-340.

[54] *New York Times*, October 13, 1957, IV, p. 9.

desegregation, all but one or two were reported to be frustrated and unhappy. [55]

These boys who initiated the Barstow strike and who chose the anti-Negro goal were ones whose lives both at home and in school had been largely unhappy and difficult. . . . They were unhappy in their relations with other boys and girls as well as with teachers and principles. This spurred them to try to build more satisfactory pictures in their own minds of what their own status was. . . . They were driven to become attention-seekers, "zoot-suiters," extremists in behavior, speech, and appearance.

Several studies seem to show some rather striking differences between the personalities of prejudiced and unprejudiced persons. Hartley, after testing several groups of college students, reports that: [56]

The *relatively tolerant personality* in this type of collegiate sample is likely to exhibit some combination of the following characteristics: a strong desire for personality autonomy associated with a lack of need for dominance, a strong need for friendliness, along with a personal seclusiveness, fear of competition, a tendency to placate others along with a lack of general conformity to the mores. He is likely to be fairly serious, to be interested in current events, to have ideas about bettering society, to be a member of a political group and to have great need for personal achievement in the vocational area. He is likely to be an accepting personality, disliking violence, able to appreciate the contributions of others, conscious of feeling that people tend to be more or less alike and adopting a nurturant rather than dominant attitude toward those younger than he. He is conscious of conflicts concerning loyalties and duties, and thinks very seriously about moral questions. His interests center about what are commonly called social studies, reading, and journalism. Although personally seclusive, he has a great need to be socially useful.

The *relatively intolerant personality* might be expected to combine in varying degrees the following characteristics: unwillingness to accept responsibility, acceptance of conventional mores, a rejection of "serious" groups, rejection of political interests and desire for groups formed for purely social purposes, absorption with pleasure activities, a conscious conflict between play and work, emotionality rather than rationality, extreme egocentrism, interest in physical activity, the body, health. He is likely to dislike agitators, radicals, pessimists. He is relatively uncreative, apparently unable to deal with anxieties except by fleeing from them. Often his physical activity has in it a compulsive component; it may be that his compulsion to be on the move, that is, constantly occupied with sports, motoring, traveling, etc., serves for him the same function that study and activities with social significance serve in the case of the individual with high tolerance.

[55] James H. Tipton, *Community in Crisis* (New York, Teachers College, Columbia University, 1953), pp. 68-69.
[56] Eugene Hartley, *Problems of Prejudice* (New York, The King's Crown Press, 1946), pp. 62-63.

This picture of the intolerant personality is quite similar to Frenkel-Brunswik and Sanford's findings that: [57]

. . . those with high scores on prejudice tests exhibit, among other tendencies, rigidity of outlook (inaccessibility to new experience), intolerance of ambiguity (they want to know *the* answers), pseudoscientific or antiscientific attitudes (more superstition, reliance on accidents as explanations, attribution of behavior to heredity), suggestibility and gullibility, and autistic thinking in goal behavior (unrealistic views of what will achieve the desired goals). Those low in prejudice, on the other hand, show more flexibility of judgment, greater tolerance of ambiguity, a more scientific-naturalistic explanation of events, greater autonomy and self-reliance, and realistic thinking about goal behavior.

From a number of such studies, Adorno constructs a picture of the basically prejudiced type of personality with these tendencies:[58]

  a. Conventionalism. Rigid adherence to conventional, middle-class values.
  b. Authoritarian submission. Submissive, uncritical attitude towards idealized moral authorities of the in-group.
  c. Authoritarian aggression. Tendency to be on the outlook for, and to condemn, reject, and punish people who violate conventional values.
  d. Anti-intraception. Opposition to the subjective, the imaginative, the tender-minded.
  e. Superstition and stereotypy. The belief in mystical determinants of the individual's fate; the disposition to think in rigid categories.
  f. Power and "toughness." Preoccupation with the dominance-submission, strong-weak, leader-follower dimension; identification with power figures; overemphasis upon the conventionalized attributes of the ego; exaggerated assertion of strength and toughness.
  g. Destructiveness and cynicism. Generalized hostility, vilification of the human.
  h. Projectivity. The disposition to believe that wild and dangerous things go on in the world; the projection outwards of unconscious emotional impulses.
  i. Sex. Exaggerated concern with sexual "goings-on."

These variables were thought of as going together to form a single syndrome, a more or less enduring structure in the person that renders him receptive to antidemocratic propaganda.

The concept of the prejudiced personality has excited much scientific interest, and scores of studies have attempted to test the hypothesis. [59]

---

[57] Else Frenkel-Brunswik and R. Nevitt Sanford, "Some Personality Factors in Anti-Semitism," *Journal of Psychology*, Vol. 20 (October, 1945), pp. 271-291; summarized in Simpson and Yinger, *op. cit.*, p. 89.

[58] T. W. Adorno and others, *The Authoritarian Personality* (New York, Harper and Brothers, 1950), p. 228. For a popularized statement, see Selma Hirsh, *The Fears Men Live By* (New York, Harper and Brothers, 1955), Chs. 2, 3.

[59] Simpson and Yinger, *op. cit.*, pp. 95-102.

For example, Kaufman found a significant association between status anxiety and anti-Semitism—persons feeling more anxious about their status were more anti-Semitic. [60] Srole found a correlation of +.43 between anomie and prejudice—those without intimate group affiliations were more prejudiced. [61] Kassof tested a group of Ukranians, finding that the prejudiced personality pattern is not limited to the American society. [62]

Many studies, then, generally agree in finding the prejudiced personality to be anxious and insecure, highly active, preoccupied with strength and toughness, non-studious, self-centered, domineering, immature, somewhat puritanical, critical of others, ethnocentric, superficial in interests and cliché-bound in thinking, whereas the unprejudiced personality is seen as more studious and serious, co-operative rather than domineering, tolerant of others, benevolent and humanitarian, and relatively free of stereotypes and rigid categories in his thinking.

It seems probable that both tolerance and extreme prejudice generally are functions of the *total* personality rather than of isolated experience. It is doubtful, however, if this can explain all prejudices. It is known that the prejudiced person generally shows similar prejudices against many groups, irrespective of his knowledge of or contact with them, but there are many exceptions—prejudiced persons who are tolerant towards certain groups and tolerant persons who are prejudiced about certain groups. It is also true that many widespread prejudices are simply learned as supposed facts (for example, "Jews have an instinct for making money," "Negroes are naturally easygoing"). Such "facts" may have no particular impact upon the personality, merely being filed away as part of one's store of information. It is probable that the social-neurosis theory may be applicable only to the extremes of the prejudice continuum, with the central group of mildly or moderately prejudiced persons explained by some other theory. It is clear beyond all question, however, that *we find the explanation of prejudice in the personality and experience of the person holding the prejudice, not in the character of the group against whom the prejudice is directed.* The utter irrelevance of the true characteristics of the victims of prejudice has been demonstrated again and again! The precise manner in which and degree to which prejudice and tolerance identify different kinds of basic personalities can be learned only through much further research.

These are the principal theories of the origin of race prejudices,

[60] Walter C. Kaufman, "Status, Authoritarianism, and Anti-Semitism," *American Journal of Sociology*, Vol. 52 (January, 1957), pp. 379-382.

[61] Leo Srole, "Social Integration and Certain Corollaries: An Exploratory Study," *American Sociological Review*, Vol. 21 (December, 1956), pp. 709-716.

[62] Allen Kassof, "The Prejudiced Personality: A Cross-Cultural Test," *Social Problems*, Vol. 6 (Summer, 1958), pp. 59-67.

although there are several others of lesser import. [63] These principal theories are more than idle speculation; each is supported by a respectable body of research. No one of them explains *all* prejudice, for prejudices are of many kinds and degrees and may have as many origins. Each helps to explain certain kinds of prejudice. Taken together, they provide a good deal of insight, and place the techniques of controlling prejudice somewhere between a science and an art.

SOME COMMON MYTHS, EVASIONS, AND RATIONALIZATIONS

A favorite way of dealing with one's guilt feelings is to change one's vices into virtues through the art of rationalization. As Myrdal insistently repeats, the conflict of the ideals of Christianity and democracy with the realities of racial discrimination produces in white folks an uneasy guilt that becomes a powerful force for change in race relations. [64] This same guilt feeling also gives birth to an elaborate folklore of myth, evasion, and rationalization that permits people to view themselves as unprejudiced without sacrificing any of their treasured prejudices. Included are such comforting beliefs as the the ones described below.

1. "It's Their Own Fault"

Minorities are variously accused of being lazy and shiftless, yet aggressive and overambitious; clannish and seclusive, yet pushy and intrusive; artful and deceitful, yet simple and trusting; miserly and grasping, yet extravagant and wasteful, and so on. The inconsistency of such characterizations seldom occurs to those who hold them. The fantastic inaccuracy of many such characterizations has been demonstrated repeatedly by cases such as this: [65]

... in Fresno County, California, where a colony of first- and second-generation Armenians has settled . . . LaPiere found that the reasons given by non-Armenians for their antipathy revealed three distinct stereotypes: (1) They are dishonest, deceitful liars. The manager of the Merchant's Association said, "I can safely say, after many years of work that the Armenians are, as a race, the worst we have to deal with." (2) They are parasitic; they do not contribute their fair share to community life and welfare. (3) They have a low moral code; they are "always getting into trouble with the law." LaPiere attempted to determine the truth of these accusations, and he could find no support for them. Far from being dishonest, the records of the Merchant's Association re-

[63] Brewton Berry, *op. cit.*, pp. 388-391.

[64] Gunnar Myrdal, *op. cit.*, pp. xli-lv.

[65] Brewton Berry, *Race Relations* (Boston, Houghton Mifflin Co., 1953), pp. 119-120; summarizing study by R. T. LaPiere, "Type-Rationalizations of Group Antipathy," *Social Forces*, Vol. 15 (December, 1936), pp. 232-237.

vealed that the credit standing of the Armenians was "remarkable." A study of admissions to the County Hospital and of the requests at the Welfare Bureau proved that the Armenians' demands for charity were very small, considering their ratio in the general population. As for their being a lawless group, LaPiere's analysis of the police records revealed that Armenians were involved in only 1.5 per cent of the cases, although they make up 6 per cent of the population.

In some cases, however, the unflattering characterizations have a measure of truth. There is no doubt that, as compared with whites, a greater proportion of Negroes are uneducated, unskilled, and unrefined. This fact may be interpreted either as a challenge to do something about it, or as an excuse for doing nothing about it. To the prejudiced person, the ignorance and poverty of Negroes serves as an excuse for preserving those conditions which keep Negroes ignorant and poor. And the stereotype of the greedy, grasping Jew becomes a basis for slights and insults that encourage Jews to become grasping and exploitative, just as a child who is repeatedly called a "bad boy" eventually becomes one. Research has clearly established the fact that groups tend to accept whatever picture of themselves the majority group keeps presenting. For example, four-year-old Negro children have already learned that white is a "nicer" color than black. [66] Herein lies the supreme importance of the unflattering minority stereotypes—not merely that they are often untrue, but that these stereotypes tend to become true by creating the conditions which make the stereotype come true. If there were no other forces at work counteracting it, the stereotype of the lazy, shiftless, sexually promiscuous Negro might already have converted all Negroes into just such persons. Any characterization of a group is not merely an inert description; it is functionally active! To describe a group as "lazy" or as "ambitious" not only affects that group's view of itself—it also affects the treatment and opportunities the group receives.

This is why the description of the supposed characteristics of any group might be termed the *self-correcting description*, for, in the absence of other counteracting forces, *any group tends to become whatever it is commonly said to be*. The greatest error of those who justify discrimination by pointing out the offensive habits of a minority is in their utter failure to realize that their own prejudices and accusations are among the causes of the traits they dislike.

2. "They Like It That Way"

Many white people confidently assert that "they know the Negro" and insist that they know exactly what pleases and displeases him. Having

[66] Kenneth B. Clark and Mamie P. Clark, "Racial Identification and Preference in Negro Children," in Theodore M. Newcomb and E. L. Hartley, eds., *Readings in Social Psychology* (New York, Henry Holt & Co., Inc., 1947), pp. 169-178.

seen that part of the Negro's personality which the Negro wished to show them, many whites feel that they understand Negroes better than Negroes understand themselves. Such whites would be much chagrined to know how deliberately and contemptuously the Negro has exploited the vanity of whites by assuming whatever pattern of outward behavior is most useful in "handling" white folk. [67] Negroes "know" white folk infinitely better than whites "know" Negroes.

The belief that Negroes like poverty and Jews prefer "their own" resorts can be supported by occasional anecdotes that make the belief sound reasonable. It is true that many Negroes show no active discontent with the poverty and squalor which have been their only experience. Some Jews prefer a segregated resort to the uncertainties and humiliations encountered elsewhere. But the belief that any American minority has been long contented with inequality is nonsense. The magnolia-scented, technicolored picture of the Old South peopled with considerate masters and contented, grateful slaves is marred by the historical fact of a succession of bloody slave revolts, [68] the 100,000 Negroes who served with Union armies during the Civil War, [69] and the steady migration of Negroes away from the South. There is no record of adequate housing remaining vacant because Negroes preferred to sleep five to a bed. In a society which trumpets the virtues of opportunity and self-advancement, no group will long be satisfied with poverty or discrimination.

3. "Discrimination Really Benefits the Minority"

Discrimination protects the minorities from disastrous competition with the dominant group, so the argument runs, and it therefore proves the dominant group's unselfishness and altruism. Segregation in particular is defended as an arrangement supposedly beneficial to Negroes; the "separate but equal" schools, churches, public services, and occupations protect them from direct competition with whites. But the economic status of Negroes is lowest wherever they are most numerous and their segregation most complete. [70] The historical fact that segregation was

[67] In Richard Wright's novel, *The Long Dream* (Toronto, Doubleday & Company, Inc., 1958), a wealthy Negro who has successfully Uncle-Tommed the white people, tells his son how to get ahead: ". . . we can handle these dumb white folks, son . . . the only way to git along with white folks is to grin in their goddam faces and make 'em feel good and then do what the hell you want to do behind their backs. . . . A white man always wants to see a black man either crying or grinning. I can't cry, ain't the crying type. So I grin and git anything I want." (Quoted from review in *New Republic*, Vol. 139 (November 24, 1958), p. 17.

[68] Melville J. Herskovitz, *The Myth of the Negro Past* (New York, Harper and Brothers, 1941), pp. 91 ff.

[69] Monroe N. Work, ed., *Negro Year Book*, 1931-1932 (Tuskegee Institute, Ala., Negro Year Book Publishing Company, 1931), pp. 327-334; Benjamin Quarles, *The Negro in the Civil War* (Boston, Little, Brown & Co., 1953).

[70] David M. Heer, "The Sentiment of White Supremacy: An Ecological Study," *American Journal of Sociology*, Vol. 69 (May, 1959), pp. 592-598.

Photo by Myron Ehrenberg

To some, this is progress. To others, it is worse than having no schools at all!

invented to protect the *whites* from competition is conveniently ob-
scured by a rationalization which permits members of the dominant
group to continue their discriminatory practices without interrupting
their professions of kindness and sympathy.

4. "They Prefer to Be with Their Own People"

Many whites are naïve enough to believe that all Negroes, of whatever social class level, will enjoy one another's company. Sophisticated
people realize that, among both whites and Negroes, social class is far
more important than race in determining with whom most people are
comfortable. An upper-class white soon finds himself more comfortable
among a group of upper-class Negroes than among a group of lower-
class whites. "Our own kind" of people are those who have the same
interests, values, ambitions, life habits, conversational topics, and so on,
that we have. Once people recover from the initial shock, they discover
that shared interests are more important than shared pigmentation as a
basis for interaction. In this sense only, Negroes prefer their own kind
of people, and the prosperous Negro who seeks to buy into an exclusive
residential area *is trying to get with his own kind of people.* Since good

housing is rarely available to Negroes in segregated areas, [71] he can get housing according to his tastes and income only by invading white areas.

5. "Whites Have Troubles, Too"

This is a device for avoiding the issue by changing the subject. Many people, confronted with the facts about Negro poverty, housing, or job discrimination, reply that there are lots of miserable white folks too, implying that if some whites are poor, Negroes should not complain. It is true, of course, that a small proportion of whites share the poverty and squalor which a great many Negroes suffer, and for reasons often beyond their control. But the proportions of white and Negro poverty, for example, are far apart because of the added handicap of race discrimination which Negroes endure. The "whites-have-trouble-too" argument shifts attention away from race discrimination as a *cause* of poverty and instead centers attention upon poverty itself; then it is another short jump to a discussion of the general worthlessness of the poor, and the original issue can then be neatly buried.

Of these and other rationalizations there is no end. It is often futile to attack them or to cite the facts which disprove them. If one's rationalizations are destroyed, he invents newer and better ones. For rationalizations are not conceived because they are demonstrably true, but because they protect and sanctify those beliefs and prejudices one is unwilling to change. But with the gradual popularization of natural and social science, it grows steadily more difficult to find convincing rationalizations, and annoying doubts persist in arising. As Myrdal repeats, this is the white man's dilemma—that he only half believes his own rationalizations. His shrill professions of innate white superiority sound less and less like a confident statement of a self-evident fact, and more and more like whistling in the dark.

MINORITY "ADJUSTMENTS" TO PREJUDICE AND DISCRIMINATION

Of all popular nonsense about race, perhaps none exceeds the nonsense of attributing racial behavior to instinct rather than to experience. People note what they see, or think they see, in a particular race or group and attribute it to their "racial nature." They fail to realize that all group behavior is a product of group experience, and all racial behavior is a

[71] Residential segregation increased between 1940 and 1950 (see Donald O. Cowgill, "Trends in Residential Segregation of Nonwhites in American Cities, 1940-1950," *American Sociological Review*, Vol. 21 [February, 1956], pp. 43-47) with practically no new housing available to Negroes at any price. In Cleveland, for example, less than one per cent of the 145,000 private housing units built between 1946 and 1956 were available to Negroes. (*New York Times*, January 3, 1957, p. 71.)

product of the conditions under which that race has lived. In a noted rabbi's remark, "I have been a Jew for a thousand years," we see that many generations of experience—of working, of struggling, of inter-action with other groups, and of traditions and legends told and retold—enter into the making of the so-called racial nature of a group.

A minority which endures discrimination and inequality in a society that professes democracy and equality of opportunity is doubly affected by this experience. The *fact* of discrimination and inequality promotes certain behavior outcomes in the minority, while the cultural *ideal* of democracy and equality of opportunity promote quite different out-comes. Consequently, there is no single racial personality for any minority in America, but a variety of personality outcomes, all of which represent minority adjustments to the conditions under which they live.

1. Acceptance

The stereotype of the contented, easygoing Negro is not entirely untrue. A considerable number of Negroes, especially in the South, ac-cept wholeheartedly the doctrine of innate Negro inferiority and view white domination as entirely proper. These are probably the most suc-cessfully "adjusted" Negroes of all, since they escape most of the frustra-tions and resentments which bedevil other Negroes. These Negroes also gain the approval of those whites who describe the Negro who is obedient, docile, and deferential as a "good nigger." This white stereotype also defines the "good nigger" as hard-working but unambitious. Such Negroes are rare, for few people will work hard and well unless driven by an ambition. In attempting to limit Negro ambition to those simple and childish goals which in no way jeopardized white status or income, whites have also deprived Negroes of their main reason for working, and have guaranteed that many Negroes would be "lazy." But if Negroes will not work hard unless motivated by ambition, many whites would prefer that the Negro be lazy, for, while the lazy Negro is an irritation, the ambitious Negro is a threat. Many whites may be unaware of making such a choice, but the effects of their choice remain. *For the Negro, laziness is a normal, intelligent, and functionally useful adjustment to his lack of opportunity.*

2. Accommodation

There is, apparently, a growing number of Negroes who resent white domination but will make expedient compromises with it in order to ad-vance themselves. Fearful of attacking the white man's prejudices, they seek to manipulate these prejudices to their own advantage. This involves the studied use of flattery, cajolery, and humble petition. It involves observing the racial etiquette and making no challenge to the racial status quo. It entails acting the way whites expect Negroes to act, and requires the use of many subterfuges to avoid disturbing any of the white man's illusions about Negroes. By preserving an outward appearance of acceptance of white domination, many Negroes have achieved a tolerable existence and even some advancement.

The accommodation pattern often includes *avoidance*, an effort by the minority to minimize contacts with the majority. The clannishness of a minority is an avoidance technique. The medieval ghetto originated as a voluntary clustering of Jews for common protection and escape from insult; only later did it become compulsory. Many Negroes travel by automobile to avoid segregated public transportation, and middle- or upper-class Negroes often shop by telephone and pay bills by check in order to avoid contacts with disrespectful whites. [72]

3. Aggression

Not all who resent discrimination are able to accommodate themselves successfully. Some find outlet for their frustrations in some form of aggression against someone—the majority, another minority, or even against each other. The many forms of aggression range from revolts, riots, and street fights to such subtle provocations as loud talk or the intentional withholding of deference. Johnson has described numerous subtle ways in which Negroes vent hostility upon whites—"talking back," quitting jobs without notice, spreading gossip, paying exaggerated courtesies, committing acts of petty sabotage, and so on. [73] In the North, Negro boasts and hints of white girl friends are an effective aggressive device; in the South, this would probably be too dangerous.

Certain members of the minority develop what has been called the *oppression psychosis*, an oversensitivity to discrimination that leads them to imagine discrimination where it is absent. Some Negro students who receive low grades because of poor work are quick to accuse the teacher of injustice. A prominent Negro explains the oppression psychosis in saying: [74]

. . . when I was a barefoot boy in Franklin County, Virginia, sometimes I stubbed my toe in the spring and it would not heal until the fall. It seemed that everything in nature, including the leaves, wind and grass, conspired to hit that toe. The children, dogs, flies, and cats always deliberately selected that toe to brush against or to trample upon. My suffering, I admit, was more

[72] See C. S. Johnson, *Patterns of Negro Segregation* (New York, Harper and Brothers, 1943), pp. 267-293, for a description of the many subtle ways in which Negroes minimize contacts with whites.

[73] *Ibid.*, pp. 294-315.

[74] A. Clayton Powell, *op. cit.*, p. 28.

psychological than physiological, for I was always expecting somebody or something to pick on that sensitive toe.

The Negro has been stubbed and snubbed so constantly by prejudice, that he not only reacts to the slightest rebuff in word or act, but he often reacts when there has been no intended action.

A person with the oppression psychosis blames all disappointments and failures upon discrimination and is likely to be highly aggressive in venting his hostilities. Such persons irritate and alienate the majority group and embarrass their own group whose complaints they exaggerate and caricature.

4. Organized Protest

Whereas aggression is merely a way to vent one's hostile feelings, organized protest is a calculated campaign to change things. Organized protest often uses aggressive devices, but only as part of a carefully organized plan. Organized protest goes beyond the humble petitions of a Booker T. Washington to include an insistent demand that the promises of the Constitution be fulfilled. The National Association for the Advancement of Colored People (NAACP) is perhaps the most effective organization in the country militantly fighting for Negro rights. It vigorously demands enforcement of existing laws and enactment of additional laws to end lynching, insure equal police protection, and reduce occupational, educational, and social discriminations against Negroes. While it has had limited success in securing new legislation, it has successfully pressed many legal actions resulting in court rulings which have weakened and reduced many kinds of discrimination.

The Congress of Racial Equality (CORE) works at the local level, seeking to open jobs and public accommodations to Negroes through persuasion and nonviolent coercion. A delegation of Negroes and whites may sit in a restaurant for many hours, patiently waiting for service. "Sit-ins," boycotts, persuasion, negotiation, publicity, and threats of court action are their weapons, but violence or provocative behavior are strictly avoided. Their techniques, which draw heavily upon Christian forbearance and upon the nonviolent methods of India's Gandhi, appear to have had some success. [75]

In organized protest, the minorities have their most effective weapon. For lack of effectively organized protest (among other reasons) the Negroes made no important gains during World War I. In World War II, however, well-organized plans for a "March on Washington" to dramatize failure to employ Negroes in defense industry—an incident which would be highly embarrassing to a nation fighting a war against

[75] See *Core-lator*, monthly newssheet of the Congress of Racial Equality, 38 Park Row, New York 38, N. Y.

fascism—resulted in President Roosevelt's establishment of the Fair Employment Practices Committee. Organized protest can be quite effective when it can appeal to a set of democratic professions such as ours. The membership of protest organizations such as the NAACP and CORE indicates that increasing numbers of Negroes are rejecting both placid acceptance and quiet accommodation in favor of organized protest as their reacton to life in America. [76]

THE SOCIAL-DISORGANIZATION APPROACH

Race problems can be viewed as products of social disorganization. Some factor—migration, population growth, technological change—disturbs an existing equilibrium between races, or between groups which are defined as races. In America, migration brought into successive contact whites and Indians, whites and Negroes, Protestants of northern and western European extraction and Catholics of southern and eastern European extraction, gentiles and Jews, and several other combinations. Each developed into a "problem." The status of the Negro aroused some debate and soul-searching from the very beginning, but not until the Civil War period did it become a major social concern. Although it is widely believed that the war was fought to free the slaves, the historical fact is that Lincoln freed the slaves in order to win the war by disrupting the South's labor force. Negroes received freedom as a bit of war strategy from a government which had no clear idea of what Negroes were to be and do after they were free. Following the war, the North more or less looted the South, ruling it with the help of the Negroes whom they gave the vote and placed in political office. [77] After a decade, the North abandoned the Negroes to the tender mercies of an embittered South as part of a deal which secured the presidency for Hayes. The South promptly disfranchised the Negro, removed him from political office, and set about returning him to servitude. [78] An elaborate etiquette devel-

---

[76] This partial list of minority reactions, largely taken from Brewton Berry, *Race and Ethnic Relations, op. cit.*, pp. 479-508, is not the only such listing. Davie finds seven Negro responses: acceptance, resentment, avoidance, overcompensation, race pride, hostility and aggression, and protest (M. R. Davie, *Negroes in American Society* [New York, McGraw-Hill Book Co., 1949], pp. 434-455.) Johnson sees four Negro reactions: acceptance, avoidance, direct hostility and aggression, and indirect or deflected hostility. (Charles S. Johnson, *Patterns of Negro Segregation, op. cit.*, pp. 244-315).

[77] See H. Donald Henderson, *The Negro Freedman: Life Conditions of the American Negro in the Early Years After Emancipation* (New York, Henry Schuman, 1952).

[78] For a brief history of the Negroes in America during the past century, see Herbert Hill and Jack Greenberg, *Citizen's Guide to Desegregation* (Boston, Beacon Press, Inc., 1955), Ch. 2, "The Negro's Changing Social and Economic Status: From Reconstruction to Desegregation."

oped to regulate all contacts between whites and Negroes [79] (for example, Negroes were never addressed as "Mr."; white and Negro children might play together only while young; Negroes never sat down in the presence of adult whites, and so on). This etiquette sought to permit close and intimate contacts but to prevent any suggestion of equality; therefore Negro servants might live on the same block or in the same house with whites, prepare their food, and even nurse white babies at their breasts, yet could not eat with whites or wear hats in their presence.

Before the war many of the skilled workmen were Negro slaves, [80] and Negroes worked in nearly all occupations except the professions. After the war, a popular classification of all jobs as either "white man's work" or "nigger's work" developed, and each postwar census showed a decline in the proportion of skilled workers among Negroes. Within a generation, Negroes were largely excluded from all but the most menial jobs.

In this way a new equilibrium developed to replace the prewar slave-oriented society of the South. Although there were many local variations and minor uncertainties, this new equilibrium did tell each person, white or Negro, where he stood and what he might do. This equilibrium persisted without great change for over half a century. Meanwhile, Negroes made some gains in education and in ownership of farms and businesses, but they made few gains and suffered some net losses in their bid for political and occupational equality. But the northward migration of Negroes, the accumulating findings of natural and social science, and the development of industrial unionism after 1933 all eventually undermined this post–Civil War equilibrium. During the 1930's the C.I.O. organized many industrial unions, which include all the workers in a particular *industry* rather than those in a given *trade* or skill (as in the A.F.L. trade unions). The industrial union cannot exclude Negroes without weakening itself, nor can it allow race animosities to disrupt union affairs. Although discrimination against Negroes has been the rule in trade unions, enlightened self-interest led most industrial unions to admit Negroes, and the national office of the C.I.O. and some locals have waged an energetic campaign to reduce prejudice and discrimination. [81]

The outbreak of World War II found the traditional race patterns be-

---

[79] See Charles S. Johnson, *Growing Up in the Black Belt* (Washington, American Council on Education, 1941), pp. 277-280; also Bertram Doyle, *The Etiquette of Race Relations in the South* (Chicago, University of Chicago Press, 1937).

[80] There were many abolitionists in both the North and South who argued that slavery penalized the great mass of whites by largely excluding them from the skilled trades, as the slaveowner found it cheaper to train a slave as a carpenter or blacksmith than to hire white tradesmen.

[81] H. R. Northrup, *Organized Labor and the Negro* (New York, Harper and Brothers, 1944); Robert Weaver, *Negro Labor* (New York, Harcourt, Brace & Co.. 1946).

ginning to weaken, and it greatly accelerated their decay. The war produced a serious labor shortage together with an emphasis upon the values of democracy and equality. Negroes and sympathetic whites took full advantage of this unique opportunity to press for minority rights. They succeeded in gaining Negro access to many job areas formerly reserved for whites and made successful attacks in the courts upon many forms of discrimination in higher education and public services. Negroes are now working in hundreds of thousands of jobs formerly closed to Negroes, attending dozens of colleges and universities which formerly excluded them, and are even being elected to some local offices in the South. The effects of such changes will be to disorganize further, and to eventually destroy the traditional pattern of race relations in all of the country. No new equilibrium is yet in sight, and it appears quite possible that relatively complete political and economic equality for Negroes may not be far distant.

The old equilibrium owed much of its stability to the fact that the status of the Negro was fully consistent with the beliefs of the period. Since nearly all people, including even the Negroes, believed that Negroes were innately different from and inferior to whites, it seemed perfectly sensible to treat them as inferiors. The "all men are created equal" dictum did not apply to Negroes, since they were "property," not men. Theories of a biblical Hamitic curse, of incompleted or separate evolutions, of geographic determinism, and of intelligence test evidences were successively employed to justify treatment of Negroes as inferiors. As long as such notions were believed—and most people did believe them—there was no inconsistency in professing democratic ideals while practicing discrimination.

But as natural and social science destroyed the intellectual respectability of such beliefs, the inconsistencies between democratic ideals and racial practice became increasingly apparent. A society which professes democracy and equality of opportunity yet practices race discrimination is to this degree disorganized. This disorganization gives whites a bad conscience and drives Negroes into frustrated confusion.

It is unlikely that such inconsistency can endure in a technologically advanced society such as ours. Only when a group is consistently trained to expect and desire the treatment it receives can that group be content. It is unlikely that any intermediate equilibrium—granting Negroes certain privileges while withholding others—will be satisfactory either to whites or to Negroes. A stable equilibrium can be secured only by bringing current practice into harmony with current beliefs, and this means either (1) admitting Negroes into full democratic citizenship, or (2) suppressing the ideas of freedom and equality of opportunity which make Negroes discontented. If whites desire an enduring racial peace with a clear conscience, they must surrender either the practice of discrimination or the ideal of democracy. They cannot enjoy both.

THE VALUE-CONFLICT APPROACH

As repeatedly implied in this chapter, the race problem is basically a moral problem—a choice of values. The existence of race discrimination is a problem only to one whose values define race discrimination as abhorrent. Although practically everyone agrees that there is a race problem, some define the problem as the task of eliminating prejudice and discrimination, while others define the problem as one of putting the Negroes back in "their place." What some hail as "progress" in race relations, others view with alarm and dismay. If all, or even most, Americans could agree upon what kind of a solution of the race problem they wished, such a solution might not be long in coming. We have enough knowledge to "solve" the problem if we shared a consensus on objectives. But there can be no agreement between those who want Negroes to be ambitious citizens and those who want them to be servile inferiors.

Even among sympathetic whites, there are difficult value choices to make. Should we seek the prevention of race conflict, the reduction of discrimination, or the reduction of prejudice? In at least the short run, these objectives may conflict. A consistently enforced segregation may reduce conflict for the present, but (aside from being uneconomic) it multiplies discrimination and perpetuates prejudice. Techniques of reducing discrimination may produce at least a temporary increase in conflict and prejudice, as the school desegregation controversy reveals. While, over the long run, it is likely that conflict, prejudice, and discrimination move together, some short-run sacrifices may be unavoidable.

THE PERSONAL-DEVIATION APPROACH

Race problems are not *caused* by deviant individuals, but deviant persons can greatly *aggravate* them. Each minority has its maladjusted neurotics who, in one way or another, increase their brothers' burdens. The aforementioned oppression psychotic, with his chip hopefully balanced on his shoulder, is an embarrassment to his fellows as he constantly confirms the worst suspicions of the enemies of his race. Another minority response which plays into the hands of the enemy is the self-hatred response. The Anti-Semitic Jew or anti-Negro Negro is a maladjusted person who seeks to escape the stigma of inferiority by agreeing with and repeating the criticisms commonly directed against his group. [82]

In the dominant group the maladjusted person is more likely to be highly prejudiced than is the well-adjusted person. Furthermore, the frustrated neurotic may be far more likely to express his prejudices in violent action than the well-adjusted person with the same prejudices. Observers of organized anti-Semitic movements (most of which are also anti-Negro)

[82] Cf. George E. Simpson and J. Milton Yinger. *op. cit.*, pp. 212-219, 333-335.

have been impressed by the numerous tight-lipped, sadistic fanatics and the almost complete absence of relaxed, genial folk among the followers. [83]

This deviant person is a noisy nuisance, making serious race problems even more explosive, yet he is not the primary cause of them. Without a background of widespread prejudice, the racial fanatic could not be effective. So both the sadistic street rioter and the well-mannered teller of the racial joke play a role in perpetuating the race problem.

The totally unprejudiced person is also a deviant, in that he has not absorbed the normal prejudices and racial stereotypes of his fellows. Racial equality may even become a "cause" to which he is fanatically dedicated. In this as in most other problems, the extremists at both ends of the continuum are likely to be deviant persons.

SUGGESTED READINGS

Since Chapters 12 and 13 form a single unit of study, the Suggested Readings and Audio-Visual Aids for both chapters will be found at the end of Chapter 13.

QUESTIONS AND PROJECTS

1. What are the scientific facts about race differences?

2. Define the "race problem" according to each of two or three different sets of values.

3. Who bears the "costs" of the race problem? In what ways?

4. What is race prejudice? Is lack of prejudice closely correlated with intelligence, knowledge about other races, or contact with other races?

5. Why do prejudiced people usually deny that they are prejudiced?

6. What are the theories of the causes of prejudice? Is any one of them adequate by itself?

7. What is the function of myths and evasions in protecting prejudices?

8. Is it possible for a member of a minority group to remain unaffected by prejudice and discrimination? What are some common minority reactions?

9. What effects does discrimination against a minority group have upon the members of the majority group? How have whites been affected by their treatment of Negroes?

10. No one is forcing Negroes to stay in the United States. Why not encourage dissatisfied Negroes to go back where they came from?

11. Why don't Negroes develop their own attractive residential areas? What difficulties would confront a Negro group seeking to develop a polite residential subdivision in your community or a nearby city?

[83] Cf. John Roy Carlson, *Under Cover, op cit., The Plotters, op. cit.;* Leo Lowenthal and Norbert Guterman, *Prophets of Deceit* (New York, Harper and Brothers, 1949).

12. Suppose all Jews in the United States were to convert to Christianity. What would happen to anti-Semitism?

13. How have race problems grown out of the disorganization of earlier arrangements? Is a new equilibrium developing? If so, what do you think this new equilibrium will be like?

14. How did World War II affect race relations in the United States?

15. In what way is every race problem the product of a value conflict?

16. Is the prejudiced or the unprejudiced person the deviant?

13

The Race Problem:
From Acceptance to Action

TECHNIQUES OF REDUCING PREJUDICE

1. Education

To MANY PEOPLE, EDUCATION is the answer to the problem of prejudice. But it is naive to expect either church or school to educate people toward beliefs and values very different from those already held by the community. Both church and school are dependent upon the community for financial support and are staffed and directed by persons who share most of the views and prejudices of the community. Angry denunciations, such as "Communist," "radical," "atheistic," "subversive," or "un-American" await the school superintendent or minister whose concern over race problems goes very far beyond the conventional platitudes. Certain church bodies, especially the National Council of Churches, have been quite active in issuing liberal racial pronouncements and supporting minority rights. Although these pronouncements may have helped promote a national atmosphere more favorable to minority rights, not much of this interest in race problems has filtered down to the local congregational level. Several studies, while inconclusive, suggest that prejudiced persons often tend to be conventionally religious, while the least prejudiced persons often showed strong, though unorthodox, religious interest.[1] There is certainly no basis for assuming that conventional or traditional religion reduces prejudice. The church remains a stronghold of discrimination, lagging far behind labor unions and professional organ-

[1] G. E. Simpson and J. Milton Yinger, *Racial and Cultural Minorities* (New York, Harper and Brothers, 1958), pp. 108-109.

izations in this respect. All major denominations have adopted national policies of integrating church congregations, but one survey found that one-third of the ministers did not even know about the national policy of their church, and relatively few local congregations are biracial. [2] Although congregational desegregation is spreading, it is still true that at no other moment during the week are white and Negro as rigidly segregated as when engaged in the worship of the "God of all Mankind."

The church reaches only part of the population, but the school reaches virtually everyone at impressionable ages. However, this strategic advantage is largely nullified by both the prejudices of the school staff and the intolerance of the community. Teachers and administrators appear to be somewhat less prejudiced than the rest of the community and, in a few places, have succeeded in introducing realistic programs of intercultural education.[3] But even these programs have a habit of dying a quiet death after the novelty wears off or their promoter moves on to a new position.

Race-relations conferences, interracial meetings, and brotherhood assemblies have little educational effect because they consist mainly of dedicated liberals busily talking to themselves. Such conferences may maintain morale among race liberals and may provide exceedingly valuable instruction in techniques of effective action, but can play no real role in the direct reduction of prejudice as long as the prejudiced people do not attend them.

2. Exhortation and Propaganda

Exhortation and propaganda form a double-edged weapon. Exhortation at the level of platitudes and generalities, like the posters, radio plugs, and sermons, saying "All men are brothers," "Prejudice is un-American," and the like, are ineffective. The prejudiced person applies them to other people, since he is unaware of his own prejudice. His own prejudices are so fully rationalized as to be immune to such slogans. In fact, such exhortation may have a negative effect, since it allows the prejudiced person to feel self-righteous, while it gives the liberal the illusion that he is "doing something" about race problems and thus serves as a substitute for more effective action.

More specific propaganda also has its dangers. Publicizing the achievement of minority members (especially Jews) may arouse jealousy rather than respect. Publicizing recent Negro gains may inspire jealousy and

[2] Lawrence K. Northwood, "Ecological and Attitudinal Factors in Church Desegregation," *Social Problems*, Vol. 6 (Fall, 1958), pp. 150-163.

[3] See Clarence A. Chatto and others, *The Story of the Springfield Plan* (New York, Barnes & Noble, Inc., 1945); Theodore Brameld, *Minority Problems in the Public Schools* (New York, Harper and Brothers, 1946); Lloyd Allen Cook and Elaine Cook, *Intergroup Education* (New York, McGraw-Hill Book Co., 1954).

insecurity among whites, while describing Negro poverty and handicaps may confirm prejudices instead of arousing sympathy. Attempts to "answer" false rumors and racial accusations may even spread the falsehood more widely. Propaganda must be used very skillfully or it will defeat its own purposes. Propaganda is seriously limited because (1) it fails to reach the right audience, since many prejudiced persons read and watch little beyond comics and sports events; and (2) the prejudiced person reinterprets propaganda in such a way that his prejudice remains undisturbed or even strengthened. [4] All in all, it is doubtful that propaganda can have very much effect in reducing the general level of prejudice.

3. Personal and Group Therapy

Since, in at least some cases, intense prejudice seems to be a function of a maladjusted personality, it might be more effective to attack the maladjustment instead of the prejudice. If the personality disorder can be cured, then the violence of one's prejudice should fade and the prejudice be far more easily removed. This approach is probably sound, but there are serious difficulties in its use. Mass psychotherapy, even on a group basis, would be fantastically expensive. Many maladjusted persons sense no maladjustment ("It's *other* people who are queer!") and have no desire for treatment. Furthermore, the problem of how to produce stable, prejudice-free personalities in a prejudice-prone environment is not easy to answer.

But psychotherapy is not always necessary. Often, a change in *situation*, by alleviating pressures and frustrations, will reduce maladjustment and lessen active prejudice. The use of *guidance* techniques by teachers, employers, military officers, and others in supervisory roles may indirectly reduce prejudices by steering pupils and adults into situations which are less frustrating.

4. Contact

Contact between peoples produces a variety of attitudes, depending upon the *kind of contact*. A mere "getting together" of whites and Negroes or of gentiles and Jews does not automatically reduce prejudices; it may even increase them. One study of an interracial boys' camp found

[4] For experimental evidence of this, see Patricia Kendall and Katherine Wolf, in Paul Lazarsfeld and Frank Stanton, eds., *Communications Research, 1948-49* (New York, Harper and Brothers, 1949), p. 158. For evidence of the boomerang effect, in which propaganda is interpreted in such a way as to strengthen the prejudice, see Eunice Cooper and Helen Dinerman, "Analysis of the Film, 'Don't Be a Sucker': A Study in Communication," *Public Opinion Quarterly*, Vol. 15 (Summer, 1951), pp. 243-264.

that the boys with the most interracial contacts also offered the most spontaneous unfavorable comments (correlation of +.83 for whites and +.67 for Negroes), and that those whose prejudices diminished were matched by an equal number whose prejudices were intensified. [5]

Certain kinds of contact, however, produce spectacular changes in attitudes. In military service, in employment, in housing projects, the integration (mixing) of Negroes and whites has not resulted in the dire predictions of "trouble" being fulfilled, but has resulted in striking reductions in prejudice with surprisingly little "trouble." Deutsch and Collins studied two integrated housing projects in which Negroes and whites were scattered indiscriminately, and two segregated projects in which Negroes and whites occupied separate sections of the project. They found that in the integrated projects, agreeable relations between whites and Negroes were ten times more common and bad relations only one-fourth as frequent as in the segregated projects. [6]

NATURE OF WHITE HOUSEWIVES' RELATIONS WITH
NEGRO PEOPLE IN THE PROJECT

Kind of relations reported	Integrated		Segregated	
	Koaltown	Sacktown	Bakersville	Frankville
Friendly relations	60%	69%	6%	4%
Accommodative relations	24	14	5	1
Mixed relations	7	11	2	3
No relations	5	0	87	88
Bad relations	4	6	0	4
Total cases	102	90	100	101

Lazarsfeld [7] reports on an interracial housing project in which:

Before they moved into the project only one out of every twenty-five whites thought that race relations would turn out well, while five times as many felt that there would be nothing but conflict between the people of the two races. After a few years, one out of every five whites said that race relations were better than they had thought they would be, while only about one-fourth as many [one out of twenty] thought they were worse than they had expected. But of the people who had anticipated really serious race conflicts, three out

[5] Irwin Katz, *Conflict and Harmony in An Adolescent Interracial Group* (New York, New York University Press, 1955).

[6] Morton Deutsch and Mary Evans Collins, "Intergroup Relations in Interracial Housing," *Journal of Housing* (April, 1950), pp. 127-129 ff., reprinted in Arnold Rose, ed., *Race Prejudice and Discrimination* (New York, Alfred A. Knopf, Inc., 1951), p. 556. It should be noted that, of those persons who reported *any* relations with Negroes, "bad" relations formed 19 per cent of all relations in the segregated group, and only 5 per cent of all relations in the integrated group.

[7] Quoted from President's Committee on Civil Rights, *To Secure These Rights* (Washington, Government Printing Office, 1947), p. 85.

of every four were willing to say that their fears had been proved groundless. Moreover, people who had worked with Negroes were considerably more willing to live in the same community with them.

A survey of attitudes in private residential areas shows that those whites living closer to Negroes are more willing to approve the idea of mixed racial housing areas than those living at a greater distance. [8] Another survey found that those who lived close to Negroes in an interracial housing project had more neighborly contacts and more favorable attitudes than other whites within the project who did not live so close to the Negroes. [9] Although the attempt to bring about mixed housing sometimes produces temporary tensions, serious "trouble" usually develops only where police encourage it by sympathizing openly with the trouble-makers. [10] Where police and prosecutors act promptly and firmly to enforce the law, "trouble" rarely develops. After the mixed housing is established, both prejudice and conflict decline.

The armed services experienced endless trouble with segregated units and found that integrated units produced less race friction and a more efficient use of manpower. [11] Owing partly to pressure from the civilian government, and partly to military necessity in the Korean conflict, [12] the armed services rather reluctantly proceeded to integrate Negro troops into white units and fill ratings and training programs irrespective of race. Integration is now virtually completed, and, to quote General Mark Clark, "Integration of Negro troops in white units on a percentage basis proved an unqualified success—against the predictions of many military men, including myself." [13] The Defense Department reports that integration has been carried out "more rapidly than had been considered possible," that "there have been no untoward incidents," and that integra-

[8] Arnold M. Rose, Frank J. Atelsek, and Lawrence R. McDonald, "Neighborhood Reactions to Isolated Negro Residents; An Alternative to Invasion and Succession," *American Sociological Review*, Vol. 18 (October, 1953), pp. 497-507.

[9] Daniel M. Wilmer, Rosabelle Price Walkley, and Stuart A. Cook, *Human Relations in Interracial Housing: A Study of the Contact Hypothesis* (Minneapolis, University of Minnesota Press, 1955), p. 95.

[10] After extended disorders at Trumbull Park housing project in Chicago, the Chicago Congregational Christian Association, representing eighty-seven Congregational Churches in the Chicago area, adopted unanimously a resolution denouncing groups fomenting racial disorder there "with apparent assurance that the law will not be enforced," and calling on Mayor Kennelly to "fulfill his duty in this regard by securing the appointment of an officer to be in charge of the police detail there who will enforce the law impartially." (*Chicago Sun-Times*, April 29, 1954, p. 30.) Another organization, the Independent Voters of Illinois, made similar charges. (*Chicago Sun-Times*, June 4, 1954, p. 12).

[11] See President's Committee on Equality of Treatment and Opportunity in the Armed Services, *Freedom to Serve* (Washington, Government Printing Office, 1950).

[12] See Lee Nichols, *Breakthrough on the Color Front* (New York, Random House, 1954).

[13] *Collier's*, Vol. 133 (February 5, 1954), p. 881.

A Southern chemical company tried out a new—and successful—way of ending one kind of on-the-job segregation. It built "separate but equal" washrooms and installed them at opposite ends of the plant. Before long, whites near the Negro washrooms began using them rather than walking the length of the factory. Later, Negroes started using the white washrooms, and soon the segregationist signs came down.

39th *Annual Report* of the American Civil Liberties Union, 1957-1958, p. 65.

tion has produced "a marked increase in over-all combat effectiveness," along with "economies in manpower, matériel, and money. . . ." [14]

The policy of complete integration was pursued only after experimentation and testing had established its practicality. After some experimental integrated units had been established, 1710 white enlisted men were asked, "Some Army divisions have companies which include Negro and white platoons. How would you feel about it if your outfit was set up something like that?" [15] Two-thirds of the white men in the mixed companies reported that they had been opposed to the idea beforehand and had expected it to fail; yet nearly all of these men agreed that it had succeeded despite their fears. When white company-grade officers and platoon sergeants involved in the experiment were asked, "Has your feeling changed since having served in the same unit with colored soldiers?," over three-fourths replied that their feelings had become more favor-

[14] "Services Abolish All-Negro Units," *New York Times*, October 31, 1954, p. 23, quoting Defense Department publication by James C. Evans, *A Progress Report on Integration in the Armed Services;* James C. Evans and David A. Lane, Jr., "Integration in the Armed Services," *The Annals of the American Academy of Political and Social Science*, Vol. 304 (March, 1956), pp. 78-85; Eli Ginzberg and others, *The Negro Potential* (New York, Columbia University Press, 1956), Ch. 4, "The Negro Soldier."

[15] Information and Education Division, United States War Department, "Opinions About Negro Infantry Platoons in White Companies of Seven Divisions," reprinted in Theodore M. Newcomb and Eugene L. Hartley, eds., *Readings in Social Psychology* (New York, Henry Holt & Co., Inc., 1947), pp 542-546.

Groups polled on Negro and white platoons serving in same company	*Percentage of white enlisted men answering: "Would dislike it very much."*
Cross section of field force units which do not have colored platoons in white companies (1450 cases)	62
Men in same division, but not in same regiment as colored troops (112 cases)	24
Men in same regiment, but not in same company as colored troops (68 cases)	20
Men in company with a Negro platoon (80 cases)	7

able. [16] When asked, "How well did the colored soldiers in this company perform in combat?", 84 per cent of the white officers and 81 per cent of the white non-coms replied, "Very well" (the most favorable answer on a four-point scale) to this question. [17] While all these percentages are based on samples too small to be highly accurate, they leave no doubt that integration produced a dramatic reduction in prejudice.

A number of other surveys support the conclusion that certain kinds of contact are likely to reduce prejudice. A study of the prejudices of four hundred merchant seamen with varying amounts of shipboard experience with Negroes shows that: [18]

... whether a man had been born in the North or the South was not important in determining whether he was prejudiced against Negroes. The extent of his education and the jobs he held before he went to sea were not important. What was important was whether the men were members of unions with tolerant policies toward Negroes; how many trips to sea a man had made; how many times he had been under enemy fire; and how many times he had been to sea with Negroes. Here again what determined whether a white man was prejudiced against Negroes was the kind and amount of experience he had with them. Where there was contact with Negroes on an equal footing in a situation of mutual dependence and common effort, prejudice declined.

Simpson and Yinger summarize our present knowledge of the effects of contact on prejudice in these four propositions: [19]

1. Incidental, involuntary, tension-laden contact is likely to increase prejudice.
2. Pleasant, equal-status contact that makes it unnecessary for the individuals to cross barriers of class, occupational, and educational differences . . . is likely to reduce prejudice.
3. Stereotype-breaking contacts that show minority-group members in roles not usually associated with them reduce prejudice . . .
4. Contacts that bring people of minority and majority groups together in functionally important activities reduce prejudice. . . . When white soldiers find Negroes fighting side by side with them, they are more likely to see them as fellow soldiers, less likely to see them as "Negroes." When white seamen shipped with Negroes, their prejudice declined, even though mixed crews were compulsory union policy, not freely chosen situations.

[16] *Ibid.* The Armed Forces study found:

Response to question, "Has your feeling changed since having served in the same unit with colored soldiers?"

	White Officers	White Noncoms
"No, my feeling is the same."	16%	21%
"Yes, have become more favorable."	77	77
No answer	7	2

[17] *Ibid.*

[18] President's Committee on Civil Rights, *op. cit.,* p. 85.

[19] *Op. cit.,* p. 757.

CURRENT TRENDS IN RACE RELATIONS IN AMERICA

1. Decline of Regional Variations in Race Attitudes

Regional variations of all sorts—rural-urban, agrarian-industrial, East-West, and North-South—are rapidly fading. Mass communication, migration of peoples, and decentralization of industry are fast dissolving the quaint provincialism of region, hamlet, and mesa. Georgia Negroes and Georgia whites not only work at the same bench and belong to the same union in Detroit; they are doing so in growing numbers in Georgia as well. The noble pose of moral superiority which Northerners are wont to strike is today losing whatever validity it may have possessed. [20] The barriers to Negroes voting in the South are rapidly crumbling, and this inevitably means better schools, more hospitals, and better jobs. The improvements now taking place in the South in Negro education at all levels and Negro success in gaining better jobs and more nearly equal pay have been remarkable. Although regional differences may never entirely disappear, they are diminishing at an impressive rate.

2. Application of Scientific Knowledge to Race Problems

Man in his earlier periods had no alternative but to wallow in his own ignorance and rely on guesswork. Our knowledge is not complete (is it ever?), but we already have enough knowledge to separate the blind alleys from the practical approaches. We now know that most racial fears are groundless, that prejudice is unnecessary, and that amity is attainable. We know how to isolate racial clashes and prevent race riots, [21] and we know the conditions necessary for racial peace. We have considerable knowledge of how prejudices are formed and how they are changed. We know something of the interrelations between prejudice and discrimination, and how it is possible to change patterns of discrimination. We can, with a fair degree of accuracy, predict the probable results of a program of action.

3. Shift from Laissez Faire to Action

Even as recently as twenty years ago, it was widely believed that any attempt to "do anything" about racial prejudice would only make

[20] See "The Negro and The North," *Life*, Vol. 69 (March 11, 1957), p. 151 ff; "Chicago's Segregation Tragedy," *Look*, Vol. 22 (September 30, 1958), pp 77-82; Fletcher Martin, "We Don't Want Your Kind," *Atlantic Monthly*, Vol. 202 (October, 1958), pp. 51-55; Morton Grodzins, "Segregation in the North," *The Progressive*, Vol. 23 (June, 1959), pp. 66-70.

[21] Alfred McLung Lee, *Race Riots Aren't Necessary*, Public Affairs Pamphlet, No. 107 (New York, Public Affairs Committee, 1945).

things worse. Social scientists who privately desired action were paralyzed by the prejudiced person's threat of "trouble" (usually a threat that someone else would make trouble). [22] Thus the prejudiced would blackmail the unprejudiced into inaction, while proceeding to fix the status of minorities according to their own prejudice. In this way the tolerance of the unprejudiced was neutralized and largely wasted as they were reduced to talking to one another and expressing hopes for the future.

Today this is changed. Social scientists have become increasingly aware of the ineffectiveness of talk unless supported by action and have learned how action—legislation, political pressure, and organized publicity —can be effectively used. Today, people who desire a reduction in discrimination are busily promoting legislation and planning local campaigns to break down discrimination in local employment, in restaurants, barbershops, and other public services. Action has replaced hopeful waiting as the program of race liberals.

4. Shift from Attack Upon Prejudice to Attack Upon Segregation

Social scientists long accepted the popular assumption that segregation was necessary to prevent race conflict in a prejudice-ridden society. Only after prejudice had declined, it was believed, could segregation be relaxed and equality be achieved; meanwhile, the races might enjoy "separate but equal" facilities and opportunities. People interested in minority rights were urged to tolerate and work within segregation—to seek to reduce prejudice first, after which discrimination and segregation would disappear.

One of the significant discoveries of the past two decades is the discovery that attempts to reduce prejudice while retaining segregation and discrimination are ineffective. For segregation prevents the sorts of contacts that reduce prejudice and, instead, channels the races into the kinds of contact that create and reinforce prejudice. To seek to reduce prejudice by exhortation and propaganda is largely futile when segregation is so busily creating it. Segregation even fails in its primary objective of preventing conflict, at least in a society in which democratic values make segregation frustrating to Negroes and embarrassing to whites. The President's Committee on Civil Rights sums up the matter: [23]

The separate but equal doctrine stands convicted on three grounds. It contravenes the equalitarian spirit of the American heritage. It has failed to operate, for history shows that inequality of service has been the omnipresent consequence of separation. It has institutionalized segregation and kept groups

[22] See Gunnar Myrdal, *The American Dilemma* (New York, Harper and Brothers, 144), pp. 19, 580, footnote, 831.
[23] *Op. cit.,* p. 87.

apart despite indisputable evidence that normal contacts among these groups tend to promote social harmony.

Sociologists generally support these views in statements such as this: [24]

It has been pointed out again and again that segregation produces ignorance and superstition, and that it perpetuates the status of minority groups and makes it impossible for them to participate fully in the main stream of American life. Instead of producing social order, it produces chaos. In the Detroit race riot, Negroes and whites who lived close together as neighbors, those who were fellow students at Wayne University, and those who worked side by side in the Detroit war plants, showed no disposition to fight. Disturbances occurred in segregated residential areas and segregated plants.

Today, in both the North and South, efforts to change race relations focus directly on the attempt to reduce segregation. Both through legal means discussed in later pages, and through organized pressure of various sorts, segregation is under attack. At the local, state, and national levels, voluntary organizations—NAACP, CORE, National Urban League, American Civil Liberties Union, Anti-Defamation League of B'nai B'rith, many local human-relations councils, and other organizations—are highly active. In addition to supporting civil rights legislation, such groups publicize local instances of discrimination; they use persuasion and pressure upon business concerns to accept minority members as employees and as patrons; they put unions and professional organizations on the spot and urge them to abandon discriminatory practices. Especially in local public services—hotel and restaurant, commercialized recreation, and so on—local groups have sometimes been able to reassure proprietors that their businesses will not suffer if they cease to discriminate.

With the fear of attacking segregation removed by recent knowledge, the attack is being vigorously pressed wherever segregation is found. And segregation and discrimination are crumbling with a speed which few if any social scientists, two decades ago, would have predicted.

5. Shift from Education and Conciliation to Legal and Administrative Action

In the days of Booker T. Washington, conciliation was perhaps the only practical approach open to the Negro. To *demand* anything from whites would only infuriate them; but to *petition* whites—to appeal to their sympathy, generosity, and vanity—was sometimes effective in getting schools, hospitals, and other benefits which did not seriously disturb the status quo. But today a better educated and more restive Negro group

[24] A. M. Lee and N. D. Humphrey, *Race Riot* (New York, The Dryden Press, Inc., 1943), p. 17.

faces a less self-satisfied white group which has been repeating the slogans
of democracy so fervently it almost believes them. The present minority
leaders, aided by many members of the dominant group, are making a
determined legal attack upon every form of segregation. Although
Negroes are the main beneficiaries of this movement, Jews, American
Indians, Americans of Mexican or Oriental ancestry, and other minorities
share in the gains made against prejudice. The legal approach involves:
(a) enforcing existing laws; (b) seeking court interpretations which extend the coverage of existing laws; and (c) passing additional laws.

a. *Enforcing existing laws.* Many rights legally guaranteed to Negroes
(and other minorities) are in fact unavailable. The rights to vote, to use
public facilities, and to equal protection of the law have often been
denied. Violence and threats of violence often deterred Negroes from
claiming their legal privileges. Negroes seeking service in hotels and
restaurants were often met by a bland refusal of proprietors to obey
the law, or else by evasion, inattention, and humiliation. Law-enforcement officials were likely to stall when legal action was sought. Such
situations are now changing. The NAACP, the Civil Liberties Union, and
other organizations often prod local law-enforcement officials into action
when necessary. The proprietor who refuses service to Negroes, in one
of the states in which such discrimination is forbidden by law (21 in
1960), now knows that a lawsuit is an actual possibility. Hundreds of
legal actions have been pressed for the sole purpose of demonstrating
that noncompliance with the law will not be accepted without complaint.
While not yet entirely successful, the effort to gain enforcement of existing laws has produced a great many changes.

b. *Extending interpretations of existing laws and constitutional provisions.* Civil rights organizations, mainly the NAACP, have pressed many
court cases seeking legal ruling that a particular discriminatory practice
is contrary to law, or is in violation of some guarantee of the Fourteenth Amendment. Almost every year there are one or more Supreme
Court rulings which extend the legal rights of Negroes. One decision
held that Jim Crow segregation on interstate trains and buses was unconstitutional; another had the effect of requiring the admission of
Negroes to tax-supported university, graduate, and professional schools
of most Southern states; another ruled that restrictive racial covenants
(preventing resale of real estate to Negroes or other undesirables) are
unenforceable, and so on. This approach has been quite successful and
has greatly weakened segregation in housing, education, and certain
public facilities.

c. *New laws against discrimination.* After a half century of comparative inactivity, recent years have brought a flood of proposals for new
legal curbs upon discrimination. The first federal civil rights legislation
of this century was passed in 1957, empowering the Attorney General to

aid any person who is denied his voting rights, and establishing a federal Civil Rights Commission to investigate voting abuses and make recommendations to Congress. This commission presented its report in 1959, calling for federal laws to provide for appointment of temporary federal election registrars wherever local officials prevent Negroes from registering. [25] The early passage of added federal legislation to protect Negro voting rights now appears to be practically certain. In a single year, no less than 149 bills opposing discrimination were introduced into state legislatures, and as this is written, thirteen states are considering laws to forbid discrimination in the sale or rental of housing. [26] Much of the new legislation deals with the two areas of housing and employment.

Fair Employment Practice Legislation

Although efforts to extend employment opportunities of minorities are not new, agitation for fair employment practice legislation is a postwar development which received its initial impetus from the wartime Fair Employment Practice Committee. After much pressure and the threat of an embarrassing Negro March on Washington, [27] President Roosevelt established, in 1941, a Fair Employment Practice Committee (FEPC) [28] by executive order No. 8802 under his war powers as president. All federal departments and agencies "concerned with vocational and training programs for defense production" were ordered to administer these programs without discrimination, and all defense contracts were to include a "provision obligating the contractor not to discriminate against any worker because of race, creed, color, or national origin." After some confusion and further extension of authority, [29] the FEPC operated throughout the war. The committee was empowered to receive complaints, conduct investigations, hold hearings, issue subpoenas, issue findings of fact, and make recommendations. It could impose no legal penalties or fines but could threaten an employer with loss of manpower priorities or

[25] United States Commission on Civil Rights, *With Liberty and Justice For All* (Washington, Government Printing Office, 1959), p. 96.

[26] John H. Burma, "Race Relations and Antidiscriminatory Legislation," *American Journal of Sociology*, Vol. 55 (March, 1951), pp. 416-423; *Civil Liberties*, monthly newsletter of the American Civil Liberties Union, April, 1959.

[27] Louis Ruchames, *Race, Jobs, and Politics: The Story of* FEPC (New York, Columbia University Press, 1953), pp. 17-21; Herbert Garfinkel, *When Negroes March* (Glencoe, Ill., The Free Press, 1959).

[28] The abbreviations, FEPC and FEPA have become widely used to refer to *all* fair employment practice legislation. FEPC originally referred to the federal Fair Employment Practice Committee which was discontinued in 1945, and FEPA referred to a national Fair Employment Practice (Act) law which was rejected by Congress under Truman's administration. Fair employment practice laws are enacted by states, and some of them have retained the same title which accounts for the continued use of these abbreviations; however, some states use different names for their fair employment practice laws and commissions.

[29] Executive Order 9343 (1943).

a striker with loss of draft deferment. It could recommend cancellation
of a defense contract, but never did so lest the war effort suffer. [30] Despite
these limited powers, the committee was successful in helping promote
an enlargement of Negro employment opportunities. "Between July,
1943, and December, 1944, the committee docketed a total of 5803 complaints of discrimination which, at first glance, seemed to be valid. Of
these, about 64 per cent were dismissed soon after docketing because of
lack of merit, insufficient evidence, and other causes. The remaining 36
per cent were satisfactorily adjusted." [31] The proportion of Negroes
among workers in war production nearly trebled, and the proportion of
Negroes in the more highly skilled jobs showed striking increases. [32] In
1938, 90 per cent of Negro government employees in Washington were
doing custodial work; this figure fell to 40 per cent, indicating that 60
per cent were in other (often better) jobs. Dozens of industries which
had employed no Negroes, or who limited them to unskilled jobs, began
hiring Negroes for many sorts and grades of service. During four years
under the FEPC, the Negroes made more progress towards occupational
equality than they had made in the preceding half century. The wartime
labor shortage, the wartime emphasis upon democratic values, and the
FEPC were all essential to this accomplishment; but, without the FEPC,
little change would have been likely. The violent and bitter attacks upon
the FEPC [33] appeared only after its success became apparent.

Following the end of the FEPC in 1945, a revival of discriminatory
practices began [34] which stimulated proposals for permanent legislation.
Although both Republican and Democratic parties supported fair employment practice legislation in their campaign platforms of 1944 and
1948, and numerous bills have been presented in the federal Congress,
none has ever yet come to a vote. There is more than a suspicion that
certain members of both parties have been more interested in fair employment practice as campaign bait than as a legislative objective. [35]

By 1960, sixteen states and over thirty cities had enacted some sort
of fair employment practice legislation. Fourteen states have such laws
with commissions which are empowered to enforce them. [36] Two states,
Indiana and Kansas, have commissions with conciliatory powers only.
The city ordinances vary widely in scope and provision for enforcement.

Unless fair employment practice legislation includes provision for
enforcement, including legal penalties and procedures for court action,

[30] See Louis Ruchames, *op. cit.*, Ch. IX, "The Committee in Structure and Function."

[31] *Ibid*, p. 159.

[32] *Ibid.*, p. 159-163.

[33] *Ibid.*, Chs. V, VI.

[34] *Ibid.*, pp. 134-136.

[35] *Ibid.*, Ch. XIII.

[36] New York, New Jersey, Massachusetts, Connecticut, New Mexico, Oregon,
Rhode Island, Washington, Colorado, Michigan, Minnesota, Pennsylvania, Wisconsin,
and Alaska.

the laws are relatively ineffective. All successful fair employment practice action relies heavily upon publicity and persuasion, [37] but these are likely to be effective only when backed by the implied threat of real penalties. Such penalties need rarely be used, if it is known that they *can* be used. In over 5,000 complaints investigated by several state commissions, there have been only five public hearings and only four court actions. [38] Purely voluntary and conciliatory programs are ineffective, as the Cleveland experience illustrates. After a thirteen-month trial of a voluntary program which the Cleveland Chamber of Commerce planned, directed, staffed, and financed at a cost of over $30,000, the Chamber of Commerce agreed that it was a failure and joined in support of a compulsory fair employment practice ordinance. [39]

Business management strongly opposed fair employment practice legislation when first proposed. Like all other groups, businessmen include a share of prejudiced persons busily rationalizing their prejudices. And the businessman's traditional dislike of "government interference" and his fear that these laws would provoke "trouble" and disrupt production led him to prefer to drop the entire matter. These fears have proved to be largely groundless. The expected "trouble" did not materialize, and there is little business opposition and considerable business support for fair employment practice legislation in those places where it has been tried. A survey of employers reported in 1950 by *Business Week* revealed that "employers agree that FEPC laws haven't caused near the fuss that opponents predicted. . . . Personal friction hasn't been at all serious . . . even those who opposed an FEPC aren't actively hostile now." [40] Employers find that such laws "get management off the hook" and help them in dealing with those who threaten "trouble." [41]

Organized labor support has varied. In general the industrial unions (CIO) do not practice discrimination and have supported fair employment practice legislation. The trade or craft unions (AFL unions, railway unions) often practiced discrimination, and unions have been the respondents (offenders) in 10 per cent of the complaints made to the New York Commission. [42] Many of these trade unions have shown little enthusiasm for this antidiscriminatory legislation. Numerous church groups, racial conciliation groups, and assorted liberal groups have strongly supported fair employment practice laws. Public opinion appears to be generally favorable, with one survey showing that even in the South,

[37] Louis Ruchames, *op cit.*, pp. 143 ff., 154, 183.
[38] John A. Davis, "Negro Employment: A Progress Report," *Fortune*, Vol. 46 (July, 1952), pp. 102 ff; James Rorty, "FEPC in the States: A Progress Report," *Antioch Review*, Vol. 18 (Fall, 1958), pp. 317-329.
[39] John A. Davis, *op. cit.*
[40] "Does State FEPC Hamper You?" *Business Week*, No. 1069 (February 5, 1950), pp. 114-117.
[41] John A. Davis, *op cit.*
[42] "FEPC: New York Version," *Fortune*, Vol. 42 (September, 1950), pp. 50 ff.

the supposed citadel of discrimination, 48 per cent of the workers favor fair employment practice acts. [43]

School Desegregation: An Experiment in Social Change

In the most important decision affecting Negroes in decades, the Supreme Court in 1954 declared segregation in public schools to be unconstitutional. In a unanimous decision written by Chief Justice Warren, the Court declared that, even though physical facilities and other "tangible" factors might be equal in segregated Negro schools, [44]

To separate them [Negroes] from others of similar age and qualifications solely because of their race generates a feeling of inferiority as to their status in the community that may affect their hearts and minds in a way unlikely ever to be undone. . . .

A sense of inferiority affects the motivation of a child to learn. Segregation . . . has a tendency to retard the educational and mental development of Negro children and to deprive them of some of the benefits they would receive from a racially integrated school system. . . .

We conclude that in the field of public education the doctrine of "separate but equal" has no place. Separate educational facilities are inherently unequal.

The Court did not order the *immediate* end of school segregation, but ruled that the states must end compulsory racial segregation in the public schools "with all deliberate speed."

Five years later (1959) found 802 of the 2,909 biracial school districts desegregated. Some 783 of these desegregated districts were in the border states (Delaware, Kentucky, Maryland, Oklahoma, Texas, West Virginia), 19 were in the mid-South states (Tennessee, Arkansas, Virginia, and North Carolina), and none in the deep South. Of almost 3,000,-000 Negro children in southern and border states, 140,000 were attending mixed schools in 1959, while 439,000 Negro children lived in school districts where some degree of desegregation had been accomplished. [45]

This is an impressive development, in view of the massive obstacles to desegregation. Arrayed against it were the traditions and prejudices of centuries. Perhaps more important is the fact that Southern Negro children average lower in school achievement and in socioeconomic status than white children. Wholesale school integration would mean that large numbers of academically retarded, uncouth Negro children would attend classes with white children, proportionately fewer of whom were similarly underprivileged. Thus, this race problem, like so many others, is found to be basically a *class* problem. These lower-class characteristics of so

[43] Conducted by McGraw-Hill Research Department, reported in "What the Worker Thinks," *Factory*, CVII (November, 1949), p. 105.

[44] *New York Times*, May 18, 1954, p. 15.

[45] *Southern School News*, Vol. 5 (May, 1959), p. 1. This monthly paper was established in 1954 to report factually and objectively on developments in the segregation controversy.

I don't think the people understand our present-day situation concerning public education in Virginia. It's not the education of our children that's so important. It's states rights.

State Senator Charles L. Moses, of Appomatox, Va., quoted in *Harper's Magazine*, August, 1959, p. 24.

many Southern Negroes, which are the results of past discrimination, become an excuse for perpetuating that discrimination.

A number of districts became desegregated voluntarily and without incident. In other districts, the usual procedure is for some Negro parents whose children have been denied admission to the schools to file suit in

United Press International Photo

First day at school—Little Rock, 1957

their district federal court; the court then orders the school board to admit the Negro children. This is a cumbersome way to promote a major social change. It makes a succession of court actions necessary in every community which resists desegregation, and invites white reprisals against the Negroes who start court actions. It advertises the localities where desegregation is being resisted, thereby inviting opponents to collect from a wide area for mob action. The courts have no police powers and cannot enforce their orders, but must rely on other governmental agencies to do so. Other agencies have given little assistance. State and local agencies have often been used to frustrate rather than to enforce the orders of the federal courts. The federal government took no action until faced with virtual insurrection in Arkansas in 1957. President Eisenhower declined to endorse the decision of the Supreme Court or to appoint a national commission of eminent persons to promote orderly desegregation. The Department of Justice offered no assistance of any sort until after 1957, while Congress declined to pass a resolution which would have eliminated debate over whether desegregation was really required by the law of the land." [46] Local school boards and school administrators were ordered to desegregate, but had no power to carry out the order when faced with organized segregationist opposition. [47]

Where a strong *external* authority in control of the schools ordered desegregation, as in Washington, D.C., on army posts, and in Catholic parochial schools, they were integrated quietly and without incident. [48] Wherever the local school leaders, in co-operation with church and community leaders, made careful preparation for desegregation, while law enforcement officials let it be known that they would tolerate no disorder, desegregation has taken place with very little disorder. Lack of careful community preparation increases the possibilities of disorder, while any lack of firmness by law enforcement officials practically guarantees violence. [49]

There are, in any community, a number of frustrated, resentful persons, filled with hostilities and antagonisms, who are ready to work off their aggressions in a good fight. They will join in any riot handy, and, since they fit the "prejudiced personality" pattern, racial violence is especially satisfying. Lurid *predictions* of bloody violence, like those of Gov. Faubus in Little Rock, [50] easily stimulate this group into action. But firm police power promptly cools off this group, who enjoy violence only as long as someone else does the suffering. [51]

[46] See Albert P. Blaustein and Clarence Clyde Ferguson, Jr., *Desegregation and the Law* (New Brunswick, Rutgers University Press, 1957).

[47] See Virgil Blossom, *It Has Happened Here* (New York, Harper and Brothers, 1959), for a detailed account of the Little Rock, Arkansas, desegregation controversy.

[48] Bonita Valien, *The St. Louis Story: A Study in Desegregation* (New York, Anti-Defamation League of B'nai B'rith, 1956); Carl F. Hansen, *Miracle of Social Adjustment: Desegregation of the Washington, D. C., Schools* (New York, Anti-Defamation League of B'nai B'rith, 1957); Omer Carmichael, "The Louisville Story," *New York Times Magazine*, October 7, 1957, pp. 12 ff.

[49] See *Field Reports on Desegregation in The South*, pamphlets published at various dates describing developments in particular localities by the Anti-Defamation League of B'nai B'rith, 515 Madison Avenue, New York 22, N. Y.

[50] See *New York Times*, August 30, 1957, p. 1; September 3, 1957, p. 1; September 5, 1957, p. 1; September 7, 1957, p. 1.

[51] For example, in Fairmont, West Virginia, picketing activity by mothers ended when the judge warned, "I'll fill the jails until feet are sticking out of the windows" (*New York Times Book Review*, December 1, 1957, p. 44). See also, "Little Rock's Finest," *Time*, Vol. 74 (August 24, 1959), pp. 14-15.

No desegregation has taken place in the public schools of the deep South, and practically none in the mid-South. [52] By 1958, the eleven Southern states had passed a total of 196 laws intended to prevent or delay desegregation, either by closing the public schools, by cutting off state funds to any desegregated school, by providing for state-aided private schools, and many others. [53] The NAACP has been harrassed by laws making it a crime for the NAACP to bring cases into court, [54] forbidding teachers and other public servants to belong to the NAACP, or requiring it to reveal its membership list so that its members are then subject to reprisal. [55] Most of these laws are unconstitutional, but may operate during years of litigation before they are declared so. White Citizens' Councils have appeared in most parts of the South, to impose economic reprisal upon anyone, white or Negro, who supports desegregation. Through these activities, moderates have been silenced in many parts of the South, where to challenge segregation is to invite dismissal or economic ruin. In many areas, organized action by Negroes or in support of their interests has halted.

For the southern churches, desegregation is a painful dilemma. A majority of the clergy, both Catholic and Protestant, favors desegregation, [56] while a majority of church members are opposed. Thus, the churches are torn between the moral imperatives of the Christian ethic and the practical necessities of operating an institution. Of six Protestant ministers who actively supported desegregation in Little Rock in 1957, four were transferred or removed within a year, [57] and in Columbus, Georgia, a minister who supported desegregation was dismissed with the explanation that ". . . the voice of the pulpit should be the voice of the congregation." [58] Consequently, most clergymen have placed congregational peace above racial reform and have handled the issue mainly by publicly "praying for guidance." [59] Even so, church leaders are virtu-

[52] See John Bartlow Martin, *The Deep South Says Never* (New York, Ballantine Books, Inc., 1957).

[53] *New York Times*, September 7, 1958, IV, p. 6.

[54] See "Inciting Legislation," *Race Relations Law Reporter*, Vol. 3 (December, 1958), pp. 1257-1277. This law journal was established in 1956 to report on the many new laws and court decisions dealing with race relations.

[55] See "Attack on the NAACP," *Race Relations Law Reporter*, Vol. 4 (Spring, 1959), pp. 224-236

[56] The *Pulpit Digest* reports a survey showing four out of five Protestant ministers in seventeen Southern states favoring compliance with the desegregation decision, with at least 50% or more supporting compliance in every state. (*Time*, Vol. 72 [October 27, 1958] p. 74). See also, Statement of Catholic Bishops, "A Call to Action on Negro Rights," *United States News and World Report*, Vol. 45 (Nov. 21, 1958), pp. 74 ff; "312 Atlanta Clerics Ask South to Obey Integration Decision," *New York Times*, November 23, 1958, p. 1, 81.

[57] *Time*, Vol. 72 (September 15, 1958), p. 53.

[58] *Time*, Vol 73, (June 22, 1959), p. 47.

[59] Ernest G. Campbell and Thomas F. Pettigrew, "Racial and Moral Crisis: The Role of Little Rock Ministers," *American Journal of Sociology*, Vol. 44 (March, 1959), pp. 509-516.

ally the only group in the South which has voiced any public support of desegregation.

Discrimination against Negroes is greatest where Negroes live in large numbers and is weaker where Negroes are proportionately fewer. [60] Resistance to desegregation is strongest in regions which are rural, agricultural, impoverished, poorly educated, and those which have large Negro populations. Resistance to desegregation weakens as we move toward areas which are more urbanized, industrialized, prosperous, better-educated, and those which have a smaller proportion of Negroes. [61] Massive resistance to desegregation is rapidly crumbling in the more urbanized, prosperous sections of the border South, for economic, not ideological, reasons. Desegregation fights are costly. New industries and government contracts are not attracted to communities with closed schools, as Little Rock has learned. [62] *Every* device for frustrating desegregation is, in some way or other, costly to whites. The proposal to evade desegregation by state-aided private schools would be impossibly expensive, cumbersome, and, probably, unconstitutional. [63] The South cannot possibly continue its march toward becoming a productive, prosperous, progressive region while pursuing the measures necessary to preserve segregation. [64] The border South is now facing this fact and is proceeding to permit a limited degree of desegregation. In time, the deep South will become unwilling to preserve segregation at the cost of isolating itself—economically, politically, and culturally—from the rest of the nation.

Housing Segregation: The Skeleton in the Northern Closet

The North secures a large measure of school segregation through housing segregation, with school district boundaries drawn to coincide

[60] H. M. Blalock, Jr., "Per Cent Non-White and Discrimination in The South," *American Sociological Review*, Vol. 22 (December, 1957), pp. 677-682.

[61] Melvin J. Tumin, *Resistance and Readiness* (New York, Anti-Defamation League of B'nai B'rith, 1957); Melvin J. Tumin, Paul Barton, and Bernie Burrus, "Education, Prejudice, and Discrimination: A Study of Readiness for Discrimination," *American Sociological Review*, Vol. 23 (February, 1958), pp. 41-49; W. H. Haltzman, "Attitudes of College Men Towards Non-Segregation in Texas Schools," *Public Opinion Quarterly*, Vol. 20 (Fall, 1956), pp. 559-569; Thomas F. Pettigrew, "Demographic Correlates of Border-State Desegregation," *American Sociological Review*, Vol. 22 (December, 1957), pp. 683-689.

[62] Little Rock's industrial growth stopped abruptly with its school disorders in 1957. Two years later, no new industries had located there; only six firms reported increased earnings, and two of these were moving firms. (*Time*, Vol. 74 [August 24, 1959], p. 45) Also, "Little Rock Finds Business Harmed," *New York Times*, February 1, 1959, p. 74.

[63] Donald R. Green and Warren E. Gauerke, *If The Schools Are Closed* (Atlanta, Southern Regional Council, 1959).

[64] J. Milton Yinger and George E. Simpson, "Can Segregation Survive in an Industrial Society?" *Antioch Review*, Vol. 18 (Spring, 1958), pp. 15-24.

with racially segregated residential areas. Residential segregation of Negroes has *increased* in recent decades, [65] and was encouraged by the government's policy of granting FHA and Veterans Administration loans on houses in only homogeneous (that is, segregated) neighborhoods. [66] However, these practices are now changing. [67] A number of myths are invoked to justify housing segregation—that Negroes do not take care of property; that Negro invasions cause property values to fall; that any area invaded by Negroes soon is taken over by them; that a property becomes unsalable to whites once Negroes enter the area; and so on. Every one of these beliefs is demonstrably untrue—proved untrue by repeated investigations—yet is widely believed. The facts are that Negro invaders are nearly always of a higher social class than their white neighbors; that Negro owner-occupants generally maintain their property as well as, or better than, their white neighbors; that property values more often *rise*, rather than fall, after Negroes enter in large numbers; that whites *will* buy into mixed neighborhoods if the areas show promise of stability. [68] Some Negro invasions are deliberately promoted by "blockbuster" realtors, who move a highly offensive Negro family into a neighborhood, hoping to panic the whites into selling out at a loss; then he resells these properties at high prices to Negroes. [69] Where whites refuse to panic, the self-fulfilling prophesy that prices will fall and Negroes overrun the neighborhood does not materialize. [70]

By 1959, laws forbidding discrimination in sale or rental of housing had been adopted by fourteen states and 32 cities, including New York. Single sales are exempted, but realtors and large scale operators are forbidden to discriminate because of race or religion. Antidiscrimina-

[65] Donald O. Cowgill, "Trends in Residential Segregation of Non-Whites in American Cities," *American Sociological Review*, Vol. 21 (February, 1956), pp. 43-47.

[66] Davis McIntire, "Government and Racial Discrimination in Housing," *Journal of Social Issues*, Vol. 13, (No. 4, 1957), pp. 60-67.

[67] *38th Annual Report of the American Civil Liberties Union, 1957-1958*, pp. 60-63.

[68] See Charles Abrams, *Forbidden Neighbors: A Study of Prejudice in Housing* (New York, Harper and Brothers, 1955); Luigi Laurenti, "Bureau of Business and Economic Research Project," *The Appraisal Journal*, Vol. 20 (July, 1952), pp. 314-329; Thomas F. Gillette, "Effect of Negro Invasion on Real Estate Values," *American Journal of Economics and Sociology*, Robert Schalkenbach Foundation, Vol. 16 (January, 1957), pp. 151-162; Eunice and George Grier, "Market Characteristics in Interracial Housing," *Journal of Social Issues*, Vol. 13 (No. 4, 1957), pp. 50-59; Center for Sociological Research, Western Michigan University, *Research Report on Integrated Housing in Kalamazoo* (Kalamazoo, W. E. Upjohn Institute for Community Research, 1959); George and Eunice Grier, *Privately Developed Interracial Housing in the United States* (Berkeley, Cal., University of California Press, 1960); Davis McIntire, *Residence and Race* (Berkeley, Cal., University of California Press, 1960).

[69] Eleanor P. Wolf, "The Invasion-Succession Sequence as a Self-Fulfilling Prophesy," *Journal of Social Issues*, Vol. 13 (No. 4, 1957), pp. 7-20.

[70] See Ellsworth E. Rosen with Arnold Nicholson, "When a Negro Moves Next Door," *Saturday Evening Post*, Vol. 231 (April 4, 1959), pp. 32 ff.

tory housing legislation will probably follow the same course as Fair Employment Practice legislation. A "highly controversial" law will be passed in some places; most of the predicted "trouble" will not materialize; then a general trend to pass and enforce such laws will develop and housing discrimination will be considerably reduced.

The Legal Approach to Discrimination

How successfully can prejudice and discrimination be reduced by law? The cliché, "you can't prevent prejudice by passing a law," is true, but the *expression* of prejudice can be controlled by law. No law can force Catholics and Protestants to like each other, but laws do prohibit them from burning each other's churches; and, by discouraging the violence upon which hatred feeds, the law indirectly encourages Catholics and Protestants to like each other better. Wherever law can reduce the *expression* of prejudice, the prejudice itself tends to decline.

A law is enforceable in a free society only when backed by a preponderant public opinion. In civil rights legislation, the problem is one of determining what measures will receive enough support to be enforceable. A proposal, such as a FEP Act, might find the people of an area divided roughly into five groups:

    a. Strong supporters, who will contribute time and money to pass a law, and actively press for its enforcement.

    b. Passive supporters, with definite approval but limited interest; will not become active unless prodded and organized by others.

    c. The indifferent, with little interest and no definite convictions; likely to follow course of least resistance and side with the majority.

    d. Passive opponents, with definite disapproval but limited interest; will not become active unless prodded and organized by others.

    e. Strong opponents, who will contribute time and money to defeat a proposed law, and will actively seek to prevent its enforcement.

The possibility of passing and enforcing a law depends upon the relative size, and the power and influence, of groups *a* and *b* compared to groups *d* and *e*. Law can easily check the intolerant when the actively intolerant form a relatively small minority. But in the absence of law, *this intolerant minority can nullify the good will of the majority* by insisting that all social policy be fitted to their prejudice. A bigoted 5 per cent, by loudly refusing to work beside Negroes, can neutralize the good will of the remaining 95 per cent. If one-tenth of the hotel guests object to Jews, they are permitted to outvote the 90 per cent who do not object. The absence of law allows an intolerant minority to coerce the majority into acceding to their prejudices, and forces the liberal into the role of the busybody who stirs up trouble.

The passing of an antidiscrimination law, if accompanied by publicity, machinery for enforcement, and a determined effort at enforcement, alters this picture dramatically. (1) *It reverses the troublemaker role;* the intolerant person now becomes the troublemaker when he hints darkly of trouble or demands that the employer or restaurateur evade the law. (2) *The burden of action is shifted;* it is now up to the bigot to start something, and experience has shown that in most cases the dire predictions of the bigots peter out into futile grumbling. (3) *The pattern of conformity behavior is changed;* nondiscrimination becomes the approved status quo, and all those who follow the course of least resistance now find that nondiscrimination is the least bother. While it is often possible to evade the law through various subterfuges, this may become such a nuisance that compliance with the law is the lesser inconvenience. For all these reasons, a carefully drawn law with machinery for enforcement *changes the balance of power* between tolerant and intolerant groups. In the outline above, if groups *a* and *b* are larger than, or even as large or influential as, groups *d* and *e*, it should not be difficult to enforce the law under consideration. Groups *a* and *b* will actively support the law; group *c*, the indifferent, will go along with the law because that has become the course of least resistance. These three groups now comprise an overwhelming majority, whereas *d* and *e* are the deserted minority. Group *d*, the passive opponents, will grumble, but are unlikely to take obstructive action in the face of a determined effort to enforce the law. Trouble is likely to develop only when law-enforcement officials betray a disinterest in energetic enforcement. Group *e*, the strong opponents, find themselves a small and lonely minority, hesitant to start anything without support.

Where a proposed antidiscrimination law finds those who are actively opposed to be more numerous or influential than those who support it, that law is obviously unenforceable and probably will not even be enacted. We have generally been quite conservative in passing antidiscrimination laws, for we have usually overestimated the opposition to their enforcement. Recent efforts at enforcing such laws have produced remarkably little of the trouble hopefully predicted by the intolerant and uneasily feared by the tolerant. [71]

The Administrative Attack Upon Discrimination

In a "folk society," people behave according to the attitudes and values they have absorbed through primary group association. In the modern mass society, however, much of one's behavior consists of playing a designated role as a member of some secondary group. Behavior in

[71] See Jack Greenberg, *Race Relations and American Law* (New York, Columbia University Press, 1959), for a detailed and well documented analysis of the possibilities of changing social behavior by legislation.

secondary-group relationships is impersonal and segmental, dictated less by personal attitudes and feelings than by the formal obligations of one's role. Thus, the teacher, salesman, and porter regularly display behavior which is contrary to their private feelings, because such behavior is part of their job; it is demanded as part of the role they fill. In the mass society, deliberately organized collectives—labor unions, professional organizations, administrative officials of business organizations and governmental departments, and others—define the behavior expected of personnel in specific situations.

This helps explain many inconsistencies in racial attitudes and behavior. The teacher is, as a teacher, expected to treat Negro and white pupils alike, but as a homeowner is likely to support other homeowners in seeking to protect the neighborhood against Negro invasion. Studies have shown little or no statistical correlation between acceptance of Negroes as fellow workers and acceptance of Negroes as neighbors. [72] Many other inconsistencies may be due to the fact that people increasingly act in specific situations in terms of their respective roles as workers, homeowners, merchants, and so on.

Such an analysis suggests that a person's race attitudes and prejudices may be less important than his role obligations in controlling his behavior. [73] Instead of trying to change his over-all race attitudes and prejudices, it may be more effective to ignore these and simply redefine his expected behavior in specific situations. The National Maritime Union has been successful in a policy which bluntly tells its members, in effect, "Feel as you wish, but if you refuse to ship out with Negroes, you don't ship out." [74] Police in several cities have been highly successful in preventing racial incidents from blossoming into violence, [75]

. . . after a program of training of the police, which stressed their role and responsibility in the maintenance of law and order without reference to their personal feelings and beliefs. . . . The training of the police was not designed to effect changes in their personal attitudes and prejudices but solely to redefine and set forth their role as professional law-enforcement agents in the implementing of public policy.

It is uncertain just how far it is possible to alter racial behavior by redefining roles and ignoring race attitudes. Presumably, there are limits to the degree to which collective or administrative redefinition of roles

---

[72] Joseph D. Lohman and Dietrich C. Reitzes, "Note on Race Relations in Mass Society," *American Journal of Sociology*, Vol. 58 (November, 1952), pp. 240-246.

[73] *Ibid.*; Melvin L. Kohn and Robin M. Williams, Jr., "Situational Patterning in Intergroup Relations," *American Sociological Review*, Vol. 21 (April, 1956), pp. 164-174; Melvin L. DeFleur and Frank R. Westie, "Verbal Attitudes and Overt Behavior," *American Sociological Review*, Vol. 23 (December, 1958), pp. 667-673.

[74] *New York Times*, May 27, 1946, p. 3. "The State of the N.M.U. on Discrimination" is stated in the union's publication, *Equality For All*.

[75] Joseph D. Lohman and Dietrich C. Reitzes, *op. cit.*

can be expected to overpower traditional habits and attitudes. To date, however, the combination of legal and administrative redefinitions has been highly effective in altering racial behavior, and continued use of these techniques may be expected. Since there is evidence that each change in racial behavior has an eventual effect upon race attitudes, thereby reducing the potential resistance to further changes in racial behavior, it is conceivable that this technique may eventually "solve" the race problem in the United States.

FUTURE PROSPECTS

In a highly dynamic society, race relations cannot possibly remain static. For a half century or more, educational opportunities for Negroes were steadily being extended while occupational opportunities were being contracted. This paradox put explosive pressure behind the Negro demand for equality of treatment. The growing insistence of Negro demands, the destruction of the popular theories supporting discrimination, the wartime labor shortage, the wartime emphasis on democratic values, and the election of two highly sympathetic presidents (Roosevelt and Truman) all combined to create a period of the most rapid Negro advance in our history. Between 1939 and 1959, the gap between Negro and white school expenditures was reduced by two-thirds, [76] the median income of Negro workers grew from 40 to 58 per cent of the median income of white workers, [77] and the proportion of Negroes employed in "semi-skilled and skilled" jobs rose from 19 per cent in 1940 to 40 per cent in 1956. [78] This is far from equality, but it is an impressive change of status in less than a generation.

How long the present equalitarian wave will continue is uncertain. A business depression with serious unemployment would almost certainly reverse the present trend towards more and better jobs for Negroes. Only those who feel relatively secure themselves are likely to feel generous toward minorities. Tension and warfare between America and fascist countries, noted for their persecution of minorities, stimulated America to emphasize the democratic values of political freedom and equality, but tension with Communist countries seems to be having an opposite effect. In most Communist countries, persecution on a basis of *race* has virtually ceased, and Communist propagandists talk expansively about racial equality and justice. This means that tension with Communist countries—since we emphasize our *differences* from them—does not particularly encourage our movement towards racial equality. It may even retard it, since those who are actively supporting racial equality then come under attack as

[76] See Chapter 12, footnote 31.
[77] *New York Times Magazine*, February 14, 1960, p. 80.
[78] *New York Times*, January 17, 1960, X, p. 12.

No full-fledged solution is possible unless . . . equal opportunity . . . is considered to be indivisible. If the nonwhite American
is granted one equal opportunity, say, education, and then denied
the choice of a job and a house commensurate with his education
and achievement, the inner core of his motivation for self-im-
provement is destroyed. If he achieves education, professional
status, and the vote—three equal opportunities possible in some
sections of America—and still is constrained from living where
his heart desires and his means and achievement permit, then the
stigma of second-class citizenship is still visited upon him and
his family. I see no answer to this total problem unless human
judgments and evaluations be made by reason of the quality, not
the pigmentation, of the human person.

John S. Battle
Former Governor, State of Virginia
Report of the United States Commission on Civil Rights

pro-Communist. [79] In these respects, the next decade looks far less favorable for racial advance than the last two decades.

Then again, there are other forces more favorable to minority rights.
The popularization of the scientific facts about race and race prejudice
continues to demolish the belief in white superiority [80] which, year by
year, grows more tattered and disreputable. The momentum of the drive
for racial opportunity will not abruptly subside. Negroes and their friends
have a taste of victory and are gaining the income and status from which
to press effectively for further improvements. The rapidly growing
Negro middle class—prosperous, educated, and skillfully aggressive—
shatters white stereotypes while providing effective leadership for Negro
action programs. [81] The impressive courage and self-discipline shown by
Negro parents and children in recent actions have further undermined the
white stereotype of the Negro as a contented ignoramus. [82] The prob-

[79] Every major organization seeking to advance minority rights in the United
States has been accused of "Communism" by one or more of the Congressional
committees which claim to be "exposing Communism." In the South, the NAACP
is regularly accused of being communist and all desegregation activities denounced
as communist-inspired.

[80] The National Opinion Research Center reports that the percentage of Southerners believing that Negroes are as intelligent as whites has risen from 21 per cent
in 1942 to 58 per cent in 1956. (*New York Times Magazine*, December 1, 1957,
p. 132.)

[81] See E. Franklin Frazier, *Black Bourgeoise: The Rise of a New Middle Class in
the United States*, (Glencoe, Ill., The Free Press, 1957); Wilma Dykeman and
James Stokely, "New Southerner: The Middle-Class Negro," *New York Times
Magazine*, August 9, 1959, pp. 11 ff.

[82] See Martin Luther King, Jr., *Stride Toward Freedom: The Montgomery
Story* (New York, Harper and Brothers, 1958); also, Minnejean Brown, as told to
J. Robert Moskin, "What They Did To Me in Little Rock," *Look* (June 24, 1958),
pp. 30 ff.

ability that no national administration will permit a severe depression to develop is a measure of protection of present Negro gains. The industrialization of the South, and the industrial unions which will follow, are possibly the most important single factor promoting Negro advance in the South. The economic development and rising prosperity of the South give her greater means with which to finance better schools and public services for Negroes. Most important of all, recent experience has shown that it is not necessary to purchase racial peace at the price of supine inaction, for we now know that there are areas where segregation and discrimination can be attacked directly, and that such an attack will result in reducing prejudice and conflict.

For all these reasons, it is likely that the present trend towards racial equality will continue for at least another decade or more. Should the segregationist effort to suppress the NAACP and halt Negro gains be successful, then genuine radical Negro movements might be expected, [83] but this is most unlikely. The segregated past is irretrievably gone, and the present generation is learning to live in an increasingly nonsegregated society. As a distinguished Southern newspaper editor writes, "Segregation is on its way out, and he who tries to tell the people otherwise does them a great disservice. The problem of the future is how to learn to live with the change." [84] Although these changes are deeply disturbing to many persons, and conflict increases temporarily, [85] the trend of race conflict turns downward after segregation and discrimination are reduced. Even though these developments are primarily concerned with whites and Negroes, the problems involving the other minorities—Jews, American Indians, Americans of Oriental or Mexican ancestry, and others—differ only in detail, and the developments are likely to be much the same.

Whether viewed on a local or a world scene, the race problem is both America's Achilles heel and her opportunity. Which we choose to make it is a choice between values, with moral confusion, economic waste, and international debility the price we must pay for protecting our prejudices. As Myrdal sums it up: [86]

If America in actual practice could show the world a progressive trend by which the Negro became finally integrated into modern democracy, all man-

---

[83] Such as a group of at least 70,000 Negroes who call themselves "The Moslems," and are dedicated to black supremacy and total hatred of whites, saying, ". . . there is no good in white men. All are children of the devil." See "The Black Supremacists," *Time*, Vol. 74 (August 10, 1959), p. 24-25; also, Wilson Record, "Extremist Movements among American Negroes," *Phylon*, Vol. 17 (March, 1956), pp. 17-23.

[84] Ralph McGill, editor of the *Atlanta Constitution*, quoted in *Time*, Vol. 62 (December 4, 1953), p. 51.

[85] The American Friends Service Committee counted 530 violent race incidents in 1955-1958—killings, beatings, bombings, and mob actions—including only those reported in the press. The peak in numbers was reached in 1957, although the 1958 incidents were more serious. (*New York Times*, June 21, 1959, IV, p. 7).

[86] *Op. cit.*, pp. 1021-1022.

kind would be given faith again—it would have reason to believe that peace, progress, and order are feasible. And America would have a spiritual power many times stronger than all her financial and military resources—the power of the trust and support of all good people on earth. *America is free to choose whether the Negro shall remain her liability or become her opportunity.*

SUGGESTED READINGS

ALLPORT, Gordon W., *ABC's of Scapegoating* (New York, Anti-Defamation League of B'nai B'rith, 1948). A concise pamphlet describing the scapegoat theory of race prejudice.

BENEDICT, Ruth and WELTFISH, Gene, *The Races of Mankind*, Public Affairs Pamphlet, No. 85 (New York, Public Affairs Committee, 1943). Probably the finest brief summary available of the scientific facts about race, interestingly written in nontechnical language.

BERRY, Brewton, *Race Relations* (Boston, Houghton Mifflin Co., 1951). A highly stimulating and readable textbook in race relations.

DAVIS, Allison, and DOLLARD, John, *Children of Bondage* (Washington, American Council on Education, 1940). Uses the case-analysis method to reveal the differing effects of racial experience upon Negro children in the South.

FRAZIER, E. Franklin, *The Negro in the United States* (New York, The Macmillan Co., 1949). A history of Negroes in the United States, and of their progress and frustrations in American society.

GINZBERG, Eli, and others, *The Negro Potential* (New York, Columbia University Press, 1956). A short book telling how Negro manpower is wasted and might be used more efficiently.

GRIER, George, and GRIER, Eunice, *Privately Developed Interracial Housing in the United States* (Berkeley, University of California Press, 1960). Interesting accounts of successful attempts to develop interracial housing.

HALSEY, Margaret, *Color Blind* (New York, Simon and Schuster, Inc., 1946). An entertaining account of a nonsegregated service men's club operated successfully by the author during the war.

KING, Martin Luther, Jr., *Stride Toward Freedom: The Montgomery Story* (New York, Harper and Brothers, 1958). How Negroes organized a successful boycott against segregated bus seating in Montgomery, Alabama.

RUCHAMES, Louis, *Race, Jobs, and Politics* (New York, Columbia University Press, 1953). A history and evaluation of fair employment legislation in the United States.

SIMPSON, George E., and YINGER, J. Milton, *Racial and Cultural Minorities* (New York, Harper and Brothers, 1958). An encyclopedic textbook in race relations; useful as a secondary source on almost any racial topic.

AUDIO-VISUAL AIDS

All the Way Home (Dynamic Films, Inc., 112 W. 89 St., New York), 29 minutes, sound, black and white. A community is aroused when an owner considers selling his home to Negroes. Brings out many facts and issues.

Burden of Truth (United Steelworkers of America, 1500 Commonwealth Building, Pittsburgh 22, or from local steelworkers' union), 67 minutes, sound, black and white. Shows discrimination against an educated Negro family in an unnamed Northern city.

Crisis in Levittown (Dynamic Films, Inc., 112 W. 89 St., New York), 31 minutes, sound, black and white. Residents of a community into which a Negro family moves express strong and conflicting opinions in a series of filmed interviews.

The High Wall (McGraw-Hill Book Company, Text-Film Department, 330 West 42 St., New York), 32 minutes, sound, black and white. A case study showing how a young bigot became "infected" and how his home life encouraged his prejudice.

Picture in Your Mind (McGraw-Hill Book Company, Text-Film Department, 330 W. 42 St., New York), 16 minutes, sound, color. A beautiful and imaginative film depicting the tribal roots of prejudice and the manner in which distorted images of other groups arise.

Roots of Prejudice [1954] (Audio-Visual Center, Indiana University, Bloomington), 30 minutes, sound, black and white. Demonstrates how prejudices are formed and maintained through selective memory.

Wanted—A Place to Live (Anti-Defamation League of B'nai B'rith, 515 Madison Ave., New York), 15 minutes, sound, black and white. Three university students argue over accepting as roommate a student of another ethnic group.

QUESTIONS AND PROJECTS

1. Discuss the proposition: "Education is the best answer to the race problem."

2. To what extent is race prejudice reduced by spreading the scientific facts about race and race difference?

3. What difficulties are met in attempting to reduce prejudice by propaganda?

4. Under what conditions is increased social contact between races likely to lead to a reduction of prejudices?

5. Why were race liberals so long fearful of taking any action in race relations? How and why has this attitude changed within recent years?

6. Which is more effective: to reduce prejudice by first reducing discrimination, or to reduce discrimination by first reducing prejudice? Why?

7. Is segregation a successful way of dealing with race relations? What are its results? What value judgments are involved in answering this question?

8. Is passing laws an effective means of changing race relations?

9. What value judgments are implied by Fair Employment Practice Acts? In the doctrine of "separate but equal" facilities?

10. Why do extremist social movements so often include violent race prejudices in their ideology?

11. Do race relations in the United States automatically "get better" as time passes?

12. In what ways is it costly to whites to preserve prejudice and discrimination? What is it costing the South to fight desegregation?

13. What is a "self-fulfilling prophesy?" Cite several illustrations from race relations.

14. Discuss the implications of each of the following answers to the question, "How would you like to have a Negro family move in next to you?"

   a. "I would encourage them to stay with their own kind of people."

   b. "I have nothing against Negroes, but hate to see my property depreciate in value."

   c. "I don't know. Show me the Negroes, and then I'll decide."

   d. "I would move quickly, before the entire neighborhood was taken over."

15. Is the race problem primarily a Southern problem? Does Southern action about race affect the North? Does Northern action affect the South? Must there be a national racial policy, or can there be a variety of local policies?

16. Numerous studies (for example, King's *Stride Toward Freedom*) show how whites may bitterly fight to preserve a particular discriminatory practice, yet, when it is actually abolished, they may quite calmly accept its loss and decide that it was not very important after all. How do you account for this?

14

Problems of Urban and Rural Communities

❧❧❧

. . . today, for the first time in this hemisphere, more than 27,000,000 people are living under urban conditions in a continuous area stretching more than 600 miles from Boston to the far tip of Fairfax County, Virginia. This is a 1950 census figure; estimates of the current figure reach 32,000,000.

Luther Gulick, head of the Institute of Public Administration, offers this prediction for the next fifty years: "There will be a solid settlement extending from Boston perhaps as far south as Newport News, Va. It will sprawl westward at least to Chicago, possibly to Kansas City, with manufacturing centers in what are now forests of Kentucky and Tennessee." [1]

. . . From samples of Los Angeles air (collected on both smoggy and clear days), the experimenters filtered out the chemicals. They painted the resulting gook on the backs of black mice. In little more than a year, 29 per cent of the surviving mice developed malignant tumors. [2]

. . . at the last count, only a fraction of 1 per cent of the available office space was unoccupied. But people who remember Frank Lloyd Wright's prophecy that cities will die and grass grow in the streets are worried about the new office buildings choking the midtown area. Grass may never grow in the streets, but it may some day grow on the roofs of the cars caught in the daily 5 o'clock traffic jam. [3]

. . . a representative in Connecticut's lower house . . . [has] only 130 constituents while a fellow member represents 88,000. A California state senator representing 14,000 rural citizens sits beside a senator who casts his vote for more than four million urban dwellers. Tiny New Hampshire's . . . lower house . . . boasts a member with exactly 16 constituents, and Vermont has one district with a population of 49, another with 33,000 inhabitants.

[1] *The New York Times*, January 27, 1957, p. 72.
[2] Reprinted from *Time;* copyright, Time Inc., 1954.
[3] Reprinted from *Time;* copyright, Time Inc., 1954.

. . . In California only 12 per cent of the voters, overwhelmingly rural, can elect a majority of the state senate; in Connecticut less than 10 per cent of the state can elect a majority to the lower house. [4]

. . . At 5:30 one frosty Indiana morning . . . , Farmer Warren North, 45, rolled out of bed to get at his chores. . . . In the barn, North stepped up to an instrument panel as intricate as a ship's, began pushing buttons and pulling switches. All around, the barn came to vibrant life. From one silo dropped ground corn, from another, silage, from a third, shelled corn.

By pushing other buttons, Farmer North shot in supplementary vitamins, mineral and hormone nutrients. . . . At regular intervals, trap doors automatically distributed the individual animal's feed (400 cattle, 500 hogs). . . .

Ten minutes later, Farmer North was through with a job that would have taken five men half a day working with buckets and pitchforks.

. . . The result of all this is that farm productivity is soaring at a rate that once nobody believed possible. From 1938 to 1957, over-all farm labor productivity rose at an annual average rate of 4.7% (vs. 2.2% for the rest of the economy). Even more significant, productivity is increasing at an accelerating rate. . . . [5]

THE INHABITANTS OF AN URBANIZED AREA of 27 million people live in a virtual sea of humanity that the traditional forms of social organization were not designed to manage. Such things as county commissioners, neighborhood planning, zoning, and civic spirit apply readily to cities of 25,000 people, or even of 250,000 people, but become almost meaningless in a city of 8 million. And even as urban living has changed, living in the country has changed also. The self-sufficient family farm probably is the rural equivalent to the small city in urban society, and is becoming less typical of rural living. Corporation management, research specialists, and automation seem natural enough in the city, but strange indeed on the farm. Moreover, important changes either in urban or rural areas upset the relations between them. Throughout these changing ways of life familiar symptoms of social problems appear.

THE TREMENDOUS GROWTH OF CITIES

The city itself is not new, for ancient history revolves around such cities as Rome, Athens, Jerusalem, and Constantinople. What *is* new is (1) the great size of modern cities, (2) the tremendous number of cities, and (3) the rapidly increasing proportion of the population that lives in cities.

Great Size

The cities of ancient and medieval times were not very large by modern standards. London in 1400 had only about 35,000 inhabitants and

[4] *The Progressive*, November, 1958, p. 7.
[5] Reprinted from *Time;* copyright, Time Inc., 1959.

was the largest city in Europe. Modern cities by contrast are behemoths. If we consider only that portion of the city population living within the corporate limits, the United States has five urban centers each with more than a million people. New York, Chicago, Detroit, Los Angeles, and Philadelphia together contain more than 17 million people. To define as urban, however, only the population living inside the corporation limits is grossly unrealistic. Many of the people who are functionally a part of large cities actually live outside the city limits. New York City contains approximately 8 million people, but greater New York contains over 12 million people. In 1950, for the first time, the United States Census reported "urbanized areas," including as "urban" all of the people who are a part of urban life. There were *twelve* Standard Metropolitan Areas in the United States, *each with over a million population* in 1950, and the 1960 census will add several more to these: [6]

TABLE 14-1.   Standard Metropolitan Areas in the United States

New York-Northeastern New Jersey	12,911,994
Chicago	5,495,364
Los Angeles	4,367,911
Philadelphia	3,671,048
Detroit	3,016,197
Boston	2,369,986
San Francisco-Oakland	2,240,767
Pittsburgh	2,213,236
St. Louis	1,681,281
Cleveland	1,465,511
Washington, D. C.	1,464,089
Baltimore	1,337,373

* Each area had over a million population in 1950.

The Number of Cities

There is a tendency to equate urban life with that which exists in New York or Chicago, but there are 4741 "urban" places in the United States! [7] Most of these are incorporated places of 2500 or more population, but also included are some smaller incorporated places and some unincorporated areas, around cities, that are definitely urban in character. The United States is not organized primarily around any one city, any five cities, or any hundred cities. Certain industries and certain products may be identified with a particular urban center, for example, automobiles in Detroit and garmentmaking in Philadelphia and New York,

[6] U.S. Bureau of the Census, *Statistical Abstract of the United States: 1958* (Washington), pp. 15-16.
  [7] *Ibid.*, p. 20.

but there are at least several hundred cities serving as primary sources for employment, commerce and trade, public utility services, newspaper publication, and many other goods and services that are an essential part of modern life. The early part of the present century saw unparalleled growth and centralization in the largest cities, and more recent decades have brought increases in the numbers of smaller cities. The present 4741 urban places represent a gain of 1277 over 1940 and a gain of 1576 over 1930. [8]

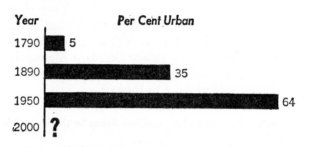

SOURCES: Data from *Historical Statistics of the United States*, 1789-1945, p. 25; and U. S. Bureau of the Census, *Statistical Abstract of the United States:* 1954 (Washington, Government Printing Office), p. 27.

FIG. 14–1. The United States becomes an urban nation.

Population in Cities

In 1790 only 5 per cent of the United States population was urban. New York had less than 60,000 people. By 1950, 64 per cent of the population was defined as urban. The urban portion of the population ranged from less than half in the South to almost four-fifths in the Northeast. Five separate states had more than four out of every five inhabitants living in urban areas, and thirty states had half or more of their population living in urban areas. [9] One-fourth of the total United States population resides in the twelve urbanized areas of a million or more population listed in the preceding section, and over half of the total population lives in Standard Metropolitan Areas. [10] The United States has become predominantly an urbanized nation. Large central cities and extensive metropolitan areas are a fundamental part of modern life. The development of such urban centers has created a whole series of new social problems.

[8] *Ibid.*

[9] "The Urban Population of the United States, 1950 Census of Population: Preliminary Counts," in Paul K. Hatt and Albert J. Reiss, Jr., eds., *Reader in Urban Sociology* (Glencoe, Ill., The Free Press, 1951), p. 59.

[10] Standard Metropolitan Areas contain at least one, and sometimes more than one, city of at least 50,000 population plus an adjacent county or counties meeting specified criteria of urban character. *Ibid.*, pp. 63-67.

THE PROBLEMS OF CITIES

The census usually defines places as *urban* if they are incorporated or have over 2500 people. This kind of definition is not adequate for all purposes. Even the census is moving toward a *social* definition of city, toward a definition which recognizes the peculiar qualities of urban life as well as the number of people included. The classic sociological definition of *city* is, ". . . a city may be defined as a relatively large, dense, and permanent settlement of socially heterogeneous individuals." [11] Many of the special problems of cities result from large numbers of unlike persons living very close together.

Heterogeneity and Anonymity

Birth rates vary markedly from one part of a city to another but for a city as a whole they are quite low. City people do not have enough children to replace themselves, let alone enough to account for the continuous growth characteristic of many cities. Most sizable cities, consequently, include large numbers of persons who were not born there—people who have come from the most varied of backgrounds and with widely divergent expectations of urban life. Moreover, these migrants move into certain areas of the city with sufficient regularity that the city takes on a *pattern* defined by the types of people and the types of living that characterize each area. The pattern will vary in detail from one city to another according to the type of economic base, special features of topography, the age of the city, and still other factors. If these limitations are kept in mind, however, it is possible to specify some of the dominant features of each area as one moves outward from the center of the city. [12]

The major areas indicated by Roman numerals in Figure 14-2 are somewhat self-explanatory. The central business district generally has few or no permanent residents. Some permanent residence begins in Zone II amid the manufacturing and wholesale businesses frequenting that area. Moving outward from Zone II, dingy rooming houses, flats, and apartments are gradually replaced by better single houses with larger yards and relatively more absence of business establishments. As one approaches the periphery, large open spaces, farms, new housing developments, and heavy industry may appear to disrupt and distort the pattern. Often, too, features most characteristic of Zones II and III may extend outward in a narrow belt well into Zone IV and even Zone V. [13]

[11] Louis Wirth, "Urbanism as a Way of Life," *The American Journal of Sociology*, Vol. 44 (July, 1938), p. 8.

[12] Robert E. Park, Ernest W. Burgess, and Roderick D. McKenzie, *The City* (Chicago, University of Chicago Press, 1925).

[13] The radial pattern of urban development outlined here has been verified empirically in Chicago, Illinois, Rochester, New York, and St. Louis, Missouri.

Superimposed upon this general pattern are likely to appear all and more of the features designated by Arabic numerals in Figure 14-2. Generally it is the areas closest to the center of the city that are most heterogeneous, most anonymous, and least affected by social controls. Family and neighborhood ties found in the suburbs are often weak or lacking altogether. Landlords don't ask questions, and frequent moving discourages the establishment of close friendships. The high ratio of men to women,

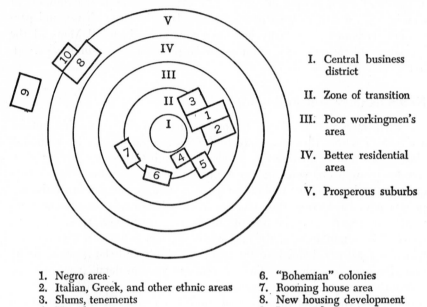

I. Central business district

II. Zone of transition

III. Poor workingmen's area

IV. Better residential area

V. Prosperous suburbs

1. Negro area
2. Italian, Greek, and other ethnic areas
3. Slums, tenements
4. Homeless men area
5. Red-light district
6. "Bohemian" colonies
7. Rooming house area
8. New housing development
9. Large industry
10. Shopping center

FIG. 14–2. Social and spatial plan of the modern city.

with the limited incomes of both sexes, discourages the normal drift into marriage and respectability, and increases the proportion of temporary illicit unions. [14] Thus, the curious paradox that the most densely populated areas of the city are often the loneliest. Deviant persons of all sorts drift into the area because of the protection which its anonymity affords. Those residents who are fairly conventional persons see the deviancy all around them and gradually become more vulnerable themselves. Hetero-

---

Research in other cities suggests other patterns of land use identified by such terms as "sector growth" and "multiple nuclei." See Walter Firey, *Land Use in Central Boston* (Cambridge, Harvard University Press, 1947), and Homer Hoyt, *One Hundred Years of Land Values in Chicago* (Chicago, University of Chicago Press, 1933).

[14] Caroline F. Ware, *Greenwich Village, 1920-1930* (Boston, Houghton Mifflin Co., 1935).

geneity and anonymity not only draw deviants; they produce deviants. [15]

Not only is there extreme heterogeneity within the central areas of the city, but there are wide differences between these and outlying areas. There is little social contact between persons living in different areas. Most suburb-dwellers know little and care less about the problems of the slum-dwellers and vice versa. Common values and goals shared by all the population are conspicuous by their absence. The population of a city is an aggregation or a conglomeration; rarely is it an *organization*. The importance of the absence of ties among the various areas of the city will become evident in a later section.

Blighted Areas

Certain areas of the modern city may be likened to malignant growth on a living organism. They develop through the same processes that give life to the city as a whole, but they are largely parasitic, continuously growing, and they drain more and more of the city's life-blood. These are the blighted areas—the areas undergoing, or having undergone, deterioration. Crime, poverty, delinquency, prostitution, gambling, drug addiction, mental illness, tuberculosis, infant and maternal mortality, all are concentrated here. Rat-infested slums, filthy streets, crumbling buildings long since declared firetraps and frequently condemned, pawnshops, secondhand clothing stores, taverns, and "greasy spoons"—these are the physical habitat. Such blighted areas literally prey upon the rest of the city. The run-down buildings of the area pay relatively little in the way of taxes, though landlords often charge extremely high rents and reap fantastic profits. The cost of providing police and fire protection, borne by the city at large, may be ten or twenty times as high as in other areas. The proportion of gainfully employed people is painfully low, and "relief" payments of all sorts flood into the area. [16] Children play in the streets; there is no other place provided for them. [17] Graduation from grade school is frequently followed by "matriculation" at reform school. Then it is an easy step to prison, all at the cost of $1200 or more each year which is furnished by taxpayers. Health needs, if met at all, are handled by public health departments and by "free" clinics which are exorbitantly expensive for the public to maintain. Slum clearance and low-cost public

[15] Robert E. L. Faris, and H. Warren Dunham, *Mental Disorders in Urban Areas* (Chicago, University of Chicago Press, 1939).

[16] Multiproblem families abound in this area. See pp. 183-185, and Bradley Buell and associates, *Community Planning for Human Resources* (New York, Columbia University Press, 1952).

[17] William F. Whyte, *Street Corner Society* (Chicago, University of Chicago Press, 1958); and Frederick Thrasher, *The Gang* (Chicago, University of Chicago Press, 1936).

housing is an additional form of subsidy. The modern slum embodies all that is un-American. The Promised Land?—a cruel joke! Faith in the future?—resignation and despair! Responsibility for self and family?—at the mercy of economic conditions and charitable agencies! A benefit of democracy?—ready-made propaganda for the totalitarian world!

Congestion

Death by strangulation! Both literally and figuratively the metropolis bodes to be choked out of existence.

DEPLETION AND CONTAMINATION. As it expanded upward the city stacked industry upon industry, apartment upon apartment, store upon store, and people upon people. Little thought was given to two human necessities—air and water. For many decades they seemed unlimited. To-day, both air and water are sometimes in short supply. The potential shortage of water was the first to be recognized.

Cities over much of the nation have been faced by two uncomfortable facts: tremendously increased needs for water, and a dropping water table. [18] Modern industry uses water in prodigiously increasing quantities. The location of many modern plants depends as much upon an adequate water supply as upon the proximity of raw materials and labor. And many cities no longer have water to spare. Even a slight drought lowers many reservoirs to the danger point. The summer pastime of sprinkling one's lawn has occasionally become a matter for legal regulation, and toward evening the water pressure may lower noticeably. Nor is it just a matter of inadequate storage facilities. Wells must be drilled deeper and deeper and communities struggle bitterly for their fair share of river and lake water. Parts of the West and South have already found their programs to encourage growth and industrialization frustrated by inadequate water resources. The rest of the country is not much better off.

Obviously, there is no shortage of air in the absolute sense. But cities are increasingly reducing the available uncontaminated, "breathable" air. As long as twenty years ago it was fashionable to point out that the lungs of urban adults tended toward a dirty black, whereas those of rural adults remained a healthy pink. The soot, dust, and grime of city life showed up here even if they did not materially shorten the life span. Twenty years ago this observation was largely a matter of amusement. Today, however, it has become quite serious. The most serious incident to date was the great London "smog" of 1952 which, directly and in-directly, caused the deaths of 4,000 people. The United States does not have fogs comparable to those of England. True. But just as this is being written a new term, "smaze," has come into our vocabulary. A

[18] Only three states—Idaho, Mississippi, and Rhode Island—have not yet re-ported water shortage problems. In 1956, President Eisenhower submitted to Congress a program designed to nearly double the available water supply in 1975—to increase it from 200 billion to 350 billion gallons per day.

pall of smoke, dirt, pulverized asphalt and rubber, "fly ash" and haze, hanging for several days over New York City resulted in thousands of cases of respiratory irritation, created a need for greatly increased medical attention, and kept people indoors to protect their health. Los Angeles is now as famous for its "smog" as for its sunshine, and when one is driving towards a city, a murky cloud ahead on the highway is often one of the first signs of approaching it. In scattered instances, the clouds over industrial cities have been directly, though temporarily, lethal. [19] Investigating commissions have been appointed to reduce the possibility of such occurrences in the future. Yet they promise to increase both in severity and number in the years to come. Cities are, literally, showing signs of strangulation.

TRAFFIC CONGESTION. The spread of cities outward has encouraged strangulation of another sort. The development of the automobile and other rapid transportation encouraged people to live at some distance from the city's center where substantial proportions of them work, shop, and do business. Early in the morning they pour through highways and streets into the city's center. There they merge with the heavy flow of commercial traffic which keeps business and industry operating, and in the evening they fight their way back out again. Until recently, the system worked fairly well. The same streets that once accommodated horse and wagon movement handled automobile traffic, and great superhighways were constructed to move traffic quickly from one city to another. But the city itself has proved the bottleneck. Central city streets fronted by ten-story buildings cannot easily be widened and it is no longer merely a joke that pedestrians move more rapidly than automobiles.

One problem is that of parking. Practically all cities face a shortage of convenient parking space and in large cities the thousands of cars milling around and jockeying for parking places greatly increase the overall congestion. The problem is complicated by two factors: first, land values are so high in the city's center that the woefully inefficient traditional parking garage frequently does not pay its way financially; and second, the motorist demands parking space convenient to his destination. One estimate states that if he has to walk over a thousand feet, the average motorist would rather park in a restricted area and take a chance of getting a ticket. [20] Many city-planning specialists believe that part of the answer to the problem is a yet-to-be-invented, satisfactory, automatic parking garage. The increased efficiency of an automatic system that would take automobiles off the street and disgorge them again at a rate of several per minute would make it a paying proposition. Varying numbers of strategically placed "parketerias" would largely solve the parking problem.

[19] One such cloud, over Donora, Pennsylvania, in 1948, caused the deaths of twenty persons and made half the population ill.
[20] William Zeckendorf, "Parking in the Sky," *Atlantic Monthly*, Vol. 191 (June. 1953), p. 34.

Homeward-bound commuters in traffic-strangled New York.

Unfortunately, the parking problem cannot really be solved if isolated from the larger traffic problem. Even if automobiles could be quickly taken off and put back on the streets again, the roadway system could not handle the volume of traffic. Within minutes the superefficient parking garage would grind to a halt because of the traffic jam in the street before it. Some means of rapidly shuttling tremendous numbers of cars out of the central city is essential. Limited-access, express roadways seem to be the only answer. But effecting these is not so simple. Many expensive buildings would have to be condemned and torn down, the cost of the roadway system alone would be tremendous, and opposition would be forthcoming from myriads of vested interests who derive profit from present conditions. We can only conclude that any large-scale solution to these problems is many years in the future. Some cities will solve them faster than others, and here and there a specific parking or roadway system will be held out as a shining example, but parking and traffic will remain a major urban headache.

That extreme concentration of facilities and population around a single urban center is not an unmixed blessing is indicated by the course of events of roughly the past thirty years. Up to 1930, growth was most rapid in the largest of cities. But the 1930 census indicated the start of a new trend—suburbanization. Some of the population was literally forced outward by the density farther in, but there also appeared a positive ideology in favor of suburban living. The desire to escape soot, grime, noise, and traffic, to have yards, gardens, and an allegedly healthy place to raise children helped create a new urban pattern. Between 1900 and 1950 surburbs grew one and one-third times as fast as central cities. Between 1940 and 1950 the rate was two and one-half times as fast. Between 1950 and 1955 the suburbs grew seven times as fast! [21] Moreover, service facilities, shopping centers and the like, and even industry, have followed the population outward. Many suburban centers today are almost as self-sufficient and as heterogeneous as the central city. Some of them are incorporated separately, some are within the central city limits, some fall within two or more political subdivisions, and most of them keep spreading outward into politically rural territory. This transformation and expansion aggravates some existing problems and helps create new ones.

Suburban Sprawl

The basic idea of suburban living now is more than half a century old. Early city planners who saw the terrifying implications of uncontrolled urban growth developed the "garden city" plan for creating model communities in formerly rural areas. Such garden cities would be care-

[21] Philip M. Hauser, "Exploding Metropolis," *Chicago Sun-Times*, March 30, 1959, p. 4.

fully laid out to provide ample living and yard space for each family, would have all essential services, would have enough carefully segregated industry to provide economic livelihood, and would be separated from surrounding areas by broad "green belts" of park land that would preserve their idyllic rural character. The garden-city movement resulted in a few trial communities but never became seriously operational. The basic ideas behind the movement, however, have remained to influence our concepts of what desirable suburban communities should be.

The first real moves toward suburbanization probably came as the automobile and electric power made it feasible for wealthy families to move outward from the city's center. Until the 1930's, suburbanization most characteristically meant the building of areas of expensive homes in attractive physical settings. With the development of highways, the rush to move out from the city was on. Roadside businesses ranging from taverns and hot dog stands to garages and filling stations sprang up. Housing, generally unregulated either as to cost or construction, mushroomed. Then developments of less expensive houses and factories arrived in the suburbs almost simultaneously. Since World War II, virtually all of the traditional urban features have literally exploded into the countryside. Cities of 50,000 population have appeared in what ten years earlier were potato fields. Some of these cities have no industry at all; others are almost completely industrial. Areas of $10,000-homes are sandwiched between areas of $50,000-homes and oil storage tanks may come to loom over both. This tremendous unplanned, unregulated growth has created new problems. City-dwellers who sought to escape to the suburbs soon find that the old urban problems of congestion and heavy taxation are back with them again. Moreover, arduous commuting to the city takes much of the joy out of suburban living. Land values vacillate crazily and developments of paperboard houses threaten to turn into slums as unattractive as city tenements.

Suburban sprawl also is drastically changing the ethnic and racial character of residential communities. Characteristically, ethnic groups enter the city in the disorganized areas near its center and gradually disperse into surrounding zones over a period of two or three generations. The spill into suburban areas is, however, almost exclusively of white people. Between 1940 and 1950 suburban areas in the United States received a total of 7,200,000 migrants of whom 6,900,000 were white and 346,000 were nonwhite (principally Negro). Central cities, by contrast, had an immigration of 1,300,000 nonwhites and lost 2,500,000 whites to the suburbs. Thus, central cities traded whites for nonwhites. If this trend continues, a wholly new pattern of residential segregation may be established that will do much to defeat desegregation efforts on the education front.

Political and Economic Problems

It is unrealistic in many ways to define the city as existing within the corporation limits. Yet, *legally*, the city is just that. Actually, large open spaces may lie within the city limits, and the urban population may extend for many miles beyond them. The power of the city to legislate and to regulate is determined by the location of the corporation limits, not by the location of the population.

GOVERNING PROBLEMS. American cities have rarely been known for good government. On the contrary they have been fountainheads of graft, corruption, and inefficiency. To be a city official has more than occasionally been a forerunner to public disgrace and even to imprisonment. [22] Names such as Hague and Kelly symbolize the city bosses and the intricate *sub rosa* structures they represent. The internal corruption characteristic of so many cities is further complicated by their inability to enforce the law outside the city limits. Where suburbs are incorporated separately or two central cities exist side by side, there are two or more sets of laws and law enforcement agencies in a single urban area; a metropolitan area like Chicago has over fifty. "Businesses" and practices, such as gambling, liquor sales, and prostitution, vigorously prosecuted in one area, can simply move "across the line" where the laws are more lax and operate virtually unmolested. Even when there is no conflict of policy among the separate municipalities, rarely is there sufficient co-operation among them to make effective law enforcement feasible. Every major metropolitan area has one or more "wide open" communities. Communities quarrel over "who is to blame?" and the illicit activity goes on and on.

FINANCING PROBLEMS. City taxes have generally shown large increases over the past fifteen years. Real estates taxes have risen; city income taxes have been adopted; city automobile taxes and city sales taxes have appeared; school taxes have been increased; personal property levies have been raised; and so on. Life has become increasingly expensive for urban residents; yet many cities are in dire financial straits. The suburban trend is a major factor in this situation.

Urban facilities such as banks, businesses, theaters, and streets serve the neighboring suburban and rural populations as well as that of the central city. Large proportions of the noncity population work in the city, drawing sustenance from it, helping deteriorate its streets, contributing to its traffic and police problems, benefiting from its administrative machinery, but paying no taxes to cover the cost of maintenance. Even the groups who do not *work* in the city generally use it for shopping and

[22] James M. Curley, *I'd Do It Again: A Record of All My Uproarious Years* (Englewood Cliffs, N. J., Prentice-Hall, Inc., 1957).

recreation. Many persons are suburb-dwellers precisely *because* it gives them all the urban advantages without the city's disadvantages and expense. As the proportion of suburbanites increases, the proportion of non-paying city-users increases. No wonder many suburbs can afford well-kept streets, new schools, and garbage collection twice a week. On the other hand, the population of some central cities, and consequently the tax base, has actually declined while the financial burden has been getting heavier. In many areas considerable strife has developed as central cities seek to regain financial solvency and as suburbs resist being drawn into the "city's" problems.

RURAL PROBLEMS

For many people the illusion persists that while the city is a polyglot mixture of variant social and personal types, the rural environment is homogeneous. The facts do not support this belief. The rural environment includes fifty-thousand-acre cattle ranches in Texas, thousand-acre wheat farms in Kansas, and ten-acre turkey farms in Ohio; it includes mining camps in Colorado, logging operations in Washington, oil fields in Oklahoma, shanty towns scattered in all sections, housing for migratory labor, trailer parks, and many other factors.

The relative size (though not the absolute size) of the rural population has been declining from 95 per cent of the total population in 1790 to 43 per cent in 1940, and to 37 per cent in 1957. [23] Traditionally, the census has divided the rural population into two broad categories—*farm* and *nonfarm*. According to this distinction, nearly three-fifths of the *rural* population is engaged in occupations other than farming. Some rural people live in villages and towns, but large numbers of them differ from urban residents chiefly in that they do not live within the corporate limits of a city. One of the effects of improved transportation and suburban sprawl has been to almost obliterate the old distinction between urban and rural. It is no longer possible to tell what people do for a living by knowing where they happen to live, and even less can be told about their attitudes and interests. Urban values have infiltrated the countryside to such an extent that the old rural way of life hardly exists any more. The transition is not complete, however, and the problems of rural and urban areas are still not identical. The most marked contrast is to be found between urban living and farming.

Low Living Standards

The price paid for rural residence can be measured in many ways, for almost any index of material living standards shows up the inferior posi-

[23] U. S. Bureau of the Census, *Statistical Abstract of the United States: 1958* (Washington), pp. 47.

tion of country people. If cash income is used as a criterion, the median income of farm families in 1956 was only $2375, whereas in urban and nonfarm areas the average was $5061. [24] In 1950, 98.8 per cent of urban residences had electricity, but only 77.7 per cent of farm homes had it. Mechanical refrigeration is found in 86.1 per cent of urban homes, but in only 62.7 per cent of rural ones. [25] And whether the criteria used are bathtubs or inside bathrooms, telephones, radios, television sets, central heating, or any number of others, the comparisons are the same.

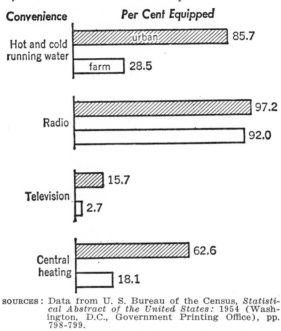

Convenience	Per Cent Equipped
Hot and cold running water	urban 85.7 / farm 28.5
Radio	97.2 / 92.0
Television	15.7 / 2.7
Central heating	62.6 / 18.1

SOURCES: Data from U. S. Bureau of the Census, *Statistical Abstract of the United States:* 1954 (Washington, D.C., Government Printing Office), pp. 798–799.

FIG. 14–3. Disadvantages in farm living.

Many people reply to such comparisons by saying, in effect, "Ah, but look at the advantages of rural living. It's a healthier place in which to live and rear children." The intangibles of living are, of course, hard to measure. Moreover, everyone would not agree as to what is desirable as a way of life. There is considerable evidence, however, that the nostalgia that many people feel for rural living is a matter of stereotype and of prior conditioning as much as of rational choice.

In the matter of health facilities, there is approximately one doctor for every 650 people in urban areas but only one doctor for every 1700 persons in rural areas. [26] There are over 28,000 physicians in greater New

[24] *Ibid.,* p. 318.

[25] U. S. Bureau of the Census, *Statistical Abstract of the United States: 1954* (Washington), pp. 798-799.

[26] David E. Lindstrom, *American Rural Life* (New York, The Ronald Press Company, 1948), p. 315.

York City, and there are hundreds of square miles of rural territory without even one doctor. In the matter of personality adjustment, Mangus presents some carefully qualified evidence from one county that, "The proportion of children of superior personality adjustment was found to be highest among farm and village children and lowest among city children." [27] He goes on to say, however, that, "The proportion of children classified as very poorly adjusted was not significantly different among farm, village, and city children." [28] Some additional evidence derived from draft rejection rates during World War II when farm youth had the highest rejection rate for physical, mental, or educational defects of any occupational group. [29] It can only be concluded that the evidence is very fragmentary and subject to varied interpretation. Most important of all, many comparisons have never been made.

Unfavorable Age Structure

One of the most pervasive of rural problems is born of the customary pattern of migration from rural to urban areas. Rural birth rates, particularly farm birth rates, are well above replacement requirements whereas urban centers fall short of reproducing themselves by approximately 25 per cent. Moreover, productivity per man-hour on the farm is steadily increasing, requiring consistently fewer farmers to feed the same urban population. As a consequence of these two factors, there is a steady stream of migration from rural to urban areas. Predominantly, the migrants are young adults. Children ordinarily cannot migrate alone, but once they are of age or have completed school, many of them trek into the cities to find employment.

The problem is not migration, per se, but the fact that it is heavily concentrated among the young adult age groups. The high rural birth rates mean a relatively *large dependent population* which must be fed, clothed, housed, and educated. The burden of supporting this large number of children falls upon the productive adults whose ranks are seriously depleted via urban (or suburban) migration. Not only are the rural areas poorer to begin with, but they bear a disproportionate amount of the cost of raising future urban adults. Each young man or woman who migrates represents a lost investment to the country and a financial gain to the city. Thus, rural areas inadvertently subsidize urban life.

The Development of Agricultural Business

Until recently, farms in the United States were almost exclusively family farms. Farming was considered to be more a way of life than just

[27] A. R. Mangus, "Personality Adjustment of Rural and Urban Children," *American Sociological Review*, Vol. 13 (October, 1948), p. 575.

[28] *Ibid.*

[29] Lindstrom, *op. cit.*, p. 309.

a way of earning a living. It was a way of life that was widely admired and just as widely recognized as fraught with financial hazard. Cash income generally was low and any income at all often was contingent on a favorable combination of weather and market conditions with abundant hard work. Boys learned to be farmers by serving apprenticeships with experienced fathers and neighbors whose folk skills and folk wisdoms had accumulated for generations and were generally adequate in a society where farm families were almost as numerous as city families.

Urban conditions were changing, however. Industrialization brought undreamed-of productive efficiency. Living standards climbed. More and more people were drawn to the city. Considerable control was gained of market conditions. In the country, the process was slower. Some farmers increased their efficiency more rapidly than others and did well financially. The concept remained, however, that farmers were at the merciless control of market and weather. During the depression of the 1930's, the philosophy of government assistance to farmers through price supports, crop controls, and other forms of subsidy became thoroughly established.

The application of modern technology to farm production has in many ways defeated the purposes of these programs. First of all, it has drastically changed the nature of farming itself. While relatively small family farms are probably still in the majority, production of farm products has become increasingly concentrated in the hands of large producers. These large producers would no more tolerate the relative inefficiency of the old family farm than would a modern factory tolerate hand-loom methods. Farm production is planned on the basis of market forecasts and makes maximum use of machine methods and even automation. The efficiency of these operations is so great that even under acreage controls production increases rapidly. Under controls designed to limit production tremendous agricultural surpluses are built up; the surpluses grow from year to year and present increasingly costly storage problems. A huge share of the government support funds, intended originally for small family farms, goes to large producers whose cash incomes challenge those of large, profitable businesses. All available signs indicate that "agri-business" will become increasingly dominant on the rural scene as the old family farm slips into obscurity.

THE SOCIAL-DISORGANIZATION APPROACH

Rural Disorganization

The United States has been becoming more and more urbanized; and the proportion of persons living in rural areas and engaged in farming has been steadily dropping. Until recently, however, most rural areas actually have been gaining population. The whole population has been growing so rapidly that rural areas could gain millions of people in a decade and still decline in proportion to the urban increases. So long as the rural-urban difference was purely a matter of *relative growth*, there was little general rural disorganization. Evidence of disorganization appeared as the rate of rural growth declined and some areas actually began to lose population.

To select any one date as the point where depopulation became disruptive of rural social organization would be to artificially break a long-term process. Nevertheless, it seems clear that the period of the 1930's both aggravated and served as a further causal factor in the rural decline. The great depression of the early 1930's actually reversed the usual flow of migration and sent many city persons scurrying back to the farms where they could at least grow some food to eat. But at the same time the depression dealt a serious body blow to the prestige and security of farming as an occupation. Foreclosures were frequent and tenancy rapidly increased. When economic conditions finally bettered, the appeal of immediate high wages in the city often seemed more attractive than years of struggle to build up a farm again, only, perhaps, to have it destroyed in the next crisis. The 1930's also saw several years of severe drought, especially in the Middle West. A vast dust bowl spread over parts of several states where sun and wind destroyed the land. The mass migrations to California and elsewhere were part of the first large-scale decreases in local rural populations. Then the increased mechanization of farming in most areas during the 1940's and 1950's led to fewer but larger farms, with more rural depopulation. The introduction of modern technology literally changed the conditions of rural living faster than rural people and rural institutions could adapt to the changes.

Community institutions by and large must be supported by the local population. Schools and churches, the Granges, police and fire protection, medical and legal services, mills, elevators, feed stores, groceries, clothing stores, and all the rest must be paid for. In a growing community this is relatively easy for, in a sense, the population can mortgage its future inhabitants. Services of all sorts are attracted to the community because of the promise of the future. But when growth stops, the burden shifts. Each existing family unit must bear a larger share of the costs. The mortgage for a contemplated new church, or even the minister's salary, becomes a much more serious problem. When the population actually begins to decline, the maintenance of *existing* services becomes difficult. Churches may have to double up and share a single minister's salary. Physicians drift away in search of patients, and the local grain elevator "merges" with one thirty miles away. Meanwhile, good roads and automobiles have drained away the economic lifeblood of smaller rural trading centers wherever larger towns are nearby. The decline renders the community a less attractive place in which to live and compounds itself. An increasing number of rural communities probably will face this kind of decline in the near future. Eventually, if large-scale corporate farming becomes the norm, it appears likely that the traditional rural institutions may disappear altogether. As rural society becomes increasingly urbanized, its institutions will approximate an urban or regional character.

Urban Disorganization

Urban disorganization stems more frequently from growth than from depopulation; and from shifts in population and institutions within the city. Disorganization appears (1) in the physical conditions of life, and (2) in city government and administration.

(1) In addition to urban pollution and congestion, there are other symptoms of urban breakdown. Just outside the city's central business district there generally lies an area of utmost dilapidation. It has the misfortune to be cast between the high land values of the business district and the lower values of residential districts, and between the land use of a former day, and, hopefully, that of the future. It has been largely deserted by its wealthy former residents and has been eagerly seized upon by businesses that cannot afford the high-rent district. Landlords hope that the high-rent district will expand outward and that, consequently, their properties will multiply in value. It is a short-run venture that has a way of seeming to become permanent. In the meantime the smellier, dirtier, noisier businesses, knowing full well that the area will go to ruin, move in, in anticipation of one day selling the land at a large profit. When, and *if*, that day arrives, the existing buildings will have to be torn down anyway to make room for more modern structures. Therefore, why bother to maintain them? Besides, taxes will be lowered as the buildings deteriorate and, since it is primarily the location which tenants are paying for, rents will not suffer.

Not all of this area is converted to business use. People also live in it. The processes are the same. The smells and dirt accumulate. Disgust, resentments, and antisocial tendencies are fostered. There, too, are tenements, warehouses, and all the symptoms of blight discussed earlier in this chapter. The processes involved are as normal as those that create the new suburbs. The old patterns of land use have broken down and new ones have not yet appeared, unless, of course, the present patterns become permanent. When new patterns do appear, the blighted areas probably will move a little farther out.

(2) Nearly sixty years ago in *Shame of the Cities*, [30] Lincoln Steffens described the graft, corruption, and maladministration typical of large United States cities. So these are not new. Showing the sagacity that made him famous, Steffens drew upon the Old Testament and said in

[30] New York, P. Smith Co., 1904.

The Inevitability of City Growth

. . . But grey though Shanghai became, it was still gayer than the rest of China. Thousands of "volunteer" workers were shipped out to forced labor, but hundreds of thousands of desperate peasants poured in. The population leaped from 5,000,000 to 7,000,000. By 1956, the baffled Reds gave up trying to reduce Shanghai. Factories were restored, new industries developed. Satellite towns housing 200,000 workers grew up on the city's expanding outskirts.

---

effect, "The cause of sin was not Adam nor Eve, *but the apple!*" Had he been more social scientist than journalist he might have gone on to explain. The factors that keep men honest (including, among others, the unavailability of anything worth stealing, the high probability of being caught, and the searching eyes and souls of moralistic primary groups) are frequently absent in the city's governing circles. "Gangbusters" to the contrary, this kind of corruption often does pay—and handsomely. And, as Steffens concluded, as long as it pays it will exist.

Yet conditions already may have changed enough to make such corruption less blatant. The modern city boss appears to rely more on decent government than heretofore and less upon doing favors for poor immigrants and the distribution of patronage. Moreover, the spotlight of public observation that was directed toward city administrations a few decades ago has more recently revealed a similar order of corruption in so-called "clean" rural areas.

A further set of problems arises from the underrepresentation of urban populations in state legislatures. Representation in the legislatures of most states was established when the states were much more heavily rural than they are today, and the rural majorities in those legislatures have often killed all efforts to achieve representation more in accord with the present-day distribution of population. The rural-dominated legislatures are frequently reluctant to assume state responsibility for urban problems, forcing the cities to turn to the federal government for what they cannot get at their state capitals. Hence, traditional rural conservatism, coupled with rural minority control of state legislatures, is a major factor in the growth of federal bureaucracy.

THE VALUE-CONFLICT APPROACH

Price Supports

Since the early 1930's, the United States government has been committed to a program of price supports for farm products. The details of the program and the method of its administration have varied, and both have been rather continually embroiled in conflict. Basically the goal has been to keep farm prices at or near parity. *Parity* is a measure of the relationship between farm prices and the prices of goods and services which farmers must purchase. To maintain farm prices at parity means to raise them when the prices of other commodities go up and to lower them when other prices fall. Most farmers and their supporters have been enthusiastically behind the idea, at least, of price supports. Many other groups have been bitterly opposed to it, attacking the program as "favoritism" and frequently, "socialism." To place floors under farm prices, they argue, is to give unfair protection to one segment of the economy, to nullify the operation of supply and demand, and to encourage overproduction. These groups generally call for the elimination of all price supports and a return to a completely free economy.

The advocates of price supports reply that the above arguments involve gross distortions of fact, that farm production and industrial production are not comparable, that industry does not operate in a free economy, and that industrialists are seeking only to preserve their own special advantages. First of all, they point out, industrial production is frequently concentrated in the hands of relatively few producers who arbitrarily restrict output in order either to maintain or to raise prices. On the other hand, there are millions of farmers and no few farmers control even a small fraction of the market. The farmer must produce and sell in a market over which he has no control. Farm produce cannot be held from the market indefinitely until prices rise. Without price supports, individual farmers chance ruin with each small adjustment in the market. Furthermore, they claim, industry has long enjoyed its own protection through tariff barriers, and more recently in the form of fast tax write-offs and rapid depreciation allowances on plants and machinery. The "free" economy advocated by business interests, they assert, is one in which industry would be free to profit and farmers would be free to go bankrupt!

Objectively, the issue seems to be not whether any kind of market protection exists but how much and what kind of protection is desirable for farmers. That farm conditions have changed materially since the introduction of price supports cannot be denied. Whether farmers have now become a privileged group in relation to business, industry, and labor is a matter of violent debate.

Education

The distorted age structures and usual patterns of migration from country to city already have been described. Rural areas have both larger numbers of dependent young children and less cash income with which to educate these children. Furthermore, large numbers of them will migrate to the city as soon as their education is completed. Which area should bear the costs of their education?

As indicated in the chapter on education problems, education, traditionally, has been the responsibility of the local community. The different states vary widely, however, in their financial ability to provide adequate educational facilities, and federal aid to education has been proposed as a technique for reapportioning the costs of educating the nation's children. A similar problem and conflict of financial interests exists between the rural and urban communities within each state. Urban communities resist taxation to help support schools in the backward rural areas and point with pride to the fine job they are doing of educating their own children. Rural communities, on the other hand, are likely to point to their higher per capita expenditures for education and to remind the cities that many rural children are future urban residents. In this case it is the communities which are prone to turn to the state government and even to the federal government for aid.

The basic issue questions the whole theory that education is primarily a matter of local concern—a doctrine founded in an era of isolation and self-sufficiency which for the most part has disappeared. The present era is becoming one of mobility and interdependence. The conflict rages around whether the traditional values are appropriate for the new conditions or whether they must give way to new definitions.

THE PERSONAL-DEVIATION APPROACH

Rural

Deviation can be meaningfully discussed only in terms of the standards or norms of a *particular* group. Any given kind of deviancy—thievery, Bohemianism, homosexuality—becomes meaningful only as the group gives it approval or disapproval. Such deviation from group norms must be distinguished from cultural variability, or the variation in norms themselves from one group to another.

Considerable cultural variability is to be found in both rural and urban areas. Amish settlements, Ozark mountaineers, and snake-worshipping religious cults are all a part of rural culture—and all play a role in the creation of certain social problems. The Amish refusal to bear arms in time of war, their insistence that formal education cease with the completion of the eighth grade, and their rebellious adolescents with secretly acquired "jalopies" pose police problems at the very least. Mountain-cultivated patterns of distilling moonshine, the exacting of personal vengeance for actual or alleged wrongs, religious frenzies accompanied by floggings, self-mutilation, and even death—these rural activities make headlines in urban newspapers, reflect urgent preoccupations of the people involved, and forecast the clash of cultures. These practices all represent variability in group norms and the contribution of such variability to problem situations. They tell us little about deviation within each of these groups or of the role of *personal* deviation in rural and urban problems.

One of the most striking characteristics of rural culture is its tendency to suppress deviation *within* the group. Rural communities are generally small, particularly in terms of the number of people involved; ties to the land tend to give them a highly permanent and stable population; and relations between country families are informal and personal rather than formal and impersonal. The group typically is quite homogeneous in religious and economic background, in attitudes, feelings, and beliefs, and in definitions of right and wrong. Constant pressure is brought to bear upon the individual to make him conform to the expectations of the group. Conform he must, for there is nowhere to go and no one to whom to turn to escape the social pressure. Rebellion is impractical for it is quickly discovered and easily punished. Complete conformity to group expectations cannot be secured, of course, but no group sanctions can be expected to support deviant behavior and every effort is made to minimize its effect on the community as a whole.

Statistics on such matters generally show deviant behaviors—crime and mental illness, for example—to be relatively infrequent in rural areas. There are fewer recorded arrests, fewer trials, fewer jail sentences, and fewer admissions to mental hospitals. The burglaries and larcenies *are* fewer in number precisely because of the closer regulation of individual behavior. But the means of handling violations that do occur make them seem to happen even less frequently than they actually do. A teen-ager apprehended in a minor violation is likely to be turned over to his parents for "correction" rather than to be "booked" and to appear before a judge. The community is law-enforcement officer, judge, and penal agency all rolled into one—and an effective one at that. Whether mental illness is less prevalent in rural areas is open to serious question. In the country, there *is* more likely to be an extra room for the "not-quite-right" relative, and the distances involved prevent him from bothering neighbors and other people. Besides, rural families are supposed to take care of their own members. The whole of rural culture is oriented toward the discouragement of deviant personal behavior and, then, toward the elimination of its disruptive effects.

Urban

Variability among group norms is at least as common in urban as in rural areas—probably more so. Large urban centers are the characteristic locations of many ethnic and racial groups. The Little Sicilies, the Greek towns, the Ghettoes, the Harlems—all signify diverse cultural patterns. Americanization battles between the first, second, and third generations of immigrant families, the encroachment of one group upon another's territory, restrictive covenants, and the like, are all parts of typical intergroup conflict.

But, more important perhaps, the city is also a haven for *personal* deviation. It provides protection for many persons whose common denominator is the rejection of group norms and the determination to evade them.

The anonymity and impersonality of the city are the keys to its attraction as a haven for deviancy. Urban residents are perhaps no more tolerant of deviancy *within their own groups* than are rural residents. But in the city, one's face-to-face primary group associations are limited to a very small proportion of the total population. There is no one set of mores or other accepted definitions, and each small group is unconcerned with the other's activities unless directly and seriously threatened by them. In a small rural area any deviant behavior is likely to bring censure, for " 'most everyone knows" and " 'most everyone cares." In the metropolis, on the other hand, it is not too difficult a matter to find other persons who share one's problems and to congregate with them in areas unmolested save by curiosity-ridden tourists and the law. Most large cities embrace local counterparts of the Bowery and Greenwich Village. Though these names identify actual places in New York City, they have come to identify patterns of deviant behavior which extend far beyond their geographical boundaries.

The Bowery (or Skid Row, or the Area of Homeless Men, or Hobohemia) welcomes illiterates and Ph. D.'s, the always-poor and the former-rich, generally middle-aged and older men with one thing in common: failure! Each has been unable or unwilling to continue to meet the requirements of his personal life or his stratum in society. An intolerable marriage, public disgrace, too much responsibility, sexual deviation, drug addiction, and alcoholism are all among the factors frequently found in their backgrounds. Each has found his way into an environment of flophouses and sheltered doorways, of soup kitchens and missions, of cheap wine and liquor, and of anonymity. No one will ask where the failure is from, or what he has done, or why.

Bohemianism has come to mean, among other things, economic and political radicalism, free love and tolerance of sex deviation, and patronage of the arts. Young unmarried men and women, students and clerks, aspiring musicians, writers, and artists dwell in the shabbiness of nondescript rooming-houses where landlords are unconcerned about the informal sleeping arrangements of many of their tenants. These practically nameless young people make a fetish out of being emancipated, but at the same time are precariously dependent upon being able to conform to bohemian mores. For weeks or months or years they dwell in a world apart. Theirs is a way of life wholly foreign and almost unbelievable to most outsiders.

Homeless men die and are buried, bohemians marry and raise children, but the patterns continue. Replacements are always headed toward each of the city's characteristic areas. The city provides the areas of refuge and torment.

FUTURE PROSPECTS

Inexorable time already has drastically altered the relation between city and country. The very terms *city* and *country* are no longer adequate to connote housing conditions, standards of living, occupations, political attitudes, or recreational patterns. Farmers now include trips to the grocery among their "chores" and many city people have large gardens. The rural residents who can be identified on the street by their dusty and dilapidated automobiles, by the uncomfortable Sunday-dress appearance of their clothes, and by their twangy or drawling speech are a small minority. The labels "rube" and "city-slicker" are hardly applicable any longer. One can drive for miles along many highways and never be quite sure whether he is in the city or the country, and it would take this entire page to describe all the types of settlements which the census now defines as urban.

High-speed transportation and transmissible electric power have done much to urbanize the entire nation. Together they reduced the need for cities to be concentrated around a single center and stimulated suburbanization. They made it possible for urban residents to move outward and for rural people to have daily contacts inside the city. The rate of growth of the largest cities has slowed appreciably while satellite cities around the central ones are growing at a furious rate. Urbanized areas are expanding, and the number of farmers required to feed a given urban population steadily declines. There is every reason to believe that these trends will continue—at least for the near future.

The central city will probably be one of the big problems of the next few decades. As its buildings and streets deteriorate, the unwillingness to pour large amounts of capital into reconstruction will foster slum conditions. The suburban movement narrows the tax base but increases the tax load, which somehow must be redistributed. Soot and grime will become greater enemies, and vehicular traffic may have to be banned from the city's center.

Traffic problems in general threaten to grow worse before they get better. Much of the nation's street and highway system is in need of improvement or replacement, and even the most adequately planned thoroughfares are overcrowded almost from the time of completion. Again, large capital outlays will be required. How these improvements are to be financed already is a matter of bitter conflict among trucking interests, railroads, city, state, and federal governments, plus "John Q." automobile driver. The carnage of life and property from accidents is hardly recognized as yet, but probably will come to the fore relatively soon.

A multiplicity of overlapping political and economic units can be expected. Many small communities, incorporated and unincorporated, rural and urban in varying degree, and with varying dependence upon larger communities are coming to be the rule. As people dwell in one area, perhaps work in a second, and seek recreation in still a third, residence-based communities become more difficult to maintain. Police, financial, and administrative problems are not coextensive with community boundaries. Action taken by one administrative or police body directly affects neighboring ones and interferes with the efficiency of both. Adequate representation of interested parties becomes almost impossible.

These are but some of the undesirable conditions now being created of which we are gradually becoming "aware;" however, no wholly satisfactory techniques have yet been invented for the solution of them.

SUGGESTED READINGS

DUNCAN, Otis D., and REISS, Albert J., *Social Characteristics of Urban and Rural Communities, 1950* (New York, John Wiley & Sons, Inc., 1956).

Editors of *Fortune, The Exploding Metropolis* (New York, Doubleday & Company, Inc., 1958). A readable account of the changing city and its reaction to changing problems.

GEE, Wilson, *The Social Economics of Agriculture* (New York, The Macmillan Co., 1954). A mine of information on rural life and rural problems. Designed for textbook use in courses in rural sociology and agricultural economics.

HATT, Paul K., and REISS, Albert J. Jr., eds., *Cities and Society; The Revised Reader in Urban Sociology* (Glencoe, Ill., The Free Press, 1957). Comprehensive and sophisticated readings in urban sociology. For the serious student.

PARK, Robert E., BURGESS, Ernest W., and McKENZIE, R. D., *The City* (Chicago, University of Chicago Press, 1925). A pioneer treatise on the city by three experts in the study of urban problems.

WIRTH, Louis, "Urbanism as a Way of Life," *American Journal of Sociology*, Vol. 44 (July, 1938), pp. 1-24. A classic statement of the nature of urbanism and a definition of the field of study of urban sociology.

ZECKENDORF, William, "Parking in the Sky," *Atlantic Monthly*, Vol. 191 (June, 1953), pp. 34-35. An imaginative attack on a growing problem, by one of America's leading real-estate magnates.

AUDIO-VISUAL AIDS

America's Disinherited (Brandon Films, Inc., 200 West 57 St., New York), 33 minutes, sound, black and white. Produced for the Southern Tenant Farmers Union. Aims to portray the plight of the Negro and white share-cropper in the South and their efforts to organize for more equitable conditions. Shows the Delta co-operative farm as one of the possible remedial measures.

Farm and City (United World Films, Inc., Government Films Department, 1445 Park Ave., New York), 8 minutes, sound, black and white. Classroom version of a longer film produced by the U. S. Department of Agriculture in 1939. Shows the relation of farm to city and how the economic status of one affects the other.

A Place to Live (Brandon Films, Inc., 200 West 57 St., New York), 18 minutes, sound. A schoolboy leaves his classes and walks home through city streets and back alleys infested with rats. There in a "band-box house" (three rooms, one above the other) his mother awaits him. Scenes follow of their squalid way of living and we learn of their hopes for a better place to live. No over-all solution is offered but several suggestions are made.

Water for the City (University of California, Extension Division, Visual Department, 2272 Union St., Berkeley), 30 minutes, sound, color. Shows how watershed areas act in receiving and storing water and in releasing it for future use; the interaction between the water cycle and the various parts of the watershed. Intended to acquaint the city-dweller with the importance of California's watershed in providing water for use in the city.

QUESTIONS AND PROJECTS

1. What proportion of the United States population is now defined as *urban?*

2. Explain the need for a social definition of the word *city*.

3. Describe the blighted area of a large city. What is the social significance of such blighted areas?

4. Discuss several ways in which congestion has become a major urban problem.

5. Explain the seeming paradox of more pressing financial problems in cities even though city tax rates have been rising steadily.

6. Is rural life synonymous with farming as an occupation? Why or why not? Illustrate your answer.

7. Comment upon the alleged superiority of the rural way of life.

8. How does the age structure of the rural population augment the problems of rural living?

9. Depopulation contributes to rural disorganization in some areas of the country. Explain.

10. Evaluate the statement, "There is less personal deviation in rural than in urban areas."

11. The proportion of the population classified as "rural" by the census rose from 36 per cent in 1950 to 37 per cent in 1957. How can this be true if cities are growing and the number of farmers is decreasing?

12. It is often assumed that city people are wicked and corrupt while rural people are honest and virtuous. Is this true? Are "downstate" politics more honorable? Look up rural and urban rates of venereal disease, illegitimacy, rape, and other sex offenses. Check Kinsey's rural and urban comparisons.

13. Take a field trip to the slum area of a modern city and visit one or more of the social agencies there. Inquire of the persons in charge concerning the nature of the problems they encounter. How are the agencies financed? What portion of the costs is paid by the people who receive the agency services?

14. See if you can locate the rural counterpart of the above mentioned slum in your area. In what ways are living conditions better in the rural area? In what ways are they worse? What agencies exist to provide aid for poverty-stricken rural inhabitants?

15

Mass Communication: Control, Content, Censorship

Now the whole earth had one language and few words. And as men migrated in the east, they found a plain in the land of Shinar and settled there. . . . Then they said, "Come, let us build ourselves a city, and a tower with its top in the heavens, and let us make a name for ourselves, lest we be scattered abroad upon the face of the whole earth."

And the Lord came down to see the city and the tower, which the sons of men had built. And the Lord said, "Behold, they are one people, and they have all one language, and this is only the beginning of what they will do; and nothing that they propose to do will now be impossible for them. Come, let us go down, and there confuse their language, that they may not understand one another's speech."

So the Lord scattered them abroad from there over the face of all the earth, and they left off building the city. Therefore its name was called Babel, because there the Lord confused the language of all the earth; and from there the Lord scattered them abroad over the face of the earth. [1]

Germany had surrendered; Japan had been left to fight alone, and the American forces had moved in their relentless steppingstone advance all the way to Okinawa. Out of the Potsdam Conference held in defeated Germany there came on July 26 the Potsdam Declaration, signed by the United States, Britain, and China—a demand that Japan surrender or be crushed.

The Allied world waited for Japan's answer. Two days later . . . the word flashed that Premier Kantaro Suzuki and his cabinet had decided to "ignore" the Potsdam Declaration.

The rest is familiar history. Within three weeks the Japanese turned about and accepted the Potsdam terms. But in those three weeks two events took place which were to have a profound effect on the history of the world. Atomic

[1] Genesis, 11:1-9.

bombs were dropped on Hiroshima and Nagasaki—giving birth to the atomic age—and Russia declared war on Japan and sent her troops sweeping south and east into Manchuria and Sakhalin—thus vastly strengthening her position in the Far East.

Japan, in fact, had been on the verge of collapse, [and] her leaders had been negotiating desperately for many weeks with the then neutral Russians in an effort to surrender. . . .

The almost unbelievable fact seems to be this: the Japanese cabinet decided to accept the Allied ultimatum, but by a mistake the Prime Minister made an announcement that was taken to mean the opposite! . . . The Premier told the Japanese newspapermen that his cabinet was holding an attitude of *mokusatsu*, a word that is difficult to translate directly into English. He meant that the cabinet was withholding comment on the ultimatum, that a decision was not yet to be announced. But the Domei News Agency, in translating Suzuki's statement into English for shortwave broadcast to the West, put the wrong meaning on *mokusatsu* and mistranslated it as "ignore." The Allied Powers— waiting for Japan's answer to Potsdam—were informed that the Suzuki cabinet was "ignoring" the surrender ultimatum. On the basis of this apparent rejection, the final effort to crush Japan was launched and the surrender came nearly three weeks later, *after* the atomic bombs had been dropped and Russia had entered the war. [2]

WITHOUT a common language, the builders of the tower of Babel could not proceed. Because of the imperfect translation of a word, the war with Japan may have been prolonged, the world balance of power altered, and the atom bombs needlessly dropped. Without communication, human social life becomes impossible. It is by the nature and quality of our communication processes that the character of our social life is molded.

THE COMMUNICATIONS REVOLUTION

IN THEIR EFFECTS UPON THE DAILY LIVES of the people, the processes of communication have probably changed more in the last fifty years than in the preceding five thousand. At the turn of the century, radio and television were unknown, the motion picture was a laboratory curiosity, and telephone and telegraph were largely confined to business use. Books rarely reached below the upper middle-class, while the muckraking era was beginning to produce the mass magazine. Newspapers, though many in number, were limited in scope and had just begun to reach a sizable fraction of the population. It is difficult for today's college student, who has been immersed in the mass media of communication since birth, to visualize the atmosphere of local isolation, provincialism, and homemade recreation of his grandparent's childhood.

[2] W. J. Coughlin, "The Great Mokusatsu Mistake," *Harper's Magazine*, Vol. 206 (March, 1953), pp. 31-40.

1. The Press

From the publication of the first daily newspaper in 1783, the number of daily English-language newspapers in America rose to a peak of 2600 in 1909 and has settled to a present figure of about 1770. Daily circulation totals about 57 million—more than one for each household in the United States. [3] Once a medium devoted to news and opinion, the modern newspaper is primarily a medium for advertising and entertainment. Advertising occupies much of the space and supplies two-thirds of the income. Although the modern newspaper prints more news more accurately than in earlier periods, newspaper circulation campaigns stress "features"— syndicated columns, comics, sports sections, style shows, lovelorn columns, and the like—more than news coverage, and many news stories are selected for oddity or "human interest" rather than for social significance. Opinion, once scattered through the news stories, is now (theoretically) limited to the editorial page and to the signed columns of the commentators.

Over 8000 periodicals are now published, ranging from mass magazines like the *Reader's Digest* (circulation 11,390,000) and *Life* (5,960,000) to many tiny, obscure journals. In 1958, there were 39 magazines with circulations of over one million copies per issue. Book publishers currently print over 13,000 new books each year, while an unknown number of booklets, pamphlets, tracts, leaflets, and handbills appear in constant succession.

The complexity of the press is revealed in its tremendous variety of publications. Newspapers include not only the mass-circulation daily and Sunday press but some 10,000 weekly and semiweekly papers, while included in the totals are the foreign language press, the labor press, the Negro press, and several other publications. Different magazines are aimed at every level of age, occupation, class, and region, and every variety of religious, political, intellectual, and recreational interest. Hundreds of trade journals cater to the special interests of each industry or trade association. A relatively new type of magazine, the *house organ*, has mushroomed into an estimated ten or twelve thousand publications. Often a single corporation publishes many different journals, one, or more, for its salesmen, customers, managers, stockholders, foreign employees, domestic employees, teen-age daughters of domestic employees, and so on. DuPont alone publishes seventy-five. Usually distributed free (at a cost to the companies of over $100 million a year), the main purpose of the house

[3] N. W. Ayer & Sons, *Directory of Newspapers and Periodicals, 1959* (Philadelphia, N. W. Ayer & Sons, 1959). Most statistics in this chapter are given in round numbers. They are not entirely reliable, for the data are constantly changing and different sources compile and classify data differently, so that figures are not always comparable.

organ is to promote prestige and good will and to mold attitudes. With a combined circulation far greater—possibly twice as great—than that of all daily newspapers, the house organ has quietly developed into a potent medium for the shaping of social and political thinking. [4] This paragraph only hints at the great diversity of the American press, which, after all, reflects the complexity of the society it serves.

2. The Motion Picture

The motion picture, born about the turn of the century, reached its peak of popularity during World War II. Since the advent of television, movie attendance has fallen off by one-half, to about once a month for the "average" American, who also watches old movies over television several hours a week. Movie studios now produce about two hundred theater films a year plus several thousand shorter films for television showing. Thus, for many hours each week, the average American is exposed to this medium which is tremendously effective in shaping attitudes and conditioned responses. [5]

The motion picture medium also includes: (1) the *newsreel*, with its abbreviated but intensely dramatic capsules of information and commentary; (2) the *educational* film, whose use in schools, colleges, and adult education groups is steadily expanding; (3) the *promotional* film, loaned out by vested interests—corporations, trade associations, labor organizations—and containing a mixture of education and propaganda.

3. Radio Broadcasting

The radio in a third of a century has developed from a novel toy into an industry with 3400 standard broadcast stations, nearly 800 FM stations, over 300,000 special-purpose radio stations (aeronautical, marine, public safety, industrial, experimental, disaster communications), and nearly 200,000 amateur stations and operators. No other communications medium reaches as many people as does radio, which enters about 98 per cent of all homes (with nearly two sets per home) and is found in three-fourths of the automobiles. Although the advent of television brought some decline in radio listening, the number of stations and receiv-

---

[4] "How To Play the House Organ," *Fortune*, Vol. 46 (October, 1952), pp. 144 ff.

[5] Several studies have established that motion pictures can produce striking changes in attitudes and beliefs. See Solomon P. Rosenberg, "Change of Socioeconomic Attitudes under Radical Motion Picture Propaganda," *Archives of Psychology*, No. 166 (New York, Columbia University Press, 1934); L. L. Thurstone, "Influence of Movies on Children's Attitudes," *Journal of Social Psychology*, Vol. 2 (August, 1931), pp. 291-305; Herbert Blumer, "Molding Mass Behavior Through Motion Pictures," *Publications of the American Sociological Society*, Vol. 29 (1934), pp. 115-117; also the twelve volumes of the Payne Fund studies. So conclusive were these earlier studies that little recent research in this area has been published.

ing sets in use continues to rise, and it seems assured that television will supplement and not replace radio.

4. Television

Telecasting has grown even more rapidly than radio. By 1959 there were 52 million sets in use, in 85 per cent of all homes in the nation. There were 609 television stations on the air and 117 more under construction. Television is still growing so rapidly that these statistics will be out of date before they are published.

Television has affected all the other media. Movie-going and radio-listening have been cut in half. Reading has shown some decline: fiction and entertainment reading has fallen off greatly, and newspaper reading has shown a slight decrease;[6] reading for information and intellectual stimulation shows no drop. Highbrow magazines have doubled in circulation since the war, middle-brow magazines have grown by about one-half, while the lowbrows (pulps, confessions, Westerns) have shown no growth during this period of growing population and rising income.[7] General-interest magazines have shown little growth, while special-interest and how-to-do-it magazines have shown the greatest growth. One would speculate that readers seeking entertainment and escape have turned to television, while others are reading more than ever. One noted writer suggests that television may drive out the cheap novel by monopolizing its audience, and indirectly encourage the writing of better literature.[8]

The *communications revolution,* however, consists of the ways in which these media have altered the lives and feelings of the people. The average American now spends about thirty-five hours a week with the mass media (newspapers, magazines, movies, radio, and television) as against about four hours a week, over his lifetime, spent in school.[9] He spends five or six as much of his lifetime watching television alone as he spends in both church and school. A century ago, the average person's free time was probably spent, in declining order, in (1) conversation, (2) games and participation sports, (3) spectator sports and organized, or commercialized, "entertainment," (4) mass communication. Today this order has been approximately reversed. Robert M. Hutchins has even suggested that conversation may become a lost art, as television may convert us into "a high order of plant life."

For many people the mass media appear to have created an imaginary world more vivid and "real" than the real one. Many children become so

[6] Wilbur Peterson, "Is Daily Newspaper Circulation Keeping Pace with the Nation's Growth?" *Journalism Quarterly,* Vol. 36 (Winter, 1959), pp. 12-22.

[7] Leo Bogart, *The Age of Television* (New York, Frederick Ungar Publishing Co., 1958), p. 148.

[8] James C. Michener, in *Chicago Sun-Times,* May 9, 1959, p. 23.

[9] Leo Bogart, *opt. cit.,* p. 66.

absorbed while reading comic magazines that they become utterly unaware of what goes on about them. [10] Many adults agonize over soap-
opera tragedies as though they were genuine. The TV series, *The
Millionaire*, showing the benefactions of a fictitious philanthropist, gets
an average of 200 letters each week asking for real money. So real do the
comic-strip and soap-opera characters become that a "wedding" brings in
truck loads of gifts for the imaginary couple, a "funeral" inspires a soggy
mountain of tearful letters, and cartoonist Chester Gould is prodded (by
uncomfortable Chicago law-enforcement officials) into explaining to his
readers how Dick Tracy can drive a Cadillac and live in a $100,000 mansion
on a policeman's salary. [11]

The mass media of communication have an effectiveness and dramatic
impact unknown to our predecessors. Through mass media, one's eye
and ear can roam the universe of time and space, and experience the
recreation of spectacles which far surpass even their originals in dramatic
intensity. Few battles, seen in person from a single viewing point, are as
dramatic as a battle in Cinemascope. [12] Seldom is the "real-life" hero so
godlike or the villain so demoniac as the celluloid one! The famous Orson
Welles "Invasion from Mars" broadcast sent millions of people into a
panic such as even the wartime reality of falling bombs and crashing
buildings does not produce. [13] Of course, the fear of the theater patron
shrinking into his cushion differs from the feelings of the soldier pinned
down by enemy fire. The point is that the mass media which claim so
much of our attention have a tremendous capacity either to inform or to
inflame. Neither capacity has been fully exploited, perhaps the one because it is too unprofitable, and the other because it is too dangerous.

PROBLEMS OF MASS MEDIA

As each new medium appeared and grew, it raised both hopes and
fears—hopes that it would checkmate tyranny and arm justice, that it

---

[10] Paul F. Lazarsfeld and Frank N. Stanton, *Communications and Research, 1948-
1949* (New York, Harper and Brothers, 1949), p. 23.

[11] He "pinches his pennies." (*Time* [November 26, 1951], p. 57.)

[12] In an early attempt at film realism, D. W. Griffiths and a camera crew accompanied Pancho Villa, the Mexican bandit, on an actual military campaign. Unknown to Griffiths, Villa accommodatingly arranged to inject realism by having
some thirty or forty prisoners actually massacred in one battle scene. The resulting
picture was so dull that it had to be padded out with studio shots before it could be
released. "Real life" is seldom dramatic in its entirety; only when carefully selected
bits and pieces of "real life" are skillfully arranged (as in the documentary film)
does "real life" become dramatic and compelling to watch.

[13] Long before the broadcast had ended, people all over the United States were
praying, crying, fleeing frantically to escape death from the Martians. Some ran to
rescue loved ones. Others telephoned farewells or warnings, hurried to inform neighbors, sought information from newspapers or radio stations, summoned ambulances
and police cars. At least six million people heard the broadcast. At least a million of
them were frightened or disturbed." (Hadley Cantril, *The Invasion from Mars*
[Princeton, N. J., Princeton University Press, 1940], p. 620.)

would bring to the masses the benefits of learning and culture, and unify a people; fears that it would become an instrument of tyranny, that it would adulterate learning, degrade culture, and promote social unrest. Each medium has been an object of social concern and controversy almost from its inception. Among the topics of concern are: (1) monopoly or concentration of control, (2) bias and responsibility, (3) content, or culture versus commerce, and (4) miscellaneous related problems.

1. CONCENTRATION OF CONTROL

The development of the mass media illustrates both the ideal of vigorous competition and the tendency towards noncompetitive practice which pervades our economic system. As in all forms of modern business and political organization, the pressing problem is, What degree of centralized organization and management is in the public interest?

a. The Press

The doctrine of the "freedom of the press," protected by the First Amendment, implies that books, magazines, and newspapers may be published and distributed by anyone, without any official permission or censorship. This freedom to publish was considered the indispensable bulwark of democracy. Through the free press, tyranny would be challenged, corruption exposed, and a market place provided for the free competition of ideas, in which truth would finally prevail. This passionate faith in the eventual triumph of truth through the free competition of ideas lies behind Jefferson's statement, "Were it left to me to decide whether we should have a government without newspapers or newspapers without a government, I should not hesitate to prefer the latter."

This free competition of ideas is complete only when the publication of conflicting opinions is politically *and economically* possible. In the days of the hand-operated press, a paper could be established quite cheaply, and a large paper had little competitive advantage over its smaller competitor. Even more recently, E. W. Scripps stated that none of his papers cost over $30,000 to establish, and declared, in 1911, that any two young men with brains, ambition, and a little money could found a successful newspaper. [14] Today, newspaper publishing is a big business. To establish a new competing newspaper in a small town is virtually a commercial impossibility; to establish one in a large city requires an investment of millions, with probable losses of millions more before it becomes self-supporting. [15]

[14] Quoted in Frank Luther Mott, *American Journalism* (New York, The Macmillan Co., 1950), p. 548.
[15] The only new large-city dailies in the past twenty years have been financial rat-holes. Marshall Field's *Chicago Sun* lost millions until virtually liquidated in a merger with the *Times*. Norman Chandler's Los Angeles *Mirror* lost millions, and

Changing technology and the advantages of large-scale operation have steadily reduced the number of newspapers from the 1909 figure of 2600, serving a population of 90,000,000, to its present 1770, for a population of 175,000,000. By 1945, daily newspaper competition had disappeared from all but 117 American cities; by 1954, this number had fallen to 74, and by 1959 to 42, while the remaining 1600 cities were either one-newspaper towns, or had two newspapers under a single management. By 1959, there were 26 states in which no city had competing daily papers. In one year, 22 dailies were merged or suspended, and one prominent publisher predicts that soon no city under half a million will have more than a single paper. [16] In a great deal of America, local newspaper competition has disappeared!

The amount of effective newspaper competition is further reduced by absentee-ownership of many papers. Over one-fourth of our newspaper circulation is attained by a few newspaper chains. Except for purely local news, most of the news that reaches print passes through one of the two major newsgathering services—the Associated Press, a co-operative to which most papers belong; the United Press International, affiliated with the Scripps-Howard and Hearst chains. Most newspapers rely on syndicated features both for entertainment—comic strips, lovelorn columns, fashion features, and the like—and for their columns of news interpretation and opinion (Walter Lippmann, Joseph Alsop, Roscoe Drummond, and others). Even the editorials are sometimes "canned," supplied by the chain owner or some other nonlocal source.

In magazine publishing, although over 8000 periodicals are published by 2200 publishers, the top five publishers with ten magazines account for about one-fifth of the total circulation. The top ten of these 2200 publishers employ one-third of the total persons employed in the industry and supply nearly half the weight of second-class mail carried in the country. Although the magazine publishing field is fiercely competitive, the need for a large circulation makes it hazardous and expensive to launch a new general-interest magazine. In book publishing, although the top dozen publishing houses dominate the field, the relatively modest cost of having a book privately published makes it fairly easy to get one's ideas into print. But book distribution is another matter! Unless a new book is reviewed and discussed in the "book review" section of newspapers and magazines, it is usually doomed to remain unsold and unread; therefore the promotional "connections" of a major publishing house assume great importance.

The total picture of the press is one that is far from freely competitive in the traditional sense, yet is far from a complete monopoly. The degree of concentration in the industry vests in a relatively small number of per-

---

". . . is still losing at the rate of an estimated $20,000 to $30,000 a week." (*Time* [June 21, 1954], p. 79.)

[16] *Time* (June 21, 1954), pp. 79, 80.

sons a great power to determine what shall reach the presses. If most of them should chance to think alike on some issue—and sometimes they do—other points of view may have difficulty getting into print and distributed so that many people will see them.

b. Motion Pictures

Although the five largest production studios dominate the industry, the smaller studios and the independent producers are highly active, and movie-making is highly competitive. In film distribution, ownership of chains of first-run theaters by the major studios gave them a monopolistic advantage, until antitrust action forced them to dispose of their theater chains.

c. Radio and Television

Since its infancy, radio has been subject to some governmental regulation, arising from the need for assigning frequencies in a spectrum that has room for only a limited number of stations. Since the limitations upon the number of stations that can operate are technical rather than economic, broadcasting is not viewed as a strictly free enterprise, but as a sort of public utility. The law creating the Federal Communications Commission (FCC) establishes the principle that the air waves belong to the public, that a station operator may own the studio equipment but does not own the frequency upon which he broadcasts, and that licenses to operate a station are to be granted only "in the public interest, convenience, or necessity." FCC rules allow one person or company to own no more than seven television stations, seven FM stations, or seven AM (standard broadcast) stations.

Concentration in broadcasting, therefore, rests less upon station ownership than upon network affiliation and program sponsorship. Most of the 3400 standard broadcast stations belong to one of the four national or several regional networks. Most local stations give little time to locally originated programs, especially during good listening hours, and most of the broadcast material consists of network shows or of phonograph records separated by commercials. [17] Practically all network broadcasts are sponsored by advertisers. In a very literal sense, *the advertisers control radio broadcasting*, for the advertising agency not only supplies the commercial but supplies the entire show, with the station operator merely a supplier of radio time. White interviewed forty radio executives of whom only two challenged the thesis that advertisers run broadcasting. [18]

[17] Federal Communications Commission, *Public Service Responsibility of Broadcast Licensees* (Washington, Government Printing Office, 1946), p. 37.
[18] Llewellyn White, *The American Radio* (Chicago, University of Chicago Press, 1947), p. 94.

A few large advertisers, operating through a still smaller number of advertising agencies, supply the bulk of network income. A 1959 study found that over 90 per cent of all broadcasting during prime evening hours originated with two networks and the nine stations they own and operate. [19] In perhaps no other medium does so small a group have as great power to control what the people may see and hear.

The advent of FM radio and television has broadened the medium, but has not greatly affected the pattern of ownership and control. When FM radio developed, the FCC sought to establish policies that would attract new blood to broadcasting, but was defeated by industry opposition. [20] Aside from those granted to schools and colleges, most of the FM licenses are now held by operators of AM stations, who effectively discouraged outside competition by carrying their AM radio commercials and sponsored shows over their FM stations without added expense to the advertiser. [21] This made it difficult for an independent FM station to earn any advertising income, and helped reduce the total number of FM stations from a high of 733 in 1950 to a low of 530 in 1957. In television's earlier years, heavy financial losses were absorbed by the established radio industry. As television became profitable, the competitive advantages enjoyed by an established, experienced broadcaster enabled the existing radio station owners to retain control of most of the television stations.

d. Interlocking Concentration

When radio appeared, many predicted the death of the newspaper, but what followed was union, not conquest. Today nearly one-third of the radio and television stations are affiliated with newspapers under common ownership or control. In over one-third of the cities with only one radio station, that station is associated with the only newspaper, giving an absolute monopoly of local news.

e. Significance of Concentration

Concern over concentration is nothing new. Jefferson complained of the great trading towns, that "though not one-twenty-fifth of the nation, they command three-fourths of its public papers." [22] In 1941, the FCC, finding 90 per cent of nighttime broadcast power in two network systems (NBC and CBS), forced NBC to dispose of one of its two networks. A

[19] Bernard Schwartz, "FCC and the Networks," *The Nation*, Vol. 188 (May 23, 1959), pp. 473-475.

[20] Charles A. Siepman, *Radio's Second Chance* (Boston, Little, Brown & Co., 1947), pp. 244-251.

[21] *Ibid.*

[22] J. A. Pollard, *The Presidents and the Press* (New York, The Macmillan Co., 1947), p. 75.

1957 study by the FCC revealed that in the top twenty-five market areas of the country, 71 per cent of the TV stations were held in multiple ownership (several stations owned by a single owner), 20 per cent were owned by newspapers, and only 9 per cent had single, independent owners. [23] Nearly every serious study of ways of "improving" the mass media includes recommendations for reducing concentration. In a society in which the mass media have replaced the town meeting and the cracker barrel, it is argued, freedom of speech has little meaning unless it includes the practical opportunity for each group to get its ideas into print and on the air. This freedom, many critics feel, is gravely weakened by the highly centralized managements of a motion-picture industry intent upon avoiding everything controversial, a broadcast industry seeking to offend nobody, and a press largely devoid of local competition. Critics also complain that centralized control imposes upon the media a dead level of mediocrity, squeezing out the next-to-the-last drop of diversity, originality, and imagination. Most serious of all is the charge that an unhealthy degree of power is shared by too small a group. MacIver writes, "Of all such monopolies, the most immediately fatal to democracy is the monopoly of the media of opinion, or any approximation to it." [24]

No doubt centralization does pose a certain threat to freedom and to diversity, but the effects of centralization are not entirely pernicious. "Yellow journalism" was a product of the circulation wars of a half-century ago. Hearst's circulation battle with Pulitzer probably caused the Spanish-American War, [25] and his circulation battle with McCormick is widely agreed to have helped establish Chicago gangdom. [26] As one liberal journal comments editorially, "Too much competition can sometimes reduce all publishers to the lowest common denominator of sensationalism; whereas monopoly can sometimes encourage independence, letting a publisher feel that he can afford to put out a good paper." [27] One study found little difference between competing newspapers and those without local competition; they were equally good—or bad— irrespective of competition. [28] The large broadcast networks bring us countless hours of vacuous mediocrity, but they also bring us many

---

[23] Roscoe I. Barrow, "Network Broadcasting—The Report of the FCC Network Study Staff," *Law and Contemporary Problems*, Vol. 22 (Autumn, 1957), pp. 611-625.

[24] R. M. MacIver, *The Web of Government* (New York, The Macmillan Co., 1948), p. 221.

[25] Frank Luther Mott, *op. cit.*, Ch. 31, "Yellow Journalism and the War with Spain."

[26] Ferdinand Lundberg, *Imperial Hearst* (New York, Equinox Co-operative Press, 1936), pp. 151-173.

[27] *The Reporter*, Vol. 11 (August 17, 1954), p. 5.

[28] Raymond B. Nixon and Robert Jones, "The Content of Noncompetitive vs. Competitive Newspapers," *Journalism Quarterly*, Vol. 33 (Summer, 1956), pp. 299-314.

artistic productions which no local studio could produce. [29] Whether partial centralization of control of the mass media has done more harm than good remains debatable; meanwhile, any attempt to alter greatly the present pattern of control would probably be economically difficult and politically impossible. Large-scale activities are a necessity in modern society, and rather than try to destroy concentration, it may be more realistic, as Brady suggests, to develop forms of democratic participation in guiding them. [30]

2. BIAS AND RESPONSIBILITY

a. The Press—Free to Inform and to Misinform

The *New York Times* proclaims as its motto, "All the news that's fit to print," and is generally agreed to come very close to fulfilling its pledge. For certain other papers, a more descriptive motto might be, "All the news that fits the publisher's biases."

Bias is not easy to measure and is difficult to establish. Bias is practically universal among the human species, for all persons have their value preferences, and most thinking is colored by personal values. It is almost inevitable, therefore, that the biases of those who control the mass media should affect their content. One would hardly expect the *CIO News* to be fully objective in reporting labor-management affairs, the *Democratic Digest* to be impartial in reporting political affairs, or the *Lutheran Witness* and the *Catholic World* to agree in appraising the film, *Martin Luther*. Although each is expected to refrain from falsehood or slander, it is expected that each will eloquently plead the cause which it was established to promote.

To a lesser degree, bias is charged against those media which are supposedly independent and neutral. Some papers, such as the *New York Times* and the *Christian Science Monitor*, are widely respected for maintaining a high degree of objectivity. Some others have a notorious record of twisting the news to fit the views of the publishers. As a striking example, an article in *Harper's Magazine* reproduces a news story from a well-known newspaper and lists 112 inaccuracies and unwarranted inferences found in this single item, in the opinion of the article's writer. [31]

There is little doubt that the economic philosophy of newspaper editors and publishers, broadcast station owners, and movie producers is

[29] Richard S. Salant, Thomas K. Fisher, and Leon R. Brooks, "The Functions and Practices of a Television Network," *Law and Contemporary Problems*, Vol. 22 (Autumn, 1957), pp. 584-610.

[30] Robert A. Brady, "Monopoly and the First Freedom," *Hollywood Quarterly*, Vol. 2 (April, 1947), pp. 225-411.

[31] Milton Mayer, "How to Read the *Chicago Tribune*," *Harper's Magazine*, Vol. 198 (April, 1949), pp. 24-35.

overwhelmingly conservative. Men of wealth and power are, understandably enough, defenders of the social system which allows them to hold that wealth and exercise that power. As veteran newspaperman Quincy Howe writes, "To criticize a newspaper because it supports the system under which it operates, or because it strives to please its advertisers and readers, is to criticize a bee because it stings or a dog because it barks. That is the nature of the beast." [32] A distinguished editor, Virginius Dabney of the Richmond *Times-Dispatch*, writes: [33]

Today newspapers are Big Business, and they are run in that tradition. The publisher, who often knows little about the editorial side of the operation, usually is one of the leading business men in the community, and his editorial page, under normal circumstances, strongly reflects that point of view. Sometimes he gives his editor a free hand but far oftener he does not. He looks upon the paper primarily as a "property" rather than as an instrument for public service. . . . (He) considers the important part of the paper to be the business management. . . . Of course, such a publisher sees that the editorials in his paper are "sound," which is to say that they conform to his own weird views of society. . . .

Every survey known to the authors reinforces the picture of the general conservative bias of the press. *Fortune* a few years ago stated that "the United States press is prevailingly capitalistic and overwhelmingly conservative," and quoted Oswald Garrison Villard, a one-time Associated Press Director, as having "declared the (Associated Press) service constitutionally incapable of doing justice to the underprivileged." [34] Child labor legislation, public housing, social security legislation, securities exchange regulations, the Wagner Labor Relations Act, and wage-and-hour legislation were enacted despite opposition from the majority of the press. Newspaper publishers are employers, and news unfavorable to unions seems to get far more space than National Labor Relations Board findings of "unfair labor practices" against employers. Some papers have refused to sell advertising space to unions which felt that the editorials and news columns were unfair, and the consumer testing organizations, *Consumers' Research* and *Consumer Reports,* have generally been unable to buy advertising space. Bias is also charged against consumer co-operatives, food and drug legislation, Federal Communications Commission orders, and Federal Trade Commission efforts to suppress fraudulent advertising. Even the comic strip may reflect a social philosophy allegedly conservative, at least in the case of "Little Orphan Annie." [35]

[32] Quincy Howe, *The News and How to Understand It* (New York, Simon and Schuster, Inc., 1940), p. 39.

[33] Virginius Dabney, "What's Wrong with Newspaper Editorials?" *Saturday Review,* Vol. 28 (February 24, 1945), pp. 7-9.

[34] "Associated Press," *Fortune,* Vol. 15 (February, 1937), pp. 89 ff.

[35] Donald Auster, "A Content Analysis of 'Little Orphan Annie'," *Social Problems,* Vol. 2 (July, 1954), pp. 21-32.

It takes a big person to do "little" things. I once saw Michigan's Governor Williams on his hands and knees picking up apples for a woman when her paper sack broke. Other "gentlemen" just stood around. . . .
Ann Landers, as printed in many papers, June 4, 1959.

It takes a big person to do "little" things. I once saw the Governor of a great state on his hands and knees picking up apples for a woman when her paper sack broke. Other "gentlemen" just stood around. . . .
Ann Landers, as printed in *Grand Rapids Press*, June 4, 1959.

In the last several presidential elections, a tremendous majority of the press has given editorial support to the Republican candidate—about 90 per cent of the nation's newspaper circulation in 1956. [36] One columnist has remarked, "Whenever I dug up dirt on the Democrats or Harry Truman, the publishers cheered and ran my story high on the page, but when I do the same about the G.O.P., they kill the story and scold me." [37] Democratic spokesmen and friends have repeatedly complained about what they call the "one-party press," charging that not only are the papers Republican editorially, but that they also favor Republican candidates and policies in their news stories and pictures. [38]

Such charges are easy to hurl but difficult to evaluate. In theory the news story is written "straight," while editorial opinions are confined to the editorial page. There are many subtle ways in which bias can be expressed in the news story, but it is difficult to establish or measure this bias.

1. *Space*—the favored cause or candidate may receive detailed reporting whereas the opponent gets little attention.

2. *Location*—favored candidates may be front-paged and headlined, and opponents buried in the inside pages.

3. *Selection*—the news story may quote the most moving and popular phrases of the favored candidate and spotlight the blunders of his opponent; or it may play up a trifling comment of a speaker and ignore his main theme.

4. *Headlines*—the headline may support and confirm a candidate's position, or may undermine it; the headline may focus attention on his main theme, or upon some irrelevance.

5. *Supporting quotations*—the favored candidate's quoted statements may

[36] Frank Luther Mott, *op. cit.*, p. 719; Nathan B. Blumberg, *One-Party Press?* (Lincoln, University of Nebraska Press, 1954), pp. 14-17; Arthur E. Rouse, *Slanted News* (Boston, Beacon Press, Inc., 1957).

[37] Drew Pearson, quoted in the Wells newsletter, *Between the Lines* (152 Madison Avenue, New York 16), May 15, 1956.

[38] Nathan B. Blumberg, *op. cit.*, pp. 11-19; Robert Lasch, "Pride and Prejudice: The Fourth Estate," *The Reporter*, Vol. 7 (November 25, 1952), pp. 9-11; Arthur E. Rouse, *op. cit.*

be followed by supporting quotations from other respected persons, whereas his opponent's statements may be followed by opposing quotations from others, or by reminders of unpleasant events for which he is blamed.

6. *Audience reaction*—the audience may be described as highly enthusiastic, or as apathetic, or hostile.

7. *Juxtaposition*—a news story or picture concerning a candidate may be placed next to a story or picture that will color the reader's reaction.

8. *General news selectivity*—the general news stories may play up news developments which are embarrassing to the party in power (for example, unemployment, taxes, debt, corruption, foreign troubles), or play up developments favorable to the party in power (for example, tax cuts, prosperity, administration accomplishments).

9. *Picture selection*—may be folksy, appealing, heroic, or may be routine, nondescript, or even ludicrous. [39]

10. *Loaded words*—is he "able" or "clever?" "farsighted" or "calculating?" "bold" or "reckless?" It is a "crusade" or a "plot"; a "program" or a "scheme," and so on.

It is difficult to see how a democracy could long survive a genuine "one-party press," and these charges of political favoritism in news handling are not to be taken lightly; neither are they to be accepted without conclusive evidence. At present, there is no comprehensive, reliable survey to warrant a conclusion. Following the 1952 presidential election, the national journalism fraternity, Sigma Delta Chi, called for such a survey, but met strong opposition from newspaper publishers. [40] *Editor and Publisher* also called for a survey, but the American Society of Newspaper Publishers and the American Newspaper Publishers Association were uninterested in any attempt to have the facts about newspaper bias clearly established. [41]

Two independent surveys were attempted. One studied the amount of space which 35 major newspapers gave to both parties in the 1952 election campaign, and concluded that over half the papers gave equal space to both parties. [42] The other studied the treatment of two news stories by 31 large papers in the 1952 campaign. It concluded that all but the *New York Times* slanted the news treatment in the direction of the editorial policy, which in all but three cases supported the Republican candidate. This study also concluded that, while bias can easily be detected by an

[39] To editorialize with pictures makes for very interesting journalism, but almost necessarily produces biased journalism. This is shown in a letter to the author from *Time* magazine which states in part, "Every *Time* cover (portrait) is in the nature of *a subjective comment*. . . . Our cover portrait is as interpretative, and is meant to be, as the cover story itself. We are trying to convey to the reader *our idea* not only of a man's appearance but *of his character* and personality." (Italics mine: letter dated May 2, 1957, signed by Gwyneth Kahn, for the Editors.)

[40] *New York Times*, December 21, 1952, p. 18; Nathan B. Blumberg, *op. cit.*, pp. 20-25.

[41] Nathan B. Blumberg, *op cit.*, pp. 23-25; "Problems of Journalism," *Proceedings of the American Society of Newspaper Editors* (1953), pp. 184-185.

[42] Nathan B. Blumberg, *op. cit.*, p. 44.

TIME CHANGES THINGS

The Income Tax

This week once again the great American taxpayer . . . was working over his income-tax return. He did not do the job happily, or . . . even very patriotically.

Time, March 10, 1952, p. 25

George Allen

. . . the President (Truman) eased his croniest crony, George E. Allen, into the Board of Directors of the Reconstruction Finance Corporation . . . George is all the more remarkable because, to the naked eye, George is a clown . . . a fixer and a puller of wires.

Time, January 28, 1946, p. 19, August 12, 1946, p. 18.

Presidential Message

President Truman flapped open his leather notebook and began in his usual flat tone to read his message to Congress on the State of the Union. When he finished 45 minutes later, he had made little news.

Time, January 21, 1952, p. 15.

Presidential Intentions

The subject of Harry Truman's 1952 intentions came up again in his weekly press conference. The President wasn't saying, just acting deliberately mysterious. It has become an unprofitable inquiry and a stale joke. . . .

Time, July 23, 1951, p. 7.

The Income Tax

. . . 60 million American have by this week signed their 1954 income-tax forms . . . They did this, wonderful to tell, without riots of protest . . . It has become more and more unfashionable to criticize the income-tax level.

Time, April 18, 1955, p. 23

George Allen

The President, however, chatted quietly with . . . a group of golfing companions (including) . . . George Allen, Washington lawyer and friend of Presidents . . .

Time, December 6, 1954, p. 26.

Presidential Message

President Eisenhower's 1955 State of the Union speech had sweep and calm and balance . . . it elaborated the obvious. Perhaps that was precisely what the nation needed.

Time, January 17, 1955, p. 21.

Presidential Intentions

. . . he (Eisenhower) has skillfully refused to commit himself on 1956. . . . Adroitly, he fielded questions about a second term.

Time, January 24, 1955, p. 9, July 11, 1955, p. 15.

Adapted from an article by Milton B. Gwirtzman in the *Harvard Crimson*. (Students may recall that it is possible to distort by quoting out of context, and may wish to check the above quotations to see whether they accurately reflect the tone of the articles from which they are quoted.)

informed reader, there is no possible way to *measure* bias, since there are so many subtle means of biased presentation. [43]

The mass-circulation magazines appear to show much the same patterns of bias as do the newspapers. The smaller journals, however, show a great variety of viewpoint, from the right-wing journals like *American Mercury* or *Freeman* to such liberal journals as *The Reporter, The Nation, The Progressive*, or *New Republic*. There is no important segment of American thought which is not represented in magazine form. Comparative circulation figures, however, show that the liberals are talking mainly to one another, for the four above mentioned liberal journals combined require nearly a full year to circulate as many copies as the more conservative *Saturday Evening Post* circulates each week. There is little evidence of bias on the part of book publishers as a whole. Certain publishers have their preferences, but, with a few possible exceptions, any manuscript likely to command a respectable sale is not difficult to market.

b. The Motion Picture—Image or Caricature of Life?

Whereas the press proudly proclaims itself a medium of public enlightenment, the motion-picture industry frankly announces that its primary purpose is to sell entertainment at a profit, not to stimulate social criticism. As one movie executive remarked, "Messages are for Western Union; I sell entertainment." Movie makers have avoided controversial plots and have sought to delete anything that might give offense to anybody. But this technique has not avoided the problem of bias, for a variety of biases are claimed against the movie industry. They include the following:

1. *Race Bias.* The important, ambitious, successful people in the movies are almost invariably white Anglo-Saxons, with Negroes, Indians, and other minority members depicted in servile, stereotyped roles. [44]

2. *Class Bias.* Most pictures deal mainly with persons in the upper income brackets and in executive or professional occupations, with the life of working-class people, when shown, often depicted unfavorably.

3. *Nationalistic Bias.* In pictures involving foreign locales or persons, the Americans are usually the heroes and the foreigners either villains or simpletons, whom any red-blooded American can easily dispatch by the score. [45]

[43] Arthur E. Rouse, *op. cit.*

[44] In recent years, movies have rarely shown minority members in highly offensive roles, but the old films resurrected for television and seen, perhaps, by more people than the new movies, often reflect a strong racial bias.

[45] See Dallas W. Smythe, "Reality As Presented by Television," *Public Opinion Quarterly*, Vol. 18, No. 2 (Summer, 1954), pp. 143-56, for a content analysis of 86 TV dramas, finding that only 44 per cent of the Italian characters shown were law-abiding. Europeans accounted for 24 per cent of the villains and 10 per cent of the

4. *Militaristic Bias*. It is charged that movies promote militarism by idealizing combat, glorifying force, belittling negotiation, and presenting military service in a colorful, glamorous, and adventuresome setting.

5. *Conservative Bias*. It is charged that movies promote conservatism in two ways: (*a*) by avoiding all controversial themes, especially anything which suggests social criticism or calls attention to social problems; (*b*) by presenting all problems as *personal* problems, caused purely by bad luck or bad people, not by defective social organization. An example is contained in a letter written to Samuel Goldwyn by Joseph Breen, production code administrator, regarding the 1937 picture, *Dead End*. [46]

We would like to recommend, in passing, that you be less emphatic, throughout, in showing the conditions of the poor in tenements and those of the rich in apartment houses. Specifically, we recommend you do not show, at any time, or at least that you do not emphasize, the presence of filth, or smelly garbage cans, or garbage floating in the river, into which the boys jump for a swim . . . such scenes are likely to give offense.

A prominent movie executive suggests that today's producers are still more cautious, saying, [47]

Hollywood has rarely ventured far into the field of films concerned with political or economic conditions. Nevertheless, one or two features of this type have appeared almost annually, providing a striking contrast to the mass of strictly escapist material that constitutes the industry's major contribution to American life. Even this small trickle has now dried up. One of the distributors of *Mr. Smith Goes to Washington* recently assured me that a remake of this fine picture, which showed some of our lawmakers in a less than favorable light, could not possibly be undertaken today. Even the mild legitimate comedy *Affairs of State* was passed up as potential dynamite by all the major picture companies.

Old movies as well as new stories are being shelved. After Harry Warner emerged from testifying before the House Un-American Activities Committee, he decided to issue instructions to take out of circulation, even by the educational film libraries, three great social documents that had made his company famous: *I Am a Fugitive from a Chain Gang*, *The Story of Louis Pasteur*, and *Emile Zola*.

The student of social problems realizes that many personal difficulties are produced by social and cultural pressures, and that a realistic treatment requires social changes. But in the movies, with exceedingly rare exceptions, blame rests upon the people, not upon the system, and the

---

heroes, while white Americans provided 83 per cent of the heroes and only 69 per cent of the villians.

[46] Reprinted from *Freedom of the Movies* by Ruth A. Inglis with permission of The University of Chicago Press, p. 182.

[47] Arthur Mayer, "A Movie Exhibitor Looks at Censorship," *The Reporter*, Vol. 10 (March 2, 1954), pp. 35-40.

problem is solved when the bad people are located and destroyed. In this way, the movies discourage social criticism and social reform and lend tacit approval to the status quo.

c. Radio and Television

Most of the comments made about movies also apply even more strongly to the entertainment aspects of radio and television. The other aspects of radio and television—news broadcasting, discussion programs, political broadcasts, and the sale of time—involve some different problems. Since the air waves have room for only a limited number of stations— often only one to a locality—the FCC imposes upon the broadcast industry a special obligation to be impartial. Time must be given or sold to all major political parties on the same terms, and a station is expected to provide balanced discussion of any controversial issues that are aired. Most station operators appear to have wholeheartedly accepted this obligation and make an honest effort to grant all points of view and equal opportunity to be heard.

There are, however, complaints that radio's impartiality is more apparent than real. The mere avoidance of controversy may, unintentionally, become a device for supporting the status quo. Lazarsfeld and Merton comment: [48]

> Since our commercially sponsored mass media promote a largely unthinking allegiance to our social structure, they cannot be relied upon to work for changes, even minor changes, in that structure. It is possible to list some developments to the contrary, but upon close inspection they prove illusory. A community group, such as the PTA, may request the producer of a radio serial to inject the theme of tolerant race attitudes into the program. Should the producer feel that this theme is safe, that it will not antagonize any substantial part of his audience, he may agree, but at the first indication that it is a dangerous theme which may alienate potential customers, he will refuse, or will soon abandon the experiment. Social objectives are consistently surrendered by commercialized media when they clash with economic gains. Minor tokens of "progressive" views are of slight importance since they are included only by the grace of the sponsors and only on condition that they be sufficiently acceptable as not to alienate any appreciable part of the audience. Economic pressure makes for conformism by omission of sensitive issues.

More direct forms of bias are also claimed. Until 1945, the code of the National Association of Broadcasters condemned sale of time to labor unions for any sort of program, although manufacturers and trade associations bought time with no difficulty. Quincy Howe has remarked that sponsors prefer conservative news commentators, asserting that

[48] Paul F. Lazarsfeld and Robert K. Merton, "Mass Communication, Popular Taste, and Organized Social Action," in Lyman Bryson, ed., *Communication of Ideas* (New York, Harper and Brothers, 1948).

". . . . sponsors snap up the news programs with a conservative slant as they never snapped up the programs with a liberal slant." [49] *Variety*, a highly respected magazine of the entertainment world, appraised thirty radio news reporters and analysts some years ago, and reported a definite conservative imbalance, classifying 5 as reactionary or extreme reactionary, 7 as conservative, 6 as middle-of-the-roaders, 7 as very cautious or middle-of-the-road liberals, 1 as an independent liberal, with 4 unclassified. [50] Several well-known radio newscasters have left the air protesting that they were pushed off because of their liberalism, whereas few conservative commentators have met such a fate. [51] Such charges of newscaster bias—difficult to evalute—are aimed mainly at advertiser-sponsored newscasters. The news reporters sustained by the radio networks themselves enjoy a reputation for greater objectivity and balance.

d. Bias

To summarize the data on bias is not easy. Charges are many, but evidence is scattered and conclusions must be tentative. It is clear that the degree of objectivity and responsibility of the mass media have greatly increased over earlier periods. With the possible exception of England, no other major country has a press as responsible and objective as ours. It also appears inescapable that a pronounced conservative bias pervades most of the mass media—which may be either a menace or a blessing, according to one's values. Although to some extent due to the pressure of advertisers, [52] who supply two-thirds of newspaper and magazine income and nearly all of the radio and television income, bias appears primarily as a consequence of the social and cultural values of those limited groups who own and control the media. As the famous editor William Allen White said, a few years ago, in words which also apply to the owners of the other media, [53]

The publisher associates on terms of equality with the bankers, the merchant princes, the manufacturers, and the investment brokers. His friends unconsciously color his opinions. If he lives with them on any kind of social terms in the City Club or the Country Club or the Yacht Club or the Racquet Club, he must more or less merge his views into the common views of other capitalists. The publisher is not bought like a chattel. Indeed he often is able to buy

---

[49] Quoted in Siepman, *op. cit.*, p. 89.

[50] *Variety*, June 25, 1945.

[51] Siepman, *op. cit.*, pp. 91-92.

[52] For example, *Editor and Publisher* (March 20, 1948), attributes the financial failure of Marshall Field's *Chicago Sun* partly to a boycott from some national advertisers who disliked Marshall Field's liberal editorial policies.

[53] William Allen White, in *Chicago Times*, June 2, 1939; quoted in George L. Bird and Frederic E. Merwin, *The Press and Society* (Englewood Cliffs, N. J., Prentice-Hall, Inc., 1951), pp. 74-75.

those who are suspected of buying him. But he takes the color of his social environment.

He is pretty generally against organized labor. He is too often found opposing the government control of public utilities. He instinctively fears any regulation of the stock exchange. The right to strike seems to the rich publisher and his Chamber of Commerce friends to be sheer anarchy. It is inevitable that the managing editor and the editorial writers who want to hold their jobs take their professional views from their boss, the man who signs the payroll check.

Bias is not ended by denouncing or explaining it. It is unlikely that bias will be ended at all. Perhaps the most effective control lies in sensitizing students to the problem of bias, so that they will recognize that one cannot hope to be intelligently informed on any public issue by reading a single paper (with a few exceptions), or even a dozen papers reflecting the same viewpoint. Only by reading and comparing sources reflecting opposing biases is one likely to find the complete truth about any controversy.

3. CONTENT—CULTURE VERSUS COMMERCE

a. Media Content

As each new means of mass communication developed, it was hailed as the key to cultural salvation—the ignorant could be enlightened and the uncouth refined. These bright—and perhaps unrealistic—visions have not materialized. Despite occasional exceptions, each medium is largely geared to bring entertainment to the public and profits to the owners. To those who demand mass improvement from the mass media, this is outrageous. Lee DeForest, whose inventions made modern radio possible, has attacked the radio broadcasting industry, saying, [54]

What have you gentlemen done with my child? He was conceived as a potent instrumentality for culture, fine music, the lifting of America's mass intelligence. You have debased this child, you have sent him out on the streets in rags of ragtime, tatters of jive and boogie-woogie, to collect money from all and sundry for hubba-hubba and audio-jitterbug. You have made of him a laughing stock to intelligence, surely a stench in the nostrils of the gods of the ionosphere. . . . Soap opera without end or sense floods each household daily. . . . Murder mysteries rule the waves by night and children are rendered psychopathic by your bedtime stories. This child of mine, now thirty years in age, has been resolutely kept to the average intelligence of thirteen years. Its national intelligence is maintained as moronic, as though you and your sponsors believe the majority of listeners have only moron minds. . . .

Who has the right to say what the press shall print, movies show, and radio shall broadcast—the owners, the public, the government? The public

[54] Quoted in "The Revolt Against Radio," *Fortune*, Vol. 35 (March, 1947), pp. 101 ff.

overwhelmingly favors leaving primary control of the mass media right where it is—with the private owners. [55] But to the critics, this merely proves the truth of George Bernard Shaw's dictum that "if we do not get what we like, we shall grow to like what we get."

What *do* we get? Detailed up-to-date surveys of media content are not available. In general, newspapers give us news, comment, and editorial opinion, and a variety of "features" that are entertaining and sometimes mildly informational. Books and magazines give us a great choice, with ample opportunity for everyone to gratify his tastes. Movies are almost entirely devoted to entertainment, either light, frothy entertainment or rootless melodrama that carefully skirts all serious themes or challenging issues. The most recent detailed study of radio content (1946) shows that about three-fourths of all broadcast time was devoted to entertainment-type programs, about one-sixth to informational programs, and the remainder to programs classed as "orientational." [56] Most commercial FM radio broadcasting duplicates the programs carried on affiliated AM stations. A recent survey of TV program content finds a third of the evening program time devoted to drama, another third to comedy and variety shows, and the remainder divided among quiz and audience participation shows, music, news, and sports events. [57]

How well do people like what they get? The more highly educated people are the more critical. They watch and listen less, and are far more interested in classical music and discussions of public issues, of which broadcasting now offers comparatively few. Persons who are critical of one of the mass media are far more likely to be critical of the others, showing that a significant minority is clearly dissatisfied with the mass media in general. [58] Just what do they dislike about them?

b. Criticisms of Media Content

Critics indict the mass media on three main counts: that much of the content is either (1) *trashy,* (2) *harmful,* or (3) so *limited in variety* that the public has little choice but to learn to like trash.

TRASH—WHERE AND WHY? The charge of "trashiness" involves a value judgment—by whose values is *trash* to be defined? This charge is rooted in the fact that most media content is scaled to mass tastes, to the dismay of those who view mass tastes as vulgar. Each of the media (excepting books and specialized magazines) seeks to attract as large an audience as possible for each issue, show, or broadcast. This means *scaling the content*

---

[55] Paul F. Lazarsfeld and Patricia L. Kendall, *Radio Listening in America,* (Englewood Cliffs, N. J., Prentice-Hall, Inc., 1948), pp. 89, 144.

[56] Kenneth Baker, "An Analysis of Radio's Broadcasting," in Paul F. Lazarsfeld and Frank N. Stanton, *op. cit.,* p. 58.

[57] Leo Bogart. *op. cit.,* p. 50.

[58] Kenneth Baker, *op. cit.,* pp. 10, 83, 136, 140.

to the least common denominator of audience acceptability. Since the average American adult has completed a fraction over nine years of schooling, the local newspaper can gain circulation by containing little that cannot be read and understood by a 15-year-old child. Since nearly everyone likes "human interest" stories whereas few will read a column about foreign trade, the serious, but undramatic, news must make room for lurid scandal and sentimental trivia. When Old Bob, the coon dog, got lost in a cave near Bedford, Indiana, he was on or near the front page of several papers for a full week—at a time when the war in Korea was in its most tense phase and the country was involved in a hasty mobilization, price inflation, a political crisis, and a basic reorientation of foreign policy. In the search for excitement, newspapers tend to emphasize the bizarre, the exceptional, and the illicit, while sober but serious news developments get buried in the back pages. At times, newspaper treatment of crime may make impossible a fair trial of the accused, a situation that occasionally leads to judicial rebuke of the press. [59]

The least-common-denominator approach is most clearly revealed in movie and broadcast content. The crime-sex-adventure trio of themes accounts for most movie plots because movie makers are under no illusions as to which kinds of pictures make money. [60] Despite occasional exceptions, serious drama and genuinely artistic films rarely make money, and no producer can afford to make many films like *The Treasure of Sierra Madre*, widely acclaimed as an artistic triumph, but a box-office failure (no love interest!). Films involving social criticism and intellectual challenge are both commercially doubtful and politically dangerous. Dancing girls, horse operas, and "who-dun-its" are both safer and more profitable.

A similar situation is found in radio and television broadcasting. Most broadcast time during the best listening hours is sponsored by an advertiser who buys the time, and chooses and presents the entire program. Although an occasional sponsor who is seeking to create an institutional image may sponsor a prestige program of limited appeal (such as the Metropolitan Opera or the New York Philharmonic Orchestra), most sponsors try to attract the largest possible audience to hear the commer-

[59] For example, see "Free Press and Fair Trial," *Time* (April 23, 1951), pp. 78-79; also Edwin H. Sutherland, *Principles of Criminology* (Philadelphia, J. B. Lippincott Co., 1947), pp. 187-189.

[60] It is revealing to note upon what assumptions some highly successful producers operate. Leonard Goldstein, described in *Time* as "Hollywood's top money-making producer," avoids sophisticated comedy and includes among his rules of operation: "avoid 'downbeat' (depressing) pictures—nobody ever bought tickets to watch inmates of a mental institution," and "adults are grown-up children, and should be entertained as such." (*Time* [April 28, 1952], p. 96.) Another producer, Hal Roach, Jr., who has been highly successful in making films for television, "accounts for his new success with the explanation that televiewers have even lower I.Q.'s than movie-goers." (*Time* [October 29, 1951], p. 48.)

cial. This produces a great deal of entertainment and—except for news broadcasting—little else. The drama is mostly second- or third-rate, for serious drama requires an intelligent audience and most programming is based, according to many television writers, on ". . . the proposition, popularly held by networks and advertising executives, that most people who listen to radio or watch television are moronic." [61] Furthermore, serious drama is difficult to stage successfully in a 26-minute program with one or two breaks for commercials. Variety shows offer something for everybody and not much of anything for anybody. Quiz shows provide a brisk contest along with many tiny fragments of unrelated information. The forum or discussion show attracts a mass audience if it is a good fight, while a discussion which reaches agreement and conclusion is less exciting. The "confrontation" show offers the morbid a peek over the emotional transom of other people's lives. Although some educational and artistic values may occasionally emerge from this diet of entertainment, it is unrealistic to expect the sponsor to cater to minority tastes.

Commercial sponsorship *must* scale the program to mass tastes if the sponsor is to sell his product and earn dividends for his stockholders. Therefore several "rules," rarely violated, guide the sponsor in selecting program material. [62]

(1) It must suit mass tastes. When Ed Sullivan found that his ratings dropped when opera stars appeared on his program, off they went. [63]

(2) It must not leave the viewers sad or depressed. They must be left in a sugary glow, receptive to the commercial.

(3) It must not offend anyone. Sponsors are pathologically fearful that program annoyances will be transferred to the product. [64] Television writers have the frustrating task of writing interesting drama in a social vacuum—drama which touches on no controversy, involves no interest or pressure group, and entails no social criticism. [65]

(4) It must not be *too* absorbing. Surveys found that viewers of mediocre shows remembered the commercials better than viewers of top-rated shows. [66] Shows rated most highly by critics, such as Playhouse 90 (praised for originality, imagination, artistic effort), generally have sponsor trouble. [67]

[61] Goodman Ace, quoted by Melvin Maddocks, in *Christian Science Monitor,* October 18, 1958, p. 2.

[62] See Jack Gould, "Control By Advertisers," *New York Times,* July 12, 1959, II, p. 11.

[63] *Chicago Sun-Times,* March 1, 1957, p. 50; Also E. Coleman, "Trial By Trendex: Ed Sullivan," *Theatre Arts,* Vol. 41 (May, 1957), pp. 78 ff.

[64] See Ray Kammerman, "The Scared Comedians: No Laughing Matter for Public Relations," *Public Relations Journal,* Vol. 13 (September, 1957), pp. 4 ff; Richard A. Smith, "TV: The Light That Failed," *Fortune,* Vol. 58 (December, 1958), pp. 78 ff.

[65] Rod Sterling, noted TV writer, says, "I love TV, but writing is mostly just discouragement. Sponsor taboos are still the big bugaboo." (*Time,* Vol. 68 [October 22, 1956], p. 87.

[66] Vance Packard, *The Hidden Persuaders* (New York, David McKay Co., Inc., 1957), p. 155.

[67] Jack Gould, "Uphill Fight," *New York Times,* January 18, 1959, II, p. 15.

(5) The *preceding* program must also suit mass tastes. Over half the viewers carry over from the preceding program, so it, too, must aim at mass tastes. The Voice of Firestone, a sponsored program of classical music, was dropped in 1959 after thirty years on radio and television, because no network wanted a "weak" program in its lineup during prime evening hours. So ABC dropped it and added Elvis Presley. [68] Thus, the occasional sponsor who wishes to broadcast to the minority audience may even be prevented from doing so.

These limitations are inherent in the system of commercial sponsorship. The result is to penalize artistic creativity and social relevance and to reward mediocrity, monotonous sameness, and triviality. One critic remarks that ". . . the television medium operates in a uniquely protective barrel: no one has yet seen the bottom." [69] If this be true, the blame—or praise, according to one's tastes—rests not with the sponsor for acting as sponsors must, but with the system wherein commercial sponsors determine program content.

A further explanation for the allegedly poor quality of much movie, radio, and television drama lies in their fantastic appetite for story material. The movie studios, with a combined production of perhaps three-hundred-hours showing time a year, have real difficulty finding enough suitable story material. Jerry Wald, production director at Columbia, is quoted as saying, "If you get six decent books in one year, it's a miracle. . . . We'd make a hundred more pictures this year if we could find the stories." [70] The radio and television studios, with the four major networks programming about five hundred hours a *week*, have an even greater problem. The entire content of a quality magazine that appears once a month would not run a television studio for a single evening. All the Pulitzer Prize novels and plays ever written would not fill the broadcast schedules for more than a few days. A vaudeville routine, once usable for several seasons, is now gone in a few minutes. The insatiable appetite of modern media makes it inevitable that *as long as the emphasis is on newness and entertainment of the mass audience*, the average quality of output will be mediocre.

MEDIA CONTENT—HARMLESS OR VICIOUS? The second criticism—*that much of the content is actively harmful*—is easy to hurl but difficult to test. The newspapers are accused of glamorizing crime and cultivating a preoccupation with sex through their lurid reporting. The movies, since their first appearance, have flickered in the baleful glare of those who distrusted their influence. Many studies, particularly the Payne Fund Studies, established that the movies had great influence on people, without clearly establishing whether that influence was "good" or "bad." As each new medium spreads, critical attention shifts to it, and at present television and comic books are the major culprits. Child interest in comic books ap-

[68] *New York Times*, April 19, 1959, II, p. 11; *Time*, Vol. 73 (May 18, 1959), p. 48.
[69] Jack Gould, in *New York Times Magazine*, September 28, 1958, p. 65.
[70] *New York Times Magazine*, June 20, 1954, p. 43.

pears to reach its peak at eight or nine years, declining slowly thereafter, but still outranking all other magazine reading at junior-high-school level and comprising about one-fourth of total magazine reading at senior-high-school level. Research findings on the effects of comics upon children vary widely. One group claims that comics fill genuine child needs for fantasy, adventure, and identification with heroes, and do no particular damage to children. Heisler compared excessive comic-book readers with nonreaders, finding no significant differences in mental age, educational achievement, socioeconomic status, or social and personal adjustment. [71] Witty finds little difference in the amount or kinds of general reading by those who read comic books extensively and those who seldom read them. [72] After reviewing numerous studies, DeBoer concludes that "good books and magazines can compete successfully with comic magazines when children and youth have easy access to a great variety of reading materials." [73]

But other experts view comic books as highly injurious. Wolf and Fiske, after dividing comic book readers into "fans" and "moderate readers," find that very few fans are normal children, while "a marked correlation is revealed between neuroticism and being a fan." They feel that comics not only attract neurotics, but actually *produce* neuroticism, saying, [74]

That the fan does indeed become a neurotic, i.e., that the habit and characteristics of comic reading gradually engulf his life and affect his entire behavior pattern, is empirically verifiable from the children's responses to interview questions. The fan is seen (1) to be interested only in the general aura of the story, as manifested by its triumphant conclusion; (2) to deliberately lift comic reading to a position superior to that of other activities, including eating; and (3) to extend to other activities the habits of thought characteristic of comic reading.

The well-known psychiatrist, Dr. Frederic Wertham, has been the most persistent and uncompromising critic of comic books, considering them highly injurious even to normal children, because of their continuous glorification of violence, crime, and sadism. [75] The consensus of recent research and opinion seems to be swinging to the belief that comic books are harmful, but there is no clear agreement upon a solution. Parental ob-

[71] Florence Heisler, "A Comparison of Comic Book and Non-Comic Book Readers of the Elementary School," *Journal of Educational Research*, 40 (February, 1947), pp. 458-461.

[72] National Conference on Research in English, *Education and the Mass Media of Communication* (Chicago, National Council of Teachers of English, 1950), p. 20.

[73] *Ibid.*, p. 22.

[74] Katherine M. Wolf and Marjorie Fiske, "The Children Talk about Comics," in Paul F. Lazarsfeld and Frank M. Stanton, *op. cit.*, p. 29.

[75] Frederic Wertham, "What Parents Don't Know About Comic Books," *Ladies' Home Journal*, Vol. 70 (November, 1953), pp. 50 ff; *Seduction of the Innocent* (New York, Rinehart & Company, Inc., 1954); *The Circle of Guilt* (New York, Rinehart & Company, Inc., 1956); *New York Times*, September 2, 1957, p. 27.

jections are generally evaded by the children, [76] industry self-regulation has thus far proved ineffective, [77] and any legal ban or censorship raises a number of other objections.

In the sale of violence, television is a brisk competitor. A one-week monitoring survey in New York counted 221 killings and 192 attempted killings. [78] A one-week survey in Los Angeles, covering the hours before 9:00 P. M., counted 161 murders (up 500 per cent in five years), 192 attempted murders, 60 "justifiable" homicides, 83 robberies, 15 kidnappings, 24 conspiracies to commit murder, 21 jail breaks, and various other criminal acts. [79] During the early days of television, when broadcast time was cheap and the industry was seeking acceptance, many highly regarded children's programs were developed. As the industry became established and time became salable at good prices, children's programs waned; children's drama, for example, dropped in New York from 30.4 per cent of total television time in 1951 to 6.7 per cent in 1953, and virtually to zero by 1959. [80] Even a high audience rating does not save a children's program, since children are not a very profitable market. [81]

How does all this violence affect children? Wertham is certain that they are greatly harmed; [82] others argue the matter. [83] A very careful British study concludes that television does not change children very much, while giving them a more interesting life; [84] but it must be noted that British television is far less gory than ours. Bogart reviews many studies and concludes that television violence may have a "trigger" effect on disturbed children but probably does not create antisocial impulses or damage normal children. [85]

LIMITED CHOICE—THE TRIUMPH OF MONOTONY. A third criticism is the charge that the media—mainly radio and television—fail to offer the public that wide range of choice which is supposed to be a special virtue of free enterprise. Each sponsor, with occasional exceptions, tries to draw the same mass audience and to keep it from switching stations; therefore each sponsor tends to offer at a particular hour a program of the same

[76] Katherine M. Wolf and Marjorie Fiske, *op. cit.*, pp. 37 ff.

[77] See "Reform of Comic Books Is Spurred by Hearings," *New York Times*, June 13, 1954, IV, p. 6.

[78] Richard A. Smith, *op. cit.*

[79] "TV: Dial Anything For Murder," *Newsweek*, October 13, 1958, p. 65.

[80] Diane Shipler, "Murder for Moppets," *The Progressive*, Vol. 18 (March, 1953), pp. 28-29; also, "NAEB Seminar on Children's Television Programs," *Saturday Review*, Vol. 42 (February 28, 1959), p. 26.

[81] *Time*, Vol. 73 (May 18, 1959), p. 48.

[82] See footnote 75.

[83] See "Case of Television vs. the Children: Symposium," *National Parent Teacher*, Vol. 52 (November, 1957), pp. 4-7, 34 ff; Paul Witty, "TV And Today's Children," *Today's Health*, Vol. 35 (November, 1957), pp. 20 ff; "NAEB Seminar on Children's Television Programs," *op. cit.*

[84] Hilde T. Himmelweit, A. N. Oppenheim, and Paula Vince, *Television and the Child* (New York, Oxford University Press, Inc., 1958).

[85] Leo Bogart, *op. cit.*, pp. 273-289.

type as scheduled on competing stations. This means that at a particular hour, the listener may have very little choice as to *type* of program.

The minority audience is neglected most of the time. There are a number of small minority audiences whose tastes may run to classical music, to pure jazz, to literary readings, to book reviews, to leisurely dramatizations of the classics, and so on. For these people, the broadcast industry offers very little. On Sunday afternoon, the "intellectual" may watch television; presumably, he is reading books the rest of the week.

In theory, radio stations are expected to offer something for everyone by carrying sustaining (nonsponsored) programs during some good listening hours, since sponsors obviously cannot afford to cater to minority tastes. In this way program balance can be achieved. [86] In practice, much of the industry has failed to do this. Although the networks and some individual stations have developed some sustaining programs of high quality and great popularity, these programs have rarely been offered during good listening hours, have often been shifted around whenever a sponsor wanted the hour involved, or unaccountably dropped. Network sustaining programs are often not carried by local stations. [87] Fewer than half the local CBS stations carried Khrushchev's first American television appearance. [88] It would appear that sustaining programs are used mainly to fill in any leftover time which no sponsor wants at that moment.

Attempts to secure a more balanced offering runs into a fundamental obstacle—sustaining programs are not profitable. In applying for a license or a license renewal, the applicant must state how he will divide his broadcast time, achieve program balance, and serve the public interest. [89] Once the license is granted, these promises are almost universally disregarded, and one FCC commissioner recently suggested that the FCC should cease asking that licensees make any promises. [90] The FCC remarks,[91]

> The most immediately profitable way to run a station, may be to procure a network affiliation, plug into the network line in the morning, and broadcast network programs throughout the day—interrupting the network only to insert commercial spot announcements, and to substitute spot announcements and

[86] The FCC states, "The sustaining program is the balance wheel by means of which the imbalance of a station's or network's program structure, which might otherwise result from commercial [sponsor's] decisions concerning program structure, might be redressed. . . . Stations have been asked on renewal, to set forth the average amount of time, or percentage of time, devoted to entertainment programs, agricultural programs, religious programs, educational programs, fraternal programs, etc.; and the Commission has from time to time relied upon the data thus set forth in determining whether a station has maintained a well-balanced program structure." Federal Communications Commission, *op. cit.,* p. 13.

[87] See Federal Communications Commission, *op. cit.,* pp. 12-32.

[88] Richard P. Goldman, "The Good TV Shows That Don't Get Seen," *The Reporter,* Vol. 18 (June 12, 1958), p. 31.

[89] Federal Communications Commission, *op. cit.,* pp. 3-9.

[90] *New York Times,* January 30, 1958, II, p. 13.

[91] Federal Communications Commission, *op. cit.,* p. 39.

phonograph records for outstanding network programs. . . . Some stations are approaching perilously close to this extreme.

Efforts of the FCC to secure greater diversity and balance in programming have been generally ineffective, and have been sharply denounced by the industry and by much of the press as a government attack upon freedom of speech and free enterprise. [92] The development of FM radio raised hopes of increased experimentation and variety of offerings, but most commercial FM stations are jointly owned and operated with AM stations and broadcast the same programs. The industry opposed and defeated the FCC's proposed requirement that two or more hours of FM broadcast time each day should broadcast programs different from their standard AM broadcast schedule. [93] FM radio has increased the number of commercial outlets without changing the general character of the programs, except for a few stations in the larger cities which specialize in classical music.

Dissatisfaction with the programs offered by commercial stations has resulted in several attitudes among the critical listeners. Some of them have gazed longingly at the British and Canadian Broadcasting Systems where there is a mixture of public and private enterprise. [94] Government broadcasting systems operate alongside private, commercial systems, with a far greater range of program choice offered to the audience. Minority audiences in America have turned to noncommercial stations wherever they are available. Serious music listeners in particular have turned to noncommercial FM radio and to phonograph records for classical music. Recent improvements in record making and reproducing have produced a spectacular growth in the record industry, with an equally spectacular expansion in the repertory of music available on records. Thus, the minority audiences have largely abandoned commercial radio.

There are, of course, conspicuous exceptions to the general program pattern. Some stations come closer to program balance than others. A number of commercial stations, such as WQXR and WFMT, located in large cities have frankly catered to the minority audience with highbrow fare. [95] New York City's publicly owned WNYC, two or three listener-sponsored and supported stations (WCFM, KPFA), [96] and over

[92] Llewellyn White, *op. cit.*, p. 84.

[93] Charles A. Siepman, *op. cit.*, pp. 244-247.

[94] See UNESCO, *World Communications* (New York, UNESCO, 1956), pp. 222-223, 99-100; Andrew Roth, "British TV: Low-Budget Highbrow," *The Nation*, Vol. 176 (March 26, 1953), pp. 297-299. In England, commercial television has been permitted only since 1954, and has captured the mass audience. While "commercials" are sold, commercial *sponsorship* is forbidden so that sponsors do not control program content. See *Time*, Vol. 72 (July 28, 1958), p. 45; John T. Suchy, "How Does Commercial Television Affect British Viewers?" *Journalism Quarterly*, Vol. 35 (Winter, 1958), pp. 65-71.

[95] *Time*, Vol. 70 (October 14, 1957), pp. 91-92.

[96] *Time*, Vol. 71 (February 24, 1958), p. 63.

one hundred stations operated by schools and colleges add considerable variety to the total radio programming available in certain areas.

No choice of content will please everybody. American radio and television aim to please the masses, but they alienate the intellectuals; British broadcasting has its Third Programme to delight the highbrows, [97] while commercial television entertains the masses. It would appear that only a variety of sources, catering to the full range of interests, will come close to pleasing everybody—and this is not easy to arrange.

4. —AND STILL OTHER PROBLEMS . . .

Still other aspects of mass communication arouse concern and debate. The *problem of censorship* has excited continuous debate for over four centuries. To some, censorship appears as a *solution* for the defects of the mass media, whereas to others, censorship is part of the *cause* of those defects and a hindrance to be overcome. [98] Government security classifications sometimes prevent disclosure of facts embarrassing to the political party in power. [99] Movie censorship makes it impossible to film some of the greatest works of literature, or to deal honestly with certain social issues. Various private groups have sought, by censorship, pressure, and intimidation, to prevent expression of any view of life and liberty which differs from their own. A widely circulated private black list, coupled with the timidity of movie makers and broadcast sponsors, barred from employment in movies and broadcasting practically anybody whom practically anybody has ever called communist. [100] The story of Robin Hood is branded as subversive by a member of a state textbook commission, and in a state library, John Bunyon's *Pilgrim's Progress*, Jules Verne's *20,000 Leagues Under the Sea*, and Hans Christian Andersen's fairy tales are reserved for "adults only." [101] In Alabama a children's book is banned from the library shelves when someone notices that the author carelessly allowed the little black rabbit to marry the little white rabbit. [102] These and many other incidents ranging from the serious to the absurd are evidence of the concern over censorship.

[97] John Morris, "Britain's Case For Egghead Radio," *New York Times Magazine*, December 9, 1956, pp. 19 ff.

[98] R. V. A. Lee, "Censorship: A Case History, Martin Luther," *Christian Century*, Vol. 74 (February 6, 1957), pp. 163-165; G. Seldes, "Climate of Fear," *Saturday Review*, Vol. 40 (October 26, 1957), p. 28; Reply, Robert Moses, *Saturday Review*, Vol. 40 (November 30, 1957), p. 21; "TV Censorship on the Rise," *America*, Vol. 100 (March 14, 1959), p. 676.

[99] Kent Cooper, *The Right to Know*, (New York, Farrar, Straus & Cudahy, Inc., 1956).

[100] John Cogley, *Report on Blacklisting*: Vol. I, *Movies*; Vol. II, *Radio and Television* (New York, Fund For The Republic, 1956).

[101] *New York Times*, November 14, 1953, p. 1; *Time*, Vol. 63 (February 15, 1954), p. 66.

[102] "Of Rabbits and Races," *Time*, Vol. 73 (June 1, 1959), p. 19.

The effects of mass communication upon modern man have become a fashionable new anxiety. [103] Some fear that modern man is being turned into a puppet, manipulated by words and slogans instead of wires. It is widely assumed that man is nonrational and nonlogical, guided by all sorts of hidden fears, longings, and impulses, which "motivation research" seeks to identify so that they can be exploited by advertisers. [104] Some experiments with subliminal advertising, where the ad is flashed on the screen so briefly that the viewer is unaware of having seen it, have aroused considerable anxiety, even though it is not certain whether subliminal advertising is effective. [105] Wiretapping and other means of electronic eavesdropping now make it possible to strip one of his privacy from his office to his boudoir. [106] In political campaigns, candidates are "merchandised" like laundry soap. [107] The head of one public relations firm, after seventy successful campaigns, remarked that he "could have won almost every one of them . . ." for the other side, had they been his clients. [108] Are political campaigns becoming simply a contest to see who has the most money and the best publicity agents, or are the mass media merely revealing more candidly the strengths and weaknesses of our political system? [109] In George Orwell's chilling novel, *1984*, he visualizes a society in which the mass media, monopolized and censored by a totalitarian party, strip the people of all privacy and independence and transform them into automatons conditioned mechanically to accept and enjoy their servitude. Is this the ultimate destiny of our inventiveness? Probably not; yet there are those who wonder.

THE SOCIAL-DISORGANIZATION APPROACH

Without the technological revolution in communication, the social problems concerning communication would be few and simple. As long as books were few and expensive, and owned only by the wealthy, their rulers saw little need for censorship. When printing made books and

[103] William H. Whyte, Jr., "Groupthink," *Fortune*, Vol. 45 (March, 1952), pp. 114 ff.

[104] Vance Packard, *op. cit.;* Pierre Partineau, *Motivation in Advertising: Motives that Make People Buy* (New York, McGraw-Hill Book Co., 1957).

[105] Guy Talese, "Most Hidden, Hidden Persuaders," *New York Times Magazine*, January 12, 1958, pp. 22 ff.; "Secret Commercial," *Time*, 70 (July 1, 1957), p. 65.

[106] Bernard B. Spindle, "Who Else is Listening?" *Colliers*, June 10, 1955, p. 25 ff.; Samuel Dash, *The Eavesdroppers* (New Brunswick, N. J., Rutgers University Press, 1959).

[107] William Lee Miller, "Can Government be Merchandised?" *The Reporter*, Vol. 9 (October 27, 1953), pp. 11-16.

[108] Irwin Ross, "The Supersalesmen of California Politics: Whitaker and Baxter," *Harper's Magazine*, Vol. 219 (July, 1959), pp. 54-61; "The Partners," *Time*, Vol. 66 (December 26, 1955), pp. 11-12.

[109] See Charles A. H. Thomson, *Television, Politics, and Public Policy* (New York, The Brookings Institution, 1958).

handbills so cheap that they could be widely circulated among the common people who had less of a "stake" in the status quo, rulers began to fear books and demand censorship of printed matter. When newspaper publishing was small-scale, minority views could quite easily find expression; when the publisher must necessarily be a wealthy man, conflicting views reach a wide audience only by his grace. When the primary means of communication was face-to-face conversation, and the town meeting or country store was the main forum, freedom of speech was secure if the government kept hands off. Today, the press, radio, and television have become the main public forum, and effective freedom of speech—the chance for all groups to share in a discussion of all vital issues—is neither greater nor less than their controllers decree. Under these conditions, *the protection of freedom of speech sometimes requires the intervention, rather than the abstention, of government.* Yet each governmental attempt to protest this freedom actively—an antitrust suit to keep a newspaper from throttling a competitor, [110] a senatorial proposal to reserve part of the radio frequencies for noncommercial stations, [111] or an FCC effort to require FM stations to broadcast some original material [112]—is denounced by the industry as an attack upon freedom. A widespread confusion as to what freedom of speech means and how it functions lies at the root of many current controversies.

This technological revolution is not ended. Television is still in its childhood, the facsimile newspaper is in prospect, and still other inventions affecting freedom of speech will be developed. And certain it is that each will bring new problems in the continuous process of adjusting the mass media to the needs of a changing society.

THE VALUE-CONFLICT APPROACH

The value conflicts of society are the cause of the arguments over the mass media. Each group wishes to use the media to propagandize its own values, and often seeks to deny use of the media to its opponents. Liberals wish the media to give more discussion to social problems and social reforms: conservatives wish the media to support the status quo. Highbrows deplore the taste of the masses, while the masses snort at the highbrows. The persistent concern over obscenity in literature is largely a representation of middle-class disapproval of lower-class tolerances. As long as values differ so widely, as they must in a changing, highly differentiated society, it is difficult to please everybody.

Perhaps the most fundamental value clash concerns the basic question, What are the media for? Should the mass media be primarily (*a*) a profit-

[110] See "Unfair Competition," *Time*, Vol. 59 (June 9, 1952), pp. 64-67.
[111] Llewellyn White, *op. cit.*, pp. 155-156.
[112] Charles A. Siepman, *op. cit.*, pp. 244-247.

making business enterprise, (*b*) a means of entertainment, or (*c*) an instrument of mass improvement? Although these objectives are not entirely incompatible, the choice of any one of them definitely limits the others. Owners generally favor the first, the masses prefer the second, while educators and highbrows usually choose the third. Underneath most arguments and criticisms of the media are such basic value judgments as these.

THE PERSONAL-DEVIATION APPROACH

This approach contributes relatively little to an understanding of communication problems. There are deviant persons who are somewhat of a nuisance—those who write crank letters to the editor, and who pester radio stations with complaints and demands—but they are no serious problem. At times a deviant person may secure leadership of a respectable local or national organization—a veterans' organization, labor union, chamber of commerce, a DAR chapter—and use the power of this position in an effort to intimidate the media into airing only his own neurotic viewpoints; but such persons cannot be effective for long unless they also express the character and viewpoint of the members of the organization. Occasionally, a deviant person will secure control of a newspaper or radio station and seek to use it to promote his intemperate views. In radio, such behavior may soon get him into trouble with the FCC.[113] In the newspaper world, the neuroticism of an owner, or of a columnist, probably accounts for some of the most notorious abuses of press responsibility.

But even if all editors, writers, newscasters, and private citizens were perfectly adjusted personalities, communications problems would remain very much the same. Social change always disorganizes, and values differ even among well-adjusted persons. Deviant persons may complicate communications problems, but they do not cause them.

IMPROVING THE MASS MEDIA

Although the owners and operators of the mass media have generally argued that they should be permitted to run their own affairs like any other business enterprise, some critics contend that the mass media owe a special obligation to the public, differing from the obligations of other business enterprises. For *the private citizen is forced by circumstance to support the mass media, whether or not he wishes to do so.* Of each dollar he spends, a few cents go for advertising, which provides two-thirds of the income of magazines and newspapers and nearly all of the income of radio and television. As a taxpayer, he shoulders the expense of carrying

[113] Charles A. Siepman, *Radio, Television, and Society* (New York, Oxford University Press, Inc., 1950), p. 234.

newspapers and magazines through the mails at less than cost, giving the publisher an indirect subsidy which, for a very large publisher, runs into several million dollars a year. Each radio and television station is a partial monopoly; since the air waves are limited, the FCC, in granting a limited number of licenses, also protects each station from having unlimited competition. As a result, the radio industry has enjoyed monopoly profits. In 1939, the net profit rate of the entire radio broadcasting industry averaged 125 per cent on depreciated investment; in 1944, this had risen to 315 per cent, but by 1958 was only 23 per cent, while in 1958 the Television broadcast industry earned 51 per cent on its depreciated investment. [114] Such profit rates, far higher than those earned by competitive businesses, are possible only because the public grants to a limited number of operators the free use of the air waves. Meanwhile, the public's investment in receiving sets is over 30-times as great as the industry's investment in broadcasting stations, and the public spends far more in operating these receivers than the industry spends in operating the broadcasting studios and transmitters. Far from receiving the products of modern communication free, the public pays the entire cost in one way or another, often in ways over which they have no individual control. In citing these facts, *it is not necessarily implied that this situation is "bad."* It may be (and probably is) in the public interest to subsidize the media in various ways, for the public's subsidies to the press, and the gift of the air waves which have earned such handsome profits for radio, have greatly aided in their development and expansion. Furthermore, they lay the basis for viewing communications as a *public utility*, answerable to the public for their standards of performance.

Criticism of the communications media, especially of the broadcasting industry, reached a new peak in 1959-1960 with the revelation that "rigged" quiz shows, "payola" and "plugola," and "cheat-shot" commercials had become a common industry practice. One noted columnist called this ". . . an enormous conspiracy to deceive the public . . . (making television) the creature, the servant, and indeed the prostitute of merchandising." [115] Not all were angered; for example, nearly half of a large sample of high school students saw nothing wrong in payola. [116] Others professed to see the practice, and toleration, of such deceptions as alarming evidence of the moral weakness of modern society. Many proposals for improvement have been offered, most of them falling into the categories which follow.

---

[114] Federal Communications Commission, *op. cit.*, p. 50; Federal Communications Commission, *25th Annual Report for Fiscal Year 1959* (Washington, Government Printing Office, 1959), pp. 76-79.
[115] Walter Lippman, *Syndicated newspaper column*, October 29, 1959.
[116] *New York Times*, February 21, 1960, p. 54.

1. Antimonopoly Action

Practically every set of proposals includes measures designed to preserve and increase competition or infuse new blood into the media. Specific proposals include: vigorous application and prosecution of the antitrust laws, [117] government encouragement to new ventures in communications, sponsorship of new ventures by philanthropic foundations, encouragement to noncommercial radio and television stations, control of radio program content by stations rather than advertisers, [118] and many others.

To find the most widely acceptable balance between the efficiency of large-scale operation and the presumed benefits of competition is not easy. Any decision involves a value judgment, and rearranges an array of vested interests. At present, the trend towards concentration of control appears to be continuing with the consent of the FCC. [119] Whether it is either desirable or politically possible to reverse it is a moot question.

2. Censorship

Almost every important book ever written, from the *Holy Bible* to *Lady Chatterley's Lover*, has been banned at some time or place. [120] Present proposals and attempts at censorship and various forms of pressure and intimidation are too numerous to catalog. Wertham wants to prohibit

[117] Emanuel Celler, "Antitrust Problems in the Television Broadcasting Industry," *Law and Contemporary Problems*, Vol. 22 (Autumn, 1957), pp. 549-571; Victor R. Hansen, "Broadcasting and the Antitrust Laws," *Law and Contemporary Problems*, Vol. 22 (Autumn, 1957), pp. 572-583; Roscoe L. Barrow, "Network Broadcasting— The Report of the FCC Study Committee," *Law and Contemporary Problems*, Vol. 22 (Autumn, 1957), pp. 611-625; Bernard Schwartz, "Antitrust and the FCC," *University of Pennsylvania Law Review*, Vol. 107 (April, 1959), pp. 753-795.

[118] See Edward R. Murrow, "A Broadcaster Talks To His Colleagues," *The Reporter*, Vol. 19 (November 13, 1958), pp. 32-36.

[119] All government regulatory agencies established to protect the public interest tend in time to become so imbued with the industry point of view that, eventually, they regulate the industry in the industry's interest, not in the public interest. At the time of writing (1959), the FCC illustrates this transition. It has made no serious effort to enforce program balance, but has renewed licenses regardless of station performance. (See Roger Kennedy, *op. cit.*) In 1954 it increased the number of stations a single owner might own, and its recent chairman publically stated that "Concentration does not frighten me. . . ." (See Bernard Schwartz, *op. cit.*) It failed to carry out the antimonopoly recommendations of its own study committee. (See Roscoe L. Barrow, *op. cit.*) Its powers to protect the public interest are unused, while concentration and program unbalance increase without FCC protest. See also, "Economic Injury in FCC Licensing: The Public Interest Ignored," *Yale Law Journal*, Vol. 67 (November, 1957), pp. 135-150; Anthony Lewis, "FCC Prestige at Record Low," *New York Times*, November 16, 1958, IV, p. 8; "Recommendations of House Interstate and Foreign Commerce Subcommittee on Special Legislative Oversight," *Congressional Quarterly*, Vol. 17 (January 9, 1959), p. 49.

[120] Anne Lyon Haight, *Banned Books* (New York, R. R. Bowker Co., 1955).

the sale of comic books to children under fifteen, [121] and Mannes suggests that "the shot and the knockout" be prohibited on television shows for children. [122] Several private organizations are busily branding those textbooks which they consider unfit for student consumption. Several states and a number of cities have legal censorship boards which must approve of any motion picture before public showing. In a number of cities, more or less official boards inspect the newsstands for obscene material. Sometimes the censorship efforts are directed at the author or producer rather than at the content. Two states now have laws requiring that for each text in use, the publisher must supply anti-Communist oaths from the authors and all others quoted therein. The Postmaster-General, from time to time, bans from the United States mails any books or magazines he thinks are obscene, and is frequently overruled by the courts. [123] The editor of the influential *Christian Herald* has called for "a new crusade" against obscenity. [124] Such examples could be added indefinitely. Dozens of state bills and hundreds of local ordinance proposals for censorship are offered each year and arouse bitter controversy. A California survey finds nearly one-third of the school librarians reporting that they habitually avoid "controversial" material when making new purchases. [125] The American Library Association and the American Book Publishers Council have expressed alarm, feeling that our basic freedom to read is in danger. [126]

Censorship has several fundamental limitations. (1) It is purely negative. Although it may eliminate "bad" content, it cannot produce "good" content. To censor obscenity does not produce noble drama; instead, it is more likely to produce a studious playing at the fringes of the obscenity code. (2) There may be a boomerang effect. Nothing stimulates the sale of a book like being banned in Boston. A considerable number of third-rate books and shows have been rescued from commercial oblivion by the censors. [127] To be fully effective, censorship must be imposed *before* publication or production. (3) To define unsuitable content is difficult. Sheer nudity is less provocative than gossamer covering. There has *never yet been a satisfactory definition of obscenity*, for every possible definition involves a subjective judgment, and eventually becomes, "If I think it's obscene, then it's obscene." [128] Innocent dialogue may become obscene

---

[121] Frederic Wertham, *op. cit.*

[122] Myra Mannes, *op. cit.*

[123] Alvin Shuster, ". . . Nor Gloom of Censorship," *New York Times Magazine*, August 2, 1959, pp. 11 ff.; James C. N. Paul and Murray L. Schwartz, *Federal Censorship* (Glencoe, Ill., The Free Press, 1959).

[124] *New York Times*, July 26, 1959, p. 47.

[125] Marjorie Fiske, *Book Selection and Censorship* (Berkeley, University of California Press, 1959).

[126] "The Freedom to Read," *Time*, Vol. 62 (July 6, 1953), pp. 62-64.

[127] See Dick Meister, "How 'Howl' Became a Best Seller," *The Progressive*, Vol. 22 (February, 1958), pp. 36-37.

[128] See Norman St. John-Stevas, *Obscenity and The Law* (London, Secker & Warburg, 1956).

through gesture or inflection. [129] Obscenity codes may produce a sophisticated sort of sexual innuendo which makes people even more sex-conscious than would frank sexuality. To define obscenity so as to prevent the cheap exploitation of sex without also preventing literary realism and artistic integrity seems to be impossible. To define subversion so as to prevent the deliberate undermining of the social system yet permit mature social criticism is still more impossible. In fact, many attempts to censor subversion are basically attempts to prevent the expression of any social criticism. (4) It is hard to place limits upon censorship. The power to censor indecency also includes the power to censor *ideas* personally offensive to the censors—and sooner or later, this usually happens. For these reasons, scholars and intellectuals seem generally to feel that censorship represents a treatment more dangerous than the disease. [130]

Supporters of censorship and antismut campaigns *assume* that bad literature promotes bad behavior. Is this assumption correct? There have been no satisfactory studies of the relation between the reading or viewing of obscene material and unacceptable behavior, with the result that *nobody really knows* what effects obscene literature has upon people. There are many *opinions,* including that of a noted psychiatrist who claims that ". . . people who read salacious literature are less likely to become sexual offenders than those who do not, for the reason that such reading often neutralizes sexual interests they may have." [131] None of the scientific studies of crime, delinquency, or sexual deviation has pointed out reading or viewing material as a factor in their development. [132] In one study, asking a co-ed sample what stimuli aroused them sexually, they reported that reading material and pictures were unimportant, while the main stimulus was "Man"—who, though he may deserve censure, is unlikely to be suppressed. [133]

[129] Stan Freberg's recording, *John and Marsha,* contained only the two words, "John," and "Marsha," repeated over and over with various inflections and hesitations. It was banned from the airwaves as too suggestive. See Daniel Dixon, "Laughing at Madison Avenue for Fun and Profit," *Esquire,* Vol. 51 (February, 1959), pp. 55 ff.

[130] See Richard McKeon, Robert K. Merton, and Walter Gellhorn, *The Freedom to Read* (Published for National Book Committee by R. R. Bowker Company, New York, 1957).

[131] Benjamin Karpman, quoted in *Censorship Bulletin* (New York, American Book Publisher's Council, Inc.,) August, 1958, p. 3; See also Marie Jahoda, *The Impact of Literature: A Psychological Discussion of Some Assumptions in the Censorship Debate* (New York, Research Center for Human Relations, New York University, 1954); Eberhard and Phyllis Kronhausen, *Pornography and The Law* (New York, Ballantine Books, 1959), especially pp. 261-289, "The Psychological Effects of Erotic Literature," in which they state, ". . . it is our view that instead of the comics, 'lewd' magazines, or even hard core pornography causing sex murders and other criminal acts, it is far more likely that these 'unholy' instruments may be more often than not a *safety valve* for the sexual deviate and potential sex offender." (pp. 273-274).

[132] See Frederick M. Thrasher, "Do Comic Books Promote Juvenile Delinquency?" *Congressional Digest,* Vol. 33 (December, 1954), pp. 303 ff.

[133] See *Censorship Bulletin. op. cit.*

Until carefully controlled scientific research has established the effects of salacious literature upon people, the informed citizen will consider all such censorship proposals as premature. Meanwhile, practical people who would not switch brands of toothpaste without "scientific evidence" will call for sweeping censorship programs without any *knowledge* of whether they are useful or of what they should prohibit.

3. Development of Noncommercial Media

Although very few people in America oppose private ownership and commercial development of mass media, there are many who favor supplementing this system with some noncommercial facilities. It has been suggested that philanthropic foundations, educational institutions, local governments, labor organizations, co-operatives, farmer organizations, and other groups might engage in the operation of mass media, thereby reducing concentration of control and increasing the variety of choices and opinions. Support for noncommercial radio and television stations is particularly widespread.

The history of educational AM radio is not encouraging. Of over two hundred licenses for educational stations granted since 1921, only thirty-four remained in operation in 1950. Some languished for lack of faculty interest; some died for lack of financial support; some were crowded out when commercial applicants wanted their frequencies. [134] Many commercial stations offered time to schools and colleges for educational broadcasts; often this time was not used, either because the schools lacked funds or interest, because good listening hours were not offered, or because the irregularity and uncertainty of the time offered prevented orderly programing and audience-building.

The appearance of FM radio and the perfection of tape recording opened new opportunities for educational radio, and by 1959 there were 154 educational FM stations in operation. Local broadcasts are supplemented by a wide variety of tape recordings interchanged through the National Association of Educational Broadcasters, which also distributes many tape recordings of British Broadcasting Corporation programs. The programs are, for the most part, not *educational* programs, but are programs for educated people—classical music, discussion, drama, literature, and so on.

The FCC has reserved 257 television channels for educational stations. By 1959 there were forty-three stations on the air, an increase of fifteen since 1958, with a number of additional stations in various stages of completion. Over a hundred colleges and universities were producing television programs, using both commercial and educational stations, and over

[134] Llewellyn White, *op. cit.*, pp. 103-109.

four hundred different college credit courses were being offered. [135] One university is televising a complete freshman program, with students appearing on campus for consultation and examination. [136] Programs of widespread interest are kinescoped and distributed nationally through the Educational Television and Radio Center at Ann Arbor, Michigan.

Many enthusiasts predict a glowing future for educational television, [137] while some even suggest that it may relieve the teacher shortage. [138] One proposal calls for a National Educational Television Authority to assist states in setting up a national educational television network to conduct college credit courses. [139] While such ideas are intriguing, past experience would suggest that educational television will be used mainly to enrich the educational experience rather than to replace the classroom teacher.

A number of people, including the noted columnist, Walter Lippmann, have suggested that commercial broadcasting be supplemented by a nationwide, noncommercial network, operated as a public service, and subsidized and endowed like a university. [140] This would give us a mixed broadcasting system somewhat like those in Canada and England. While appealing to highbrows, this seems unlikely to be attempted.

Meanwhile, a number of noncommercial outlets greatly increase the variety of total broadcast offerings in some localities without greatly impairing the commercial broadcast industry's freedom of action or opportunities for profit. In the movie industry, noncommercial films are largely limited to classroom educational films, or to the propaganda films of vested interest groups. In the press, the labor press offers a forum to a group which feels itself mistreated by the commercial press, while a small liberal press opposes the bias of the commercial press with a bias of its own, receives little advertising revenue, loses money steadily, and survives only through voluntary contributions of its supporters. All in all, the media gain some variety and diversity through the existence of some noncommercial and semicommercial facilities.

[135] Franklin Dunham, Ronald R. Loudermilk, and Gertrude G. Broderick, *Television in Education* (Office of Education, Bulletin 1957, No. 21 [Washington, Government Printing Office, 1957], pp. 8, 72).

[136] *Research Report*, No. 581 (Ann Arbor, University of Michigan Press, Educational Television and Radio Center, July 31, 1958), p. 4.

[137] John C. Adams, C. R. Carpenter, and Dorothy R. Frank, eds., *College Teaching by Television* (Washington, American Council on Education, 1958); Charles A. Siepman, "The Case For TV in Education," *New York Times Magazine*, June 2, 1957, pp. 13 ff; John L. Scanlon, "The Expanding Role of Television in Education," *Journal of Educational Sociology*, Vol. 32 (May, 1959), pp. 413-420.

[138] E. Stasheff and W. C. Varnum, "Can Television Help Solve the Teacher Shortage," *Senior Scholastic*, Vol. 74 (February 20, 1959), pp. 13T-14T.

[139] John E. Ivey, Jr., "Television, Educational Quality, and Dollars," *Educational Record*, Vol. 40 (January, 1959), pp. 53-61.

[140] Syndicated newspaper column, October 29, 1959.

4. Self-Regulation

Each set of proposals includes a suggestion that the members of each industry develop and follow a set of standards for the self-regulation of the industry. Self-regulation, with its accompanying codes of performance, can be an effective means of regulating a medium, or it can be a smoke screen to confuse and disarm critics. Often it is the latter. The most idealistic code of ethics is of little effect if compliance is voluntary; the comic-book industry, for instance, is accused of having one of the most highly praised and rarely followed codes in existence. [141] On the other hand, a self-regulation system with penalties and machinery for enforcement of the code upon violators is easily subject to abuse and is rarely popular within the industry. The only highly effective program of industry self-regulation has been in the motion-picture industry, which established the "Hays office" [142] to stem the rising tide of legal censorship. Its Production Code Administration (now headed by Goeffrey Shurlock) inspects scripts before filming and may recommend changes or disapprove the entire script. Lack of approval makes distribution of the completed film difficult, and practically all producers abide by the Administrations recommendations. This movie self-regulation has eliminated many offensive features and enabled the industry to avoid the further spread of legal censorship. Some censorship laws have remained in effect, however, and the Legion of Decency and other private groups keep the movies under careful scrutiny.

Experience seems to indicate that self-regulation is effective only when an industry feels the public breath hot upon its collective neck. Whether purely voluntary codes without machinery for enforcement accomplish anything is debatable. They may persuade an industry towards a greater sense of social responsibility, or they may retard this development by lending an implied sanction to certain dubious but widespread practices within the industry. The deceptive practices revealed in the recent TV "scandals" were no surprise to anyone within the broadcast industry, and only when public outcry arose did industry leaders show any concern. It may be unrealistic to expect that self-regulation will stop any practice which is profitable to the industry, or that it can elevate standards of performance above the level of bare public toleration.

[141] See "Reform of Comic Books Is Spurred by Hearings," *New York Times,* June 13, 1954, IV, p. 6.

[142] Officially the Motion Picture Association of America, which was first headed by prominent churchman and public official, Will H. Hays, Jr.

5. Other Proposals

a. More stringent regulation of broadcasting in the public interest is urged by those who charge that the FCC has neglected its duty. If the FCC would merely enforce its own rules and regulations, and hold broadcasters to their promises, better programs would result. [143] The FCC might also enforce some new rules, such as requiring every station to carry sustaining (nonsponsored) programs for a certain number of prime evening hours each week. [144] This is a simple, workable proposal with only one defect—it would reduce profits. And, as already pointed out, government regulatory bodies have a way of becoming servants of the industries they are supposed to regulate.

b. Pay-television, for which viewers would drop a coin in the slot for each pay-television program, is a hotly debated proposal whose effects are difficult to predict. [145] The broadcast industry is bitterly opposed to this method, and Congress and the FCC are at present unsympathetic to it.

c. A national broadcasting authority is proposed by one critic, to be financed by fees of 10 or 15 per cent of the annual income of local stations. [146] This authority would then produce top-quality public service programs which all networks and local commercial stations would be required to carry during desirable broadcast time. This proposal would face certain industry opposition, making its adoption unlikely.

d. New Legislation. Widespread deception and fraud was revealed in 1959 by the investigations of the House Committee on Legislative Oversight. This committee not only charged the FCC and the Federal Trade Commission with failure to use their powers to protect the public interest, [147] but called for a number of new laws which would: (1) make it a criminal offense to deceive viewers with deliberately fraudulent presentations; (2) forbid undercover payola and plugola payments; (3) grant licence renewals only after a hearing in which the station's performance "in the public interest" is evaluated; (4) permit *temporary* license suspensions as a penalty for failing to operate in the public interest (since

[143] Bernard Schwartz, "Antitrust and the FCC," *op. cit.;* Roger Kennedy, *op. cit.;* John Fisher, "TV and its Critics," *Harper's Magazine,* Vol. 219 (July, 1959), pp. 10-14; Jack Gould, "Forgotten Clues To The TV Crisis," *New York Times Magazine,* December 13, 1959, pp. 9ff; "Where, May We Ask, Was The FCC?", *Consumer Reports,* Vol. 25, (January, 1960), pp. 9-11.

[144] See *New York Times,* December 13, 1959, IV, p. 1.

[145] Dallas W. Smythe, "The Position of Pay-TV," *Illinois Business Review,* Vol. 14 (August, 1957), pp. 6-8; "Can TV Exist Half-Free?" *Sponsor,* Vol. 11 (November 2, 1957), pp. 37-39; "Debate on Pay-TV," *Business Horizons,* Vol. 1 (Summer, 1958), pp. 39-51.

[146] John Fisher, *op. cit.*

[147] "House Unit Asks Penalties to End Radio and TV Frauds," *New York Times,* February 7, 1960, p, 1.

a *permanent* licence revocation has proved to be so severe a penalty that it is never used). [148]

As this is written, none of these has yet been enacted into law. The effects of such law would hinge upon energetic action by the FCC, and would vary according to the changing membership and viewpoint of the commission.

SUMMARY

Changes in the technology and business organization of communication have revolutionized the interchange of ideas and the formation of the public opinion by which democracy operates. To many responsible critics, the performance of the media and the vitality of democracy are threatened (1) by tendencies toward monopoly and concentration of control of the media, (2) by their biases and occasional irresponsibility, (3) by the limited variety and low cultural level of content, (4) by threats of censorship, and (5) by other problems. Critics also feel that the public, due to its indirect investments in and subsidies to the media, has a legitimate right to a voice in shaping their policies. The numerous suggestions for improvement include: (1) action to reduce the degree of concentration of control, (2) censorship, (3) development of noncommercial facilities to supplement commercial media, (4) industry self-regulation, and (5) other proposals.

To maintain the opportunity for all groups to be heard on vital issues in a period of mechanized, large-scale communication will require a steadily expanding sense of social responsibility on the part of the owners of the media, a changing concept of the role of government in protecting freedom of expression, and an enlarged interest and activity on the part of the public.

This chapter may give to the student an unjustifiably critical impression of the over-all operation of our media of communication. Since it is only the alleged defects of the media that arouse discussion and concern, any presentation of communications problems will be mainly a recital of these criticisms. Yet, the critics of the media readily concede that they see much improvement. The press is greatly more accurate, impartial, and responsible than in earlier decades. Movies have become more artistically produced, and now offend the moral sensibilities of fewer people. Radio has admitted certain groups which it formerly barred, and noncommercial radio and television are helping to provide greater diversity than ever before. The mass media have helped to elevate the level of popular taste, so that by 1951 we were buying more admissions to symphonic concerts than to baseball games.

[148] "Recommendations of House Study Unit Into Broadcasting Practices," *New York Times*, February 7, 1960, p. 62.

There is a present tendency throughout the media to avoid controversial issues and curtail minority viewpoints. Whether this tendency continues will depend upon what happens to the general intellectual atmosphere of our society. If this atmosphere grows steadily more repressive and authoritarian—as it appears to have done in recent years—all discussions of press freedom will become purely academic. But if such curbs are avoided, there is reasonable prospect that the performance of the media will grow steadily more satisfactory to public and critics alike.

SUGGESTED READINGS

BOGART, Leo, *The Age of Television* (New York, Frederick Ungar Publishing Co., 1958). A comprehensive textbook on television and its role in society.

Commission on the Freedom of the Press, *A Free and Responsible Press* (Chicago, University of Chicago Press, 1947). An authoritative report on the performance of the press, with recommendations for improvement.

Federal Communications Commission, *Public Service Responsibility of Broadcast Licensees* (Washington, Government Printing Office, 1946). A statement of standards of public service for radio, with data on the industry's degree of fulfillment.

JACOBSON, David J., *The Affairs of Dame Rumor* (New York, Rinehart & Company, Inc., 1948). A popularly written, highly entertaining account of how rumors arise and are circulated.

MacDOUGALL, Curtis D., *Hoaxes* (New York, Dover Publications, Inc., 1958). An interesting collection of fakes and frauds in history, literature, journalism, and elsewhere.

McKEON, Richard, MERTON, Robert K., and GELLHORN, Walter, *The Freedom to Read* (New York, R. R. Bowker Co., 1957). An examination of the problem of censorship.

MURROW, Edward R., "A Broadcaster Talks to His Colleagues," *The Reporter*, Vol. 19 (November 13, 1958), pp. 32-36. A criticism and plea that the broadcast industry should develop higher standards of public service.

PACKARD, Vance, *The Hidden Persuaders* (New York, David McKay Co., Inc., 1957; Pocket Books, Inc., 1958). A severely critical examination of efforts at nonrational manipulation of people by advertisers and merchandisers.

SIEPMAN, Charles A., *Television and Our School Crisis* (Toronto, Dodd, Mead & Co., 1958). An enthusiastic appraisal of the possibilities of television in education.

AUDIO-VISUAL AIDS

Freedom to Read (Columbia University, Center for Mass Communications, New York), 14 minutes, sound, black and white. Dramatizes the issue of whether a library should remove controversial books from circulation.

Rumor (Columbia University, Center for Mass Communications, New York), 8 minutes, sound, black and white. A case history of a rumor, showing its origin, spread, and consequences. Poses the question of how to deal with rumors.

QUESTIONS AND PROJECTS

1. Why is modern society more dependent upon mass media than ever before?

2. Our founding fathers apparently felt that the only serious threat to freedom of speech and the press came from government. Is this view sound today?

3. Should newspapers suppress news which is "harmful" to the community? What further questions are raised by this issue?

4. Should the mass media give the public what it *wants* or what it *needs?* What are the difficulties in trying to give the public what it "needs"?

5. Why does the commercial broadcast industry make relatively little effort to cater to minority tastes? Why is it easier for noncommercial broadcasting to do so?

6. What explains the generally conservative bias of the mass media?

7. What are the advantages and disadvantages of mass media which have a generally conservative bias?

8. How does the avoidance of controversial issues result in bias? What kind of bias?

9. What would be the effects upon society if the mass media generally reflected a liberal bias?

10. Why has self-regulation been more effective for the movies than for the other media?

11. What is meant by the "least-common-denominator" approach to programming? What are its results?

12. Why is broadcasting the only medium which is subject to much government regulation? How effective is this regulation?

13. One critic remarks, "There is a Gresham's Law of television—'Bad programs drive good programs off the air.'" Do you agree?

14. Divide the class into small groups and let each group formulate a definition of *obscenity*, such as might be used in a local ordinance. Then subject each definition to class criticism.

16

The Personal Pathologies

Not long ago, a study showed that more people per 1000 . . . are receiving treatment for mental illness in Manhattan than in New Haven, Connecticut. The difference does not reflect a special predisposition to mental illness on the part of New Yorkers. . . . A major factor in the difference is the concentration of psychiatrists and psychiatric-treatment facilities in the big city. Psychiatrists and clinics in Manhattan treat patients from many communities, including a substantial number from New Haven! [1]

. . . there is little question that the number of alcoholics (by any definition) runs into millions; that annual fatalities in automobile accidents alone, where alcohol is involved, exceed our annual deaths in the Korean war; and that our jails and workhouses the country over exist primarily for the temporary restraint of those found guilty of drunkenness. [2]

People don't understand how slot machines can be illegal in Illinois while the Federal government collects a tax of $150 per year on each machine. The lawyer can explain the difference between the gambling laws of Illinois and the revenue laws of the United States. The average citizen, however, naturally assumes that when a machine has been properly registered with the Collector of Internal Revenue and the tax has been paid, the owner is entitled to use it. The owner is indignant when gambling devices on which he has paid the Federal tax are confiscated and destroyed under state law. [3]

About a year ago—with memories of committee publicity still implanted in her mind—a high school student told her father, "Why, Daddy, boys at school are taking dope." This information was relayed to police chief Howard W. Hoyt who talked to the girl. She named several students as the dope users. . . .

[1] *Mental Health: A Ford Foundation Report* (New York, The Ford Foundation, n. d.), p. 20.
[2] Robert Straus and Selden D. Bacon, *Drinking in College* (New Haven, Yale University Press, 1953), p. 16.
[3] Governor Adlai E. Stevenson, "Who Runs the Gambling Machines?" *Atlantic Monthly*, Vol. 189 (February, 1952), p. 35.

Thomas (the school principal) had already begun an investigation, but the only result was more rumors. . . . Pinned down, most students finally admitted they had heard from someone else who had heard from someone else that someone was an addict. . . .

Then there was the case of a few high school boys who acquired a case of beer and proceeded to demolish the contents in a short period of time. These neophyte topers became mildly and carelessly intoxicated. In this condition, they met several high school girls and with a familiar teenage bravado they explained their inebriated actions saying, "We been smoking marijuana."

. . . Dr. W. B. Prothro, city-county health director, is among those who pronounced the teen-age "menace" greatly exaggerated. "In all the time I have been here I have not known of a teen-age addict," Dr. Prothro said, "nor have I been informed of a single commitment for treatment" . . . [4]

Arrested by the vice squad of the first precinct, 9-20-40, in a large northern industrial city. . . . The charge was pandering. The complainant was Simone Potter, twenty-six years, white, separated from husband. Simone claimed that she prostituted for Helen Bleeker about nine months. She met her when defendant [Helen Bleeker] came to a beer garden where she was employed. On 9-4-40 she passed the defendant's home and defendant called to her. During the conversation the complainant told defendant she was looking for work. Defendant said, "Come and work for me. I need a girl." [5]

EACH OF THE ABOVE QUOTATIONS illustrates a social malady—and a personal affliction. Each problem may be considered in the abstract—gambling, alcoholism, prostitution—just as urbanization, social class, and population problems can be. But when one speaks of gamblers, alcoholics, or streetwalkers, there is an added implication. There is something wrong with such people. Urbanization, social class, and population problems do not depend upon individual wrongdoing; nor are they cases in which the individual succumbs to forces which many think should have been resisted. One may be born in an urban slum, but ordinarily he is not born a gambler or a pimp. He may *become* one of these in subsequent years. The problem inheres both in the *conditions* that lead people into such pathological patterns and in the *persons* who become involved. Those who yield to temptation need to be rehabilitated. Even more basic is the need to *prevent* these aberrations as well as to *cure* them.

MENTAL ILLNESS

The diagnosis and treatment of mental illness is the province of other professional groups—psychiatrists, clinical psychologists, and psychotherapists generally. Sociologists are interested in mental illness as a symp-

---

[4] *The Gazette*, Kalamazoo, Michigan, March 30, 1952.

[5] Walter C. Reckless, *The Crime Problem* (New York, Appleton-Century-Crofts, Inc., 1950), p. 241.

tom of social disorganization and in the attitudes and social policies that influence the diagnosis, care, and treatment of the mentally ill.

Magnitude of the Problem

There are no reliable statistics on the number of people who need hospitalization for emotional problems, but we know that the need is great. The available statistics tell us more about existing facilities for

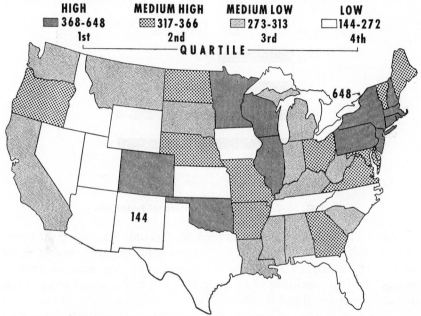

SOURCE: *Statistical Bulletin,* Metropolitan Life Insurance Company, Vol. 39 (May, 1958), p. 5, by permission.

FIG. 16-1. Geographic variation in hospitalization for mental disease. Resident patients in public hospitals for long-term care per 100,000 population in each state, 1957. (Patients in state and county hospitals at end of fiscal year and in Veterans Administration hospitals, allocated to State of residence, as of November 30, 1956.

dealing with the mentally ill than about the magnitude of the problem. Commitment rates to mental institutions, for example, vary directly with the adequacy of hospital facilities. States with the fewest hospitals tend to have the lowest commitment rates and states with the most hospitals per unit of population have the highest rates. All but the expensive private sanitaria are tremendously overcrowded. The number of people admitted depends not upon how many people need treatment but upon how much room is available.

In 1955 there were 631,503 people in mental hospitals in the United States. [6] Approximately 150,000 new patients are admitted each year. Mental patients occupy over half of all hospital beds—more than are required for the treatment of all physical illnesses and injuries combined. About one out of every twenty persons in the United States spends at least part of his life in a mental institution. Yet these appallingly high figures still reflect available facilities more than they do actual need. A more accurate picture of the incidence of emotional illness among a restricted age and sex group is provided by the draft rejection rates during World War II. Over 1 ½ million men were rejected because of personality

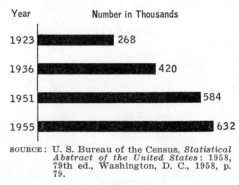

Year	Number in Thousands
1923	268
1936	420
1951	584
1955	632

SOURCE: U. S. Bureau of the Census, *Statistical Abstract of the United States*: 1958, 79th ed., Washington, D. C., 1958, p. 79.

FIG. 16–2. More people in mental hospitals.

disorders—12 per cent of all men called up. [7] In addition, during the three-and-one-half years from January, 1942, to June 30, 1945, over 550,000 men were discharged from the army and navy for neuropsychiatric causes. [8] Perhaps one-third of all manpower lost to the armed services was due to mental-emotional problems.

The total burden of mental illness is almost beyond belief. In states with better hospital programs, such as New York, nearly one person out of ten encounters hospitalization during his lifetime. Two recent studies indicate that the percentage of people seriously enough disturbed so that they would benefit from formal treatment may be as high as 25 per cent. [9]

[6] U.S. Bureau of the Census, *Statistical Abstract of the United States: 1958*, 79th ed. (Washington, D. C., 1958), p. 79.

[7] Carl Binger, M.D., "What is the Psychiatrist's Job?" *McCall's Magazine* (October, 1946), p. 211.

[8] Daniel Blaine, M.D., and John H. Baird, M.D., "The Neuropsychiatric Program of the Veteran's Administration," *American Journal of Psychiatry*, Vol. 103 (January, 1947), pp. 463-466.

[9] *Mental Health, A Ford Foundation Report*, n.d., reporting on research projects under the direction of Alexander H. Leighton, Cornell University.

Nature of Mental Illness

Some time ago a lady beyond middle age remarked to this writer in the course of a casual conversation that her husband was "crazy as a loon." And she meant it. She said it as casually as if she had said, "My husband has a club foot!" She meant to convey only that she could not expect very much from her husband and that in many ways he was a nuisance. It did not occur to her, apparently, that he was "ill" or that anything might be done about his condition. Her ignorance of the true nature of mental illness is quite typical; her blasé acceptance of it, quite atypical. Most people are frightened into near silence by any mention of mental illness. They are ashamed of its presence in themselves, their families, or their friends, almost as they would be of syphilis. They feel, somehow, that the individual is to be blamed for becoming ill, and that it is the result of depravity and inferiority. These definitions are not unexplainable since they reflect directly the accumulated ignorance of the past. They are, however, grossly unrealistic and bear little relation to the true facts.

All of us are potential victims of mental illness. Undoubtedly, some persons are more susceptible than others, but no one is immune. It is rather well established that most types of mental illness are not directly hereditary, though a hereditary tendency toward certain types of mental illness has not been ruled out. Equally important, mental illness develops through experience just as more normal behavior does. Moreover, normality shades off into illness by almost imperceptible degrees. Checking two or three times to make sure that the door is locked or that the gas is turned off, blaming others for our own failures, and wondering if we are being talked about, are all behaviors which in slightly more exaggerated form would be regarded as pathological. Illness is frequently a matter of degree rather than of kind. Temporary conditions of great stress such as the death of a loved one, a divorce, the marriage of one's child, losing one's job, getting a big promotion, or moving to another city may bring on temporary or even permanent signs of illness in persons who otherwise seem to be reasonably well adjusted. In the light of these facts, the usual distinction between those people who are "crazy" and those who are not is not very useful. We need definitions that will cover the whole range of behavior from the very normal to the most bizarre and dangerous.

Psychotherapists generally use the terms "neurosis" and "psychosis" to indicate both varying *degrees* and *types* of emotional illness. Neurotic behavior ordinarily is less disabling and less serious, covering the whole range from almost normal to that which is serious enough (possibly incurable) to warrant institutionalization. Psychotic behavior is usually characterized by a more complete break with reality. The psychotic person may have delusions, that is, believe himself to be another person, believe that he has some kind of sacred mission to perform, or that he is being persecuted by other people; or he may suffer hallucinations, that is, hear voices or see visions.

Psychotics may be declared by courts of law to be insane, insanity being a legal status and not a type of illness. Persons defined as insane may be forcibly committed to mental institutions, and thus it is primarily psychotics who populate our mental hospitals and who provide most of the statistics offered at the beginning of this discussion. Not all psychotics, however, are in institutions. Most of us come into occasional contact with one or more of them during our routine activities.

Social Factors in Mental Illness

Though no one is immune to mental illness, research has shown that the probability of one's being diagnosed as mentally ill is greatly influenced by where he lives and by the groups of which he is a member. Similarly, what happens following the diagnosis of mental illness depends not only upon the character of the illness but also upon a number of social factors influencing the treatment accorded the mentally ill in general and specific groups of the mentally ill in particular.

DIAGNOSIS OF MENTAL ILLNESS. Most studies of the amount and distribution of mental illness have been based upon the study of persons admitted to mental hospitals. [10] In general, these studies have shown that men are more likely to be committed than women, single persons are more likely to be committed than married persons, urban persons are more often committed than rural persons, commitment rates for urban persons decrease as one moves outward from the center of the city, [11] and commitment rates are higher among Negroes and among the foreign-born.

Two general hypotheses are suggested by these generalizations. First, mental illness is more likely to be diagnosed among persons living under social circumstances involving considerable stress. Presumably, men, in the course of having to earn a living, are subjected to strains not completely shared by women, single persons have generally less satisfactory living conditions than married persons, and special stress is associated with inadequate income, living under the undesirable conditions near the center of cities, and with minority group status. Second, even if actual rates of mental illness do not vary with these social factors, mental illness leading

[10] A large number of studies have been conducted. For a bibliography listing sixty-five studies, see Arnold M. Rose and Holger R. Stub, "Summary of Studies on the Incidence of Mental Disorders," in Arnold M. Rose, ed., *Mental Health and Mental Disorder* (New York, W. W. Norton & Company, Inc., 1955), pp. 87-116.

[11] Differences have been found here for different types of psychosis. The manic-depressive psychoses do not seem to fit the pattern indicated but show an almost random distribution throughout the city. See Robert E. L. Faris and H. Warren Dunham, *Mental Disorders in Urban Areas* (Chicago, University of Chicago Press, 1939).

to institutionalization is more likely to occur where they are present. Because of the social contacts required by their occupations, mental illness in men may become more obvious. Because they do not have spouses to protect them, mental illness in single persons may become more troublesome, and, along with the other inequities suffered by the economically disprivileged and minority groups, they may be more quickly committed to mental hospitals.

There has been a good deal of speculation concerning the reasons for the drop in hospital commitment rates with increased distance from the city's center. One theory has it that emotionally unstable people, because of their inability to adjust satisfactorily, tend to move frequently and thus they gradually drift into the socially disorganized areas around the city's center. There they live in relative impersonality and anonymity until they become difficult enough to be committed to an institution. If this "drift" theory is correct, then conditions of life near the city's center do not necessarily cause mental illness any more than conditions of life elsewhere.

Another theory has it that, while there may be some movement of maladjusted people into the zone of transition, the conditions of life there actually cause a disproportionate amount of mental illness. One study of catatonic schizophrenics showed that they were self-conscious, timid persons who were unable to cope with the harsh, crude, individualistic, and competitive conditions of life in crowded areas. [12] There may be some justification for each of these positions: disorganized areas may both produce and attract deviants.

Very recently, studies have been undertaken to study the incidence of mental illness from samples of the general population rather than from hospital admissions. One study of all persons from the urbanized area of New Haven, Connecticut, who were receiving psychiatric treatment during the latter half of 1950 showed an inverse relationship between social class status and the probability of one's being under psychiatric treatment. Proportionately fewer high status persons and proportionately more low status persons were psychiatric patients. [13] This finding supports the weight of evidence from earlier studies based upon hospital admissions.

Two other studies that are still in progress are concerned with the incidence of all mental illness in all persons, not just those who are in hospitals or who are receiving psychiatric treatment. One is a study of a sample of 170,000 people living in mid-town Manhattan, and the other is a study of a rural county of 20,000 people in an Atlantic coast province of Canada. Both studies have shown a high incidence of mental illness—one

[12] H. Warren Dunham, "The Social Personality of the Catatonic-Schizophrene," *American Journal of Sociology*, Vol. 49 (May, 1944), pp. 508-518.

[13] August B. Hollingshead and Fredrick C. Redlich, *Social Class and Mental Illness: A Community Study* (New York, John Wiley & Sons, Inc., 1958), pp. 194-217.

approaching 25 per cent. Surprisingly, the studies show no substantial differences between city and country in the amount of mental illness. The inverse correlation between economic status and mental illness holds up but is found to reflect such disorganizing conditions as broken homes and loss of social status rather than income alone. [14] These studies highlight the questionable nature of available statistics on mental illness and the difficulty in determining where normality leaves off and mental illness begins.

TREATMENT OF MENTAL ILLNESS. Social factors influence the treatment of mentally ill persons in at least three ways. First, there is evidence that the kind and amount of treatment received depends upon the patient's position in the class structure. Second, widespread public unwillingness to provide adequate financial support for the treatment of mental illness results in inferior, ultimately more costly and less effective treatment. And, third, resistances to expansion in the training of psychiatrists threatens to make an already acute shortage of psychotherapists still more serious.

The study of all persons from New Haven, Connecticut, receiving psychiatric treatment showed that patients' class positions make real differences in *where*, *how*, and *how long* they are treated. Individuals from the three highest social classes are treated primarily by psychiatrists in private practice, persons from Class IV are treated in about equal numbers in private and public agencies, and persons from Class V go primarily to public agencies.[15] In chronic cases, only Class I persons make continued use of private hospitals, Class II and III persons gradually shift from private to public hospitals, and Class V persons are completely dependent upon public agencies from the beginnings of their illnesses. [16] The form of treatment, particularly for neurotics, also varies with social class. The more highly regarded psychotherapies are used almost universally with Class I and II patients but with only 59 per cent of Class V patients. The less widely approved organic and shock therapies are used far more commonly with lower-class patients. [17] Lower-class patients in psychotherapy receive less of the psychiatrist's time and are treated for a shorter period. Ninety-four per cent of Class I patients saw their therapists for a fifty-minute hour, while only 45 per cent of Class V patients got that long, and 36 per cent of them had interviews lasting less than thirty minutes. [18] Also 40 per cent of Class I and II patients had been in continuous treatment for more than three years while not one Class V patient had received any form of treatment for as long as two years. [19]

[14] Both studies are under the direction of Alexander H. Leighton of Cornell University. Reported in *Mental Health: A Ford Foundation Report* (n. d.), pp. 21-22.

[15] *Op. cit.*, p. 261.

[16] *Ibid.*, p. 263.

[17] *Ibid.*, pp. 266-267.

[18] *Ibid.*, p. 270.

[19] *Ibid.*, p. 271.

Much additional evidence could be introduced to document the relation between class status and treatment for mental illness but the pattern already is quite clear. Many factors stemming from the social class backgrounds of both patients and psychiatrists combine to influence the amount and kind of treatment received. Persons from higher social class backgrounds not only can afford prolonged treatment of the more expensive types but, because of their attitudes and habits of dealing with their problems verbally, probably are objectively better candidates for psychotherapy. Lower-class persons, who lack both financial and social resources, are more likely to receive abbreviated, inferior treatment. The therapists themselves are frequently middle-class, upwardly mobile persons and undoubtedly are sometimes unwittingly influenced in their professional judgments by their own class backgrounds and those of their patients.

One of the most serious limitations on the rehabilitation of mental patients has been the general unwillingness to spend enough public money to develop adequate treatment programs. Most mental hospitals now hold at least 25 to 50 per cent more patients than they were designed to accommodate. The American Hospital Association reported that in 1953 the average daily cost of hospital care was $21.09. The average daily cost of mental hospital care was $2.83 per patient. [20] Conditions are frequently unsanitary and personally degrading. Patients are quartered in hallways and corridors, sit on the floors for lack of adequate furniture, and occasionally are even without clothing. And there is constantly pressure on the staff to make room for more. Persons for whom commitment orders have been obtained are denied admittance because there is no room. Even more serious, patients who are not cured are often discharged with the "hope" that they will not "get into trouble again." [21]

The state governments (especially legislators) which generally administer and finance the hospitals are frequently unaware of and insensitive to their needs. Mental patients cannot complain effectively when they are denied adequate care. The salaries provided for staff members are so low that it is practically impossible to obtain and to hold competent personnel. Attendants, particularly, include large numbers of unintelligent, sadistic, and otherwise maladjusted persons. When a state does decide to put more money into its mental institutions it is likely to insist that the funds be put into buildings or something that is tangible for the public to see. The very rare multimillion dollar buildings provide a shiny new front for the same old barbarously inadequate care—custodial care by an underpaid, frequently disgruntled, skeleton staff.

Hospitals are supposed to be treatment centers. But overcrowding

[20] *New York Times*, April 18, 1954, p. 10.

[21] For an authoritative account of the deplorable conditions prevalent in state mental hospitals, see Albert Deutsch, *The Shame of the States* (New York, Harcourt, Brace & Co., Inc., 1948).

and understaffing combine to make effective treatment the exception rather than the rule. "Treatment" often consists of administering a battery of tests to the patient when he is admitted to the hospital in order to "classify" him, and then of incarcerating him with a group of similarly classified patients. Psychotherapy which offers the greatest possibility for actual rehabilitation is rarely used. Occupational therapy *may be* available to one patient out of twenty. Only the least effective and most drastic treatments are at all widely used. Hydrotherapy, which consists of soaking the patient in a tub of warm water or swathing him in wet blankets, makes him easier to handle for a few hours, but does little more. Electric or chemical shock treatments are widely used and widely con-

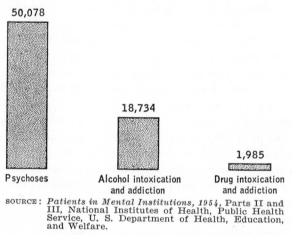

SOURCE: *Patients in Mental Institutions, 1954,* Parts II and III, National Institutes of Health, Public Health Service, U. S. Department of Health, Education, and Welfare.

FIG. 16-3. First admissions to public and private hospitals, 1954.

demned. Certainly, patients hate and fear them. The most debatable of all is the wide use made of surgical operations which sever some of the higher brain centers. Advocates of such methods insist that following the operation, patients are generally less violent, less inclined to bizarre thoughts and behavior, and, therefore, "better adjusted." Critics claim that, by destroying part of the patients' affective capacity, they are rendered less capable of any kind of thought or emotion.

Under such conditions the number of patients in mental hospitals has risen steadily over the years and the problem of mental illness has appeared increasingly insoluble. Recently, however, actual evidence has begun to accumulate that better medical care, which is possible when treatment funds are available, can bring about a significantly larger number of cures and materially reduce the size of the mental hospital population. The state of Kansas, in a six-year drive to treat all cases of mental illness as intensively as possible, upped its daily per-patient expenditures from $4.19 to

$4.39 and lowered its ratio of patients per full-time employee from 2.21 to 2.11. As a result, the number of patients in Kansas state hospitals dropped from 4551 in 1954 to 4462 in 1955 even though more patients were admitted during this period than previously. [22]

In 1956, for the first time, the increase in mental patients was reversed on the national level. There were about 7000 fewer patients in mental hospitals in 1956 than in 1955, again in spite of a record number of hospital admissions. [23] This change followed upon a trend toward increased per patient expenditures from $1.06 in 1945 to $3.26 in 1956. The impact of tranquilizer drugs has, of course, helped to increase the number of discharges from mental hospitals. Between 1956 and 1958, the number of institutionalized patients per 100,000 U.S. population dropped from 335.7 to 319.3.

Rapid progress in the cure and prevention of mental illness is still rendered difficult by the shortage of well-qualified, trained personnel. There are approximately 6000 psychiatrists in the United States—it would take three to four times that many to handle the potential case load recognized at the present time. Moreover, the prospects for rapidly increasing the number of psychiatrists in the near future seem dim indeed. Medical schools are set up to provide for the training of only a relatively few psychiatrists at a time, and their training is exorbitantly expensive. Both the medical schools and the medical associations oppose rapid expansion of training facilities, presumably upon the grounds that the quality of training would thereby be lowered. That much of conventional medical training is largely irrelevant to the successful practice of psychotherapy does not swerve them from their stand. From the standpoint of the prospective psychiatric trainee, psychiatrists, even after their long period of training, often earn less than general practitioners with good practices. Moreover, the medical associations vigorously oppose the right of any group other than psychiatrists to practice psychotherapy. At the present time, training facilities are slowly being expanded and numerous groups are challenging the medical profession's self-declared monopoly on the treatment of emotional problems, but it will take many years under the most ideal conditions before even a barely adequate number of therapists can be trained.

ALCOHOLISM

Magnitude of the Problem

Americans spend more money for alcohol each year than they spend upon the education of their children. The direct economic cost of alco-

---

[22] *Time* (January 9, 1956), p. 62.
[23] *Time* (January 28, 1957), p. 79.

holism alone in the United States is estimated at one billion dollars per year. An estimated two-thirds of all adults drink, some 60-80 million people in the United States. [24] Most people are *social drinkers*, or at least they start out that way. They begin the drinking pattern as a part of the organized social life in which they participate. What they drink, where, when, and in what quantities, depends upon the social context. Beer, wine, whiskey, bourbon, scotch, and brandy have different appeals at different social levels. In some groups men drink with men; in other groups men and women drink together. In one situation the goal is to get rapidly and boisterously drunk; in another, two drinks before dinner are usual with three or four drinks after dinner. Certainly "well-bred" people do not become intoxicated—that is, *too* intoxicated! But in all cases it is the consumption of alcohol which counts. The intoxication may be genteel or crude, but generally it is some degree of intoxication.

Intoxication may be of two sorts—acute or chronic. It may be the temporary result of too much celebrating or a too successful party. This kind of intoxication is sandwiched between longer or shorter periods of relative sobriety. Or it may be a fairly continual pattern. When the periods of sobriety in between become shorter and the intoxicated state becomes the generally preferred one, the intoxication has become chronic. The amount of drunkenness, both acute and chronic, is exceedingly difficult to measure, as is even the number of people who are drinkers. The best estimates available, however, indicate a pool of 4 to 5 million problem drinkers out of the total 60-80 million drinkers. Most of these 4 or 5 million people would be termed chronic alcoholics. Approximately 13,500 of them are the victims of alcoholic psychoses. [25] Over 200,000 people are arrested by the police each year and charged either with drunkenness or disorderly conduct—more than five times the number charged with gambling, drug addiction, and prostitution combined.

The Alcoholic Pattern

Drinking is a recognized part of American culture. One need not look for aberrant personality factors or unresolved frustrations to explain why most people begin to drink. A recently completed study of the drinking habits of over 15,000 college students indicated that 80 per cent of the men and approximately 60 per cent of the women engage in some kind of drinking. [26] Moreover the study reveals that knowledge of the students' backgrounds and their present social situation provides some basis for predicting how many of them will be drinkers, what they will drink, and

[24] Robert Straus and Selden D. Bacon, *Drinking in College* (New Haven, Yale University Press, 1953), p. 9.

[25] "The Scientific Approach to the Problem of Chronic Alcoholism" (The Research Council on Problems of Alcohol, New York, 1947), pp. 5-6.

[26] Straus and Bacon, *op. cit.*, p. 47.

how much and how often they will drink. The probability that an individual will imbibe apparently is greater if he attends a private nonsectarian college, if his family has a substantial income, if he does not belong to the Mormon church, if his parents drink, and if his close friends drink. Moreover, most of the students who are drinkers began before they entered college and took their first drinks in their own homes. [27] The study in general, however, does not support the stereotype of widespread *excessive* drinking among college students. Chronic drinking and alcoholism appear to develop somewhat later in life.

Once drinking has begun there is always the risk that it will get out of control. The antisocial chronic alcoholics of tomorrow are to be found, by and large, among the social drinkers of today. One study of chronic alcoholics revealed that only 10 per cent of them began as solitary drinkers. [28] Instead, there is a steady path from moderate, controlled drinking to uncontrollable alcoholism. It is a path of demoralization and decay, involving loss of self-respect as a minimum price and, often, loss of job, home, and even family as a part of the process.

Acute intoxication appears to be the first step. In the study of college drinking patterns referred to above, 80 per cent of men drinkers and 49 per cent of women drinkers admitted to having been tight at least once. [29] Occasional acute intoxication is almost inevitable if drinking is continued over any period of time. Probably most drinkers succeed in limiting themselves to this first stage. Only one out of every sixteen drinkers becomes an alcoholic and there is some evidence that most of the others could not become alcoholics even if they tried. [30] For that one person out of sixteen, some loss of control over future drinking tends to follow the experience of intoxication. In the aforementioned study of chronic alcoholics, loss of control followed the first intoxication by two years. [31] Other studies have indicated that the average time to the bottom ranges from seven to about eighteen years. [32] The intoxication becomes chronic. The next step is the "blackout," where following a drinking spree the individual can remember little or nothing that happened while he was under the influence of alcohol. Sobriety brings torment. No one approves of such extreme intoxication. It is disgraceful. What did one do and say? How could one have so completely lost control? Intoxication, itself, comes

[27] *Ibid., passim.*

[28] E. M. Jellinek, "Phases in the Drinking History of Alcoholics," *Quarterly Journal of Studies on Alcohol,* Vol. 7 (June, 1946), pp. 1-97.

[29] Being "tight" was defined as "suggests unsteadiness in ordinary physical activities, or noticeable aggressiveness, or oversolicitousness, or loss of control over social amenities or of verbal accuracy, or slight nausea." *Op. cit.,* p. 131.

[30] Milton Golin, "Alcoholism: Robber of Five Million Brains," reprinted from *Journal of the American Medical Association,* in *Best Articles and Stories,* Vol. 3 (June-July, 1959), p. 48.

[31] E. M. Jellinek, *op. cit.*

[32] Golin, op. cit., p. 52; and *Time* (May 4, 1959), p. 52.

to afford the only relief from shame and doubt. Sneak drinking sets in. One must always keep a bottle nearby in case it is needed. But the need implies dependence—one cannot get along without it! Such a sorry state must be concealed from the eyes of others. Drinking becomes solitary. Self-protection demands isolation and the individual becomes antisocial. The first drink is taken upon awaking in the morning, and drinking continues. Complete intoxication becomes more frequent and lasts longer. The alcoholic goes on "benders" that last for days at a time during which period his personal life goes to pieces. Demoralization is practically complete. There seems to be no escape and no solution.

Alcoholics Anonymous

The seemingly hopeless plight of most alcoholics has led many persons to refer to alcoholism as a disease. While such broad usage of the term *disease* is questionable, it does stress the fact of uncontrollable dependence upon alcohol. Alcoholism parallels drug addiction in that both psychological and physiological dependence develops. Efforts at cure must break that dependence. One of the most successful efforts to date is the growing movement called "Alcoholics Anonymous."

Alcoholics Anonymous makes use of the terror of alcoholism and the understanding of alcoholics by former alcoholics. It is, in fact, an organization of former alcoholics committed to aid others to rehabilitation. The movement, which began in 1934, stresses unlimited personal aid to the person who is attempting to stop drinking, combined with a kind of nonsectarian religious fellowship shared by all members of the group. The tenets of that fellowship to which each member subscribes are:

1. To admit that one is powerless over alcohol—that he has lost control of his life.
2. To believe in a higher Power who can restore men to sanity.
3. To will to turn one's life over to God, as one understands Him.
4. To make a searching and fearless inventory of himself.
5. To admit to God, to himself, and to another human being the nature of his wrongs.
6. To be ready to have God remove these defects of character.
7. To humbly ask God to remove one's shortcomings.
8. To make a list of all persons one has harmed and to be willing to make amends to them.
9. To make amends wherever possible.
10. To continue to take personal inventory and to admit all wrongs.
11. To seek contact with God, as one understands Him; through prayer and meditation to know His will and to have the power to accept His will.
12. To carry this message to other alcoholics and to practice these principles in all of one's affairs.

Any member who begins to feel that he may succumb to the desire for alcohol in spite of these tenets has only to contact other members who, day or night, will come to his aid and remain with him until the period of danger has passed.

While not a universal solution, Alcoholics Anonymous has proved its usefulness. From its beginning, primarily among business and professional groups, it has spread into almost all levels of society and currently numbers some 7000 groups with 200,000 members in the United States and foreign countries. [33] The exact proportion of its successes and failures is not known, but estimates indicate that some 50 per cent of cases are cured, probably one-fourth of the "cured" alcoholics have relapses, and that with the remaining 25 per cent it fails altogether. [34] This rate of success is spectacularly higher than has been achieved by any other means. Psychotherapists are quick to admit that most alcoholics successfully resist treatment and traditional medical procedures. Even the new antialcohol drugs, such as Antabuse and Temposil, have not proved adequate to the task of reducing alcoholism.

There appear to be sound sociological reasons for the success of this organization. In Alcoholics Anonymous the alcoholic finds a group in which his affliction does not stigmatize him, but is actually the means of his gaining status and group support. He maintains and increases his status by staying "on the wagon." In the meantime, he gains a sense of personal worth by helping others, and has a new and absorbing pattern of activity to absorb the energy that formerly went into seeking alcohol. These factors of group identification and group support may be more important in accounting for A. A.'s successes than are the formal propositions to which A. A. members subscribe.

Cultural and Personal Factors in Alcoholism

There are no completely acceptable explanations for why alcoholism is much more of a problem in some societies than in others or why some drinkers become alcoholics while others do not.

In the United States, where alcoholism is a serious problem, Jews have a very low alcoholism rate. [35] Only 13 per cent of Jews as compared to 21 per cent of Roman Catholics and 41 per cent of Protestants are teetotalers. Moreover, Jews drink more regularly than either of the other two religious groups. But, judging from admissions to hospitals for alco-

[33] *Alcoholics Anonymous Comes of Age*, by a cofounder (New York, Harper and Brothers, 1957).

[34] Anonymous, "My Return from the Half-World of Alcoholism," *Readers' Digest* (January, 1946), p. 34.

[35] Charles R. Snyder, *Alcohol and the Jews* (Glencoe, Ill., The Free Press, 1958); and David M. Liberson, "Causes of Death Among Jews in New York City in 1953," *Jewish Social Studies*, Vol. 18 (April, 1956), pp. 83-117.

holism, Jews are almost completely out of the picture. [36] Mormons in the United States ban the consumption of alcoholic beverages altogether and experience almost no alcoholism. Apparently more Canadians than Americans drink, but the alcoholism rate is twice as high in the United States. France has an extremely high alcoholism rate, but in Italy, despite almost universal drinking, the alcoholism rate is very low. Among the Aleut Indians, heavy and extended drinking appears to result in no true alcoholism and there are practically no guilt feelings associated with drinking or drunkenness. [37] Both the use of alcohol and the incidence of alcoholism vary widely over the world.

Clues to the reasons for this extreme variability can be found in the way in which the drinking patterns fit into the over-all culture patterns. Where drinking is associated with manliness and virility—as among the Irish, the French, and even in the United States—alcoholism appears to be common. The Jews and the Mormons, on the other hand, appear to have strong taboos against excess—and have very little alcoholism. Among the Italians, drinking appears to fit into the nutritional pattern and, unlike the French, the Italians do not often drink apart from their meals. It has also been suggested that alcoholism is more common in countries with a strong Puritan ethic. [38] Thus, "where the social group withdraws its approval from drinking, it becomes either a solitary vice or a wickedness covertly shared with a few boon companions. [39] The alcoholism rates of Sweden and the United States, both of which have tried prohibition, are among the world's highest.

Considerable effort also has been put into attempting to discover why some persons are more susceptible to alcoholism than others. A large body of research has sought the causes of alcoholism in physiological conditions such as endocrine disorders, vitamin deficiencies, and hormone imbalances. These efforts have been so unprofitable as not to warrant detailed discussion. More recently considerable research has centered on the rate of absorption, oxidation, and elimination of alcohol from the body. [40] Knowledge of average rates of the assimilation of alcohol tells us little, however, about variations in the effect of alcohol consumption from one person to another. Unfortunately the search for personality factors related to alcoholism also has been rather unsuccessful. [41] One recent study, comparing alcoholics with moderate drinkers, found that alcoholic men were gen-

[36] Snyder, *op. cit.*

[37] Gerald Berreman, "Drinking Patterns of the Aleuts," *Quarterly Journal of Studies on Alcohol*, Vol. 17 (September, 1956), pp. 503-514.

[38] Article in the *British Medical Journal*, quoted in *Time* (November 26, 1951).

[39] *Ibid.*

[40] Leon A. Greenberg, "Alcohol in the Body," in Raymond G. McCarthy, ed., *Drinking and Intoxication* (Glencoe, Ill., The Free Press, 1959), pp. 7-13.

[41] Leonard Syme, "Personality Characteristics and Alcoholic: A Critique of Current Studies," *Quarterly Journal of Studies on Alcohol*, Vol. 18 (June, 1957), pp. 288-302.

erally less "masculine" than men who were moderate drinkers. [42] As tentative as they are, hypotheses on cultural and social factors in alcoholism seem more promising than those which seek causes in physiological and psychological differences.

GAMBLING

Nature and Extent

Probably gambling is the most difficult of the personal pathologies to define and to describe with precision. Basically, gambling involves a dependence upon chance—dependence upon the turn of a card, the roll of dice, the appearance of a certain combination of numbers or symbols, or the winner of a race. Uncertainty and the possibility of benefiting or losing as the uncertainty is translated into reality are inevitably a part of gambling no matter what specific form it may take.

We easily recognize certain forms of gambling that are commercialized and which utilize establishments and/or devices arranged specifically for that purpose. These would cover the usual run of "gambling joints," roulette wheels, gaming tables, and so on down to the private card game in the back room of a local tavern or pool hall. Not always recognized as gambling are the policy or numbers rackets, lotteries, and pin-ball machines which pay off in the form of cash, merchandise, or only "free" games. Even less widely recognized are raffles and bingo games used by church, civic, and charitable groups to raise money for worthy causes. If carried much further gambling becomes truly indistinguishable from the normal elements of chance that are a part of living itself. Speculation on the stock market and commodity or future markets is now rather widely recognized as gambling, but what about the large or small investor who merely hopes that his securities may undergo a modest increase in value in addition to providing dividends or interest? Where does gambling cease and legitimate business investment begin? Consider the man who takes a chance by parking his automobile in a restricted zone, who underinsures his house, or even who crosses a busy street away from the intersection? These activities are not gambling in the conventional sense, but they contain similar elements of chance.

Sociologically, gambling can be differentiated from the normal operation of chance in our lives by two criteria. First, gambling exists when the individual hopes or works for extraordinary gain—gain out of proportion to the money invested or to the effort exerted. The gambler typically hopes to "make a killing." Second, gambling serves as an escape

[42] Frederick B. Parker, "A Comparison of the Sex Temperament of Alcoholics and Moderate Drinkers," *American Sociological Review*, Vol. 24 (June, 1959), pp. 366-374.

—an escape from the predictability or the routine or, possibly, the frustration of everyday life. At least temporarily, the gambler sees the opportunity to be freed from some of the restrictions that he ordinarily faces. If he is lucky he may be able to avoid experiencing those restrictions again. Seldom, if ever, is he that lucky, of course, but even the act of gambling may afford him temporary relief. He may "live beyond himself" for as long as the gambling lasts and may come to depend on the process of gambling as formerly he did upon the hope of winning.

For the very reasons that gambling cannot be precisely defined, the number of gamblers and the financial cost of gambling to society are difficult to estimate. Probably the majority of adults participate in professional gambling of some kind. The risk of being arrested for gambling ordinarily is not great. More arrests are made for gambling than for narcotics violations or prostitution, but gambling arrests do not number one-tenth of those for drunkenness. Much gambling, obviously, is done in very private circumstances, but even in public places the police are likely to look the other way unless there is general disorderliness or unless too many people complain.

The financial costs of some limited forms of gambling have been estimated. Betting the horses, for example, costs the American people more than a billion dollars annually. [43] The policy or numbers rackets have an estimated "take" of approximately a billion dollars each year, and slot machines take another billion dollars from the gambling public. Altogether, the American public may wager as much as 30 billion dollars a year. [44] Bloch reports an estimate to the effect that gambling profits are greater than the combined profits of the hundred largest manufacturing concerns in the United States, including such giants as General Motors, General Electric, and the United States Steel Corporation. [45] These are merely *some* of the *monetary* costs of gambling. The personal costs may be far greater.

Legal Status

Gambling in the United States ordinarily is illegal. Only one state, Nevada, has completely legalized gambling and put it under government regulation. The importance of gambling in the Nevada economy is indicated by the fact that an estimated 15 per cent of all state revenue is derived from taxes on the gambling "take" and from the licensure of gaming establishments and devices. [46] In the other forty-nine states gam-

[43] Albert H. Morehead, "What Makes Men Gamble?" *New York Times Magazine,* January 13, 1946, p. 24.
[44] T. F. James, "Gambling Boom in America," *Cosmopolitan* (July, 1958), p. 26.
[45] Herbert A. Bloch, *Disorganization, Personal and Social* (New York, Alfred A. Knopf, Inc., 1952), p. 473.
[46] *Ibid.,* p. 474.

bling generally operates without the sanction of law but is frequently un-molested. There are some genuine efforts to stamp out gambling in certain localities, but these rarely meet with any degree of success. For one thing, gambling is profitable and, on the local level at least, gamblers often wield political power far out of proportion to their numbers. Again, gambling is often an adjunct to businesses which are not themselves illegal. The law can attack the gambling but not the businesses that nurture it. Finally, the existence of gambling is tacitly supported by a sizable proportion of the population, including some of the very people who are charged to elimi-nate it. The public sentiment, which is translated into antigambling laws, simply is not very effective on the enforcement level.

One of the least understood aspects of the problem is the seemingly conflicting policies and authorities of various governmental units in rela-tion to gambling. The division of power between the federal, state, and local governments provides part of the basis for this confusion. Gambling ordinarily is regulated by the separate states but the Constitution gives to the federal government certain broad powers to raise revenue and to regu-late the flow of commerce among the states. Since gambling is so profit-able and since it is not prohibited by federal law, the federal government has often seen fit to tax it. The statement by the former governor of Illinois, quoted at the beginning of this chapter, shows how the federal government can tax activities that are illegal in the localities where they operate. Payment of the federal tax does not render the gamblers immune to prosecution under the local laws, but instead may render prosecution easier by identifying the gamblers and providing records of their activ-ities. The most recent of these taxes, and probably the most threatening to professional gamblers, is the federal tax of fifty dollars per year upon the gambler himself. If he pays the tax the gambler opens himself to local prosecution; if he does not pay it he may be prosecuted by the federal government for violation of the revenue laws. The two-way squeeze is making professional gambling operations increasingly hazardous.

Personal Demoralization

The gravest cost of gambling cannot be measured in purely monetary terms. The tremendous sums of money wagered represent a loss in pro-ductive effort to the society and represent a kind of social parasitism, with the professional gamblers drawing sustenance from, but not con-tributing to, the labors of others. But what is more tragic is what happens to the personal lives of many persons who become inveterate gamblers.

It is unlikely that many of the persons who gamble for the first time do so out of purely neurotic inclination or even out of a passionate desire to increase their holdings. Most persons become acquainted with gambling through ordinary daily routine. Many children's games involve the roll of dice, or the drawing of cards, or otherwise include a large chance element. Family card games, church raffles, and so on, are known to most of us. The excitement of anticipating the unknown and the pleasure of being rewarded for being lucky are common experiences. It is only a short step then to gambling in adult life. Bridge parties, poker games, football pools, playing the numbers, and wagering on the outcome of elections grade into playing the horses and sitting at the gaming tables. For most persons gambling remains, however, a pleasant diversion. Knowledge of "the odds" usually discourages serious dependence on gambling and occasional small losses strengthen that conviction.

There is little reliable knowledge as to why some persons become chronic, compulsive gamblers. We do know that with some people the pattern takes hold with an emotional force akin to those involved in alcoholism and drug addiction. Winning becomes very important, the stakes get larger and larger, and everything is subordinated to the need to gamble. In the long run, of course, the odds are against the gambler and he loses. Home, job, family, and respectability may be sacrificed in the process. Some psychiatrists believe that the compulsive gambler is always neurotic. [47] Supposedly, he actually has an unconscious need to lose, in spite of his conscious efforts to win. The unconscious need to lose stems from a need to rebel against the parents and ends in rebellion against the total society. Unfortunately, such a theory is very difficult to test and no adequate tests of it have yet been made. Even if one does not accept the theory *in toto*, it is plausible that anxious, insecure persons and those who experience more than ordinary frustration in their lives may be somewhat more vulnerable to the escape that gambling provides.

Likewise, the area of social and cultural determinants of gambling has hardly been explored. Surveys have shown that men gamble in only slightly greater numbers than women, for while men play cards and bet the races, women are greater lottery and raffle fans. Gambling is primarily an urban phenomenon, becoming more common with each increase in city size. Higher educated persons are more likely to gamble than lesser educated ones, young people gamble more than older people, and Catholics and Jews gamble more than Protestants. [48] There is undoubtedly some protection against gambling in the rural community which offers fewer opportunities, and in the urban environment the factor of "differential association" [49] may be important. People who, by virtue of the groups

[47] Edmund Bergler, "The Gambler: Misunderstood Neurotic," *Journal of Criminal Psychopathology*, Vol. 4 (January, 1943), pp. 379-393.

[48] Tabulations of data from the American Institute of Public Opinion made by Edward C. Devereux, Jr., *Gambling and the Social Structure: A Sociological Study of Lotteries and Horse Racing in Contemporary America*, Ph.D. dissertation, Harvard University (Cambridge, Harvard University, 1949), pp. 1044-1054.

[49] Edwin H. Sutherland, *Principles of Criminology*, 4th ed. (Philadelphia, J. B. Lippincott Company, 1943).

they belong to, are thrown into continuous contact with other people who gamble may run greater risk of becoming involved themselves. The Protestant values of frugality and hard work, combined with definitions of gambling as sinful, appear to make of Protestantism a hard core of resistance to the pattern.

DRUG ADDICTION

Incidence

No one knows exactly how many drug addicts there are in the United States. The available evidence indicates, however, that the number is probably smaller than is generally believed and is decreasing with the passage of time. Many estimates have placed the number of probable addicts at something over a hundred thousand. The Federal Bureau of Narcotics, on the other hand, estimates that there are currently only about 45,000 addicts in the United States. [50] This is less than one-twelfth the number of chronic alcoholics. Moreover, the vast majority of addicts apparently are concentrated in several of our largest cities: New York, Philadelphia, Chicago, Washington, Detroit, Baltimore, New Orleans, and Los Angeles. [51] New York State is estimated to have some 20,000 addicts, while Illinois and California have approximately 6,000 each. [52]

That addiction is less common today than formerly is not surprising. Federal regulation has taken narcotics out of general sale, whereas a generation ago many narcotic drugs could be bought without medical prescription. During the first World War, one out of every 1,500 draftees was found to be an addict, but the figure dropped to only one out of every 10,000 selectees during World War II. [53] The post-World War II period brought public attention to the problem and congressional investigation of the drug traffic was begun. There have been sporadic increases in the number of narcotic arrests since the war, but these probably reflect more rigid enforcement of the laws rather than an increase in the use of drugs.

The monetary costs of drug addiction are phenomenally high. The total money cost to Americans is about $350 million per year. Even if we omit the proportion of ordinary police work that goes into suppressing the drug traffic, governmental costs alone will amount to over $5 million per year. The two federal narcotics hospitals cost $3 million per year to run, and the Narcotics Bureau is likely to spend over $2 million

[50] Dr. H. J. Anslinger, United States Commissioner of Narcotics, reported in the *New York Times*, March 22, 1959.

[51] John Gerrity, "The Truth About the Drug Menace," *Harper's Magazine*, Vol. 204 (February, 1952), p. 28.

[52] Anslinger, *op. cit.*

[53] Gerrity, *op. cit.*

each year. [54] Added to these figures, the average addict must spend from $15 to $75 per day to support the habit. Using the minimum figure, 45,000 addicts would spend over $235 million per year for drugs.

Addiction and Demoralization

As with the other personal pathologies, the greatest costs of drug addiction must be measured in terms of broken lives. The path to addiction is the path to demoralization and despair.

Persons apparently begin to use drugs in one of two principal ways. They may use them consciously and deliberately for the intoxicating or euphoric effects the drugs provide. Or, drugs may first be used for the relief of pain while under medical treatment. However it is begun, the use of drugs is habit forming. The user seeks to repeat the "kick" or "jolt," or to relieve the pain again. With some drugs, tolerance develops with use. That is, it begins to require more of the drug to produce the same effect provided by the initial doses. As increased use develops, the body begins to adjust to the presence of the drug and physiological functioning is altered. At this stage, withdrawal symptoms appear. As the drug begins to wear off, his body, which has become dependent upon its presence, causes the user great distress. The symptoms may range from excessive perspiration and dilation of the pupils of the eyes to violent trembling and vomiting. As soon as the user connects his distress to withdrawal of the drug and seeks more narcotics to relieve the discomfort, he is "hooked." [55] He is an addict. The lurid conceptions of confirmed addicts, supposedly "high" on narcotics, are far less accurate than those which picture addicts as tormented souls continually on the verge of physical distress and struggling desperately to maintain an adequate supply of drugs.

Social and Personality Factors in Addiction

Distortion and misinformation comprise much of the "knowledge" that people have of the nature of narcotic addiction. The specter of innumerable shady characters loafing around street corners and schoolyards, hoping to induce high school students to become addicts, is almost pure fantasy. Not that an occasional high school student does not become addicted—some do. In fact, some forms of addiction, at least, are most common among very young adults. Occasionally, these groups may initiate a high school acquaintance into the use of drugs, but the facts

[54] Alden Stevens, "Make Dope Legal," *Harper's Magazine,* 205 (November, 1952), p. 42.

[55] Alfred R. Lindesmith, *Opiate Addiction* (Bloomington, Ind., Principia Press, 1947).

of this situation are a far cry from the supposed exposés luridly detailed in newspapers and magazines.

New York and Chicago have more than three-fourths of all teen-age addicts. [56] One study to determine some of the characteristics of neighborhoods in New York City with high drug incidence found that drug use among adolescent males was concentrated in a few low income neighborhoods, [57] in which the educational levels were extremely low, and the rate of family breakdown quite high. Dr. George Stevenson, medical director of the National Association for Mental Health, describes drug addiction as a symptom of rebellion against discrimination, futility, and frustration, with the great majority of teen-age addicts coming from minority groups living in slum areas where life is bleak. [58]

Considerable attention has been given to the relation between drug addiction and crime. Usually drug addiction is portrayed as a cause of criminal behavior. Since few addicts can earn the fifteen or more dollars per day necessary to purchase drugs, the addict often turns to "boosting" (shoplifting) and to forging checks to get money. And, since addicts usually get at least part of their drug supply through legitimate trade channels, they may steal physicians' prescription forms to forge the prescriptions. The study of teen-age addicts in New York showed that the areas high in drug use were also high-deliquency areas. Most of one hundred heroin users were introduced to the drug by youthful friends, and, contrary to the popular stereotype, not by adult "pushers." On the other hand, a study of eighteen street gangs did not reveal any organized drug-selling activity, and the gangs were not found to be an important source of recruitment into addiction. Rather than being a special cause of addiction, the gangs appeared to bring together a high concentration of socially and personally maladjusted boys. [59] Another recent study of addicts indicated that a large proportion of them were involved in criminal behavior *before* their addiction. [60]

Much has been written about personality factors as a cause of drug addiction. The Chief of the Addiction Research Center at the Public Health Service Hospital at Lexington, Kentucky, writes that addicts include, "nervous, tense individuals with a great deal of anxiety and many somatic complaints . . . [some] are irresponsible, selfish, immature, thrill-seeking individuals who are constantly in trouble. . . ." [61] A medical study of atypical reactions to the administration of narcotics showed

[56] Elizabeth L. Wheeler, "Facts About Drug Addiction," *National Educational Association Journal*, Vol. 42 (March, 1953), p. 142.

[57] Isidor Chein, "Narcotics Use Among Juveniles," *Social Work*, Vol. 1 (April, 1956), pp. 50-60.

[58] Wheeler, *op. cit.*, p. 143.

[59] Chein, *op. cit.*

[60] The Board of Correction, *Narcotics in California*, February 18, 1959, pp. 8-9.

[61] Harris Isbell, M.D., *What To Know About Drug Addiction*, No. 94 (Washington, Public Health Service Publication, 1958), p. 2.

the atypical reactors to be relatively aimless, drifting types who had demanding fathers and overprotective mothers. [62] The theory is that such persons, when exposed to dope, readily become addicted, while more normal people do not become addicted even following experimentation with drugs. [63]

Treatment

Treatment for addiction is both unpleasant and not very successful. Withdrawal of the drug must be accomplished whether it be sudden or gradual, with or without the temporary assistance of other drugs. The two federal narcotics hospitals, one at Lexington, Kentucky, and the other at Forth Worth, Texas, accept both patients forcibly committed by the courts and those who voluntarily apply for treatment. In either case, recidivism is common and the proportion of permanent cures is low. Public policy with regard to the treatment and prevention of addiction is a subject of violent debate and will be treated later in the chapter.

SEXUAL PATHOLOGY

The point at which sex deviation becomes sex pathology is hard to locate. If the laws governing sex behavior are used as the standard, then most adults are sex offenders (see Chapter 7, pp. 191-192). The various studies of American sex behavior that have been done over the past thirty years, however, indicate that a wide variety of sex behaviors apparently are consistent with good personal and social adjustment. [64] Patterns of sex behavior, widely engaged in throughout the population apparently without harmful consequences, would not fit the definition of pathology used in this chapter. In a few instances, however, patterns of sex behavior do have the unfavorable social and personal consequences that merit their treatment here.

Prostitution

The "red light" districts in most American cities are less extensive, less well known, and probably less well organized than they were a

[62] Reported in *Time* (April 18, 1955), p. 93.

[63] Jerome Leon, M.D., Director, Riverside Hospital (for teenage narcotics users), New York City, as reported in the *Kalamazoo Gazette*, November 16, 1952.

[64] In addition to the studies of the Kinsey group, the following are relevant: Dorothy D. Bromley and Florence H. Britten, *Youth and Sex* (New York, Harper and Brothers, 1938); Katharine B. Davis, *Factors in the Sex Lives of 2200 Women* (New York, Harper and Brothers, 1929); Robert L. Dickinson and Lura Beam, *A Thousand Marriages* (Baltimore, The Williams & Wilkins Co., 1931); Gilbert V. Hamilton, *A Research in Marriage* (New York, Albert & Charles Boni, Inc., 1929); and Leslie B. Hohman and Bertram Schaffner, "The Sex Lives of Unmarried Men," *American Journal of Sociology*, Vol. 52 (May, 1947), pp. 501-507.

generation ago. This does not necessarily mean that prostitution is less common today; however, what little evidence is available supports that belief. [65] It does mean that the *pattern* of prostitution has changed.

It would be erroneous to believe that law enforcement has been really effective in controlling prostitution or even that public opinion is solidly behind the efforts at control. Yet, together with the Mann Act that prohibits transporting a female across state lines for immoral purposes and the May Act that prohibits prostitution near military establishments, these forces have at least accomplished some dispersal of the prostitutes. Whereas formerly much of the organized prostitution was concentrated in one portion of the city, it is now spread over a much wider area. The development of rapid intracity transportation has both permitted the pattern to disperse under "outside" pressure and has yet kept prostitution readily available.

Just how much prostitution exists today is extremely difficult to say. At what point, for example, does promiscuous behavior cease merely to be promiscuous and become prostitution? The courts in most states are prone to interpret any relatively permanent relationship between a man and woman as something other than prostitution. If the couple do not live together and the man only "visits" occasionally, the relationship is apt to be more difficult to define satisfactorily, but is still not likely to be regarded as prostitution. In other cases the woman may accept gifts from one or more men, gifts which are not very well disguised payments for sexual favors. In still other cases the woman may ocasionally prostitute for money but derive most of her income from some legitimate employment. Finally, there is the widely recognized prostitute who depends upon prostitution to make her living. One estimate states that there are perhaps 600,000 women in the latter category in the United States. [66] The same writer would add another 600,000 women as occasional prostitutes. [67]

THE PATTERN. There are several somewhat distinct groups and patterns of operation among habitual prostitutes. In a sense, prostitutes form a kind of hierarchy according to the social class they come from and the class status of their patrons, and according to their age, general attractiveness, and the length of time they have been in "the life." At the base of the pyramid exist the brothel, or house, prostitutes who are usually employees of the madam or procurer and who accept all comers. They are likely to be physically and personally unattractive and to have a history of arrests, venereal disease, and often alcoholism. The second category, of street-

[65] Kinsey and his associates found that, though the proportion of males who had patronized prostitutes had not changed over the last generation, the importance of prostitution in their sex patterns had declined somewhat. *Sexual Behavior in the Human Male* (Philadelphia, W. B. Saunders Co., 1948), pp. 410-413.
    [66] *Encyclopedia Americana*, "Vice, Regulation of," Vol. 28, 1945, p. 58.
    [67] *Ibid.*

walkers, is very similar to that of brothel prostitute except that this second group often operates alone, making their contacts in bars and on the street and then taking their patrons to their rooms or to rooms that are rented specifically for prostitution. "Call girls" generally have an arrangement with bellhops or other hotel personnel who summon the prostitute by telephone to the man's room. The call girl's clientele is somewhat more limited than that of the above categories and generally she must protect herself against extreme demoralization. For when she becomes too degenerate she can no longer be tolerated in or around hotels and she tends to gravitate downward into the streetwalker and brothel categories. Probably the highest prostitute category is composed of professionals who are of middle-class background and who maintain residences or apartments away from the central part of the city. Such women cater to upper-class men who are referred or brought to them by taxi drivers or others who, of course, receive some payment for their services. Some of these women are able to be rather selective in regard to their patrons, to charge high prices, and to resist the tendency toward complete demoralization. Others of this group tend to move downward into the lower categories as they become victims of venereal disease, increasing age, and decreasing attractiveness.

SOCIAL AND PERSONAL FACTORS. How do women become involved in prostitution? And how are prostitutes different from other women? There is virtually no evidence to support the popular stereotype of innocent young girls being lured into prostitution by unscrupulous men. Probably very few women are initiated into sexual experience through prostitution. Rather, some previous sex experience seems to be almost a prerequisite to entering the profession. The same conditions that encourage sex experience outside marriage and relatively promiscuous sex behavior are favorable to entrance into prostitution. The more promiscuous the woman and the more contact she has with persons involved in prostitution, the more likely she is to resort to prostitution. Many women in dire economic circumstances and essentially without occupational skills may find prostitution the path of least resistance. Wartime experience which finds large numbers of women, without histories of promiscuity, resorting to prostitution under conditions of great hardship indicates that social factors may play an important role in its causation.

Yet only some women, even under conditions of great stress, will yield to prostitution. Presumably there are some personality differences involved. One recent study, in New York City, of twenty-four high-priced call girls showed that every one of them had suffered emotional deprivation in childhood. [68] None of the women had been tied to their families with bonds of love and affection. All of them apparently sought emotional security in promiscuous behavior before becoming call girls,

[68] Harold Greenwald, *The Call Girl* (New York, Ballantine Books, Inc., 1959).

but they got little satisfaction out of sex. Most of them regarded them-selves as being unhappy and many of them depended upon their pimps for companionship. Whether similar studies of lower class prostitutes would show the same personality factors is unknown.

Homosexuality

In spite of the wide variation in sexual practice in the United States, the society is officially very intolerant. When sex offenders are known they are apt to be subjected to the most ruthless kind of treatment. With no group is this more true than with homosexuals. Known homosexuals are likely to be fired from their jobs, divorced by their spouses, beaten and robbed by vandals, arrested by the police, and to be shunned by all others.

Kinsey and his associates found approximately 4 per cent of their male subjects and from 1 to 3 per cent of their female subjects to be true homosexuals. [69] If their statistics were representative of the general popula-tion, this would mean some three million male and possibly one and one-half million female homosexuals in the United States. There would have to be added to these figures an undetermined number of persons of both sexes who are *bisexual,* who, under appropriate circumstances, can respond sexually to members of either sex. Probably most bisexuals tend to give up their homosexual patterns as regular heterosexual outlets become available. Bisexuals often marry, rear children, and live out their lives without en-countering any major difficulties. There is an additional group of persons of both sexes who have the capacity for homosexual attachment but who never become actively involved in overt homosexual relationships. Thera-pists refer to such persons as *latent* homosexuals.

More startling than the above statistics are the Kinsey findings that *at one time or another* in their lives approximately 37 per cent of their male respondents and 13 per cent of their female respondents had had a complete homosexual experience. [70] The etiology of homosexuality is not well understood, but it seems for the most part to result from early emotional conditioning. A sizable proportion of all persons have some exploratory homosexual experience, as indicated above, in the process of growing up. Unless the early emotional conditionings have been un-favorable, however, they go on to make the transition to adult hetero-sexuality. The role of biological and endocrine factors in causing some cases of homosexuality is still uncertain, but such cases are believed to be definitely in the minority.

[69] *Sexual Behavior in the Human Male,* p. 651, and *Sexual Behavior in the Human Female,* p. 488.

[70] *Sexual Behavior in the Human Male,* p. 623, and *Sexual Behavior in the Human Female,* p. 493.

Traditionally, homosexuals have been arrested under the law and punished for their misbehavior. This probably still is the usual practice. Recently, however, several states have enacted "sexual psychopath" laws which define homosexuals as victims of illness rather than as criminals. Such laws generally provide for hospitalization and treatment in the hope that the homosexual needs may be eliminated and the individual returned to society as a useful citizen. Though such laws are not yet widespread, and though their administration is often crude and uneven, they mark a radical departure from earlier practice.

Other Sex Pathologies

Just as prostitution and homosexuality appear to result at least partly from personality disturbance, a variety of other sexual pathologies— exhibitionism, voyeurism (Peeping Tom), fetishism, and the sexual molestation of children—have been thoroughly studied. A number of studies, however, tie these various patterns to inadequate socialization and resulting personality disturbance. One study at Sing Sing prison, comparing sex criminals with criminals convicted of other kinds of offenses, found that the sex criminals were typically submissive and effeminate, withdrawn, timid persons. [71] Their sexual interest in children and adolescents stemmed, not from a fatal attraction for women but, rather, from their inability to sexually approach adult women. The so-called child "victims" of these men often were not completely innocent either. Some 23 per cent of the victims had actually solicited or seduced the offender while another 37 per cent were quite co-operative. Another study of sex offenders, done at the University of California Medical School, showed sex offenders to be generally shy and religiously inclined, with a strong tendency to be conscience-stricken about their offenses. [72] The offenders, themselves, often had been seduced in childhood by older men and many came from either physically or emotionally broken homes.

THE PERSONAL-DEVIATION APPROACH

Each of the preceding sections has dealt with a specific type of personal deviation. Each describes the problems of a particular group of people who are *different enough* to be regarded by others, and often by themselves, as problems. All members of the society would not agree precisely on what the problems are but few would deny that something needs to be done in relation to each of these pathologies. Before we can

[71] Study by Dr. Bernard C. Glueck, Jr., for the State of New York. Reported in the *Kalamazoo Gazette*, May 16, 1957, p. 34.
[72] Study by Dr. James Marsh. Reported in the *Kalamazoo Gazette*, July 21, 1954, p. 8.

evaluate the conflicting policies recommended, we must seek further to understand the nature of these personal deviations.

In most cases the pathology has a history of development. Eventually the drinker may become an alcoholic, the gambler may find that he cannot quit, and the drug user that he is hooked. Such pathologies develop through experience; they do not spring full-blown from the germ plasm. In a small minority of cases there does seem to be a kind of presocial causation involved. The small proportion of psychotics in whom there are associated physical symptoms and, possibly, some homosexuals are problems for medical and biological scientists, rather than social scientists to analyze. Practically all alcoholism, gambling, drug addiction, and most mental illness and sexual pathology are primarily social problems. They must be explained, if at all, in terms of the history or experience through which they develop.

The history of development is one of gradual loss of control and increasing demoralization. In the beginning stages the behaviors seem not to differ significantly from the normal. Rationalizing, blaming others, drinking, gambling, experimenting sexually, and even using drugs are common enough in this culture so that almost anyone may be introduced to them. It is not necessary to assume that one must be "different" *to begin with,* in order to be introduced to any of these things. The *probability of becoming involved does vary* with the social groups to which one belongs. Drug addiction, for example, is primarily an urban pattern; the chances that a rural person will become an addict are slim indeed. Nor are playing the horses and prostitution widespread rural patterns. Some types of mental illness, such as schizophrenia, tend to be concentrated in certain family lines and the probability of being committed to an institution, at least, depends upon where one happens to live. The individual is more likely to drink and gamble if drinking and gambling are common among his friends and associates. Once the behaviors are started, the stage for eventual personal destruction has been set. As they explain away one's failures, drinking, gambling, using drugs, and illicit sexual activity are all "escapes." These practices provide at least temporary satisfaction without the necessity to meet societal expectations. So long as recourse to them is seldom and not extreme, the pattern may not become progressive. But the potential for progressive involvement is always there. It becomes easier and easier to seek the escape. And each time it is more difficult to resist. The individual finds himself caught in a grip he cannot escape and demoralization begins.

The most important question that remains unanswered is why, when so many are exposed, some persons succumb and some do not. Part of the explanation undoubtedly lies in the conditions under which exposure occurs. Some persons are exposed only occasionally and temporarily, while for others the exposure is relatively constant and continuous. Some

persons are exposed before they have had opportunity to develop convictions which would sustain them against involvement. Children who
witness these patterns within their families and among their friends may
come to accept such behaviors long before they are able critically to
evaluate them. Others are exposed at times when they are particularly
vulnerable to disorganization. Personal and family crises such as a death
or the loss of one's job may reduce temporarily the capacity to resist
an "easy" escape. If exposure should come immediately following such
crises even very resistant persons might yield. Common-sense experience
recognizes ". . . the straw that breaks the camel's back"; we must recognize
that the capacity to resist demoralization depends partly on one's psychic
condition and habit patterns when exposed to it.

The other part of the equation that cannot be ignored is the individual
himself. Some persons resist strains that would crush many others; some
persons crumple under the slightest pressure. Why the difference? At
least two separate sets of personality factors must be considered. One
of these is the extent and character of the moral definitions the individual
makes. The more adamant he is in defining drinking, gambling, prostitution, as morally wrong the less the probability that he will participate
in them. Such strong convictions are a source of protection against
gradual, unwilling involvement. Moral definitions alone, however, do not
provide an adequate explanation, for some persons become involved
despite moral proscriptions to the contrary, and extreme moral rigidity is
occasionally an indication of mental illness—one of the very pathologies
being considered. The second important variable is the degree to which
the individual has met and successfully conquered past frustrations and
problems. Nothing succeeds like success. And nothing is better preparation
for meeting future temptations than past temptations which have been
successfully resolved. Persons whose past experiences have taught them
to feel quite secure in themselves and in relation to others have little
need for the relief provided by invidious escapes. On the other hand,
insecure and anxious people are prone to any behavior which affords
temporary well-being, even though the consequences of that behavior
may be disastrous. These two factors of moral definitions and general
adjustment in the individual, combined with the nature of the stresses
to which he is subjected, hold the key to whether discernible deviance
develops.

THE VALUE-CONFLICT APPROACH

In any area major conflicts may develop over whether or not a
problem exists, over what the nature of the problem is, and, finally, over
what should be done about it. There is fairly general agreement that what
we have called personal pathologies *are* social problems. But beyond this

point agreement tends to break down. When it comes to in *what way* gambling, prostitution, and so on, are social problems and to *what means* we should use in dealing with the problems, major value differences appear. How should society view the alcoholic or the psychotic? Is he to be scorned, pitied, punished, or helped? What can be done to stamp out drug addiction and prostitution? Or, *can* they be eliminated?

Legalization versus Extermination

Many people believe that vices such as gambling, prostitution, and narcotic addiction are inevitable; that no matter how much we try to eliminate them, they will continue to exist. Some people, of course, do not want them eliminated. Millions of Americans enjoy gambling and millions more take part in, or profit from, the other pathologies. Many in these permissive groups, along with others who thoroughly disapprove of them, will proclaim that much of the harm which attends these practices derives not from the practices themselves but from the fact that they are illegal.

Prostitution and gambling, they declare, are even socially somewhat useful. Both act as safety valves, draining off tensions which might otherwise be expressed in even more antisocial behavior. They may insist, generally without evidence, that if the houses of prostitution are closed the number of Peeping Toms will increase. Furthermore, they continue, one of the chief evils of prostitution—venereal disease—could be made less common if prostitution were made legal and the registration and frequent medical examination of prostitutes were required. Gambling, it is pointed out, is a tremendously profitable business—so profitable, in fact, that in most localities organized criminal gangs seek to monopolize it. Once the monopoly is established it is a simple matter to rig the odds so that gamblers have little chance of winning. And, because gambling is illegal, the government is denied one of its most lucrative possibilities for taxation. The same kind of reasoning is used to argue for the legalized sale of drugs. Since drugs cannot be obtained legally, their cost is many times higher than it would be on the open market and the addict virtually is forced into forgery and thievery. Moreover, if drugs could be obtained legally from physicians, some addicts could be induced to break the habit through medical treatment. Additional evidence could be mustered, but by now the viewpoint is probably clear: these pathologies are inevitable; they are mixed blessings; they would be less harmful and in some cases would even be less antisocial were they made legal and subject to strict governmental regulation.

Other powerful and articulate groups are violently opposed to giving legal sanction to any of these practices. Such vices are, it is pointed out, both morally wrong and personally degrading. To legalize them would be to encourage their continuance and to increase the toll of human misery which they already exact. The arguments of those who favor legalization, they hold, are merely rationalizations; the not too plausible rationalizations of people who in reality do not want to see such vices eliminated. Effective regulation, they state, is virtually impossible. The examination of prostitutes to control venereal disease would have to be done every day, and even then it would not work. To make cheap narcotics available would tremendously increase the number of users. To legalize gambling would multiply the opportunities for graft and corruption as well as sanction the robbery of countless people of money needed to feed, clothe, and house their families. The logical solution to these problems in the eyes of most of those who oppose legalization is unrelenting enforcement of the laws until the practices are completely eliminated. That elimination may be difficult is no excuse for compromising human dignity.

That these opposing philosophies can be completely reconciled is doubtful. That either one will soon completely win out over the other is similarly unlikely. The law in most states now reflects the views of those who favor vigorous suppression. Though the zeal with which the laws are enforced varies widely from one location to another, the past few decades probably have seen enforcement in general become somewhat more effective. There are no signs, however, that any of the pathologies are nearing extinction.

Punishment versus Rehabilitation

Perhaps more significant than the trend toward more effective law enforcement has been the appearance of a relatively new and controversial philosophy of treatment for deviant persons of many sorts—the mentally ill, sex deviants, alcoholics, gamblers, and addicts.

Traditionally the aim has been to punish those who were guilty of "wrongdoing." Theoretically, if the punishments were made severe enough, offenders would be forced to give up their deviant practices. Heavy fines and long jail sentences were relied upon to accomplish this end. In the case of the mentally ill, the aim was not so much to punish as to remove offenders from society. As indicated earlier, the concept of mental *illness* with prospects for curing that illness is of very recent origin. As long as the mentally ill were defined as *abnormal* and generally incurable, they were treated very much like criminals. Much of the American population even today considers institutionalization to be the most satisfactory answer to such problems. Deviants should be jailed, they say, until such time as they are willing to conform to societal expectations; and if they show no inclination to reform, then institutionalization should be permanent.

An increasing number of people attack this philosophy as being barbaric and medieval. [73] Advancements in knowledge, they claim, have long since invalidated the simple pain-pleasure principle upon which the philosophy is based. Deviants, it is pointed out, are frequently *unable* as much as *unwilling* to change. Punishment alone will do little good and, moreover, the very institutions to which deviants are committed tend to produce deviancy as much as to eliminate it. Deviants should be *helped* rather than punished. In many cases some temporary institutionalization may still be necessary to protect society and the deviant himself while treatment is carried out. But primarily, they say, the emphasis should be on treatment. The aim should be to return the individual to a useful life as soon as there is reasonable probability that he will be able to adjust satisfactorily.

The present trend in the United States probably is toward the latter philosophy but majority practice is still in terms of the former one. People are slow to give up vindictiveness where social codes have been violated. The rehabilitation philosophy gradually is being mirrored in law and administrative procedure, but public and private opinion often demand vengeance. Even where the new philosophy is accepted in principle, it is often virtually inoperative because of the lack of trained personnel and general unwillingness to appropriate funds for their hire.

THE SOCIAL-DISORGANIZATION APPROACH

Personal deviation is measured from either social or biological standards. No matter what the accepted standards are there are always some persons who are inadequate. But the amount and kind of inadequacy derives from the nature of the accepted standards as well as from individual differences. What the society demands, and the help it provides in meeting those demands, have much to do with the nature and amount of deviancy.

Increasing Demands

By former standards modern life is tremendously complex. The youth of today participate in a variety of groups and manipulate an array of machines unknown to previous generations. The period of formal training required to prepare them for adult life has lengthened considerably and new levels of intellectual, social, and mechanical competence constantly are being attained. There were always some persons who were inadequate even under the old standards of behavior—some who did not have sufficient mental capacity and some who broke down under the

[73] Alfred R. Lindesmith, "Federal Law and Drug Addiction," *Social Problems,* Vol. 7 (Summer, 1959), pp. 48-57.

strain, resorting to some pathological pattern. Logically, one might expect increasing standards to result in increased numbers of inadequate persons. The greater complexity of modern life might be a major factor in raising the incidence of the personal pathologies.

Indeed, many persons have assumed such a causal relationship. The constantly increased numbers of persons committed to mental institutions are pointed out as evidence. More people presumably are succumbing to the increased demands placed upon them. Unfortunately for the theory, the committment rate is not a good index of the rate of mental illness. It is impossible to say whether more people are ill or merely whether more of the ill are being committed. Nor is there adequate evidence that other personal pathologies are increasing. In the case of narcotic addiction and prostitution there is even some evidence that law enforcement has succeeded in somewhat reducing the size of the problem.

The relative strain placed upon people from one time period to another is not a simple thing to measure. Certainly, the requirements of farm life and of a machine technology are different. But by what objective standards can the one be said to be more difficult than the other? A common assumption is that there are limits to the amount of adjustment and learning of which man is capable and that the limits are being rapidly approached. The assumption remains unproved, however. The same assumption, in fact, has been made for many centuries past. On the other hand, such limits undoubtedly do exist, and if and when they are approached the rate of personal breakdown probably will increase. The present rate of increase in personal breakdown remains a matter for speculation.

Breakdown of Controls

Personal pathologies indicate individual inabilities to adjust but they also indicate failure of the social structure to protect the individual against disorganization. Ideally, each person should be so indoctrinated with the prevailing group values that he will not be tempted to engage in disapproved behavior, and the social structure should provide sufficiently adequate interpersonal relationships that he will not be driven to disapproved behaviors for compensation or escape. Traditionally, family and other intimate group ties have performed these functions. The family is the primary agency entrusted with the indoctrination of the young and is also their primary source of refuge throughout life. Community institutions, particularly the church and school, play strong supporting roles. Occasionally, these agencies fail in their respective tasks, but it is quite significant that the incidence of personal pathologies is lowest where family and community life are most satisfactory. Conversely, personal pathologies are most common in areas and situations where family and community life are not well organized.

It has already been pointed out in earlier chapters that community life functions most smoothly in rural areas, where there is not much mobility, and that the anonymous, heterogeneous, mobile character of urban life is disruptive of many of the more traditional kinds of human relationships. Institutional committments and arrests for gambling, drunkenness, prostitution, and homosexuality are all unusually high in urban blight areas, around military installations, and in communities which undergo boom-town conditions. Social isolation and extreme mobility of the population are statistically associated with increased evidence of personality disorganization.

The exact extent to which the breakdown of close interpersonal relationships produces personal pathology is not known. Certainly arrest and commitment rates mushroom under such conditions but, again, such rates may not reflect accurately the increased incidence of pathology. One alternative explanation is that the pathology, when it does appear, is less tolerable when family and friends are not available to close ranks and protect both the afflicted one and society at large from its manifestations. Persons living in deteriorated areas probably are more subject to arrest *as well as* to pathological involvement itself. An additional complicating factor exists in the high mobility rates in such areas. Deviants may be *drawn* to deteriorated areas because of the slight protection which their anonymity affords. The most reasonable conclusion seems to be that the recognized tendency for social isolation to foster personal pathology is augmented both by decreased ability to care for deviant persons under these conditions and by a tendency for already deviant persons to gravitate to areas where isolation is possible.

SUMMARY

Mental illness is the greatest single health problem in the United States today. Over half of all hospital beds are occupied by mental patients and there are more mentally ill people outside than inside the hospitals. Studies show that social factors are important in determining who receives psychiatric treatment, who is committed for institutional care, and what kind of treatment patients receive. Facilities and personnel for the care of the mentally ill are woefully inadequate.

Alcoholism, gambling, drug addiction, and sexual patholgy are all escapes from the demands of normal social living. The less extreme patterns which open the way for the individual to succumb to these pathologies are not in themselves pathological, however. They are to be found in one form or another as common elements of American culture. These personal pathologies have a history of development. Involvement tends to become progressive and eventually the individual finds that he has lost control of himself. Continued participation leads to complete personal demoralization.

The probability of becoming involved in pathological behavior varies from one social group to another. The more prevalent such patterns among one's associates the greater the likelihood of becoming involved. Some persons are able to resist involvement; some are not. Inadequate socialization, resulting in personality disturbance, appears to make one vulnerable to these pathologies. Moral definitions which prohibit any participation in such patterns are ordinarily a protection against involvement, and crisis situations tend to render individuals temporarily more vulnerable.

At least two major conflicts rage over how to deal with the pathologies. One faction argues that they are inevitable and that, in the long run, less harm would result if the practices were legalized and subjected to strict government regulation. The opposing faction clamors for vigorous suppression and eventual elimination. The second dispute concerns whether the individuals involved should be defined as wrongdoers and be punished for their actions, or whether they should be defined as ill and aided to recover their capacity to resist. There is, at present, something of a tendency toward the latter definition.

Certain factors in society at large contribute to the existence of the personal pathologies. The complexity of modern life subjects individuals to great strain and perhaps heightens the tendency to seek escape measures. The relative strains to which people are subjected in different time periods is extremely difficult to measure, however, and caution is suggested. The incidence of pathology is greater under conditions of social isolation and mobility. Probably such conditions also attract deviants and render their presence more apparent.

SUGGESTED READINGS

AUSUBEL, David P., M. D., *Drug Addiction: Physiological, Psychological, and Sociological Aspects* (New York, Random House, 1958). A relatively brief volume that includes sections on the treatment and prevention of drug addiction.

BACON, Selden D., ed., special issue on "Understanding Alcoholism," *Annals of the American Academy of Political and Social Science* (January, 1958). Excellent symposium covering the nature and extent of the alcohol problem, physiological, psychological, and cultural factors in alcoholism, and the medical and nonmedical treatment of alcoholism.

BERGLER, Edmund, M.D., *Homosexuality: Disease or Way of Life?* (New York, Hill and Wang, Inc., 1956). A psychiatric interpretation of homosexuality as a disease. Author believes that the disease can be cured through public education and proper psychiatric treatment.

DEUTSCH, Albert, *The Mentally Ill in America*, 2nd ed. (New York, Columbia University Press, 1949). One of the best treatments of the whole problem of treatment for the mentally ill. Discusses history, trends, and problems.

HOLLINGSHEAD, August B., and REDLICH, Fredrick C., *Social Class and Mental Illness: A Community Study* (New York, John Wiley & Sons, Inc. 1958). Report of an investigation into the relationships between social stratification and mental illness in New Haven, Connecticut. General findings that each social class exhibits definite types of mental illness and reacts to the fact of mental illness in predictable fashion. Treatment by psychiatrists also varies with the social class of the patients.

LINDESMITH, Alfred R., *Opiate Addiction* (Bloomington, Ind., Principia Press, 1947). Contains the most satisfactory schema yet devised for explaining the phenomenon of opiate addiction.

PLOSCOWE, Morris, and LUKAS, Edwin J., eds., special issue on "Gambling," *Annals of the American Academy of Political and Social Science* (May, 1950). Includes articles on the legal status of gambling, the various forms gambling takes, the professional gambler, and gambling in other countries.

ROSE, Arnold, ed., *Mental Health and Mental Disorder: A Sociological Approach* (New York, W. W. Norton & Company, Inc., 1955). An excellent book of readings on the present status of research and theory on social aspects of mental health and mental illness.

STRAUS, Robert, and BACON, Selden D., *Drinking in College* (New Haven, Yale University Press, 1953). A study of the drinking histories and drinking patterns of approximately 16,000 college students in twenty-seven colleges and universities.

"Symposium on Alcoholism," *Social Problems*, Vol. 5 (Spring, 1958), pp. 292-338. Contains four articles on social organization and alcoholism, the ecological correlates of alcoholism, the "wino," and drinking among high school students.

WARD, Mary Jane, *The Snake Pit* (New York, Random House, 1946). A best-selling novel which highlights the antitherapeutic aspects of the environment of mental hospitals. Fascinating reading.

AUDIO-VISUAL AIDS

1. *Howard Street* (Kinesis, Inc., 566 Commercial St., San Francisco), 10 minutes, sound, black and white. A documentation of life on the street which is the home of the personal dregs—the alcoholics, the unemployables, the lost individuals. There is no editorial comment. The sound employed was recorded directly on the scene.

2. *Mental Hospital* (International Film Bureau, Suite 308-316, 57 E. Jackson Blvd., Chicago), 20 minutes, sound, and black and white. Sponsored by Oklahoma State Dept. of Health and Oklahoma State Dept. of Mental Health. The day-to-day story of the treatment received by a mental patient from the time of admission to the hospital until he is discharged.

3. *The Lonesome Road* (Columbia University Center for Mass Communications, New York). Eight 15-minute, 16-inch, 33⅓ rpm transcriptions. Transcriptions prepared especially for sale to radio stations. The series uses, dramatically, the actual voices of alcoholics from Skid Row and the shaded lawns of residential areas, as well as voices of law enforcement

officers, doctors, and psychologists. A complete, compelling exposition of the alcoholism problem.

4. *This is the United Nations*, No. 6, United Nations Laboratory Aids Fight on Opium Smuggling (United Nations, Films and Visual Information Division, New York), Black and white.

QUESTIONS AND PROJECTS

1. Explain the difficulties inherent in estimating the amount of mental illness in American society. How generally adequate are facilities for the treatment of mental illness?

2. How does the factor of social class position impinge upon the diagnosis of mental illness, the probability of commitment for mental illness, and the amount and kind of treatment received therefor?

3. Trace the route from moderate social drinking to confirmed alcoholism. What evidence is there concerning causative factors in alcoholism?

4. Give an adequate sociological definition of gambling. Is there a gambling parallel to the pattern referred to in the previous question? What personality factors appear to be associated with chronic gambling?

5. How widespread is drug addiction in the United States? Does the evidence indicate that the number of addicts is increasing rapidly?

6. Describe the process of demoralization experienced by a typical prostitute. Assess the role of social and personality factors in the production of sexual pathology.

7. Explain the statement: "Most cases of personal pathology have a history of development."

8. Give as many arguments as you can in favor of the legalization of gambling and the sale of narcotics. Give contrary arguments in favor of exterminating gambling and narcotic addiction.

9. Assess, critically, the argument that the rate of personal breakdown is increasing in modern society.

10. Take a field trip to one of the state hospitals for the mentally ill. How many persons was it designed to accommodate? How many persons are located there? What techniques of therapy are used to aid the patients? Ask one of the officials there to give you a brief history of the institution, citing the improvements that have been made both in the care and treatment of patients. What plans have been made for further improvement?

11. Contact the local police department to see what facilities exist for the control of narcotic addiction in your community. Do the police believe that there is much of a problem? Does any other evidence exist to indicate that there is or is not a problem? If a problem exists, to what extent does it approximate the lurid accounts of drug addiction in newspapers and magazines?

17

Health and Medical Care

❲❲❲❲❲❲❲❲❲❲❲❲❲❲❲❲❲❲❲❲❲❲❲❲❲❲❲❲❲❲❲❲❲

With five children to support, Michael D., 42, a telephone operator, had to mortgage his home to pay doctor's bills during his wife's long illness. Last year, when Mrs. D. died, Mr. D.'s aged mother moved in to run the household and his oldest daughter, Florence, now 18, went to work to help meet expenses. Despite her financial aid, the D.'s lost their home and had to move to an apartment. Three months ago Mr. D.'s mother died.

But this loyal family is still undefeated. Trudy, 14, and Philip, 13, have taken over much of the housework and marketing under their father's direction and try to look after Bobby, 9, and Anne, 6. Bobby, however, requires special attention. Grieving for his mother, he has grown apathetic in school and complains of deafness. Several times lately he has barely escaped being run down in traffic because of his apparent inability to hear cars approaching.

Unable to afford private medical care for Bobby, harassed Mr. D. has appealed to the [social casework] agency. The counselor will arrange clinic tests for Bobby and psychiatric treatment, if that proves necessary, but in the coming year Mr. D. will need continued guidance in handling all of the heavy family responsibilities alone.[1]

. . . what keeps the great majority of people well is the fact that they can't afford to be ill. That is a stern harsh dictum and we readily admit that under it a certain number of cases of early tuberculosis and cancer, for example, may go undetected. Is it not better that a few such should perish than that the majority of the population should be encouraged on every occasion to run sniveling to the doctor?[2]

Undue reverence for authority as such, a serene satisfaction with the status quo, and a fatuous objection to change have often retarded the progress of medicine. In every generation, in every country, there have been, and ever will

---

[1] "New York's Hundred Neediest Cases," *New York Times*, December 7, 1952.
[2] Editorial, "License For Illness," *New York State Journal of Medicine*, Vol. 49 (September 15, 1949), pp. 2129-2130.

be . . . men in high places who lent the weight of a complacent conservatism to bolster up an ineffectual attempt to stay the progress of a new idea.[3]

ILL-HEALTH IS PROBABLY THE GREATEST SINGLE CAUSE of human suffering in modern society. It is doubtful if any other single circumstance produces so much poverty and dependency, so much family disruption, or so much economic inefficiency as illness. In an average day in the United States, nearly two million persons of working age have no jobs because of disability, nearly another million with jobs are absent because of illness, and roughly one-fourth of the rest are working at less than full efficiency because of nondisabling illness. We are now spending over $23 billion a year for medical care and health services, and wages lost through ill-health add another $5 billion to our health bill. Although by no means can all illness be prevented or cured, our present mores define *any* ill-health as undesirable and as a problem to command our concern.

AMERICA'S HEALTH—HOW GOOD IS IT?

Many Americans have comfortably assumed that as the wealthiest and, admittedly, the most progressive nation on earth, we must also be the healthiest. Whether we actually are the world's healthiest nation is debatable. We have many more doctors and hospital beds per 1000 people than any other country [4] and, according to the American Medical Association (AMA), our doctors are better trained and more competent than those of any other country. Yet health statistics for the leading nations are so close together, and so imperfectly comparable, that it is impossible to say any one nation is the "healthiest" in the world. We certainly do not lead the world in health by the margin that our greater wealth and technical resources make easily possible.

Our country's health standing has, however, been rapidly improving. A half century ago, we were far behind other modern nations. Even in 1938, we ranked eighth in infant mortality, twenty-second in maternal mortality, fifth in tuberculosis deaths, seventh in diphtheria deaths, and ninth in deaths from all causes. [5] Recent reductions, however, have been spectacular. Between 1930 and 1957, our maternal mortality rate fell from 67 to 4 deaths per 10,000 live births, our infant mortality rate fell from 65 to 26 per 1000 births, while the expectation of life at birth rose from 59.7 years in 1930 to 69.6 years in 1956.

Although these are impressive accomplishments, it is notable that

[3] Sir William Osler, Bt., M.D., *F.R.S. Aequanimitas with other addresses* (Philadelphia, P. Blakiston's Sons, 1932).

[4] Except Israel, with a large number of refugee doctors, mainly from Germany.

[5] Carl Malmberg, *140 Million Patients* (New York, Reynal & Company, Inc., 1947), pp. 4-7. This ranking should be viewed in the light of the fact that differences in population composition and in methods of reporting make exact comparisons more or less misleading.

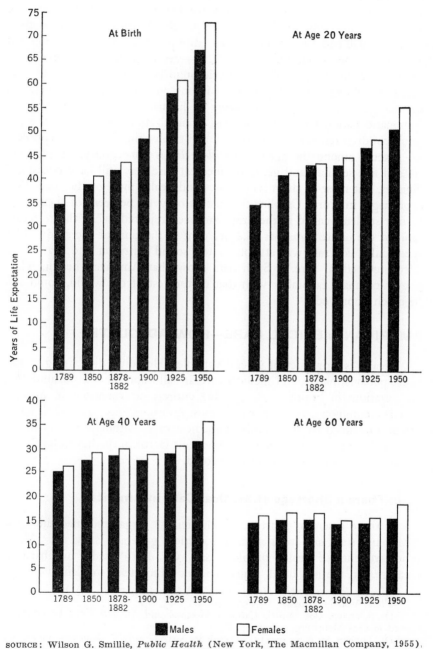

SOURCE: Wilson G. Smillie, *Public Health* (New York, The Macmillan Company, 1955).

FIG. 17-1. Do people live longer than they used to live? Why has the expectation of life at age 60 years shown no real increase?

in 1957, New Mexico had an infant death rate more than twice as high as New Hampshire, while a Negro mother in the United States was more than four times as likely to die in childbirth as a white mother. Between 1920 and 1957, typhoid cases dropped from 36,000 to 1,300 and diphtheria cases from 148,000 to 1,200—yet *all these 1957 cases were preventable*. In 1959, cases of paralytic polio were running two-and-one-half times above 1958, [6] higher than in any year since polio vaccination became general; but after five years of haphazard vaccination with no systematic national program of mass immunization, nearly half the nation's children remained unprotected, and twelve times more susceptible. [7]

Except among the aged, *most ill-health is unnecessary*. People who eat and live sensibly and get good medical care may still have occasional illnesses, but most of them will be in good health most of the time. Five orphanages in North Carolina found that only 1.4 per cent of their 1,138 former students called in the draft had been rejected, while the rejection rate for the entire state was 56.8 per cent at the time of the study. This spectacular contrast was attributed to "sound nutrition and reasonably adequate medical care." [8] Such data show that America's health, while it may compare favorably with that of the rest of the world, could still be much improved.

AMERICAN MEDICAL CARE—HOW ADEQUATE?

Health is a product of several variables. Heredity, diet, living conditions, personal habits, and medical care are all important. To assume that all variations in health levels are due entirely to variations in medical care is a common error. Yet with almost no exceptions, low health levels are accompanied by low levels of medical care. Although by no means the sole factor, medical care is an important factor in the health level, and the one to which this chapter is devoted.

1. Is There a Shortage of Medical Care in America?

Is there a serious shortage of physicians? Organized medicine (the AMA and state and local medical societies) generally says, no. [9] Many other students of health problems say, yes. But "needs" are hard to measure. On the one hand, many illnesses which used to claim hours of

[6] *Weekly Report, Public Health Service*, Vol. 8 (August 21, 1959), p. 1.

[7] *Time*, Vol. 74 (August 31, 1959), p. 52.

[8] Dr. Clarence Poe, North Carolina Hospital and Medical Care Commission, quoted in Carl Malmberg, *op. cit.*, p. 27.

[9] Dr. Dwight H. Murray (1957 President, AMA) says, "A sufficient number of physicians is being produced to handle the nation's health needs adequately." See "The President's Page," *Journal of the American Medical Association*, Vol. 163 (March 30, 1957), p. 1143; also "Shortage of Doctors? Debate is Growing," *U. S. News and World Report*, Vol. 44 (May 9, 1958), pp. 66-74.

the doctor's time are now prevented entirely, or treated in minutes instead of hours and cured in days instead of weeks. On the other hand, rising incomes and growing health-consciousness have increased people's demand for medical services.

How these two trends balance is not clear. There has been no comprehensive, authoritative survey of medical needs and resources since the reports of the President's Commission on the Health Needs of the Nation in 1953, which predicted a 1960 shortage of 30,000 physicians, 50,000 nurses, and similar shortages in other health personnel. [10] We now have 132 physicians per 100,000 people, a ratio which has shown little change since 1921, but this ratio will drop steadily unless medical education is expanded beyond present plans, [11] and medical educators are predicting grave shortages. [12] At last count, medical school staffs were short 330 teachers, while over 2,000 American medical students are studying

TABLE 17-1. Expected supply of Physicians and Dentists, 1950-1975

	Physicians		Dentists	
	Number	*Per 100,000 population*	*Number*	*Per 100,000 population*
1950	203,400	134.0	89,441	59.0
1955	218,061	132.0	97,529	59.0
1960	239,350	132.9	100,266	55.6
1965	259,950	132.8	106,735	54.5
1970	279,000	130.5	112,881	52.8
1975	296,100	125.9	118,142	50.2

At presently-expected rates of growth, the number of physicians and dentists per 100,000 people will decline steadily. Meanwhile, our people grow more prosperous and health-conscious. Without a massive increase in expenditures for medical and dental education, which will probably require federal grants, an acute shortage appears probable. (Source: Markley Roberts, *Trends in the Supply and Demand of Medical Care,* Joint Economic Committee, Congress of the United States, 86th Congress, 1st Session, 1959.)

[10] President's Commission on the Health Needs of the Nation, *Building America's Health* (Washington, Government Printing Office, 1953).

[11] "Shortage of Doctors? Debate is Growing," *op. cit.*

[12] Dr. Grayson Kirk, President of Columbia University, says that by 1975, ". . . our present and projected medical schools will be able to turn out only about two-thirds of the number of doctors of all kinds that will be needed. Moreover, this estimate does not make any provision for any further rise in medical care standards." (*Ibid*). See also, Lois R. Chevalier, "Crisis in the Supply of Doctors," *Medical Economics,* Vol. 35 (March 31, 1958), pp. 67-73. See Surgeon General's Consultant Group on Medical Education, *Physicians for a Growing America, Public Health Service Publication, No. 709* (Washington, Government Printing Office, 1959), for an official estimate that we must double our expected rate of increase in medical education to maintain our 1959 ratio of physicians (p. 59), and a recommendation for federal grants in aid to medical students on a merit basis with federal grants to medical schools (p. 63).

Medical men got a bad press in Suffolk County, N. Y.,
recently when a man died of a heart attack "while police
phoned more than twenty doctors" in vain. A medical society
officer observed, "I thought (our emergency call system) was
working very well." But local police were quoted thus: "This
sort of thing happens about once a month."

Medical Economics, Vol. 36, July 20, 1959, p. 2.

---

abroad. [13] In 1957, over 8,000 of the 30,000 hospital positions were vacant, [14] and nearly 2,000 towns asked the AMA for help in securing doctors. [15] The classified advertising section of any issue of the *Journal of
the American Medical Association* lists numerous vacancies for physicians
with promises of starting salaries of $15,000 to $20,000 or more. It would
have required 13,500 more dentists in 1957 to bring all states up to the
dentist-to-people ratio of the twenty-four leading states. [16] The numerous vacancies in all health fields, and the total absence of any unemployed
personnel, are proof of a shortage to all except those with a vested interest
in denying its existence.

2. Does Anyone Lack Medical Care?

The medical profession takes pride in the fact that, with relatively
few exceptions, medical services are given to everyone who reaches the
doctor or hospital and asks for treatment. This record is a generous one,
but it overlooks these important facts: (1) some people are unable to
reach or locate a physician or hospital bed when needed; and (2) many
people, for one reason or another, do not ask for the medical services
their health requires. There are at least three major groups whose medical
needs are only partly filled.

a. Those living in medical shortage areas get less and poorer medical
care. Although some concentration of medical facilities in the larger cities
is efficient, the present urban concentration goes far beyond considerations of medical efficiency. The greater metropolitan centers have nearly
four times as many physicians per 1000 people as the isolated rural areas.
Furthermore, these rural small-town physicians are older, less well trained,
and work longer hours; nearly one-third of the physicians in rural areas
are semiactive physicians over 65 years of age, contrasted with 12 per cent
of the urban physicians. Of the 757 "medical service areas" into which

[13] "Shortage of Doctors? Debate is Growing," *op. cit.*
[14] *New York Times*, June 2, 1957, p. 65.
[15] William Barry Furlong, "Vanishing American—The Country Doctor," *New York Times Magazine*, September 7, 1958, pp. 90 ff.
[16] *Public Health Reports*, Vol. 73 (March, 1958), p. 244.

the AMA divides the country, the number of physicians in 1950 varied from one for each 380 persons to one for each 5100 persons. There were 75 areas with more than 2000 persons per physician, and 262 areas with more than 1500 persons per physician. [17]

People often travel outside their immediate locality for medical care, but still must find it within their general region. In 1955, for every 100 physicians, dentists, and nurses (per 100,000 people) in the northeastern states, the southern states had 64 physicians, 47 dentists, and 51 nurses,

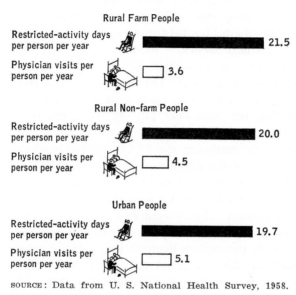

Rural Farm People

Restricted-activity days per person per year — 21.5

Physician visits per person per year — 3.6

Rural Non-farm People

Restricted-activity days per person per year — 20.0

Physician visits per person per year — 4.5

Urban People

Restricted-activity days per person per year — 19.7

Physician visits per person per year — 5.1

SOURCE: Data from U. S. National Health Survey, 1958.

FIG. 17-2. Farm people have more illness, but less medical care.

while the north central states had 73 physicians, 77 dentists, and 73 nurses. [18] Eleven per cent of our population—19 million people—live in areas having no public health department, while local public health departments have shown no expansion since 1950. [19] Such data help explain why Alabama and South Carolina have diphtheria rates eighteen times as high as New York or Michigan. [20]

Other medical facilities show similar geographic variations—hospital beds, nurses, paramedical personnel, and public health facilities. The most obvious reasons are economic. The number of physicians and hospital beds per 100,000 people corresponds quite closely to the per capita income of each region. But other important reasons include: (a) physicians'

[17] Frank G. Dickenson, *How Bad is the Distribution of Physicians? Bulletin*, 94B (Chicago, American Medical Association, 1954).

[18] *Statistical Abstract*, 1958, p. 75. (Data for nurses are for 1950, latest date available).

[19] Barkew S. Sanders, "Local Health Department: Growth or Illusion," *Public Health Reports*, Vol. 74 (January, 1959), pp. 13-20.

[20] *Public Health Reports*, Vol. 72 (June, 1957), p. 539.

dislike for practice in isolation from their fellow practitioners; (*b*) physicians' dislike for practice where hospital, laboratory, and specialist services are limited or inferior; (*c*) medical graduates' tendency to establish practice either in their home towns or in the area where they attended medical school. All these factors favor the urbanized areas and the prosperous regions, and those areas which are already medically well equipped attract a disproportionate number of each year's medical graduates.

    b. Low-income groups. Medical care is costly. The average American family in 1953 spent either $110 or $207 for personal medical services, depending upon whether the median or mean is taken as an "average;" [21] this rose to $294 (mean) by 1958, with most of the increase due to a greater use of medical service. [22] Medical costs are claiming a rising share of our incomes—from 3.7 per cent in 1929 to 5.3 per cent of all consumer expenditures in 1958. [23] The proportion of persons who see no physician during the year is three times as high for families with incomes under $1,200 than for those over $10,000, while less than one in five families with incomes below $1,000 has any health insurance, compared with five out of six families in the $7,500—$10,00 bracket. [24] A survey in a small New York town found that, as compared with upper incomes, the low-income group had over twice as many illnesses, each of which lasted nearly twice as long, but was only three-fifths as likely to be fully treated by a physician. This low-income group was less than half as likely to have a family doctor, only one-third as likely to have any health insurance, and only one-sixth as likely to have a family dentist. [25] Almost endless statistics of this sort could be cited to show that low-income people need more medical care, but get less of it, than more prosperous people.

    Some of this disparity may be due to a lack of effort by low-income people who are not educated to seek medical treatment, but to "blame" *all* untreated illness among low-income folk on lack of effort would be a crude evasion of facts. For while the amount spent for medical care rises with income, the *proportion* of income spent for medical care is larger for the lower incomes—14 per cent for incomes under $1,000 against 4.5 per cent for incomes over $10,000. [26] Although low-income

    [21] Odin N. Anderson, *National Family Survey of Medical Costs and Voluntary Health Insurance* (New York, Health Information Foundation, 1954), p. 25.

    [22] *Time,* Vol. 75 (February 22, 1960), p. 62, quoting data from Health Information Foundation.

    [23] *Ibid.*

    [24] Maurice E. Odoroff and Leslie Morgan Abbe, "Patterns of Hospital Prepayment Coverage in the United States, 1956," *Public Health Reports,* Vol. 74 (July, 1959), pp. 573-580.

    [25] Earl Lomon Koos, *The Health of Regionville* (New York, Columbia University Press, 1954).

    [26] "Consumer Spending for Medical Care," *Progress in Health Services,* monthly bulletin of Health Information Foundation, December, 1958.

people waste much of their money on quack practitioners and self-medica-tion, it is a reasonable measure of the *effort* of low-income people to get treatment for their illness.

Low-income people also receive free medical care from various sources. Local public health departments provide some free health services to many low-income people; but 30 million people live in areas with no full-time local health department. Medical-school hospitals and clinics provide many free services to low-income persons within the surrounding area. Federal, state, and local government provide certain services for certain groups of people and categories of illness. Physicians give about one-tenth of their time for free services. [27] A number of voluntary health organizations provide treatment for specified illnesses, and private social agencies provide some medical services. Out of this confusing patchwork of agencies, a good deal of free medical care appears. *Some* of the low-income people have *some* of their medical care needs fulfilled. Many others are missed—because the services they need are not locally available to them, because their pride prevents them from accepting "charity" medical care, or because they do not recognize their medical needs and seek medical care. A few years ago, of two national surveys, one showed 29 per cent and the other 31 per cent of the population reporting that they "put off going to a doctor because of cost." [28] And much free medical service is wasted because of lack of co-ordination and continuity. In some areas, a person who is self-supporting is ineligible for free services and can obtain them only by waiting until he becomes unemployable and goes on relief, whereupon he becomes an eligible "indigent." [29] Those who are barely self-supporting usually have greater difficulty in obtaining medical care than those who are already on the relief rolls.

The aged generally have low incomes, yet have more illness than other age groups. The members of Health Insurance Plan of Greater New York HIP, for whom the cost barrier had been removed by their insur-ance, received the following services:

Age	Physician visits per person per year	Hospital days per 100 persons per year
15-44	4.9	65.3
45-64	5.5	87.3
65 and over	7.3	159.5

[27] *Medical Economics,* Vol. 36 (May 11, 1959), p. 69.
[28] Clarence A. Peters, *Free Medical Care* (New York, H. W. Wilson Co., 1946), pp. 94-95.
[29] See Odin W. Anderson and Harold Alksne, *An Examination of the Concept of Medical Indigence,* Research Series, No. 8 (New York, Health Information Foun-dation, 1957).

But only one in three persons over 65 has any kind of health insurance, compared with over two-thirds of the people in their productive years. [30] Only two in five of the unemployed and only one in four of the agricultural laborers has any health insurance. [31] Practically none of the 750,000 members of migrant farm workers' families have any health insurance or any dependable access to health facilities. [32] The federal government spends more to protect the health of migratory birds than it spends on the health of migratory children!

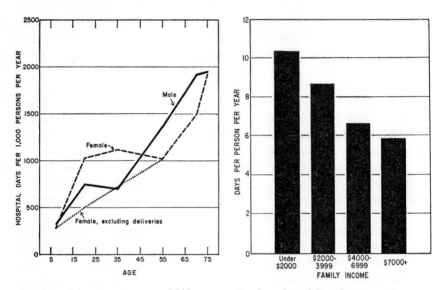

Number of hospital days per 1,000 persons per year by sex and age.

Number of work-loss days per person per year by family income for "usually working" persons.

SOURCE: U. S. National Health Survey, 1957-1958.

FIG. 17-3. Illness most often strikes the old and poor.

Some of the medical care received by low-income people is also wasted because they lack funds to continue treatment to its completion. One small pilot study of persons who felt that their medical needs were not met revealed that one-fifth of them had seen a physician and received prescriptions but had not filled them because of lack of funds.

c. Racial minorities. It is sometimes stated that America's *white* population is more healthy than the population of any other country on earth —that it is the low health level of our Negroes, Indians, and Mexicans that pulls down our health standing. No doubt a very rosy picture of our

[30] Odoroff and Abbe, *op. cit.*
[31] *Ibid.*
[32] Otis W. Anderson, "The Migrants and the Rest of Us," *Public Health Reports,* Vol. 72 (June, 1957), pp. 471-477.

nation's health could be presented by excluding sickly groups, but the amount of illness is not thereby reduced. As compared with our white population, our nonwhite population is only one-half as likely to have any health insurance, but has illness rates and death rates which are 50 per cent higher. [33] The infant death rate of Negroes is twice as high as that of whites, while only one-fourth as many Negroes have early pre-natal care, and maternal mortality among Negroes is four times as high. [34]

The disparity is greatest for precisely those diseases which medical care can prevent or cure. Nonwhite death rates are five times as high for typhoid and syphilis, four times as high for whooping cough and dysen-

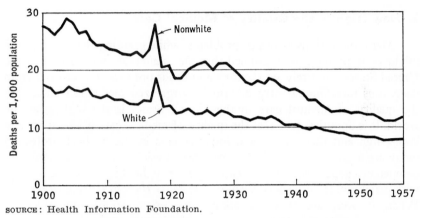

SOURCE: Health Information Foundation.

FIG. 17-4. Mortality by color, United States, 1900-57.

tery, three times as high for diphtheria, tuberculosis, and diseases of preg-nancy, twice as high for pneumonia and diarrhea, and ten times as high for "unknown or unspecified causes" (a term which usually indicates a lack of medical attention either before or after death!). For the less easily preventable diseases, such as cancer, diabetes, or arteriosclerosis, the white population's death rate is higher than that of the nonwhites—because most nonwhites do not live long enough to develop these diseases!

Most of our nonwhite population is in the lower income brackets, and much of it lives in those areas where medical facilities are least adequate. Discrimination reduces further the medical facilities available to minori-ties. Health insurance premiums are usually higher for minority groups, if they are eligible for them at all. There are many localities, even fair-size cities, where no dentist will accept Negro patients. Negroes report great difficulty in getting physicians to make after-hours house calls. Although one-tenth of our people are Negroes, fewer than one-fiftieth of

[33] "The Health of the Nonwhite Population," *Progress in Health Services* monthly newsletter (New York, Health Information Foundation, April, 1958).

[34] Ödoroff and Abbe, *op. cit.*

the physicians are Negroes, and the proportion has been declining for a quarter century. Negro entrance into the medical profession is limited by the inadequacy of the pre-medical education available to Negroes in many areas producing a shortage of academically qualified Negro medical students, by the high cost of medical education, by the lack of medical schools accepting Negroes in some parts of the country, and by many discriminatory practices in granting hospital internships and appointments, and medical and specialty society memberships. [35] Considering all these factors, it is not surprising that tuberculosis kills proportionately twice as many Negroes and eight times as many Indians as whites.

3. How High Is the Quality of Medical Care?

Many discussions of health problems, while granting that distribution might be imperfect, have assumed that the *quality* of medical care in the United States is entirely satisfactory and needs only to be protected from dangerous meddling. It may be true, as organized medicine claims, that the quality of medical care in the United States is the highest in the world. It is doubtless true that the quality of medical care has been rapidly improving, and that quacks and incompetents in the medical profession today are a rarity. It may also be true that physicians may be individually competent, generous, and dedicated, yet may be kept from practicing with maximum effectiveness *because of the way their practice is organized.* What, if any, are these situations and organizational imperfections which limit the effectiveness of the medical services which our people receive.

a. Isolation of practitioners. According to a Subcommittee on Medical Care of the American Public Health Association, "The greatest single deterrent to good service is the isolation of the individual practitioner from his colleagues." [36] Modern medical science is exceedingly complex and rapidly changing. The highest levels of medical care require the close co-operation of general practitioners, specialists, hospitals, laboratory technicians, and all other medical and paramedical personnel. Lone practitioners, practicing in scattered private offices, cannot make efficient use of many kinds of expensive and highly specialized equipment. It is more inconvenient to arrange consultations with other practitioners or to arrange for laboratory tests, and the patient's time is wasted as he trots from place to place. Most important of all, the physician loses the exchange of knowledge and the stimulus toward professional excellence that comes from a close working association with his fellows. A widespread recogni-

[35] See Dietrich E. Rietzes, *Negroes and Medicine* (Cambridge, Harvard University Press, 1958; Lois E. Chevalier, "New Light on Medicine's Color Line," *Medical Economics,* Vol. 36 (January 19, 1959), pp. 171 ff.

[36] Subcommittee on Medical Care of the American Public Health Association, "Quality of Medical Care in a National Health Program," *American Journal of Public Health,* Vol. 39 (July, 1949), pp. 700 ff.

tion of these facts by the medical profession is partly responsible for the current spread of the group practice of medicine, and for the growing tendency to organize medical services around hospitals and clinics rather than in independent offices.

b. The fee-for-service system of payment is widely accused of increasing costs while lowering the quality of medical services. Under this method, the patient pays a separate fee for each item of service he receives; under the *capitation* method, the physician receives a stated fee for each person to whom he provides whatever services are needed over a period of time; or the physician may be paid on a *salary* basis. According to the above subcommittee of the American Public Health Association, [37]

The fee-for-service method puts emphasis upon sickness rather than health and upon quantity rather than quality. It hinders appropriate referral of patients because it provides an economic incentive for the physician to retain his patient [rather than referring him to another physician better qualified to treat the particular disorder]. This factor, in addition, seriously limits the effectiveness of regional centers for necessary consultant services. . . . By removing or minimizing the incentive for quantity inherent in fee-for-service, the [ideal] program could make careful, deliberate work, rather than the multiplication of services, the principal motivation for a physician to improve his professional and economic status.

The fee-for-service system is also said to discourage early diagnosis and treatment, and to provide less incentive for preventative medicine or health education than the other methods of payment. [38]

c. Ghost-surgery and fee-splitting are two additional abuses which the fee-for-service system encourages. "Ghost-surgery" exists when the patient pays for the services of a highly regarded surgeon but, without his knowledge, is operated upon by another surgeon who receives only a part of the fee the patient has paid. Fee-splitting exists when the specialist or surgeon shares part of his fee with the physician who referred the patient to him. Both practices are classed as unethical by the AMA and nearly all state and local medical societies because they tempt the physician to refer his patients to the specialist or surgeon who gives the largest split rather than the one who is most competent. Although less widespread than it used to be, fee-splitting is still a common practice in some areas, and an official of the American College of Surgeons writes, ". . . in some areas of the middle west [fee-splitting] is practiced by the great majority of general practitioners and general surgeons. . . ." [39] The

[37] *Ibid.* (This report was published for discussion only and is not an official pronouncement of the American Public Health Association.)

[38] President's Commission on the Health Needs of the Nation, *op. cit.*, Vol. IV, pp. 104-105.

[39] Greer Williams, "Unjustified Surgery," *Harper's Magazine*, Vol. 208 (February, 1945), pp. 35-41.

American College of Surgeons has been campaigning against fee-split-ting, [40] and one official charges the medical societies with failing to co-operate in its elimination. [41] Although twenty-three states have laws forbidding fee-splitting, there is no record of a prosecution.

d. *Limitation of hospital privileges* reduces the effectiveness of many physicians and surgeons. In some instances the denial of hospital appoint-ments is based upon a physician's incompetence or unethical behavior, but this does not explain why in some large cities nearly half of all general physicians do not have hospital affiliation. "A lot of doctors complain that they cannot get on a hospital staff and cannot practice proper medicine unless they do." [42] In many areas, Negro physicians have extreme diffi-culty in securing hospital affiliation, without which they cannot treat their patients within the hospital. Some excellently trained young physi-cians and surgeons are barred from hospital affiliation by less-well-trained older physicians who fear their competition. [43] Meanwhile, some in-competent and unethical physicians, who are justifiably barred from the hospitals, proceed to open their own unsupervised hospitals and sanatoria, where many of the most appalling examples of malpractice are found.

e. *High cost of medical services* prevents some paying patients from getting all the services that might aid them. As Paul de Kruif writes, [44]

The cost of really complete medical care is . . . bearable only by the rich. For all others . . . the doctor must be on the watch to avoid sending his sick patient from the frying pan of disease into the fire of subsequent worry about unbearable medical debt. This is medicine's tragedy: where doctors are indi-vidual business men dealing with the average individual sick man, they dare not sell all the science they have to offer. Their regard for the average indi-vidual's pocketbook makes it necessary for them to withhold the full power of that science. They must go easy on X-rays, blood chemistry, special nursing, new chemical treatment, complicated operations—expensive procedures that, limitless, may make the difference between life and death.

His first sentence is probably an exaggeration, and, for persons with health insurance, the rest is less true than when de Kruif penned it; yet for millions of people, this situation has not changed. It remains true that

[40] *Bulletin of the American College of Surgeons,* Vol. 37 (September-October, 1952), p. 233.

[41] Dr. Fred Rankin, former president of the American College of Surgeons, not long ago "accused the AMA of subtly opposing the efforts of surgeons to root out exorbitant fees, kickbacks, and unnecessary operations." ("Surgeons Questions AMA's Sincerity," *Chicago Sun-Times,* October 10, 1953, p. 7.) At the 1953 convention of the AMA "eleven resolutions of censure were introduced, not against fee-splitting, but against Dr. Paul Hawley for having discussed fee-splitting in a public interview." (Richard Carter, *The Doctor Business* [Garden City, Doubleday & Company, Inc., 1958], p. 123).

[42] Dr. Russell V. Lee, in President's Commission on the Health Needs of the Nation, *op. cit.,* Bol. V, p. 204.

[43] J. D. Ratcliff, "Give Young Doctors a Break," *Woman's Home Companion,* LXXV (October, 1948), pp. 32-33.

[44] Paul de Kruif, *Kaiser Wakes the Doctors* (New York, Harcourt, Brace & Company, 1943), pp. 36-37.

when a patient of modest means is ineligible for free medical care or his pride will not let him accept it, the physician often must find a compromise between prescribing everything that might help him and prescribing what the patient can afford.

  f. *Lack of continuity and of co-ordination* reduces the effectiveness of much medical care. Because of the costs, some prescriptions remain unfilled and some courses of treatment are not carried through to completion. Many medical services are ineffective because of lack of co-ordination with the services of a medical or psychiatric social worker, who works with the patient and his family on living conditions, health habits, diet, and emotional understanding. The fact that from one-half to three-fourths of all physical illnesses involve emotional causes calls for a co-ordination of medical and psychiatric practice which is largely lacking in our health service organization.

  g. *Overwork* in the medical profession is a constant drain on its effectiveness. Physicians in general practice work an *average* of about 60 hours a week—meaning that some work far longer—and their hours are irregular and their rest broken. Physicians have an expectation of life several years shorter than other professional groups. A study of drug addiction among physicians—whose addiction rate is 100 times the national rate—concluded that the physician's greatest need was for a good night's sleep, more vacation time, and some release from tension. [45] Their heavy duties make it difficult to find time for vacations, for periodic advanced study, or even to keep up with a changing field. A distinguished surgeon and medical educator writes that of the thirty doctors he knew intimately, only five kept abreast of medical progress, while the other twenty-five read little or no scientific material and merely treated symptoms instead of making diagnoses. [46] A large publisher of medical books reports that less than 15 per cent of the practitioners buy new medical books with any regularity. [47] The occasional tragic errors of even the best practitioners can often be attributed to sheer exhaustion. It is simply an impossibility for an overworked profession to maintain the highest level of professional service at all times.

  h.—*And still others* . . . The physician's memory is overburdened by the drug houses' practice of producing a standard drug under dozens of different competing names. [48] Dr. Paul Hawley, an official in the American College of Surgeons, says, "Today, one half of the surgical operations in the United States are performed by doctors who are inadequately trained

[45] J. DeWitt Fox, "Narcotic Addiction among Physicians," *Journal of the Michigan State Medical Society*, Vol. 56 (February, 1957), p. 214 ff.

[46] Caleb Smith, "How Good is Your Family Doctor?" *Atlantic Monthly*, Vol. 186 (August, 1950), pp. 43-48.

[47] Dr. James Peter Warbasse, "Doctors and Dollars," *The Progressive*, Vol. 14 (November, 1950), pp. 12-14.

[48] See "The High Cost of ℞ Drugs," *Consumer Reports*, Vol. 23 (November, 1958), pp. 597-599.

to undertake surgery," and places the blame on health insurance plans which do not check the qualifications of the physicians they pay. [49] New York City's Committee of Interns and Residents charges that an ". . . alarming deterioration of medical care" has hit many of New York's city-owned hospitals. [50]

Perhaps the most authoritative recent study of the quality of medical practice was made by a research team of physicians from the medical school of the University of North Carolina. This team spent months in an on-the-spot examination of the professional practice of eighty-eight

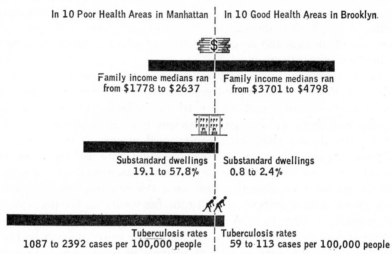

In 10 Poor Health Areas in Manhattan | In 10 Good Health Areas in Brooklyn.

Family income medians ran | Family income medians ran
from $1778 to $2637 | from $3701 to $4798

Substandard dwellings | Substandard dwellings
19.1 to 57.8% | 0.8 to 2.4%

Tuberculosis rates | Tuberculosis rates
1087 to 2392 cases per 100,000 people | 59 to 113 cases per 100,000 people

SOURCE: Anthony M. Lowell, "TB and the Environment," Bulletin of the National Tuberculosis Association, 43 (January, 1957), pp. 3-4.

FIG. 17-5.   Health, housing, and income go together.

general practitioners in North Carolina, where conditions might approach a national average. This team concluded that of the 88 physicians, only seven were fully competent and professional, practicing as good physicians; 15 more came very close to this level; 27 were mediocre; 23 were decidedly inferior; and 16 were grossly careless and incompetent. [51] They found no association between the size of a physician's income and the quality of his medical practice.

Many factors enter into the quality of medical care, and not all are easy to measure. As this list suggests, a number of conditions keep the quality of medical care lower than it might be. [52] It is not suggested that

[49] *Medical Economics,* Vol. 36 (July 6, 1959), p. 38.
[50] *Medical Economics,* Vol. 36 (July 20, 1959), p. 3.
[51] Lois Hoffman, "How Do Good Doctors Get That Way?" in E. Gartly Jaco ed., *Patients, Physicians, and Illness* (Glencoe, Ill., The Free Press, 1958), pp. 365-381. Report originally published as supplement to the *Journal of Medical Education,* 1958.
[52] See also Richard Carter, *op. cit.,* Ch. 7, "Medical Delinquency."

any person or group is necessarily "to blame" for them; they are perhaps better interpreted as a *culture lag in the organization of health services.* For, as the President's Commission on the Health Needs of the Nation states, "The genius for organization, so characteristic of American life in general, is conspicuous in health services by its absence. By organization is meant the process of putting together people and facilities, and utilizing them in the most efficient manner." [53] It is clear that a more efficient organization of medical services could measurably improve the quality of medical care in the United States.

To the student, especially if he has a relative who is a physician, this section may seem overly critical and entirely negative in tone. The American medical profession undoubtedly deserves great admiration. However, this section is not concerned with physicians as individuals, but with the way their practice is organized. And it is concerned with the *problem aspects* of medical practice. A recital of alleged imperfections may seem unkind, but is needed if problems are to be explored.

DEFINITION OF THE PROBLEM

As with all social problems, people disagree upon whether there is a "problem" of medical care, upon its exact nature, and upon its seriousness. At least four levels of definition can be recognized.

1. Some feel that there is *no serious health service problem;* that while there may be certain small imperfections, these are now being taken care of by the medical profession. This is the attitude of most of the spokesmen for organized medicine. [54] To these persons, the problem is mainly one of protecting an "excellent" system of medical care from "dangerous" attempts to modify it. The membership of the medical profession is divided; a significant minority feels that there *is* a serious medical care problem and is active in promoting changes in medical organization.

2. Some view the problem as mainly one of *providing for catastrophic illness.* American families pay an average of 5 per cent of their incomes for medical care—enough to cover ordinary illnesses. But 7 per cent spend over $500 a year. Each year a million families pay over 50 per cent of their income for medical care and a half-million families pay more than their entire year's income. [55] Some people define the problem as one of providing insurance protection against these unbearable costs of catastrophic illness, assuming the most people can meet purely routine medical needs without assistance.

3. Others see the problem as one of *insuring medical care for all,*

[53] *Op. cit.,* Vol. I, p. 29.

[54] See President's Commission on the Health Needs of the Nation, *op. cit.,* "Doctors Speak," Vol. V, pp. 193-256.

[55] Odin W. Anderson, *National Family Survey of Medical Costs and Voluntary Health Insurance* (New York, Health Insurance Foundation, 1954), p. 25.

since it is clear that many who need medical care do not get it. Some feel that the problem is met if medical services are available to all who *ask for them*. Others, noting that ignorance or pride keep many from asking for free medical services, believe that the problem includes the need for an educational and promotional campaign to encourage these people to ask for the medical care they need.

4. The most inclusive definition of the problem includes all these objectives in demanding a sweeping *reorganization of the administration of health services*. Some critics believe that the quality of medical care could be improved and its cost lowered through a rational reorganization of health services administration. They define the problem as partly one of promoting such a reorganization.

THE SOCIAL-DISORGANIZATION APPROACH

The genial country doctor with his familiar black bag was fairly adequate for the medical needs of our great-grandparents. He didn't know much medicine, because there was not much medical knowledge for him to learn. But most of the patients got well anyway, and his earnest efforts and his long nightly vigils earned him the respect and affection of his neighbors.

The spectacular growth of medical knowledge is revolutionizing the arrangements of medical practice. With the discovery of how disease is transmitted has come the realization that disease anywhere in the community is a threat to the health of all of the community. [56] This realization leads to the demand that health services be made equally available to all. Modern medical care involves many specialized fields and skills, and the traditional method of solo fee-for-service practice comes under fire as a major obstacle to high quality medical care. The constant stream of new medical discoveries and treatments enables doctors to save many today who yesterday would have died—and also makes good medical care so costly that traditional methods of payment became unsatisfactory and new ones are appearing.

Changes in the society also disorganize the traditional administration of health services. The growth of large-scale industry has led to industrial health service plans that sometimes infringe upon private practice. The changing age distribution of our population, due mainly to our lower birth rate, calls for changes in medical emphasis and organization. The tendency to offer public assistance to practically all who fail to support themselves makes those who are unemployable because of illness a heavier economic burden on the entire society than they once were. One study of

[56] For example, the AMA recently announced that the major source of infection for tuberculosis is found among skid row bums, who often work as cooks and dishwashers in restaurants. (*Chicago Sun-Times*, July 10, 1954, p. 15).

relief clients found that one-third of them became relief clients through illness, while another one-fifth had illness as a contributing factor. [57] In many ways, current experiments in the organization of health services are reflecting the familiar "change-disorganization-reorganization" cycle.

THE VALUE-CONFLICT APPROACH

Many of the value conflicts in this problem are found lurking behind the opposing statements of alleged "facts." Defenders of the medical status quo point out that few who ask for free treatment are denied. Critics point out that the medical status quo discourages many from asking for the treatment they need but feel they cannot afford. Both facts are true, and each implies a different value judgment. *How important is it that all should be offered complete medical care under conditions that strongly encourage all to ask freely for it? How important is it to preserve the current system of practice which a majority of the doctors seem to prefer?* These questions of value lie at the heart of current medical controversy.

Is ill-health among those too ignorant or too indolent to seek treatment a social problem? Some say, "No it is their own fault!" Some say, "Yes, they must be educated to recognize their need and to demand treatment." These answers imply several value judgments about personal versus public responsibility, about taxes and public expenditure, and about the degree to which we should be our "brothers' keeper."

Many other values compete with health values. Overeating is said to be the greatest single cause of death. Many people who cannot "afford" medical care can easily afford new cars and sporting goods. Recent scientific data about cigarettes and health made no real dent in cigarette use, showing that people would rather enjoy life than prolong it. [58] We spend more each year on chewing gum than on health research. It is easier to get federal appropriations for the health of brood sows than for expectant mothers—farmers are organized and fathers are not! Pure food and drug laws mediate the bitter clash between the right of a business to seek a profit and the people's need for protection against dangerous, worthless, or misrepresented products. [59] There are many points where choices must be made between health and other values.

[57] Herbert Wolkin, *Health Research Opportunities in Welfare Records,* Research Series, No. 8 (New York, Health Information Foundation, 1959), p. 5.

[58] See Charles F. Connell and James C. MacDonald, "The Impact of Health News on Attitudes and Behavior," *Journalism Quarterly,* Vol. 33 (Summer, 1956), pp. 315-323; Harold F. Dorn, "Tobacco Consumption and Mortality—From Cancer and Other Diseases," *Public Health Reports,* Vol. 74 (July, 1959), pp. 581-593.

[59] See James Cook, *Remedies and Rackets: The Truth About Patent Medicines Today* (New York, W. W. Norton & Company, Inc., 1958); Oscar E. Anderson, Jr., *The Health of a Nation: Harvey N. Wiley and the Fight for Pure Food* (Chicago, University of Chicago Press, 1958).

THE PERSONAL-DEVIATION APPROACH

Of the many persons who practice poor health habits and are unaccustomed to seeking medical services, only a few are deviant persons. The rest are merely reflecting the normal behavior of persons in their social environment. The members of some groups or cults raise religious objections to medical services—these persons are conforming members of deviant groups.

When the deviant person is also an emotionally disturbed person, as he frequently is, he is less likely to remain physically healthy for a long period. Various medical estimates define from one-half to three-fourths of all physical disorders as being wholly or partly caused by emotional disturbances. Today there is scarcely any disorder—not even cancer—from which emotional factors are definitely excluded as being of no importance. Of course, not all deviants are disorganized or emotionally disturbed. But deviation often carries emotional tensions, anxieties, confusions, and resentments that become active causes of a long list of physical ailments. [60] Much chronic illness is emotional in origin, and an endless succession of ailments strongly suggests emotional causation. When one is unconsciously using illness for an escape from responsibility, an appeal for affection, or a means of revenge, the "curing" of one ailment merely forces the patient to develop another. In this way, personal deviation is responsible for a certain proportion of our ill-health.

Many deviant persons are attracted by health fads, quacks, and absurd causes and controversies. Antivivesectionism (opposition to the use of animals in medical research experiments) cannot be explained on any rational basis; some emotional need must motivate the antivivesectionist. Fluoridation of the public water supply is considered by scientists to be a harmless, effective, economical way to reduce tooth decay. Yet a determined, uninformed, highly emotional opposition has arisen in many places, with fluoridation proposals defeated in two-thirds of the local referendums in recent years. [61] Personal deviation helps to explain a great deal of irrational behavior.

PROPOSALS FOR IMPROVING THE ADMINISTRATION OF HEALTH SERVICES

Whether a particular proposal is good or bad depends upon the values which are used in measuring it. In 1948, the National Health Assembly, some eight hundred representatives of professional organizations and

[60] See Helen Flanders Dunbar, *Mind and Body: Psychosomatic Medicine* (New York, Random House, 1947).
[61] "Fluoridation," *Public Health Reports*, Vol. 74 (June, 1959), pp. 511-520.

public and private agencies concerned with health matters, adopted the following criteria for evaluating the effectiveness of prepayment plans (whose members pay a weekly or monthly premium to become eligible for certain services) in meeting the medical care needs of the people: [62]

1. The extent to which a prepayment plan makes available to those it serves the whole range of scientific medicine for prevention of disease and for treatment of all types of illness or injury.

2. The proportion of the population of its area—local, state, or national, as the case may be—covered by a plan (cost in relation to ability to pay, restrictions on enrollment imposed by actuarial considerations, income level, age, conditions of employment, means of securing enrollment and collecting premiums).

3. The degree to which a plan makes use of and encourages the development of a high quality of medical care for its subscribers (standards of personnel and facilities, organization of services, emphasis on prevention of disease, promotion of health, health education).

4. The degree to which freedom and willingness to experiment with methods of payment and operation are encouraged in a plan.

5. The degree to which a plan succeeds in arranging amounts and methods of payment and conditions of participation that are satisfactory to physicians, hospitals, and others serving the plan's subscribers.

6. The extent to which sound financing, efficiency, and economy in the operation of a plan are achieved and encouraged by its basic policies and its administrative techniques.

7. The extent to which the individuals or board members who carry the ultimate responsibility for a plan represent the interest of those entitled to service and those who are paying the cost, as well as of the physicians, hospitals, or others who are providing the services.

These tests of "adequacy" might be abbreviated as (1) comprehensive medical care, (2) universal enrollment, (3) high quality, (4) freedom to experiment, (5) satisfactory methods of payments, (6) economy and efficiency, and (7) consumer participation in control. This is not the only set of criteria which might be used, and this one is not entirely acceptable to organized medicine, but it may serve as a useful guide for comparing the several alternative proposals which follow.

1. Group Practice

Although group practice is not a method of prepayment, it has attracted wide support as a pattern of organization. In group practice, [63]

A number of physicians combine their practice, utilize the same offices and other facilities, which are owned in common, refer patients to one another ac-

---

[62] National Health Assembly, America's Health (New York, Harper and Brothers, 1949), p. 222-223.

[63] New York Academy of Medicine, *Medicine in the Changing Order* (New York, The Commonwealth Fund and Harvard University Press, 1947), p. 137.

cording to the patient's needs, and share by agreement in the expenses and the net income. The group includes specialists and, if it plans to extend complete medical care, general practitioners.

Advocates of group practice claim that it offers a higher quality of service at lower costs than traditional practice. The New York Academy of Medicine stated in 1947: [64]

There are obvious scientific, financial, and professional advantages in well-organized group practice. . . . Besides offering more inclusive service the group can extend medical care quantitatively by lowering charges and distributing them more evenly. Overhead expenses are relatively low. . . . Close association with colleagues in such groups tends to maintain both ethical and technical standards. Solo practitioners, on the other hand, are "on their own" in these matters. It is one of the weaknesses of prevailing general practice that there is no means for maintaining standards, save within the broad limits set by licensure and the laws against malpractice. . . . But . . . outside pressure is not likely to prove effective and would certainly be resisted by physicians as being coercive. The merit of group practice is that it provides for some control of standards within the professional family. . . . Close association with colleagues also proves stimulating to the individual members.

To sum up, group practice . . . affords a better quality of care to patients and improved professional conditions for physicians. Most important, it is more adaptable than solo practice to comprehensive voluntary prepayment plans, and so facilitates a wider extension of medical care.

The President's Commission on the Health Needs of the Nation comments that with group practice: [65]

The patient benefits through having his entire health service concentrated in one place. This gives greater unity and continuity to his care, encourages consultation whenever it is needed, and minimizes travel. The patient also gets more service per dollar spent through the economy of group practice.

Physicians working together in a group continue the best features of their training period throughout their professional lives—the stimulation to keep up with medical progress through constant appraisal by informed colleagues and ready access to consultations and technical assistance. On the personal side the physician in group practice has greater opportunity to take time off for study and vacation in addition to a more stable income throughout his years of practice.

These features of group practice may account for its steadily growing popularity, for group practice is replacing solo practice all over the world. [66] A small but steadily growing fraction of American physicians are engaged in group practice, and an AMA survey in 1957 found a

[64] *Ibid.*, pp. 137-139.
[65] *Op. cit.*, Vol. I, pp. 33-34.
[66] Leo C. Brown, "The Economic Future of Medical Practice," *Social Order*, Vol. 8 (June, 1958), pp. 269-279; Harry Eckstein, *The English Health Service* (Cambridge, Harvard University Press, 1959).

majority of these physicians believing that they practiced better medicine than they could in solo practice. [67] Group practice appears to have no inherent disadvantages, yet certain problems have limited its expansion. Some physicians are too individualistic to enjoy group practice. The large cash investment required for offices and equipment has been an obstacle. Some groups failed because the controlling physicians sought to exploit the underpaid, younger physicians in the group. And, "in many parts of the country, organized medical bodies have been distinctly hostile to group practice" [68] and have impeded its growth.

Advocates of group practice do not claim that it is a solution to the entire problem of medical care. They merely claim that group practice is an efficient way of organizing medical practice. Problems of financing, of providing care for low-income groups, and of shortages in isolated areas would still remain. But because group practice is considered more efficient and economical, its expansion is a central feature of practically every proposed plan for comprehensive health services.

2. Voluntary Health Insurance (Limited Coverage)

Over 123 million people, or over two-thirds of the civilian population, had some form of health insurance protection by the end of 1958.[69] Nearly half of these were insured with Blue Cross plans, and the other insurance was divided among industrial and union programs, independent plans, and commercial insurance company policies. *Comprehensive* health service plans, covering most of a family's medical costs, were held by about 6 million persons, or about 5 per cent of the people. Most persons with health insurance receive *limited* services, mostly hospital services and perhaps certain surgical and medical services while in the hospital. There is sharp disagreement upon which services should be covered by health insurance. Most medical society spokesmen and Blue Cross officials have maintained that routine medical expenses—house calls, office calls, occasional treatment of minor ailments—are certain to be needed by everyone, and for this reason are noninsurable; they state that health insurance should seek to cover only the heavier costs of the catastrophic illness. [70]

There is a wide variety of health insurance plans in operation. Commercial insurance companies have long sold health and accident policies which pay specified cash benefits to individual policyholders. As a means of meeting medical costs, these policies are costly and inefficient; ad-

[67] Richard Carter, *op. cit.*, p. 148.

[68] President's Commission on the Health Needs of the Nation, *op. cit.*, Vol. 1, p. 34.

[69] *13th Annual Survey*, Health Inurance Council (New York, 1959).

[70] President's Commission on the Health Needs of the Nation, *op. cit.*, Vol. IV, pp. 50, 77, 79.

ministrative costs consume nearly half of each dollar, and the size of the cash benefit bears no necessary relation to the cost of treatment. Commercial insurance companies are now promoting the sale of group health insurance policies, on which administrative costs are much lower, and which usually provide medical service benefits instead of paying cash benefits. For all health insurance plans combined, administrative costs in 1956 averaged 20 per cent of premiums. [71]

A national network of Blue Cross Hospital Care plans is operated by nonprofit organizations largely controlled by hospital administrators. Local Blue Cross plans vary somewhat in rates and coverages. Michigan

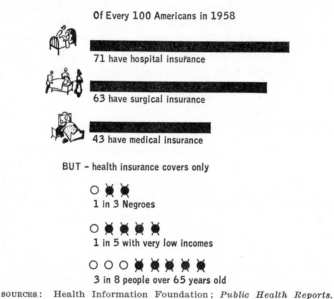

Of Every 100 Americans in 1958

71 have hospital insurance

63 have surgical insurance

43 have medical insurance

BUT – health insurance covers only

1 in 3 Negroes

1 in 5 with very low incomes

3 in 8 people over 65 years old

SOURCES: Health Information Foundation; *Public Health Reports.*

FIG. 17-6. Health insurance coverage in the United States, 1958.

Blue Cross, for example, covers costs of ward bed or semiprivate hospital room for 120 days during the year for each person covered. Certain other items, such as operating room use, drugs and dressings, laboratory services, special diets, and most other hospital expenses are covered. The annual premium (1960) with semiprivate hospital room is $56 for one person and $138 for a full family, with rates a little less for ward bed service. Some variations are offered at somewhat lower premiums: an "economy" plan with only thirty days hospital service, a $50 deductible plan in which the patient pays the first $50 of each hospital bill. Members join in groups, and premiums are often paid through payroll deductions. Individuals, retired members, and dependents can also be covered, but at somewhat higher rates. [72]

[71] *Statistical Abstract*, 1958, p. 76.

[72] Data from 1960 promotional materials of Michigan Blue Cross, 441 East Jefferson, Detroit 26, Michigan.

The Blue Shield Medical-Surgical Care plans are organized and indirectly controlled by the medical societies, and are usually sold together with Blue Cross Hospital Care plans. The Michigan Blue Shield plan covers most costs for medical services while in the hospital, and for surgical services in the hospital or doctor's office. Obstetrical care, anesthesia, emergency first aid, and certain other costs are covered. The plan pays the physicians and surgeons for each unit of service, following a fee schedule which is graded according to the member's income bracket. Unless the family income exceeds $7,500, the physicians may not bill the patient for any additional fees for the services included in the coverage. Annual premiums range from $22 to $29 for one person and from $67 to $92 for a family, depending upon their income. The combined Michigan Blue Cross—Blue Shield package thus costs from $77 to $85 for one person and from $144 to $230 for a family, or somewhat less if one of the economy forms is chosen. The Blue Shield plans in other areas vary from this, but offer much the same services at roughly comparable rates. [73]

Many other voluntary insurance plans offering similar coverages are operated by industries, unions, and commercial insurance companies. All have certain exclusions and do not try to cover *all* of a family's medical costs. Their purpose is to cover that part of a family's medical expense which comes in a sudden, unbearable flood. If these limited-coverage health insurance plans are evaluated according to the National Health Assembly's criteria, their achievements and limitations become apparent.

a. Comprehensive medical care is not provided by most Blue plans or other comparable plans. The home and office calls which make up the bulk of the average family's ordinary medical expenses are defined as "noninsurable." Either a time limit or a dollar limit is placed on practically every kind of service provided.

b. Universal enrollment—the insuring of everybody—is unattainable under purely voluntary insurance. Most plans have an upper-age limit or special, more costly provisions for the aged, and only three in eight people over 65 years old have any health insurance. Most plans insure only *groups* of people, or accept individual members at considerably higher premiums. This is done because group enrollment cuts administrative costs and secures a more normal assortment of health risks, whereas individual enrollment loads the plan with people who expect heavy medical expenses. The AMA is now promoting the organization of cut-rate health insurance plans for the aged, with the physicians accepting a reduced schedule of fees for persons insured under these plans. [74] The success of this venture cannot yet be measured. But it is doubtful whether voluntary insurance plans can ever reach more than three-fourths of the

[73] *Ibid.*

[74] Gunnar Gunderson, "American Medical Association Report," *Public Health Reports,* Vol. 74 (July, 1959), pp. 615-620; *Medical Economics,* Vol. 36 (March 30, 1959), p. 3.

population, which would still leave 45 million people—heavily concentrated among the aged, the poor, the unemployed, racial minorities, and migratory and seasonal workers—with no prepaid health services.

c. The *quality* of medical services secured through limited-coverage voluntary health insurance is neither better nor poorer than that generally available under private medical practice. Group practice is not particularly encouraged and its special advantages are not secured. Health education and preventive medicine are not included. Most of the kinds of services involved in early detection and diagnosis are not covered, although the coverages do aid in prompt treatment of some disorders when they are discovered.

d. *Freedom to experiment* is present to some degree in voluntary health insurance. Different plans vary somewhat in coverage and charges.

e. *Methods of payment and conditions of participation* have been quite satisfactory to physicians and hospitals, since they control the plans. The hospitalization plans were largely developed by hospitals, partly to stabilize their income during the depression, and are largely controlled by hospital representatives. [75] The Blue Shield plans are controlled by the medical profession and use the fee-for-service system of payment. [76] Some physicians have objected to Blue Shield attempts to set a uniform fee schedule. [77]

f. *Costs* remain high and *efficiency* of practice is not greatly improved under limited voluntary health insurance, since there are no important changes in the organization of practice. Inasmuch as the fee-for-service system is retained, the tendency may be to *increase* costs rather than reduce them. The physician is tempted to recommend unnecessary services, since the patient does not himself pay for them. There is evidence that much unnecessary surgery takes place, partly from mistaken diagnosis but partly for mercenary reasons. [78] The schedule of *maximum* fees which the insurance plan will pay for specified operations tends to become the *minimum* which surgeons charge, and sometimes the surgeon adds an additional fee for the patient himself to pay, a practice which the AMA discourages. [79] There are even instances of physicians billing the insurance plan for services never performed. [80] An insurance company study found

[75] Louis S. Reed, *Blue Cross and Medical Service Plans* (Washington, United States Public Health Service, 1947), pp. 81-85.

[76] Oscar N. Serbein, Jr., *Paying for Medical Care in the United States* (New York, Columbia University Press, 1953), p. 134.

[77] *Medical Economics*, Vol. 36 (May 25, 1959), p. 4.

[78] Dr. Paul Hawley, Director, American College of Surgeons, says, "Unjustified surgery goes on in many parts of the country, and we run into it every day. . . . Some of these are performed because of bad judgment, and some for mercenary reasons." (*Time*, Vol. 63 [February 15, 1954], p. 72).

[79] *Journal of the American Medical Association*, Vol. 148 (March 22, 1952), p. 1036.

[80] Milton Silverman, "The High Cost of Chiseling," *Saturday Evening Post*, Vol. 230 (June 14, 1958), pp. 36 ff.

that 70 per cent of the physicians raised their fees when patients joined a major medical expense insurance plan, boosting over-all costs by 17 per cent. [81] Patients often seek hospitalization for services which could easily be handled outside, but which are covered by insurance only if performed in the hospital. For this and other reasons, almost 20 per cent of the Blue Cross dollar is spent on unnecessary hospitalization, according to a survey by the Michigan State Medical Society. [82] Wisconsin Blue Cross reports "substantial overcharging" in nineteen of thirty hospitals. [83] Costs have mounted so rapidly that New York Blue Shield lost $40 million in 1958, asked for a rate boost of 34 per cent, and dropped its smaller groups. [84] The recent president of Connecticut Blue Shield comments, "Blue Shield is the only [nonprofit concern] that's controlled by the people for whom it's a source of income. It cannot logically remain so." [85] In these ways, limited-coverage voluntary health insurance using fee-for-service payment tends to maintain and increase the cost of medical care and the somewhat inefficient organization of health services.

g. *Consumer participation* is largely lacking in the control of these plans. In 1933 the House of Delegates of the AMA approved the organization of voluntary health plans under the control of the medical profession. The medical societies sponsored legislation, since passed in about half the states, insuring that control of voluntary health organizations would remain with the medical profession. Even in states without such legislation, pressure and intimidation by medical societies has largely prevented the organization of consumer-controlled health insurance organizations.

In summary, limited voluntary health insurance provides the majority of the American people some protection against heavy medical expense. It has undoubtedly made good medical care more easily available to a great many people than it used to be. In the view of most medical society spokesmen, voluntary health insurance, plus public health services, free medical care for the indigent, and certain other grants and programs, provides a satisfactory solution for any medical care problem which may exist in the United States. In the view of its critics, however, voluntary health insurance with limited coverage and fee-for-service payments is inadequate and basically unsound, because, [86]

Voluntary insurance plans not only fail to provide adequate insurance protection but they do not, and apparently can not, provide needed additional

[81] *Medical Economics*, Vol. 36 (May 11, 1959), p. 29.

[82] Milton Silverman, *op. cit.*

[83] *Medical Economics*, Vol. 36 (April 13, 1959), p. 4.

[84] "Blue Shield Drops Coverage; Other Plans Pick It Up," *Medical Economics*, (May 25, 1959), pp. 47-48; *New York Times*, June 28, 1959, p. 1.

[85] *Medical Economics*, Vol. 36 (February 2, 1959), p. 3.

[86] I. S. Falk, quoted in President's Commission on the Health Needs of the Nation, *op. cit.*, Vol. IV, p. 67.

financial support for personnel and facilities and for educational and related resources. They hinder at least as much as they help the development of group practice arrangements required for advancement of quality of care. They encourage segmented and categorical services, with excesses in various directions, rather than co-ordinated care. They impede as much as they support modern preventative medicine. They are inherently more expensive than comprehensive insurance can and should be. And some of them encourage financial exploitation by practitioners and progressive commercialization of health services.

3. Comprehensive Medical Care Plans

In 1946, the Co-operative Health Federation of America was organized to become "the national voice and spokesman for democratically controlled co-operative and group health plans throughout the country." It has grown steadily and now numbers about 20 organizations caring for over 750,000 people. Its basic principles are: (a) prepayment, budgeting the costs of medical care, (b) comprehensive medical and health care— preventive and curative, (c) group medical practice, (d) management of facilities by members, and (e) democratic control. Most of the comprehensive plans are sponsored by consumer co-operatives (such as Group Health Association, Washington, D.C., or Elk City, Oklahoma), or by community nonprofit organizations (such as Health Insurance Plan, New York) or by labor unions and employee mutual benefit associations.

Group Health Association (Washington, D. C.) provides hospital care without dollar limits or any limit upon the number of days care, and provides practically all hospital "extras" (operating room, dressings, special diets, etc.). It also provides unlimited medical and surgical care, including unlimited office calls, specialist services, home calls ($5 charge for the first home call of an illness), and certain other services. It is a "closed panel" system, meaning that the patient may choose only from among those physicians who have contracted with the association to provide services to its members. These services cost from $87 a year for a single person to $226 for a family of five or more. For an additional payment of $25 for a single person or $64 for a family of five or more, the association will also provide all laboratory services, private duty nursing, and 80 per cent of the cost of all medicines and drugs over $25 a year. [87]

Health Insurance Plan of Greater New York (HIP) is quite similar except that HIP does not include hospitalization, which the members secure through Blue Cross or elsewhere. Medical care is centered in thirty-two medical centers, and covers medical, specialist, and surgical services without dollar limits. Service is given in medical center, hospital, or home. Laboratory and diagnostic procedures, maternity care, and most other special services are included. Preventative medicine is encouraged,

[87] Data from 1960 promotional materials of Group Health Association, 1025 Vermont Avenue, N. W., Washington 5, D. C.

with the result that HIP members have 25 per cent fewer hospital admissions than other Blue Cross members. [88] Annual fees in 1960 ranged from $43 for one adult to $128 for a family of three or more, plus about 21 per cent additional if the family income exceeds $7,500 a year. To these fees should be added the costs of basic hospitalization insurance. [89]

An evaluation of comprehensive medical care plans according to the National Health Assembly's criteria reveals characteristics quite different from limited-coverage health insurance plans.

a. Comprehensive health care is provided as the main function of such plans. Some exclusions are necessary, but the coverage is far more extensive. Office calls are covered at little or no charge and home calls at nominal charge. There are no dollar limits on coverage for surgery or for medical service in office, home, or hospital.

b. Universal membership has not been approached by comprehensive care plans, with only about 5 per cent of the people having comprehensive coverage. The growth of comprehensive plans has been retarded by the difficulty of financing the necessary facilities, by restrictive legislation, and by the opposition of organized medicine. Furthermore, *no* form of voluntary health insurance will reach *all* people, for the unemployed, the low-income groups, the migratory workers, and many of the aged would never be covered unless someone else paid their premiums.

c. The *quality* of medical care provided by comprehensive plans is, according to its advocates, *higher* than that ordinarily obtained by most other people. Group practice is used to provide the continuity of care, ease of consultation, and stimulus towards professional excellence that are claimed to inhere in group practice. Preventive measures such as health examinations and immunizations are usually covered, and health education is actively promoted. Members appear to be generally well satisfied and complaints are few. [90] In 1959, an AMA committee studied many comprehensive medical care plans in great detail, concluding that "Medical service rendered by these plans was good; physicians were qualified, felt adequately paid, and were not overworked." [91]

d. Freedom and willingness to experiment are usually encouraged in the charters of the plans, but restrictive legislation and the opposition of organized medicine sharply limits the range of experimentation that is possible. The earlier plans faced bitter opposition from medical societies.

[88] Edwin F. Daley, "Medical Care Under the Health Insurance Plan of Greater New York," *Journal of the American Medical Association*, Vol. 170 (May 16, 1959), p. 273.

[89] Data from 1960 promotional materials of Health Insurance Plan of Greater New York, 625 Madison Avenue, New York 22, N. Y.

[90] "Comprehensive Medical Insurance," *Progress in Health Services*, monthly newsletter (New York, Health Information Foundation, June, 1959).

[91] "Report of the Committee on Medical Care Plans," *Journal of the American Medical Association*, Special Issue, (January 17, 1959), p. 28.

Physicians serving the plans were denied membership in the local medical societies, barred from hospitals, denied referrals of patients, and generally classed as medical outlaws—exceedingly grave penalties for any physician to face. Several celebrated court battles ended with the Supreme Court ruling that such medical boycotts were a violation of law; [92] nevertheless, opposition continued. But in 1959 the AMA officially dropped its opposition to closed panel plans, [93] and this presumably will end a long and bitter struggle. In several areas, including Detroit and Southern California, comprehensive closed panel plans are now being organized with strong labor union support. [94]

e. *Methods of payment and conditions of participation* have been relatively satisfactory to the participating physicians. The comprehensive health plans report that resignations by staff physicians have been remarkably few, and the Co-operative Health Federation of America has received more applications from physicians seeking positions than it could place. [95] Physicians like the regular hours (they take turns on night duty), opportunities for advanced study, relief from office chores, and the stimulating professional atmosphere of group practice. [96] Payment is usually by salary for full or part time, a method agreeable to the employed physicians but disliked by organized medicine, since it departs from the fee-for-service system.

f. *Efficiency* is high and costs are lowered under these plans. Group practice raises efficiency in the use of facilities, in arranging consultations, and in use of the physician's time. Costs are also reduced through the removal of the incentive for unnecessary services. Overutilization, the demanding of unnecessary services by neurotic or malingering patients, has not been a serious problem. [97] A study made several years ago revealed that the medical services received at a cost of $118 by the average family under the [Kaiser employees] Permanente Health Plan would cost $167 at private rates. [98]

[92] James Howard Means, *Doctors, Dollars, and Government* (Boston, Little, Brown & Co., 1949), Ch. X, "Legislation and Litigation"; Horace R. Hansen, "Group Health Plans: A 20-Year Review," *Minnesota Law Review*, Vol. 42 (March, 1958), pp. 527-548.

[93] The AMA now officially ". . . recognizes the patient's right to select the type of medical care plan he wants—including a closed panel plan." *Journal of the American Medical Association*, Vol. 170 (July 25, 1959), p. 155.

[94] *Medical Economics*, Vol. 36 (March 30, 1959), p. 3; Vol. 36 (August 17, 1959), p. 2; Walter Reuther, "Medicine and Labor in These Changing Times," *Journal of the Michigan State Medical Society*, Vol. 56 (October, 1957), pp. 1293-1298.

[95] James Howard Means, *op. cit.*, p. 135.

[96] "Report of the Committee on Medical Care Plans," *op. cit.*, p. 33.

[97] President's Committee on the Health Needs of the Nation, *op. cit.*, Vol. III, p. 268; Robert A. Rothenberg, Karl Pickard, and Joel E. Rothenberg, *Group Medicine and Health Insurance in Action* (New York, Crown Publishers, Inc., 1949), Ch. X, "Utilization of Services."

[98] President's Committee on the Health Needs of the Nation, *op. cit.*, Vol. IV, pp. 360-363. See also, "Groups Give Patients More for Their Money," *Medical Economics*, Vol. 35 (May 26, 1958), pp. 84-90.

Comprehensive medical care plans can make substantial savings in the cost of drugs and medicines, which form a steadily rising part of the costs of medical care. Recent congressional investigations have shown that the profits of the drug industry are very high—higher than for any other major industry—and that their methods of sales promotion are exceedingly costly. [99] For every fourteen physicians in practice, there is a drug company "detail man" who calls on physicians to inform them of new products and push his company's brands. Many drugs are sold under their chemical or generic name for a fraction of their price under their brand name—for example, "Reserpine" costs $1.75 per hundred, unless brand-named "Serpasil," when it costs $5.50. Also, there may be several different drugs, priced differently, which are equally effective for a particular ailment. The well-informed physician can save a lot of money for his patients by the way he writes his prescriptions. Comprehensive care plans try to do this, and may also buy drugs in wholesale lots for dispensing to their members.

g. *Consumer participation in control* is provided by most of the comprehensive medical care plans, although some are controlled by physicians or employers. In all cases physicians retain complete control over all *medical* matters—what treatment to give, what drugs to prescribe, when to operate, and so on. It is the *administrative* matters—coverage, charges, methods of payment, and the like—which laymen control in many of the plans.

In summary, the comprehensive medical care plans present a means whereby many people can get good medical care at considerably less cost than at present. Largely because of determined opposition from organized medicine, these plans have been available to only a few people, but they may grow more rapidly now that medical opposition is relaxing. Yet, even if fully developed, these plans would still be unavailable to millions of people because of mobility, unemployment, and low income.

4. National Health Insurance

Every modern nation except the United States has some form of comprehensive medical care financed by taxation. [100] Compulsory health insurance has twice been seriously considered in the United States, just

[99] See "The Drug Industry: What It Is and How It Operates," *New York Times*, December 13, 1959, IV, p. 8; "Big Pill Bill to Swallow," *Life*, Vol. 48 (February 15, 1960), pp. 97-103; "The High Cost of ℞ Drugs," *Consumer Reports*, Vol. 23 (November, 1958), pp. 597-599; also, *Time*, Vol. 74 (December 21, 1959), pp. 70-72; *New York Times*, December 13, 1959, pp. 1ff.

[100] Harry Eckstein, *The English Health Service* (Cambridge, Harvard University Press, 1959); Leona Baumgartner, "A Doctor Diagnoses Soviet Medicine," *New York Times Magazine*, May 17, 1959, pp. 42 ff.; Milton L. Roemer, "Socialized Medical Services in Saskatchewan," *Social Research*, Vol. 25 (April, 1958), pp. 87-101; Max Awner, "Freedom and Security in Denmark," *The Progressive*, Vol. 22 (February, 1958), pp. 27-28; also *New York Times*, November 9, 1958, p. 84; March 3, 1959, p. 6.

before and after the First World War, and, again, during the Truman administration. [101] The more recent proposal called for a national system of compulsory health insurance, built on the framework of the Social Security administration and covering all persons who now make payments into or receive benefits from federal insurance systems, together with their dependents—about 85 per cent of the people. Other persons might join voluntarily. Payments equal to 3 per cent of income would be collected, using the same machinery that now collects social security payments. Benefits would include all necessary services of dentists and physicians, including specialists, hospital care, home nursing care, laboratory and related services, and the more expensive appliances and medicines. All practitioners and facilities would be free to participate if they desired. Special measures would deal with shortage areas and annual grants would be made to medical schools, with maintenance grants to medical students and grants for medical research. National administration would be vested in a national board and advisory council which would determine policy and allocate funds; local administration would be handled by local boards composed of laymen and physicians. The recommendations and proposed bills have included many specific guarantees, including: [102]

. . . the right of all qualified practitioners, hospitals and other facilities to participate and be paid for services to insured persons; the right of . . . voluntary health service insurance plans to participate; free choice of doctor, hospital, etc., by the insured persons; freedom of the doctor, dentist or nurse to practice where he chooses; no intrusion into the management of hospitals; payments to practitioners by the methods of their choice, at rates sufficient to yield adequate annual incomes; full cost reimbursement to hospitals; and preservation of the confidentiality of personal records.

Since national health insurance is a *proposal* rather than a plan in operation in the United States, it is difficult to be certain what it would accomplish. An attempted evaluation according to the National Health Assembly's criteria might describe it as follows:

a. Comprehensive care is promised, somewhat limited at first, but expanded as rapidly as personnel and facilities could be provided.

b. Expected *enrollment* of 85 per cent of the people does not include everyone but is more extensive than any other single plan is likely to become. The remaining 15 per cent, some of whom would be migratory workers and other low-income people, would need other provisions if their medical needs were to be met.

---

[101] George Rosen, *A History of Public Health* (New York, MD Publications, Inc., 1958), pp. 439-463; Oscar E. Ewing, *The Nation's Health: A Ten Year Program* (Washington, Government Printing Office, 1948).

[102] I. S. Falk, in President's Commission on the Health Needs of the Nation, *op. cit.*, Vol. IV, pp. 68-69.

c. Quality of care is heatedly debated. Advocates point out that in many ways—better distribution of personnel and facilities, elimination of financial barriers to treatment, co-ordination and continuity of care, and others—the quality of care *might be improved* by national health insur- ance. Dissent comes from two groups. (1) Opponents of "socialized med- icine," as they term it, insist that quality of care would deteriorate terribly because of political interference and corruption, bureaucratic incompe- tence, malingering on the part of patients, and other abuses. [103] (2) Some supporters of the national health insurance principle object that the recent proposals do not go far enough in promoting group practice and the salary method of payment to secure possible gains in quality of care.

d. Freedom to experiment would be substantial, as administration would be decentralized with state and local units retaining considerable freedom of action.

e. Payment methods and conditions of participation satisfactory to medical personnel are specifically guaranteed in the proposal. Whether they would be realized is a matter of dispute. The medical societies and hospital associations are guaranteed a major voice in these matters, but not the sole control which organized medicine feels it should have.

f. Costs and efficiency levels are also disputed. Costs of collection, using the existing social security machinery, should be extremely low, but other costs are not accurately predictable. Most plans, both public and private, have found that costs exceeded original estimates. Opponents of "socialized medicine" predict astronomical costs and disgraceful ineffi- ciency. [104] Some supporters of the national health insurance principle claim that, since this particular proposal permits solo practice and fee- for-service payment, costs would be unnecessarily high, and the present alleged inefficiencies of medical practice would only be continued and compounded.

g. Consumer participation in all levels of policy-making is provided through membership in the various administrative boards.

5. Special Grants and Categorical Services

Governmental and private philanthropic agencies promote many kinds of *categorical* programs, meaning that each deals only with certain specified disorders or only with a designated group of people. Volun-

[103] For example, an AMA pamphlet, "The Voluntary Way is the American Way," published about 1950 (n. d.), states, ". . . the historical record of every great country to try politically controlled medicine, is a record of: deterioration of medical education, training, and research; degeneration of medical standards, and of medical care; steady decline of the people's health." (p. 9.)

[104] An AMA pamphlet states, "The medical bill of the average family would be doubled, if not trebled." "America would require a million and a half non- medical employees . . . siphoning off medical funds. . . ." (*Ibid.*, pp. 4, 5.)

TABLE 17-2. Government assumes growing responsibility for the nation's health

(Millions of dollars)

	1929	1940	1950	1958
General hospital and medical care.	215.0	415.0	1,174.0	1,881.5
Defense Department facilities	30.0	45.0	332.0	584.7
Medicare				86.6
Veterans' hospital and medical care	30.0	72.0	582.2	794.1
Public assistance medical care				320.2
Workmen's compensation medical benefits	25.0	90.0	193.0	370.0
Temporary disability insurance medical benefits			2.5	31.9
Medical vocational rehabilitation		.4	7.4	14.9
Maternal health and child health services	5.0	13.7	29.7	122.7
School health programs	9.0	17.9	30.6	87.8
Medical research		3.1	55.0	237.5
Other public health activities	100.0	179.5	373.7	386.6
Medical facilities construction	99.0	55.1	585.0	525.2
Total	513.0	891.7	3,365.1	5,443.7

Public spending for health and mental care, selected fiscal years, 1929-58.
SOURCE: Social Security Administration, *Research and Statistics Note No. 26-1959*

tary private agencies like the National Tuberculosis Association and the National Foundation for Infantile Paralysis provide treatment and promote research in certain diseases. Federal, state, and local governments spent $5.4 billion for health services in 1958, one-fifth of our nation's $23 billion medical bill. [105] Services are given to a wide variety of groups—Indians, drug addicts, the crippled, the indigent, tuberculosis victims, and others. Federal grants are made for numerous definite purposes: to aid state and local governments in conducting certain programs, for hospital construction, for research, and many others. [106] It is clear that we already have a partly socialized system of medical care, and that it has been a major factor in health gains we have already accomplished. If government financing of health services is "socialized medicine," then the issue is not *whether* to socialize medicine in the United States, but *how much further* to socialize medicine in the United States.

[105] *Time*, Vol. 75 (February 22, 1960), p. 62, quoting data from the Health Information Foundation.
[106] See Oscar N. Serbein, *op. cit.*, Part V, "Governmental Programs," for a detailed, though no longer complete, description of governmental health activities.

Whether grants and categorical services are a more practical approach to health problems than a wholesale reorganization of medical practice is a debatable issue. Grants and categorical services result in a medical patchwork with many gaps, considerable overlapping, and little co-ordination. On the other hand, such programs can be started cheaply and expanded gradually, and excite less opposition than sweeping reorganization proposals. One of the ways of getting a program into operation is to provide federal grants to the states, which must set up their programs and provide some matching funds in order to claim the federal grants. In recent years, federal grants for health research have been greatly increased—from $57 million in 1951 to $418 in 1960. [107]

THE "SOCIALIZED MEDICINE" CONTROVERSY

With the aggressive support of President Truman and various health officers of the federal government, the proposal for national health insurance aroused one of the most bitter political battles in decades. Supporters included most labor organizations and co-operatives, consumer organizations, and a number of physicians and medical educators organized into Physicians' Forum. Opponents included the medical and hospital associations, the American Legion, the DAR, national business and commercial associations, and many other politically conservative groups and organizations.

In addition to charges that costs would be staggering and quality of care poor, the AMA and its supporters lodged charges that doctors would be regimented, and their freedom of practice and their incentives for improvement destroyed; medical careers would become unattractive and medical school enrollments would decline; private practice would be eliminated; the medical privacy of the patient would be invaded; the patient's "free choice of physician" would be limited; the patient-doctor relationship would suffer; politicians might threaten to withhold medical services from persons who did not support the party in power; health insurance would be socialistic and communistic, and merely a first step to the regimentation of all the professions and the destruction of free enterprise. Lenin was widely—and incorrectly—quoted as having said that "socialized medicine is the keystone to the arch of the socialist state," [108] and the motives of the supporters of national health insurance were liberally impugned. The British National Health Service was de-

[107] *Congressional Quarterly*, Vol. 17 (June 26, 1959), p. 857.

[108] This alleged Lenin quotation, widely used in AMA campaign material, was first "quoted" by Lawrence Sullivan in *The Case Against Socialized Medicine* (Washington, Statesman Press, 1949), but neither Mr. Sullivan nor anyone else has given an exact citation of this "quotation" in any of Lenin's recorded writings or speeches. Although no doubt Lenin favored state medicine, there is no evidence that he ever made this particular statement.

picted as an alarming example of what national health insurance would bring to the United States. [109]

Some of these charges no doubt expressed real possibilities and dangers. The possibilities of political manipulation, of graft and corruption, and of red-tape-entangled bureaucracy are too real to be ignored. Other charges have been quite unrealistic in view of the provisions and specific guarantees in the proposed bills. In particular, the flagrant misrepresentation and distortion of the British National Health Service presents a remarkable study in irresponsible propaganda. Many pamphlets, paid advertisements, and articles in mass magazines have pictured medical care in Britain as disgraceful and British health as rapidly deteriorating. British medical journals have protested repeatedly against the misleading caricatures drawn by Americans who study Britain's Health Service "with the idea of finding out everything bad about it so they can make their compatriots' flesh creep when they go home." [110] The facts appear to be that the sudden expansion of their National Health Service in 1948 overloaded it for a time, and that some initial errors were made, but by 1952 public opinion polls were showing 85 to 90 per cent of the public well satisfied with the health service. Nearly everyone in Britain today, including over 80 per cent of the physicians, approves the principle of national compulsory health insurance, although both doctors and laymen often complain about certain details of its operation. [111] The general success of Britain's National Health Service is now an established fact— which does not, of course, imply that we should necessarily copy it, for our needs and traditions are different.

Several public opinion polls between 1942 and 1946 revealed that some system of national health insurance was acceptable to a majority of our people. [112] In the ensuing socialized medicine controversy, public support apparently declined and the bill was easily defeated in Congress. Public discussion has faded, and it appears highly improbable that any such legislation will be passed in the near future.

Piecemeal socialization of medical care, however, will continue to grow. Congress is now (1960) seriously considering a proposal to expand the social security system to provide comprehensive medical services for

[109] See such AMA pamphlets, such as "The Voluntary Way is The American Way," "Compulsory Health Insurance," and "Pickpocket Medicine," and see Melchior Palyi, *Compulsory Health Insurance and the Welfare State* (Chicago, National Institute of Professional Services, 1949), for detailed statements of these charges.

[110] Sir Henry Ogilvie, M. D., in *British Medical Journal* (March 25, 1950), pp. 714-715. A recent editorial in the British Medical Journal accuses the AMA of deliberate misrepresentation, acidly advising the AMA ". . . to find out how far American medicine falls behind in its services to the great American public" (*Chicago Sun-Times* [October 5, 1959], p. 16).

[111] Harry Eckstein, *op. cit.;* Leona Baumgartner, *op. cit.*

[112] See Carl Malmberg, *op. cit.*, pp. 230-232, and Clarence A. Peters, *op. cit.*, pp. 93-104, for summary of opinion polls.

the aged. This would amount to socialized medicine for persons over sixty-five. This proposal is supported by organized labor and opposed by organized medicine. [113] New York's Governor Rockefeller has proposed compulsory major medical insurance (covering large bills but not small, and routine medical expenses) to be sold by private insurance companies under state supervision. [114] Federal grants, especially for hospital construction, are substantial and are growing larger. In some form or other, greater government activity in health services seems to be a certainty.

ISSUES CONCERNING THE HEALTH PROBLEM

Attempts to meet the health problem have been greatly confused by the persistent attention given to some unreal, or phony, issues. These issues are often misrepresented and the alternatives are incorrectly stated to the public.

1. The "socialism" issue is an unreal issue. None of the medical care proposals—not even national health insurance—would either create a socialist state or require a socialist government for its operation. Like public schools, highways, and the postal system—all once denounced as socialistic—a health service plan can be operated by any form of government. Nor would government-financed health services necessarily promote socialist philosophy. During the past quarter-century of expanding governmental services, public opinion polls have shown a steady decline in popular support for nationalization of banks, mines, and railroads—the heart of the real socialist program. [115] The interjection of the bogeyman of "socialism" and "Communism" into the health discussion serves only in an effort to replace rational with emotional thinking and to shift the basis of decision from a practical to a theoretical or doctrinaire level.

2. The "free-enterprise" issue—whether to retain or destroy "the free-enterprise system of medical care" is no real issue. Medical practice in America is not a "free enterprise" in any ordinary use of the term. Doctors are prevented by law or by professional ethics from doing many of the things which a competitive business may properly do—enter and leave the business at will, advertise, entice customers away from one another, criticize competitors' products, cut prices, hold "sales," and so on. Medical practice has privileges and obligations quite different from those of the businessman. To invoke the terminology of the market place in discussing medical practice is only confusing.

There are, however, some real issues—vital questions upon which the future direction of health organization will hinge—which deserve fuller discussion.

[113] *Journal of the American Medical Association,* Vol. 170 (July 25, 1959), p. 33.
[114] *Medical Economics,* Vol. 36 (March 2, 1959), p. 4.
[115] Four Gallup polls, taken in 1936, 1945, 1949, and 1953, show popular support for these propositions steadily declining to less than half its 1936 level. (*Time* [October 19, 1953], p. 28.)

1. How Much Shall We Sacrifice to Gain Full Health Care for All?

How much shall we spend? The government and individuals in the United States are currently spending about as much for medical services as for alcohol and tobacco; individuals spend a trifle more for health services than they spend for alcohol. Shall we increase taxes—for any major increase would need to be through taxation—in order to spend more for medical care? Shall we determine to spend *whatever is required* to provide high-quality medical services for everyone? The cost might be considerable. A recent survey in Michigan—a relatively healthy and prosperous state—found "that there were more persons in rural areas who had none of their medical needs met than those who had all of them cared for." [116] National health cannot be bought at bargain prices!

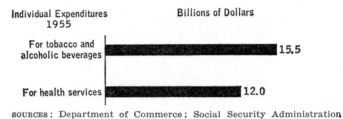

SOURCES: Department of Commerce; Social Security Administration

FIG. 17-7. Hilarity and health.

Should low-income persons be *encouraged* or *discouraged* from asking for free medical care? Should those too ignorant to recognize their medical needs be encouraged to seek services for which they cannot pay, or should we be grateful that they do not clamor for free attention? These questions are important, both for health and for government finance.

There are *some* health expenditures which eventually pay for themselves in reduced dependency. At a cost to federal and state governments of $32.6 million in 1952, some 63,682 vocationally handicapped persons were rehabilitated; their annual earnings increased by $100 million after rehabilitation; and the federal government collected an additional $9.2 millions in income taxes in the following year. [117] Vocational rehabilitation more than pays for itself. Whether all increases in government health increases would also pay for themselves is not certain.

Health is also a matter of diet, of housing, of health habits. Shall we make the determined (and costly) attack upon poverty, substandard housing, and ignorance which would be needed to reach the highest

---

[116] President's Commission on the Health Needs of the Nation, *op. cit.*, Vol. III, p. 273.
[117] *Ibid.*, Vol. IV, pp. 196-197.

health level? Or shall we use these conditions to excuse and justify the continuation of widespread unmet medical needs in the United States? All these questions are important; all involve major value choices, and each answer would impose sacrifices upon some of us.

2. Who Shall Control the Organization of Medical Services?

Organized medicine has felt that the profession itself should control all phases of medical practice—financial and administrative as well as medical—and has obtained laws in about half the states to insure such control. A number of laymen, joined by some physicians, feel that laymen should be permitted to organize medical care plans in which they control the business and financial management. Organized medicine now appears to be relaxing its insistence upon complete control, but the division of responsibility between physicians and laymen remains an issue.

3. To What Extent Shall a Reorganization of Medical Practice Be Promoted?

Many members of the medical profession feel that the present system is a good one and are rather resentful that it is under attack. But the growing trend toward group practice and salary payment and the successful operation of the comprehensive health care plans suggest that an eventual reorganization along such lines is, perhaps, inevitable. Meanwhile, should only plans fully acceptable to organized medicine be promoted, or should other plans be demanded despite medical opposition? [118]

4. What Should Be the Role of Government in Health Services?

There is no serious proposal that government should assume *direct control* of medical practice. The real issues include: (*a*) How actively should the government promote medical reorganization (such as the President's Commission's recommendation for federal grants to encourage voluntary, comprehensive, group-practice medical care plans)? Should the government, perhaps, grant medical leadership a veto power in deciding what to promote? (*b*) How much shall the government spend on health services? Should it try to discover unmet medical needs in order to meet them? (*c*) What health grants and services should the government provide, and what should it leave to individual initiative and private philanthropy?

[118] See David R. Hyde and Payson Wolff, with Ann Gross and Elliot Lee Hoffman, "The American Medical Association: Power, Purpose, and Politics in Organized Medicine," *Yale Law Review*, Vol. 63 (May, 1954), pp. 938-1022, for an objective, elaborately documented account of the political activities and pressure operations of organized medicine.

As the American people seek to grapple with the health problem, issues such as these arise, are partly answered, and then are redefined in different form to be considered again. Such is the process of policy formation in a democracy. Meanwhile, medical knowledge continues to grow, the health level continues to rise, and American medical practice continues its sometimes painful process of adapting itself to serve the changing needs of a dynamic society.

SUMMARY

Americans may be as healthy as any people in the world, but still less healthy than they might be. Health is a product of many factors—diet, housing and living conditions, health habits, sanitation, preventive medicine and medical care. All of these factors tend to go hand in hand and are closely associated with income. Health facilities are at present insufficient to provide all of the people with complete medical care and are unevenly distributed over the country. People in rural and isolated areas, low-income persons, and racial minorities receive far less medical care and have far higher illness and death rates than the national average.

The quality of medical care, while higher than in most—possibly all —other countries, is still impaired by a number of limitations: isolation of practitioners in solo practice, the fee-for-service system, fee-splitting, exclusion of some physicians from hospital privileges, high cost of medical services, lack of continuity and co-ordination, and overworking of medical personnel. Proposed improvements include group practice, voluntary health insurance, voluntary comprehensive health care plans, compulsory national health insurance, and governmental grants for specified uses. All but one of these proposals are being increasingly applied in the United States. Compulsory national health insurance has been decisively rejected, at least for the present.

The health problem can be analyzed in terms of the inability of traditional methods of medical organization and finance to handle efficiently the growing body of medical knowledge and meet changing medical needs—a social-disorganization approach. The problem can be analyzed in terms of differing value judgments concerning the extent of medical needs and of desirable ways of meeting them—a value-conflict approach. The problem can be analyzed in terms of the manner in which deviant personality organization contributes both to ill-health and to debate about the problem—a personal-deviation approach. Each approach contributes to a complete understanding of the problem.

No single proposal will solve the health problem, because a number of causes are involved. Among the major issues to be decided by the American people are these: How extensive an attack upon *all* the causes of ill-health—poverty, housing, ignorance, and medical care—should be mounted? How much tax money should be spent for health purposes? Should health services be provided, without cost if necessary, to all who *need* them or only to all who *request* them? We are now *spending enough* to provide good medical care to all who need it, but some of this expenditure is inefficiently used and some of it is totally wasted. How extensive a reorganization of medical administration should be encouraged, or even demanded? How should control of medical administration be divided between the medical profession and the public? What should be the role of government in the financing and control of medical services? The above are not questions of fact, but of value and of social policy.

There are many other aspects of health problems—dental health services, mental health, chronic illness, the health needs of the aged, the migrant-labor health problem, and others—to which this chapter gives little attention. But to completely discuss the entire health problem would require not a chapter but a bookshelf.

SUGGESTED READINGS

ANDERSON, Odin W., *Voluntary Health Insurance in Two Cities* (Cambridge, Harvard University Press, 1957). A research study showing what health insurance does and does not do for people.

CARTER, Richard, *The Doctor Business* (Garden City, N. Y., Doubleday & Company, Inc., 1958). A critical appraisal of medical organization and practice in the United States.

DAVIS, Michael, *Medical Care for Tomorrow* (New York, Harper and Brothers, 1955). A detailed survey of medical needs and resources, and a call for major reorganization.

DEKRUIF, Paul, *Kaiser Wakes the Doctors* (New York, Harcourt, Brace & Co., Inc., 1943). A brief, highly readable account of the organization and early operation of Kaiser's comprehensive health care plan for Kaiser employees.

"A Game of Wild Indians," *New Yorker* (April 5, 1952), pp. 74 ff. A true medical detective story; a highly readable account of how Department of Health officers prevented a typhoid outbreak from becoming an epidemic by tracking down and eliminating the source of the infection.

Koos, Earl Lomon, *The Health of Regionville* (New York, Columbia University Press, 1954). A research study of the health attitudes and practices of an American small town.

MEANS, James Howard, *Doctors, People, and Government* (Boston, Little, Brown & Co., 1953). A former president of the American College of Surgeons and leading medical educator in a semipopular discussion of the problem of securing better medical care for all the American people. Includes a chapter describing the history and operation of Britain's National Health Service.

PALYI, Melchior, *Compulsory Medical Care and the Welfare State* (Chicago, National Institute of Professional Services, 1949). A strong condemnation of

compulsory health insurance and the "welfare state" in general, with critical
description of compulsory health insurance systems in European countries.

ROTHENBERG, Robert A., PICKARD, Karl, and ROTHENBERG, Joel E., *Group Medicine and Health Insurance in Action* (New York, Crown Publishers, 1949).
An account of actual experience in a prepaid comprehensive medical care
plan, the Health Insurance Plan of Greater New York, written by two
physicians and an attorney active in its operation. An interesting report of
what actually goes on in such plans, with detailed suggestions on how to
establish one. The final chapter outlines an interesting plan for a National
Voluntary Health Insurance system.

SILVERMAN, Milton, "The Post Reports on Health Insurance," *Saturday Evening
Post,* Vol. 230 (June 7, 1958, p. 25 ff; June 14, 1958, pp. 36 ff; June 21, 1958,
pp. 30 ff). Three well-written popular articles appraising the achievements
and limitations of voluntary health insurance.

QUESTIONS AND PROJECTS

1. Why, in spite of medical progress, is the death rate from chronic
diseases higher than a half-century ago?

2. Why has the death rate for young people fallen so much faster than the
death rate for older people?

3. Can the death rate of an area be interpreted as a fairly accurate measure
of the quality and adequacy of medical care received by the people of that
area? Why or why not?

4. List all the factors which you think help explain the lower health level
of low-income people. Of Negroes. Of Indians.

5. Are there any common practices on the campus which are unfavorable
to good health? If so, why do they persist?

6. Why is the mean family expenditure for medical services nearly twice
as high as the median? What does this fact show about the kind of distribution curve which family medical expenditure would show on a graph?

7. Why do graduating doctors prefer to settle in urban areas? What would
be necessary to attract more doctors to small towns and rural areas?

8. Why are there so few Negro physicians? Is this a "problem" or merely
a statistical fact?

9. Do you think that, if you were a physician, you would prefer to practice
under group practice or individual practice? Why?

10. Why do you think the AMA has so strongly opposed most proposed
changes in the organization of medical practice? Is it greed? Conservatism?
Unawareness of the significance of changes in medicine? Or were they correct
in their opposition?

11. Distinguish between the *need* for medical care and the *demand* for
medical care. Which largely determines the distribution of facilities and medical personnel? Which term is evaluative and which is merely descriptive?

12. Discuss the proposition: "The main issue in the health field is whether
medicine in America shall be socialized."

13. What is your position on each of the issues stated at the end of the

chapter? What *evidence* can you cite to support your position? What value judgments did you make in taking your position?

14. Dr. James Means, in the final chapter of *Doctors, People, and Government,* proposes a plan that he believes would insure good medical care for all, without using compulsory national health insurance. Read this chapter and evaluate his proposal.

15. Evaluate the National Voluntary Health Insurance proposal in the final chapter of Dr. Robert Rothenberg and others, *Group Medicine and Health Insurance in Action.* Which aspects of the health problem would this plan affect? What opposition might be expected?

18

War and International
Organization

ჼჼ

A dying man, supporting himself on crutches, made his way to the rostrum of the National Assembly and told of his experience in Buchenwald—he had been a cripple ever since, and now, very soon, was going to die. "We Frenchmen who survived Buchenwald swore that never again should Germany be allowed to build up its military power. I have come here to renew that oath. I am going to die, Mr. President. I am going to die because of what the Germans did to me. I warn you, do not trust the Germans!" Deeply moved, the whole Assembly rose and cheered. Men had tears in their eyes as they watched George Heuillard, a Radical deputy, painfully make his way down the steps and start back to the hospital.[1]

What do you know about Hitler? Pointing his movie camera into dozens of high school classrooms, Frankfurt TV reporter Jurgen Neven-DuMont put his question to scores of German students aged 15 to 17. Telecast last week, their answers displayed a surprising ignorance of Nazi turpitude. In fact, nine out of every ten students either knew nothing at all about Adolf Hitler or thought that he had accomplished more good than harm.[2]

. . . "Most of the world," said Lawyer Rhyne (Charles S. Rhyne, President, American Bar Association), "doesn't know the International Court exists. It has fifteen judges who sit at the Hague waiting for work. It has decided only an average of slightly more than one case per year since its creation in 1945."[3]

. . . Last week in Washington the House Military Operations Subcommittee tried to stop a panicky rumor about the "dangers" of luminous watch dials, light switch markers, et cetera.

. . . In West Germany the *Hamburger Abendblatt* prints daily reports of air radioactivity. . . . As a result of such scaremongering, thousands of suggestible Germans have come down with "atomic headache." . . . The

[1] *The Nation*, Vol. 174 (March 1, 1952), p. 202.
[2] Reprinted from *Time;* copyright, Time Inc., 1959.
[3] Reprinted from *Time;* copyright, Time Inc., 1958.

Bavarian Minister of the Interior tried to convince complaining farmers that the yellowing of their pastures had nothing to do with atomic rain. . . .

In Japan, where rain is sometimes really radioactive, a new term, "radiation neurosis" has been coined to express a state of extreme nervousness which affects many Japanese after United States, Soviet, and British bomb tests. . . . In Osaka, school children are told to wear plastic raincoats with hoods. One school held drills to teach the children how to hold their umbrellas so that their hands and faces would not get spattered. . . .

In nearly all parts of the world, atomic bomb tests are blamed for unusual weather. In the United States, for instance, an article in the *Saturday Review* . . . blames bomb tests for steering hurricanes toward New England. . . . In Germany . . . in France, and Italy the public has the same conviction: the weather is unprecedented; it is the bomb's fault.[4]

THE QUOTATIONS YOU HAVE JUST READ offer a rough chronology of important public attitudes since the last major war. The first, dated just six years after World War II, shows the bitterness, the hate, the determination never to let it happen again that go with actual wartime experience. The second, from just eight years later, suggests that most of the passion has died out and that the Deputy's plea was in vain. Quotation number three reflects the unwillingness of nations to submit their disputes to international tribunals, and the final excerpt reveals world-wide anxiety over even the peacetime effects of the development of weapons for possible World War III. The threat of another world-wide war is the most ominous threat to humankind today. Unless the problem of war can be solved there may not be the opportunity—or the need—to solve any of the other problems discussed in this book.

WAR AS A CULTURE PATTERN

A wit once said, "We are such a peace-loving people that we go to war every twenty years to prove it." He was being facetious. Or *was* he? That one remark expresses an unpleasant fact that is true of Western European culture generally. Most people fervently desire peace, but wars occur with distressing frequency. There are literally dozens of organizations devoted to the cause of national and world peace, and huge sums of money are spent for the prevention of war. But these same nations express pride over never having lost a war, build countless statues of military heroes, describe history in terms of battles and wars, and form nonintervention pacts with other nations—strange behaviors for peaceful peoples. We struggle valiantly to preserve the peace, but there is a point beyond which we will not go. National honor will not be sacrificed. We will go to war if necessary, and "necessary" it has often been!

War appears early in our cultural history. The Greeks and Romans,

[4] Reprinted from *Time;* copyright, Time Inc., 1956.

who are among our remote cultural ancestors, were warlike peoples; eventually, both succumbed to the strains of war. Intermittent wars continued to spot history as the great nation-states developed in Europe, and the United States itself was born of war. The American Revolution was followed by the War of 1812, by a series of battles against the indigenous Indian population, by the Mexican War, by the Civil War, by the Spanish-American War, by World War I, by World War II, and then by the undeclared Korean conflict (with 10,000 Americans killed). Historically, warfare is a major feature of our culture pattern.

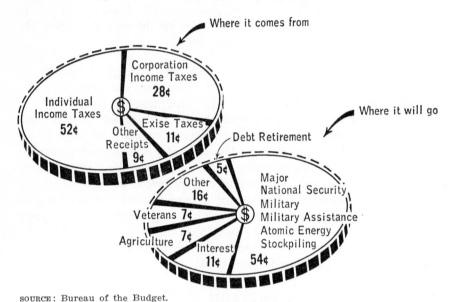

SOURCE: Bureau of the Budget.

FIG. 18-1. The United States government's budget dollar; fiscal year 1961 estimate.

The present American scene cannot help but reflect these past wars. It also reflects the current state of international tension and the possibility of future wars. Figure 18-1 shows the estimated proportion of each tax dollar spent for various military and nonmilitary purposes in the fiscal year, 1961. Current military expenditures take over 54 cents out of every tax dollar and another 5 cents is being paid to veterans of past wars. The interest on the national debt, contracted largely to finance our various wars, takes another 11 cents. Only 16 cents is allotted to all other governmental services combined. *Nearly four-fifths of the national budget is a war budget!* Whether we like it or not the American economy is overwhelmingly tied to war.

One suspects that if a true peace should "break out" the effects might be more disorganizing than war itself. The constant state of semimobilization that has been maintained since World War II has created an economy dependent upon large defense expenditures. Missile development, bomber production, and thousands of associated activities absorb over half of all government expenditures and employ millions of people. Any sudden reduction in the amount of government spending might bring wholesale unemployment and a severe economic recession. [5] It is one thing to imagine the great good that could be accomplished if all these resources were poured into education, welfare services, highways, and the like, but quite another actually to adjust the economy from a wartime to a peacetime basis. While the long-run effects of such a transition would be highly desirable, the short-run effects might approach disaster proportions.

To suggest that war is in any sense normal or to be expected is almost heresy. Most persons continue to define it as an inexcusable aberration of the relations between nations—as an evil event which somehow must be the creature of the evil intent of a few evil minds. War must be associated with villainy—Hitler, Mussolini, and Tojo being some of the most recent villains. History is written by the victors, while the villains are always leaders of the nations which *lose* the wars. Such leaders do play an important part in the initiation and conduct of wars but to identify them as *the cause* of war is to indulge in wishful thinking. Though it is comforting to think that if we can eliminate the "bad" men we will have eliminated war, history should have taught us that there is either an inexhaustible supply of bad men or that war is more than an aberration of culture! The frightening prospect is that war is deeply rooted in the culture of modern nations and that only major alterations in that culture offer much hope for its elimination.

THE DESTRUCTIVENESS OF MODERN WAR

Literature is filled with imaginary accounts of wars among preliterate peoples. Hence it is not difficult to conjure up visions of screaming hordes of savages busily impaling one another upon poison-tipped spears. Modern anthropology, however, has shown us the inaccuracy of these impressions. War is found in many preliterate societies, as it is found today, but "savages" generally fought a remarkably civilized kind of war. Total casualties in their encounters seldom reached a hundred, and to have half a dozen people killed was often sufficient reason to bring the war to an

[5] It is occasionally charged, of course, that war continues because it is profitable to munitions makers and others who prey upon the misery of mankind in general. Such explanations, in addition to being greatly oversimplified and ascribing exaggerated influence to manufacturers, provide an excellent illustration of the "social problems are caused by bad people" fallacy discussed in Chapter 1. Dependence of the economy upon defense expenditures need not imply that anybody is actually in favor of continuing the situation. Indeed, it is difficult to correct precisely, because it exists in spite of the desire of virtually everyone to eliminate it.

end. Modern man has no monopoly upon war but here, as elsewhere, he is wondrously efficient. In a single war he kills more people and destroys more property than could have been accomplished in a thousand pre-literate wars.

The history of war is one of continually increasing destructiveness. Originally, our wars probably were much like those of preliterates, but the technology of war developed apace with technology in general. Fire-arms were more efficient than thrown or hurled weapons; then automatic firearms, artillery, armored vehicles, aircraft, and, finally, nuclear weapons revolutionized warfare. In one sense the difference seems to be only a difference of degree, but in another sense it is also a difference in kind.

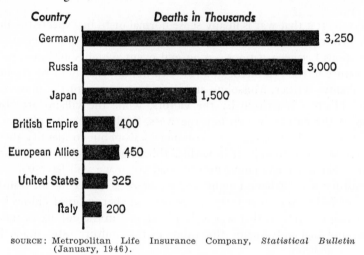

SOURCE: Metropolitan Life Insurance Company, *Statistical Bulletin* (January, 1946).

FIG. 18-2. Military deaths in World War II.

The destructiveness attained in war over the past few decades almost defies imagination. One measure of the destructiveness, of course, is the number of men killed in battle. Americans are not apt to be aware of the awful toll of human life because, relatively speaking, American casualties have not been heavy. In World War II the United States suffered ap-proximately 325,000 men killed. The individual families involved have some idea of what war means, but the majority of American families have suffered no overwhelming personal loss. The total number of military deaths in World War II, however, numbered nearly ten million! Germany and Russia each lost over three million men—each one lost ten times the American figure. Japan lost 1,500,000 men, the British lost 400,000, and our other European allies lost approximately 450,000. As if the misery and suffering caused by this mass slaughter were not enough, it will be at least a full generation before the economic life of the separate nations will recover from the loss of vigorous young manpower.

In World War II, for the first time, whole civilian populations came under attack. Up until that time the folkways of warfare had permitted the fine young men from each nation to decimate one another without too seriously disrupting life in the society at large. [6] Mass aerial bombing ended all that. Saturation raids on the city of Dresden, Germany, killed 200,000 people in a single night. In 1945, a single atomic bomb from a single airplane killed between 70,000 and 80,000 people in Hiroshima and a few days later a similar bomb killed from 35,000 to 40,000 people in Nagasaki. One estimate places the total number of civilians killed at ap-

TABLE 18-1. What an H-bomb would do to some major U.S. cities

Washington. Aiming point: the Lincoln Memorial. The perimeter of total destruction would include the entire District of Columbia and Arlington County, Va. (The Pentagon, National Airport), the suburbs of Chevy Chase, Bethesda, Silver Springs, Hyattsville, Alexandria.

New York. Aiming point: Rockefeller Center. The circle of complete destruction would extend from Spuyten Duyvil to the State of Liberty, cover all Manhattan, Hoboken, Weehawken, large parts of the The Bronx, Queens, Brooklyn and Jersey City.

Philadelphia. Aiming point: City Hall. All of the midtown and South Philadelphia areas, the Navy Yard, Germantown, Upper Darby and Camden destroyed; Chestnut Hill, Bryn Mawr, Chester severely damaged.

Boston. Aiming point: the State House. The heart of the city, Cambridge, Watertown, Brookline, most of the Newtons would be destroyed. Severely damaged: Concord, Lexington, Lynn and Quincy.

Detroit. Aiming point: Cadillac Square. Wiped out: downtown Detroit, Hamtramck, River Rouge, Highland Park, Windsor. Major blast damage: Dearborn, Grosse Pointe, Royal Oak.

Los Angeles. Aiming Point: the Hollywood Race Track. Totally destroyed: much of the business district, several major aircraft factories, Dow Chemical, M-G-M, El Segundo Oilfield and part of Santa Monica.

Chicago. Aiming Point: the International Amphitheater in the stockyards. Destroyed: the Loop, the Gold Coast, the University of Chicago, Municipal Airport, Cicero. Badly blasted: South Side steel mills and the North Shore.

Reprinted from *Time;* Copyright Time, Inc., 1954.

[6] Although of a selected group of physically superior males, those who had survived the war as veterans had more illnesses and disabilities in later life—at all ages —than non-veterans of the same age. *United States National Health Survey*, Series G-2, "Veterans' Health and Medical Care," (Washington, D.C., Government Printing Office, 1960), pp. 14-21.

proximately twelve million—more than the number of soldiers killed in combat! [7] Major wars will no longer be fought by armies but by nations, with the wholesale extermination of civilian populations as an inevitable result. Any nation on earth can now be almost completely destroyed in a matter of days!

The destruction of property and the wastage of resources during World War II are impossible to estimate accurately. One index of such destruction is pure monetary cost. Most of the war probably cost the American people in excess of $250 million per day. The United States entered the war with a national debt of $50 billion and emerged "victorious" with a debt of $260 billion. The total cost to the United States may have been as much as $400 billion, enough to have provided each

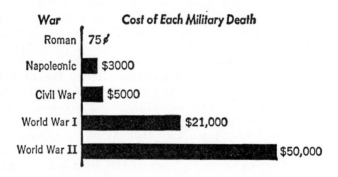

SOURCE: J.H.S. Bossard, "War and the Family," American Sociological Review, Vol. 6 (June, 1941), p. 339.

FIG. 18-3. The high cost of killing a man.

American family with a $50,000 house and two new cars a year for the next thirty years! World costs are even harder to determine, but one estimate places the total monetary cost of the war at one and a quarter trillion dollars and the total economic cost, including property destruction, at four trillion dollars. [8]

The day has passed when any nation could "win" a major war. A third world war would so deplete the earth's natural resources as to lower living standards everywhere. The financial costs would probably bankrupt the participants. And nuclear weapons undoubtedly would be used. If World War III is fought with nuclear weapons, World War IV might have to be fought with clubs! Or the atmosphere may become so poisoned that all animal life will be eliminated and the earth may be uninhabited.

[7] Mabel Elliott and Francis Merrill, *Social Disorganization*, 3rd. ed. (New York, Harper and Brothers, 1950), p. 713.

[8] Harry E. Barnes and Oreen M. Ruedi, *The American Way of Life* (Englewood Cliffs, N. J., Prentice-Hall, Inc., 1950), p. 435.

INTERNATIONAL ORGANIZATION

Like war itself, various attempts to prevent war began far back into history. Treaties have been signed, declarations made, and conferences held—but without any long-term effects. Most such efforts have involved only a few nations who were attempting to cope with a particular set of tensions or conflicting interests. Naturally these agreements provided no basis for resolving other tensions not included in the agreements, and even such limited pacts as were made contained no real provisions for enforcement. They depended upon the continued good will of the signatories. When the good will disappeared, so did the effectiveness of the pacts.

Efforts to prevent war are not new, but attempts to prevent war through large-scale international organization are relatively new. A first step was taken with the establishment of the first Permanent Court of Arbitration in 1901, as an outgrowth of the Hague Conference of 1899. The Court was never very successful in its operation—the nations of the world simply were not ready to submit their grievances to arbitration by an international body. The Court was powerless to prevent World War I. Yet the Court was important for it carried the *idea* of peaceful settlement of differences *via* an international organization through World War I to the peace conference of 1919.

The League of Nations

The plan for the League of Nations was taken to the peace conference by President Woodrow Wilson. The League was to be an instrument of international good will, providing a variety of social services and constituting a forum, aided by the World Court, for settling disputes among nations. But the League of Nations, as finally established, was ill designed to preserve world peace.

The failure of the League cannot be laid to any one force. Instead, a series of unforeseen developments combined to destroy it. One of the first and one of the most important of these was the unwillingness of the United States government to participate in the organization. President Wilson and his internationalist philosophy lost favor very rapidly as the war came to a close. By the time the peace treaty was signed the isolationist United States refused to be a party to it. Since America had emerged from the war as the world's greatest economic and military power, her unwillingness to join was a blow from which the League never recovered.

Unfortunately, too, the League was not conceived in a spirit of international co-operation but was made a part of the very harsh Treaty of Versailles. The sanctions taken against Germany and the Soviet Union included denial, for a time, of membership in the League. Thus, in addition to the United States, two of the most powerful nations in Europe were left outside its orbit. By the time they were finally admitted, the damage had already been done.

Membership in the League included approximately sixty nations. From the very beginning it proved itself most effective in dealing with social issues; problems pertaining to world health, regulation of the narcotics trade, improvement of agricultural practices, and others, were attacked most successfully. But in the crucial area of settling international disputes and preventing armed aggression the League proved impotent. A few minor disputes were settled amicably, but the League's death knell began to sound when it was unable to cope with the Japanese invasion of Manchuria in 1931. Japan's open defiance of the League was repeated with Mussolini's seizure of Ethiopia in 1935. It was only a matter of time then until World War II began. The League continued to function in its ineffectual way until the end of the war. It was then dissolved in favor of the new United Nations Organization.

The United Nations

Plans for a new and more adequate world organization were underway well before the end of World War II. The Dumbarton Oaks Conference was followed by an organization meeting in San Francisco in 1945. This time the United States played a major role in the formation of the organization and became a charter member.

The United Nations is composed of four main bodies, plus an administrative organization called the Secretariat. The hub of the organization is the Security Council. This executive organ is composed of representatives from eleven nations. There are five permanent members, the United States, the U.S.S.R., Great Britain, France, and China, and six additional members elected on a yearly basis by the General Assembly. The General Assembly is the legislative body; the Economic and Social Council is charged with continuing and improving the social services begun by the League of Nations; and the Trusteeship Council is responsible for the administration of territories under United Nations jurisdiction.

The U. N. had no sooner been organized in 1946 than major difficulties appeared. While it has a basically democratic structure, most of the U. N.'s real power centers in the Security Council, and it was there that *the major powers, including the United States,* had insisted that they must have the right of "veto." Any one of the "Big Five" could prevent the Council from taking action, and the assumption that the veto power would be used responsibly proved fallacious. The wartime harmony

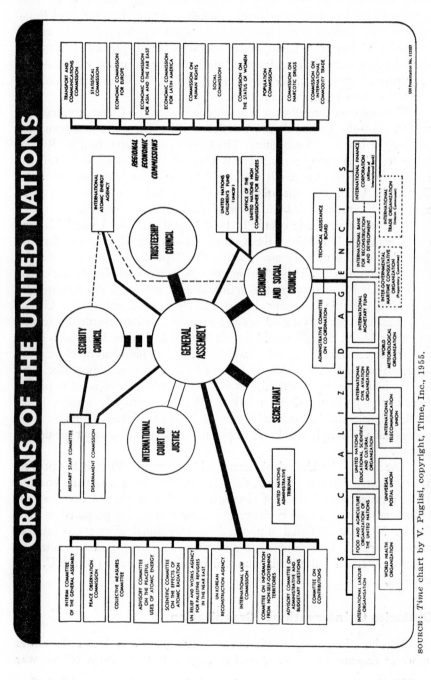

ORGANS OF THE UNITED NATIONS

UN Presentation No. 112537

SOURCE: *Time* chart by V. Puglisi, copyright, Time, Inc., 1955.

FIG. 18-4. Organization and agencies of the United Nations.

among the Allies did not carry over into the peace. American opinion repudiated the wartime agreements reached at Yalta, Teheran, and Potsdam; and the United States was launched upon a policy of "containing" the Soviet Union. The Russians, on the other hand, proved determined to consolidate their gains and seemed to demand even more. Soviet diplomacy proved aggressive, obstinate, and bewildering. Russia had used the veto forty times by December, 1949.

The diplomatic conflict was heightened when the China government, supported by the United States, was defeated in civil war and driven into exile by the Chinese Communists. The Communists, supported by Russia, demanded China's seat on the Security Council. The United States refused to recognize even the validity of the Chinese Communist government. Clearly the U. N. was not off to a good start, and many observers forecast an early grave for it beside that of the League of Nations.

A series of dramatic events in 1950 helped give the United Nations a new lease on life. When the Communist-dominated northern half of Korea launched a military attack upon the Republic of South Korea the United States acted swiftly. Rushing troops to the battlefront, she called upon the U. N. to support the action and to condemn the Communist aggression. The Soviets, who had petulantly walked out of the U. N., were unable to prevent the action and seventeen nations eventually served under the U. N. flag. Never before in history had there been such swift concerted resistance to armed attack. The Soviet Union had no choice but to return to the U. N. which by now had taken on new importance. The Korean issue is not yet settled, but the action taken there is an unprecedented step in international relations. Whereas formerly attacks upon small nations could be made with relative impunity, future aggressors will always have to weigh the threat of possible retaliation by other groups of nations.

The fate of the United Nations is still uncertain. While it has proved to be a limited deterrant to war, the resistance in Korea was made possible by an unusual combination of circumstances that might not occur again. Moreover, there is ample evidence that most nations are prepared to give the U. N. only qualified support. The traditional distrusts of supranational organizations still exist and there are important obstacles to effective international organization which may yet prove to be the U. N.'s undoing.

Obstacles to International Organization

Men have long sought, without complete success, to locate *the causes* of war. [9] Explanations have ranged through supposed "instincts" for war

[9] Morris Ginsberg, "Social Change," *British Journal of Sociology*, Vol. 9 (September, 1958), p. 210.

and "man's natural combativeness" to the theory that war results from unbridled economic competition. Of these, the first two have been rather completely discredited and the third shown to be an inadequate explanation. On the other hand, when war is recognized as a part of culture it becomes possible to locate other elements within the culture that contribute to war and make effective international organization difficult. Four such elements in modern culture are: historical enmities, colonialism, power pacts, and the concept of sovereignty.

HISTORICAL ENMITIES. The strength of the hates and fears among nations is illustrated vividly by the passage which begins this chapter. The French-German hostility is one of the most widely publicized, but it is only one hostility of many. Created by past wars, defeats, humiliations, and exploitations, animosities are not quickly forgotten. Each country vents its anxieties in bitter condemnation of the other; each strives to be militarily strong while vigorously opposing the arming of the other. Since neither opposing country will willingly face possible annihilation by a traditional enemy, efforts toward disarmament tend to give way to an armaments race instead.

The military aspects of these continuing conflicts are fairly well known. What is not widely recognized, however, is how the military patterns are supported and reinforced in the cultures at large. Government pronouncements, news reports, editorial comment, movies, literature, and even the history taught in the schools are pervaded by subtle, and sometimes not so subtle, distortions which provoke one nation to antagonism toward the other. French and German children each learn that the other is an usurper in the Saar, American youth learn that England was a despotic mother country, English youth learn that the American colonies were impetuous and ungrateful, American children learn that a few Americans can lick anybody, and even within the United States the terms *damn Yankee* and *rebel* persist. War has produced many terrible weapons, but of all the weapons that civilized nations have used against one another probably none has been quite so insidious in creating an atmosphere conducive to war as has the biased history textbook!

The decline of hostility between the North and the South, and the strong friendship between this country and Great Britain are proof enough that such enmities *may* be overcome. Within a few years after World War II, our enemies had become our allies. Yet many nations today— Egypt and Israel, Pakistan and India, the U.S.S.R. and the United States, France, and Germany—are engaged in the most intense kind of psychological warfare. Most of these countries are members of the United Nations but mutual distrusts are so deeply rooted that much of the diplomacy of each is designed merely to counter the proposals of others. This process is one of the most direct routes to open war. Only the most pervasive of re-education programs offers much hope to reverse it.

COLONIALISM. A large part of Africa, much of southeast Asia, parts of the Middle-East, and even some of Central America, are seething with discontent. Riots are easily provoked, hidden weapons abound, and lives are often in danger. The fury generally is directed at one or more of the great world powers and against local governments supported by those powers. The great powers are on the defensive against a widespread and unreasoning hatred—a hatred they helped to create.

Agence-France Presse

Native peoples openly rebel against colonial powers.

World-wide colonialism followed the period of sixteenth-century international exploration. Aided by the fruits of the Industrial Revolution, western Europe was able to dominate economically and, often, politically, much of the world. In many ways it was a beneficient domination; mineral resources were tapped, production was increased, and living standards were raised. Understandably, however, much of the wealth was drained off by the mother countries so that the domination was also exploitative. Moreover, in many areas the local European population set itself up as a caste apart, maintaining itself by prejudice and discrimination against the native peoples. Thus, the very processes that increased wealth sowed the seeds of discontent and paved the way for ultimate rebellion.

From the beginning, colonialism was bathed in war. Not only did some of the native peoples resist intrusion, but the major powers fought among themselves for the right to colonize many areas. Most of the major wars of the past three centuries have included colonial struggles. Even the two world wars have been described as wars between the "have" and "have-not" nations—between those who have colonies and those who wanted them.

The past decade has accented still another element in the colonial struggle. A long-smoldering nationalism among the native peoples has burst into flame. Compromise, in the form of quasi independence or eventual independence offered by the major powers, frequently is not enough. The U.S.S.R., a relative newcomer among the major powers which lacks established colonies herself, apparently has seen fit to encourage violent rebellion as a means of both weakening the Western powers and establishing Communist-dominated governments friendly to herself.

Colonialism, in the traditional sense, is dying. As world opinion becomes more and more hostile, the great powers gradually are being forced to give up many of their prerogatives. In colonial areas where very few Europeans have made permanent homes, control rapidly is passing to native leaders. But where substantial numbers of Europeans have settled as permanent residents, as in Algeria or Kenya, this white minority fears to relinquish authority and become a white minority in a native-governed country. They have a lion by the tail which they can no longer control, yet dare not let go. Much blood may flow before this dilemma is resolved.

POWER PACTS. Formal and informal alliances among nations are far older than the relatively recent attempts at world organization. By banding together, nations could make an attack on any one of them more hazardous and thus be somewhat protected against threats of war. England with her balance-of-power formula probably was the chief architect of this pattern. Throughout the nineteenth century she was able, by a judicious array of alliances, to make herself the crucial factor in almost any power struggle between nations. According to the formula, the threat of such massed power is the most effective deterrent to war, but should war develop, it also provides the means to win it.

Such "defense pacts," however, present something of a paradox. Presumably designed to help preserve the peace, their existence is a major stimulant toward war. Inevitably, they array groups of nations against one another. A pact designed to resist aggression by one power poses a threat to that country and encourages it to seek compensatory alliances with other nations who are then rendered parties to the conflict, and so the spiral continues. Threats mount, and either side may decide to precipitate a crisis whenever it feels that to delay might cause it to lose the advantage. Thus, the means to prevent war becomes a factor in causing war.

Both the League of Nations and the United Nations have been plagued by the existence of power pacts. The League was unable to supersede them and was, itself, destroyed in World War II. Since 1945, the Soviet Union has ringed herself with a group of satellites extending from the Baltic countries to North Korea and Communist China while the West has formed the North Atlantic Treaty Organization and is debating a European Defense Community. These preparations for defense are also preparations for war. If they continue unchecked, the United Nations is probably doomed.

SOVEREIGNTY. One of the most formidable obstacles to effective international organization is the reluctance of individual nations to give up any of their sovereign power. To yield any real authority to an international body often seems to threaten the very independence of the separate nations, and recommendations in that direction are fiercely resisted. The decisions of international courts and of arbitration bodies have been widely rejected upon the grounds that the decisions were infringements upon the sovereignty of one or more of the disputants. The League of Nations was a weak organization precisely because it had no sovereign power itself but had to deal with sovereign nations. In the same way the United Nations lacks any large measure of sovereign power because the permanent members of the Security Council have the power to veto any concerted action. Should a major crisis involving one of the Big Five arise today there is little question but what the U. N. could not handle it. The U. N. could not legally take action over a veto.

There is considerable evidence, however, that in some quarters, at least, the insistence upon absolute sovereignty is weakening. The U. N. has machinery for action which was never granted to the League, and there is frequent talk of an effort to seek to remove the obstructionist use of the veto power. Such revision is not likely to come about during the current state of international tension, but the mere fact that the possibility is being considered is some indication of progress.

On still another front, negotiations among several European nations since World War II concerning both defense and the pooling of natural resources have seen those nations yielding some sovereignty under conditions that were obviously for the common good. [10] A similar approach to the U. N. would immeasurably improve its chances to preserve the peace, but it must be recognized that the jealous guardianship of sovereignty is still a major fact and a major obstacle to lasting world organization.

[10] In 1959, France, West Germany, Belgium, the Netherlands, Luxembourg, and Italy banded together into the European Common Market to remove mutual tariff barriers, achieve common wage and tax levels, and promote the interchangeability of workers.

THE SOCIAL-DISORGANIZATION APPROACH

War Under Rules

Since the hate and destruction of war are so completely contrary to the professed beliefs of Western society, war is often considered to be the perfect example of social disorganization. Yet war is not, as is often believed, completely unregulated conflict. It is in fact the final step in the breakdown of efforts to achieve national goals through peaceful channels. Warfare is conducted not *without* rules but under a *special set* of rules.

The roots of war are to be found in the conflicting values and interests of nations and in the occasional inability to find peaceful means whereby those differences may be reconciled. Nations are in fairly continuous competition to achieve various economic and political goals. They struggle for raw materials and markets, for favored trade relationships, for land, for additional human resources, and for the right to dominate the economic and political life of other peoples. The means of competition range from offering advantageous trade relationships to manipulating currencies, infiltrating governments, and making a show of military force. Alliances with other nations and military build-up are a part of the pattern. The use of force is the ultimate means of seeking a redress of power. Whenever an impasse is reached, the use of military force becomes more and more probable. Experience has shown that higher government echelons are generally aware of an impending conflict and commit themselves to it long before hostilities actually begin. Military preparations are rushed, efforts are made to create a favorable climate of opinion in the populace at large, and the maneuvering begins. The incident which finally sets war off is, by that time, almost inevitable. The beginning of hostilities is a signal to all that the old rules are no longer in effect and that from then on the rules are the rules of war.

For the Western world, at least, the rules of war are symbolized by the Geneva Convention. Among other things, the convention outlawed the use of poison gas; it guaranteed unarmed medical corpsmen, marked ambulances, and hospitals freedom from attack; and it set up standards for the care and treatment of prisoners of war. Nations that are trying to destroy one another are urged to do it *by the rules!* Generally the provisions of the convention have been adhered to and even nations which have not ratified the agreement have permitted themselves to be bound by it. Consequently, war per se, as terrible as it is, is not the ultimate in social disorganization.

Disruption of the Rules of War

The rules of war, as with any other form of social organization, tend to break down under the influence of social change. At the time of the Geneva Convention the most lethal weapon in the war arsenal was considered to be poison gas. The development of the use of atomic energy had just begun and even the potential of airplanes could not be anticipated. Civilian populations, who could be evacuated from the front line area, were not especially endangered. The rules drawn up by the Convention were, therefore, designed chiefly to protect the actual combatants; injured combatants should not be subjected to further attack; combatants taken prisoner should not be mistreated; and all combatants should be secure against the "terrible" effects of poison gas.

These rules, appropriate to the social and technological conditions of World War I, proved increasingly inadequate during World War II, and appear to be almost irrelevant to any future global conflict. In at least two ways, technological change has almost erased the former distinction between civilians and combatants. First, the newest and most effective weapons are of such destructive power that it is not possible to destroy "military" targets without attacking the civilian population. Conventional aerial bombs used to destroy production and transportation facilities inevitably decimate the surrounding heavily inhabited areas. With nuclear energy the situation is even more obvious. Second, war has come to hinge as critically upon the efficiency of civilian production as upon the size and training of the military. When wars can be won or lost on the production line, civilians may become higher priority targets than soldiers. The surest way to defeat an army is to destroy its source of supply. Experience has shown that the people who man a production line can continue to produce goods even after many of their facilities have been destroyed and, conversely, that destruction of the morale of the work force can effectively disable facilities that remain physically intact. Under these circumstances, soldiers in future wars may be safer than the civilians whom they supposedly protect.

Modern armies, too, are ceasing to be professional armies. Except for a core of career officers and a permanent cadre, modern armies are made up chiefly of conscripted civilians. These huge impermanent armies, even if physically strong, are often psychologicaly vulnerable. The rules of the Geneva Convention, which sought principally to protect prisoners from physical abuse, failed to anticipate how the findings of modern psychology might be used to break their morale. Such brainwashing is potentially capable of producing defection to the enemy even without violating the Geneva rules. When combined with new drugs developed by the medical profession these techniques are even more effective. Already efforts are being made to discover indoctrination techniques that will immunize soldiers to brainwashing. Until such techniques are perfected, or new rules are drafted, the present *anomie* [11] will continue.

Battlefield conditions give rise to still another form of social disorganization that is not so directly linked to social change. Squads, platoons, and companies of men are suddenly cut off in a drastic sense from the controls which normally regulate behavior. With the usual restraints upon antisocial behavior removed and aggression toward the enemy encouraged, frequent unprovoked atrocities are committted. Undoubtedly armies vary in the kinds and amount of atrocities they commit and the atrocities that receive public attention are seldom the violations committed by one's own forces. But the conditions of warfare, including hates, fears, and desperations, produce some breakdown irrespective of the identification of the combatants.

In most cases of violation it is exceedingly difficult to determine the extent to which the atrocities are matters of deliberate policy and the degree to which they result from inability to regulate the behavior of small groups of soldiers. The circumstances of war differ from those of peace where there are many controls upon individual behavior. Small groups of soldiers operate in virtual isolation from their fellows. The restraining influences of families, friends, business associates and the like which normally induce the individual to suppress, redirect, or limit his antisocial impulses are largely absent. Much has been written about the supposed comradeship of men in arms but little has been written about the quasi isolation which most of them actually experience. The combined forces of isolation from any permanent relationships, the institutional encouragement of aggression toward the enemy, and the physical isolation of the battle front permit men to overstep easily the restrictions only halfheartedly enforced by the military itself. Large numbers of men of both sides commit many heinous acts that are contrary both to the rules of war and to their own moral codes. The cumulative effect of such individual atrocities is to produce a condition of widespread disregard for human life and human welfare that results in almost unbelievably wanton destruction of life and property. No other condition on earth so effec-tively brutalizes human behavior.

THE VALUE-CONFLICT APPROACH

War and the relations among nations provide almost unlimited opportunity for the study of value conflicts. A book the size of this might well deal with this aspect of international relations alone. Here we shall deal with just two value conflicts important in the American scene which are involved in the effort to prevent future wars.

[11] The French sociologist, Emile Durkheim coined the term *anomie* to refer to the confusion and demoralization associated with "normlessness."

Internationalism vs. Isolationism

The United States perhaps more than any other major nation has vacillated between active participation in and withdrawal from international affairs. Following war and in peacetime she has sought to avoid entanglement in European and Asian affairs only to be drawn into the fray again in time to participate in the next war. From these facts are drawn diametrically opposing conclusions. One group claims that our mistake lies in permitting ourselves to be drawn into conflict again while the opposing factions maintain that future wars may be prevented only if the United States takes an active role in world affairs.

ISOLATIONISM. Isolationists look to the past to buttress their position. They cite Washington's Farewell Address which warns about foreign entanglements, and the Monroe Doctrine which sought to protect the Western Hemisphere against foreign interference. Internationalism, they assert, is contrary to the principles laid down in the Constitution and adhered to by the founding fathers. In short, it is both immoral and unworkable. The isolationist position also makes two important assumptions about the modern world: first, that power struggles in the rest of the world need not concern the United States; and second, that the United States is capable of defending itself against all external forces.

Isolationists point out that all our foreign wars have been fought on alien soil, that the United States has seldom been a direct party to the underlying disputes, and that the United States has borne the major cost of such wars. Europe and Asia, they claim, with their illogically drawn boundaries, border disputes, surplus populations, currency problems, trade barriers, and power struggles, are natural trouble areas. If America persists in becoming involved in such foreign wars the continued strain upon her natural resources, her population, and her economy will eventually lead to national bankruptcy and domestic chaos.

The corollary argument is that America is capable of meeting any threat that might develop from foreign sources. First of all, the American continent is surrounded by vast oceans which provide a formidable barrier to potential invaders. Secondly, we could ring the nation with impenetrable defenses and warn possible enemies of complete destruction of their countries by guided missiles should an attack be made upon us. Not even totalitarian governments bent upon world domination could successfully wage war upon a fully armed United States, it is said, and thus there is nothing to fear and no reason to become involved in foreign wars of attrition. The tremendous productive capacity of the American system, freed of the necessity to wage and support constant wars, would raise the domestic living standard considerably and would be the most powerful inducement to other nations to imitate the American economic and political system.

INTERNATIONALISM. The isolationist arguments have periodically gained and waned in popularity, giving way increasingly to internationalist philosophy. The prime tenet of the internationalist position is that no major country can isolate itself from world affairs; that interdependence among nations is so great that both the foreign and domestic policies of each nation affect, and, hence, are the concern of, all the others.

Apart from war, it is asserted that the United States cannot afford to curtail relationships with other areas of the world. The American economy is a production economy, producing far more goods than it consumes directly and deriving part of its high standard of living by favorable trade relationships with other countries. The United States exports manufactured goods and farm products. We must import large quantities of raw materials—rubber, oil, fissionable materials, and many basic metals. These commercial needs, alone, indicate the unworkability of isolationism. Satisfactory trade relationships depend upon friendly governments; it does make a difference what faction is in power in a country that is five thousand miles away. Under these circumstances it is unrealistic to talk about not becoming involved in foreign affairs.

When the possibility of war is brought into the picture the internationalists become even more insistent. They deny the possibility of physical isolation in a world characterized by speeds faster than sound and nonstop flights around the earth. The next war, if there is one, will be fought along great circle routes over the North Pole so that the United States may be attacked without the enemy having to cross the Atlantic or the Pacific. With these new routes no American city is out of bombing range by the other major powers. Moreover, military experts agree that even the magnificent American technology could not prevent enemy bombers from getting through in the event of a mass attack. Atom and hydrogen bombs would be sure to hit American cities. The best defense, it is claimed, lies in a ring of bases thousands of miles from America so that aggression might be met very near its source. The United States must, therefore, band together with other free nations, pooling both resources and manpower to stave off the twin threats posed by insufficient mobilization and overwhelming surprise attacks.

The long-run trend in American affairs appears to be away from the isolationist view and toward the internationalist one. It is not a clear and unswerving trend, however. The climate of public opinion and official policy both continue to vacillate so that, to date, the United States has had no really *consistent* policy regarding the conduct of foreign affairs.

Sovereignty and Human Rights

An earlier section stressed the role of sovereignty as an obstacle to world organization and also indicated that awareness of this situation is becoming evident in some quarters. The United States as a nation is not in

the forefront of the movement to yield sovereignty and the implied necessity for such action has aroused bitter controversy.

Sovereignty, of course, implies "national rights" and the urge to preserve sovereignty is often associated with a presumed or actual threat to
a particular right rather than with sovereignty in a more general and
abstract sense. For example: the military alliances of World War II and
the Korean conflict established important precedents in the relinquishment of sovereign power, but these events passed virtually unnoticed
because they obviously were an aid in the attainment of United States
military goals. No direct threat to our national rights seemed to be involved. In another area, however, where the requirements of national
security are not so pressing, a seemingly minor matter recently became a
major issue.

As a part of its program of general social and economic betterment
the United Nations has been attempting to construct a Universal Declaration of Human Rights. This declaration would put all member nations on
record as advocating at least minimum standards of living, health, and
leisure for all the world's peoples. At first glance the resolution seems
harmless enough, and unquestionably it is in accord with many of our professed democratic and Judeo-Christian values. Many Americans, acting in
terms of those values have come out strongly in favor of the resolution.
Other groups of Americans, powerful and articulate, vigorously oppose it.

Opposition to the declaration stems not so much from failure to
sympathize with its goals but from fear of what its implementation would
entail. Almost everyone favors higher living standards *provided* they are
not achieved at his expense. That is the crux of the problem. Opponents
of the declaration insist, with some logic (see Ch. 11, pp. 327-328), that
the means do not exist simply to raise the standards in underdeveloped
areas. The underdeveloped areas contain the bulk of the world's population and they cannot begin to raise their standards by themselves; consequently, if standards are raised, the Western nations and, particularly,
the United States must bear the burden. The United States could not
carry such a tremendous burden of support without making drastic sacrifices in her own living standards. Objection to the declaration then becomes objection to sacrificing domestic standards in order to raise the
lower common denominator.

If the declaration should pass, the way will have been opened for
demands that the United States meet its share of the obligation. From
that point, opponents claim, it is merely a series of short steps to complete
dictation of American policy by a foreign body. All the labors of the
American people to build a superior way of life will have been sacrificed
to the lesser ambitions and lesser accomplishments of backward nations.
The 1953-54 session of Congress saw the introduction of an amendment
to the Constitution which would prevent the government from entering

into agreements that might result in curtailment of the sovereign power of the United States. By a very small margin, this amendment failed to pass, so it is likely to be an issue for years to come.

Advocates of the Universal Declaration of Human Rights generally do not dispute the difficulty of raising world standards without some sacrifice of standards at home. They deny the proposition that the declaration is merely a means to granting complete control to an international body, but they do tend to feel that *some* relinquishment of sovereignty and some general raising of world standards is essential to peaceful international relations. Further, they attack the assumption that property rights are inviolable even in the face of human suffering. They conclude, again with some logic, that sovereignty, when it is obviously related to the tax rate, will be protected to the last ditch!

THE PERSONAL-DEVIATION APPROACH

Throughout this book we have paid special attention to the ways in which deviant persons are involved in social problem situations. Generally, we have centered upon the roles that deviants play in helping to create problems. Certainly deviant personalities are not difficult to discover in war situations, so here again we shall briefly explore their function. In addition, we shall consider the reverse part of this process, namely, how war helps to produce, or at least to give prominence to, deviant persons.

Accounts of past wars devote considerable space to analysis of the personalities of various civilian and military leaders. From Hannibal through Caesar and Charlemagne to Hitler and Mussolini, the motives and needs of dictators and generals have influenced their conduct of foreign affairs. A very common pattern in the reported personalities of such leaders combines haunting feelings of personal inferiority with a thirst for power. Modern psychology suggests that the acquisition of power in such cases may be a means of compensation for feelings of inadequacy.

The power needs of the ruler strike fertile ground in the frustrations and hostilities of many of his subjects and the trappings of war help satisfy the needs of both. The period of preparation for war generally sees the emergence of some kind of "divine destiny" concept around which the nation unites. The *particular* destiny may be ". . . to rule the world," ". . . to create or perpetuate a super race," or ". . . to rid the world of a despot bent upon one of the preceding 'destinies.' " Gross distortions of fact are espoused by leaders and populace alike. In more extreme cases, the fanatic adherence to these slogans is not unlike the delusions experienced by mentally ill people. The feelings of personal importance are supported by the creation of gaudy uniforms and the employment of symbols, such as the swastika of Nazi Germany. The process of war involves the manipulation of powerful machines and an orgy of mass destruction. Conquests give great power over conquered peoples, and the frequency of atrocities committed on helpless persons provides evidence of the needs of soldiers and of armies to abuse their power. These and many other facets of war support the broad pattern of assuaging personal and group doubts at the expense of other populations.

Unfortunately for purposes of precise observation, social scientists have not yet been able to subject any of these noted personages to detailed study. We must depend instead upon the accounts of biographers and upon the observations of associates whose accounts of their former leader's behavior may be influenced both by their personal relationship to him and by the biases implicit in the demands of the conquering audience. We cannot be certain whether or not psychometric testing would show such leaders to differ significantly on inferiority feelings and power-striving from the general run of the population. The subtle interplay between the leader's personality and the influences of his position as wartime leader are difficult to disentwine.

Another question that remains to be considered is whether the personalities of war leaders differ significantly from those of peacetime leaders. Certainly wartime leaders receive more public attention and are longer remembered. Most of the students who read this book probably can name most of the United States war presidents, but how many of the peacetime presidents can they name? How many of the peacetime presidents would be remembered had it been their misfortune to be chief executive during a war? Thus we come to the disturbing question of whether a leader comes to be defined as a "great leader" because he is intrinsically a great leader or because of the characteristics of the period during which he holds office. The role played by societal factors is unquestionably great; the special personality characteristics of wartime leaders, if they are ever definitely established, may be either the cause of war or the effect of it.

Whether history ultimately defines them as great leaders or not, there is a disturbing possibility that future world peace may be no more secure than the emotional stability of the most erratic of the world's presidents or dictators. As more and more nations develop atomic weapons, there is a growing possibility of the world being plunged into total war by the head of a minor nation. Even without atomic energy there is the haunting possibility that unscrupulous leaders of small nations might deliberately attempt to cause war among the great powers in order to advance their own political causes.

SUMMARY

War is not simply a product of modern culture; its roots are deeply embedded in the history of that culture. Though widely condemned, it is one recognized means of resolving conflicts among nations. It will not just disappear, and it will only be eliminated through drastic changes in the culture in which it is intrinsic. With the prospect that a third world war would destroy entire nations and, possibly, the entire human race, war is more than a hypothetical problem. The very existence of human civilization depends upon the discovery of the means to avoid all-out conflict because of the efficacy of modern weapons.

The most immediate hope for the elimination of war probably is through international organization. The League of Nations was never adequate, and perished in World War II. Its successor, the United Nations, is now on trial. The U. N. has shown some capacity for limiting aggression but serious obstacles stand in the way of complete success.

War, despite its terrible destructive power, generally is conducted under rules. The conditions of war, however, conduce to the breakdown of those rules. The overpowering need to win the war and the loss of effective control over individual behavior combine to produce a disregard for human life and welfare not matched in any other human endeavor.

The United States stands divided on two major issues, and continued division is an invitation to blunder into another war. The first is dispute over the role America should play in world affairs and the second is division over national versus human rights.

Feelings of inadequacy and consequent strivings for power, both in national leaders and in the general population, provide fertile ground for embarking upon war. Whether or not wartime leaders differ from other people as to these traits has not yet been determined by testing.

SUGGESTED READINGS

BERNARD, Luther L., *War and Its Causes* (New York, Henry Holt & Co., Inc., 1944). Analysis of war as a social institution, and exploration of psychological, population, economic, political, geographical, and cultural causes of war. Written for the intelligent layman as well as for the specialist.

BURCH, Guy I., and PENDELL, Elmer, *Human Breeding and Survival, Population Roads to Peace or War* (New York, Penguin Books, Inc., 1948). A neo-Malthusian monograph on the role of population factors in causing war. Useful as an illustration of particularistic theories of warfare.

DOLIVET, Louis, *The United Nations: A Handbook on the New World Organization* (New York, Farrar, Straus, and Cudahy, Inc., 1952). A brief treatment of the structure and functioning of the United Nations.

DUVALL, Sylvanus M., *War and Human Nature*, Public Affairs Pamphlet, No

125 (New York, Public Affairs Committee, Inc., 1947). Refutes the notion that human beings are inherently warlike, and includes a section on education for world peace.

NEHRU, Pandit J., "The Pursuit of Peace Armaments Will Not Solve Basic Problems", *Vital Speeches of the Day*, Vol. 16, No. 2 (November 1, 1949), reprinted in John E. Nordskog, Edward C. McDonagh and Melvin J. Vincent, *Analyzing Social Problems* (New York, The Dryden Press, Inc., 1950), pp. 718-723. A speech by the Prime Minister of India in which he opposes the militant preparations for war which are common among Western nations.

ORWELL, George, *Nineteen Eighty-four* (New York, Harcourt, Brace & Co., 1949). An anti-utopian novel. Paints a frightening picture based upon extension of present patterns of warfare and totalitarian trends.

WALLER, Willard, *War in the Twentieth Century* (New York, The Dryden Press, Inc., 1940). Contains an excellent account of various modern theories of warfare. Can be readily appreciated by the intelligent layman.

WRIGHT, Quincy, *A Study of War*, 2 vols. (Chicago, University of Chicago Press, 1942). The most complete sociological analysis of war yet produced. Published early in World War II.

AUDIO-VISUAL AIDS

1. *Guilty or Not Guilty—The Nuremberg Trials* (Film Forum Foundation, 924 West 18 St., Spokane), 29½ minutes, sound, black and white. Shows pictures of the atrocities presented as evidence at the trials and raises questions regarding the moral foundations of international justice.

2. *Man in the Twentieth Century* (McGraw-Hill Book Co., Text-Film Dept., 330 West 42 St., New York), 17 minutes, sound, black and white. Sets forth the idea that although man has reached a high peak of material progress in the twentieth century, his daily routine is often one of boredom and dissatisfaction. Stresses man's desire for peace in a world split by conflicting philosophies. Presents public education and the mechanism of the United Nations as a means for securing peace and happiness for future generations.

3. *Social Revolution* (Encyclopaedia Britannica Films, Inc., 1150 Wilmette Ave., Wilmette, Ill.), 17 minutes, sound, black and white. Traces social changes during the past two hundred years. Contrasts constructive or peaceful methods of change with destructive or violent methods.

4. *A Time for Greatness* (Association Films, Inc., 347 Madison Ave., New York), 27 minutes, sound, black and white. Sponsored by the American Friends Service Committee. Expresses moral concern over the use of military force as the chief instrument of foreign policy. Surveys what the Quakers have learned about securing peace and understanding between peoples of other nations from the work of the American Friends Service Committee.

QUESTIONS AND PROJECTS

1. Explain the phrase, "war as a culture pattern."
2. What proportion of the men killed in World War II were Americans?

Evaluate the statement, "The United States does not really know what war means."

3. Will any nation "win" the next major war? Why, or why not?

4. What crucial weakness was common to all of the peace pacts made prior to the present era of international organization?

5. What role did the United States play in the League of Nations?

6. Name the major branches of the United Nations. Describe the general functions of each.

7. Evaluate the statement, "Biased history textbooks are a major obstacle to the prevention of future wars."

8. List and discuss at least three major obstacles to the prevention of war.

9. Is war ordinarily fought without rules? How does social change bring about breakdown in the rules?

10. What are the pros and cons of waging "preventive war"—of attacking a probable enemy (for example, China) before it becomes strong enough to defeat us.

11. What are the arguments used by both "nationalists" and 'internationalist" groups in the United States?

12. How does warfare help give prominence to deviant persons?

13. Read George Orwell's *Nineteen Eighty-four* and relate its message to the continued use of war as an instrument of national and international policy. Evaluate the proposition that increased tendencies toward totalitarianism are inevitable for all major nations involved in warfare.

14. Arrange a panel discussion, in class, upon the United Nations. What bases do the panelists use in their evaluation of the U. N.? How much of the evaluation derives from objective consideration of the U. N.'s successes and failures and how much of it is a function of the individual's nationalist-internationalist bias?

19

Civil Liberties and Subversion

❧❧

What Do You Think?

1. Government employees accused of disloyalty should have the right to know the sources of information against them and to cross-examine their accusers.   YES___ NO___

2. The teaching of sectarian religion should be permitted in the public schools.   YES___ NO___

3. The kind of discharge a soldier gets should be based solely on his service record, rather than upon his pre-induction political associations.   YES___ NO___

4. State universities are justified in using a quota system to limit enrollment by members of certain racial and religious groups. YES___ NO___

5. Labor unions are entitled to restrict their membership on the basis of color, religion, or national origin.   YES___ NO___

6. Police officials should have the right to listen in on the phone conversations of suspects.   YES___ NO___

7. Employers should be permitted to state their views regarding labor unions to their workers.   YES___ NO___

8. Movies, plays, or books should be suppressed if they present an offensive characterization of some racial or religions group.   YES___ NO___

9. Anyone who invokes the Fifth Amendment privilege against self-incrimination when asked if he is a Communist must be one.   YES___ NO___

10. Labor's right to picket should include the right to deny access to struck plants by force of numbers.   YES___ NO___

11. Everyone should have the right to leave any country, including his own, and to return to his country.   YES___ NO___

12. Congress should investigate political beliefs and associations in order to determine whether they are "un-American."   YES___ NO___

13. The Post Office is justified in refusing to deliver unidentified foreign propaganda material to certain addresses.   YES___ NO___

14. Tests of government employees' loyalty should be confined to sensitive positions involving military, atomic, or international affairs.   YES___ NO___

15. Students who seek federal loans under the National Defense Education Act should be required to sign a special non-
Communist loyalty oath.[1]   YES___ NO___

FREEDOM HAS BEEN A RARE FLOWER in world history. In nearly all
times and places, the dungeon, torture chamber, and gallows awaited all
who dared to question accepted authorities and values. Today, many
Americans fear that our liberties are in danger. At no time since, perhaps,
the early days of the republic have so many books and articles been
devoted to a searching analysis of freedom and the conditions of its survival. What is the American heritage of freedom, and what are the developments which seem to place it in jeopardy?

THE AMERICAN HERITAGE OF FREEDOM

We hold these truths to be self-evident, that all men are created equal, that
they are endowed by their Creator with certain unalienable rights, that among
these are Life, Liberty, and the pursuit of Happiness—That to secure these
rights, Governments are instituted among Men, deriving their just powers from
the consent of the governed—That when any Form of Government becomes
destructive of these ends, it is the Right of the People to alter or to abolish it,
and to institute new Government. . . .

The Declaration of Independence and the Constitution were the work
of men who were classical scholars. (Today, they would be called "egg-
heads.") They were acquainted with the history and literature of ancient
Rome and Greece and were fully familiar with the rationalist philosophy
of the eighteenth century. They firmly believed in *natural rights*, that governments were man-made (not divinely ordained) institutions for securing
these rights, and that when governments fail to do this they should be

---

[1] Adapted from a list of questions prepared by the American Civil Liberties
Union. After answering them for yourself, check at the end of this footnote to see
whether you agree with their views. The American Civil Liberties Union is an
organization of persons who strongly believe in the right of all people in America to
enjoy all the rights and privileges guaranteed by our Constitution and our laws,
including those Americans whom they dislike and whose ideas they detest. The
ACLU offers legal assistance to persons whose rights have been violated, and
originates publicity defending civil liberties. Those whom it aids include racial and
religious minorities, political radicals—anyone, regardless of his views or actions,
whose rights of expression or rights to a fair trial are denied. This means that the
ACLU sometimes finds itself defending the rights of unpopular and obnoxious persons,
including Communists, which has led some people to the mistaken belief that the
ACLU is a pro-Communist organization. It is difficult for some to understand that
one can detest another's views, yet defend his right to express them.
If you answered *yes* to questions 1, 3, 7, 11, 14, and *no* to the others, your views
on civil liberties agree with those of the ACLU.

altered or overthrown. They firmly believed that freedom of thought and expression were as inseparable parts of a divinely ordained natural order of things as was the law of gravity, and that any society which curtails freedom of thought and expression must suffer as surely as the person who violates the law of gravity. [2]

In framing the Constitution, and especially the Bill of Rights, these men sought to devise a government with the power to govern but without the power to oppress. These men were highly aware of social change and of the need for adapting governmental institutions to a changing society. But remembering the bitter costs of change by revolution, they attempted to devise a government with built-in provisions for peaceful change—an experiment which much of the world regarded as highly impractical. These provisions for peaceful change included not only a system of elections, but guarantees of freedom of speech, press, and religion, of peaceful assembly and freedom of political activity. In this way, the people could secure a government of their choice at all times, and resort to armed revolt would be unnecessary.

The Basic Assumptions of American Democracy

This attempt to harmonize orderly government with a free society rests upon two fundamental assumptions. The first is *the faith that truth defeats error*, that in the market place of free competition in ideas, truth will eventually triumph. Unless truth can win out over error in open contest, then it follows that we must protect truth by suppressing error. Democratic government *must* rest upon the assumption that the majority of the people, given free access to facts and unlimited opportunity to discuss them freely, will arrive at the right answers most of the time. Any attempt to prevent the expression of "wrong" ideas is a confession of doubt in the ability of the people to arrive at correct conclusions. If the majority of the people are "too dumb" to arrive at the right conclusions, then democratic government cannot endure and we may as well start considering what kind of dictatorship we prefer.

The second fundamental basis of democratic government is an implicit social contract in which *the majority gives up the persecution of the minority providing the minority gives up the practice of revolution*. The majority agrees to tolerate the criticism and dissent of the minority (or minorities), while the minority agrees to seek power only through persuasion and political activity, not through violence. Such an unspoken agreement is necessary for orderly representative government. If the governing officials representing the majority seek to outlaw opposing political

---

[2] See Milton Mayer and Mortimer J. Adler, eds., *The Tradition of Freedom* (New York, Oceana Publications, 1958), for selections from the writers who shaped American concepts of freedom and justice.

parties, jail critics, suppress critical newspapers, and so on, then it is no longer a free government, and the minority feels justified in organizing a revolution. Conversely, if any members of the minority are unwilling to rely upon persuasion, but use force and violence in attempting to gain power, they have sacrificed their claim to political freedom. Revolution, to our founding fathers, was justifiable in a republic only when the ruling powers interfered with the efforts of the minority to gain power through criticism, persuasion, and political activity; *if the government did so interfere, then revolution became a duty* ("it is their right, it is their duty, to throw off such Government. . . ."). This is the real meaning of freedom—freedom for the idea one hates as well as for the idea he embraces. Unless people are free to express unpopular opinions and to support "dangerous" ideas without sacrifice of liberty, property, or employment, *freedom* is an empty word and free government an illusion.

It cannot be too strongly emphasized that our ancestors erected these constitutional guarantees of freedom, not from any fondness for radicalism, but because they wanted *order*. Having lived through the chaos of revolution, they wanted a social order in which revolution would be unnecessary. They felt that free speech and unrestricted political agitation, even for the ideas they loathed, were less of a threat to orderly government than the seething intrigues and secret conspiracies which the denial of freedom will provoke. Such a belief, together with a confidence in the people's wisdom, is reflected in Jefferson's statement in his First Inaugural Address,

If there be any among us who wish to dissolve this union, or change its republican form, let them stand undisturbed, as monuments of the safety with which error of opinion may be tolerated, where reason is left free to combat it.

It is true that not all of our ancestors shared the faiths that lie behind our constitutional guarantees of freedom. Hamilton's famous retort, "Your people, sir, is a great beast," expressed the views of a great many of the colonial aristocracy. Aaron Burr's revolutionary conspiracies received much support from persons who disliked the notion of popular government. At no time in our history has everyone agreed that the people could be trusted with intellectual and political freedom.

Historic Violations of Freedom in America

Our practice of freedom has never fully measured up to our ideals. Racial minorities and immigrants have not enjoyed the full rights of citizenship or the full protection of the law.[3] Scores of dissenters have been tarred and feathered, and to burn the plant of an unpopular news-

[3] See John Higham, *Strangers In The Land: Patterns of American Nativism, 1860-1925* (New Brunswick, Rutgers University Press, 1955), for accounts of many persecutions of foreigners, Catholics, and other groups in America.

paper is an old American custom. Both radical political movements and efforts to organize labor unions have been opposed with injunction, intimidation, and violence. Even movements which today seem quite innocuous, such as the feminist movement, brought public ridicule and even physical danger to their promoters. Although American society has been far more tolerant of unorthodoxy and dissent than most other nations, the record shows considerably less than complete toleration.

There have been several periods in our history when waves of suppression swept over the country. The first brought the Alien and Sedition Laws, which sound strangely up to date. The French Revolution had released revolutionary ideas of equality and democracy which the upper classes throughout the civilized world correctly viewed as a dangerous threat to their power and privilege. The excesses of the Jacobin "reign of terror" added an emotional intensity to their intellectual distaste for the ideals of the French Revolution. The union of a revolutionary ideology with an aggressive military power under Napoleon filled the world's well-born with an anxious foreboding.

In the United States the Democratic-Republican Party of Jefferson, Madison, and Monroe included many who, while objecting to the excesses of the French Revolution, shared many of its ideals and tended to be "French sympathizers" in the wars of the French Revolution. The Federalist party of Hamilton, Adams, and Marshall, with many members who felt that the American Revolution had gone entirely "too far," tended to sympathize with the British who led the aristocratic opposition to the equalitarian ideals of the French Revolution. Leading members of both parties in America were deeply involved with foreign agents, to whom state secrets were handed with an abandon which, today, would put dozens of them in jail. Each group accused the other of disloyalty and treason, and name-calling ("royalist," "Jacobin," "anarchist," "atheist"), guilt-by-association, and all the other propaganda techniques had a good workout.

In this tense situation, the Federalists were trying to retain power in the face of growing Democratic-Republican popularity. The Federalists used the foreign danger as an excuse for passing the Alien and Sedition Laws, which were intended to silence domestic political opponents, to discourage the spread of dangerous ideas, and to prevent disloyalty during the expected war with France. Under these laws, practically any criticism of the Federalist administration became a crime, and a number of editors, teachers, preachers, and other citizens were jailed for "pro-French" and other "seditious" utterances. Jefferson and the Democratic-Republicans won the election in spite of (or perhaps because of) these suppressions; those imprisoned for "sedition" were freed, and the Alien and Sedition Laws expired. With the defeat of Napoleon and the establishment of conservative regimes in Europe, anxiety over "dangerous" ideas declined. This first great assault upon American civil liberties proved ineffectual both as a means of maintaining Federalist power and protecting conservative values, for it was followed by a forty-year reign of the Democratic-Republican (later known as the Democratic) party, during which many "radical" ideas became firmly established. And as a means of protection against treason and subversion, the Alien and Sedition Laws now appear in historical retrospect to have been both ineffectual and unnecessary.

Another serious curtailment of civil liberties accompanied the slavery issue preceding the Civil War. In the early nineteenth century there was a vigorous public discussion in the South over the merits of slavery. But with the increased economic value of slaves which followed the invention of the cotton gin, and with the increasingly bitter political rivalry between the North and South over control of the West, the middle decades brought a crystallization of southern opinion to the point where no doubts about slavery might safely be expressed in print, pulpit, classroom, or even on the street corner. After the Nat Turner insurrection (1831), abolitionist meetings were suppressed, the mails closed to abolitionist books and newspapers, and abolitionists were threatened with death if they crossed southern soil. The North, meanwhile, sought to avoid conflict by preventing discussion of the slavery question. Abolitionists were viewed as dangerous troublemakers; furthermore, they were often obnoxious radicals about other things. Abolitionist meeting places and printing presses were burned. Elijah Lovejoy met death at the hands of an angry mob and William Lloyd Garrison and James G. Birney narrowly escaped it. Hundreds of teachers, college professors, and ministers were dismissed in both the North and the South for expressing views that deviated from the local moral imperatives. This suppression of civil liberties, too, was a failure, for it neither preserved slavery nor prevented conflict.

Still another wave of suppression came after the close of World War I. [4] Disillusionment with the peace settlements encouraged a return to traditional isolationism, with overtones of disdain for "foreigners" and "foreign ideas." The success of the Russian Revolution stimulated radical agitation, while both the Communist ideology and the bloody extremes of the Russian Revolution aroused in some Americans an intense fear of revolutionary outbreak. Although the possibility of revolution in the United States was remote, the fear was real, and radical propaganda of any sort aroused disproportionate anxieties. In this situation, the ill and ailing President Wilson's Attorney General, A. Mitchell Palmer, ordered the arrest of hundreds of labor organizers, radicals, and agitators of all sorts. Most were arrested without proper warrants, jailed in violation of the "due process of law" specified in the Constitution, and eventually

[4] See Robert K. Murray, *Red Scare: A Study in National Hysteria, 1919-1920* (Minneapolis, University of Minnesota Press, 1955).

released without trial or without having been specifically charged. About this time, Sacco and Vanzetti, two obscure anarchists, were convicted and eventually executed in one of the most celebrated cases in American history. The charge was murder, but the evidence was so unconvincing and the trial so prejudicial that many prominent citizens believed Sacco and Vanzetti were victims of a legal lynching because they were radicals who could easily be framed for a conventional crime. [5] The effectiveness of such methods of suppressing radicalism may be deduced from Vanzetti's final statement to the court: [6]

If it had not been for these things I might have lived out my life talking at street corners to scorning men. I might have died, unmarked, unknown, a failure. Now we are not a failure. This is our career and our triumph. Never in our full life could we hope to do such work for tolerance, for justice, for man's understanding of man, as now we do by accident. Our words, our lives, our pains—nothing. The taking of our lives—lives of a good shoemaker and a poor fish peddler—all. The last moment belongs to us—that agony is our triumph.

It is to be expected that the approved values of a culture will never be fully attained. It is not surprising that the ideal of civil liberty has often been violated in practice. Throughout our history, those who sharply challenged the status quo have been persecuted for their opinions. "Republicans," "anarchists," "abolitionists," "feminists," "socialists," "bolsheviks," "Communists"—the names change but the reaction against the disbeliever and the critic remains fundamentally unchanged. In tranquil periods, suppression of dissent is largely unorganized and sporadic. In periods of national anxiety, suppression may become systematic and official, while civil liberties go into eclipse. America is today in such a period of national anxiety and is again debating the perennial question of whether some curtailment of civil liberties is necessary.

THE COMMUNIST CHALLENGE

Communists are noisy champions of the cause of civil liberty wherever they are seeking power, but allow few civil liberties whenever they succeed in obtaining it. Their raucous demand for social reform is matched only by the venom of their hatred for liberals and reformers. A brief summary of communist ideology and practice may explain these inconsistencies. [7]

[5] Felix Frankfurter, *The Case of Sacco and Vanzetti* (Boston, Little, Brown & Co., 1927).

[6] Quoted in Fred Hamlin, *Land of Liberty* (New York, Thomas Y. Crowell Company, 1947), p. 281.

[7] See Karl Marx and Friedrich Engels, *The Communist Manifesto*, published in 1848 and available in many editions, for a concise statement of classic Communist ideology. See Nikolai Lenin, *The State and Revolution* (New York, The

The Communist Ideology

There have been many versions of the communist gospel, but all share several basic propositions.

1. The *labor theory of value*, a respectable, classic economic theory, held that all value was created by labor, whereas trade and distribution were nonproductive. Communism interprets this to mean that all profits are stolen from the workers, and private capital is but an accumulation of past thievery. In expropriating private capital, the working class would merely be seizing stolen property as its rightful owner.

2. The *class-conflict* theory holds that the interests of the capitalist class and the working class are unalterably opposed, and that all history is but the record of class warfare.

3. The doctrine of *economic determinism* states that all other aspects of the culture are determined by its economic aspects. The methods of economic production and the system of ownership of the means of production (land, machines, resources) are said to shape and mold all other aspects of the culture into harmony with these economic aspects. Thus, communism teaches that under capitalistic ownership and operation of the economy, the family takes the forms and functions most profitable to capitalists; law, government, and the police are only devices for protecting the capitalists; warfare is only the effort of opposing groups of capitalists to steal resources and markets from one another; religion is but an "opiate of the people" promising them a "pie in the sky" in exchange for earthly servitude; "bourgeois" morality is merely a body of superstitions to keep the working classes servile, while occasional crumbs of charity induce the poor to kiss the hands which rob them.

4. The *progressive misery of the proletariat* (the working class) is claimed to be inevitable under capitalism, where the rich allegedly grow richer and the poor grow poorer. Monopoly destroys small business, and the independent middle class of small business and professional men becomes proletarized, or converted into hired servants of the capitalists. Eventually, the workers become aware of their misery, and this proletarized middle class comes to identify its interest with that of the workers, and capitalist rule is overthrown.

5. The *inevitability of violent revolution* stems from the refusal of the capitalist class to surrender its privileges. Political parties, elections, and the other trappings of representative government are said to be only

Vanguard Press, 1927) for a statement of the Communist technique of revolutionary action. For competent pictures of present-day communism, see William Ebenstein, *Today's Isms* (Englewood Cliffs, N. J., Prentice-Hall, Inc., 1958), Chapter I; or Warren B. Walsh, *The Soviet Crucible: Soviet Government in Theory and Practice* (Princeton, E. Van Nostrand Co., Inc., 1959).

a pretense which disguises the rule of the capitalists. When the people show signs of a serious challenge to capitalistic rule, civil liberties are promptly withdrawn, and the people may vote only as long as most of them support candidates and policies acceptable to the capitalists. Communism cannot be voted gradually or peacefully into power, for the capitalists will resort to force to prevent it. Therefore, communism will eventually gain power through a violent revolution provoked by capitalist repression.

6. Following the revolution, there is to be a temporary *dictatorship of the proletariat* which must ruthlessly exterminate all capitalist or bourgeois elements lest they sabotage the regime or promote a counter-revolution.

7. After a generation or so of this dictatorship, the *classless society* is supposed to emerge. The state, since it is only an instrument of capitalist oppression, should be unnecessary and should gradually wither away. The planning of production and other administration problems would be handled by local, regional, and national organizations of workers, and liberty and abundance would be enjoyed by all!

Evaluation of Communist Ideology

Although many details are omitted, the above are the basic ideas of communist ideology. To what extent are they true? This question is both difficult and dangerous to answer, for many will be unable or unwilling to accept an unemotional appraisal. But could a doctrine which is entirely false have the world effects which communism has produced? An unemotional answer is necessary if the growth of communism is to be understood or arrested.

The labor theory of value and the doctrines of economic determinism and class conflict are half-truths. The economic institutions have tremendous influence upon the rest of a culture, but are far from the sole determinant. Class conflict has played a major role in nearly every great social controversy, but not a lone role. Although the interests of the different classes often conflict, it is also true that their interests often coincide.

The "progressive misery of the proletariat" has not materialized. Instead of growing more miserable during the past century, the workers in Western Europe and the United States have grown more prosperous and less radical. Marx believed that capitalist industrialism must inevitably produce a growing exploitation of the working classes, with revolt as the final consequence of completed industrialization. Instead, the most fully industrialized nations have the most comfortable workers and the least successful revolutionary movements, while communism has a mass following only in the undeveloped areas and impoverished countries.

Only the communists (and some extreme anticommunists) believe that violent revolution is inevitable. It is possible that a growing communist movement would not be permitted to come into power peacefully but would be forced into revolutionary activity by the suppression of its political freedom. [8] It is even more likely that communists would attempt a violent revolution at any time they thought it might succeed. But it is most unlikely that communism can gain power through either channel in the more prosperous democracies.

The dictatorship of the proletariat and the transition to a classless society are completely unrealistic concepts. In no communist-dominated country have workers much control over their individual actions or an effective voice in national policy. Communist rule is not a dictatorship by the proletariat, but dictatorship by a small ruling elite which claims to represent the proletariat, while the proletariat is about as completely controlled as it is possible to be. Sociologists doubt that a classless society is possible, except among the simplest primitive cultures. Instead of creating a classless society, communism appears to replace the aristocracy of property owners with an aristocracy of party officials. The state shows no signs of withering away in communist countries, and it is unrealistic to expect that any complex society could function without both the bureaucracy and the police power of the state. In short, communist ideology as outlined by Marx contains a passably accurate description of the misery of European workers a hundred years ago—a misery which workers have been steadily escaping in most democratic countries. The communist interpretation of history and social dynamics is a half-truth, and its blueprint for Utopia is unrealistic and unattainable.

Communist Techniques

From the basic principles of communist ideology, certain principles of communist action emerge.

1. *Communism is nonmoral.* All conventional laws and moral codes are denounced as only tricks to protect the wealthy. Anything is "right" if it serves the interests of the party.

2. *Communists seek revolution, not reform.* [9] Khrushchev says, "Social Democrats . . . are enemies of the working class." [10] FBI chief

[8] Democratic countries have sometimes acted as the Communists predict. For example, in 1921 the New York legislature refused to seat five successful Socialist candidates. More recently, France revised its election laws so that in 1958 the Communist party, with 20% of the vote, got only 2% of the seats in the Chamber of Deputies. (*New York Times*, December 7, 1958, IV, p. 2).

[9] The official *History of the Communist Party in the Soviet Union* states, "The transition from capitalism to Socialism and the liberation of the working class from the yoke of capitalism cannot be effected by slow changes, by reforms, but only by a qualitative change of the capitalist system by revolution. Hence, in order not to err in policy, one must be a revolutionist, not a reformist." (Quoted in Herbert A. Philbrick, *I Led Three Lives* [New York, McGraw-Hill Book Co., 1952], p. 292.)

[10] Quoted in *Life*, Vol. 40 (May 7, 1956), p. 31.

J. Edgar Hoover explains, "The communists detest democratic reforms. These changes, they know, will make free government stronger, hence, less likely to be overthrown by revolution." [11] For example, the communists in Italy long clamored for land reform, but when the de Gasperi government finally produced a real program of land reform, the communists opposed it; they didn't wish their favorite propaganda theme to be destroyed. The communists hate social reforms, yet dare not oppose them openly lest their concern for the people sound insincere. Therefore, *the basic communist strategy is to "support" social reforms in ways which discourage their adoption.* They insistently demand reforms of all sorts—fair employment practice legislation, free medical care, federal aid to education, civil rights legislation, and so on—in a raucous and offensive way that alienates possible supporters. They call attention to their communist "support" of reforms and thereby bestow on them the "kiss of death" and alienate many of the sincere supporters. They reject modest reforms, to insist upon sweeping reforms which have no chance of adoption. In discussion of reforms, they are preoccupied with the "social injustices" and have little interest in planning the details of a workable reform program. They infiltrate liberal organizations, seeking either to convert them into sounding boards for communist propaganda, or to disrupt and destroy them. All this is an effort to (*a*) discourage the adoption of reforms, while (*b*) maintaining a public pose as champions of social reform and true friends of the masses. Therefore, the communists do not mind when conservatives accuse liberals of "procommunism" and attack moderate reforms as "communist ideas," for this helps the communists to achieve both the above objectives. When Southern governors denounce the NAACP as "communist-inspired," or the American Legion attacks the ACLU as "procommunist," the communists are delighted.

This helps explain why the *public* position of the Communist party, as expressed by the *Daily Worker*, is often at complete variance from the real position of the party's leaders. As an FBI undercover agent with nine years' experience in the party reports, [12]

Publicly, the party gave lip service to [price] controls, urging them as necessary to the saving of the nation's economy and in the interests of justice. This appeal drew a huge popular response. But it did not represent the party's true objective. . . .

The termination of controls over the economy, the party blueprint said, would encourage inflation through runaway prices, and bring on the depression even more quickly. The National Association of Manufacturers, the party whispered in private, was in this respect a strong ally of the communist movement. The most rabid reactionaries are invariably the Communists' best friends.

[11] J. Edgar Hoover, *Masters of Deceit* (New York, Henry Holt & Co., Inc., 1958), p. 100.
[12] Philbrick, *op. cit.*, pp. 202-203, 210.

Communists have occasionally formed a "popular front" or temporary working alliance with liberals, socialists, and other reform-minded groups when they felt it expedient to do so. During these brief alliances, their vitriolic denunciations of liberals, reformers, and socialists are suspended, but they never cease to regard the liberals and socialists as their real enemies and the capitalists as their unwitting allies. As Lenin, who directed the Russian Revolution, wrote some years ago, [13]

The millionaires of all countries are now behaving on an international scale in a way that deserves our heartiest thanks. They are hunting Bolshevism [as Communism was then termed] with the same zeal as did Kerensky and Company; they are, moreover, "overdoing" it and helping us just as Kerensky did.

When the French bourgeoisie [capitalist class] makes Bolshevism the central issue at the elections, and abuses the comparatively moderate or vacillating Socialists for being Bolsheviks; when the American bourgeoisie, having completely lost its head, seizes thousands and thousands of people on suspicion of Bolshevism, creates an atmosphere of panic and broadcasts stories of Bolshevik plots; when the British bourgeoisie—the most "solid" in the world—despite all its wisdom and experience, commits acts of incredible stupidity, founds richly endowed "anti-Bolshevik societies," creates a special literature on Bolshevism, and hires an extra number of scientists, agitators, and priests to combat it—we must bow and thank the capitalist gentlemen. They are working for us. . . .

3. *Communists prefer that capitalist governments be reactionary.* They wish the masses to feel oppressed by a "rich man's government" which is utterly indifferent to the welfare of the masses. It is the communist's dream to manipulate the situation so that the oppressed and resentful masses see no possible hope for a better life except by supporting the communists. To create such a situation, the communists need (1) a period of genuine economic distress, (2) a government which is unable or unwilling to do anything effective to relieve this distress, and (3) an atmosphere in which all reform movements have been destroyed, so that the people must choose between enduring their misery or supporting the communists. So, while communists may publicly call for liberal government, they privately consider a reactionary government most helpful to their effort to gain power.

4. *Communists seek martyrdom and invite persecution.* Like Brer Rabbit, who kept begging "Don't throw me into that briar patch" until the fox finally did so, the communists keep defending civil liberties in the hope that such liberties will be attacked. Communists eagerly seek the martyr's crown, feeling that a moderate degree of persecution is helpful to them. They publicly demand an end to Congressional investigations of un-American activities, but fervently hope that the investiga-

[13] Nikolai Lenin, "Left-Wing Communism, an Infantile Disorder," *Little Lenin Library,* Vol. 20 (New York, International Publishers Co. Inc., 1934), p. 81.

tions will continue to afford the communists an opportunity to magnify their importance, discredit liberals, and parade their martyrdom. [14] They love to see police beating up strikers, [15] and consider each suppression of the civil liberties of a communist (or if he is only an "alleged" communist, so much the better) to be the very best advertising obtainable. There may be some kinds of legislation which communist leaders genuinely fear, but most anticommunist legislation to date has been greeted by the party leaders with loud hoots of derision. [16]

These are only a few of the many subtleties of communist strategy. It is not implied that *all* one-time members of the Communist party have held the cynically opportunistic views described above. Many well-meaning persons with humanitarian sentiments joined the party briefly, especially during the 1930's and early 1940's, but left upon finding its humanitarianism was insincere. But the hard-core veterans of many years' membership are likely to reflect the cynical duplicity described above.

THE CURRENT AMERICAN REACTION

It would seem that a prosperous and democratic nation like the United States would have little fear of a communist movement which never, even during the depression, was able to poll over 100,000 votes in the entire country and whose present membership has almost vanished. But American fears of communism are nourished by several conditions: (1) the genuine possibilities of espionage and sabotage by a conspiratorial organization that specializes in these arts; (2) the possibility of a war with Russia or China, during which the dangers of communist espionage and sabotage would be even greater; (3) the fact that there *is* a conspiracy, directed from Moscow, whose declared purpose is to infiltrate free societies, discredit their institutions, and disrupt their efforts to deal rationally with their social problems; (4) a greatly exaggerated popular

[14] Philbrick quotes one party leader as saying, "The House [Un-American Activities] Committee? Bah! How much more are we helped than we are harmed? What can they do? They call us before the committee. So we put on a suitable performance. . . . Going before the House Committee is a chance for winning as many friends as we can to the party, and creating as many enemies of the American Congress as possible." Philbrick states that among the professional party workers, "there was no genuine concern that the United States was, as we told the rank-and-filers, heading straight for the fascist state! It was to the interest of the party that the country become more fascist, not less. And yet, outside of its secret councils, the Communist party posed with its own membership as the champion of antifascism." (Philbrick, *ibid.,* p. 186.)

[15] Philbrick states that the trusted party members were instructed to arrange to have new members beaten up, if possible: " 'Work them into the most precarious positions, and hope that trouble will brew,' we were told. Once a grubber [a small-fry member] gets cracked over the head with a police club, we don't have to argue with him about the existence or nonexistence of police brutality." (*Ibid.,* p. 187.)

[16] *Ibid.,* p. 258.

impression of the size and power of the communist movement in the United States. This exaggeration is encouraged by certain politicians who build their political careers upon fighting communism, and by conservative groups which find an exaggerated fear of communism a useful weapon in fighting liberalism.

There is a sound factual basis for fear of communist espionage and sabotage and for the extensive counterespionage program which the FBI is conducting. While the Communist party works openly, espionage must be done secretly by persons who are not suspected of communist sympathies. Therefore, communist espionage is conducted by "underground" organizations entirely separate from, and unknown to, the public Communist party members. [17] A person who "talks like a radical" is almost certain *not* to be a communist spy, for a real spy seeks to remain unnoticed by avoiding political discussions and acting like a completely conventional person. [18] The problem of communist espionage and sabotage

TABLE 19-1. How much civil liberty do Americans want?

	Yes %	No opinion %	No %
	ANSWERS OF NATIONAL SAMPLE OF INFORMANTS		
If a person wanted to make a speech in your community favoring government ownership of all the railroads and big industries, should he be allowed to speak, or not?	58	11	31
If some people in your community suggested that a book he wrote favoring government ownership should be taken out of your public library, would you favor removing the book, or not?	35	13	52
If a person wanted to make a speech in your community against churches and religion, should he be allowed to speak, or not?	37	3	60
Consider a man whose loyalty has been questioned before a Congressional committee, but who swears under oath he has never been a Communist. Should he be allowed to make a speech in your community, or not?	70	9	21
Suppose he is teaching in a college or university. Should he be fired, or not?	22	9	69
Suppose an admitted Communist wants to make a speech in your community. Should he be allowed to speak, or not?	27	5	68
Suppose a Communist is a clerk in a store. Should he be fired, or not?	68	6	26
Should an admitted Communist have his American citizenship taken away from him, or not?	77	10	13
Should an admitted Communist be put in jail, or not?	51	15	34

source: Adapted from *Communism, Conformity, and Civil Liberties*, by Samuel A. Stouffer. Copyright, 1955, Samuel A. Stouffer; reprinted by permission of Doubleday & Company, Inc.

[17] J. Edgar Hoover, *op. cit.*, pp. 295-296.

[18] For example, Harry Gold, a convicted spy, reports, "I was told by my superior to stay away from the Communist Party, never to read the *Daily Worker*,

is, therefore, quite separate and distinct from the problem of dealing with communism as a political movement. And communist espionage and sabotage are a police problem, not a sociological problem.

The Communist Party in the United States

Sociologists are concerned with communism as a social movement. Although organized radical activity has a long history in the United States, it is only since the Russian Revolution that we have had an active Communist party. Fully controlled from Moscow since 1923, the Communist party in the United States has never been able to attract a genuine mass membership.[19] Its program was designed to serve the changing interests of Russian domestic and foreign policy. Whenever Russian policy changed, the American Communist Party had to reverse itself, even when this alienated its American membership. For example, when Russia and Germany signed a nonaggression pact in 1939, the Communist Party in the United States ceased overnight its denunciations of fascism, a switch which lost several thousand members to the party. When Russia denounced the Marshall Plan in 1947, all national communist parties were forced to join the chorus of condemnation, and more thousands left the party. Russia's brutal suppression of the Hungarian revolt in 1956 left the party in America a shattered, demoralized remnant. Furthermore, a communist philosophy which originated in the anticlerical, class-conscious intellectual atmosphere of a rigidly stratified European society had limited appeal in a country with individualistic traditions, a relatively open-class system, and an optimistic expectation of personal advancement and social progress. The "party line" in America has been dictated by persons who had little understanding of the American character, and were unable or unwilling to fit the party program to American political needs and interests.

In forty years of intense activity, the party reached a peak of over 100,000 members during our wartime alliance with Russia, declining to a tiny fraction of that number at present, according to the FBI,[20] which

and never to read liberal literature or express liberal thoughts." Quoted in Clair Wilcox, ed., *Civil Liberties under Attack* (Philadelphia, University of Pennsylvania Press, 1951), pp. 94-95.

[19] See Irving Howe and Lewis Coser, *The American Communist Party: A Critical History, 1919-1957* (Boston, Beacon Press, Inc., 1958); Theodore Draper, *The Roots of American Communism* (New York, The Viking Press, Inc., 1957); David A. Shannon, *The Decline of American Communism: A History of the Communist Party of the United States Since 1945* (New York, Harcourt, Brace and Co., 1959).

[20] Exact membership is unknown. The FBI estimated 1955 membership at 22,600 which "further declined" by 1957 (J. Edgar Hoover, *op. cit.*, p. 5). In 1958, the *New York Post* reported a secret self-audit by the Communist Party which placed its membership at only 3,000. (Reported in Civil Liberties, monthly newsletter of the ACLU, May, 1958). David A. Shannon (*op. cit.*), also places 1959 membership

also estimates that over 700,000 people are exmembers. [21] This constant turnover of party membership shows a highly significant inability to "hold" its converts, who soon become disillusioned and leave the party. When compared with even such momentarily successful social movements as populism or the prohibition movement, or with the well-established labor movement, the communist movement in America is revealed as a spectacular flop!

At no time in forty years has the communist movement been as weak and as discredited as it is today. Yet anticommunist measures continue. The grim reality of a world power struggle with Russia makes even a small communist movement appear as a major menace and has led many to feel that vigorous anticommunist measures are necessary. These measures have taken several forms.

FORMS OF AMERICAN ANTICOMMUNIST EFFORT

1. Congressional Investigations

Ever since the birth of the House Committee on Un-American Activities in 1938, one or more Congressional committees have been investigating communism. Their main procedure has been to hear and publish testimony from witnesses who tell what they know (or claim to know) of communist operations, organizations, and membership. "Friendly" witnesses, usually ex-communists, name their former communist associates, who are then subpoenaed and questioned, required to name *their* associates, and so on. The files of the Un-American Activities Committee are said to contain dossiers on over 1,000,000 persons who have been "named" by a witness, or whose names have been found as contributors or members of organizations which have been "named" as communist organizations, or who have been seen at an allegedly communist-sponsored meeting, or something of the sort.

If a citizen ignores a subpoena or refuses to answer questions put by a Congressional committee, he can be imprisoned for contempt of Congress unless he bases his refusal upon the Fifth Amendment, which states that one may not be compelled to give evidence against himself which might be used against him in a criminal prosecution. In the present atmosphere, one who invokes the Fifth Amendment becomes a "Fifth-Amendment Communist," and faces almost certain professional ruin and social ostracism. The witness is under oath, so if he lies, he can be imprisoned for perjury.

---

at about 3,000. The House Un-American Activities Committee placed 1959 membership at 10,000, probably a high estimate, in view of the committee's tendency to magnify the party's size and power. (*New York Times,* March 8, 1959, p. 38.)

[21] Morris Ernst and David Loth, *Report on the American Communist* (New York, Henry Holt & Co., Inc., 1952), p. 33.

Violent controversy has raged over the methods of the various Congressional committees investigating communism. Since a Congressional committee is not a court, the witness has none of the legal rights of an accused person in a court trial. Because the supposed purpose of a Congressional committee is not to try prisoners but to collect information, there are practically no limits upon what questions it may ask or what statements it may publish (with immunity from libel actions). In practice, however, committees have sometimes functioned much like courts—but courts in which the "accused" is charged on a basis of secret charges, is not permitted to face or cross-examine his accusers, or to call witnesses in his own behalf, and not always permitted to be represented by counsel. Although a committee has no power to issue sentences like a court, the power to destroy careers and reputations gives them a very real power with which to punish. Many critics of such procedures, including the National Council of Churches and the American Bar Association, have suggested that committees either cease acting as courts, or adopt rules that protect the rights of the accused as in the legitimate courts. [22]

Committees frequently received testimony from witnesses of doubtful reliability and, without verifying this "evidence," made public charges against the loyalty of private citizens. Such charges make sensational newspaper headlines, whereas the accused's denial often appears later on the inside pages. The technique of public accusations based upon secret evidence places the burden of proof on the accused—a reversal of the American judicial doctrine that one is presumed innocent until proved guilty.

The evidence which committees receive often includes rumor, hearsay, opinion, speculation, and other material which would not be admitted into a court of law. As a part of its proper function of collecting information, all agree that it is entirely proper for a committee to *receive* such evidence. But whether a committee should *publish* such "evidence," without first verifying it, is another matter. Such evidence is sometimes the result of faulty recollection, of mistaken identity, or even of malice and deliberate falsehood. In every large office or bureau, there are disgruntled employees and frustrated neurotics who are happy to make grave charges against their superiors before an appreciative committee. The use of unverified hearsay evidence ("lots of people told me he was a Communist") for public attacks upon individuals has been a severely criticized practice of the Congressional committees.

The committees have relied heavily on the guilt-by-association test

[22] Jacob K. Javits, "Some Queensbury Rules for Congressional Investigations," *The Reporter*, Vol. 9 (September 1, 1953), pp. 23-25; "Congressional Investigations," *University of Pennsylvania Law Review*, Vol. 106 (November, 1957), pp. 124-127; Edward U. Condon, "Time To Stop Baiting Scientists," *Bulletin of The Atomic Scientists*, Vol. 14 (February, 1958), pp. 80-82.

of loyalty. If one's name is on a letterhead along with names of any communists, or anyone "named as" a communist by a witness; if one signed a petition which was also signed by some communists; if one delivered a lecture at a meeting sponsored, however secretly, by a communist organization—these may be listed as "evidence" of one's communist sympathies. [23] Even to have joined an organization when unaware of its communist domination, and to have withdrawn upon discovering its communist domination, is no defense against the charge of "serving" the communists, for committee members have stated that the accused should have known that there were communists active in the organization. [24] If this test were generally applied, it would paralyze the voluntary organizational activity which has been traditional in America, for it is obviously impractical to check the secret purposes of the members of every organization one joins or supports.

The methods of the Congressional committees have varied considerably, depending upon the personnel and upon the witnesses they were questioning. Many examples of both scrupulous fairness and callous disregard for decency can be found. Many witnesses have been arrogant, provocative, and insulting. Communist witnesses have deliberately sought to exasperate or "bait" the committee members, who sometimes have had excuse for losing their tempers. It may be remembered, however, that there are other persons—teachers, physicians, nurses, social workers, police officers, salespersons—who sometimes must deal with obnoxious people, but are not excused for unprofessional conduct.

Since 1957, when the Supreme Court ruled that questions asked must be relevant to the drafting of legislation, committee questioning has been less abusive. [25] The Un-American Activities Committee continues investigating, demanding names and confessions, and issuing contempt citations, but, with no new sensational disclosures, it no longer gets headlines. Meanwhile, occasional criticism of the methods of other investigating committees [26] show that the problem of responsibility and fairness in investigating committee procedure is a continuing one.

An objective appraisal will recognize that the communist movement has received both aid and injury from the Congressional investigating committees. [27] These committees have uncovered some facts which might

---

[23] See *Testimony of Bishop G. Bromley Oxnam*, Hearing Before the Committee on Un-American Activities, House of Representatives, 83rd Congress, First Session, July 21, 1953 (Washington, Government Printing Office, 1954), exhibit No. 5, and pp. 3629, 3661, 3791.

[24] *Ibid.*, pp. 3671, 3698.

[25] *New York Times*, March 1, 1959, IV, p. 2.

[26] H. Solow, "Goldfine Got a Raw Deal," *Fortune*, Vol. 58 (December, 1958), pp. 128 ff; Discussion, Vol. 59 (January, 1959), pp. 22 ff.

[27] See Telford Taylor, *Grand Inquest, The Story of Congressional Investigations* (New York, Simon and Schuster, Inc., 1955); Alan Barth, *Government by Investigation* (New York, The Viking Press, Inc., 1955).

have been overlooked. They have made people aware of the communist conspiracy and of the danger of giving undiscriminating support to organizations. On the other hand, they have played into the hands of the communists by exaggerating their power and influence, by helping them claim martyrdom, and by discrediting liberals and liberal organizations so that communists have less reason to fear that a vigorous progressive movement will weaken their propaganda.

Perhaps the greatest single weakness of the Congressional investigations has been their failure to provide any real insight into the communist movement. Why do its converts join it? What kind of personalities are attracted? What are they really seeking when they become communist members or fellow-travelers? Why do most of them become disillusioned? How may communism's attraction best be neutralized? Congressional committees, in twenty years of investigation, have produced far less insight into these questions than is found in a single small volume by Ernst and Loth. [28]

2. Antisubversive Legislation

Laws against treason and espionage have existed for generations. These offences must be overt actions, with two witnesses or documentary evidence thereof, perpetrated with the intention of injuring the United States. A number of new laws have been passed recently to deal with subversion. The Voorhis Act of 1940 requires the registration of persons and organizations who act as agents for foreign powers or organizations. The Smith Act of 1940 forbids the advocacy by speech, printed matter, or conspiracy, of the forceful overthrow of the government. Both these acts were originally aimed mainly at the Nazis, but were later applied to the communists. Over one hundred communists were convicted and sentenced under the Smith Act, although some were released following a

[28] *Op. cit.*, based on interviews with 300 ex-Communists. Ernst and Loth state, "In 109 thick volumes of Congressional testimony studied in preparation for this book, we could find virtually nothing elicited except by accident or inadvertence, to establish the fundamental facts about the types of people who join the party, their family backgrounds, why they leave, the amount and kind of education they received.

"The Congressional inquiries often have been called "witch hunts." While it would be dangerous to carry the parallel between these investigations and the Salem witchcraft trials to extremes (e.g., witches were imaginary while Communists *do* exist), there is a useful analogy. The Salem trials developed as little truth about witches as the Congressional investigations have about Communists. The hysterical courts of Salem seemed to desire only a confession, and immunity was promised to those who confessed. All of the accused preferred to burn. The Congressional committees also have been mainly concerned with confessions. They have obtained some, but the chief result has been that . . . the witness burned anyway at the bar of public opinion. In Salem no one bothered to ask how these people were drawn into witchcraft, any more than Congress has tried to learn how Communists are drawn into the party." (pp. 2, 227-228.)

1957 Supreme Court decision that "theoretical advocacy" or mere membership without overt action was not punishable under the act. [29]

The Internal Security Act of 1950, known as the McCarran Act, strengthens the espionage laws, tightens immigration and naturalization laws, provides for detention in time of national emergency of anyone considered a potential spy or saboteur, and requires both communist-action and communist-front organizations to register with the Attorney General. [30] This law has been hotly debated, and its constitutionality is still in process of being determined by the courts as this is written.

The Immigration and Nationality Act of 1952 (the McCarran-Walter Act), besides changing many immigration regulations, provides for excluding immigrants or foreign visitors and for deporting resident aliens because of "disloyal" beliefs or associations. This law made it difficult to hold international meetings in the United States, and deported a number of long-time alien residents because of their past beliefs or associations. [31]

The Communist Control Act of 1954 outlaws the Communist party or any successor of like purpose and, if upheld by the courts, will presumably prevent the party from placing candidates on the ballot, using the mails, holding bank accounts, suing in court, or engaging in any corporate activity. Anyone who becomes or remains a member "with knowledge of the purpose or objective of such organization" must register with the Attorney General or face a $10,000 fine and ten years imprisonment. The law adds a third category of communist organization—the communist-infiltrated organization—which is any group which the Attorney General determines is communist-controlled, and subjects it to the same penalties as the communist-action group. This hastily drawn and vaguely worded act was opposed by President Eisenhower, Attorney General Brownell, and FBI Director Hoover on the grounds that it was probably unconstitutional and certain to interfere with efforts to enforce the Internal Security Act of 1950. [32] This law was promoted by senators and representatives who apparently were seeking to protect themselves against campaign charges of "softness" on communism. Its enactment illustrates what sort of laws may be passed when there is a national atmosphere in which it is politically dangerous for a legislator to vote against any bill which is called anticommunist.

Congress also passed legislation in 1954 which permits the Attorney General to grant witnesses immunity from prosecution as a result of any

[29] *New York Times*, March 1, 1959, IV, p. 3.

[30] A *communist-action group* is defined as one under the domination of a foreign power and aimed at the forcible overthrow of a government. A *communist front* is a group of noncommunists which communists secretly dominate and use deceptively for communist purposes.

[31] *New York Times*, March 1, 1959, IV, p. 2.

[32] *Ibid.*, August 29, 1954, IV, p. 6.

of their confessions, so that they may no longer use the Fifth Amendment to justify refusal to answer questions of an investigating committee.

A wide variety of state laws and local ordinances have also been passed, many of them far more stringent than the federal laws, and many probably unconstitutional as well. *It is difficult to pass laws "against communism" which will also be consistent with a Constitution which was intended to protect the freedom to hold and advocate unpopular and even revolutionary ideas.*

Whether the communists are injured by anticommunist legislation is uncertain. FBI Director J. Edgar Hoover claims that prosecution of communists under the Smith Act was "a strong disabling blow," yet implies that the menace is still as great as ever. [33] The more wild proposals (such as one Congressman's bill requiring the Librarian of Congress to mark all "subversive" matter in the 9,000,000 volumes in the library) aid the communists by making the anticommunists look either ridiculous or oppressive. The laws requiring registration have probably hurt the communists by making it more difficult for them to work undetected. Yet it is significant that *the most rapid drop in communist membership occurred between 1945 and 1948, before the legislative attack on communism got under way.* It is likely that Russian behavior and our political and economic conditions have affected the communist movement more than the laws under which it has operated. It is also interesting to note that every nation which has voluntarily "gone communist" was well furnished with anticommunist legislation far more stringent than ours.

3. Loyalty and Security Procedures

In response to charges that the Democratic administration was infiltrated by communists, President Truman established in 1947 a government loyalty program designed to eliminate "potentially disloyal" persons from federal employment. Under this program, the FBI made loyalty checks on all federal employees, transmitting its information to the heads of government departments for action. Each government department had a loyalty board which ruled whether there were "reasonable grounds for belief that the person involved is disloyal." A dismissed person might appeal an adverse decision to the Loyalty Review Board for review if he wished. During the first three years of this program, loyalty checks on about 2,500,000 federal employees were completed, of whom only 202 were dismissed for disloyalty, while about 2400 resigned during the investigation. Not a single act of espionage or any other disloyal *act* was discovered by the loyalty program. [34] The failure of the loyalty program

[33] *Op. cit.*, pp. 75, 78.
[34] According to Seth Richardson, Chairman, Loyalty Review Board, cited in John C. Wahlke, ed., *Loyalty in a Democratic State* (Boston, D. C. Heath & Company, 1952), p. 54.

to find any large number of subversives was interpreted by some to mean that there were only a few subversives in the government, whereas others insisted that the administration was simply covering up for them.

In 1951, the basis for dismissal was changed from "reasonable grounds for belief" that the person is disloyal to "reasonable doubt as to the loyalty of the person involved," thereby placing the burden of proof largely upon the accused and resolving all doubtful cases against him. In 1953, President Eisenhower made further changes, abolishing the Loyalty Review Board and the employee's right of appeal and telescoping "loyalty" and "security" risk classifications into a single category of "security risk." A "security risk" may be a person of doubtful loyalty or may be one whose reliability is uncertain for any of several reasons: he may talk too freely or drink too much to be trusted with important information; he may be vulnerable to blackmail because of drug addiction, sex deviation, past indiscretions, or because he has relatives living in communist-dominated lands or relatives or friends who are, or once were, communists or radicals. Although some unscrupulous politicians of both parties have sought to equate "security risk" with "subversive," every responsible official in the security program has pointed out that not all security risks are suspected of disloyalty.

During the first two years of the Eisenhower administration, from over 2,500,000 employees, some 8008 "security separations" were made, of whom 5006 resigned while their cases were under consideration (and sometimes without knowing they were under suspicion), while 3002 were dismissals. Only 2096 were said to have in their files "information indicating varying degrees of subversive activities." [35] All this phrase actually implies, however, is that each of these security files contained one or more unverified accusations from somebody or other—perhaps that the accused was seen reading a communist paper, or once belonged to a radical organization. Consequently, there is no way of knowing how many were actually subversives. Among the entire 8008 security risks, *not one* is officially alleged to be an active communist, spy, or traitor. In 1956 the Civil Service Commissioner admitted under questioning that a great many of the security risks then being discovered were Eisenhower Administration appointees, and that statement ended publicity over "security risks" among government employees. [36]

Some difficulties inherent in a security program. The government's loyalty and security programs appear to have been, for the most part, carefully administered by conscientious, judicious, fair-minded men, but the nature of the task is such that the issue of civil liberties inevitably arises. For a security program is not an effort to locate people who *have been* disloyal, but to locate those who *may become* disloyal or untrust-

[35] *New York Times*, January 9, 1955, IV, p. 2.
[36] *Ibid.*, January 11, 1956, p. 9.

worthy at some time in the future. How can a person's *potential* disloyalty be measured? Only by probing his past associations, his beliefs, his opinions, his convictions. Only by making certain that he is so thoroughly and unquestioningly wedded to the conventional order of things that he is psychologically incapable of seeking to change it! This means that a complete loyalty investigation inevitably becomes an investigation into opinions and values, with any kind of independence or unconventionality a symptom of undependability, for independent thinkers may arrive at unconventional conclusions.

This means that one's *lack* of intellectual interests becomes a recommendation, whereas an active interest in social issues becomes a basis for suspicion. Some of the questions asked in loyalty board hearings are revealing: [37]

> Have you ever had Negroes in your home?
> There is a suspicion in the record that you are in sympathy with the underprivileged. Is this true?
> In your recollection, do you recall ever discussing any topic which might be sympathetic to Communist doctrine?
> Are your friends and associates intelligent, clever?
> Did you ever hear any political discussions at X's home?
> If you are, as you say, a loyal American, why do you persist in denying that you were a member of the Communist Party?

Although these questions are quoted out of context, they show how a security investigation becomes an inquiry into the basic mental outlook of the subject, an attempt to see whether he has the kind of interests and values which might ever lead to an unconventional judgment. To one subject who had stated that he was not a communist and did not believe in revolution but did believe that people should be allowed to *advocate* revolution, as long as there was no probability of violence, a loyalty board chairman said, [38]

> What causes us concern is your basic philosophy, which seems to go so far as to defend the right of advocacy even to overthrow the government of the United States, unless the conditions at the time are such that they would probably incite a dangerous upheaval. It is not all of these marginal things that concerns me; it's your basic philosophy that concerns me!

A loyalty or security hearing *must* become an inquiry into one's basic philosophy because it seeks to determine not what one *has done* but what he *might do*. Unlike a court trial, the burden of proof is on the suspect, who is not accused of any specific wrongdoing, but vaguely accused of "associating with communists" or "expressing agreement with communist

[37] Quoted from transcripts of loyalty board hearings, as quoted in Wahlke, *op. cit.*, p. 55.

[38] Quoted in Alan Barth, *The Loyalty of Free Men* (New York, The Viking Press, Inc., 1951), pp. 121-122.

viewpoints" at some unspecified time or place, or of being "unreliable," or of "having had a reputation as a radical." Not even the security board knows who makes the accusation, for the FBI must keep secret the identity of its informants if they are to collect further information. This makes it possible for anyone who dislikes a federal employee to denounce and possibly ruin him with false accusations, and in some instances, this has happened. [39] In one celebrated case, after a government employee had spent four years and $10,000 defending himself against charges of disloyalty and perjury, it developed that the only firm evidence against him was a joking inference he had made nineteen years earlier, to some callers as a "Communist-cell meeting"—a costly bit of humor. [40] Such cases are unusual, but the basic task of a security program makes them inevitable.

By the mid-1950's, the loyalty-security program was under severe criticism from responsible sources. The Fund for the Republic conducted a careful review of 350 random security cases, revealing on what flimsy, unreliable "evidence" many people were being labeled as security risks. [41] Responsible scientific bodies regularly criticized the security program as unfair, inefficient, and harmful to scientific advance, warning that security restrictions were helping Russia to overtake us [42] in some areas (as she soon did). Some government agencies revised their security procedures to allow persons to face and cross-examine their accusers. [43] In 1959 the Supreme Court gave a decision calling for rights of confrontation and cross-examination in the industrial security program, covering several million workers in industries holding government contracts. [44] At many points, injustices under the security program are being corrected.

Whether a security program does more good than harm to American security is a debatable question. [45] It is impossible perhaps to have a security program unless we are prepared to limit government employment and research to those who are thoroughly conventional and conformist. What effects this may have upon government service and scientific ad-

[39] See *Time* (May 10, 1954), p. 22; (September 13, 1954), p. 25.

[40] *Time*, Vol. 63 (June 7, 1954), pp. 20-21.

[41] Association of The Bar of the City of New York, *The Federal Loyalty-Security Program* (New York, Dodd, Mead & Co., 1956).

[42] See "Secrecy, Security, and Loyalty," special issue, *Bulletin of the Atomic Scientists*, Vol. IX (April, 1955); "Loyalty and Unclassified Research," report of the National Academy of Sciences, *Bulletin of the Atomic Scientists*, Vol. XII (June, 1956), pp. 227-228; "Prizewinners on Secrecy," *Time*, Vol. 73 (June 29, 1959), p. 56.

[43] *New York Times*, July 12, 1959, p. 28.

[44] *Ibid.*, July 5, 1959, IV, p. 2.

[45] Sidney Hook, "Fallacies in our Thinking about Security," *New York Times Magazine*, January 30, 1955, pp. 15 ff.; Ralph S. Brown, *Loyalty and Security* (New Haven, Yale University Press, 1958); W. E. Dillon, "Security Program Five Years After," *New Republic*, Vol. 139 (September 8, 1958), pp. 7-8; Milton Greenberg, "Loyalty Oaths: An Appraisal of the Legal Issues," *Journal of Politics*, Vol. 20 (August, 1958), pp. 487-514; Harold M. Hyman, *To Try Men's Souls: Loyalty Oaths in American History* (Berkeley, University of California Press, 1959).

vance is problematic. Brilliant, original thinkers are not always noted for their conformity.

4. Blacklists, Official and Unofficial

President Truman, in 1947, instructed the Attorney General to prepare and publish a list of subversive organizations. This list of several hundred organizations, revised occasionally, has been widely used by loyalty boards, the armed services, and the FBI as a measure of loyalty, with one's membership in any organization on the "Attorney General's list" a damning bit of evidence.

The Attorney General may list as "subversive" any organization he considers subversive, and not until 1953 were the organizations involved given a hearing in which they might protest such designation. The Attorneys General entrusted with this responsibility have, thus far, exercised it with restraint and have not indiscriminately branded organizations as subversive without some cause. What a less moderate Attorney General might do with this authority in a period of national unrest, is interesting to ponder. In nondemocratic countries it has been a common practice for the state to designate what "loyal" citizens may believe and join, but this is the first time in American history that a government official has been granted authority to determine what organizations loyal citizens may not join. That such a fundamental extension of federal authority should be accepted with so little public discussion, especially from the long-time opponents of federal controls, is a striking illustration of how readily people will surrender their freedoms in the name of anticommunism.

In 1958, four organizations were dropped from the list. After years of widespread use as a test of disloyalty, it was decided that these organizations were not disloyal after all! [46] (Persons whose careers and reputations were damaged might then start informing people that it was all a mistake!)

Many private blacklists also circulated in the 1950's. [47] Perhaps the most famous was *Red Channels*, listing the "subversive" connections of many entertainment personalities, quoting mainly from reports of various un-American activities committees, including some state committees which were notoriously inaccurate. [48] Many of those listed protested their loyalty, but as there was no court or board to appeal to, and the movie

[46] American Civil Liberties Union, "The Past Is Prologue," *38th Annual Report of the American Civil Liberties Union, 1957-1958* (New York, 1958), p. 79.

[47] John Cogley, *A Report on Blacklisting:* Vol. I, *Movies;* Vol. II, *Radio-Television* (New York, Fund for the Republic, 1956).

[48] American Business Consultants, *Red Channels* (New York, Counterattack, 1950). See Merle Miller, *The Judges and the Judged* (Garden City, N. Y., Doubleday & Company, Inc., 1952), for an ACLU-sponsored study of this blacklisting operation.

and broadcast industries wished to play it safe, these persons had little chance of avoiding professional ruin. By the late 1950's, use of the private blacklist had subsided, and some of the victims were allowed to resume their careers. [49]

5. McCarthyism

The term *McCarthyism* has recently entered the language; it was first listed in the 1955 edition of the *American College Dictionary* with three definitions: "1-Public accusation of disloyalty, especially of pro-Communist activity, in many cases unsupported by proof or based on slight, doubtful, or irrelevant evidence; 2-Unfairness in investigative technique; 3-Persistent search for and exposure of disloyalty, especially in government offices." [50] These definitions parallel the contrasting evaluations of the late Senator McCarthy. To some he was a great patriot and a scourge of the communists, [51] while to others he was their unwitting ally and a hindrance to an effective anticommunist program. [52] Many feared McCarthy as a coming fascist dictator, but while he was a skillful demagogue, he lacked self-discipline and organizational ability. He began attacking fellow Republicans, revealed his irresponsibility to the nation in a televised series of hearings, was censured by the Senate. Thereafter, the press ignored him and he lapsed into obscurity until his death in 1957. [53]

But McCarthyism was not invented by McCarthy—Titus Oates used it centuries earlier—nor is it buried with him. It is the anxieties and fears of a people which create McCarthyism, and its practitioners arise when there is a social appetite. For McCarthy to have successfully remained the nation's most prominent communist-hunter for four years while failing to uncover even *one* authenticated communist would be

---

[49] "Harmonica's Return," *Time*, Vol. 73 (April 27, 1959), p. 54; Bosley Crowther, "Hitting the Blacklist," *New York Times* (February 14, 1960), II, p. 1.

[50] *American College Dictionary* (New York, Random House, 1955), p. 754.

[51] William F. Buckley, *McCarthy and His Enemies* (Chicago, Henry Regnery Co., 1954).

[52] For example, Herbert Philbrick, the FBI undercover agent who rose higher in Communist party circles than any other counterspy whose work has been revealed, is quoted as saying, "According to the leaders of the Communist Party, McCarthy has helped them a great deal. The kind of attacks he has made do three things that the comrades like: 1—They add greatly to the confusion, putting up a smoke screen for the party and making it more difficult than ever for people to discern just who is a Communist and who is not. 2—They make the party appear to be a lot stronger than it is. 3—They do considerable damage to some of the 'stupid liberals' whom the party hates." (Quoted in *The Progressive*, Vol. 16 [March, 1952], p. 5.) See also James Rorty and Moshe Decter, *McCarthy and the Communists* (Boston, Beacon Press, Inc., 1954); *Time*, Vol. 58 (October 22, 1951), pp. 21-24; *Time*, Vol. 64 (October 4, 1954), pp. 21-25.

[53] See Richard H. Rovere, *Senator Joseph McCarthy* (New York, Harcourt, Brace & Co., 1959).

impossible unless the social atmosphere were tense, uncritical, and neurotic.

6. The Cumulative Erosion of Liberty

There has been no frontal attack on civil liberties as such, but there has been a gradual erosion of individual freedom, notably in three respects:

a. The spread of security procedures. Security procedures first appeared to protect government employees against reckless accusation. Bit by bit, they became a device for excluding nonconformists. Gradually, they were extended to cover more and more persons—defense workers, military personnel, scientists—even students seeking government loans (under the National Defense Education Act of 1958). [54] Procedures became steadily more complicated until by 1955 it required a 400-page manual to list and interpret them. [55] The Attorney General's list started out as a guide for government employees only; it eventually became accepted as a conclusive test of disloyalty, applied to people in and out of the government. Laws and administrative rulings increasingly require loyalty oaths as a condition for individuals to receive ordinary government services. Industrial security, intended to prevent subversion in defense industry, also becomes a device for dismissing aggressive union members. [56] As long as people want to play safe, security procedures tend to become more widespread and more deeply embedded in law and administrative procedure.

b. Growth of administrative punishment. The Constitution prohibits legal punishment without due process of law. In practice, a large body of punishment by administrative procedure has developed. [57] Congressional committees and security boards are not courts, and the accused has none of the legal rights of a criminal defendant. No prison sentences are imposed, yet the loss of career and reputation are very harsh punishments. When an army draftee, after serving his army without blemish, is given a less-than-honorable discharge because of beliefs and associations he had *before* he entered the army, he is being punished! [58] The denial of a pass-

[54] See "Loyalty Provisions of National Defense Education Act Meets Opposition from Educators and Congressmen," *Science*, Vol. 129 (March 6, 1959), pp. 625-626.

[55] *Internal Security Manual*, (Washington, Government Printing Office, 1955).

[56] The 1952 report on Industrial Security of the National Industrial Conference Board states, "Industrial Security . . . can rid your plant of agitators who create labor unrest, who promote labor grievances, slowdowns and strikes, and encourage worker antipathy to management." Quoted by Benjamin Segal and Joyce Kornbluh, "Government Security and Private Industry," *The Reporter*, Vol. 17 (May 2, 1957), pp. 25 ff.

[57] Walter Gellhorn, *Individual Freedom and Governmental Restraints* (Baton Rouge, Louisiana State University Press, 1956), Ch. 1, "Changing Attitude toward the Administrative Process."

[58] In 1958, following an adverse Supreme Court decision, the army ceased this practice and reconsidered many earlier discharges. See ACLU, *op. cit.*, pp. 79-81.

port because of beliefs or associations or refusal to co-operate with an investigating committee; [59] deporting an alien because of his associations twenty years earlier; denial of a job because one was a "campus radical" years ago; [60] withholding a pension because of political beliefs and associations; [61]—all these are real punishments although no laws are involved. Punishment for belief or association, forbidden to the courts by the Constitution, has been achieved by administrative procedure. [62]

c. The fear of unconventionality is the final product. It would be easy to list dozens of examples—complaints by writers that they must avoid satire and social criticism, cases of minor censorship and individual injustice by the score—straws in the wind which blew strongly in the 1950's, less strongly today. Has it left a play-it-safe legacy in our conditioned responses? Have we become less original, venturesome, and independent, with the habit of cautious conformity so deeply embedded in us that we are unaware of it?

THE BALANCE SHEET—FREEDOM IN AMERICAN AND RUSSIAN SOCIETY

A comparison of civil liberties in America with those in a totalitarian society may indicate how civil liberties are changing in America today.

1. *Absolute conformity* in belief and behavior is demanded in a totalitarian society. Disbelief is disloyalty, and controversy is suspicious, since it is an indication of doubt. Communism demands that history, literature, art, and science must all support the official orthodoxy.

No such sweeping demands for conformity are enforced in America, but there is little doubt that nonconformity is far more heavily penalized than it was a few years ago. No one is likely to be jailed for unconventional ideas alone, but one's job and reputation may depend upon avoiding unconventional thought or action.

2. *Loyalty* in a totalitarian state is measured, not by one's *motives*, but by the *effects* of one's actions. If a Soviet commissar makes a miscalculation, if an engineering project fails to work out, if a tactic of foreign policy backfires, the official responsible faces charges of disloyalty or

[59] In 1958, the Supreme Court ruled that the Secretary of State may not withhold passports for these reasons. (*New York Times*, March 1, 1959, p. 2.)

[60] The University of California faculty in 1958 voted to refuse to inform employers about the beliefs and opinions which students revealed in the classroom. (*New York Times* [November 2, 1958], p. 65).

[61] A U. S. Court of Appeals has ruled that the Veteran's Administration may not withhold a disabled veteran's pension because of his associations. ACLU, *op. cit.*, p. 76.

[62] The Supreme Court has ruled against many such practices, but many others continue, while determined efforts are now being made to pass legislation which would strip the Supreme Court of authority over antisubversive measures. See "American Bar Association Calls for Changes to Curb Court," *New York Times* (March 1, 1959), IV, p. 2; also *New York Times* (May 10, 1959), IV, p. 6; ACLU, *op. cit.*, pp. 43-44.

"I'm shocked," the President [Eisenhower] said, "that even the Soviets would do this kind of thing . . . to take an author (Pasternak, *Doctor Zhivago*) so honored by the Nobel Prize and condemn him because some things he said didn't quite coincide with their doctrines."

Chicago Sun-Times, November 6, 1958, p. 4.

Have any American Nobel Prize winners been in trouble because of things they said?

---

sabotage. The striking rarity of *live* retired officials in communist lands is eloquent testimony to the condition of "freedom" therein.

The American tradition measures loyalty according to the intention of one's actions and judgments, not according to their consequences. There have always been some, however, who sought to read disloyalty into the failures or errors of their opponents. The recent demand of some Americans to know "who was responsible for the policies which helped the communists attain power in China, etc. . . ." suggests a tendency to equate error or failure with treason. The efficiency and morale of our diplomatic service has at times been seriously damaged by the practice [63]

. . . of equating subversive intent with faulty judgment with respect to any government official left holding the bag for a policy that happens to turn sour.

If these [foreign service] officers are made to feel—as many of them do— that their honest judgments of trends and conditions in their distant posts are liable to be turned against them later, they will be bound to put caution before objectivity in their reports.

3. A totalitarian state often measures loyalty by *past* actions, evaluated in the light of *present* attitudes and knowledge. If one strongly expresses a view or joins a group which, at some later date, becomes condemned, he, too, is condemned. The only way to be safe in such a climate is to join no groups and express no views.

The American tradition measures loyalty according to *present* views and actions and evaluates past actions according to the knowledge and attitudes which prevailed at that time. Not all Americans are careful to observe this tradition, for some delight in evaluating the past actions of their victims according to the knowledge and attitudes which have developed in later years. As one government official remarked, [64]

It is very difficult for a liberal who was active in the Thirties to survive political life in the Fifties. Take my case. As soon as I became convinced there

[63] Cabell Phillips, in *New York Times* (December 21, 1952), IV, p. 3.
[64] Quoted in *New York Times Magazine* (April 12, 1953), p. 28.

was any evidence of communist control in liberal organizations I belonged to, I dropped my membership—formally and completely. But do you think that explanation would do me much good in the atmosphere of today against political opponents who wouldn't scruple to cite my "guilty record" against me?

4. A *dual system of justice* prevails in communist lands, where political offenders are dealt with differently than conventional criminals. Although conventional criminals in Russia, at least before the war, received rather mild treatment, political offenders were severely punished, with "trials" designed as a public display of guilt rather than a means of determining guilt.

In America our courts, perhaps, have been less affected by current anxieties than most other institutions. Persons tried for violation of any law receive trials in which injustice is the exception rather than the rule. But most "subversive" cases are "tried," not by a court but before a Congressional committee or a security board, where the accused has none of the rights of a criminal defendant. Another symptom of a double standard of justice is seen in the alacrity with which the accused, who lied in his own defense, was prosecuted for perjury, in contrast to the relative immunity from perjury prosecutions enjoyed by "friendly" witnesses who may have lied under oath. [65]

5. The *use of secret police in intimidating and destroying political opponents* is a characteristic feature of the totalitarian state. The secret police compile files of information on all important persons, including youthful indiscretions, past associations with persons and groups now officially suspect, accusations collected from various secret informants, and any other damaging information. These secret files can be used to blackmail the subject into any desired co-operation, perhaps in informing on others. The ruling party can dip into the secret files and publish such material as will destroy the public reputation of the subject and his associates and discredit the policies he advocates. It is this feature of the totalitarian state—the "conviction" of citizens on a basis of secret evidence supplied by anonymous informers, and not subject to public examination or judicial cross-examination—which makes the individual utterly helpless before his rulers and makes the totalitarian state so terrifying to believers in human freedom.

America has a secret police (the FBI plus, perhaps, the Central Intelligence Agency) which collects dossiers on individuals and uses secret informers—as any modern state must in order to protect itself against espionage, sabotage, and treason. But herein lies a dilemma: the collection of secret files on many individuals is probably necessary to national security, yet their existence creates for the administration in power a

[65] See syndicated newspaper columns by Joseph and Stewart Alsop, September 13, 1951; February 7, 1952; July 2, 1954; July 12, 1954.

constant temptation to use these files in attacking its opponents. Very few instances of the political use of the secret files have occurred in the United States. If it should become a common practice, political life in America would soon acquire a distinctly totalitarian flavor. [66]

This partial list of contrasts shows that there are fundamental differences between American and communistic "freedoms," but that the differences may be smaller than we sometimes imagine. It is not true, as is sometimes wildly announced, that we have "lost our freedom" or "become a fascist" state. To speak of a "national hysteria" is an exaggeration. Yet there *is* concern, as many bits of evidence attest. And we have in America *all the machinery necessary* to develop a state with little more freedom than the communist states we fear. All we would need to do would be to continue for a generation or two the trends of the past decade, for freedom can be extinguished by almost imperceptible degrees. Most college students are not old enough to recognize any trend or to realize that the civil liberties "issues" of a decade ago (such as "Should *past* membership in communist organizations bar one from government employment?" or "Should communists be permitted to teach school, provided they do not propagandize?") have now been firmly decided, whereas the present "issues" (such as "Should the Supreme Court's authority over antisubversive measures be curbed?" or "Should passport applicants be subject to a security check?") were not even issues a few years ago.

DEFINITION OF THE PROBLEM

To some, the problem is, How can we protect America against a cynical conspiracy to subvert it without destroying civil and intellectual freedom in the process? This definition is implicit in most of the recent literature on civil liberties. People who accept this definition consider many recent anticommunist activities a greater danger than the communist menace at which they are supposedly directed. As a Catholic missionary with firsthand experience with communism states, [67]

> . . . My missionary career in China ended in a communist court in which accusations were taken as facts and charges as proofs. . . . As a result of that experience, I cling desperately to the principle that . . . man is innocent until he is proven guilty. . . . If you must betray democracy in order to save it, why bother?

There are many people, however, who see no fundamental difference between communism and socialism, liberalism, New-Dealism and other varieties of reformism, all of which they consider merely steppingstones

[66] See Francis Biddle, "Ethics in Government and the Use of FBI Files," *The Reporter*, Vol. 10 (January 5, 1954), pp. 13-16.

[67] The Reverend Leon Sullivan, O.F.M., quoted in *Commonweal*, Vol. 57 (November 14, 1952), p. 143.

> I have no anxiety that the Communists will pull off a Communist revolution in the United States. That is not what happens. What does happen is that a people get annoyed and indignant over Communist sabotage of the wells of liberty. Then in a rage they go Fascist and put the Communists down by cruelty and violence. Or in milder form they go vigilante. Both these reactions are the defeat of liberty.
>
> HERBERT HOOVER, in *Collier's*, April 27, 1940.

to communism. Although some of those who denounce liberals and reformers as "communistic" are consciously and cynically trying to neutralize them, there are many who firmly believe that liberals *are* communistic, and that federal aid to education for example, *would* bring communism closer to power. The facts that communists often pose as liberals and reformers and that liberals have sometimes been naively uncritical of communism help reinforce the notion that communism and liberalism differ only in degree. People who believe this merely nod in agreement when liberals are incorrectly accused of communism and are undisturbed when liberals' jobs and reputations are destroyed. Although many of these people believe in civil liberties as an abstract value, they are easily convinced that the civil liberties of communists and procommunists should be curtailed. To these people the only threat to civil liberties comes from the communists, and the problem of civil liberties is purely one of keeping the communists from power.

This group fades imperceptibly into another group which realizes the difference between communism and social reform, but willingly uses charges of communism as a means of defeating social reforms and discrediting social reformers. It is impossible to understand some kinds of "anticommunist" activity unless it is realized that *liberalism is its real target*. This may explain why some professional "anticommunists" show no interest in developing accurate knowledge about communism and why it attracts certain people. First, their real fight is against liberalism. Second, accurate public knowledge about Communism would impair the value of their brand of "anticommunism" as a weapon against liberalism. To destroy completely the communist movement would deprive many conservative groups of their favorite weapon against liberals. Certain politicians also have a vested interest in "fighting" communism. This may be why the Un-American Activities Committee warns that, although Communist party membership keeps shrinking, the party itself remains as strong and dangerous as ever. [68]

[68] *New York Times* (March 8, 1959), p. 38.

Then there are those who do not believe in civil liberties at all. Those who have no *faith in people* distrust any civil liberties. [69] They doubt the ability of the people to make wise decisions, and feel that if communists and other "radicals" are permitted to agitate freely, too many people will be beguiled by them. They view civil liberties as a dangerous idea, and are contemptuous of the "bleeding hearts" and "sentimentalists" who are concerned about them.

Finally, there are the communists themselves, to whom civil liberties are valuable while they seek power, especially if accompanied by occasional suppressions of civil liberties, giving them an issue to dramatize. A *complete* suppression of civil liberties checks certain communist activities for as long as the suppression can be maintained, but creates an atmosphere of conspiracy and repression which communists believe helpful to their long-run objectives. *Complete freedom* of speech, press, and political activity is not helpful to communists in a prosperously contented society, as they cannot strike a heroic pose as martyrs and defenders of liberty. But a tradition of civil liberties coupled with occasional conspicuous denials of these liberties gives communists an ideal "issue." For the communists, then, the "problem" of civil liberties in a country like the United States is one of how to "bait" the society into a partial denial of its professed liberties so that they may exploit this inconsistency.

Some of these definitions overlap with one another, and some persons may vacillate between them. Possibly the largest group of people do not recognize any problem at all. Of a national sample of teen-agers, over half would permit police censorship of books, movies, and broadcasting—"to protect ourselves against improper thinking;" almost half would limit freedom of press; and one-third would deny free speech to certain groups. [70] In a recent national survey asking nearly 5000 people the question, "What kinds of things do you worry about most?" not over 20 people volunteered a worry over civil liberties. [71] Few people seem to get much aroused over civil rights until they feel that their personal freedom to act or speak as they wish is impaired. In this fact lies freedom's greatest danger.

THE SOCIAL-DISORGANIZATION APPROACH

Like Godliness and chastity, the right of civil liberties in the American republic has been a value approved in theory but often ignored in practice. Throughout our history, legal and extralegal penalties have been

[69] Morris Rosenberg, "Misanthropy and Political Ideology," *American Sociological Review* Vol. 21 (December, 1956), pp. 690-695.

[70] H. H. Remmers and D. H. Radler, *The American Teen-Ager* (Indianapolis, The Bobbs-Merrill Company, 1957).

[71] Samuel A. Stouffer, *Communism, Conformity, and Civil Liberties* (Garden City, N. Y., Doubleday & Company, Inc., 1955), p. 69.

exacted from the dissenter and the nonconformist. Although it is inconsistent with the ideal of civil liberty, vigilante action against nonconformists has been an integral part of the *organization* of American society. [72] Suppression of civil liberties, therefore, cannot be accurately described as disorganization.

But the disorganization of any aspect of the culture arouses anxieties, jeopardizes vested interests, inspires the questioning of established institutions, and stimulates many a forceful effort to silence these questionings and protect the status quo. Periods of disturbing change normally bring a crisis in civil liberties, whereas periods of relative cultural stability show fewer suppressions of liberty. The crisis of laissez-faire capitalism and the trend to a partially controlled economy during the 1930's and 1940's was a change profoundly disturbing to many Americans, and the assumption of world responsibility by an America which must remain permanently mobilized for war is another disturbing change. If tension with Russia were to subside, many civil liberties issues would dissolve overnight.

Changing technology, too, creates civil liberties problems. George Orwell's disturbing picture of a television camera policing every living room [73] seems improbable, yet the question of how widely the television camera may be used to "watch" people has already arisen. Wiretapping is a growing practice and may soon be legalized. The increasing portability of atomic bombs multiplies the potential destructiveness of the spy or saboteur, and stimulates increased security precautions. Are the "right of privacy" and the "right to travel" hazards which our advanced society cannot permit? Is the regimentation of the anthill the price we must pay for the scientific marvels of the future? Who can say?

THE VALUE-CONFLICT APPROACH

The term *subversion* implies a value conflict. If all shared the same values, there could be no subversion. But people differ in the values they wish to preserve and in the means they think proper in preserving them. As indicated earlier, some wish to check communism while promoting liberalism, some wish to check both communism and liberalism, and a very few wish to promote communism while confusing and paralyzing liberalism. Some believe in civil liberties; some do not. At one extreme are those who follow Holmes' "clear and present danger" doctrine [74]—that

[72] See John W. Caughey, *Their Majesties The Mob: The Vigilante Impulse in America* (Chicago, University of Chicago Press, 1960).

[73] George Orwell, *Nineteen Eighty-four* (New York, Harcourt, Brace & Co., Inc., 1949).

[74] Mr. Justice Holmes stated, and the full Supreme Court accepted the principle, that "The question in every case is whether the words used are used in such circumstances and are of such a nature as to create a clear and present danger that will bring about the substantive evils that [the State] has a right to prevent." (Schenck *v.* United States, 249 U. S. 47, 52.)

we should allow any *ideas* to be expressed and advocated, however repugnant, so long as there is no "clear and present danger" that violence will result. These people are likely to join the American Civil Liberties Union and defend the right of all Americans, even those they despise, to express any views, even those they detest. At the opposite extreme are those who believe—as do the communists—that only the "safe," "right," or "American" ideas are entitled to freedom of expression. When Russia's Vishinsky writes, "In our state, naturally, there can be no place for freedom of speech, press, and so on for the foes of socialism," [75] these Americans need change only the last word to be in complete agreement. Between these two extremes fall many people with a vague general belief in civil liberties except when they are afraid or confused, and who can sometimes be led into a suppression of liberty during a period of national anxiety.

THE PERSONAL-DEVIATION APPROACH

Most extremists are deviants. Most extremists show a fanatical preoccupation with their "cause," a suspicious distrust of other people in general, a disinterest in normal pursuits, recreations, and small talk, and a strong tendency to divide other people into enemies and allies. These are symptoms of an unhappy, neurotic personality. Ernst and Loth's study of American ex-communists [76] finds that most of them were young people who were not yet settled in adult life, from comfortable but unhappy homes, intelligent and well-educated, but frequently unpopular folk who had never really "belonged" until they found the Communist Party. Most suffered strong feelings of personal inadequacy and harbored hostilities or resentments against domineering parents. Many of the rank and file were idealistic, self-sacrificing, submissive, and unselfish. The total picture is that of an unhappy, insecure person who needs a cause in which to lose himself and gain a sense of personal worth. The members were not much changed by their experience, retaining more or less the same personalities they possessed before and during their membership.

The Ernst and Loth study is largely confined to short-term young members. A similar study by Almond shows the hard-core party professionals to be more cynical, ruthless, and opportunistic. [77] Their personalities, too, remain much the same as when they become ex-communists. As a communist, Whittaker Chambers viewed the world as a hostile conspiracy

[75] In *The Law of the Soviet Union*, 1948; quoted in Wahlke, *op. cit.*, p. 45.
[76] *Op. cit.*, especially pp. 1-15. See also Dean Brelis, "The Making of a Spy" [Harry Gold], *Life* (June 12, 1950), pp. 7-15; Walter White, "Portrait of a Communist," [Benjamin J. Davis, Jr.], *The Progressive*, Vol. 14 (November, 1950), p. 17.
[77] Gabriel A. Almond and others, *The Appeals of Communism* (Princeton, N. J., Princeton University Press, 1954), based on intimate studies of 221 former American, British, French, and Italian Communists.

in which the liberals, the reformers, much of the church and school, and all moderates were unwitting allies of the capitalistic oppression; after leaving the party, he saw these same groups as unwitting allies of the communists. As a communist, he saw social reform as an obstacle to revolution; later, he saw reform as a bridge to revolution. As a communist, he saw conspiracy and wicked scheming against him on every side. As a communist, he foresaw an eventual titanic struggle between communism and its enemies in which one must inevitably destroy the other; he never changed these views. [78] It is this inability of the extremists—whether of the right or of the left—to see a reasonable middle way which causes so many ex-communists, when they abandon one set of undemocratic absolutes, to embrace another. The ease with which German communists turned Nazi, and, later, Nazis turned communists, further shows how a certain type of personality can be equally at home with either form of totalitarianism.

How reliable is the information provided by ex-communist informants? It varies widely. Some informants are stable and dependable; some are neurotics who cannot tell fact from fancy; some are publicity-seekers; some are pathological liars. A number of ex-communist informers have been repeatedly caught in contradictions and inaccuracies. [79] Some have received pay as government "consultants" or as government witnesses in court trials, a practice which carries certain dangers, since they got paid only as long as they could recall incriminating evidence.

The personal-deviation approach is highly suggestive. If more "experts" on communism had studied communism as a refuge for maladjusted personalities instead of viewing it as a contagious disease, fatal upon exposure, many of our difficulties with communism as an internal social movement would have been avoided.

RATIONAL PROPOSALS FOR PRESERVING LIBERTY AND SECURITY

If it be assumed that our objective is to preserve both civil liberties and American security, then several courses of action are indicated.

1. *Recognize that communists will survive suppression.* Our recent rash of loyalty oaths, security programs, and congressional investigations mainly hurt the communists' enemies—the liberals and reformers—not the communists. How the communists protect themselves in such periods

[78] Cf. Whittaker Chambers, *Witness* (New York, Random House, 1952). See also Arthur Schlesinger, Jr., John Dos Passos, Charles Alan Wright, Richard M. Nixon, Richard B. Morris (symposium), "Whittaker Chambers and His Witness," *Saturday Review*, Vol. 35 (May 24, 1952), pp. 8-13 ff.; also Elmer Davis, "History in Doublethink," *Saturday Review*, Vol. 35 (June 28, 1952), pp. 8-9.

[79] See Joseph W. Alsop, "The Strange Case of Louis Budenz," *Atlantic Monthly*, Vol. 189 (April, 1952), pp. 29-33; also syndicated newspaper column by the Alsops, July 12, 1954.

is revealed in their "Guide for Guatemalan Communists in Guatemala" during the Armas regime: [80]

1. Abstain from defending Communist viewpoints in order to avoid suspicion.
2. All unknown members of the Party should . . . [join] anti-Communist parties . . .
3. Denounce as Communist as many anti-Communists as possible. . . .

As this shows, there are very few "anticommunist" measures which the communists cannot turn to their own advantage. To be effective, anti-communism must be intelligent. Hitler was an "anticommunist", yet his actions left half of Europe under communist rule.

2. *Accurate knowledge of communism* is necessary if it is to be opposed intelligently. This includes distinguishing between communism and liberalism, and between the genuine and the professed objectives of communism. People who do not fully understand communism often fall into the communists' trap by doing just what the communists want them to do. Conservatives do this when they smear liberals as communistic, or when they cry, "Wolf!", "Communist Wolf!" so often that reasonable men cease to listen. Liberals fall into the communists' trap when they denounce *all* anticommunist efforts as "Red-baiting," and when they are reluctant to admit that there *is* a ruthless communist conspiracy directed against American democracy.

3. *Understanding of the American heritage of liberty* is also necessary if it is to be continued. A study of past civil liberties crises is reassuring, for it shows that the present problem is not so greatly different from those of the past. Communism—and certain modes of opposing it—are the present threat to civil liberties, but the basic issue is constantly the same old question of *whether to trust the people to reach their own decisions, or to make their decisions for them.* This question is always with us, to be reargued each generation.

4. *An adequate national defense* is, needless to say, necessary in a world where an international revolutionary movement is joined with an aggressive major power. This is a military problem, not a sociological problem.

5. *Counterespionage is essential.* Highly trained professional agencies such as the FBI and the Central Intelligence Agency can do this efficiently and without endangering personal liberties of citizens. If headline-hunting congressmen, American Legion officials, or other amateurs turn G-man, they merely scare off any real spies and destroy the counterespionage efforts of the professionals. [81]

[80] Keith Monroe, "Guatemala: What the Reds Left Behind," *Harper's Magazine,* Vol. 211 (July, 1955), pp. 60-65.

[81] See statement of J. Edgar Hoover in *New York Times* (May 11, 1954), p. 18; J. Edgar Hoover, *Masters of Deceit, op. cit.,* 311-313.

6. *Reform of Congressional committee procedures* and the security program is necessary if civil liberties are to be protected. Unless committees either cease acting as courts "trying" people for disloyalty or allow the accused the safeguards long since adopted by courts to protect the accused from injustice, it is inevitable that injustice will be done.

7. *A more forgiving attitude towards ex-communists* and ex-fellow-travelers might help undermine the party. Our social and economic ostracism of the former communist or fellow-traveler discourages members from leaving the party, encourages former members to try to conceal their past associations, and encourages the former member to try to redeem himself by an orgy of denunciation. Ernst and Loth suggest that a "Communists Anonymous" organization, patterned after Alcoholics Anonymous, would help in the social and economic rehabilitation of ex-communists. [82] This would weaken one of the most powerful forces which keeps people in the party. [83]

8. *A prosperous, progressive society* is the best defense against communism or any other kind of radical movement. Sombart said fifty years ago, "All the socialist utopias are destroyed by roast beef and apple pie." Although there will probably be a few who are communists for emotional and personality reasons there is no prospect of communists gaining a mass following as long as our society is prosperous and free. The greatest tragedy recently to befall the American communists was our failure to go into an economic tailspin after the recent war. No prosperous, progressive country in the world has ever had a strong communist movement. In America the communist menace, insofar as it concerns communism as an *internal revolutionary movement*, is little more than a bogeyman for unscrupulous politicians and reactionaries to exploit in misleading the gullible. If America remains a free and prosperous society, no other defense against communism as an ideology and revolutionary movement will be necessary. [84]

A list of proposed laws is conspicuously missing from this series of proposals. The omission is deliberate. Although national security requires a vigorous enforcement of existing laws against espionage and sabotage, it is difficult to find any social scientist of repute who feels that national security requires additional *antisubversive* legislation. Laws passed *against* communism are likely to curtail the liberties of noncommunists while not greatly bothering the communists. If we have a strong, prosperous, and free society, antisubversive legislation is unnecessary; if our society does not remain prosperous and free, antisubversive legislation will probably be ineffective.

[82] *Op. cit.*, pp. 230-235.
[83] See John Gates, *The Story of an American Communist* (New York, Thomas Nelson & Sons, 1959).
[84] For a research study showing how communism appeals to workers who have lost faith in improvement under democracy, see Hadley Cantril, *The Politics of Despair* (New York, Basic Books, Inc., 1958).

SUMMARY

America is now emerging from one of its recurrent attacks of anxiety over its liberties. These liberties were written into our constitutional system at a time when our nation was weak, divided, and menaced by powerful enemies within and without—written by men who believed that good government must protect civil liberties if it is to survive.

Communism provides the current occasion for a variety of laws and activities, some honestly directed at communism, and some apparently intended to achieve other political or ideological objectives under the pretext of opposing communism. Some of these measures may actually aid the communists; at least the communists seem to think so. Many of the existing and proposed laws pose a great *potential* danger to civil liberties. If administered by moderate and judicious men, civil liberties may not be impaired; if administered by frightened or bigoted men during a period of national anxiety, our present legal machinery could easily become an instrument of widespread oppression.

It is perhaps impossible, in the modern world, to grant a government the power to govern effectively and protect the national security adequately without also granting it the power to curtail the liberties of its citizens. It is also impossible, in modern life, to prevent private organizations and communications media from possessing a great power to intimidate and punish individuals, to penalize and inhibit independent thinking, to promote a timid, conforming population.

Whether these powers are used to achieve these ends depends upon several factors. A frightened people is unlikely to remain free, and a hungry man treasures freedom less than bread. An American people intelligently informed about the genuine purposes and techniques of communism will be neither greatly attracted nor greatly frightened by communism. The possibilities of war, of sabotage, and of espionage are the continuing threats to our national security which it would be unrealistic to ignore, but which cannot be effectively averted by curbing the speech, thought, and associations of our citizens. The menace of communism as an ideology and political movement is a largely imaginary danger in any country which remains prosperous and free. And, in the long run, the communist movement in America may be far more greatly affected by what we do to ourselves in the process of opposing communism than by anything we do to the communists.

SUGGESTED READINGS

ALMOND, Gabriel A., and others, *The Appeals of Communism* (Princeton, N. J., Princeton University Press, 1954). A study of 221 former American,

British, French, and Italian Communists, to see what attracted them to Communism, and why they eventually left it.

American Civil Liberties Union, *Annual Report*, (New York, American Civil Liberties Union). An annual survey of the current state of civil liberties in the U. S.

CAUGHY, John W., *In Clear and Present Danger* (Chicago, University of Chicago Press, 1958). The piecemeal surrender of freedom in the search for internal security.

DOUGLAS, William O., *An Almanac of Liberty* (Garden City, N. Y., Doubleday & Company, Inc., 1954). An almanac listing 365 incidents in the historic and continuing struggle for human liberty.

ERNST, Morris L., and LOTH, David, *Report on the American Communist* (New York, Henry Holt & Co., Inc., 1952). A highly readable account of the kinds of people who become communists in America, why they join, why they leave, and suggestions for effectively opposing communism. Based on interviews with 300 ex-communists.

GELLHORN, Walter, *Individual Freedom and Governmental Restraints* (Baton Rouge, Louisiana State University Press, 1956). Discusses the erosion of freedom through government actions.

IVERSON, Robert W., *The Communists and the Schools* (New York, Harcourt, Brace and Company, 1959). An authoritative account of the communists' unsuccessful attempt to capture the schools.

LASSWELL, Harold D., *National Security and Individual Freedom* (New York, McGraw-Hill Book Co., 1950). Seeks to outline a detailed policy for safeguarding national security against both military and ideological dangers without destroying our civil liberties in the process.

Legislative Reference Service of the Library of Congress, *Fascism in Action*, House Document, No. 401, 80th Congress, 1st Session (Washington, Government Printing Office, 1947). A documented study and analysis of fascism as it operated in European countries.

MARX, Karl, and ENGELS, Friedrich, *The Communist Manifesto*. A brief authoritative statement of the ideology and objectives of Communism. Available in various editions and collections in any good library.

MAYER, Milton, and ADLER, Mortimer J., eds., *The Tradition of Freedom* (New York, Oceana Publications, 1958). Selections from the writings that shaped the concepts of freedom and justice in America.

PHILBRICK, Herbert, *I Led 3 Lives* (New York, McGraw-Hill Book Co., 1952). The fascinating account of an FBI counterspy's nine years within the Communist party. Gives many insights into the character and techniques and secret purposes of the Communist leadership in America.

STOUFFER, Samuel A., *Communism, Conformity, and Civil Liberties* (Garden City, N. Y., Doubleday & Company, Inc., 1955). A comprehensive study of American attitudes upon Communism and civil liberties.

AUDIO-VISUAL AIDS

The Challenge (AFL-CIO, 815 Sixteenth Street, N. W., Washington, D. C.), 28 minutes, sound, black and white. Should a school bus driver be fired for refusal to sign a loyalty oath?

Friday Is a Great Day (American Civil Liberties Union, 170 Fifth Ave., New York), 26 minutes, 33⅓ rpm transcription. An NBC broadcast to commemorate "Bill of Rights" day; dramatizes civil liberties incidents and issues.

Peaceful Assembly and Free Speech (McGraw-Hill Book Company, Inc., Text-Film Department, 330 West 42 St., New York), 22 minutes, sound, black and white. An account of a contest between the ACLU and the Indiana American Legion over whether the ACLU should hold a public meeting.

QUESTIONS AND PROJECTS

1. If Jefferson were living today, and held the same values as he did when living, what do you suppose he would approve and disapprove in our current situation? What would he say about communism? About McCarthyism? Would he be a "security risk?"

2. What did the framers of our Constitution and Bill of Rights rely on to prevent revolution in America?

3. Are the dangers of subversion greater now than they were in 1801 when Jefferson allowed the Alien and Sedition Laws to lapse?

4. Why do communists desire revolution rather than social reform?

5. Why do communists support social reforms, if they really don't want reform?

6. Whom do the communist leaders consider to be their major enemies? Why?

7. How have conservatives or reactionaries sometimes given unintentional assistance to the communists? How have liberals sometimes given unintentional assistance to the communists?

8. How can those persons and organizations which are honestly seeking social reforms be distinguished from those who seek to exploit popular interest in reform as a means of promoting communist propaganda?

9. How would the behavior of a communist spy in our government differ from the behavior of a procommunist or fellow-traveler? Which would be more likely to express the "Communist party line?"

10. How does the problem of dealing with possible espionage and sabotage differ from the problem of dealing with subversive social movements?

11. What value conflicts are involved in defining the problem of civil liberties?

12. Will there ever be a time when civil liberties cease to be a problem in the United States?

13. During a period of prosperity, communism appears to attract only those who are somewhat emotionally maladjusted. Would this still be true during a long period of depression and hardship?

14. What jobs should admitted communists be permitted to hold? If none, then what should be done with communists? Should any distinction be made between communists who admire Russia and communists (such as Titoists) who hate the Russian communists?

15. What civil liberties issues would remain even if all problems concerning communism, Russia, and China were solved?

Part **III**

REASSESSMENT
AND SOCIAL ORIENTATION

20

The Three Sociological
Approaches Reassessed

ተተተ

Part i of this book provided a definition of social problems and a body of general understandings about them. Three sociological approaches to the study of social problems were formulated and the student received some guidance in the interpretation of data. In Part II, a variety of important problems were analyzed and interpreted in terms of these three approaches. The purpose of this final section is that of synthesis. The three approaches need to be reassessed in terms of their application to the concrete data set forth of Part II. Recurrent threads—factors causing disorganization, pervasive value conflicts, and personality influences—must be organized into patterns and the patterns related to one another. The final chapter of this section will attempt to foreshadow the course of history—to hazard predictions about the course of things to come.

SOCIAL DISORGANIZATION: RETROSPECT AND PROSPECT

Social problems are in large measure products of change. The change may be a major revolution in human civilization or only a slight alteration in local conditions. Its effects may be felt for months and years before the change occurs, or for centuries afterward. The change may be one of attitude or of knowledge. But whatever the specific case, the fact of change is fundamental to the emergence of social problems.

The Effects of Change

Regardless of its nature, change requires that persons, and/or groups, and/or institutions make adjustments. Change (1) threatens vested interests, (2) interrupts habits, (3) creates distress, and (4) eventually results in the development of new patterns.

1. THREATENS VESTED INTERESTS. Inevitably, some groups in a society create for themselves, or are the recipients of, positions of special advantage. In a theocracy they might be priests; in a bureaucracy, politicians or civil servants; in a society dominated by pecuniary values, businessmen and merchants; in a gerontocracy, the aged; and so on. The prevailing values determine which group reaps which special benefits; and not one but, ordinarily, numerous groups soon come to have a special interest in maintaining the status quo. Unless they themselves initiate it, vested interest groups often view change with suspicion or with open hostility. With the multiplicity of interest groups, almost any change will prove threatening to some of them. At the first suggestion of change, interested groups mobilize their resources to do battle. The ensuing conflict increases awareness, sharpens differences, and furthers antagonism. These are the conditions of social problem situations.

2. INTERRUPTS HABITS. The various interest groups curry favor with whosoever will give them an audience and, possibly, support. Many persons take sides but most people ordinarily have no clear vested interest in a particular change. They do not stand to reap great profit or to suffer great loss. But when the change occurs, they suffer for it nevertheless. For men are creatures of habit, and change disturbs habits. A new traffic light at an intersection where one is accustomed to passing through or a new filing system at the office disturbs personal habits as surely, though perhaps not as drastically, as do major wars and depressions. Routines which had long ago become so automatic as to become unconscious and attitudes so familiar as to seem almost sacred are suddenly called back into consciousness. The individual must work at things that were formerly routine. Not only must time and energy be devoted to the changing situation, but such effort interferes with the smooth operation of other habits. When driving an automobile, one cannot plan tonight's dinner or reminisce about last night, but must concentrate on watching the traffic lights. The office worker cannot daydream about his upcoming vacation because he has to cope with a pesky new filing system. Change, because it disturbs old habits, is uncomfortable. Because it is uncomfortable one tends to resist it. To many otherwise disinterested persons, change itself becomes the problem. One feels that if only all this nonsense were stopped, one could go back to former comfortable routines.

3. CREATES DISTRESS. Because habits are so persistent the adjustment to change is often difficult. Attitudes and values, in particular, are slow to change and are frequently held too long after the conditions for which they were appropriate have disappeared. The average person does not see that his failure to adjust is an important factor in the disorganization caused by change. He knows that something is wrong, but his definition of what is wrong centers upon the breakdown of the familiar,

and what are to him the "right," ways of doing things. His feelings are apt to be expressed in such phrases as, "Remember the good old days?" "What is the world coming to?" "Such things would never have happened back in . . .", and so on. The emphasis is upon the breakdown of the old patterns and upon the resulting chaos and confusion. Obviously, many of the persons who think and feel this way are in dire distress. For no reason at all, things seem to have gone wrong and there is little that one can do about it. The husband and wife caught up in a divorce procedure, the southern white man who must send his children to a school attended by Negroes, and the devoted parishioner who hears her minister talk of the "figures of speech" in the Bible all have this one factor in common—something seems to be terribly wrong.

4. RESULTS IN NEW PATTERNS. The serious distress of countless people is not always quickly alleviated. Divorce, desegregation, and the modern gospel may be bitterly resisted for years and even for generations. But, even as the resistance continues, it is gradually being undermined. Some persons cease to venerate the past and seek to understand the present. Soon there appears a whole new generation which never knew of the old conditions and to whom the reminiscences of their elders are a sign of deterioration. Youngsters more quickly see the order in the new patterns, for their vision is uncluttered by the habit-debris of the past. And new order does exist, or at least it is in the offing. For much social change is not merely the breakdown of traditional patterns but their replacement by new, unfamiliar, and, therefore, disturbing ones. In many cases the new and the old exist side by side, with the old gradually relinquishing its ground. In still other cases, the old patterns may begin to break down before new patterns appear. Especially when change results from the imposition of elements from outside the culture or from another area of culture, there may be a time lag between the breakdown of the old and the complete development of the new. [1] The period of lag will be a period of widespread dissatisfaction, and the dissatisfaction will continue until such time as the new patterns become established.

Major Changes in Western Culture

A truly comprehensive discussion of the changes which underlie current symptoms of disorganization would have to include a complete history of Western culture as well as substantial amounts of world history. There are, however, a relatively few pervasive historical developments in the Western world, an understanding of which will aid immeasurably in putting the present scene into proper perspective. Four of these developments are: (1) the rise of science and "scientism"; (2) the Industrial Revolution; (3) urbanization; (4) and the rise of secularism.

[1] William F. Ogburn, *Social Change* (New York, The Viking Press, Inc., 1922).

1. SCIENCE AND SCIENTISM. Mastery of the techniques of science is one of the most distinguishing characteristics of Western culture. The West has gained unparalleled control over the physical world and has produced hitherto undreamed of quantities of material goods. It is not surprising that great pride should be taken in these accomplishments and that the production of more and better goods should be regarded as a hopeful prospect for the solution of many current problems. Especially where deprivation and low living standards contribute to the problem, the diffusion of technological know-how holds great promise. But there is ample evidence that there are grave shortcomings in this approach.

First, there is a strong tendency to confuse the material results of scientific investigation with the process of objective inquiry which made them possible. Many persons who sing the praises of science do not really admire *science* so much as they admire the *technology* which is a product of science. They actually oppose free scientific inquiry at every point where it might threaten some of their other values. Such persons probably encourage research, but only under conditions that prevent new knowledge from interfering with their interests. Scientists, however, have long held—and the history of scientific development supports this view— that such restriction is inimical to scientific progress; that scientists must be free to explore seemingly unpromising avenues and even extremely controversial ones. Many of the greatest scientific discoveries have followed such "impractical" investigation.

A second deficiency frequently found in this approach is the unwitting expectation that the discovery of new knowledge or inventions should make it evident how such inventions should be used and should insure their proper employment. In addition to being grossly unrealistic, such expectations betray great ignorance of the nature of science. Science itself includes no value system which guarantees that its fruits will be used to provide the greatest benefit for the greatest number of people. Science has helped both to *alleviate* and to *create* problems. It is no panacea, but provides great potential for change, which change creates the need for tremendous adjustment as well.

2. THE INDUSTRIAL REVOLUTION. Not the least of the accompaniments of scientific development was the Industrial Revolution. Together with the related revolution in agricultural methods, the Industrial Revolution resulted, perhaps, in the most far-reaching changes in Western culture since the development of written language. Within a span of only decades it had uprooted the traditions of centuries and launched the Western world upon a period of unprecedented expansion and development. Simple methods of hand production gave way to mass production and the factory system: the former luxuries of the elite became the necessities of the masses. And still more goods were produced. The resulting trade relationships and military prowess combined to permit the West to dominate much of the world.

Some aspects of almost every problem treated in this book have some of their origins in this period. The present pattern of race conflict, the demand for and ability to support universal public education, and quintupling of the world's population, the atomization of the family, and so on, are mingled in a cause-and-effect network, with the Industrial Revolution. The significance of the Industrial Revolution, however, goes far beyond the changed production methods and the improved military status of Western nations. It was part of a process of expansion and development which continues even more rapidly at the present time and which is spreading to all corners of the earth. The steam engine, the cotton gin, and the Bessemer process of steelmaking were wonderful inventions, but they must be compared with the supersonic air travel and nuclear fission of the present and with the prospects for harnessing solar energy and the possible synthesis of carbohydrates in the near future. The rate of change seems not to be decreasing but to be accelerating at a dizzy rate. According to an early Atomic Energy Commission report, the world progressed as far during the period from 1940 to the dropping of the first atomic bomb on Hiroshima in 1945 as it had travelled during the entire period from the discovery of fire to the building of the first locomotive.

To expect that such radical changes could be rapidly and effectively adjusted to is not very realistic. Those who point out the fact that social problems never seem to be eliminated ignore the fact that change constantly requires new adjustments. Even keeping up with those changes is a major accomplishment. So long as society is characterized by rapid change, there will be the lags and stresses which we call *social disorganization.*

3. Urbanization. The large cities of modern times are a very recent development. The changes sponsored by the Industrial Revolution made them both possible and necessary. Urbanization must be seen not as a condition but as a process. The United States has changed from an almost exclusively rural nation to one which is predominantly urban. Up until the third decade of the present century the pattern was one of rapid growth in the largest of cities. Huge populations clustered around single business centers. Skyscrapers appeared to concentrate more people in a given land area—congestion, contamination, slums, and tenements were all by-products. The 1930 census showed the emergence of a new trend —the trend toward suburbanization. The largest cities began to slow down in their rate of growth. Yet the number of metropolitan centers increased. The cities were built outward instead of upward. Low-cost housing developments, with shopping centers and industries on the periphery of the city became the order of the day.

The trend still continues. Since World War II, some new notes have crept in. The planned community with its winding streets, its own schools, parks, recreation, and business centers, has appeared in large numbers. "Development" houses now range in price up to $50,000 or more. A whole new highly mobile, managerial class is located in the suburbs and has complicated their structure. [2] Highway and traffic problems, taxation, and representation are the 1960 counterparts of the congestion problems of the urban 1920's. It is impossible to say how long the present era of suburbanization will continue. Already the hydrogen bomb, bacterial warfare, tax and labor problems, hydroelectric developments, and so on, threaten to alter the pattern. Urban expansion is one of the major characteristics of our time. Whatever the specific direction it takes, future urban development will definitely be involved in social problem situations ranging from racial discrimination (in housing, schools, and so on) to the detection of criminal behavior.

4. SECULARIZATION. It is not difficult to see how the processes of scientific development, industrial progress, and urbanization are intertwined. As observable trends they are a part of the more general change in fabric of Western society. At least one additional element needs to be added—the process of secularization.

The trend toward secular thinking is as revolutionary and far-reaching in its effects as any of the others, for it represents a radically new approach to the solution of human problems. Very simply, secular thinking is utilitarian thinking. It assumes that man has broad control over the conditions of his own existence and that when a problem arises he should manipulate those conditions in any manner necessary to end the problem. Secular thinking relates means to ends and judges both means and ends in terms of their usefulness in attaining other goals. Secular thinking in this sense is the polar opposite of sacred thinking, which is oriented to and judges all actions by standards coming out of the past. Sacred thinking is tradition-oriented and discourages change, secular thinking subjects the eternal verities to the withering test of practical application. [3]

Probably no society is either completely sacred or completely secular in orientation. [4] Some societies are more conservative and more tradition-bound than others. Recent centuries have seen drastic changes in the sacred-secular balance of Western society. The development of science and the revolutions in industry and agriculture have given man a degree of power he never possessed before and have encouraged him to seek more control over his own destiny. The schism in organized religion, personified by the Reformation, was a part of the process, and it contributed to the process as well. Whereas formerly much effort was directed toward explaining *why* given conditions existed and *why* they must be

[2] William H. Whyte, Jr., *The Organization Man* (New York, Simon and Schuster, Inc., 1956).

[3] For an illuminating analysis of the sacred-secular dichotomy in the wider context of social values and social action, see Howard Becker, *Through Values to Social Interpretation* (Durham, N. C., Duke University Press, 1950).

[4] *Op. cit.*

borne, we are now trying to discover *how* they can be changed to suit man's needs. The trend toward secular thinking is not complete and a major conflict relating thereto is discussed in a subsequent section. But the past and current change resulting from this trend are dwarfed only by its future potential. Modern society has come not only to accept change but to value it. The rate of social change is not apt to decline in a society which is so oriented.

Unsolved Problems in Social Disorganization

To expect that social science, or even that man himself, can succeed in eliminating disorganization from social life is as naive as for the farmer to believe that the insect problem will be eliminated once he has halted a particular invasion of grasshoppers or locusts. There are thousands of varieties of insects, all of which cannot be fought at the same time, and even those which he does combat breed new generations incessantly. Our farmer must be ever on the alert, pushing back the multitudes, repairing the damage, and shifting his attack to meet new developments. So it is also in society. Not one line of change, but many lines affect our daily lives—and while one set of adjustments is being worked out the need for others is developing. Here, too, man needs to learn to anticipate and to control his social problems so that the damage in terms of human suffering may be reduced to a minimum. The long-sought *answers* to social disorganization lie not in its elimination—which could occur only if social change were halted—but in the development of continually more efficient techniques of adjustment.

That new techniques of adjustment are constantly appearing is unquestionable; many of them are discussed in the chapters in Part II. Whether the schisms and lags of today are less numerous and less serious than those of the past, however, is open to question. In many ways it seems that distress and disaster are more prevalent today than ever before. Are we falling behind in our ability to adjust to new demands or does it only seem that way? Are we nearer to ultimate disaster, or do we merely lack perspective on problems that are near at hand? There are, in this connection, at least two basic problems in social change that remain unsolved. The first problem is the unequal rates of change in different aspects of culture, and the second problem involves the constantly heavier demand made upon individuals by accelerating rates of social change.

1. UNEQUAL RATES OF CHANGE. This is an era of unprecedented technological expansion. The process of creating material inventions appears to be cumulative. The more inventions that are made, the faster new ones appear and the more complex they become. The past fifty years have seen us move from the horse-and-buggy stage to the stage of jet and rocket propulsion. The past two decades alone have seen the develop-

ment of nuclear fission, deadly nerve gases, and bacteriological warfare. Man's tools of destruction have reached the point where the annihilation of civilization, if not of all mankind, is a grave possibility.

The danger to mankind, however, does not lie solely in the development of continually more destructive weapons. It also lies in the failure of other aspects of culture to change rapidly enough to meet the challenge presented to them. [5] Particularly, long outmoded political institutions and practices tend to persist. As outlined in the chapter on War and International Organization, nations continue to conduct their affairs as though eighteenth century conditions still prevailed. How long can this gap between material invention and social practice continue to widen? Present prospects are that another major war would result in world-wide disaster, and with each new invention the prospects become even more terrifying.

The only possible solution to this dilemma appears to lie in a rapid transformation of world political institutions. Occasionally another solution, a moratorium on further material invention, is proposed, but no competent authorities actually believe that such a "holiday from invention" could be accomplished. [6] Nor does past experience indicate that a rapid overhaul of social institutions is likely. This is the most pressing of the great unsolved problems of our time. The wrong combination of further social change and a lack of social adjustment may eliminate all social problems—permanently!

2. INCREASING DEMANDS. The gap between the rate of material invention and the rate of institutional change is a function of inertia within the social system. It is not a question of whether human beings can live under political institutions which would render war unnecessary; it is, rather, a question as to whether they *will* develop such institutions. That problem does not raise the question of ultimate human capacity to adjust to ever more rapid social change.

It is probable that ever since he became capable of reflecting upon such things, man has questioned his capacity to adjust to the new and unfamiliar. Up to the present, of course, such fears have proved groundless. There has always been, up to now, a kind of reservoir of potential which man has been able to draw upon to adjust to the new complexities that faced him. Thus, there is some justification for believing that apprehensions about the future are partially a function of our unfamiliarity

---

[5] Ogburn, *op. cit.*

[6] Bans upon the testing of nuclear weapons reflect, in part, this kind of thinking. They are also viewed as preliminary to pacts outlawing the use of such weapons. It appears that many people have been lulled into a sense of security because, under similar agreement, poison gas has not been used since World War I. One extremely important difference between these two situations is that poison gas has not yet been proved to be a very useful weapon. There is ample evidence, however, that nations continue to experiment with its development.

with new culture patterns which are appearing. Students in the next century may look back upon the present era with the same feeling of condescension which we now experience when we think of the "terrible complexity" of horseless carriages and continuous radio broadcasting.

Yet there undoubtedly are limits to man's capacity for adjustment. His brain and nervous system are wonderfully plastic but they are finite. Since the rate of human biological evolution is almost imperceptible and the rate of social change constantly increases, it is logical to assume that sooner or later the limits of man's ability to adjust to new situations will be reached. As indicated in the chapter on the personal pathologies, many persons feel that the high rate of mental-emotional breakdown in modern society is proof that the limits have nearly been reached. Unfortunately, there is no way of knowing for certain whether the actual rates of mental illness have increased or only that there is now more awareness of the problem. Present knowledge will not permit a definite answer to the question, but we are now accumulating enough data so that future trends in the rate of personal breakdown will permit some judgment as to whether society is becoming too complex. If illness rates soar and therapeutic measures prove ineffective, then the inference will be that the limits have nearly been reached. If, on the other hand, the rates do not increase appreciably, then our respect for the human organism should grow apace.

VALUE CONFLICTS: RELATIVITY AND THE SEARCH FOR STANDARDS

Social problems inevitably include value conflicts. Ordinarily, values are slowly crystallized, over time, in response to established conditions. But the very nature of social problems includes social change. Social problems are not products of static conditions and accepted definitions: they are products of change and the search for new definitions. When established values provide for no effective means of coping with a problem, then new and more adequate values must be developed. The search for new values crystallizes differences among groups which formerly had not received so much attention.

Bases for Value Conflicts

Many groups, when the issues are sharpened, differ fundamentally on important matters. The common assumption that reasonable people "can get together if they will only try" is found to be something less than completely true. A part of the remaining truth is that on social issues there are no universally accepted standards of what is right or wrong, good or bad. At best, there are surface conflicts concerning how a particular accepted solution to a problem may be implemented in practice, and, at worst, there are fundamental value differences which make any agreement at all as to whether a problem exists or what ought to be done about it virtually impossible.

The key to understanding value conflicts and their role in social problems lies in the recognition of group differences and in the attitudes that people take toward those differences. The range of group differences is almost limitless. For purposes of convenience and illustration, we will mention just four principal sources of value differences that conduce to conflict.

1. SEVERAL ECONOMIC, POLITICAL, AND RELIGIOUS SYSTEMS. The terms *Republican, Democrat, Protestant, Catholic, Jew, free enterprise,* and *government regulation* are all common terms used in every day speech. Usually in a vague sort of way it is recognized that a man who is labeled as Republican, Protestant, and an advocate of free enterprise feels, thinks, and acts somewhat differently from a man who is labeled Democratic, Catholic and a supporter of more government regulation of the economy. This series of identifications, whatever the specific combination, influences far more things than how the man will vote on, say, a proposed public power project. [7] It indicates with some predictability what he conceives to be the nature of man, the relation of man to his God, the role of government in relation to both man and God, and what he will define as good or evil in man, his works, and his society. People do differ in these fundamental definitions according to their group affiliations. The fact that Catholic and Protestant, Republican and Democrat can work together cordially in the same office, enjoy the same movies, and be equally devoted to their families does not mean that they would make the same changes in society if they had the power to do so. At countless points their preferred changes would go in completely opposite directions. Awareness of problem situations and the possibility that "something might be done" in the problem area brings these customarily glossed-over differences to the fore. Then people who are neighbors, co-workers, and even friends become embroiled in bitter conflict.

2. RACIAL AND ETHNIC VARIATION. Ethnic and racial differences are neither so subtle nor so well camouflaged as economic, religious, and political ones. Over fifteen million United States citizens are a group set apart racially, that is by physical identification, and many millions more are set apart by cultural or ethnic differences. Into the former category fall most Negroes and Orientals, together with some Indians and Mexicans. Into the latter category fall most of the European immigrant groups, who

[7] Sociologists use these group identifications to predict a variety of attitudes and actions, including voting behavior. See Paul F. Lazarsfeld, Bernard Berelson, and Hazel Gaudet, *The People's Choice* (New York, Columbia University Press, 1948), and Eugene Burdick, and Arthur J. Brodbeck, eds., *American Voting Behavior* (Glencoe, Ill., The Free Press, 1959).

have retained many European traditions, and also some small religious sects whose beliefs and patterns render them readily identifiable.

The democratic prescription against group discrimination has been notoriously ineffective in relation to racial and ethnic groups, and conflict is seldom absent in the lives of minority group members. Racial epithets of many sorts are used to express antipathy toward or from these groups. Substantial numbers of each group resent any rights or privileges enjoyed by the others, and feel themselves morally justified in, if not obligated

The New York Times

This Chinese laundry, Jewish butcher shop, and Puerto Rican grocery existing side by side dramatize the potential for value-conflict in large cities.

to, "keep the ——— in their proper place." Social problems and the solutions proposed to alleviate them often derive from or threaten to change some aspects of the relations between these groups. All of the antipathies, the conflicts of interest, and the desires for exploitation are immediately involved in a struggle to determine whose values shall prevail.

3. CONFLICTS OF INTEREST. Social life always involves a balance between those interests which persons and groups have in common and those which they do not share. In simpler societies it is often difficult to determine where the common interests end and the individual interests begin. Any tendency for an individual to shirk his obligations to others

may result in such quick and drastic retaliation that the person soon learns not to attempt it. In fact, if the society's techniques of indoctrination have functioned smoothly, it probably will not even occur to him to try it. Even in complex, modern societies it is sometimes difficult to separate the joint interest from the individual interest. The interests of labor and management, for example, often tend to be opposed, but both share in the prosperity of full employment and both suffer from prolonged strikes. This does not mean, of course, that workers and management agree on the advisability of strikes but it does stress the difficulty of clearly categorizing the separate interests of individuals and groups.

On the other hand, the larger and more complex the society the more clearly can *short-run* interests be in conflict with one another. At the present time, for instance, express highways are being planned in many parts of the nation. Traffic problems mount daily and such thoroughfares seem to be a partial solution. In the long run such highways will benefit the entire country. Yet, wherever new highway proposals are made the conflicts begin to rage. Many citizen groups in cities and towns would like to rid themselves of through traffic. But many merchants complain that express highways will hurt their businesses. Other businessmen, who hope to gain concession rights along the highway, are strongly in favor of it. Farmers oppose the highways because they threaten to isolate and hence reduce the value of certain farms. Other strategically located farmers see chances for quick profits. Concrete and asphalt manufacturing companies struggle to have their materials used in the construction, politicians vie for the right to fill the new jobs created, and so on. Although the long-run interests in increased flow of traffic, safety, and economic prosperity may be shared by all these groups, the opportunities for short-run conflict and temporary advantage are numerous.

The conflicts of interests illustrated here could be duplicated in almost any area of modern life. The number of groups and the special interests they hold almost defy imagination. These conflicting interests are both a part of, and are distinct from, the religious, racial, ethnic, political, and major economic cleavages discussed above. They help to explain why the inexorable onslaught of social change is always accompanied by emerging and continuing patterns of conflict.

4. DIVERSITY AND HETEROGENEITY. Although they are perhaps the more dramatic, not all of the value differences and incipient value conflicts in modern society derive from clear-cut clashes of interest. Nor do they all derive from group and ideological differences where prejudice and discrimination are consistently operative. A large part of the value differences are simply products of slightly different conditions of life. Such differences are far more characteristic of urban than of rural living and the larger and more diversified the city the more evident they become.

There is, first, the whole range of occupational differences: the bricklayer may have something in common with the stonemason and with certain other members of the building trades, but how much does he have in common with the druggist, the file clerk, the chiropodist, the school-teacher, and the tailor? Occupational differences are accompanied by income differences and problems of wages and salaries. Housing condi-tions, recreational facilities, transportation needs, and so on, vary almost ad infinitum. In most of these cases there are no special conflicts of in-terest so much as there is a lack of *shared* interests. There is no necessary conflict between the slum-dwellers whose housing problem includes in-festation with rats and the suburban development residents whose problem is a water-filled drainage ditch, but neither group is particularly interested in the specific problem of the other. Without the bond of immediate shared interests, such groups are, to a great extent, unavailable to one another for aid in achieving their separate goals.

When there is so little communication, either of meaning or feeling, group attempts to realize particular values may be complicated in at least two ways. First, the group may not be able to get any real support for its program. Unless the group is articulate or powerful, this is often the case. Its members frequently become antagonistic toward those per-sons who seem to frustrate their program or they become generally hostile toward other groups and their needs. The second and more significant outcome is that, in order to put its program across, the group must resort to other than purely rational appeals. It must, in effect, become a pressure group and seek to mold opinion by means of propaganda. Pressure-group tactics, of course, create conflict. Conflicts of interest are born where formerly only differences existed.

Major Issues in Western Society

Among the myriad conflicts that pervade social problems there are occasional recurrent and persistent themes. The broad course of social change in Western society that was outlined in the first section of this chapter has inevitably resulted in the re-examination of values that were formerly held uncritically. New values, themselves part of a larger pat-tern, begin to appear. In the clash between the traditional and what *may* be the patterns of the future are found the major issues of today and tomorrow.

The depth of the conflicts to be considered here is measured by the amount of emotional heat they engender. Any one of them will send many persons' blood pressures to the boiling point. For these are not mere surface conflicts with outcomes of limited significance. These conflicts involve the validity of the most basic assumptions upon which people build their lives and upon which they depend for definitions of right and wrong. Regardless of which side of an issue an individual espouses, he is not apt to be easily converted to the point of view of his opponent.

1. SACRED VS. SECULAR. By what standards should a man, a law, an

idea, or an action be judged? Any of these can, in the United States at the present time, be judged as completely praiseworthy or as absolutely reprehensible by different groups of people. Not all, or even most, of the people who make the judgments will be adequately aware of the presuppositions upon which their judgments are based. But whatever the issue, one part of those assumptions is likely to involve *where* the individuals look for standards.

To one group of persons all actions are judged externally by whether or not they conform to the beliefs and practices which come to us from the past. It is not loyalty to the past alone, however, that characterizes sacred thinking and differentiates it from secular thinking. In addition, the sacred orientation assumes that the heritage from the past is not to be questioned, and that not only the ideals of the past, but also the forms through which these ideals were met, are inherently good. Deviations from past standards are judged, not by whether the results of the deviations help satisfy other traditional values, but by the fact that they are deviations.

Secular thinking rejects the notion that deviation is inherently bad and claims instead that it is rigidity—the inability to adjust forms and practices to changed conditions—which is harmful. The secular orientation would preserve that part of the heritage from the past which is still useful and discard all the rest. It would define man's needs in terms of a set of values which is consistent within itself rather than in terms of any special ties to the past.

As indicated earlier, a marked trend toward secular thinking is a major feature of Western culture. It is too soon to say, however, how far the balance will shift and how permanent the shift will be. Just in the past few years a "back to the traditional values" emphasis in education, politics, economics, and religion has developed. Whether the balance will swing in a few more years is not certain. In any event, the conflict bodes to be a central one for many years to come.

2. Freedom vs. minimum living standards. Conflict over the developing philosophy of minimum standards is probably more acute in the United States than elsewhere in the Western world, for the conditions leading to the conflict have operated at very near maximum in this country. The conflict is a product of both rising standards of living and inequalities in standards of living. Only rather recently in the United States have inequalities in living standards come to be regarded as a problem in themselves.

The United States has one of the world's highest levels of living. The American economy is a tremendously productive one and the benefits of that productivity have been widely distributed throughout the population. Certainly the American people as a whole have a stake in the preservation and improvement of that productive capacity. At the same time, the United States has had one of the world's freest economies in the sense that both business and industry have been permitted to develop and to operate with a minimum of regulation by government. This is our philosophy of "free enterprise." Historically, at least, the two conditions of high living standards and of minimum regulation of the economy have been closely associated. In the light of this close historic association many people have asserted a direct casual relationship, for example, "It is the free economy which is responsible for the high living standards and the continuance of the high living standards depends upon the continuance of maximum freedom in the production and distribution of goods and services."

Unquestionably, this statement of the relation between living standards and free enterprise is gross oversimplification. Seldom, if ever, do we find simple, direct cause-and-effect relationships among institutional and other social patterns. High living standards in the United States *are* associated with relatively unhampered business activity, but they are *also* associated with such other plausibly causal variables as abundant natural resources, a tremendous land area, a young and vigorous population, a strategic physical location, and democratic political institutions. Just how much each of these factors has contributed to our high living standards it is impossible to say. We value each of them for itself and for the role it has played in our economic development. At the very minimum, relatively free capitalism is one of these factors and, at the maximum, it might outweigh the others to the point of being indispensable. From the most naive viewpoint to the most sophisticated, it is important to have the maximum amount of personal freedom or the minimum amount of government regulation that is consistent with the achievement of our other societal values.

The same unrestricted distribution of goods and services which has been instrumental in raising living standards has played an important role in crystallizing the minimum-standards values which are part of the present conflict. Although living standards in general were being raised, some groups were profiting hugely and others little, if at all. Thus, while economic freedom in this sense meant the freedom to make a fortune, it also meant the freedom to live in abject poverty and to be unable to share in the society's increased productivity. For many decades it was held to be the individual's own responsibility to see that he did share in the benefits, and, presumably, he could do so, according to his ability, if only he were ambitious and willing to work. More recently, as the competitive advantages of upper economic status and the competitive handicaps of lower economic status have been recognized, the philosophy has begun to develop that there are certain minimum benefits to which an individual or a family should be entitled, whether or not they are earned through direct economic competition. This philosophy assumes that society itself has the obligation to provide certain minimum benefits. The essential benefits generally are stated in terms of the right to be gainfully employed, to earn a living wage, to be assured adequate medical care and to be protected against disability, to have paid vacations, and to be assured of adequate income in retirement. The minimum standards tend gradually to be raised as living standards improve and as the philosophy itself gains greater acceptance.

Actually, it appears that the *philosophy of minimum standards* has already gained acceptance and is here to stay. The great depression of the 1930's resulted in the passage of minimum wage laws, unemployment compensation, and the social security program which are now permanent aspects of the American scene. The struggle of the present and the near future concerns the *level* at which the minimum standards should be located. The advocates of business freedom claim that they are already dangerously high and that further increases might stifle business initiative and wreck the economy. Advocates of higher minimum standards contend that business is not afraid of government interference as such, for example, tariffs, fair trade laws, and the like, and that the same forecasts of disaster have been used to oppose every step of progress that has already been made. Neither set of arguments appears to impress the other side so the conflict goes on.

3. NATIONALISM VS. INTERNATIONALISM. War is the ultimate issue in this conflict, and much of the debate centers around which philosophy offers more hope for preventing it. War is not the whole issue, however, for there are other practical, as well as moral, issues involved.

The so-called practical issues concern the whole tenor of our relationships with other peoples as well as our political and economic well-being. The nationalist philosophy in approaching these problems states in effect: "We have a superior system in practically all ways. Objective comparison cannot help but confirm that superiority. Therefore, we should encourage other peoples to become familiar with our system in order that they might imitate it. When they have patterned their systems after ours, the majority of the world's problems will have been solved." The internationalist approach on the other hand asserts: "Attempts by one nation to impose its standards on other nations are likely to incur only resentment and hostility. Even if others accept our technological superiority, it does not mean that they will wish to copy us, and they are apt to feel strongly that in other areas their way of life is clearly superior to ours. To get along adequately with other nations we must strive to understand their viewpoints and we should be prepared to compromise important differences." The nationalist philosophy sees hope for world progress only as other nations can be induced to follow our lead. The internationalist philosophy stresses the need for mutual understanding and compromise.

There is, too, a moral issue involved—that of our alleged superiority, which is reputed to be a mixture of biology and culture. Since the culture is superior, there is a strong presumption that the biological stock which produced that culture is in itself a desirable one. In matters of immigration, for example, this is presumed to be sufficient reason for preserving the basic biological composition of the American people. Opponents of this alleged superiority claim that the biological composition of the people has had little to do with the development of American culture and that the whole philosophy is contradictory to our professed democratic and Judaeo-Christian beliefs. The current struggle between those who would continue to drastically restrict the numbers of immigrants who may come to the United States from non–Northwest-European countries and those who would eliminate the favored treatment given to just a few nations is a part of the larger conflict over nationalist-internationalist ideologies.

Ultimately the issue becomes one of war or peace. Those who hold to the nationalist position stress the belligerent nature of nations, the conflict of political and economic ideologies, and the likelihood of war when any nondemocratic, noncapitalist nation believes that it has a good chance to win. From these assumptions, it would be folly to relax our guard and, thus, give a potential enemy his opportunity. Since there is a strong probability of future wars anyway, it is alleged that we must be strong enough to foredoom an attack to failure. Only in such a program of preparedness, according to nationalist philosophy, is there any real possibility of preventing future wars.

Internationalist thinking regards this nationalist rationale as one of the major forces operating to perpetuate the pattern of intermittent warfare. By assuming that war is almost inevitable, they claim, and by acting as though war will come, the efforts to prevent it actually serve to make war more likely. Only by a relatively complete break with past patterns of international diplomacy do they see much hope for breaking the cycle. The co-existence of such antithetical ideologies as capitalism and communism, democracy and dictatorship, require that all of man's resources be put into a supreme effort to discover ways whereby the differences may be either reconciled or accommodated. Past experience has amply demonstrated that armaments and alliances do not prevent wars; an all-out effort to accommodate national differences has not yet been made.

Amelioration Conflicts

Conflicts rage at each step in the definition, operation, and solution of social problems. The conflict usually begins when it is first asserted that "a condition is bad," for there are always some persons who profit by the existing condition and some who believe it to be right, proper, or inherent in the scheme of things. Then conflicts are apt to develop over whether anything can be done about the condition and which of several alternative solutions should be tried. Finally the conflict is apt to shift to the way in which the proposed solution should be put into effect. Even when all factions are agreed upon what needs to be done, there generally remains disagreement on how to do it. Thus, conflicts center about the issues themselves and about policies for dealing with the problems. In the "technique" or "policy" area, two disagreements on how to deal with problem situations recur time and again.

1. REGULATE OR SCOURGE? In many different problem situations there is continuing debate over whether the "devils" should be exorcised or whether they should be permitted to remain but with their malevolent powers curbed. In matters of family instability, racial segregation, and gambling, for example, one alternative is to strike at the heart of the matter; to forbid divorce, to eliminate segregation, and to stamp out gambling. The other alternative is to permit all three but to remove the elements in each situation which cause hardship. The trauma might be removed from divorce procedures, the desegregation orders might be vigorously enforced, and gambling might be legalized, regulated, and taxed. These are fundamentally different proposals and the proponents of each are generally scornful of the other.

Advocates of vigorous efforts to scourge the undesirable conditions frequently hold that to do otherwise is immoral. When a situation is defined as wrong there should be no compromise with it. Determination and courage are called for; to speak of regulating or controlling vice is either wishy-washy or it amounts to rationalization by those who really wish the evils to continue. The proponents of regulation and control are prone to argue that efforts to stamp out such vices are naive and un-realistic. Prostitution and drug addiction, they remind us, have existed since time immemorial. Since social change cannot be reversed and since the condemned practices *will* continue, the sensible approach is to make them available but under conditions where a minimum of harm will be done and where some incidental public good might result. The traits which are called for, they suggest, are understanding and discretion rather than fanaticism and myopia.

It seems apparent that there are some elements of validity in each of these positions and that many persons hold to each view out of the genuine conviction that it is the correct one. In some cases, however, there is also reason to suspect that the insinuations cast by each group regarding the characters and motivations of some of the other groups could bear some scrutiny. Some fanatics, whose motivations are complex, do tend to the former position and some apologists for the status quo do tend to the latter.

2. FAST OR SLOW? A closely related conflict concerns the method or rate at which any proposed solution should be put into effect. One position is that proposed changes should be instituted as rapidly as possible,

while the counterposition is that changes should be made as gradually as possible over an extended period of time. Many, though by no means all, of the persons who feel that problem conditions should be completely uprooted also feel that it should be done quickly, while many of those who favor regulation also favor going slowly in whatever is done.

The advocates of rapid change are again prone to emphasize the inconsistency between ideals and practice and to work energetically toward making the ideals a reality. They are inclined to favor change through legislation and to point to instances, such as the whole series of laws and rulings against racial discrimination, as evidence that this taking-the-bull-by-the-horns approach does work. The go-slow approach of others is again interpreted as evidence of faintheartedness or as reluctance to see the changes made.

Those who favor a cautious approach stress the importance of cultural traditions which are opposed to the anticipated change. "You can't change a whole way of life overnight," they feel, and fundamental alterations in habit and custom may require a generation or more to be accomplished successfully. Efforts to bring them about quickly are sure to meet with evasion and hostility which will make the problem more difficult rather than less difficult to solve.

The charges by each side of unrecognized or unacknowledged motivations on the part of their opponents are again not completely true nor are they totally without foundation. Personal interest and personal elements in such conflicts are discussed in the next section.

PERSONAL DEVIATION: PATHOLOGY AND VARIATION

Both social change and value conflicts may operate on a grand scale and in seemingly impersonal fashion. Nevertheless, personalities are always involved. Some persons adjust readily to changed conditions, whereas others do not; and value conflicts are products of the divergent values held by individuals and groups. Personality factors intrude into the concepts of social disorganization and value conflicts, and they play an important role in their own right. The present section re-examines the nature of these personality factors, and the mode of their involvement in social problems.

The Deviant in Social Problems

One of the first questions to be answered is just how personal deviancy contributes to the development of social problems. In answer: (1) deviants may play an important causative role, (2) they may help precipitate or aggravate the problem, or (3) they may *be* the problem.

1. *Deviants may play an important causative role.* Some of the im-

portant variables in any social situation are the needs, desires, strengths, weaknesses, and peculiarities of the persons who occupy places of leadership. The positions of leadership are multiple and varied; they include: the heads of governments, military leaders, political figures, scholars, literary experts, scientists, the officers and "bosses" of major organizations, and so on. The important consideration is whether the person is in such a strategic position that his personal peculiarities have important influence on the behavior of numerous other persons. Marked paranoid tendencies, for example, in the man on the street are not apt to have broad repercussions in the behavior of others. People may say, simply, "He's a suspicious cuss;" they may shy away from contacts with him; or, if he becomes too troublesome, they may institutionalize him. *But,* those same feelings of persecution in a major public official, or in the publisher of a large newspaper, may be instrumental in creating a climate of fear and hostility leading to religious persecution, race riots, or even war. The influence of the deviant personality is in direct proportion to the extent of the power wielded by the person so afflicted.

One need not assert that dictators and presidents, bishops and popes, physicists and inventors have *caused* the world's problems. There is always a complex web of cause and effect centering about the personalities of leaders and the social conditions that enabled them to assume leadership. Whether the social climate produces the man or whether the man creates the social climate is a kind of "chicken-or-egg-first?" question. Social problems never have a single *cause,* they have *many* causes. Some of those causes may well inhere in the deviant characters of important leaders. History from Hannibal to Hitler illustrates the point.

2. *Deviants may precipitate or aggravate the problem.* Though the personalities of leaders must occupy a conspicuous role and though most ordinary individuals wield little power and influence, the "little" man's contribution to social problems cannot be discounted. For one thing, even the exhortations of the famous must fall on receptive ears if they are to be effective. The demagogue thrives, not so much because he personally is popular, as because he mirrors, heightens, and gives focus to the insecurities and rabid strivings of the masses. Remove his fanatical following and the demagogue is doomed. Thus, in the *aggregate,* the deviancies of individuals assume an importance which separately they could never have.

In still another way neurotic persons, who are not otherwise outstanding, play a limited causative role in the crystallization of problems. They often provide the incidents that bring incipient conflicts to the point of explosion, and, once the explosion occurs, they fan the resulting flames and constantly seek to add new fuel. Such troublemakers can generally be found deeply involved in or loitering on the periphery of any pending dispute. They are extreme and intemperate in the positions they take and they deprecate compromise in favor of a violent, angry crusade to win their ends. They suppress, twist, distort, and magnify. They use, but do not accept, other persons, casting each person aside when he has ceased to be useful. With an attack upon some person or program, they often succeed in creating an issue. Drawn by the smell of blood, other deviants join the fray, revising the issue at will in order to keep the struggle alive. Possibly these issues would never develop otherwise, but neurotic persons may both trigger and intensify conflicts as well as impede their solutions.

3. *Deviants may be the problem.* Certain types of deviants are, in themselves, problems. Drug addicts, alcoholics, inveterate gamblers, prostitutes, homosexuals, the mentally ill—the whole range of personal pathologies—are subjected to public scrutiny and to efforts at reform. The problem is probably never as simple as "Here are some errant persons who must be cured," for there are more than personal factors involved. Many of the pathologic behaviors are tolerated and even approved by some groups. Many deviants shade off from accepted social behavior by almost imperceptible degrees. There are questions of treatment and care which go far beyond the handicapped persons themselves. The deviant persons are not *all* of the problem but they are the *heart* of the problem. Were it not for the tendency of the deviants to get in trouble, the associated social issues would not be regarded as problems at all.

Personal Variation

Most of the deviant persons involved in social problems are not noticeably limited either in intelligence or in general ability. They have sufficient innate capacity to behave as they are expected to behave, but they do not conform. They remain "different." These are the persons who, if they occupy influential positions, may play an important causative role in social problems and who, if they do not have great power or prestige, often help to precipitate or to aggravate problems. It is important to recognize that such individual variation: (1) is learned, (2) is partly a product of diverse norms, and (3) derives much of its significance from the social context.

1. *Deviation is learned.* The deviant person is deviant because of experiences that he has had in the past. He learns to hate, to fear, to mistrust, to aspire, to envision, and to covet just as less deviant persons learn these same things in more moderate form. Just how and why *some* persons learn *some* things in much more extreme form than most other persons do is a fascinating and complex problem which has not been completely solved. In some cases it seems to be a matter of overlearning which interferes with subsequent learning. The boy-grown-to-manhood who still so reveres his mother that he cannot adjust to a wife, and the "completely honest" man

who insults his friends and ruins his business by being candid are both cases in point. In still other cases, persons block or resist what seem to be normal learnings for them and acquire deviant and often disapproved patterns instead. The boy from a "nice" home may rebel murderously because, though the home provides all wanted material goods, it fails to meet his emotional needs.

Whatever the variant pattern assumed, the deviant seldom is completely antisocial. More frequently, his rejection of one set of norms is accompanied by acceptance of a different set of norms.

2. *Deviation is partially a product of diverse norms.* Sociologically, variation in norms and practices is entirely normal. Though some small, homogeneous societies may possess but a single set of standards, all large, complex societies have multiple systems of values which conflict at many points. Among various elements of the society there even exist entire culture patterns which stand opposed to those values which are accepted by the society as a whole. The codes of delinquent street-corner gangs and the loyalties of subversive groups are illustrations. It is characteristic of many deviants (in fact, this is one way in which deviancy is defined) that they have rejected loyalty to certain values of the larger society in favor of the generally disapproved values which are accepted in minority groups.

The generally disapproved values which are accepted by deviant groups are sociologically just as much a part of the culture as are the universally accepted ones. Widespread condemnation does not necessarily mean that these are elements soon to disappear from the culture. Indeed, some of the widely held values of today may be persecuted in the future, when they are replaced by some of today's radical notions.

3. *Deviation and the social context.* The mere fact of deviation is not intrinsically important. At least equally important is the way in which the deviation fits in, or does not fit in, with the important issues of the day. There are at all times numerous deviant persons whose deviancy brings them no great attention and who never become involved in major public conflicts. Probably most such persons are regarded by their associates as somewhat eccentric or strange, and there the matter rests. However, when the eccentricity centers in an area of public dispute or perhaps slightly anticipates the direction of social change, the person may be lifted into prominence and even into a position of leadership. Although the process whereby leadership develops is not well understood, there is abundant evidence that the long-term significance of a particular leadership is determined by the course of history as well as by the personal qualities of the leader himself. From dictators and presidents down through minor leaders of all sorts, the social climate of the period has had much to do with both the rise to power and with the ultimate definition of the man. Deviation is both created and defined by the social milieu.

SUMMARY

Social change is the forerunner of the appearance of social problems. Change inevitably threatens vested interests, interrupts habits, creates distress, and, finally, results in the development of new social patterns. Major alterations in Western culture which have contributed a great deal to current social problems are: the rise of science and scientism; the Industrial Revolution; urbanization; and the rise of secularism.

Social change generally sharpens conflicts of values. The bases for conflict exist in the facts of economic, political, and religious differences, in racial and ethnic variation, in conflicts of interest, and in the diversity and heterogeneity which characterize complex societies. Major conflicts in Western society include sacred versus secular thinking, the ideology of business freedom versus the ideology of minimum standards, and nationalist versus internationalist approaches to world affairs. Important conflicts also rage over the proper approach to social problems, over whether they should be merely regulated and controlled, and whether they should be solved rapidly or gradually.

Personal deviation is a third element found in all social problems. Deviants, when they occupy important positions, often play a causative role in the development of social problems. Deviants in less critical positions help to precipitate and to aggravate problems. When the deviation is sufficiently great, the deviants may even be a considerable part of the problem. Social deviation is learned, is partially a product of diverse norms, and derives much of its significance from the social context.

SUGGESTED READINGS

BARNES, Harry E., *Society in Transition* (Englewood Cliffs, N. J., Prentice-Hall, Inc., 1939). Detailed description of the influence of the Industrial Revolution upon modern American society. Includes treatment of urbanization and secularization of modern society.

BECKER, Howard, *Through Values to Social Interpretation* (Durham, N. C., Duke University Press, 1950). Revised collection of essays on the role of values in science. Includes analysis of the sacred-secular society concepts.

CLINARD, Marshall, *Sociology of Deviant Behavior* (New York, Rinehart & Company, Inc., 1957). Contains extended discussion of the nature of personal deviation and analyzes deviation in several problem areas.

OGBURN, William F., *Social Change* (New York, The Viking Press, Inc., 1922). Stresses the disorganizing influences which are felt when some aspects of culture change more rapidly than others. Assigns a determinative role to technology.

WHYTE, William H., Jr., *The Organization Man* (New York, Simon and Schuster, Inc., 1956). Penetrating analysis of the way of life a whole new managerial class in American society. Highlights the challenge of social change to traditional standards.

WRIGHT, Richard, *Black Boy* (New York, Harper and Brothers, 1945). Powerful, autobiographical novel which reveals the development of deviant personality characteristics through subjection of the author to racial prejudice and discrimination.

QUESTIONS AND PROJECTS

1. Social breakdown often appears more evident to mature adults than to young adults and youth. Explain. How is this difference related to the appearance of new culture patterns?

2. List four major changes in western European culture which play major roles in the development of many current social problems.

3. Differentiate between science and scientism.

4. Define *secular thinking* and differentiate it from *sacred thinking*.

5. Why is it unrealistic to expect that disorganization will soon be entirely eliminated from social life? Illustrate your answer.

6. Discuss the thesis that unequal rates of change in different aspects of culture pose a grave threat to human civilization.

7. Do you see any connections between the sacred versus secular, and the freedom versus minimum-standards, controversies? Could you predict how most persons would feel on one of these issues through knowledge of their feelings on the other issue?

8. Defend the policy of attempting to regulate or control problem conditions as opposed to the policy of attempting to stamp them out completely.

9. How many deviant persons play an important causative role in producing social problem situations?

10. What classes of deviants are often considered to *be* a problem in themselves?

11. How may deviancy appear through overlearning? Illustrate your answer.

12. Explain the statement, "Widely disapproved values are part of the culture."

13. How does the social context influence the definition given to deviant personality characteristics? Give several illustrations.

21

The Orientation of American Society

ꞏꞏ

This is not the time for superficial solutions and everlasting elocution, for frantic boast and foolish word. For words are not deeds, and there are no cheap and painless solutions to war, hunger, ignorance, fear, and imperialist communism.

ADLAI E. STEVENSON

WE COULD EASILY ADD A SECOND VOLUME to this textbook without touching again on any of the social problems already discussed. Many other problems—housing, immigration, politics, labor relations, poverty, depressions, natural resources—are among those a second volume might treat. But neither the college term nor the student's patience lasts forever. At some point, one must simply stop, recapitulate, and attempt to assess prospects for the future.

One cannot accurately predict either the exact nature of future problems or our future action toward them. But, aware of the continuity of culture, we may assume that most of the established trends in American society will continue, and that future social problems and social action will be shaped by these trends.

TRENDS IN AMERICAN SOCIETY

Important trends in American society which are well enough established to need no documentation include the following:

1. *Increasing productivity and rising standards of living.* Our productivity per man hour has increased by about six times during the past

century. If this rate of increase continues for another century, our average worker in 2050 will produce and earn as much in one 7-hour day as he now does in a 40-hour week, and as much as he produced in 1850 by working more than three weeks for 70 hours a week. [1] The Editors of *Fortune* magazine predict that productivity per man-hour will continue growing by about 3 per cent a year, [2] giving the United States a national product of $750 billion (at 1958 price levels) by 1970. [3] In the past 50 years, national production rose by $1,450 per person (at 1958 prices); it is expected to rise by $900 per person during the next 10 years. [4] Productiv-

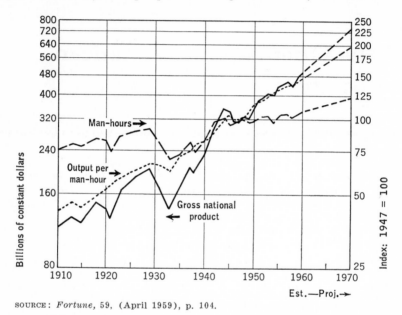

SOURCE: *Fortune*, 59, (April 1959), p. 104.

FIG. 21-1. The rising tempo of American economic growth.

ity is rising all over the world, even faster in some countries than in the United States. [5]

This modern explosion of productivity is a tremendously important social fact. Throughout fully 99 per cent of recorded history, most of the world's people lived at or near the level of bare subsistence; most of the world's people still do. At nearly all times and places, high birth rates and low worker productivity made poverty normal and inescapable, and social problems were so insoluble that such situations were not even

[1] J. Frederic Dewhurst and associates, *America's Needs and Resources: A New Survey* (New York, The Twentieth Century Fund, 1944), p. 942.

[2] Charles E. Silberman and Sanford S. Parker, "How the United States Can Get 50 Per Cent Richer," *Fortune*, Vol. 59 (March, 1959), pp. 107 ff.

[3] Gilbert Burck and Todd May, "The Good Uses of $750 Billions," *Fortune*, Vol. 59 (April, 1959), pp. 104 ff.

[4] *Ibid.*

[5] Silberman and Parker, *op. cit.*

defined as *problems*. It is only in the United States and a few other nations where we *can produce enough* to make possible such luxuries as public assistance to the indigent, universal education, and widespread health services. This high and rapidly rising productivity and the rising standards of living it makes possible are among the most significant social facts of modern life.

2. *Increasing leisure.* Most of the people of the world follow a daily routine, in the words of Galsworthy, of "get up, work, go to bed, sleep." Until very recently in Western civilization, leisure was an upper-class monopoly. Ours is the first civilization in which the masses of the people enjoy leisure in any appreciable amounts. Although the mass enjoyment of leisure may not be an unmixed blessing, its development is a social fact of tremendous significance.

3. *The democratization of comforts.* [6] It may be no accident that the most highly productive peoples are those with a comparatively small gap between the living standards of the very rich and of the masses. A social system which produces such stupendous adornments as the Taj Mahal, the Pyramids, or the palace city of Versailles does not reward its workers with the high standard of living that encourages maximum productivity. The democratization of luxuries and comforts also tends to make political conservatives of the masses who have acquired a vested interest in a social system that provides these comforts. It is, furthermore, a potentially explosive factor, since a population accustomed to a high standard of living will not quietly surrender it.

4. *Increasing economic security.* A little over twenty years ago, our society awakened to the fact that the shift from a folk society to an urban-industrial society had greatly reduced the economic security of the individual. It also became clear that in an increasingly interdependent economy, the economic hardship of any major group—business, labor, farmers—had depressing consequences upon the entire economy. It appears that government has abandoned its "neutral" role and that, regardless of political party, government will accept responsibility for maintaining prosperity and protecting each major economic group from severe hardship. Labor now has minimum wage laws, unemployment insurance, and union contracts; business has a wide variety of government aids and subsidies; farmers have price supports. Each group seeks governmental assistance for itself (while deploring this tendency among others). A continuing determination of every group in the United States to seek protection against economic adversity through group action is one of the inescapable social and political facts of modern life.

5. *Growing power of pressure groups.* In a mass society, the individual has no voice except through his group connections. The unorganized mass is inarticulate and politically ineffectual. Even *democratic*

[6] See Sanford S. Parker and Lawrence A. Mayer, "The Decade of the Discretionary Dollar," *Fortune*, Vol. 59 (June, 1959), pp. 136 ff.

decision-making in a mass society cannot be a mere counting of heads, but inevitably becomes a counting of organizations. The number of interest groups which maintain formal lobbying machinery grows rapidly, and the pressure group becomes the real center of political power in the United States.

6. *Growing international interdependence and vulnerability.* Economically we grow steadily more dependent upon other nations. Our high-grade iron ore deposits approach exhaustion, and advancing science and technology transform one after another of the 102 known chemical elements from laboratory curiosities into an industrial raw material. Far more dramatic, however, is the collapse of geographic defenses in a day of intercontinental bombers, guided missiles, and atomic weapons. The knowledge that half our cities and a fourth of our people may be destroyed in a single hour is a Damoclean sword under which we have learned to live with surprising equanimity. Yet our anxieties over possible wars and revolutions fomented by communist nations now dominate our social controversy. It is difficult to discuss any social problem without considerations of national defense, security, and subversion arising. Technology is not reversible, and each nation grows steadily more vulnerable to every other technically advanced major nation. This is perhaps the most significant political fact in the world today.

7. *World spread of Western technology.* For perhaps the first time in history, every society in the world is rapidly changing at the same time. Pastoral folkways everywhere are giving way to modern industrial discipline. The traditional society—rooted in custom, based on localism and small group life, and resistant to change—is in convulsive change all over the world. [7] Women everywhere are emerging from seclusion and subordination. Juvenile delinquency is rising all over the world, as traditional controls are undermined and the temptations and uncertainties of adolescence multiply. The tremendous patience of the world's poor is fading away as the ancient rationalizations crumble before the dawning hope of a better existence. If this hope is not fulfilled, and quickly, we may see a tremendous anger which will feed the fires of political demagoguery. Whoever can say, with Egypt's Colonel Nasser, "I took away their despair," will lead the underprivileged. [8]

CURRENT TENSIONS AND ISSUES

These social trends are not likely to be interrupted or reversed in the near future. They outline roughly the kind of world within which Amer-

[7] See Daniel Lerner, *The Passing of Traditional Society* (Glencoe, Ill., The Free Press, 1958).
[8] Osgood Caruthers, "What Drives the New Arab 'Saladin'?" *New York Times Magazine* (August 24, 1958), pp. 10 ff.

ican social problems will be considered during the next several decades. These trends produce a variety of social tensions and raise vital questions about policy for which there is no easy answer. The following three issues would appear to be of transcendent importance:

1. How to provide for national security and national defense, including protection against espionage and sabotage.

2. How to maintain national prosperity in a society which desires both economic security and political freedom.

3. How to divide the national income among the various groups which claim it—management, stockholders, workers, farmers, teachers, pensioners, the indigent, and others.

ORIENTATIONS IN AMERICAN SOCIETY

There are many other current social issues, but the above three are central to nearly all social problems. The manner in which they are dealt with at any particular moment in history depends largely upon the pattern of social organization dominant at the time. Among the many possible patterns of social organization for a technically advanced mass society, the following three appear to be the most likely alternatives for our society.

1. *The democratic state.* Despite many imperfections and occasional derelictions, the ethos of American culture has been predominantly democratic. Our history shows an almost unbroken effort to democratize opportunity, to preserve individual dignity, and to diffuse widely among our people the necessities and comforts of life. It can be argued that the process of decision-making is more widely diffused than at any time in our history—one of the consequences of the proliferation of pressure groups. [9] Although these features of American life may or may not be blessings, according to one's values, they are undeniably democratic.

A democratic state is unlikely to be indifferent to social problems. Democratic values inevitably define many conditions as "social problems" and encourage action on them. Democratic traditions encourage voluntary association in order to promote reforms, raise funds, and devise plans for dealing with problems. If democratic social organization persists, our society will probably continue to define and treat social problems much as it has been doing.

Whether democracy will persist is less clear. The development of a

[9] There is also an opposing point of view—that the organization of the pressure group enables a small leadership clique to impose its views upon the large membership, and that the centralization of industry, finance, and mass communication gives a narrowing group of decision-makers a growing power to determine social policy. See Floyd Hunter, *Community Power Structure* (Chapel Hill, University of North Carolina Press, 1953).

mass society activated by pressure groups, [10] the lack of a strong unifying core of universally held values, [11] the expanding role of government in economic and social life, the expansion of highly centralized systems of mass communication, and the effort to insure national security in an increasingly insecure world—each of these factors carries a potential threat to democracy. It is possible that democracy is a pattern of social organization that can appear and flourish only under certain rare combinations of historic circumstances. If so, its replacement by some other alternative may be expected.

2. *The garrison state.* When a modern society faces a military crisis which lasts for decades, its transformation into a garrison-police state becomes more than a theoretical possibility. A long-term military crisis requires that all other interests and values be subordinated to the requirements of national security. Civil liberties become a nuisance in dealing with suspected traitors and are likely to be curtailed. The pressure for mounting military expenditures requires that all public services not directly related to defense—national parks, conservation, civilian education, and others—must be curtailed. The functions and authorities of the government expand in a hundred directions, from the stockpiling of raw materials to the conduct of psychological warfare. The historic privacy of the individual is steadily narrowed, as his friends, organizational memberships, reading habits, and presumed philosophical views come under security scrutiny; his telephone conversations are tapped and taped; and official guesswork as to his future loyalty becomes an accepted prerogative of government. The number of jobs requiring security clearance grows, the procedural safeguards of personal privacy in identifying security risks are reduced, and the tests of security become steadily more stringent. Private intelligence services provide security information to employers, and private detective services begin to specialize in spying on employees. The industrialist's decisions about factory location, plant layout, raw material utilization, choice of personnel and employees, and many other business matters become increasingly dominated by defense and security needs as each such decision is cleared with the proper government official. Passports, scholarships, research grants, and university teaching staffs all come under police surveillance and are conditioned upon security considerations. Art, music, and literature cease to be nonpolitical, and both the political orthodoxy of the production and the alleged political views of the artist, writer, actor, or composer become a basis for determining the acceptability of his work. The atmosphere of suspicion grows and deepens until privacy, independent thinking, and

[10] See Stuart Chase, *Democracy Under Pressure: Special Interests vs. the Public Welfare* (New York, Twentieth Century Fund, 1945).

[11] See Robert C. Angell, *The Integration of American Society* (New York, McGraw-Hill Book Co., 1941).

spontaneity of association become, in themselves, suspicious and incriminating.

The government withholds information it feels the people should not have, and the news agencies become dependent upon official handouts in many areas of public policy. Political parties join in a bipartisan approach that removes certain vital issues from any public discussion of alternatives. In numerous areas of public policy, the technical expert announces the defense "needs"—a specified radar screen, a certain number of missile platforms, a certain amount of money to develop a new sensor system, and so on. The legislators and civilian administrators, who cannot be given free access to the facts upon which such decisions are based, are almost forced to accept and approve these decisions.

In these and many other ways, a prolonged military crisis can transform a democratic society into a garrison state. Some of the more subtle aspects of this transformation are outlined by a distinguished political scientist: [12]

This transformation would come about gradually as men abandon their former roles and take up new ones, which are thought of as temporary. The owner, or active head, of a business notes that he is losing able associates to the civil or military services. Sensing that his own activities are becoming more stereotyped, the executive may himself "put on a suit" [join the civil or military service]. A credit manager connects with the political police because of his knowledge of the network of industrial information contacts across the nation. A trades-unionist joins up [as a secret informer] in order to spy on communists and supposed fellow travelers in the labor movement. It is on the basis of thousands of choices of this kind that the transformation of American society would take place. At any given moment the currents appear to be running, as usual, in all directions. Closer inspection would show drift away from the activities comparatively untouched by the crisis into operations immediately involved. The garrison-police state is both a "state of mind" and a "state of readiness." It is when the state of mind gets set that the transformation is well along.

The garrison state is not a purely theoretical possibility, as indicated by the fact that many of the tendencies described above are clearly operative to some degree in present American society. [13] It may be that a prolonged military crisis makes the garrison state an inevitability. Whether America becomes a fully developed garrison-police state depends both upon the duration and severity of the crisis in American-Russian relations and upon the vitality of our democratic value heritage. There are some

[12] By permission from *National Security and Individual Freedom*, pp. 47-48, by Harold D. Lasswell. (New York, McGraw-Hill Book Co., 1950.)

[13] See Aldous Huxley, *Brave New World Revisited* (New York, Harper and Brothers, 1958), in which Huxley argues that the nightmare described in his *Brave New World* (Garden City, N. Y., Doubleday & Company, Inc., 1932), is becoming a reality.

countries, such as Finland, which appear to have remained relatively democratic during a fairly long period of national insecurity which is far greater than ours. Possibly a study of their experience would be revealing.

In a garrison state, social problems are defined largely according to security criteria. Crime, mental illness, and personal pathologies continue to be defined as problems. Ill-health and certain kinds of educational deficiency might receive an increased attention; subversion becomes a leading problem while civil liberties become a nuisance; and the problem in mass communication is how to organize the media to transmit only the approved propaganda most effectively.

The treatment of social problems in the garrison state emphasizes state action rather than private initiative. Experimentation by voluntary organizations is not encouraged, and agitation for reform is distinctly dangerous. Membership in any but officially sanctioned organizations is extremely hazardous, so much of the sort of private activity now devoted to social problems would be greatly curtailed. It is likely that well-established voluntary organizations (for example, the Red Cross) would conduct fund drives with semiofficial endorsement and carry on noncontroversial activities consistent with defense needs, while all controversial voluntary organizational activity would disappear.

The garrison state will inevitably become a "welfare state" to a degree as it assumes welfare services that contribute to national strength. These might include free health services, elementary education of the functionally illiterate, support of technical and professional education in certain areas, and perhaps others. The garrison state is highly active with respect to social problems, although both its definitions and its responses differ greatly from those of the democratic state.

3. *The fascist state.* [14] If America's international tensions could be resolved, a number of problems would be simplified, but others might be aggravated. With the economic props of a large military program removed, the problem of maintaining economic prosperity would probably become *the* great problem. As this is written, our nation has had no "normal" peacetime prosperity for a quarter-century. Certain institutional machinery erected during this period and intended to prevent the recurrence of another great depression has had no real test and its effectiveness is undemonstrated.

A major depression would accentuate many of the tensions and cleavages in American society. Racial antagonisms would probably become more tense as Negro and white competed for scarce jobs. Radical social

[14] The term *fascist* is not currently fashionable. Communism has replaced fascism as "the enemy," and the communists have so freely applied the term *fascist* to everyone and everything they dislike that others have shied away from its use. But as a term to describe a particular kind of society, it has a certain usefulness. For a concise analysis of fascist states, past and present, see William Ebenstein, *Today's Isms* (Englewood Cliffs, N. J., Prentice-Hall, Inc., 1958), Ch. 2, "Totalitarian Fascism."

movements would gain in strength and conservative fears of radicalism would mount accordingly. Since people who are insecure find it easy to blame any plausible scapegoat, every division of class, race, religion, or occupation could become a potential point of antagonism to be exploited by those who crave power. [15]

A major depression, or some other similar set of developments, can create a situation in which the people are divided into hostile, warring camps. They lack common values and are unable to agree upon a common course of action. This results in paralysis of effective governmental functioning. The outcome is endless talk and interminable legislative bickering but indecisive action, because *no* particular action will please more than a minority of the people. Demagogues flourish, to rouse false hopes by promising the impossible, and to foment dangerous passions by denouncing error as evil and indecision as cowardice. Eventually, people may grow weary of indecision and lend support to the strong man or party that promises to bring order out of chaos. Although no two fascist states are exactly alike or come to power in exactly the same way, this is the general manner in which fascism gained power in both Germany and Italy. [16] In each case there was widespread economic distress, an indecisive government in which the people had lost confidence, and a popular craving for prompt, decisive action. In each case, a multiplicity of political parties helped contribute to the parliamentary confusion of which the people grew weary. In each case, recent military defeats and sweeping social changes had reduced and weakened the core of unifying values which all revered in common. In each case, the absence of a firm democratic tradition made it easy for the people to exchange a half-understood freedom for a deeply desired order. [17]

A fascist state, having gained power, tends to become a garrison-police state as well. To maintain order and prevent bickering, the suppression of dissent is soon required. Censorship, police surveillance, security certification, outlawing of any real political opposition, demands for political conformity in the arts, removal of "disloyal" teachers and preachers—all these inevitably follow from the attempt to solve social problems by imposing an authoritarian pattern of control upon the so-

[15] See Lawrence Dennis, *The Coming American Fascism* (New York, Harper and Brothers, 1936), for an unabashed statement of the thesis that America should, and inevitably will, become fascist.

[16] See Calvin B. Hoover, *Germany Enters the Third Reich* (New York, The Macmillan Co., 1933); Erica Mann, *The Lights Go Down* (New York, Farrar and Rinehart, Inc., 1940); H. R. Knickerbocker, *The German Crisis* (New York, Farrar and Rinehart, Inc., 1932); Robert A. Brady, *The Spirit and Structure of German Fascism* (New York, The Viking Press, Inc., 1937); Frederick L. Schumann, *The Nazi Dictatorship* (New York, Alfred A. Knopf, Inc., 1935); John Strachey, *The Menace of Fascism* (New York, Covici Friede, 1933); Giuseppe Borgese, *The March of Fascism* (New York, The Viking Press, Inc., 1937).

[17] See Milton Mayer, *They Thought They Were Free: The Germans, 1933-1945* (Chicago, University of Chicago Press, 1955).

ciety. Whereas the slogan of the French Revolution—Liberty, Equality, Fraternity"—eventually helped produce a democratic society, the slogans of fascism—"Order, Discipline, System"—call for actions and policies which inevitably destroy democracy.

The fascist state emerges from a society's inability or failure to deal effectively with its social problems. No nation has become fascist (or communist) as an end result of too bold or sweeping (or "socialistic") an attack upon social problems. Fascism and communism are more likely to gain power following prolonged attempts to postpone dealing realistically with social problems. Once installed, the fascist state attempts to solve social problems in a manner consistent with its authoritarian philosophy. Its definitions of problems reflect the philosophy of the fascist state; the problem of civil liberties vanishes while the problem of "loyalty" grows, and the problems of education and mass communication become those of insuring (not of preventing) the conversion of these activities into agents of official indoctrination. Solutions emerge not from public discussion and agreement but from the counsels of the elite, which then imposes these solutions upon the society. Social problems receive a great deal of attention in a fascist state, and the solutions sought are often so drastic that they arouse bitter opposition that must then be forcefully suppressed. Many of the "solutions," however, are likely to be showy palliatives rather than fundamental solutions, for the fascist state must constantly dazzle the population with its accomplishments, in order to make their surrender of freedom appear as a good bargain.

In this discussion of alternatives, the communist state is omitted. Although there are parts of the world where communism has powerful appeal, it would be difficult to find a social scientist who believes that communism, as a political movement, has any prospect of gaining power in the United States. If communism were to attract a considerable following in the United States, the probable result would be, not a communist state, but a fascist state established to "save" the country from communism.

WHICH ALTERNATIVE?

Will democracy survive in the United States? Within which framework will social problems be defined and considered? This question cannot be answered positively. Actions of other countries will greatly affect the outcome. Our success in maintaining economic prosperity is a crucial factor; it is unlikely that democracy could survive repeated or prolonged economic crises, for idle and despairing men are not rational social analysts. Unless economic problems are met fairly successfully, there can be no rational atmosphere for consideration of any other problems.

Assuming reasonable success in maintaining prosperity and in avoid-

ing wars or war fevers, the survival of democracy may depend upon the
vitality of our value heritage. There is no doubt that there are powerful
currents of antidemocratic thought in America, [18] but there is also a value
heritage highly favorable to democracy. As long as these values survive,
our approach to social problems is likely to remain democratic.

THE AMERICAN VALUE HERITAGE

Among the many values which comprise our value system in the
United States, the following are conspicuous:

1. *Pleasure.* Most people appear to feel that life should be pleasant
and enjoyable, now, in this world.

2. *Property.* Most people desire property and demand a social order
that protects the right to acquire and enjoy it.

3. *Freedom.* Most people resent being pushed around, insisting upon
thinking and acting much as they wish with a minimum of arbitrary
restraints.

4. *Fair play.* Most people feel that people in general should have
equal opportunities, that the strong should not bully the weak, and that
deception, insincerity, and entrapment should be confined to harmless
games and rituals.

5. *Education.* Most people consider education desirable and a mark
of individual achievement and cultural advance.

6. *Religion.* Most people consider religion necessary for a good society, and many also consider a personal religious faith essential.

7. *Science and technology.* To most people, applied science and
technology hold great prestige as the source of our high standard of living
and as the means of national survival in the atomic era. Pure science and
the ideals of scientific objectivity and freedom are less widely understood
and less highly valued.

8. *Progress.* A desire for progress and a belief in its attainability is
almost universal in American society. The definition of *progress*, however, varies widely and reflects the total value system of each individual.

9. *Democracy.* For a great many people, *democracy* is a major value.
Although the varied meanings they give to the term are a reflection of
their individual value systems, some ideals of freedom, equality, and fair
play are nearly always implied.

If this describes correctly the major value system of most Americans,
it is clear that social problems will not disappear. These values inevitably
define as social problems many situations which our rapidly changing
(disorganized?) society will continue to produce.

Failure to meet these problems with some degree of success would

[18] See David Spitz, *Patterns of Antidemocratic Thought* (New York, The Macmillan Co., 1949).

eventually destroy a democratic society. Totalitarianism, either of the left (communism) or of the right (fascism), awaits a democratic society that cannot or will not deal effectively with its social problems. That these totalitarianisms, so much alike in many respects, promise no real *solutions* as defined by democratic values, is perhaps true but irrelevant. Recent history clearly reveals that the disorganizing effects of rapid social change inevitably produce social tensions fatal to democracy unless they are resolved by constructive social policy.

KNOWLEDGE FOR WHAT?

If a rapidly changing society can remain reasonably tranquil and orderly only by continuously and consciously reorganizing itself, high levels of knowledge, rationality, and unselfishness are essential.

The *knowledge* needed to deal effectively with social problems is available to a considerable degree. We do not know all the answers about any problem, but we do know *some* of the answers. We are steadily learning more of them. The use of expert consultants in developing and administering social policy appears to be increasing. Today, it is easy to find many examples of both brilliant use of knowledge and spectacular evasions of knowledge in dealing with social problems.

Rationality is needed if knowledge is to be useful. Unless one can consider various alternatives objectively, viewing each proposal on its merits, no rational approach is possible. Where thinking has frozen into rigid, inflexible dogmas, a rational analysis is impossible. Many people who are fond of telling what practical people they are, insist upon discussing proposed reforms at a theoretical level. They refuse to consider the facts of a situation and the detailed workings of a proposed policy, but talk only of "states rights," "bureaucracy," "socialism," "free enterprise," and other vague and transitory concepts. Or, if they are left-wingers, they talk of "the contradictions of capitalism," "opiates of the masses," "bourgeois sentimentality," and so on. Slogans and catchwords are impressive substitutes for thought.

Unselfishness is a homely virtue that still plays a leading role in meeting social problems. It is historically true, of course, that action on many problems came only when an interest group was persuaded to redefine its vested interest, that is, persuaded to support a reform or policy by being shown how it would benefit the interest group itself. Public fire departments replaced privately operated fire companies when the National Board of Fire Underwriters, after the disastrous Chicago fire drove many fire insurance companies into bankruptcy, called for public fire departments to save insurance companies from ruin. One reason corporations contribute to the Community Chest is because they consider it "good business" to do so. C.I.O. unions oppose racial discrimination partly be-

Question asked of a group of prominent Americans: "What worries you most about America today?

One answer: "The tendency to overinvest in things and underinvest in people. This is a serious disproportion which we are far from correcting. It is epitomized by our magnificent steel plants and our seedy schools, parks, playgrounds, and hospitals.

John Kenneth Galbraith, in *Esquire*, Vol. 51 (February, 1959), p. 50.

cause racial discrimination weakens the union and depresses white wages. Much of the motivation for treating social problems stems from an enlightened self-interest.

But not all motivation is selfish in an ordinary sense of the word. *Solutions always cost somebody something!* For each solution, taxes must be collected, contributions offered, profits trimmed, opportunities for exploitation surrendered, power shared, prestige sacrificed, prejudices suspended, cherished values compromised—someone always has to give up something or other. These sacrifices do not always pay off financially, at least not soon enough to do the maker any good. The successful treatment of a social problem nearly always requires that a number of persons be willing to make some personal sacrifice in order to achieve some larger public benefit. By whatever name it is called—brotherly love, Christian charity, social consciousness—such a spirit of unselfishness is not a saccharine sentimentality but a major force in social action. Whatever stimulates or inhibits this spirit of unselfishness—religion, education, unique personal experience—becomes an indirect determinant of success in treating social problems.

CONSENSUS UPON VALUES

When people share the same values, even though they may be ignorant and clumsy, they can usually arrive at workable agreements. When their values differ, no amount of technical knowledge and parliamentary finesse can produce more than a tolerable compromise. Most important decisions eventually resolve themselves into a choice between values.

How to spend one's life (how to kill oneself, for that is the ultimate price of living) is answered only by one's choices between values. To this most important of all questions, science has no complete answer. Values are matters of preference, not matters of factual knowledge. Any attempt to say which values people ought to hold makes one a philosopher, not a scientist.

Social scientists may, however, guide people in their value choices in at least three ways.

1. *Science may show the implications of alternative values.* Science may show what each value choice involves. If national unity, or equality of opportunity, or "free enterprise" is proposed as the primary value, social scientists may show what social arrangements each choice requires. If people object (and some do) to materialism as a primary value, the social scientist can show some of the institutional rearrangements which would be needed in order to replace materialism with some other value. It is likely that many who listened approvingly to Hitler in the early 1930's had no clear idea of the kind of society which Hitler's values would *necessarily* produce. If social science can *show people what the results of their choices will be* when they make value choices, much social conflict could be averted.

2. *Science may show the relation between values.* Certain values, such as "democracy" and "caste," are incompatible and cannot coexist without many cumbersome evasions and compromises. Other values, like "freedom of speech" and "equality of opportunity," are mutually supporting so it is difficult to separate them. Since, in adopting one major value (for example, "democracy," "discipline," or "rugged individualism,") one implicitly accepts the other values and institutional arrangements that go with it, knowledge about the relations between values and their concomitants should reduce confusions and social tensions.

3. *Science can indicate which values are functionally useful in a particular social setting.* This is as close to "choosing" values for people as the social scientist can come. For example, the social scientist can point out how certain frontier values do not fit an urbanized, industrialized, interdependent society. A value like "thrift"—spending only the bare minimum and saving the balance—was useful to a society with a capital shortage, but would be economically disastrous if widely followed in a mass-production economy such as ours. A tolerant attitude toward cultural differences, unnecessary in an isolated frontier hamlet, becomes highly useful in an interdependent heterogeneous modern world. Early marriage and high fertility are useful cultural ideals in a frontier society, in a society with a high death rate, or a society organized for warfare; for a peaceful society with an ample population and a low death rate, a far lower birth rate is conducive to an orderly society. To value retribution in dealing with criminals is incompatible with scientific knowledge of its consequences. Although this test of functional utility for a given social setting will not resolve all value choices, it will, in some cases, indicate which values are likely to produce satisfactory results.

Will these contributions of science to the selection of values produce an American consensus upon values and thereby simplify the treatment of social problems? Not necessarily. Values emerge from the social experience of groups of people and are not adopted on a basis of sociological suggestion. But to the extent that people gain insight into their value choices and are aware of the social significance of their value judgments, their social experience *is* modified. Social experience has *meaning* only as it is interpreted by individuals and groups, in the light of their knowledge and insight. To some degree, therefore, the scientific study of values may contribute to a rational consensus upon values, and thereby simplify the task of reaching agreements upon social problems and their treatment.

SUMMARY

There is no way to finish a social problems textbook. Each attempt at a conclusion succeeds only in raising additional questions. But this is the way of all science—no field of inquiry is ever exhausted. All scientific truth is tentative and the search for it is unending; each conclusion affords an intermission, but is not a finale.

In the opening chapter the authors expressed the hope that students might be helped to develop (1) *awareness* of present social problems, (2) some *factual knowledge* about them, (3) some understanding of their *sociological origins*, (4) some awareness of the roles of *theory and practice*, (5) a balanced *perspective* upon social problems, (6) an appreciation of the *role of the expert*, and (7) an intelligent *personal involvement*. Perhaps there is no better way to conclude this volume than to repeat this hope and append the further hope that, long after this volume's bits and pieces of data are forgotten, some fragments of sound habits of social analysis may be retained and used.

SUGGESTED READINGS

Bain, Read, "Our Schizoid Culture," *Sociology and Social Research*, Vol. 19 (January-February, 1935), pp. 266-276. A classic sociological essay: a pungent statement of many of the value conflicts and inconsistencies in American social life.

Ebenstein, William, *Today's Isms* (Englewood Cliffs, N. J., Prentice-Hall, Inc., 1958). A penetrating description and comparison of communism, fascism, socialism, and capitalism. Chapter 3, "Democratic Capitalism," is especially recommended.

Galbraith, John Kenneth, *The Affluent Society* (New York, Harper and Brothers, 1958). A critical analysis of the ways in which the world's richest society is using—or misusing—its riches.

Huxley, Aldous, *Brave New World Revisited* (New York, Harper and Brothers, 1958). A brilliantly written, pessimistic view of modern man's march towards the status of robots in an overpopulated and overmanaged world.

LUNDBERG, George, *Can Science Save Us?* (New York, Longmans, Green & Co., Inc., 1947). A somewhat pessimistic view of the prospects for the rational guidance of society.

LYND, Robert, *Knowledge for What?* (Princeton, N. J., Princeton University Press, 1939). An eloquent plea for the use of scientific knowledge in directing society. A vivid contrast to the above Lundberg volume.

MANNHEIM, Karl, *Freedom, Power and Democratic Planning* (New York, Oxford University Press, Inc., 1950). An attempt to show how social planning can reconcile conflicting social forces in a democratic society.

REIMER, Svend, "Social Planning and Social Organization," *American Journal of Sociology*, Vol. 52 (May, 1947), pp. 508-517. A stimulating discussion of the prospects for rational control of a society which has not yet accepted the rational ideology of planning.

RIESMAN, David, with GLAZER, Nathan, and DENNEY, Reuel, *The Lonely Crowd* (New Haven, Yale University Press, 1950); abridged pocket edition (Garden City, N. Y., Doubleday & Co., Inc., 1953). A study of the changing American character in a mass society in which people are guided by interiorized values and goals rather than by custom and tradition.

AUDIO-VISUAL AIDS

Man In The Twentieth Century (McGraw-Hill Book Company, Inc., Text-Film Department, 330 West 42 St., New York), 17 minutes, sound, black and white. Modern man is prosperous but bored, fearful, and dissatisfied. How is he to gain peace of body and mind in the twentieth century?

QUESTIONS AND PROJECTS

1. When will all social problems be solved? Why?

2. What are the trends in American society mentioned in this chapter? Are there any others which should be added? What reason is there to believe that these trends will continue?

3. Criticize this statement: "The easiest way to settle the question of how to divide the national income is simply to give everyone a fair share of it."

4. Toward what values is the democratic state oriented? The garrison state? The fascist state?

5. Would a transition to a garrison or a fascist state be gradual and imperceptible or abrupt and dramatic? Or are both kinds of transition possible?

6. Why is the communist state not included among the alternatives?

7. Of what importance is the American value heritage with respect to social problems?

8. To what extent can science guide people in choosing values?

9. Why is a society's value consensus important in dealing with social problems?

10. Social problems can be dealt with either by seeking to solve them, or by redefining the situations so that they are no longer problems. Can the latter course be followed without modifying our value heritage?

11. What are some possible policies or solutions upon which many people have such an inflexible attitude that no rational evaluation is possible?

12. Is enlightened self-interest a rational reason for supporting social action? Can support for practical solutions always be secured by appeal to enlightened self-interest? If not, what other means are sometimes effective?

13. Evaluate and rank in order of importance the following factors in the modern world's failure to achieve harmony and happiness:

a. Lack of knowledge needed to solve social problems.

b. Failure to use present knowledge.

c. Lack of established consensus upon values.

d. Individual imperfections and defects in human character.

14. Suppose that you were granted full authority to select and impose, regardless of opposition, the policies needed to solve *one* of our social problems:

a. Which problem would you elect to solve? Why this one?

b. What policies would you impose to solve it?

c. Would the solution of this problem create any new problems?

Index of Names

Subject Index

Addiction Research Center, 491
Agriculture, big, 95, 97
 see also Rural areas
Agricultural Adjustment Act, 95
Aid to the blind and to dependent children, 102
Alcoholism, 469-470
 alcoholic pattern, the, 480-482
 Alcoholics Anonymous, 482-483, 613
 arrests for, 480
 in college, 480-481
 cultural and personal factors in, 483-485
 magnitude of the problem, 478-480
 treatment for, 500-501
Alien and Sedition Laws, 580
American Association of University Professors, 291, 301
American Bar Association, 592
American Book Publishers Council, 302, 460
American Civil Liberties Union, 52, 77, 377, 378, 576, 586, 610, 615
American Civil Rights Congress, 52
American College of Surgeons, 519, 521
American Council of Christian Churches, 222, 224
American Education Association, 52
American Federation of Labor, 80, 92, 94, 363, 381
American Federation of Women's Clubs, 207
American Hospital Association, 477
American Legion, the, 77, 130, 541
American Library Association, 302, 460
American Medical Association, 77, 207, 509, 510, 512, 513, 519, 524, 528, 531, 532, 533, 535, 536, 539, 541
American Mercury, 441
American Newspaper Publishers Association, 439
American Public Health Association, 518, 519
American society, Ch. 21
 alternatives for, 652-653
 orientations of, 647-652
 tensions and issues in, 646-647
 trends in, 643-646
 value-heritage of, 653-654
American Society of Newspaper Publishers, 439
Anti-Defamation League, 377
Antisubversive legislation, 594-596, 613
Antitrust laws, 90, 120, 121, 459
 see also Sherman Antitrust Law *and* Clayton Act

Associated Press, 432

Behavior, learned nature of, 29
Bell Telephone System, 86
Birth Control
 changing mores, 229
 and Malthusian theory, 244
 and world population policy, 264-265
Birth rates
 decreases in U. S. before 1940, 247-248
 increases in U. S. since 1940, 248-250
 among migrants, 260
 social class variation in, 256-257, 259
Bohemianism, 420-421
British Broadcasting System, 453, 462
British National Health Service, 541, 542
Business,
 and free contract, 89
 growth and concentration, 90-91
 and monopoly, 90-91
 and private property, 89
 separation of ownership and control, 91-92
 as a vested interest, 88-92

Canadian Broadcasting System, 453
Catholic World, 436
Causation, and association, 65-67
Censorship, 454, 459, 462, 464
Central Intelligence Agency, 605, 612
Chamber of Commerce of the United States, 79, 80
Character disorder, 34, 129-130
Chicago Area Project, 169
Chicago Tribune, 51
Christian Herald, 460
Christian Science Monitor, 51, 436
CIO News, 436
Cities, Ch. 14,
 blighted areas, 403-404, 415
 congestion of, 404-407, 422
 education in, 418
 future prospects, 421-422
 great size of, 398-399
 growth of, 397-400, 416
 heterogeneity and anonymity of, 401-403, 630-631
 medical facilities in, 411-412, 512-514
 metropolitan areas, 399-400
 number of, 399-400
 personal deviation in, 420-421
 political and economic problems of, 409-410, 415-416, 422
 problems of, 401-410
 proportion of population in, 400